21/7

WILLIAM J. WALSH
Archbishop of Dublin

WILLIAM J. WALSH

Archbishop of Dublin

By
PATRICK J. WALSH, M.A.

Longmans, Green and Co.
London · New York · Toronto
1928

LONGMANS, GREEN AND CO. LTD.

39 PATERNOSTER ROW, LONDON, E.C.4
6 OLD COURT HOUSE STREET, CALCUTTA
53 NICOL ROAD, BOMBAY
167 MOUNT ROAD, MADRAS

LONGMANS, GREEN AND CO.

55 FIFTH AVENUE, NEW YORK
221 EAST 20TH STREET, CHICAGO
TREMONT TEMPLE, BOSTON
210 VICTORIA STREET, TORONTO

PRINTED IN IRELAND
AT THE TALBOT PRESS
DUBLIN

Prefatory Note

THE chief sources used in writing this biography are letters and other documents preserved in the archives at Archbishop's House, Dublin. Use has also been made of documents in the diocesan archives of Cashel, Limerick, and Westminster. To the Prelates who so kindly granted permission to consult their archives the writer acknowledges his indebtedness and expresses his thanks.

The following pages deal mainly with the activities of Dr. Walsh as a public man. His purely pastoral work does not receive the fulness of treatment which might naturally be looked for in the life of a prominent churchman. This defect will, it is hoped, be supplied in another volume.

The writer was intimately acquainted with Dr. Walsh, to whom he acted as secretary, and with whom he lived during the last fifteen years of the Archbishop's life.

P. J. W.

1st September, 1928.

Prefatory Note

The chief sources used in writing this biography are letters and other documents preserved in the archives of Archbishop's House, Dublin. Use has also been made of documents in the diocesan archives of Cashel, Limerick and Waterford. To the Prelates who so kindly granted permission to consult their archives the writer acknowledges his indebtedness and expresses his thanks.

The following pages deal mainly with the activities of Dr. Walsh as a public man. His purely pastoral work does not receive the fullness of treatment which might naturally be looked for in the life of a prominent churchman. This defect will, it is hoped, be supplied in another volume. The writer was intimately acquainted with Dr. Walsh, to whom he acted as secretary, and with whom he lived during the last fifteen years of the Archbishop's life.

P. J. W.

1st September, 1928.

CONTENTS

CHAPTER I

viii

CHAPTER IX

CHAPTER X

CHAPTER XI

CHAPTER XII

x

xi

List of Plates

Illustrissimo ac Reverendissimo

GULIELMO J. WALSH

Archiepiscopo Dublinensi

Quinque lustra summo Pontifici plurimam optamus salutem.

Auguste Praesul pontificum decus
Fidique semper dulcis amor gregis,
   Iam quinque lustrorum superbis
    Ingenii radias triumphis.

Immensus ergo cum citharae modis
Prorumpat omni pectore fervido
   Concentus, ingentique plausu
    Nunc resonent hilares Camoenae.

Quantum patrono debeat indigens
Semper benigno pauperies tibi,
   Quantumque tutori potenti
    Relligio pietasque supplex;

Quantum supinae commoda patriae
Certantis aequa lege resumere
   Abrepta longinquos per annos
    Iura, malos reparare casus;

Doctrina quantum debeat inclyta
Demum resurgens omine tam bono
   Cultuque tam claro, quid omnis
    Tam studiosa cohors iuventae;

Testantur aegris undique conditae
Sedes opimae, culmina divitum
   Erecta templorum, scholarum,
    Rura per et plateas frequentes;

Testatur aedes omnibus artibus
Apte docendis nata recentior,
  Auctore primo te magistro,
  Plena piis iuvenum catervis.

Felix amicis praesidium tuis
Longo superstes tempore floreas,
  Longosque producas triumphos,
  Magne Dei patriaeque vindex.

Gratae perennis gloria patriae
Regnare pergas usque valentior,
  Tutela, custos, laus Iernes,
  " Dulce decus columenque rerum."

—N. J. Brennan, C.S.Sp.,
Blackrock College.

IV. *Non. Aug.*, MCMX.

WILLIAM J. WALSH

ARCHBISHOP OF DUBLIN

CHAPTER I

EARLY YEARS

ARCHBISHOP WALSH was a native of the city of Dublin. At the time of his birth his parents, Ralph and Mary Walsh, resided at 11 Essex Quay, Dublin, where, on January 30, 1841, the future archbishop was born. The child was baptised in his parents' house—a practice common enough among Irish Catholics in those days—and received the name of William. The record of his baptism is preserved in the Baptismal Register of the parish of SS. Michael and John, and shows that "William, son of Ralph and Mary Walsh, was baptised according to the rite of the Catholic Church, on the 2nd day of February, 1841, the sponsors being Hugh O'Flaherty and Eliza Pierce." At his Confirmation he took the additional name of Joseph, and throughout his life he generally signed his name " William Joseph Walsh." He was an only child.

Ralph Walsh came from an old and respected stock of farmers and shopkeepers, whose home was in the County of Kerry. Born at Tarbert, he was apprenticed as a youth to a watchmaker at Tralee. Later, after a sojourn of some years in the city of Waterford, he moved to Dublin, where he established his home, and opened up business as watchmaker and jeweller at Essex Quay. Here he married Mary Pierce, whose family was connected with Galway.

In the parish of SS. Michael and John, Mr. Walsh was prominently identified with various religious and charitable works.   Among the charitable organisations in which he was actively interested was the society known as " The Malachean Orphan Society," of which he was a prominent member.   One of the Archbishop's earliest recollections was his being brought by his parents to the old Queen's Theatre to witness a performance in aid of that charity.   Ralph Walsh knew Daniel O'Connell intimately, and, hailing as he did from the Kingdom of Kerry, he was naturally a staunch and zealous supporter of the great Liberator.   His son, William, was born in the year in which O'Connell was Lord Mayor of Dublin, and as early as the 2nd of November, 1841, the boy, then nine months old, was enrolled, by his father, as a Repealer in the books of the Repeal Association.   In 1844 Mr. Walsh acted as Honorary Secretary to the committee formed by O'Connell to oppose the Bill, then introduced by Sir Robert Peel in the House of Commons, for the establishment of a Board which should have exclusive control of " Charitable Donations and Bequests" in Ireland.   The voluminous correspondence in connection with the agitation against the Bill remained in the Secretary's possession, and at his death passed to his son, ultimately to find a place in the diocesan archives of Dublin.

At the age of five young Walsh was presented to O'Connell, and he distinctly remembered not a few occasions on which he was present at political conversations between his father and the Great Tribune.   Thus at an early age he was introduced to matters in regard to which he was destined to figure prominently in later life.

After some years spent in the house on Essex Quay, Ralph Walsh moved his business to 19 (now No. 30) Parliament Street, where he resided up to the time of his death, which took place in April, 1867.   After the death of her husband, Mrs. Walsh lived at Booterstown Avenue, and later at 6 Royal Terrace, Dun Laoghaire (Kingstown), where she died, in her 72nd year, in April, 1875. She was buried beside her husband in Glasnevin Cemetery; and in the same grave her sister, Eliza Pierce, William's godmother, was laid to rest, in October, 1887. In the meantime, after Mr. Walsh's death, the business premises in Parliament Street had passed into other hands; but the name of Ralph Walsh may still be seen on a brass plate outside the old shop window.

William Walsh passed his boyhood in Parliament Street, in the parish of SS. Michael and John. He attended regularly the parish church, where he used to serve Mass. It was while he was a Mass-server that he was first brought into close personal relations with the Rev. C. P. Meehan, a priest of the parish, who exercised no small influence on his early life. Father Meehan was a man remarkable in many ways. He possessed considerable literary powers. He was well versed in Irish history, and was the author of *The Fate and Fortunes of the Earls of Tyrone and Tirconnell*, and other historical works. He was a constant contributor to the *Nation*, and numbered among his intimate acquaintances Thomas Davis, Denis Florence McCarthy, Dalton Williams, James Clarence Mangan, and other literary figures prominent in the Young Ireland movement.

Father Meehan was always an oddity. Small in stature, of spare and meagre build, and somewhat strange in manner and gait, he was for over fifty years a notable and familiar figure in Dublin. Eccentric and choleric and not devoid of humour, he was gifted with a caustic tongue and mordant wit. He mocked and lashed the philistines among his acquaintances, lay and clerical. Indeed, " He made a mock of all save God," for, though whimsical and testy, yet he was pious and ascetical, and towards the poor and the unfortunate he was charitable to a fault. James Clarence Mangan was a constant object of

Meehan's care and of his bounty; and many another
hapless victim of drink or misfortune recounted tales of
the little priest's kindliness and liberality. When roused
to opposition he had a characteristic trick of adjusting his
monocle and darting a look of withering contempt on the
object of his wrath, while he rapped out his biting sarcasm
or sardonic wit. His copious store of apt invective and
ready command of grim contumely made Meehan the
delight and the terror of friend and foe alike. His anger,
however, was generally short-lived—

Irasci celerem, tamen ut placabilis essem.

On pedants he poured out the vials of his wrath, and his
attitude towards the prig who spoke wearisome platitudes
was that of the man in *Ebb-Tide* who used to look at
strangers with the air of asking, " Did God create you ? "
and of finishing with the command, " Get off the earth."
A lifelong friend of Meehan's, Father James Healy, the
parish priest of Little Bray, used to tell how, when he
had on an occasion provoked the little man's fiery glance,
he soothed his ire by quoting at him Tennyson's lines :—

> " And curving a contumelious lip
> Gorgonised me from head to foot
> With a stony British stare."

Meehan was placated and playfully replied : " No more of
that, James, an thou lovest me."

An incident which Ralph Walsh witnessed, and
which he used to recount with amusement, gives
an inkling of Father Meehan's fiery temperament.
When Canon O'Connell, the incumbent of SS. Michael
and John's, and Meehan's parish priest, was being
promoted to the parish of Irishtown, some of his admirers
determined to present him with a carriage. A committee
was formed for the purpose of obtaining subscriptions.
Some members of the committee called on Father Meehan
to solicit his co-operation. He received them in his room

at the Presbytery, and, as soon as he ascertained the object of their visit, he immediately snatched up a battered farthing that lay on his table, and, glaring in characteristic fashion at his visitors, exclaimed : " Subscribe for a carriage for Dean O'Connell ! Why, if that rap could secure for him the reversion of Elias' fiery chariot, I would not give it."

Meehan early conceived a liking for young Walsh, to whom, at all times, he continued to be kind and considerate. He lent him books and directed his early reading. The boy in turn used to help the priest in many little ways, reading his proof sheets, copying extracts, and rendering other similar services. Meehan's influence on William's mind was very considerable. He early stimulated in him an interest in Irish history and archaeology, and evoked his enthusiasm for Mangan's poems and Davis's patriotic verse. Indeed, William's first literary efforts in print appeared in the columns of the *Nation* to which, at Meehan's suggestion, he contributed occasional articles while he was still an ecclesiastical student at Maynooth. Meehan owing to his eccentricities, was never promoted to be parish priest. When the Mass-server of former days had become Archbishop, he found Father Meehan still at SS. Michael and John's, where his curacy lasted for a period of well over fifty years (1835-1890).

William Walsh received the elements of knowledge in his own home. When he was about eight years old he was sent to a private school in Peter Street, conducted, as he used to say, on very polite lines by a Mr. Fitzpatrick. As in the case of most children of the middle class in Dublin, music and singing formed part of his early training. For music he had a natural bent, and, as he had little interest in boyish pastimes, he devoted to his music lessons much of the time that boys are wont to give to outdoor games. Thus he acquired early and rapidly a sound knowledge of the theory and practice of music; and in after life music

was to him a never-failing source of interest and recreation.
Following his educational training at the hands of
Mr. Fitzpatrick, he became a boarder for some years at
St. Lawrence O'Toole's Seminary in Harcourt Street.

At Harcourt Street the boy studied with success and
distinction. In the report of the Distribution of Prizes
of July 1855, we find that William Walsh was a first-prize
winner (*solus*) in Algebra, in Geometry, and in Italian; he
was first (*ex aequo*) in Latin and in German; and he was
awarded second prizes in the subjects of Greek, French,
Ancient History, and Elocution. It was on the occasion
of this distribution of prizes that he first spoke to Cardinal
Cullen, who was then Archbishop of Dublin.

Dr. Cullen in presenting to the young prize-winner
a copy of Manzoni's *I Promessi Sposi*, recommended him
to read the story through during the holidays, then commencing, and intimated that after the vacation he would be
glad to see him again, and discuss with him in Italian the
various episodes of that celebrated romance. Thus began
between the actual and the future Archbishop of Dublin
an intercourse that ripened into a friendship which lasted
down to the Cardinal's death in October 1878. William
Walsh always entertained sentiments of reverence and
admiration for the Cardinal; and for the remaining twenty
years of his life Dr. Cullen continued to hold his young
friend in high esteem, and to evince a deep and friendly
interest in all his affairs. In 1855 William J. Walsh passed
from St. Lawrence O'Toole's Seminary to the Catholic
University of Ireland, which had just then ventured on
the first steps of its arduous struggle for existence.

The Catholic University had been founded to supply a
crying need and to meet an existing danger in the matter
of the higher education of Irish Catholics. When Walsh
entered upon his university studies, there were two State
Universities in Ireland, Trinity College and the Queen's
University. Trinity College was still, for all practical

purposes, an institution of the Established Church; its honours and emoluments were reserved almost exclusively for Protestants; the other existing system, the Queen's University, with the affiliated Queen's Colleges, was for Catholics inadequate from the point of view of justice, and dangerous from the point of view of religion.

The Queen's Colleges had been established by an Act of Parliament passed in 1845, during the ministry of Sir Robert Peel, as the initial step towards a university in which the full benefits of university education should be available for Catholics, and for Presbyterian and other Protestant dissenters. Three non-residential colleges of higher education were set up, one at Belfast, one at Cork, and one at Galway. Parliament voted a grant of £100,000 for the erection of the necessary buildings, and provided a yearly endowment of £7,000 for each college by placing an annual sum of £21,000 on the Consolidated Fund. The colleges were opened in 1849; in the following year, " The Queen's University in Ireland" was incorporated, and was by Royal Charter empowered to confer degrees on the students of the Queen's Colleges.

The " costly and fantastic scheme" of the Queen's University with its constituent colleges failed utterly to meet the claims of the Irish Catholics for higher education. In principle and in plan it was altogether unacceptable to the Catholic bishops. Based on the system of " mixed" education—of ill-repute in Ireland, and opposed to Catholic discipline—the colleges were strictly " non-sectarian" in character; they were open to students of any religion or of none; no religious instruction might be given; no religious topic might be admitted to their teaching; the power of appointment and dismissal of professors was vested in the Crown, and professors were appointed without any reference to their religious beliefs, even in such departments as Philosophy and History. The system was denounced at its inception, by Sir Robert Inglis within the House of Commons, and by O'Connell without, as a " gigantic system of godless education," and was condemned by the Irish bishops as " intrinsically dangerous to faith and morals." The condemnation was confirmed in a Rescript from the Holy See, October 1847, and in two further Rescripts, October 1848, and April 1850. At the Plenary Synod of the Irish Church held in Thurles in 1850, the Queen's Colleges were finally and unreservedly condemned by the assembled bishops. This condemnation was formally promulgated in the bishops' pastoral letter addressed to the clergy and laity of Ireland in September 1850.

With the view of securing for Irish Catholics a system of higher education in conformity with Catholic principles, the Holy See, in the Rescript of 1847, and again in 1848, had urged on the Irish bishops the project of founding a Catholic University in Ireland and suggested as a model to be followed the University then recently founded at Louvain. The matter was taken up at the Synod of Thurles, and the Fathers decided to adopt the suggestion of the Holy See, by establishing a Catholic University at Dublin. A committee styled " The Catholic University Committee" was appointed by the Synod " to examine into the details of this most important project, and to carry it into execution." The Chairman of the committee was the Most Rev. Paul Cullen, then Archbishop of Armagh and Papal Delegate, subsequently (June 29th, 1852) Archbishop of Dublin. Dr. Cullen sought the advice and assistance of Dr. John Henry Newman of the Oratory, as to the most effective steps to be taken in furtherance of the project, and in July 1851 he made to the distinguished Oratorian the proposal that he should allow himself to be nominated Rector of the new institution. After some delay Newman accepted the offer (November 14, 1851), and the appointment was confirmed by the Holy See.

It was not, however, until three years had elapsed that

the Rector was installed in his office. The long delay was due in large measure to causes inseparable from a project of such magnitude, undertaken under difficult circumstances. The delay was also attributable to misunderstandings and disagreements that arose between Archbishop Cullen and Dr. Newman. The Archbishop exercised a close vigilance on all the actions of the Rector. He insisted that the Rector should keep him fully informed of the successive stages of progress, and give him definite information as to various details of organisation. The question of professorial appointments provided a chief bone of contention. The Archbishop had to be advised as to the steps that were being taken to secure competent teachers, and frequently he made suggestions as to the personnel of the professorial staff. These suggestions were ill-received by Newman, who regarded Dr. Cullen's action as an unwarrantable interference with his own rights as Rector. Suspicion and jealousy arose, and relations between the Archbishop and the Rector became very strained. On hearing that Dr. Cullen was having inquiries made on his own initiative with a view to securing suitable professors, Newman wrote to him, protestingly :

August 14th, 1852.

It will never do, if things are done, or begin to be done from distinct sources of action. There must be Unity—nothing can be done without it. I cannot help being jealous of these initial inquiries, even on the part of your Grace, and for the simple reason, that unless your Grace undertakes everything, you will only lose time which can ill be spared . . . And what is true of these initial movements, is still more certain as regards the government of the nascent institution, when it first comes into operation.*

Newman was anxious and eager to get his professorial staff together without loss of time, and to set the work of the University going somehow; while Dr. Cullen, with his

* Cf. *My Campaign in Ireland,* pp. 271 and ff.

(D 700)   B 2

habitual caution, was adverse to sanctioning the details of
a scheme still in a state of immaturity until he was satisfied
as to their ultimate implications and possibilities.   Disagreements occurred, delays ensued, letters sometimes
remained unanswered, and Newman, disappointed and
chagrined, offered to resign.

At length some definite progress was made.   The
Rector was formally installed on the Feast of Pentecost
1854, and the University was ready to begin its work
in November of the same year.   At the same time
the beginnings of three Colleges of the University were laid
down.   These Collegiate Houses, as they were called, were
St. Patrick's at 86 St. Stephen's Green, St. Mary's at 6
Harcourt Street (the Rector's house), and St. Lawrence's
at 18 and 19 Harcourt Street.   On the Feast of
St. Malachy (3rd November), 1854, the University was
open for students in the faculties of Philosophy, Letters,
and Theology; and the young institution entered on its
career.

The worries endured by Newman at this period, owing
to Dr. Cullen's procrastinations, suspicions and inquiries,
are recounted in many of his private letters, and in *My
Campaign in Ireland*.   The grounds of the Archbishop's
caution and mistrust in his dealing with Newman have not
yet been published, but an explanation may be found in
Cullen's early training and in the policy and procedure of
Newman from the time of his appointment as Rector of the
University.

Newman was an Englishman, high-souled and patriotic
it is true, but yet an Englishman, proud of his country,
and full of faith in the destiny of his imperial race to rule
and govern.   Dr. Cullen, during his long residence in
Rome, had ample opportunities of learning how Englishmen rarely let slip an opportunity of forwarding their
country's interests.   In fact he had developed an instinctive distrust of Englishmen in all matters wherein the

interests of their country were concerned; and, as Newman was an intensely patriotic Englishman, he was, to Dr. Cullen's way of thinking, infected with the " *peccatum originis*," and, like the rest of his race, to be watched even while he was being trusted.

The truth is that Newman and Cullen had fundamentally opposed notions of what the scope and purpose of the Catholic University ought to be. With Newman the main thing was to have a Catholic university centre for the English-speaking world. Dr. Cullen would have the University a distinctively national institution—a centre of Irish tradition, culture, and learning. He was determined that the new institution should not become an instrument for the anglicisation of Ireland—a development that he thought he had serious reason to apprehend. This is clear from Cullen's unpublished correspondence; but, without drawing at length upon that abundant store of information, it will be sufficient to mention here a few pertinent facts.

1. Newman withdrew from the University in 1858, because, as he said, "the hope of the University being English as well as Irish was [then] at an end."*

2. The original staff of the University was composed largely of Englishmen, and Newman jealously resented any interference with his discretion in the selection of professors, lecturers and tutors.

3. He had vigorously endeavoured to secure that the University should be intimately connected with England by recruiting students (as well as professors) from among the Catholics in England.

4. He exerted all his efforts to have Cardinal Wiseman, Archbishop of Westminster, nominated first Chancellor; and Wiseman in turn had striven to have Newman made a bishop, so as to render him practically independent of the Irish episcopate. Newman himself has left it on record that he was much chagrined when he realised that the Irish

* Cf. *My Campaign in Ireland*. Intro., p. iv.

bishops alone, to the exclusion of their English brethren, were to be his ecclesiastical superiors during his term of office in Ireland.

5. The persistent efforts of Englishmen to gain a controlling influence in the University are attested by contemporary witnesses. From amongst others one may be selected. Dr. Quinn, a member of the University, and a friend of Newman's, writing to Dr. Cullen (November 6, 1858), numbers Newman " among those Englishmen who take it for granted they are the only people qualified to conduct the University." " For Newman," he adds, " I entertain great respect and regard, and would desire to see him continue Rector under certain circumstances, but it is my conviction that the interests of the University are in inverse ratio of present English influence."

At this infant institution, beset with the very many difficulties of its incipient life, but strong in hope of a successful development, young Walsh, then in his fifteenth year, entered on his studies in the sphere of higher education. Here he continued to give evidence of the application and ability of which he had shown such brilliant promise at the school in Harcourt Street. His course of studies covered a wide and varied field. He attended the Science lectures of Professors Henry Hennessey, F.R.S., Edward Butler, and W. K. O'Sullivan; and lectures in the Faculty of Philosophy and Letters by Professors David B. Dunne (Logic), Signor Marani (Italian), Abbé Schür (French and German Literature), Robert Ornsby (Greek and Latin Literature), James Stewart (Greek and Latin Languages), and Eugene O'Curry (Irish Archaeology). He studied with great industry and with marked success. He had a special taste for Mathematics. The *University Calendar* for 1856 records that in that year a mathematical exhibition was awarded to William J. Walsh. The exhibition, value for £25 and tenable for two years, was awarded for proficiency in the subjects of Euclid, Algebra, Plane Trigonometry and Conic Sections. During this time he resided in the Collegiate House of St. Lawrence; and was one of those who drew special praise from Newman in one of his reports :

Among the students of St. Lawrence's Collegiate House, meritorious from the first, are now to be found some of the most promising youths of the University.*

His time at the University almost coincided with Dr. Newman's term of office. He attended some of Newman's public lectures, and was present at the eight sermons preached by the Rector in the University Church between the time of its opening (Ascension Day, May 1, 1856) and Newman's resignation in 1858. His recollection of the sermons was that they were read by Father Newman in a clear musical voice, unimpassioned and well modulated, and that they were listened to with rapt attention by fashionable and cultured congregations. But beyond occasional conversations of an incidental nature he had little personal intercourse with the Rector. Sometimes, indeed, he was examined by Newman as to his proficiency in his studies, but these examinations were not searching and were very informal.

For the space of three years he continued his studies at the Catholic University. At the close of the session which ended in July 1858, when he had attained the grade of " Scholar," he left the University to take a decisive step which he had long been contemplating.

From an early age, when as a boy he used to serve Mass at SS. Michael and John's, he had conceived the idea of becoming a priest. In the atmosphere of his pious Catholic home, this growing purpose developed and strengthened, to the great satisfaction of his parents, who noted with quickening joy the first faint signs of the divine call, and

* *My Campaign in Ireland,* p. 69.

did all in their power to encourage and foster it. The boy himself was endowed with qualities that promised the realisation of their yet unexpressed hope. He was bright in manner, pious, talented, studious in habits, and upright in character; a most marked feature in him was an inborn purity of soul that found, perhaps, its most conspicuous manifestation in a loathing of all things coarse, whether in life or literature, and in a fastidious propriety of speech —traits that were characteristic of him all through life.

During his school days at Harcourt Street he became definitely convinced of his call to the priesthood, and, long before the completion of his studies at the University, his mind was definitely formed on the matter. His choice of a career was approved and encouraged by Dr. Quinn, the head of the House, who informed Archbishop Cullen of his young friend's purpose, and assured him that he had all the marks of a true vocation for the priesthood.

It was decided that young Walsh should be sent to Rome for his ecclesiastical studies, but when it was represented to the Archbishop that he was an only son, and that the long separation would be a severe trial to his parents, Dr. Cullen consented to his prosecuting his studies in Ireland. As the diocesan seminary of Dublin, Holy Cross College, Clonliffe, was not then quite ready for the reception of students, he was sent to commence his ecclesiastical course at St. Patrick's College, Maynooth, where on August 25, 1858, he matriculated in the Class of Logic.

His scholastic career at Maynooth was one of rare distinction. He has left a record of academic honours that has seldom been rivalled in that great college. Gifted with great powers of concentration and with remarkable physical endurance, he studied with great industry and diligence. His position as a student soon became prominent. His intellectual interests were many and various. He entered with enthusiasm into every department of the intellectual and social life of the college though he took little part in the outdoor amusements or physical exercises.

On one occasion his thirst for knowledge was very nearly attended by serious consequences. Among the professors of Maynooth at that time whose achievements shed lustre on the college, was Dr. Nicholas Callan, whose name is well known to scientists in connection with his discoveries in the departments of electro-magnetism and galvanic electricity. He constructed what was called " Callan's Coil," the forerunner of the Ruhmkorff Coil, which at the time was the most effective and inexpensive of all devices for producing a constant supply of electricity for purposes of light and chemical analysis. Mr. Walsh, always interested in Mathematics and Physics, used frequently to assist Dr. Callan in his experiments, and on the occasion of one of these experiments he had a narrow escape from death, through receiving a terrific shock from the electric coil.

But while his academic interests led him into many fields there was about him little of the dilettante. He was never satisfied with a superficial knowledge of a subject. It was characteristic of his thoroughness that, taking up the study of Irish shortly after his entrance to the college, he carried off the prize awarded annually for the best original essay in that language, though many of his competitors were native speakers and advanced students of the language. The College Calendars do not go back quite to the beginning of Dr. Walsh's student days, but in the available lists his name invariably occupies first place. He is *primus inter pares* except when he stands alone.

In 1863 he was ordained deacon, and in 1864 he had completed the fourth year of his theological course, but, as he had not yet reached the canonical age of twenty-four years, he could not be admitted to the priesthood. In the meantime he was called to pursue a course of higher theological studies within the College in the Dunboyne

Establishment. Here he devoted special attention to the study of Canon Law and of Hebrew. After two years of study in the Dunboyne Establishment he was called to the priesthood. His ordination took place on May 22, 1866, He was then in his twenty-sixth year.

One who was a fellow-student of Walsh's in those days described him to the present writer as follows. In stature he was below medium height; his frame was strong and well knit; his deportment and bearing dignified, and though not athletic he was active and agile in movement. When walking he leaned slightly forward, which gave to his gait a suggestion of eagerness; even at this time he showed a slight tendency towards a stoop which became quite perceptible in his later years. A fine massive head covered with thick black hair, and a broad, lofty forehead gave to his otherwise homely features an unmistakable air of distinction, while his grey-blue eyes looked out beneath thick bushy eyebrows, lighting up his countenance and imparting to it an expression of great intelligence. Endowed with a strong baritone voice, pleasant though not musical, he spoke with singular clearness of enunciation in an unemotional tone, relieved by the faintest trace of a lisp. He had a well-shaped mouth, regular teeth, a strong upper lip, rounded chin, a straight nose slightly too short, ears that were very small and shapely, hands smooth and soft and dimpled like a child's, with straight and beautifully shaped fingers. His highly-strung nervous constitution betokened great sensibility, but he had a firm control of his countenance; and, as his features were not mobile, his facial expression was not always a sure index to his thoughts and feelings. In moments of lighter mood and pleasant social intercourse he sometimes assumed a quizzical look, and on occasion he could almost emulate the feat of Piso, who could " fetch one of his brows up to his forehead, and bend the other down to his chin."

Always popular, though never a prime favourite with his

fellow-students, he was undoubtedly one of the most admired and respected of their body. His temperament was sanguine and his manner alert and somewhat impetuous. His naturally quick temper was kept under perfect control, and he carried himself with an air of reserve and quiet confidence. In company he was bright, and often buoyant, interesting and easily interested, a good talker and a good listener. The vein of his humour was not rich, it is true, and his mental texture showed but a pale shot of wit, yet he was quick to perceive and appreciate humour and wit in others; the ludicrous always appealed to him, and he was himself possessed of an impish playfulness. Though he was not without ambition to excel in matters of mind, conscious and perhaps a little vain of his talents, he was not at all inclined to be jealous of his student rivals, and it is worthy of note that his closest competitor for academic honours at Maynooth—Thomas J. Carr, afterwards Archbishop of Melbourne—was all through life one of his dearest friends.

Apart from his predilection for music, he had few aesthetic tastes. Music was to him a source of never-failing interest, and of high-class music he had early acquired a good critical appreciation. But in the pictorial and plastic arts he was something of a philistine : he did not " envy poets and painters and artificers in works wherein he had not a vein to excel." It was so with him all through life. While he would linger with delight over Murillo's ragged boys or Jan Steen's boisterous topers, he would scarcely look at a Ruysdael or a Metzu, and would do little more than glance at a Fra Angelico, a Dürer, or even a Raphael. He was stirred much more by intellectual argument than by appeal to imagination; and while he could be roused to enthusiasm over a mathematical conundrum or legal argument, or the decodification of a cypher-system, the reading of the choicest imaginative literature left him cold. Aristotle he preferred to Plato, and it is scarcely an overstatement to say that he preferred a blue-book to either.

He gave early and convincing evidence of great versatility. He had a rare capacity for rapidly acquiring a grasp of abstruse and difficult subjects or complicated schemes. His orderly and methodical mind was receptive rather than constructive, and with his patient and persistent diligence he was constantly stocking his ready and retentive memory with fresh and varied stores of knowledge. He was deeply interested and well informed in mathematical science. He became an expert canonist and a theologian of repute. He had a turn for the positive sciences and for the classical and modern languages; later he displayed such a capacity for administrative work that it might have been all-in-all his study. But, though his mental equipment was rich and elaborate, he seems to have lacked inspiration; he had little gift of fancy, and his literary style was devoid of charm. Long afterwards, when he had become Archbishop and was in the full maturity of his powers, John Morley said of him, " though he was very talented, Dr. Walsh was not gifted with genius, notwithstanding his capacity for taking pains."

CHAPTER II

PROFESSOR OF THEOLOGY

MR. WALSH remained at Maynooth after his ordination to complete his course of higher ecclesiastical studies in the Dunboyne Establishment. During this period he continued to apply himself to his studies with unremitting energy. His exuberant vitality found vent in study. Amongst a group of brilliant students he gained the prize offered for a theological essay; the subject was *De Infallibilitate Romani Pontificis*. He excelled his colleagues in Sacred Theology, Canon Law, Ecclesiastical History, and Hebrew. During this period he was called upon from time to time to act as lecturer in the theological faculty of the College, in the absence of Professor Henry Neville. When Dr. Neville resigned his chair in 1867, the student-lecturer who had been his capable substitute was marked out by common consent as his worthy successor, and on October 23, 1867, Mr. Walsh was appointed by the College Trustees to the Chair of Moral and Dogmatic Theology. It is noteworthy that the appointment was made without *concursus* —a very exceptional procedure in those days. Thus, in his twenty-seventh year, he took his place on the professorial staff as the colleague of his former teachers and superiors.

At the time of Mr. Walsh's promotion to a theological chair, the faculty included four professors who conducted the ordinary course of Dogmatic and Moral Theology in the college. Amongst them were two at least whose reputation as theologians had travelled beyond Ireland, and whose names were held in reverent esteem by generations of Maynooth students. These were the Rev. Patrick

Murray and the Rev. George Crolly. Dr. Murray was the author of a treatise *De Ecclesia* which was used extensively and highly prized by the Fathers of the Vatican Council. The work was in its day a promptuary on the subject, and is still a valuable book of reference. Dr. Crolly was then engaged on his treatises, *De Justitia et Jure* and *De Injuria et Restitutione*, which were published in three large volumes—a work of outstanding merit for its informative character and exhaustive treatment of the principles of justice and their application to the various forms of contract in English law; but unfortunately its utility was lessened by a lack of order and scientific method which was calculated to baffle the most patient and diligent student. The fourth professor of the group, the Rev. Gerald Molloy, was interested more in the positive sciences than in theology. He devoted his attention chiefly to treating of the relation of theology to physical science. He was a man of very orderly mind, gifted with considerable literary power and a faculty for expounding an abstruse and complex subject in charming, simple language. He was pragmatic in manner, and was known among the students as " the Expounder." His books, *Geology and Revelation* and *Gleanings in Science*, may be read with interest and profit even at the present day. For over a quarter of a century his popular lectures on the discoveries of science delighted cultured audiences in Dublin and throughout the British Isles. Subsequent to his leaving Maynooth he became Rector of the Catholic University, and at the time of his death he was also Vice-Chancellor of the Royal University of Ireland.

In those days at Maynooth, the practice among the members of the theological faculty was for each professor to lecture in both Dogmatic and Moral Theology, devoting to each subject a prescribed portion of each year. Mr. Walsh commenced his professorial work in 1867 by expounding the fundamental principles of Morals in the

tract *De Actibus Humanis*; and from 1867 till 1871 he
lectured on the tracts *De Actibus Humanis*, *De Conscientia*,
De Legibus, *De Peccatis*, and on the dogmatic tract *De
Locis Theologicis*.

He was a capable and successful professor. His strong clear
voice could be heard distinctly in every part of the largest
lecture-hall in the college; his impressive personality, no less
than the clearness of his exposition, secured for him the
respect of the students; his style as a lecturer was vigorous
and stimulating, and his enthusiasm and delight in his work
were infectious. His lectures were always prepared with
scrupulous care, and his numerous references to authorities
and copious quotations from the great theological classics
evinced wide reading and an intimate acquaintance with the
literature of his subject.

He was vigilant and tactful in dealing with his auditory,
quick to perceive among his listeners any signs of flagging
interest, which he met by deftly introducing apposite and
carefully thought-out illustrations. Thus he managed to
revive and stimulate interest. Rarely, if ever, did he
resort to anecdote, and he was seldom lured away from
his theme by the interrogations of insidious questioners.
He was a strong believer in opportune iteration of the
question under discussion, and throughout his lectures he
aimed at keeping the attention of his students fixed on
certain pivotal positions of the particular tract or treatise
he was expounding, and these propositions recurred with the
frequency and prominency of the *leit motif*, linking his
themes and theses into one harmonious whole.

Earnest and conscientious in everything concerning his
work, he was capable of great concentration of mind, and
of intense and sustained effort. *Quodcunque facere potest
manus tua, instanter operare* (Eccles. 9, 10) was the motto
inscribed in many of his notebooks at this time, and in every
work which he undertook throughout his life it was his
custom to " do it with might." Firmly convinced that

there is no royal road to learning, and that knowledge is attainable by industry alone, he imitated Sir Walter Scott (with whose works he had an intimate acquaintance) in his " infinite diligence in the work of preparation."

It was his practice to write out beforehand a scheme of each lecture, and to have prepared a number of lithographed copies sufficient to be distributed to the students of his classes. As he wrote a neat and well-formed hand the lithographs were easily legible. Soon he began to enlarge the schemata by filling in the outlines; and later he had the " Notulae" of his lectures printed, the pages containing the day's work frequently arriving by the morning train of the same day from his printers in Dublin. Most of the students found the schemata helpful as a preparation for the developed treatment of the particular subject by the professor in the class-hall. Others, however, especially those who were not dowered with great ability or energy, set little store by the schemata. Before the lithographed or printed notes were introduced, these weaker men used to deplore their hapless lot, condemned as they were to the drudgery of constant note-taking. But for many of them the " Notulae" provided a still more trying task—so many were the headings, divisions and subdivisions, references and cross-references. While making due allowance for Lazyman's criticism, it was not without a substratum of truth; for Professor Walsh's passion for exhaustiveness in treating a subject oftentimes led him into excessive minuteness and attention to detail. All, however, agreed that he had an unusual faculty for clear, orderly exposition; and even on the most difficult questions of theology and philosophy he generally made himself easily intelligible to the average student. Outside of lecture he was easily accessible to his students, and was sympathetic to all who consulted him in their difficulties. But he had always a marked predilection for brilliant men. Intellectual ability he always held in the highest esteem; and one of his strongest terms of disparage-

ment was " stupid." Indeed it was facetiously remarked
that stupidity was the only *peccatum irremissibile* in
Dr. Walsh's eyes.

In 1872 a slight change was introduced in the system of
the theological school. Thenceforward two of the professors
conducted all the classes in Moral Theology throughout the
entire academic year, while the other two dealt altogether
with Dogma, the lecturers in Morals in one year becoming
the lecturers in Dogmatics in the following year; so that
each professor lectured in Dogmatic and Moral Theology in
alternate years. In 1872 the classes in Dogma fell to
Mr. Walsh, the subject matter being *De Vera Religione, De
Locis Theologicis, De Ecclesia et Romano Pontifice.* At
this time he began to write a treatise on Apologetics, but
soon abandoned the work. In the year 1873-74 he lectured
once more on the fundamental principles of Morals. It was
then that he began to prepare a Latin treatise on *Human
Acts.* Towards the end of 1874 he received the degree of
Doctor of Divinity from the University of Propaganda.

When the treatise on *Human Acts* was finished, he had
it printed with a view to publication. Not being satisfied,
however, with the order he had followed, and desirous
especially to improve the latinity of the book, he carefully
revised the printed sheets with the assistance of two of his
colleagues, re-wrote the treatise in its entirety, and had it
printed anew. The work was published in 1880 and met
with a favourable reception by qualified critics. In the
opinion of Fr. Lehmkuhl, the distinguished Jesuit professor
and author of the well-known *Theologia Moralis*, Walsh's *De
Actibus Humanis* was "Opusculum ... in quo [auctor] acute
et profunde diversas quaestiones pertractat."* Cardinal
Manning considered it to be both " learned and minute."
Cardinal Newman called it "a learned and serviceable addition to other works on the subject." " What has struck me
at once," he added, "which though accidental and secondary

* *Theol. Moralis.* Ed. ix., vol. ii, p. 854.

is a real merit (and I hope not an impertinence in an old
man to notice) is that your latinity is very good."—(Dec. 1,
1880). When Cardinal McCabe was giving permission to
affix his *Imprimatur* to the work, he wrote to its author :

> You can put my Imprimatur on your *Human Acts*. I
> was going to say, on all your acts, but that might be too
> large a range to take . . . as yet.—(Oct. 15, 1880).

Dr. McCabe personally presented the book to Pope Leo
XIII, soon after its publication. The Pope availed himself
of the occasion of the presentation to make minute inquiries
about the author, the college, and its curriculum. Writing
to Dr. Walsh from Rome on December 8, 1880, Dr. McCabe
says :

> On Sunday evening I presented your book to the Holy
> Father who inquired . . . what your course is, how many
> professors are in the college, how far Maynooth is from
> Dublin, do I often go to the college, and how the professors
> stand towards me. When he heard that the *Summa* [of
> St. Thomas Aquinas] was adopted as the text-book, he
> asked me was there any difficulty in having it accepted, and
> he seemed very pleased when I told him there was none.

The interests and activities of Professor Walsh were not
confined to the peculiar matter of the lecture-hall. Even
before he was called upon to share officially in the administration of the college he took a deep and active interest in
promoting the study and the proper rendering of the sacred
music and of the ecclesiastical chant. When the college
organist was absent—as sometimes happened—Mr. Walsh
was always ready to take his place at the organ. Later,
when he was President of the college, he compiled and
published (1885) a *Grammar of Gregorian Chant* for the use
of the students. It was a plainly-worded exposition of the
principles of the ecclesiastical chant, together with a collection of liturgical chants for use at High Mass, Vespers,
Compline, and on various special occasions. Many years
afterwards, when he had become Archbishop of Dublin, he

prepared an edition of the Requiem Chant for the use of his priests.

During his years as professor, Mr. Walsh was one of the favourite confessors with the students of the college. One is scarcely prepared to hear of the eager young professor being selected as spiritual director by a number of the students, and of his taking a deep paternal interest in fostering their piety and moulding their character. Yet such is the description given of him by not a few venerable clerics, hoary-headed now, with the frosts of many winters on their heads and their brows furrowed by the harrow of time, who in reminiscent mood recount tales of the kindly confessor who, in the seventies of the last century, smoothed away the wrinkles of care from their brow, assisted them in their difficulties and scruples, and confirmed them in their vocations to the priesthood.

Almost from the time of his ordination he was a regular contributor to the theological reviews, to the *Irish Ecclesiastical Record* in particular. For that review he acted as expert adviser on the theological questions submitted to the editor for discussion and solution. He had a flair for journalism, and he soon became a skilled controversialist. Indeed he revelled in controversial discussions and sometimes prolonged them unduly. Many of the theological questions mooted anonymously in the papers of the *Record* during this period were the products of his pen. Generally, however, he preferred to write over his own name, being conscious of his power and anxious to come under public notice, for, as Tacitus says of Mucianus, " he had the showman's knack of attracting attention to anything he would say or do." In controversy he was skilful and formidable; on occasion he could be aggressive and scathing. He wielded with skill the weapons of his warfare, often selecting the club of mace in preference to the rapier, in his controversial combats. At times, of course, he received a Roland for his Oliver, but he took his punishment with a good grace and returned to the attack with undiminished courage.

The quiet tenor of his academic life at Maynooth was interrupted for a while in the July of 1875, when he was called on to give evidence in a famous lawsuit which attracted widespread notice at the time. The case—described by Mr. Justice Barry as " A great Irish Ecclesiastical Cause"—concerned a series of actions for libel and slander instituted in the civil courts by the Rev. Robert O'Keeffe, Parish Priest of Callan in the diocese of Ossory, against Cardinal Cullen, Dr. Walsh (Bishop of Ossory) and his Vicar-General, and other ecclesiastics. In the last of the series of legal actions—*O'Keeffe* v. *McDonald*—Dr. Walsh was called on to give evidence as an expert witness in Canon Law. The trial, which was a remarkable one in itself, was an event of paramount importance in Dr. Walsh's career. The manner in which he gave his evidence, as well as the acumen and scholarship that he displayed, earned for him a name as canonist and theologian, and placed him thenceforward in an outstanding position before the Irish public, both lay and clerical. The account of this famous cause, which exercised such a decisive influence on Dr. Walsh's career, we reserve for subsequent pages.

In the autumn of the same year (1875) the Second Plenary Synod of the Irish Church convoked since the Reformation was held at Maynooth. Cardinal Cullen, who had presided at the First Plenary Synod held at Thurles in 1850, was again deputed by the Holy See to summon the Synod and preside at its deliberations. The sessions of the Synod lasted from Monday, August 30, till Monday, September 20. Dr. Walsh, who accompanied Dr. Moran, Bishop of Ossory, as his theological adviser, was appointed by the Fathers to act as one of the Secretaries of the Synod. He was present at all the Sessions and General Congregations, and had a considerable part in drafting the Statutes.

One chapter at least—the chapter *De Vicariis Generalibus et Foraneis* (Cap. xx.)—was written by him under peculiarly pressing circumstances. When the question of the offices of Vicar-General and Vicar-Forane came up for discussion there was considerable disagreement among the bishops as to the form in which the statutes dealing with the matter should be drawn up. It was finally decided to refer the matter to the Cardinal, who undertook to submit to the bishops on the following morning an outline on which it was hoped agreement would be reached. After dinner that evening the Cardinal consulted with Dr. Walsh about the subject and invited his assistance. Dr. Walsh set to work at once; he wrote the whole chapter and prepared lithographed copies for each of the prelates, completing his task about 4 a.m. on the following morning. When the draft was submitted to the bishops the same morning it met with unanimous approval.

Drs. Walsh and Molloy were entrusted with the duty of keeping a record of the proceedings of the Synod and of compiling an accurate précis of the discussions on the various topics dealt with. Of the very full summary of these discussions—which at times were very lively—and of the divergences of opinion that were occasionally expressed, very little trace will be found in the printed *Acta* published along with the Statutes of the Council. Almost the only inkling of divergence of view recorded in the *Acta* is Dr. McHale's protest against the treatment of Irish in the Catholic University.

Dr. Walsh's work at the Synod enhanced the reputation he had lately gained by his evidence at the O'Keeffe trial. So impressed were the members of the Synod by his ability that he became the theological adviser to many of the Irish bishops, and from that time he was frequently engaged in correspondence on questions of morality and Canon Law.

Of this extensive correspondence one sample shall be

referred to here, as of special interest. It concerned a
subject which was later to claim much of his attention—the
question of Irish land tenure. The correspondence dealt
with the morality of certain reforms of the system of land
tenure in Ireland which were being advocated by Isaac
Butt in 1876-'77. Butt was pressing for the amendment of
Gladstone's Land Act of 1870, and was especially insistent
on the extension of what is known as the Ulster Custom* to
Irish tenants generally. So revolutionary, however, and of
such doubtful justice did Butt's programme seem in the
eyes of Dr. Moriarty, Bishop of Kerry, that he felt that he
ought to inhibit his clergy from taking part in the meetings
which were being held in his diocese in support of that
programme. Before taking such a serious step he wished
to ascertain Dr. Walsh's views on the morality of the question at issue. Dr. Moriarty wrote (January 23, 1877) :

You have seen how many priests at meetings and elections
go in for what is commonly called Butt's Land Bill. Now,
the morality of this proceeding seems to be very doubtful.
One part of this Bill purposes to take from the landlord the
right he now possesses of selling a tenancy, or call it the
goodwill, of a farm, on acceptance of a fine, which is now
offered by bidders to very large amounts, and to transfer
that right and advantage to the occupying tenant. I
would admit, of course, that if public policy—the *salus
reipublicae*—demanded such an expropriation it might be
done *vi alti dominii*, but with full compensation, of which
no mention is made or notion entertained. The most
Radical political writers, such as J. S. Mill, when advising
such a transfer of property, stipulate for compensation.
And the notion of *altum dominium* I have gathered from
Theology supposes the same, unless in the absolute necessity of the Commonwealth.
I put my argument in practical shape : It would not be
competent for the legislature to take from the Ulster
tenant the right he now possesses to sell his tenancy, and
to transfer that right to the Ulster landlord. Why should
it then be competent for the legislature to take the same

* For meaning of " Ulster Custom " see p. 97 *infra*.

right from the Munster landlord, and transfer it, without compensation, to the Munster tenant ?

Mind, I would admit that property in land may be fairly restricted by the State, and the contracts concerning it subjected to conditions, especially as, with us, these contracts are not really free on one side. But why give to the tenant the right, unlimited, of taking the highest price he can get, though he has not acquired that right by purchase or prescription ?

It pains me to see priests without any reflection taking up every project set forth by the newspapers, or by men as ignorant of political economy as they are of theology. Yet, they may be right and I may be wrong. I ask your opinion, even glad that I were wrong. Though I confess that I do not like the position of antagonism taken by the priests.

Dr. Walsh sent a lengthy reply to the Bishop (February 7, 1877) :

I know very little about the Land Question in its economic or social aspects, and almost everything I hear or read about it, from time to time, brings out some phase of it for which I was altogether unprepared. So that I can have but little confidence in the few opinions I have formed about it.

I do not know the provisions of what they call " Butt's Land Bill." But as he prides himself on being able to frame his proposals, no matter how advanced, on principles more or less conservative, I should be surprised at his putting forward any Bill that could not at least with some probability be cleared of the charge of Communism.

I believe, however, that he does propose to establish *Fixity of Tenure* by means of leases for ever, at rents which, though variable in accordance with the varying market prices of the various articles of farm produce, would be fixed by a Tribunal other than the landlord and his agent.

If this be his proposal, it would in my opinion amount to a transfer from the landlord to the tenant of property which is *pretio aestimabile*. And—if, as I understand, the Bill proposes to do this without making any direct compensation to the landlord for the portion of his property which is taken from him, I think it equally beyond question that it is at variance with the principles of justice.

But then I would add, that as far as I can see, it is only a question of degree, and by no means one of principle, between the Act passed by the Gladstone Ministry and the Bill now proposed by Butt.

I never could understand how the Gladstone Bill was accepted so quietly by the landlords of the Gladstone Ministry. The Act, no doubt, leaves it open to a landlord to evict any tenant to whom he has not voluntarily given a lease; but it obliges a landlord to pay a large sum of money to the tenant (and this for mere disturbance, over and above the question of improvements) if he chooses to exercise his right. I cannot see any difference—except in degree—between the two measures. It is, no doubt, an exercise of the *altum dominium* to make over to the tenant the permanent right of occupancy. But it is equally an exercise of it to oblige the landlord to choose between *relinquishing that right and paying to the tenant* a large sum of money for the exercise of it. Yet, in the Gladstone Bill no compensation was provided for the landlords of Ireland.

Now, let us see is there any way in which Mr. Gladstone's Bill can be cleared of the charge of being a measure of confiscation. I know only one—the way indicated by Butt himself in that most interesting tract of his, the *Irish Querist*, a copy of which I send Your Lordship. Look especially at questions 10-13, 21-2, 36-9, 43, 47-9, 77-83, 94, 146, 159, 212-4, 250, 310, 316-9, 324-6. I cannot even conceive any other justification for what was done by the late Ministry. And if their Act has failed in accomplishing its avowed object, and if that object can be attained without introducing into the legislation any new *principle*, why should not the same sort of compensation be deemed sufficient in the case of the new measure also?

All this on the hypothesis that the Gladstone Land Act was not a measure of confiscation.

But, as I believe that it was, I should not make much use of the view that I have put forward, except as an *argumentum ad hominem* against liberal landlords who gave their support to the late Ministry in passing that Act, or who in some way approved of it. I would, however, suggest it as worth considering whether if this view be fairly sustainable, much could be made of the conduct of ecclesiastics advocating the Butt Land Bill, seeing that bishops and priests all over the country have been for years publicly extolling what Gladstone has done in this respect,

My own opinion—so far as I have any settled opinion on the merits of the question itself—is that no Land Act could be regarded as consonant with the principles of justice which would not give the landowners *direct* compensation as in the case of land taken for the making of railways. No one surely would dream of taking land for that purpose without compensation, on the ground that the advantage of having a railway in the neighbourhood would *raise* the letting value of the *farms all through the district*, still less on the ground that the landowner would derive sufficient compensation for the *general improvement* and *increased prosperity* of the *whole country resulting from the introduction of railways*.

Again, I should not think any measure justifiable which would make this transfer of the property from landlords to tenants *universally* throughout the country. To give fixity of tenure to those who happen to possess the land just now would be in fact to give a very substantial premium to the people whose dealings in land have brought about those very evils which a Land Bill would be required to remedy. *Melior est conditio possidentis* is a very excellent principle, but there are limits to its application.

But *exceptis excipiendis*—and I think this exception would be a very substantial one—I do not see why Parliament, on the principles laid down by Gladstone, would not be fully justified in enacting—and consequently every person in the community calling on Parliament to enact—a measure which would on the plan of the Ulster Tenant Right, or in some similar way, secure the occupying and working tenant in possession of his holding.

As to the compensation, it seems to me that it ought to be paid by the people who are directly to benefit by the new measure. When a railway is to be made, the State does not make the requisite compensation to the landowners; the railway company pays them, and the travelling community subsequently pays the railway. So, too, if the occupying tenants are to get this great advantage of Fixity of Tenure —which on the showing of its advocates will unquestionably be a most substantial boon to them—they ought unquestionably to pay for it. The means of doing so could easily be provided by a loan, on the principle of the Board of Works' Loans, or those arranged by the " Bright Clauses" of the Gladstone Act,

It is only when limited in this way that I should think that any measure such as the one proposed, could be regarded as just, or as a fair subject for advocacy, whether in or out of Parliament.

THE famous case of *O'Keeffe* v. *McDonald*, which was the occasion of bringing Dr. Walsh's name into prominence throughout Ireland and Great Britain, was tried at Wicklow in July, 1875. The case, however, had a long antecedent history, which it will be necessary to recall in order to understand the issues that were involved and the great public interest that it aroused. In view of the remarkable character of this celebrated case, and of its important bearing on the subject of this memoir, it is right to tell the story at some length.

The Rev. Robert O'Keeffe was a parish priest of the diocese of Ossory who had been promoted to the parochial charge of Callan in 1863, by the Bishop, the Most Rev. E. Walsh. He was a man of considerable ability, a capable and zealous pastor, active and energetic, but of a somewhat bustling and restless temperament. From the time of his appointment as parish priest he had made many improvements in his parish, especially in the matter of education. He had introduced the Christian Brothers, and established the Callan Academy, a secondary school for boys; and, anxious to make provision for the better education of the girls of his parish, he decided on establishing at Callan a religious community of teaching Sisters, members of the Congregation of the Sacred Heart of Mary, who were then living in a convent at Béziers in the diocese of Montpellier.

Before the community could be canonically established in the parish, ecclesiastical discipline required the sanction of the Bishop of the diocese as a necessary condition precedent, and this sanction Bishop Walsh withheld. For reasons which seemed to him sufficient, the Bishop was strongly opposed to the introduction of the Sisters. This and other causes of disagreement led to much misunderstanding and various disputes between the parish priest and his bishop. The parish priest, who had obtained from the Sisters a sum of £500 or £600, which he had expended 'in fitting up Callan Lodge as a suitable residence for the community, endeavoured to have the Bishop's decision overruled at Rome, and strove in various ways to outwit and defeat the opposition and to carry through his own cherished project, but without success. Failing in these efforts, he resorted to bullying and worrying tactics to force the Bishop's consent, but the Bishop was adamant. Very strained relations ensued, and the tension was further heightened by the appointment as curate of Callan, of a Fr. Neery, between whom and Fr. O'Keeffe there existed an instinctive and deep-rooted antipathy.

A crisis soon arose. The Bishop, speaking officially to Fr. O'Keeffe in the presence of his two curates and a canon of the diocese about some of the matters of disagreement, used language which Fr. O'Keeffe considered slanderous, and for which, when writing to the Bishop on the following day, he demanded an apology. The Bishop in his reply informed Fr. O'Keeffe that the words of which he complained were devoid of any such offensive construction as he had chosen to put upon them. This repudiation by the Bishop did not satisfy Fr. O'Keeffe, who thereupon began his career of litigation in the civil courts by bringing an action against the Bishop for slander, claiming damages to the extent of £5,000. This was in May, 1869. Owing, however, to friendly intervention, this action was compromised. The Bishop undertook, for peace' sake, to reimburse Fr. O'Keeffe—and incidentally the Sisters—for the outlay of £500 incurred in repairing Callan Lodge, and also to pay him £50 to cover the costs that he had incurred in the action. The stipulated sums were paid over to Fr. O'Keeffe, and the action was withdrawn.

But, unfortunately, the troubles did not end here. Very shortly after, disputes broke out between Fr. O'Keeffe and his curates. Some injudicious statements made by the curates in the course of their Sunday addresses to the people gave him great offence. These statements were a public contradiction of an announcement made by Fr. O'Keeffe on the previous Sunday when he had assured the congregation that he had the approval of the Bishop for various projects in connection with the schools and some other parochial buildings. As a matter of fact the Bishop had not approved of the arrangements in question; but the method adopted by the curates in publishing this information was a decided indiscretion, and was calculated to give grave annoyance to the parish priest. Accordingly, Fr. O'Keeffe had recourse to the civil courts a second time.

He took an action for slander; but, curiously enough, he sued, not the curates who had spoken the alleged slander, but the Bishop, who, he assumed, had instigated them to make the offending statements. When the case came into court, in July 1870, it was clearly proved that the Bishop had not enjoined, though he might have allowed or authorised, the curates' statements; and Fr. O'Keeffe was nonsuited.*

For having impleaded his Bishop in the civil courts, Fr. O'Keeffe was suspended by the Vicar-General of the diocese, Dr. McDonald, in October 1870. The Vicar's letter, written on October 10, but not dated, ran :

In punishment for the action-at-law taken by you against the Right Rev. E. Walsh, Roman Catholic Bishop of Ossory, I, vested with the requisite power, do hereby suspend you from office.

* Cf. Baron Dowse's *Charge,* p. 59

To rectify the informality of the absence of date in his first letter, the Vicar addressed to Fr. O'Keeffe a second letter (October 13) in which he stated : " I repeat the sentence of your suspension."

To these communications Fr. O'Keeffe replied in vigorous fashion, repudiating Dr. McDonald's " insolent assumption of power" to suspend him, adding that " you must be very silly indeed to think that I can take your word for the absurd statement (that you had such power), or you must suppose me to be as ignorant as you appear to be yourself of the course of proceeding to be followed in the infliction of censures," and reminding him that " it is as true now as it was when written three hundred years ago, that :

> ' Man, proud man,
> Dressed in a little brief authority,
> Like an angry ape,
> Plays such fantastic tricks before high heaven,
> As make the angels weep.' "

Fr. O'Keeffe's letter wound up with a threat that, if Dr. McDonald or anyone else should assail him publicly on behalf of Bishop Walsh, he would print and publish certain letters written by Fr. O'Keeffe himself to Cardinal Cullen and others, wherein he charged Bishop Walsh with having for forty years led an infamous life of simony and nepotism, and with having slandered his predecessor.

Following up his letters of suspension of October 1870, the Vicar-General on November 17, formally cited Fr. O'Keeffe to appear before him " to show cause against being declared to have incurred, and being again visited by, the censures of the Church, or, failing to do so, to offer such satisfaction as will appear sufficient."

The citation was disregarded by Fr. O'Keeffe, who meanwhile had instituted civil actions for slander against his curates Frs. Walsh and Neery. The action against Fr. Walsh was to be tried in Dublin at the end of 1870. Dr. McDonald was cited as a witness in the case, and on receiving the subpoena commanding his presence he wrote to Fr. O'Keeffe (December 10, 1870) admonishing him that it was a violation of Canon Law to take a brother priest before a civil tribunal, and that, with a view to stopping such flagrant violation of ecclesiastical discipline, he commanded him to withdraw the case *Robert O'Keeffe* v. *John Walsh* from the civil court, " under pain of suspension *ab officio et beneficio* to be *ipso facto* incurred the moment your counsel begins to state the case to the court and jury." The cases against the curates were proceeded with, and damages for slander were awarded against them both.

As Fr. O'Keeffe had flouted and scoffed at the Vicar-General's suspensions of October and December 1870, and had failed to offer any justification of his conduct, or to appear in answer to the citation of November 17, 1870, Bishop Walsh, on January 11, 1871, suspended Fr. O'Keeffe in the form known as suspension *ex informata conscientia*. The Bishop's letter was in the following terms :

As you have disregarded the ordinary mode of procedure, I, after mature deliberation, send you hereby a suspension *ex informata conscientia ab ordine, officio et beneficio*. You are aware, that from this suspension there is no appeal : and that should you violate it, you will incur an irregularity.*

The reply, addressed to the Bishop on an open postcard, was terse and trenchant. It ran :—"The Rev. Mr. O'Keeffe can hold no private correspondence with a man who is capable of throwing his private and confidential letter on the table of a public court." The letter referred to was that of October 15, addressed by Fr. O'Keeffe to the Vicar-General, which contained the threat of exposure of simony, nepotism, and slander.

---

* Irregularitas est impedimentum canonicum prohibens ne quis clero adscribatur, vel ad ordinem superiorem ascendat, vel functiones ordinis suscepti exerceat. Hoc exercitium ordinum susceptorum prohibet irregularitas indirecte tantum et per consequens; directe et per se hoc praestat suspensio. (Cf. Suarez, B.P. vii, 402.)

In the early months of 1871, Fr. O'Keeffe found himself
in a very sea of troubles. One difficulty followed fast upon
another, but he faced them all with undaunted courage.
He had a lawsuit with Fr. Neery, a vigorous dispute with
the Commissioners of National Education, a voluminous
correspondence with the Prefect of Propaganda,* with
Cardinal Cullen and others. But the severest trial of all was
a schism which broke out among his people at Callan.

In the month of March 1871, the Bishop, in view of Fr.
O'Keeffe's continued disregard of ecclesiastical authority,
withdrew the curates from the parish church, and transferred them for the discharge of their duties to the church
of the Augustinian Order in Callan, which had been placed
at the disposal of the diocesan authority by the Superiors of
the Order during the continuance of the sad state of things
that had arisen. An open feud arose between the supporters
of these rival churches, and soon the town of Callan became
the scene of much confusion and even of riotous disorder.

Amidst all these anxieties, Fr. O'Keeffe did not lose sight
of the Vicar-General, and on June 10, 1871, he filed
an action for libel and slander against Dr. McDonald. The
alleged libel was held to have been contained in the
letters of October 1870, in which the Vicar-General had
stated : " I, vested with the requisite power, do hereby

---

* The Sacred Congregation of Propaganda (*de propaganda
fide*), a department of the Roman Curia, was established in 1622,
by the Constitution *Inscrutabili* of Gregory XV, to conduct the
work of the foreign missions. The congregation is administered
through a Cardinal Prefect, assisted by a Secretary, Under-
secretary, and several minor officials. The Congregation of
Propaganda has jurisdiction over " missionary territory "—i.e.,
over countries where the hierarchy is not established, or where,
owing to persecution, the normal work of the hierarchy is
impeded. Ireland, as well as England and Scotland, remained
subject to " Propaganda " down to 1908, when by the Constitution *Sapienti Consilio* of Pius X several countries were withdrawn from its jurisdiction.

As part of the same general scheme, the " College of Propaganda " was instituted by Urban VIII (1623—1644), for the
education for the priesthood of students from every nation, and
its management entrusted to the Congregation.

suspend you from your office," and again :—" I repeat the
sentence of your suspension"; the alleged slander was held
to have been contained in words spoken to divers persons
to the effect that " Fr. O'Keeffe has been suspended."

Owing, however, to a new and startling development in
the campaign, Fr. O'Keeffe did not pursue the action
against Dr. McDonald at this juncture. Cardinal Cullen,
armed with the fullest powers from Rome, was about to
take up the case against the parish priest of Callan; consequently, Fr. O'Keeffe abandoned for the time the contest
with the Vicar-General to measure swords with a more
formidable opponent.

Cardinal Cullen's association with the Callan troubles
dated back to August 1869. On hearing of the feud that
existed between Fr. O'Keeffe and his Bishop, and the
scandal that it occasioned, the Cardinal wrote to Fr.
O'Keeffe urging him to try and compose his differences with
the Bishop and set himself right with God and the Church,
and so prevent further scandal. Fr. O'Keeffe in reply
thanked the Cardinal for his letter and for "the fatherly
advice contained therein"; but he went on to inveigh
against the Bishop. " Your Eminence," he added, after he
had enumerated the shortcomings of the Bishop, " has
presumed the Bishop to be right and me to be wrong in the
difference that has occurred between us; I want to destroy
that presumption in your mind." Anxious to win the
Cardinal to his side, he suggested that His Eminence should
send a commissary to Callan to inquire into the true state
of affairs; even after his suspension by the Vicar-General
and by the Bishop he pressed the Cardinal to intervene.
Such intervention, however, even had he desired to intervene, was not within the ordinary competence of the
Cardinal.

In 1871 the Holy See directly intervened in the dispute.
On May 31 of that year, by order of Pope Pius IX, a
decree was issued to Cardinal Cullen, directing him to take

the case in hand and deal with it as delegate of the Holy
See. The decree invested him with the fullest powers, and
in addition, Pius IX, in a personal interview, conferred on
him all the power of the Pope himself to deal with the
matter either by way of paternal mediation or by a judicial
process, according to his discretion. On receipt of the
decree the Cardinal wrote to Fr. O'Keeffe that he was
" now in a position to attempt to restore peace" in Callan,
and that he would " make every effort to obtain so desirable
a result."

During the months of July and August Cardinal Cullen,
in a paternal and friendly way, and with great patience,
endeavoured to induce Fr. O'Keeffe to submit to his
Bishop. But as these efforts proved unavailing he wrote
on September 8 to Fr. O'Keeffe : " Much against my own
inclinations, I have been deputed by His Holiness to put
an end to the present state of things (in the parish of
Callan), and to repair, if possible, the evils produced by
recent feuds amongst the faithful.

" In obedience to the Supreme Pastor of the Church, I
will apply myself to this difficult task with a deep sense of
the responsibility placed upon me."

In reply Fr. O'Keeffe informed the Cardinal that he
required the removal of his two curates as a preliminary to
any inquiry into his conduct, or into the question of the
validity of the censures passed on him.

The Cardinal made another effort to compose matters
informally, and wrote again on October 2 :

The Holy See has given me the amplest powers in the
case, but I am anxious not to be placed under the necessity
of using them. Hence I would wish for a conference with
you on the matter.

Fr. O'Keeffe declined to take any part in such a conference, even with the Delegate of the Holy See, unless the
curates were first removed, declaring that " the humblest

man in the Church may sometimes have to say, as well as its Supreme Head, *non possum.*"

As all hopes of a settlement by informal negotiation had vanished, the Cardinal resolved on holding a regular judicial inquiry; and on October 21 he wrote to Fr. O'Keeffe informing him that he was about to send him a formal citation to appear before him at his house in Dublin, on Friday, October 27, with the view of inquiring :

(1) Whether Fr. O'Keeffe had incurred any suspension or excommunication ;

(2) Whether he had incurred irregularity ;

(3) Whether any, and if so, what penalty was to be inflicted upon him for having disregarded the ecclesiastical penalties previously inflicted, and

(4) Concerning other matters connected with the unhappy state of Callan.

Fr. O'Keeffe consented to appear before the Cardinal on the day appointed; and he wrote : " In order to save your Eminence's valuable time, as far as I can, *I send you my defence.*"

The inquiry took place at the Cardinal's house, Rev. Dr. Laurence Forde, " an expert canonist and a learned man in every way," acting as assessor to the Cardinal. The Cardinal commenced the inquiry by asking Fr. O'Keeffe if he had taken a civil action against his Bishop in 1869; if he had taken another action against the Bishop in 1870; if he had taken actions against the curates Frs. Walsh and Neery; and if he had commenced an action against the Vicar-General. To each of these questions Fr. O'Keeffe replied in the affirmative. Being questioned about the suspensions by the Vicar-General he replied that he had received the suspension, but that he did not observe it; that he despised and violated it, " and called the Vicar-General an ape and a fool, or some such words, and he deserved it."

After the various other pertinent matters had been fully investigated, Dr. Forde proposed, on his own initiative, that the whole case should be submitted for judgment to the Cardinal Prefect of Propaganda, and that, as it would take some weeks before a decision could be looked for, something should be done to restore calm and peace in Callan. With a view to securing that most desirable end, Dr. Forde suggested that Cardinal Cullen should remove the two curates, and that, pending a reply from Rome, Fr. O'Keeffe, while continuing to be parish priest, should withdraw from the parish for the purpose of making a retreat; that in his absence the administration of the parish should be entrusted to some worthy priest of the diocese of Ossory to be suggested by Fr. O'Keeffe himself, as one on whom he could rely to safeguard his interests; and that a mission, to be conducted by the Vincentian Fathers, should in the meantime be held in the parish.

This proposal was accepted by the Cardinal and by Fr. O'Keeffe, and the latter agreed to attend on the following morning to have the agreement embodied in a formal document. But when the morning came, Fr. O'Keeffe would not agree to leave the parish. When the Cardinal pointed out that that was an essential condition of the agreement, Fr. O'Keeffe replied that " it would take three regiments of Her Majesty's soldiers to put him out of Callan."

Dr. Forde's proposed arrangement broke down, and the session came to an end. Fr. O'Keeffe accepted the situation in cavalier fashion, which he describes himself : " I put my hand to my hat, I took my stick in my hand, I said ' Good-morning to you, my Lord Cardinal,' and I walked away." He did not again appear before the ecclesiastical tribunal, disregarding two formal canonical citations subsequently sent to him by the Cardinal.

Owing to his contumacious disregard of the citations, he was proceeded against *in absentia*. There was no difficulty in such a mode of procedure. The facts were of public notoriety, and had been admitted by Fr. O'Keeffe.   Fr.

O'Keeffe's defence was already in the Cardinal's hands. It set forth, under ten heads, the various grounds on which he based his contention that he had not transgressed the law of the Church (*a*) by instituting civil proceedings against the Bishop, the Vicar-General, and the curates, or (*b*) by disregarding the censures imposed on him by the Vicar-General and the Bishop.

The Cardinal, having considered the case in all its bearings, found that Fr. O'Keeffe had transgressed a disciplinary law of the Catholic Church forbidding an ecclesiastic to implead another ecclesiastic in the secular courts on an ecclesiastical matter; that by the common law of the Catholic Church such misconduct was a crime which made the delinquent liable to be visited with condign ecclesiastical punishment. The Cardinal subsequently felt it his duty to inflict on Fr. O'Keeffe for his repeated violations of ecclesiastical law and for his open resistance to ecclesiastical authority—even to the authority of the Holy See from whose tribunal he had contumaciously absented himself—the twofold penalty of suspension and deprivation of his parochial office.

The sentence inflicting these penalties was published at Callan, and the document containing the sentence was affixed to the door of the Augustinian Church in that town. By the publication of the Cardinal's sentence on November 26, 1871, Fr. O'Keeffe ceased to be parish priest.

As Fr. O'Keeffe disregarded the decree of suspension and deprivation, the Cardinal appointed a priest to administer the parish of Callan, and in the hope of withdrawing the faithful from attending the ecclesiastical ministrations of their former parish priest, he placed the parish church under interdict. The decree of interdict was published in Callan in December 1871.

Almost immediately after the publication of the Cardinal's decree of suspension and deprivation, Fr. O'Keeffe served his Eminence with a writ of libel, and, on December 3, he issued an appeal for funds to enable him to bear the costs of the contemplated legal proceedings. This appeal was published in several English newspapers, including the *Times*. It contained, *inter alia*, the following :—

I care not who blames me for seeking redress in one of the Queen's Irish Courts ... I have served a writ on Cardinal Cullen, and if I can provide the necessary funds, I shall certainly follow up the proceeding. My solicitor thinks the case will end in the House of Lords. I appeal to the public, therefore, Catholic and Protestant, for support. An attempt is made to introduce a discipline into the Irish Catholic Church which would make the laity the slaves of the clergy, by screening the latter from the consequences of their illegal acts, and which would make the clergy the slaves of the bishops by visiting them with the censures of the Church, if they dared remonstrate against episcopal tyranny. My cause is the cause of freedom from unjust and tyrannical laws, at least as far as these countries are concerned. To exempt the clergy from the jurisdiction of civil courts may suit the circumstances of other countries ; but in this free country the clergy generally would, I believe, themselves indignantly disclaim such privileges, even though they were not to be used against them, as has been attempted to be done in my case.

The Protestants of these countries, of course, on principle, care nothing for Papal excommunications ; yet Cardinal Cullen would maintain stoutly that the censures of the Bull *Apostolicae Sedis* (Oct. 12th, 1869) as of the *Bulla Coenae* affect them quite as much as they do the members of his own Church. His Eminence has been educated in a school of divinity where the *Bull of Adrian IV* in 1156, making over this island to Henry II of England, and the *Bull of Pius V* in 1570, absolving the people of these countries from their Oath of Allegiance to Queen Elizabeth, are held in reverence. Will the people of these free countries, Protestant or Catholic, I care not, tolerate a Papal assumption of temporal power in the 19th century, which our ancestors in the 16th denounced as an invasion of the rights of the monarch, and an unwarrantable tampering with the duties of the subject, and which the Irish of the 12th century resisted in arms, until reduced to subjection by the superior strength of the English nation ? If Cardinal Cullen succeeds in exempting the Irish clergy from the jurisdiction of the civil courts, what redress will a Catholic have if ill-treated by a priest or bishop?

My case proves that none need be expected, at least where the bishop is the delinquent; but, if I get from the public the support I require, I will baffle with ease all attempts to put the brand of slavery on the clergy or laity of the Irish Church.

The appeal met with a ready response. A committee of prominent sympathisers was formed for the purpose of promoting it. Amongst the members of the committee were several peers including the Earl of Harrowby and Earl Russell, some of the members of the House of Commons, and many prominent Protestant clergymen including such men as Dean Stanley of Westminster.

To ensure the success of the appeal no means of exciting the sympathies of the Protestant public was left untried. Fr. O'Keeffe was held up to the admiration of liberty-loving Englishmen as the courageous champion of British law—a brave man assailed for his championship of that law by an overbearing prelate, a Cardinal of the Church of Rome, whose aim it was to curtail the jurisdiction of the Queen's courts by withdrawing from their control the bishops and clergy of the Catholic Church of Ireland, who were thenceforward to be subject only to the jurisdiction of ecclesiastical tribunals set up for the administration in Ireland of the Canon Law of Rome—in fact, a new Papal aggression had begun.

Fr. O'Keeffe himself in a letter to the *Times* (October 28, 1872), did not shrink from declaring that the only ecclesiastical offence with which he had been charged, and for which he had been punished under the Canon Law by Cardinal Cullen, was that he was faithful to his "Oath of Allegiance," and had refused " to acknowledge the temporal supremacy of the Pope." This seemed to many to open up a prospect no less alarming for the laity than for the clergy; that it should be so regarded could be in no way displeasing to Fr. O'Keeffe, for at a later stage of the case we find him writing, in an appeal for further subscriptions : " If might can overpower right in my case, *what subject of this realm can say that he lives in a free state?*"

The appeal succeeded in bringing in a sum of well over £1,500. This sum, together with £500 which the Sisters of Béziers had advanced, and other monies subsequently subscribed, was all spent before the end of the action against Cardinal Cullen.

Fr. O'Keeffe, having obtained the requisite funds, took steps at once to follow up the proceedings against the Cardinal Delegate. He impleaded the Cardinal in the civil courts. The action began on February 26, 1872, and lasted for three years. The grounds of Fr. O'Keeffe's legal action were the two ecclesiastical sentences that had been published in Callan by direction of the Cardinal. Alleging them to be libels, he claimed damages, setting forth his claim under four heads or counts. Under each count he claimed £2,500 damages—in all £10,000.

Three of the counts dealt with the sentences of suspension and deprivation. The fourth dealt with the interdict.

The first count set out that " the suspension conveyed that Fr. O'Keeffe had been guilty of such conduct as to render him unfitted to discharge the duties of his office of Parish Priest of Callan." The innuendo put upon the sentence of deprivation was that " it conveyed that Fr. O'Keeffe was not fit to fill the office of Parish Priest, and had so misconducted himself as to render himself unfitted for the said office, and that he ought to be deprived of the same."

The second count dealt with the sentence of suspension only, the innuendo being that Fr. O'Keeffe had been " legally" suspended.

In the third count, the two sentences of suspension and deprivation were set out simply as libellous in themselves, without any innuendo.

In the fourth count, which dealt with the decree putting

the parish church under interdict, there were innuendoes to
the effect that the interdict, as worded, conveyed " that
Fr. O'Keeffe was a person who disregarded the rules and
discipline of the Catholic Church, and refused to be bound
by the same, and that he was legally suspended."

The Cardinal's defence was a denial in all four counts.
He pleaded that the words complained of as libellous were
not written or published by him; that they were not written
or published in the defamatory sense imputed to them; and
that they were not libels. The effect of these general
denials was to put upon the plaintiff the *onus* of proving the
fundamental facts of the case. In addition to these
" general defences" there were two " special defences" put
in plea. The special defences were, that the words complained of were " privileged" communications, and that the
words were " justified."

It may be well to explain the legal meaning of a
plea of " privilege" and of a plea of " justification," in
reference to the law of libel. A communication is " privileged" if its subject-matter be one in which the person
making the communication has a legitimate interest, or in
reference to which he has a duty—legal, religious, or moral
—to discharge, and if, moreover, the communication is
made to somebody having either a duty to perform in the
matter or a legitimate interest in it. To sustain a plea of
" privilege" a defendant need not prove that the communication complained of is true; but he must prove not only
that the communication in question was made on a
" privileged occasion," but also, that, in making it,
he was acting " *bona fide*, without malice, and
believing the same to be true." " Privilege" so
understood is a good defence to an action for libel.
" Justification" in the legal sense simply means that the
statement complained of as defamatory is true. It is not
necessary to show that there was provocation or any special
circumstances to justify the defendant in publishing the

defamatory matter. If the truth of the statement, no matter how defamatory, can be proved by evidence, the statement is " justified," and the defence to an action for libel is complete. Either " justification" or " privilege" is a complete defence.

The Cardinal's special defence, then, was a plea of " privilege" on all four counts, and a plea of "justification" on counts two, three, and four. "Justification" was not pleaded on the first count, the reason apparently being that the language of the innuendo put in that particular count on the sentence of deprivation was rather strong, and might be taken to refer to " misconduct" of a kind that was not at all imputed to Fr. O'Keeffe.

The Cardinal, in effect, undertook to prove (*a*) that throughout the entire case he had acted with proper authority; that in suspending Fr. O'Keeffe, in depriving him of his benefice, and in placing the parish church under interdict he was acting legally; that in order to carry out the Papal Commission with which he had been entrusted it was his " duty" to publish the sentences of suspension, deprivation, and interdict; that he had an " interest" in doing so; and that he had published these sentences " *bona fide,* without malice, and believing the same to be true." He also undertook to prove alternatively (*b*) that Fr. O'Keeffe was a person who had disregarded the rules and discipline of the Catholic Church; that by so doing he had made himself liable to the punishment of suspension and deprivation; that, in fact, he had been legally suspended and deprived; and that the parish church had been legally placed under interdict.

Fr. O'Keeffe's counsel contended that the Court could take no cognisance of the provision of the Canon Law forbidding an ecclesiastic to implead another ecclesiastic in a civil court on an ecclesiastical matter, because, as such provision was an attempt to oust the jurisdiction of the civil courts, it was contrary to public policy and illegal.

This contention failed; for the court decided that the Catholic Church in these countries—being in the eye of the law a tolerated Church, or society composed of members voluntarily associated together, professing the same religion—is competent to make regulations for enforcing discipline within its own body. The court also decided that the rule prohibiting ecclesiastics from impleading one another is in no way immoral, or against the public good, or illegal.

The court, at the same time, laid down that no ecclesiastical prohibition could oust the jurisdiction of a court of law. A law of the Church might prohibit ecclesiastics from bringing a particular class of cases into a civil court of law; but if an ecclesiastic, in violation of that prohibition, did bring such a case into court, the court would be in no way fettered in its action by such a prohibition. At the same time, a court would not ignore the existence of such a regulation : it would inquire if such a prohibition existed, and if it existed the court would take cognisance of it.

With regard to the counts (2 and 4) in which it was set out that Fr. O'Keeffe had been " legally suspended and deprived," his counsel construed the words as meaning " suspended and deprived according to the *laws of the realm*," in the sense that the suspension and deprivation were valid and binding according to those laws, and should be enforced by the civil court, if the ecclesiastical superior were to appeal to the civil judge to carry into effect the sentence of the ecclesiastical judge. The Cardinal's lawyers accepted that meaning of "legally suspended and deprived"; and though they might fairly have held that " legally suspended" meant suspended according to the rules of the Catholic Church, for certain reasons they did not choose to do so.

Fr. O'Keeffe's counsel then proceeded to argue that, as the Cardinal, all through the case, had been acting, not in virtue of his ordinary jurisdiction as Archbishop of the ecclesiastical province of Dublin, but in virtue of a jurisdiction delegated to him by the Pope, such a jurisdiction could not be regarded by a court of English Law as of effect for any purpose whatever, for it was a jurisdiction delegated by the Pope in contravention of a statute* enacted in the reign of Queen Elizabeth, which made unlawful any exercise of Papal jurisdiction within the realm.

The court, composed of four judges sitting *in banco*, by a majority of three to one, held that the statute of Elizabeth had not been " even impliedly" repealed, and that consequently the jurisdiction delegated to the Cardinal by the Holy See had been delegated to him contrary to the law of the realm, so that nothing done by him in the exercise of that jurisdiction within the realm could be said to have been done " legally."

The effect of this decision was to rule out the plea of justification as a defence in reference to the second and fourth counts; and, as justification had not been pleaded as to the first count, there remained only the third count in which justification might be pleaded in defence. This third count had set out the two decrees of suspension and deprivation as libellous in themselves and apart from any innuendo; and the court decided that the legal construction of the third count was that Cardinal Cullen had suspended and deprived Fr. O'Keeffe " in conformity with the laws, ordinances, and discipline of the Catholic Church."

The defence, then, was reduced ultimately to a plea of " justification" on the third count, and to a plea of "privilege" on all four counts.

In regard to the jurisdiction exercised in this case by the Cardinal, it is well to draw attention to the difference in the views held by the Church and by the civil law.

According to Catholic doctrine the jurisdiction exercised by Cardinal Cullen, when acting as ecclesiastical judge in the case was, of course, a jurisdiction delegated to him by

---

* 1 Eliz. c. 2, Ir.

the Chief Pastor of the Church of Christ, in whom, as successor of St. Peter, the supreme ecclesiastical authority of the Church, whether doctrinal, legislative, or judicial, is vested by divine institution. But no court of English law could view the Cardinal's jurisdiction in that light, for, in the eye of the civil law, Cardinal Cullen was simply exercising a " consensual" jurisdiction, the meaning of which will appear forthwith.

The Catholic Church in Ireland was, in the eye of the law, merely tolerated as a lawful society composed of members voluntarily associated together, and as Fr. O'Keeffe was, and claimed to be, a member of the Catholic Church, he was to be regarded as consenting to be bound by whatever was done in the due execution of a commission such as that entrusted by the Pope to Cardinal Cullen.

The authority to decide the case, conferred on the Cardinal by the Pope's commission, like the Pope's own authority to interfere at all in the case, was viewed by the civil law as an authority conferred by the parties to the suit (Fr. O'Keeffe on the one hand and Bishop Walsh and other ecclesiastics on the other) who explicitly or implicitly agreed to accept the Pope or his delegate as an arbitrator by whose award they were willing to abide. For, in the eye of the law, the Pope is for Catholics the supreme arbitrator in all differences concerning matters of ecclesiastical jurisdiction.

A court of English law, then, was bound not only to take cognisance of the award of an arbitrator, such as Cardinal Cullen was in the case, but also to enforce such award, provided that it was made in accordance with the laws, ordinances, and discipline of the Catholic Church. But, as such laws, ordinances, and discipline were no part of the system of English law, the civil court had no cognisance of them. They were technically " foreign law," and like all " foreign law" had to be proved before the court. As the ordinary means of proving " foreign law" is by producing

witnesses expert in that law, witnesses expert in the Canon
Law were consequently produced in court.

The witnesses expert in the Canon Law who were produced in the case were Fr. O'Keeffe on one side, and on
the other Cardinal Cullen, Dr. Leahy, Archbishop of Cashel,
Dr. McEvilly, then Bishop of Galway and subsequently
Archbishop of Tuam, Rev. Angelo Jacobini, at that
time Professor of Canon Law in Rome and an official in
Curia, and subsequently Cardinal Secretary of State to
Leo XIII, Rev. Cesare Roncetti, another Roman canonist,
afterwards Papal Nuncio at Munich, and Rev. Henry
Neville, ex-Professor of Theology at Maynooth and subsequently Rector of the Catholic University of Ireland and
Dean of Cork.   Professor Walsh, an expert witness in
reserve, was not called upon at this stage to give evidence,
but he appeared later on, as will presently appear.

The case was tried by Chief Justice Whiteside in Dublin,
and the trial lasted from the 15th to the 27th of May, 1873.
The trial was remarkable in many ways.

In the first place, it showed how very imperfect was the
measure of emancipation enjoyed by the Catholic Church
in Ireland, nearly half a century after the passing of the
Catholic Emancipation Act of 1829.   For, in deciding an
issue that had to be determined before the case could be
heard, the court held that there was still in force the penal
enactment of Elizabeth which made unlawful any exercise
of Papal jurisdiction within the realm.*

It was remarkable, in the second place, for bringing
prominently to the notice of the public in Ireland and Great
Britain for the first time since the Protestant Reformation,
the fact that in the Catholic Church there exists a highly
developed system of ecclesiastical jurisprudence, and an
elaborate code of disciplinary laws which must be administered in strict accordance with a specific and accurately
defined procedure.   The trial showed conclusively that

* 1 Eliz. c. 2, Ir.

ecclesiastical censures may not be hurled indiscriminately at the heads of inoffending clerics, or inflicted by rule of thumb according to the whims of tyrannical prelates. The O'Keeffe case also made it clear that in the Catholic Church there exists a highly organised and developed body of laws which compare favourably with the laws of England. It became evident that the Common Law of England had its counterpart and compeer in the Common Law of the Catholic Church, both, as one of the judges pointed out, being the embodiment of legal tradition. It was shown, moreover, that the Canon Law embodied in the law of England had its roots in the Canon Law of Rome, and for its development was mainly indebted to the Catholic Church.

The trial was remarkable, in the third place, for the array of distinguished canonical experts who appeared in court to state the Church's law—perhaps the most famous assemblage of highly skilled Roman lawyers in these countries since the days of Campeggio and Wolsey.

In the fourth place, the trial secured for itself a bad eminence owing to the attitude taken up by the judge who allowed his judgment to be clouded by personal prejudice, and whose misdirection forced the jury to bring in a verdict for the defendant, Fr. O'Keeffe, who was awarded a farthing damages. The verdict was at once challenged, and in due course—a very long course it proved to be—was set aside as wrong, owing to Justice Whiteside's grossly illegal misdirection of the jury. The judgments setting aside the verdict were delivered on the 13th and 15th of February, 1875.

Fr. O'Keeffe made a show of preparing for a new trial of the action against Cardinal Cullen, but he quickly abandoned the idea. He did not, however, abandon litigation, for, very soon after, he took up again the action against the Vicar-General, Dr. McDonald, which had lain in abeyance since July 1871.

Fr. O'Keeffe's action against the Vicar-General, Dr. McDonald, was a civil action for libel and slander. There were two counts of libel, and on each he claimed £1,000 damages. Libel is defamatory *written* matter; slander is *spoken* defamation.

The libel, relied upon in Fr. O'Keeffe's first count, was alleged to be contained in the letter written to the plaintiff by the defendant on October 10, 1870. The words complained of as libellous were : " I, vested with the requisite authority, suspend you from your office." In the second count the alleged libel was found in the letter written three days subsequently, October 13, to O'Keeffe, which contained the words : " I repeat the sentence of your suspension." The innuendo placed on the words in each of these counts was the same, namely, " that the plaintiff had been guilty of such conduct as would render him liable to be suspended from the office of Parish Priest."

Fr. O'Keeffe's case broke down on these two counts of libel owing to his failure to prove the publication of the words. But, as he succeeded in proving publication of the words on which the charge for slander was founded, he was able to proceed on that count.

In the count dealing with the slander it was averred that in the presence of divers witnesses (on occasions not specified, but subsequently determined to have occurred before the month of June 1871) Dr. McDonald had *spoken* the words, " Fr. O'Keeffe has been suspended." The innuendo put upon these words had a threefold implication : (1) that Fr. O'Keeffe had been guilty of some offence for which he might properly be suspended; (2) that he had been, in fact, suspended and " legally" suspended; and (3) that he had thus become incapable of exercising the functions of his office of parish priest.

Dr. McDonald's defence to the action of slander was a plea of " justification." He had consequently to prove that Fr. O'Keeffe had committed an ecclesiastical offence

for which—according to the laws, ordinances, and discipline
of the Catholic Church—the ecclesiastical penalty of suspension could properly be inflicted. The offence in question
was the impleading of an ecclesiastic by an ecclesiastic in
the civil courts in reference to an ecclesiastical matter. He
had to prove, moreover, that Fr. O'Keeffe had been
" legally" suspended. The court took the word " legally"
suspended to mean suspended according to the laws of
the realm. That is to say, the phrase did not
mean that the suspension had been inflicted by a civil
judge or magistrate administering the law of the realm and
following a procedure prescribed by that law, but it meant
that the suspension inflicted on Fr. O'Keeffe by the Vicar-
General in October 1870, and the suspension *ex informata
conscientia* inflicted on him by Bishop Walsh in January
1871, were valid and binding according to the laws of the
realm, and should be enforced by the civil court, if the
ecclesiastical superior were to appeal to the civil judge to
carry into effect the sentence of the ecclesiastical judges.

As Dr. McDonald and Bishop Walsh in inflicting the
suspensions complained of as slanderous, had acted not by
virtue of a jurisdiction delegated in contravention of the
Statute of Elizabeth, but in the exercise of the ordinary
diocesan jurisdiction, there was no difficulty such as had
arisen in Cardinal Cullen's case. And so the only questions
to be dealt with were whether the suspensions inflicted by
the Vicar-General and by the Bishop were or were not
inflicted in accordance with the laws, ordinances, and
discipline of the Catholic Church; and whether such suspensions rendered the plaintiff incapable of exercising the
functions of his office of parish priest. The matters,
therefore, to be proved, in order to establish the plea of
" justification" were : (1) that the impleading by Fr.
O'Keeffe of his Bishop, or of any other ecclesiastic, in the
civil courts in reference to an ecclesiastical matter was an
offence against the laws, ordinances, and discipline of the

Catholic Church; (2) that such an offence could, according to Catholic discipline, be punished by suspension; and (3) that in the infliction of the suspension on Fr. O'Keeffe the forms prescribed as essential by the ecclesiastical law had been observed.

To prove to the court what were the laws, ordinances, and discipline of the Catholic Church—the " foreign" law, as it was called—witnesses expert in the "foreign" law, were summoned to give evidence. These witnesses, expert in the Canon Law, included Fr. O'Keeffe, who gave evidence on his own behalf; and for Dr. McDonald the witnesses were Cardinal Cullen, Right Rev. Monsignor MacCabe, then Vicar-General of Dublin, afterwards Auxiliary Bishop to Cardinal Cullen, and finally, Cardinal-Archbishop of Dublin, and Professor Walsh, then professor at Maynooth, himself also destined to be in time Archbishop of Dublin.

The evidence given by Dr. Walsh evoked the high encomiums of those who heard him, including Baron Dowse, the judge who tried the case. Speaking of Dr. Walsh's evidence, Baron Dowse, in his address to the jury, said :

With reference to the evidence of Dr. Walsh, I must say that I have never heard evidence given more clearly and distinctly in a court of justice. He appeared to me to be eminently master of his subject. It is a matter of sincere pleasure to me to see my countrymen excel in any position or walk of life, and when I hear people say there are not as good men now as there were forty years ago, my answer is, that every generation brings its own men to suit the circumstances of the time. If Maynooth in former days was distinguished for great scholars—and no one can doubt that it has been—and if Dr. Walsh is a specimen of those of the present day, all I can say is the glory of the present will not be overshadowed by that of the past. Some people seem to assume that the Roman Catholic clergy of this country are ignorant men. But this case would of itself be sufficient to disabuse their minds forever of that idea—that is, if they had minds that were capable of being disabused of anything.*

Of Cardinal Cullen, Baron Dowse said in the same charge :

> Regarding the alleged rule or disc_iine of the Roman Catholic Church, Cardinal Cullen stated the Canon Law [on the point.] He tells us that he has made the Canon Law his study; and no person who heard His Eminence could doubt his profound learning in that branch of the law. I take the liberty of saying, that if anyone could entertain a doubt of it, the doubt would arise solely from the modesty with which he expressed himself. Anything more free from pride, arrogance, or presumption in the way he gave his evidence in this court, I never witnessed ; but it is only what I should expect from a prelate of his eminent position.

It may not be out of place to mention that Baron Dowse was a Protestant.

Only a few points of Dr. Walsh's evidence will be adverted to here, but the reading of his whole evidence is interesting and illuminating. Indeed, the evidence of all the canonical experts, Roman and Irish, who were examined in this " great Irish ecclesiastical cause," will repay the close scrutiny of anyone who is interested in the study of the administration of Canon Law in Ireland.†

The case *O'Keeffe* v. *McDonald* was tried at Wicklow in July-August 1875, before Baron Dowse, the going judge of assize, and a special jury of the county. The trial lasted three days. Both judge and jury (many of whom were prominent Protestant gentlemen of the county) sympathised with Fr. O'Keeffe, and did not refrain from expressing their sympathy from Bench and jury-box. Nor did the Cardinal fail to show his sorrow at Fr. O'Keeffe's plight. Fr. O'Keeffe, in his opening statement, enlisted the

---

* In this eulogium the judge included Dr. MacCabe, who received his education in the same great institution.

† *Report of Trial, O'Keeffe* v. *Cullen,* Eyre & Spottiswoode, London, 1874.

jury's sympathy by telling them that he would have to conduct his own case, as he was unable to fee counsel. For, owing to his previous prolonged litigation, all his money—the £1,500 subscribed in England, the £500 which should have gone to the Sisters at Béziers, and every pound that he possessed—was gone, and all prospect of securing further funds had vanished. The case, as he told the jury, was to him one of vital importance; their verdict would either consign him to a union workhouse for the rest of his days or restore him to the position which, he added, he had held for thirty years without stain or reproach.

The judge, while expressing his disappointment that professional help was not available for Fr. O'Keeffe, proffered to do everything he possibly could to secure that Fr. O'Keeffe should not suffer thereby. Indeed, the judge gave him great latitude in the conduct of the case, and heartened him in his difficult task, reminding the jury that Fr. O'Keeffe had shown that he had the courage " To beard the lion in his den, the Douglas in his hall."

It will be remembered that the grounds of the alleged slander were the words spoken in the presence of the Rev. John Walsh by Dr. McDonald : " Fr. O'Keeffe has been suspended." Fr. O'Keeffe held that these words were slanderous, because—

(1) He had been guilty of no canonical crime; and even if he had been,

(2) the Vicar-General was not competent to suspend him inasmuch as (a) he had not got a special mandate authorising him to do so; and even if he had had a special mandate (b) he could not act as judge in his own case. Furthermore, even if the Vicar-General had authority from the Bishop to suspend him,

(3) such suspension was of no avail (a) because it was inflicted under the authority of the *Bulla Coenae* and of the Constitution *Apostolicae Sedis*, which were never received in Ireland and not binding in that

country; (*b*) because there was no formal citation; (*c*) and no regular trial. Further, he contended that (4) he had been deprived of his parish in direct violation of the Bull of Pope Martin V, issued at the Council of Constance in 1415.

Dr. Walsh, when directly examined, stated that the Vicar-General, even without a special mandate, had power to inflict suspension; that there was a law of the Roman Catholic Church, binding in Ireland, which forbade a priest to implead his Bishop in a civil court, that that disciplinary law was part of the Canon Law of the Church, and existed independently of the *Bulla Coenae* or of any other Apostolical Constitution; that the *Bulla Coenae* and the Constitution *Apostolicae Sedis* could have no reference to the slander action instituted by Fr. O'Keeffe, inasmuch as they dealt not with suspension but with excommunication only; that the suspension inflicted by the Vicar-General without a special mandate was valid; that the citation was unnecessary where a crime was notorious or the offence undeniable; that the suspension *ex informata conscientia* was valid. He explained that suspension might be *ab ordine* or *ab officio* or *a beneficio*—three distinct things.

Fr. O'Keeffe began his cross-examination by asking twittingly, " Do you belong, Doctor, to the Ultramontane School ? " To which the witness answered, " Yes ; and when I say I belong to the Ultramontane School I mean that I hold the doctrine of the Pope's infallibility."

Father O'Keeffe then proceeded to read a number of statements from a book which he himself had written—*Ultramontanism versus Civil and Religious Liberty*—and asked the witness's opinion about them. Whereupon the judge interposed and said : " As far as I can see this is utterly irrelevant. Perhaps you want to cross-examine as to the credit of the witness ? " " I want, my Lord," said Fr. O'Keeffe, " to show his ignorance." Before long, how-ever, it was evident that, however ignorant Professor Walsh might be in other respects, he was certainly not ignorant of Canon Law. For, in his answers, he not merely stated canonical principles with clearness and explained their meaning exactly, but he applied those principles to the case with such cogent and merciless logic that Fr. O'Keeffe, wincing under the witness's relentless onset, exclaimed : " If you had all Serjeant Armstrong's fees,* you could not be more bitter against me."

Fr. O'Keeffe : You say that the vicar-general has power to suspend me *ab ordine, officio, et beneficio*. But is it not laid down in the Statutes of my diocese of Ossory that the vicar-general cannot take away a parish ?

Witness : It is laid down that the vicar-general cannot take away a parish (" *nequit auferre*"). But surely you ought to understand by this time the difference between *suspending* a priest from his benefice, and *taking the benefice away*. (To the court) I fear, my Lord, there may be still some confusion about this point, plainly as it already has been explained. And so, with the permission of the court, I will explain.

Suspension is merely an ecclesiastical *prohibition* to do certain acts, for instance to say Mass, to hear confessions, to preach. It makes it *unlawful* for the priest to do these things ; it does not take from him *the power* of doing them ; indeed, the power of Orders cannot be taken away. And thus a suspension from benefice does not deprive the priest of the benefice ; it is merely a prohibition, while the suspension lasts, to do certain things—to receive the emoluments, or to take part in the temporal administration of the benefice. In such a case the parish priest still continues to be parish priest, though he becomes a suspended one. If a person were writing to him he ought, notwithstanding the suspension, to address him as parish priest ; for he still retains the benefice, that is, the parish. It could be taken from him only by another process—*deprivation*, which is thus a more severe penalty than mere suspension. Suspension and deprivation are perfectly distinct things. Suspension may regard only Orders and office, and may not touch the benefice at all. But, moreover, a suspension *a beneficio* does not take away the benefice, deprivation does.

* Serjeant Armstrong was the leading counsel for the defence.

When it is laid down in the diocesan statutes of Ossory that the vicar-general cannot take away a benefice (*nequit auferre beneficium*), this merely withholds from him the power of depriving priests of their benefices; it does not affect his power of inflicting suspension.

BARON DOWSE : The distinction is perfectly clear.

WITNESS : I feel that I ought to apologise, my lord, for having explained the distinction at such length, but it seemed really necessary to do so . . . Father O'Keeffe seems to have failed to grasp this obvious distinction. Indeed at the trial in the Queen's Bench (before Chief Justice Whiteside) although the distinction was fully and clearly explained, it was altogether lost sight of by the judge. In his charge to the jury, the judge confounded suspension and deprivation, and did not seem to be aware of the distinction at all. But I am sure there is no fear of that occurring with your Lordship.

FR. O'KEEFFE : Devoti is a canonist of repute; his hand-book is used as a text-book at Maynooth. Now Devoti teaches that a vicar-general cannot, without special mandate, deal with criminal cases (such as the inflicting of censures), where the person convicted of guilt should be *severely* punished. Is not suspension a severe punishment?

WITNESS : Suspension is a severe punishment, but Devoti says nothing of the kind that you attribute to him. Devoti wrote in Latin. His words are : "In quibus in reum criminis *gravius* est animadvertendum." You have simply mis-translated Devoti. Were you not teaching Latin for a number of years, and is it possible that you do not see the mistake even now?

FR. O'KEEFFE : There is no mistake; it is a perfectly good translation.

WITNESS : It is, perhaps, better to clear up this point. What Devoti says is, that the vicar-general cannot act where any of *the more severe* penalties are to be inflicted " *in quibus gravius est animadvertendum.*" Now, suspension, though undoubtedly a severe penalty in itself, is not regarded and cannot be regarded as one of the *more severe penalties* of the Canon Law, especially suspension from Orders and from office. Suspension from a benefice would be a more severe penalty, excommunication or interdict more severe still; so also deprivation of office, deposition, or degradation. Hence, I say, although suspension is a severe punishment, it is not one of the more severe. And

Devoti does not deny the competence of the vicar to inflict a punishment, though he does deny his competence to inflict any of the more severe ones.

Fr. O'Keeffe : Well now, Doctor, we will pass from the canonists to the Canon Law itself. Take this (handing witness a volume of the *Corpus Iuris Canonici*) and read from the *Sextus Decretalium* of Boniface VIII, Cap. I. Tit. *De Officio Vicarii*.

Witness : This is the well-known chapter, *Licet*. " *Licet* in Officialem episcopi per commissionem officii generaliter sibi factam causarum cognitio transferatur, potestatem tamen inquirendi, corrigendi, aut puniendi aliquorum excessus, seu aliquos a suis beneficiis, officiis, vel administrationibus amovendi, transferri nolumus in eundem, nisi sibi specialiter haec committantur."

Fr. O'Keeffe : Now, Doctor, there is nothing about the " more severe" punishments there. *Puniendi* is the word : the vicar-general cannot inflict punishment at all.

Witness : So you say, but it is, unfortunately for you, only another case of mistranslation. My Lord, I am afraid it will not be so easy to explain this point as clearly as the last one. But I will try. I suppose I had better translate the passage. " Although the cognizance of the cases is transferred to the Official"—the official and the vicar-general were one and the same person in the diocese of Ossory—" of the bishop by the general commission of his appointment to his office, we do not wish the power to be communicated to him of instituting inquiries, of administering correction, or of punishing the excesses of any persons, in other words, of removing them from the benefices, offices, or administrations unless those powers are made over to him by special commission."

There are two different words in Latin to express "or"— *aut* and *seu*. Their meaning is quite distinct. They are both used in this chapter ; and if we attend to the difference of meaning, we shall see that the text is very far from denying to the vicar the power of inflicting such a punishment as suspension. It clearly excludes a power of inflicting certain punishments ; but it clearly has no reference whatever to the power of suspending.

One of these words—*aut*—is used when we speak of two *different* persons or things, meaning one or the other ; as, for instance, if I wished to say, "the judge or his registrar," I should use *aut*. But if I were speaking of the same person or thing under different names, as, for example, if I were to say, " the judge or his lordship or Baron Dowse," *seu* would be the appropriate word.

BARON DOWSE : So far the distinction is perfectly intelligible. One of the two words—*aut*—we may say is disjunctive; the other—*seu*—is explanatory.

WITNESS : Yes, and in fact in translating the chapter I used the form of expression "or in other words." Now bearing in mind that difference of meaning between the two words, if we look at the chapter again, we shall see that it merely denies to the vicar the power of *punishing* excesses by *deposition* or *deprivation*; the vicar cannot punish so as to depose. So we have here nothing more than what Devoti says : the vicar cannot inflict any of the *more severe* punishments, or, as it is put in the statutes of the diocese of Ossory, he *cannot take away a benefice*, or punish by *deprivation*.*

FR. O'KEEFFE : If the vicar-general had power to suspend me on October 10th and 13th, what was the use of that paper ? (handing witness a document)† Is not that a *speciale mandatum* ? Was a special mandate necessary to give him the power that he had by virtue of his office of vicar ?

WITNESS : I must take your questions one by one. You ask me what was the use of this special mandate, if Dr. McDonald had already the power to suspend you. Well, it might have been considered useful in many ways. For instance, when this document was given to the vicar, it might have been in contemplation to inflict some of the

---

* " Then, gentlemen, we had a reference to some passages of the Canon Law, one of which, undoubtedly, at first seemed to deny the authority of the vicar to inflict punishment at all, and consequently to inflict suspension. But Dr. Walsh, with an accuracy of critical knowledge which I have never seen surpassed, showed at once that by attending to the difference of meaning of two Latin words—*aut* and *seu*—which occurred in the passages in question, its true meaning was not in any way at variance with what he has told us regarding the vicar-general's power to inflict such a punishment as suspension."— Baron Dowse. Cf. Baron Dowse's *Charge*.

† The document was as follows :—" To the Very Rev. Mr. McDonald, Vicar-General of Ossory. Very Rev. Sir—To you, as our Vicar-General in virtue of your office, we grant power to absolve from cases reserved to us; to hear and determine criminal cases, inflict censures, and *do all such things as require special authority*. Given at Kilkenny, 25th October, 1870.— ✠ Edward, Bishop,"

more severe penalties on you. Although, as I have said, the vicar was competent to excommunicate you, or to impose an interdict, or——

Fr. O'Keeffe : But did Dr. McDonald think he had power to suspend me at all ?*

Witness : Oh, really, Father O'Keeffe, you cannot expect me to give evidence about Doctor McDonald's thoughts.

Fr. O'Keeffe : Now, Doctor, I will take another point. If an invalid suspension is inflicted on a priest, is he bound to take any notice of it?

Baron Dowse : As far as I can see, we have nothing to do here with the question of appeal. But I won't interfere to stop you.

Witness : I have no objection, of course, to answer the question. A priest is bound, in the case proposed, to submit to the sentence, until its invalidity is declared by competent authority.

Fr. O'Keeffe : He is? Just read that—(handing witness a volume of the *Corpus Iuris Canonici*).

Witness : I shall translate it :—" A sentence inflicted contrary to the laws or canons, although it may not be suspended by an appeal, is nevertheless——"

Fr. O'Keeffe : Not suspended by an appeal? Is that what you say?

Witness : Yes, and the words cannot be translated in any other way. " *Sententia . . . licet non sit appellatione suspensa*," and——

Fr. O'Keeffe : Well, listen to this from Devoti——

Witness : Please allow me to finish my explanation. I was about to say that the passage you asked me to read, so far from bearing out your view, goes to some extent against it. There are two sorts of appeal, my lord; we call the one *suspensive*, and the other *devolutive*. The *suspensive* appeal has the effect not merely of transferring the case to the tribunal of the superior judge—say, from the bishop to the archbishop of the ecclesiastical province —but it suspends the operation of the authority of the inferior; so that, pending the decision of the question by

---

* Cardinal Cullen in his evidence suggested another explanation of the *speciale mandatum* of October 25—*viz.*, that Dr. McDonald was a simple man, who was frightened by Fr. O'Keeffe's vigorous opposition into seeking for a *special mandate*, to make assurance doubly sure.

his superior, he is incompetent to exercise any jurisdiction in the matter, and his acts, if he persist in acting, may be disregarded. A *devolutive* appeal does not suspend the operation of the sentence from which the appeal is made; it merely transfers the case to the tribunal of the superior judge who is called upon to adjudicate upon it. Now, in the passage from which Father O'Keeffe has asked me to read, it is merely stated, that, in the case contemplated, the appeal, even if made, is not *suspensive*. In other words, then, pending the appeal the sentence must be observed.

FR. O'KEEFFE : Now listen to this from Devoti : " Nihil attinet appellare cum sententia nulla est, quoniam appellatio pertinet ad sententiam quae iniqua quidem est sed tamen *valet* . . . ergo inutilis est appellatio si ab incompetente judice, aut a competente quidem sed neglecto iuris ordine, aut contra expressam legem, bonosve mores, sententia lata sit."*

I quote all that in Latin. There is no mistranslation here, Doctor. Does not Devoti say in this passage that if the sentence be invalid it is not necessary to appeal at all?

WITNESS : He does. Now, my lord, as this is one of the plainest instances of what I have repeatedly stated with regard to the quotations in Father O'Keeffe's book,† I must ask your lordship's permission to explain the matter fully.

BARON DOWSE : Of course.

WITNESS : I have no doubt that Devoti says all that Father O'Keeffe ascribes to him, although, unfortunately, here in Wicklow I have not been able to refer to that third volume of his work from which Father O'Keeffe's quotation is taken. But, to understand the meaning of such a statement, we must bear in mind that the canonists distinguish very carefully between several sorts of remedy which are available in the case of a censure or other ecclesiastical penalty improperly inflicted. Thus, in the case of suspension *ex informata conscientia*, although no appeal lies

---

* " When a sentence is invalid it is altogether out of place to *appeal:* for an appeal has reference to a sentence that is *unjust* but *valid* . . . . therefore it is useless to appeal from the sentence of a judge who was not competent to issue it, or from the sentence of one who acted without observing the order of the law," etc.—*(Devoti Instit. Canon.* Lib., 3 tit. xiv n. 6.)

† *Ultramontanism versus Civil and Religious Liberty.*

D

from the bishop to the archbishop, there does lie a *reference* to the Holy See, which to all intents and purposes is an appeal, though not called so. The remedy against an unjust censure inflicted *ex informata conscientia* is technically styled *recursus* and not *appellatio*.

So, too, in the case of a sentence where the person who feels himself aggrieved alleges that he has not merely been too harshly dealt with, but that the sentence is absolutely null and void, the reference to the superior judge in such a case is not called an appeal (appellatio) : it is designated by the special and appropriate name of *querela* or *oppositio nullitatis*—a complaint or allegation of invalidity.

Hence the canonists most truly say that, in such a case, it is not necessary to *appeal*, that in fact an appeal would be altogether out of place. But they do not say, and Devoti does not say, that on the grounds of a sentence being regarded as invalid, or of its being invalid in reality, the person on whom it has been passed is at liberty to disregard it. The canonists, on the contrary, teach that, except in one special case, which unquestionably does not arise here, the sentence must be obeyed until its invalidity, if it be invalid, has been pronounced by competent ecclesiastical authority.

(After quoting from a manual of Canon Law—*Praelectiones Iuris Canonici habitae in Seminario Sancti Sulpitii*—the witness continued :)

The writer from whom I have quoted deals in the first place with the remedy known as allegation of invalidity (*oppositio nullitatis*). He says that the invalidity of a sentence may arise either from the want of competent authority in the judge, or from the omission of some formality essential to the observance of the judicial form; these are the very cases contemplated by Devoti as quoted by Father O'Keeffe. In either case, he says, the sentence so pronounced is invalid; and he quotes the very text of the law which Father O'Keeffe asked me to read a few moments ago. He then adds that although the sentence be invalid, yet unless it be so manifestly invalid that its invalidity is plain to all men (*nullitas manifesta omnibus appareat*) it must be regarded as valid so far as the external submission to it is concerned, until its invalidity be established by the decision of competent authority; for the sake of obtaining such a decision, he says, the application—that is, the *oppositio nullitatis*—is to be laid before the judge by whom the sentence was originally pronounced, or before a superior judge, as in the case of appeal.

So that pending the decision of the question, the censure or sentence must be observed, just as in the case of a *devolutive* appeal. It is plain that no man is at liberty, in the ecclesiastical any more than in the civil courts, to disregard a sentence on the mere ground that he *himself* regards it as invalid.

FR. O'KEEFFE : At all events I was not bound to appeal against an invalid sentence?

WITNESS : If you believed that the sentence was invalid you were bound, not exactly to *appeal* from it, but to lodge an *oppositio nullitatis,* and pending the decision of the question, you were bound externally to act as if the suspension were valid. The one exceptional case of which I spoke a moment ago does not arise in your case, for, no matter what your own theory may be about the suspensions which have been inflicted upon you, at all events you cannot contend that their *invalidity is plainly recognised by all (nullitas manifesta omnibus appareat).*

FR. O'KEEFFE : Suppose the foreman of the jury sent me a paper purporting to suspend me?

WITNESS : You would be justified in utterly disregarding it, for in that case " nullitas manifesta omnibus apparet."

FR. O'KEEFFE : If Cardinal Manning sent me a suspension—Cardinal Manning has no jurisdiction over me.

WITNESS : Cardinal Manning has no ordinary jurisdiction over you, but he might have received delegated jurisdiction. And if Cardinal Manning sent you a suspension you should, of course, presume that so eminent an ecclesiastic would not do so ridiculous a thing as to presume to inflict punishment on you, if he had not jurisdiction for that purpose. That, at all events, is the view that the majority of people would take. So that, even if you did not yourself believe that His Eminence had received jurisdiction, your course would be to lay allegation or *oppositio nullitatis* before the proper tribunal, and pending the decision of that question, you should submit to the Cardinal's suspension as binding on you.

FR. O'KEEFFE : Listen to this (reading) : " I should advert——"

BARON DOWSE : What is it you are reading now?

FR. O'KEEFFE : The report of the judgment of Chief Justice Whiteside.

BARON DOWSE : I do not wish to embarrass you, but I must tell you that you cannot read that as a statement of the law binding on anyone. The judgment was overruled by the court.

FR. O'KEEFFE : Do you hold that the *Bulla Coenae* was in force in Ireland up to 1869 ?

WITNESS : Yes, at least in many parts of Ireland. It certainly was in force in the diocese of Ossory. The *Bulla Coenae*, however, has nothing to do with this case. The *Bulla Coenae* deals with excommunications only, and no one has stated that you are excommunicated.

The witness then explained fully the nature of the *Bulla Coenae* and whence it derived its name, and gave a lengthy historical statement in reply to Fr. O'Keeffe's question. When Professor Walsh pointed out that the *Bulla Coenae* was superseded by the Constitution *Apostolicae Sedis* in 1869, Fr. O'Keeffe interjected, " But that Constitution excommunicates even laymen who implead an ecclesiastic in the civil court." Professor Walsh replied that that was not so : that Fr. O'Keeffe had again obviously failed to grasp the meaning of the clause *contra dispositiones canonicas* exempting laymen, at least in Ireland.

FR. O'KEEFFE : I could not be suspended unless I was guilty of some offence.

WITNESS : Oh, certainly not. But evidence has been given to show that you committed a very grave offence against the discipline of the Church by impleading your bishop, by bringing an action against him in the civil court.

A JUROR : Evidence has been given that it is an offence against ecclesiastical discipline for an ecclesiastic to bring an action against his bishop in the courts. Mr. O'Keeffe denies that there is any such law. Is there any law which can be produced in which it is forbidden ?

BARON DOWSE : It is not at all necessary to produce the text of such a law.

WITNESS : But, my Lord, there is no difficulty in producing abundant evidence of it . . . I shall have great pleasure in quoting the relevant canonical enactments.

BARON DOWSE : Very well, Doctor Walsh, but I want the jury clearly to understand how this matter stands. The

Canon Law of the Catholic Church is to a great extent (as Professor Walsh has pointed out earlier) like the Common Law of England—traditional. For, like the Common Law, it is the growth of centuries of use, and exists altogether independently of a code of written statutes. You may find it set forth in books, but its authority does not come from those books or from the sources in which you may find it written. These written records are merely evidences of the tradition. Now, you have the evidence of eminent, able and learned canonists, that the impleading by an ecclesiastic of the bishop in the civil courts is an offence against the Canon Law of the Catholic Church—an offence for which the punishment, at all events of suspension, may be inflicted by a competent ecclesiastical superior. Now, Dr. Walsh.

Professor Walsh then enumerated disciplinary enactments dealing with the punishment of an ecclesiastic who impleads his bishop. He referred to the Council of Chalcedon (*can.* 9, an. 451), to the Council of Carthage (*can.* 9 an. 397), to the Council of Milevis (an. 589) to the Canon *Inolita* of the third Council of Toledo (*can.* 13, an. 447), to the famous *Decretal* of Innocent III (1199-1216), to the Council of Bourges (1336), to the Council of Toulouse (1590), and to the Council of Trent (1545—1563). Coming to ecclesiastical discipline in Ireland, Professor Walsh quoted the Synod of Cashel (1685) which embodied statutes made at two National Councils, one held at Waterford in 1643, and the other held at Kilkenny in 1644, to a Council held at Armagh in 1670, to a diocesan Synod held in Dublin in 1686, under Dr. Russell, an Archbishop of Dublin under whom a great many such synods were held.

Professor Walsh then dealt with the Bull of Martin V, *Ad reprimendas*, which Fr. O'Keeffe said excommunicated all persons, whether laymen or priests, who brought ecclesiastics into court; and he pointed out that Fr. O'Keeffe's view was quite erroneous, as all such prohibitions as regards laymen had gone into disuse.

It is unnecessary to pursue further the cross-examination,

at the end of which Fr. O'Keeffe's case was utterly shattered. Two incidents, however, may be mentioned— one illustrating Fr. O'Keeffe's resourceful humour, even in his hour of trial, the other showing Professor Walsh's alertness and nimbleness.

When Dr. Walsh, in enumerating the conciliar enactments dealing with the offence of impleading a bishop in the civil courts, mentioned the Council of Milevis (*Concilium Milevitanum*), Baron Dowse, who by that time had been impressed by Dr. Walsh's extensive and accurate knowledge, asked : " Where is Milevis, Dr. Walsh ?" " In Africa," he replied, " but I don't know the precise locality." " Well, I can enlighten you both," said Fr. O'Keeffe. " Milevis is a town on the banks of the Nile, and the modern name is Melvis." This was an invention of Fr. Robert's. It was pure bluff on his part, and his *audace* succeeded for the time. In point of fact, Milevis was an episcopal city in the kingdom of Numidia, situated very near its western borders, several hundred miles from the Nile. Its modern name, Milah, is the name of a small town not far from Constantine in Algeria.

The other incident occurred when Fr. O'Keeffe gave a wrong reference to the *Corpus Iuris Canonici*, in connection with the power of a vicar-general to inflict censures. Dr. Walsh immediately pointed out that the passage indicated had no reference to the matter in question; and with the deftness of the skilled fencer he seized on the opening left by Fr. Robert's blunder to send a shrewd thrust home. " This seems," he said, " a strangely inappropriate reference for Fr. O'Keeffe to give, for the whole passage deals exclusively with the forms to be observed in the investigation of any serious charge *against a Bishop*, and the whole passage expresses in the strongest terms the respect due to bishops on account of their great dignity, ' standing as pillars'—to use the words of the chapter—' set forth by the

Lord to sustain the Church, and therefore not to be rudely assailed by irreverent hands.' "

At the end of the evidence in the case of *O'Keeffe v. McDonald*, the judge delivered an able and impartial charge to the jury.* The verdict was in favour of the defendant. The jury found that the statement " Fr. O'Keeffe has been suspended" was true and therefore legally justified. The verdict was the *coup de grace* to Fr. O'Keeffe. He left the court a broken man and retired to Ossory, but not to take charge of his parish at Callan.

Cardinal Cullen's kindness followed him into retirement. The interdict was removed from the parish church at Callan, and Fr. O'Keeffe in time set himself right with God, and got absolution from the censures and irregularities which he had incurred. Long before he died he was reconciled to the Catholic Church, from whose teaching on faith and morals he had never swerved, but whose disciplinary code he had for years flagrantly and persistently violated. Dr. Walsh, too, always spoke kindly of Fr. O'Keeffe, and gave practical help in assuaging the misery which had been brought upon him by his misguided zeal. After the Wicklow trial Fr. O'Keeffe vanished from the forum, and we see him no more, but in fancy we behold him a lonely and pathetic figure, chafing in the enforced retirement in which he passed the remaining years of his sojourn—a saddening example of a spirit eager and forthright, but venturous and overbold, which was lured to ruin by a zeal that was not tempered by prudence or exercised according to knowledge. He died in 1879.

* Cf. *O'Keeffe* v. *McDonald. Charge of the Right Hon. Baron Dowse.* (Browne & Nolan. 1875.)

CHAPTER IV

VICE-PRESIDENT AND PRESIDENT AT MAYNOOTH.

THE appointment of the Rev. Daniel McCarthy, D.D., to succeed Dr. Moriarty in the bishopric of Kerry (May 1878), opened the way for Dr. Walsh's advancement to an administrative post in the college. Dr. McCarthy, at the time of his elevation to the episcopate, was Vice-President at Maynooth, having held that office since September 1872. For nearly a quarter of a century he filled the chair of Sacred Scripture in the college and bore the reputation of an able and painstaking professor. His study of *The Epistles and Gospels of the Sundays*,* published in 1868, is a work of sound and accurate scriptural scholarship, and his *Collections of Irish Church History*,† which he edited and issued in 1861, is a most useful work on that subject. He was appointed Bishop of Kerry at the first Congregation held at Propaganda after the accession of Pope Leo XIII.

Cardinal Cullen, who attended the Congregation, wrote to Dr. Walsh from Rome (May 7, 1878) :

I write to tell you *confidentially* that the Congregation yesterday appointed Dr. McCarthy, Bishop of Kerry. This election is subject to the approbation of the Pope. Of course he will confirm it, but it is well not to publish anything about it until the Pope shall have sanctioned it on next Sunday, or about that time. The Congregation of yesterday was the first held since Pius IX's death.

The Pope is well but he is thin and weak-looking, and he works a great deal too much. Probably he will have much to suffer, but he is a man of great courage and firmness. I

---

* *The Epistles and Gospels of the Sundays with Notes, Critical and Explanatory,* Dublin, 1868.

† *Collections of Irish Church History,* Dublin, 1861.

fear the confinement in the bad air and heat of the Vatican during the coming months will try him severely. For more than thirty years, while Bishop of Perugia, he enjoyed every summer the fine climate and fresh breezes of the beautiful hills of Umbria. The change to the Vatican must affect him very much.

Writing again from Rome, Cardinal Cullen says (May 15, 1878) :

I send you a photograph of His Holiness which is like him. He does not at all fill the big chair which was small enough for Pius IX. I suppose the Brief of Dr. McCarthy's appointment will not arrive before June, so there will be no difficulty about the affairs of the college. I expect to be home in the beginning of June, and to be present at the meeting of the Board.

The Cardinal did not return to Ireland till after the middle of June, but meantime he was in communication with some of the Irish bishops about the appointment to the impending vacancy in the vice-presidency at Maynooth. Among these correspondents was Dr. Moran, Bishop of Ossory, who wrote to Dr. Walsh (June 3, 1878) :

I have had some correspondence about the appointment of Vice-President for your college, and myself and others are of opinion that you are the person that should be appointed to that post. As it will be necessary to concert the matter before the meeting of the Board, I am anxious to learn from you, will you give any opposition to such an appointment.

There will be so many new Professors now coming in, and the President being infirm, unless the Vice-President be a person who will take a deep interest in the students, the college will go to the bad. I presume, too, the President cannot continue to hold his post for more than a few months, and, of course, the Vice-President will take his place. I need hardly say that the views which I have expressed harmonize entirely with those of His Eminence.

Dr. Walsh must have informed the Bishop of Ossory that he would not " give any opposition " to the contemplated

appointment, for Cardinal Cullen soon after wrote to
Dr. Walsh from Liverpool (June 16, 1878) : " I hope your
appointment will be unanimous and that it will do a great
deal of good.   However, there will always be difficulties to
be contended with, and nothing else can be expected where
the community is so large.   But please God, everything will
go on well."

Dr. Walsh was appointed Vice-President by the College
Trustees at their meeting on June 25, 1878, and as the
President, Dr. Russell, was then incapacitated as the result
of an accident from which he never recovered, the Vice-
President had to bear the main responsibility for the
administration of the college until Dr. Russell's death.

On the same day on which Dr. Walsh was appointed
Vice-President, the Rev. Michael Logue was appointed to a
theological professorship.   Dr. Logue resigned his professorship in the following year on being elected by the Holy See to
the bishopric of Raphoe.   About the same time, Dr. Walsh
was compelled by the pressure of administrative work in
the college to relinquish his chair.   The vacant professor-
ships were filled by the Rev. John Healy (afterwards
Archbishop of Tuam) and the Rev. Patrick O'Donnell
(subsequently in turn Bishop of Raphoe and Cardinal-
Archbishop of Armagh).

One of the earliest subjects to occupy the attention of
Dr. Walsh as Vice-President of Maynooth was the new
departure in secondary education arising out of the Intermediate Education (Ireland) Act, which was passed into
law, August 16, 1878.   By the new Act an Intermediate
Education Board for Ireland was established, consisting of
seven unpaid commissioners and two salaried assistant
commissioners.   Its purpose was to promote intermediate
secular education (1) by holding public examinations of
students, (2) by awarding exhibitions, prizes and certificates
to successful candidates, and (3) by paying " results

fees" to the managers of schools. Of the seven unpaid commissioners only three were Catholics—Lord O'Hagan, Chief Baron Palles, and The O'Conor Don. The necessary funds were provided by the allocation of a sum of £1,000,000 out of the surplus fund of the Disestablished Church, yielding an annual income of £32,000.

The Intermediate Examinations were to bring the secondary schools into public competition for the first time. The head-masters of these schools took steps, immediately after the passing of the Act, to meet the new situation that had been created. The Protestant masters were the first to take concerted action. They formed an organisation to safeguard and protect their interests, and they invited some of the Catholic headmasters to join their body. This invitation was declined, chiefly on the advice of the Rev. William Delaney, S.J., and the Rev. Edward Reffé, C.S.Sp. Fr. Delaney was Rector of the Jesuit College at Tullabeg, and Fr. Reffé was Prefect of Studies of the French College, Blackrock, Dublin—the college so successfully conducted by the Fathers of the Holy Ghost.

These two most capable and energetic educationists took a leading part in organising the Catholic schools. They met at first with considerable apathy. But as the matter was urgent—for it was expected that the first examinations would be held in the following June—they redoubled their efforts. Many of the older generation of Catholic masters, and some of the bishops, feared that in public competition the Catholic schools, labouring under severe handicaps, would be altogether outdistanced by their Protestant rivals. The Protestant schools had the advantage of being long established; many of them were in the enjoyment of rich endowments; their professors, drawn mainly from Trinity College, had a tradition of classical learning; many of their schools were well-equipped with scientific appliances, so necessary for the proper teaching of the positive sciences; and the mathematical school at Trinity

College, which at that time stood in high repute, provided them with capable mathematical teachers. The Catholic schools, on the other hand, were for the most part but poorly equipped, and had a hard struggle to carry on their work under financial and other disabilities. It was greatly feared that the disadvantages under which they laboured would be an enormous and decisive handicap in the competition.

Dr. Walsh did not share this despondent view. While fully aware of the many drawbacks which hampered the Catholics, he was of the opinion that by organisation much could be done to remedy their disadvantages. The superiority of the classical teaching in the Protestant schools he regarded as a myth, and the deficiencies of the Catholic schools in the department of science could, he thought, be easily remedied. He was in entire sympathy with the views of Father Delaney and Father Reffé as to the urgent need of organisation and co-operation, and he promptly took action to achieve those ends. He communicated with the bishops who had preparatory seminaries or other secondary schools in their dioceses, asking if they would be willing to send representatives to a conference of Catholic masters that he proposed to summon for the purpose of taking common counsel in the matter. By many of the bishops his proposal was received with approval and encouragement; from some it elicited a chilling reply. The Bishop of Elphin, Dr. Gilhooly, approved of the idea of a conference, but regarded it as presumptuous for Dr. Walsh to take on himself the responsibility of summoning such a conference. Dr. Moran of Ossory deprecated the proposal, and was with difficulty persuaded to give it any countenance. He wrote to Dr. Walsh (September 4, 1878):

As you persist in thinking that the conference will do some good, I will permit Fr. Murphy to go to it. However, my own opinion remains unchanged. I think it is a mistake for twenty or thirty good priests to hold a conference together on a matter that they know very little about.

Dr. Walsh persevered in his purpose of summoning the conference, and addressed to each of the bishops the following letter, outlining the objects that he hoped to attain :

St. Patrick's College,
Maynooth,
September 27, 1878.

MY LORD,—I have been for some time thinking over a project bearing upon the working of the new Education Act, which I trust will meet with your Lordship's approval.

It seems to me essential that if our Catholic schools and colleges are to have any share in the benefits to be derived from successful competition under the Act, something in the way of organisation must be done, and done at once.

I have already mentioned this matter to such of the bishops, and of the heads of colleges or schools, as I have happened to meet during the past few weeks; and, so far, I have met with nothing but encouragement.

My idea, then, is that we should at once hold a conference of the heads or representatives of all those Catholic schools or colleges in Ireland which are under ecclesiastical management.

The objects to be aimed at in such a conference are, as I conceive them, *four* :

First : Mutual communication and interchange of ideas, as regards :

(*a*) Methods of teaching.

(*b*) The best school books to use.

(*c*) The special training required in preparing students for examinations conducted on the system which we may anticipate will be adopted by the Examiners under the new Board : and here I may mention that already some heads of colleges, whose experience and success in connection with similar examinations will render their assistance most valuable, have kindly promised me to attend the conference in case I succeed in bringing it together.

(*d*) The changes which it may be advisable to suggest to the bishops at your Lordships' meeting in October, as regards the programme of our Entrance Examinations here, so as to secure that, especially during the first year of the working of the new Board, the double duty may not be imposed on the professors and students of the Diocesan Seminaries, of preparing for two examinations, in two distinct sets of authors or subjects.

Secondly : The careful consideration of the " rules" of the new Act, as at present framed, with a view to seeking their amendment so far as may be thought advisable in the interests of our Catholic colleges and schools. In reference to these, as your Lordship is aware, very large powers are given to the Commissioners : and there is every reason to believe that the Board, as constituted, will favourably consider any practical suggestions offered by a thoroughly representative conference such as I contemplate. As an instance of the class of points to which I thus refer, I may suggest the " *limits of age*," as fixed by the present rules ; some statistics bearing upon this point, compiled from the baptismal certificates of over 100 candidates who presented themselves at our Entrance Examinations this year, will, I think, be of some use in the consideration of this topic.

Thirdly : The formation of a standing committee, to serve as a medium of communication between the various schools and colleges, in reference to the points I have already specified, and to any others that may be brought into prominence by the working of the Act.

Fourthly : The establishment of communication between our Catholic schools and colleges on the one hand, and the leading publishers of school books on the other. I have no doubt that when the nature of our organisation is put before these publishers, they will gladly avail themselves of so easy a means of placing specimen copies of their publications in the hands of those whose favourable notice will ensure a large and constant demand.

I had intended waiting till the meeting of the Maynooth Board in October before bringing my proposal under the notice of your Lordship ; but I have received two letters— one to-day from a priest, the head of a very large educational establishment—from which I learn that the heads of the chief Protestant schools are already at work. My correspondent has himself been written to by a representative of the organisation which they are endeavouring to establish. They wish to form a committee ; and they seem to consider it an act of great liberality, that they will admit a certain number of Catholics—of course a minority—to take part in it.

My friend, on receipt of their letter, writes to me urging the necessity of prompt action.

"As I anticipated," he says, "the Protestants are organising; and we are still, and I fear likely to be, scattered units, without a plan or a policy. The Protestant masters will have their scheme ready for the Board, backed by a majority on that Board, and by the weight of the whole body of Protestant masters. Our Commissioners, already a minority, will represent only their own, perhaps not fully matured, ideas; and so the scheme threatens from the very start to be shaped so as to suit the Protestant schools, and to shut out Catholic schools practically from any chance in the competition—and we are looking on with our arms folded, without any attempt to forestall the danger or to help ourselves.

"What say you?" he asks, "and what can we do to dispel the lethargy?"

My answer is this letter to your Lordship.

I trust that in the circumstances it will not be thought strange that the initiative in such a movement should be taken by me. There are, I think several reasons, any one of which your Lordship will, I trust, regard as sufficient.

In the first place I have already received many assurances of co-operation of the most practical kind.

Secondly, in no other ecclesiastical establishment in Ireland, except Maynooth, is there a possibility of receiving, for the two or three days that the conference will probably last, the twenty or thirty priests whose presence may be counted on.

Besides, the work of the conference ought, I think, to comprise the consideration of our Maynooth Entrance Programme.

And finally and chiefly, while the work seems absolutely necessary to be done, in the interests of Catholic education, there seems to be no prospect of its being done at all, if it be not done, as I suggest, in our college of Maynooth.

May I request your Lordship, then, at your earliest convenience, to do me the honour of letting me know whether you consider it advisable that the Heads of any colleges or schools in your Lordship's diocese should be invited to take part in the proposed conference, and also the names of the priests whom I should invite? I fear that I must limit the number to one from each college or school.

It is hardly necessary for me to ask your Lordship to observe that I do not contemplate any arrangement which would have the effect of placing any controlling power in the hands either of the conference itself, or of the standing committee.

Earnestly hoping that the project will meet with your Lordship's approval, and that we may have the assistance of your blessing on our work.

I have the honour to remain,
Your Lordship's most obedient servant,
WILLIAM J. WALSH.

P.S.—As it would obviously be impossible to ascertain by correspondence what day would suit the convenience of all, I think it the most practical course to name the 8th and 9th of October.

The conference was held at Maynooth, under the chairmanship of Dr. Croke, Archbishop of Cashel, and produced important and practical results. An organisation was formed which proved of valuable service to the Catholic secondary schools during the early years of the Intermediate system. In this organisation Dr. Walsh was the prime mover and dominant influence, having as his first lieutenant Fr. Delaney, who was proud, he said, to work under Dr. Walsh, the founder and director of the organisation.

The results of the first year's Intermediate examinations, published in September 1879, justified the hopes of Dr. Walsh and the existence of the new organisation, and at the same time gave gratification and encouragement to the Catholic schools. In the public competition the Catholic students outclassed their rivals, and a Catholic boy, Charles F. Doyle (now a distinguished Irish judge) of the College of the Sacred Heart, Limerick, headed the list of the successful candidates. Dr. Walsh was glad to be the first to announce the good news by telegram to the Rector of the school where Master Doyle had been taught. The success of the Catholic schools in this instance was not a casual victory. The superiority which they evidenced in the first test of public competition has since been consistently maintained, and during the half-century of the Intermediate Board's existence the Catholic schools and colleges have always secured the lion's share of the money which is annually distributed by the Board.

The year 1880 witnessed the revival of the *Irish Ecclesiastical Record*. It was mainly the exertions of Dr. Walsh which made it possible to revive the periodical, and it was he who arranged that thenceforward it should be edited and issued from Maynooth. The *Irish Ecclesiastical Record*—a monthly journal under episcopal sanction—was founded by Cardinal Cullen in 1864. In a foreword to the first number, which appeared in the month of March of that year, the programme of the periodical was clearly set forth. The *Record* was intended in the first place to be a link between Ireland and Rome. It would likewise serve to connect the clergy of Ireland with their foreign brethren, and not only enable Irish priests to know what was being done abroad in theology, in history, in the philosophical and natural sciences, and in the actual life and warfare of the Church, but would at the same time bring under the notice of foreigners the doings and achievements of the Church in Ireland. It was also to be a bond of union and a medium of communication between the priests of Ireland themselves.

The *Record* had for its first editor the Rev. George Conroy, D.D., who was assisted by a " Society of Clergymen" formed in Dublin and extending over the country. Chief amongst the assistants was the Rev. Patrick Moran, D.D., who then was Vice-Rector of the Irish College, Rome. Shortly after the foundation of the *Record*, Dr. Moran had returned to Dublin as Secretary to his kinsman, Cardinal Cullen, and became joint-editor of the *Record* with Dr. Conroy. In the year 1871 both Dr. Conroy and Dr. Moran were promoted to the episcopacy. Thereupon Dr. Conroy's direct connection with the *Record* came to an end. Dr. Moran, however, continued to edit the periodical, and with the assistance of Drs. Verdon and Tynan, of Clonliffe College, Dublin, he managed for some time to keep it in life and vigour. In 1875, Dr. Moran, finding that it was no longer feasible for him to continue as editor, proposed that Dr. Tynan should take his place. The latter, however, declined. For, as at that time he was not only professor of theology at Clonliffe but also held the onerous office of Secretary to Cardinal Cullen, he felt that it would be impossible for him to devote to the *Record* the time and care which it demanded. Besides, the undertaking was not—then, at all events—successful from a commercial point of view. Eventually, at the end of 1875, the *Record* was handed over, in a moribund condition, to Dr. Walsh. Though Dr. Walsh was never formally appointed editor, he edited the journal for about a year and managed to keep it alive till the volume for that year was completed in December 1876. At least one whole number published at that time was written exclusively by himself. But he could not continue such a task unaided, and for the next three years the publication of the *Record* lapsed.

With a view to reviving the periodical, Dr. Walsh wrote (1879) to each of the Irish and English bishops soliciting their approval and support. The new Archbishop of Dublin, Dr. McCabe, warmly approved of the project. So, too, did Dr. Moran, Cardinal Manning, Dr. Hedley, and Dr. Herbert Vaughan. Archbishop McCabe urgently requested Dr. Walsh to become editor, but he declined, recommending instead the name of Dr. Carr, who accordingly was appointed to the editorship. The first number of the resuscitated periodical was published in January 1880, and from that time to the present the *Record* has continued to be issued from Maynooth, the editor being appointed by the Archbishop of Dublin. From 1869 till 1921, Dr. Walsh was a constant contributor to its pages, and some of the most valuable articles which it contained were written by him. Scores of its articles and thousands of its pages are from his pen.

During the time that Dr. Walsh was Vice-President at Maynooth, an event occurred which caused great excitement in the college and attracted much public notice and sympathy throughout Ireland. This was a serious outbreak of fire which destroyed a large portion of the buildings. The fire occurred on the morning of November 1, 1878. It was first noticed about half-past eight in the morning, in the portion of the college known as St. Mary's, and it was at a point adjoining the senior oratory and reading-room, and not far from the college library, that the fire originated. The flames spread with great rapidity, the corridors being soon filled with dense volumes of smoke. Some of the students, in their efforts to save the furniture of the college and their own personal belongings, narrowly escaped with their lives. One student who had been rendered insensible by the blinding and suffocating smoke was heroically rescued by his companions; another narrowly escaped a fearful scalding—the molten lead from the roof actually scorching a portion of his clothing. Dr. Walsh, who was immediately apprised of the outbreak, acted with great promptness and decision. He at once despatched three telegrams—one to the Dublin fire-brigade requesting their assistance, another to the Lord Mayor of Dublin asking his permission for the brigade to leave the city, and another to the railway authorities at the Broadstone terminus asking them to have in readiness a special train to convey the brigade to Maynooth. Pending the arrival of the train from Dublin, recourse was had to every available means of staying the progress of the flames. The students and servants of the college gave willing and valuable help, aided and directed by the professors and superiors. Dr. Walsh, with a devoted band of students, busied himself in an endeavour to save the library. Thousands of volumes flung through the window escaped unharmed, or with injuries that were reparable. The arrival of the fire-brigade gave an assured hope that the havoc of the flames would soon be stemmed. The firemen devoted their first efforts to saving the library by severing the connection between it and the oratory and reading-room. In this they were successful. After hours of most vigorous effort the spread of the fire was completely checked, but all endeavours to save the building in which the outbreak originated were futile.

The damage, which amounted to thousands of pounds, was covered by insurance, and in addition to the money which was devoted to the restoration of the damaged buildings, a considerable sum was available for rebinding and rebacking thousands of the volumes which had been damaged in their hurried ejectment.

The trustees of the college at a special meeting held on November 4, after expressing to Dr. Walsh their warm appreciation of his prompt and resourceful action, passed a cordial resolution of thanks to all who had assisted so effectually in saving the college.

The outbreak of the fire occurred on a Friday. The firemen who reached Maynooth about 11 a.m. were strenuously engaged for some hours after their arrival in getting the fire under control, and when in the afternoon they were free to partake of some much-needed refreshment they found themselves seated at tables with joints of beef and mutton set before them. Dr. Walsh explained to the men that, although the day was Friday, owing to the lack of abstinence fare and to the fact that the men themselves had been so strenuously engaged in exhausting work, they might without scruple partake of the flesh-meat with which they were being served. A theological student who was present—a young man who had been studying the treatise *De Ieiunio et Abstinentia*—quietly asked

Dr. Walsh if he were justified in granting a general dispensation in the ecclesiastical law of abstinence. The Vice-President explained that he had not dispensed, but had merely declared the men exempt from the ecclesiastical law —that it was a case of *Epieikeia*.* A fireman who had overheard the remark turned to Dr. Walsh, and said : " Your reverence, what kind of a case did you say it was ?" " A case of *Epieikeia*," he replied. " Well, Father," said the man, " I don't care what it means; but even if it was a case of whiskey, I could not bring myself to break the fast by eating meat on a Friday." And he remained fixed in his determination.

Early in 1879, some months after the great fire, Her Imperial Majesty the Empress Elizabeth of Austria visited the college. The ill-fated Empress was passionately fond of hunting and was a spirited and accomplished horsewoman. She came to Ireland in the early spring of 1879, travelling as the Countess of Hohenehms, and with a small retinue took up residence at Summerhill in the county of Meath. Summerhill was chosen because of its position in the midst of a hunting country within easy reach of the Meath, the Kildare, and the Ward Hunts. On Monday, February 24, the Empress hunted with the Ward hounds. A stag which was enlarged at Batterstown gave a fine run through Meath and Kildare, and about three o'clock in the afternoon the hunt reached Maynooth. The stag made his way into the college grounds through a temporary gateway which had been left open by a workman. The staghounds followed, and, close on their track, a huntress on a dark bay mount. It was the Empress. By the time that the main body of the hunt was arriving in scattered fragments, the stag had been rescued from the dogs and the Empress had dismounted. Meantime the residents of the college had been apprised of

* *Epieikeia* is a technical term used by theologians. It means a reasonable presumption that the legislator does not intend that the law should bind in certain circumstances.

the adventure, and the Vice-President, Dr. Walsh, had come to invite the illustrious lady to partake of some light refreshment. The Empress, whose appetite had been whetted by her fine run in the cool February air, gladly accepted the proffered hospitality. Apprehensive of catching a chill, as she was heated by her strenuous exertions, Her Imperial Majesty asked if she might have a wrap or shawl to put about her shoulders, whereupon Dr. Walsh divested himself of the light academic gown which he wore over his soutane, and the Empress having donned the gown remarked that it suited her admirably. When the Empress was leaving the college, the Vice-President, informally, perhaps, but cordially, invited her to come another time. Her Majesty graciously acceded to the invitation, and on the following Sunday she came again to Maynooth. It was her wish, however, that there should be no departure from the customary routine and ways of the college, and that her attendance at Mass should be marked by an absence of display of any kind. Her wishes were respected. She assisted at Low Mass which was celebrated at eleven o'clock in the Junior Chapel, and at which there assisted, besides the Empress and her suite, the Vice-President and Staff and the junior students of the college. After the Mass, Benediction of the Blessed Sacrament was given by Dr. McCabe, Vicar-Capitular of Dublin. The Empress then made an inspection of the library and other buildings of the college.

In memory of this visit she sent to Dr. Walsh from her Austrian capital a magnificent gold ring, with an olivine stone inset, which he treasured until his death. She also invited him to visit the Austrian Imperial Court where, she said, she would have much pleasure in presenting him to the Emperor. She also sent to the college as a souvenir of her visit, a splendid equestrian statue of solid silver, weighing four hundred and sixty ounces. The statue represents the conflict of St. George and the Dragon—St. George being the best-known equestrian saint. The figure of the rider is excellently wrought, holding a drawn sword in act to strike; beneath, the writhing dragon with open jaws and scaly folds is vividly reproduced. The whole statue is three feet high, and is mounted on an ebony pedestal curiously inlaid with silver. The Empress's presentation was announced to Dr. Walsh in the following letter from Herr Linger, her controller :

Vienna,
September 12th, 1879.

To the Most Rev. President of the College at Maynooth.
Most Rev. Sir,

I have the honour to communicate to you that Her Majesty the Empress of Austria, in remembrance of her visit to the College at Maynooth, has been greatly pleased to dedicate to your church a small statuette representing St. George, which I send herewith to the address of the above-named college.

Hoping for the safe arrival of this gift and that you would be good enough to acknowledge briefly to me the reception of same, I have the honour to remain,

Most Rev. Sir,
Your obedient servant,
KARL LINGER.

The following year the Empress was again at Summerhill and repeated her visit to the college. After this visit she presented to the college a beautiful and costly set of cloth of gold vestments. The embroidery—almost exclusively of shamrocks worked in green silk—is of the richest description. The fringes are of gold lace through which tiny shamrocks, to be counted by thousands, are deftly interwoven. In front of the chasuble beneath the cross, stand three shields bearing the arms of Austria, Bavaria, and Lorraine, richly wrought in appropriate heraldic colours, and surmounted by the Imperial Crown in gold. Within, on the satin lining of the chasuble, are embroidered in green and gold, the names of the Imperial donor and the date of the visit so graciously commemorated—" Elizabeth 1880." These vestments were first used in June 1886 when Dr.

Walsh, as Archbishop of Dublin, officiated for the first time at the general ordinations in the college.

An amusing incident happened to Dr. Walsh on the occasion of the Empress's second visit to Ireland. After it was known that she was in residence at Summerhill, Dr. Walsh drove over from Maynooth to pay his respects by writing his name in the visitors' book. The door was opened by a tall man-servant who wore the livery of the Imperial household. The Vice-President, speaking in German, explained the purpose of his visit and asked for a book in which to write his name. The man looked confused and somewhat scared. " Wo ist das Buch?" pressed Dr. Walsh, and immediately the man precipitately disappeared. In a moment he returned with Herr Linger, who explained to Dr. Walsh that the janitor was an Irishman who knew not a word of German.

In the winter of 1879 Dr. Walsh found himself defending the reputation of his college in a public controversy. The early theological teaching at Maynooth had been severely arraigned in an article which appeared in the October issue of the *Dublin Review*, under the title " Theology, Past and Present, at Maynooth." The writer of the article was the Rev. Henry Neville, Rector of the Catholic University of Ireland, himself an ex-professor of theology at Maynooth.

Gallicanism* in dogma and in moral doctrine, according

* It may not be out of place to mention here that by Gallicanism is usually meant the teaching set forth in what are termed the *Gallican Liberties,* which are contained in four propositions drawn up by the French clergy in 1682.

The first proposition denies that St. Peter and his successors have received any power from God extending to temporal and civil affairs, declares that kings are subject to no ecclesiastical power in temporals, and denies the deposing power of the Pope.

The second insists on the supremacy of General Councils over the Pope.

The third affirms that laws and usages in the Gallican Church and also in other churches, should subsist with variation.

The fourth is as follows : " The Pope has the principal share in questions of faith; his decrees regard all the churches and every church in particular; nevertheless, his judgment is not irreformable, unless the consent of the church be added."

to Dr. Neville, flourished at Maynooth in the early decades
of the nineteenth century, under the influence of French
professors. For Maynooth got her first professors from
France, when the ecclesiastical seminaries there were suppressed, and their staffs expatriated, towards the end of
the eighteenth century. These French professors were
distinguished scholars, and their services were a valuable
asset to the recently founded Irish college; but, unfortunately, they were imbued with the Gallican tradition, and
they brought their Gallicanism with them to Maynooth.
For nearly half a century the theology of Maynooth was
" the Gallicanism of the Sorbonne, the Gallicanism of the
Clerus Gallicanus." From the same source Maynooth took
her ethics—a moral system of exorbitant rigorism, harsh,
narrow, intolerant. Under this alien influence Maynooth
became " a hot-bed of Gallicanism," and the Irish clergy
became " Gallican to the core." The Gallicanism of
Maynooth, however, was but a passing phase. The innate
orthodoxy of the Irish mind presently asserted itself; the
clear thought and right moral sense of the Irish student
penetrated the darkness of French error, and within half a
century the dangerous doctrines inculcated by professors of
the stamp of Delahogue—refugee professor of dogma—were
superseded by the clear teaching on the prerogatives of the
Roman Pontiff which found concrete expression in Murray's
De Ecclesia. With the sounder dogmatic teaching came a
milder system of moral doctrine, and text-books which a
short time before were proscribed in an *index prohibitorius*
became favourite books of reference with the students. No
violent causes were responsible for this revolution in
thought—simply, the Irish mind had triumphed over the
influence of Gallican teachers.

So contended Dr. Neville.

Neville's article, though written professedly in a detached
and friendly spirit, was resented in many quarters in
Ireland. The assertion that Maynooth for nearly half a

century was a hot-bed of Gallicanism, and had Gallicanised the Irish clergy, was felt by the friends and patrons of the college to be an arraignment unwarranted and undeserved. Dr. Walsh protested at once in the columns of the *Tablet* against the substance of the article, and challenged the unsupported statements of the writer.

A futile correspondence, lasting over weeks, followed. Neville reiterated his assertions (which Dr. Walsh as vigorously denied) and expressed surprise at the note of resentment that had been sounded : he had innocently intended " to exalt Maynooth," " to do honour to the living without reflecting any discredit on the dead." Many friends of the college deplored the incident and advised Dr. Walsh to drop the matter and let an unpleasant incident be speedily forgotten.* Others, more abundantly zealous for the honour of their college, urged him to publish a comprehensive reply to Neville's allegations. After much hesitancy he adopted

---

* A characteristic note (marked *private and confidential*) was written to Dr. Walsh by Dr. Croke about the matter (Dec. 5, 1879) :

" I wish all parties concerned expressly to understand, that though I am in most things a man of peace, I am by no means averse to a fair fight, and rather like, than otherwise, a trial of strength between such skilled buffers as yourself and the rector.

" I must, however, honestly confess that if I felt assured that you would hammer the rector well, and put his ' facts ' down his throat, causing him to keep the same to himself for evermore, I should be immensely gratified and exultant.

" But folk supposed to be learned in things pertaining to this controversy, have put it somehow into my head that the weight of the evidence is against you, and that certain depositions made by quondam professors, such as Slevin and Crotty, and others, in anno 1826, or so, whereof printed copy is kept in divers places, and easy of access, go conclusively to prove that Maynooth, up to the epoch aforesaid, was a hot-bed of Gallicanism, and that the clerics who issued therefrom were Gallicans ' to the heart's core.' Sic audivi. So honestly my solicitude is about you.

" To be sure, I do not think the controversy can serve any useful purpose, and may lead to ugly revelations. But if it must be for all that, let it be.

" So ' liberavi animam meam.'

" *Entre nous,* and confidentially, Ossory (Dr. Moran) thinks you a very young man to engage in such a weighty controversy."

the latter course, and in the following issue of the *Dublin Review*, January 1880, he replied to Dr. Neville in a lengthy article.

The article, which was hurriedly prepared, was a clever and able defence. Dr. Walsh dealt severely with the contention of Dr. Neville that his statements contained no reflection on the Irish clergy of his own day : Maynooth was founded about eighty years before (1795) and many of the existing Irish clergy—priests and bishops—were students of the college within the period under discussion. There existed in abundance living testimony to disprove the Rector's charges. Plainly, neither Maynooth nor the Irish clergy were then (1880) affected with Gallicanism; nor were they so affected thirty years previously—this on the Rector's own admission. The same could be proved true of the earlier decades of the century. Some of the senior Maynooth professors, who had completed their theological studies in the college within the period specified—one of them as early as 1827—had assured Dr. Walsh that in those days if any professor were so wanting in loyalty to the Holy See as to teach Gallican doctrines, he would, unquestionably, have been removed from his professorial office. Moreover, a venerable member of the existing hierarchy, John McHale, Archbishop of Tuam, who was a student of the college as early as 1808, in his sworn evidence before the Royal Commission of 1826, denied the alleged Gallicanism of Delahogue and his associate professors. These testimonies, Dr. Walsh contended, should in themselves be sufficient to close the case against Dr. Neville. But he went further. Although Neville, on whom the burden of proof properly rested, had adduced no proofs for his assertions, Walsh undertook to show that there were in fact no solid grounds to justify them. From a critical analysis of Delahogue's published works, and of the evidence given by the early professors—French and Irish—at the Royal Commission of 1826, he argued that the French professors did not obtrude Gallican principles (if they held them) and that Gallican doctrine was not contained in the suspect treatises of Delahogue. In confirmation of this conclusion he appealed to the verdict of the *Quarterly Review* of March 1828, which from the same evidence had concluded : " No more we think may be said to prove that the Irish Church does not, as a body, admit these [Gallican] articles, or permit them to be taught."*

Dr. Walsh readily admitted the rigoristic character of the early moral teaching at Maynooth. But this rigorism, he pointed out, was not derived from the imported French professors. It was due directly to Roman influence, and was in harmony with the contemporary teaching in the Roman schools and in general use throughout the Church. In fact its adoption at Maynooth was countenanced and even encouraged by the Roman authorities; after the foundation of Maynooth the Cardinal Prefect of Propaganda actually presented the college with a generous number of copies of Antoine—an anti-probabilist theologian of exceptional rigorism.

The article, an interesting example of polemical method, while it affords a fair illustration of Dr. Walsh's style and method as a controversial writer, is one of the rare instances in which he overstated his case. In refuting the charge that the French professors had Gallicanised Maynooth, and in defending the orthodoxy of the Irish clergy, he bases his case on weighty arguments which he uses to their full value and with telling effect. In his case regarding the early moral teaching at Maynooth he is also on solid ground. But when he endeavours to acquit the French professors of a Gallican leaning he is not convincing. His analysis of Delahogue's treatises and of the evidence given before the Royal Commission is a feat of skilful advocacy, which does not, however, compel the conviction that he claimed for it. His support from Delahogue is chiefly negative; the

* Cf. *Quarterly Review*, March, 1828.

replies of the early professors at the Commission, even in his judiciously chosen excerpts from their evidence, are very guarded and not always free from ambiguity. Though the evidence is skilfully arrayed and presented with great plausibility, the flaws in the argument emerge, and on this point, at least, he fails to establish his case against Dr. Neville.

At the end of the article in the *Dublin Review* Dr. Walsh expressed regret that the duty of replying to Dr. Neville's charges could not have been undertaken by one who seemed marked out for the task by his official position and long association with the college, as well as by his literary powers. He referred to Dr. Russell, the President of Maynooth, who at the time was dangerously ill. Three years previously he had been incapacitated as the result of a serious accident. He was thrown from his horse and suffered concussion of the brain, and though he lived a considerable time and was able to resume his duties, he never fully recovered from the shock, nor fully regained his physical or mental energy.

Russell was a man of recognised literary powers, and of high critical acumen. He co-operated with Wiseman in founding the *Dublin Review* (1836), and for a long period was one of its chief supporters. For years he contributed learned and interesting articles to almost every number of it. His papers on the English sonnet, which appeared in its pages, attest the fineness of his literary sense, and his exhaustive knowledge of the subject. In both Ireland and England Russell exercised considerable religious and social influence. His influence with Newman in his Anglican days had much to do with the great Tractarian's conversion, and is recorded in the *Apologia*.* His main interests, however, were centred in the college of Maynooth, where

* *Apologia pro Vita Sua,* p. 194.

he passed the greater part of his life, and where he was President for nearly a quarter of a century.

He died on February 26, 1880. His death opened the way for the promotion of Dr. Walsh, who was appointed President on June 22 of that year.

CHAPTER V

LAND TENURE REFORM

THE Bessborough Commission marks an important stage in the history of Irish Land Legislation. The Commission, of which Lord Bessborough was chairman, had been appointed in 1880 by Gladstone's ministry, to inquire into the Irish land system and to take evidence regarding the conditions of the tenure of land that prevailed in Ireland. The inquiry was held during the height of the Land League agitation and the findings of the Commission helped in no small degree to vindicate the justice of the claims of the tenant farmers of Ireland.

Dr. Walsh was perhaps the most important witness* who appeared before the Commission. Soon after he had been appointed President of Maynooth, the Trustees of the college deputed him to appear before the Commission to give evidence on their behalf regarding a farm from which the college had been recently evicted by the Duke of Leinster. His evidence dealt with the refusal of the Irish bishops, as tenants of the Duke of Leinster, to sign the " Leinster Lease"—a form of agreement under which it was sought to induce or to compel tenants to "contract themselves out" of the protection which was afforded them by the Land Act of 1870. By his evidence regarding the trans-action which resulted in the eviction of the bishops by the Duke, Dr. Walsh had a definitive share in influencing the minds of the Commissioners, and thus indirectly in impressing on Gladstone the need for a speedy introduction of the

* The *Tablet* (April 16, 1921) speaks of Dr. Walsh as the *decisive witness* at the Bessborough Commission.

Land Bill of 1881. He had also a direct part in the shaping of that measure, for, in his evidence before Lord Bess-borough, he had shown such an intimate knowledge of the Irish Land Question that the Gladstone Ministry consulted him when they were drafting their Bill. The chief channel through which his views were conveyed to Gladstone and his colleagues was H. C. E. Childers, who was Secretary of State for War in Gladstone's Cabinet.

In order to understand the bearing of Dr. Walsh's evidence it will be well here to draw attention to certain features of the system of land tenure in Ireland. Since the Legislative Union in 1800, the highest ideal of English statesmanship was to give Ireland what were called equal laws with England. The land laws which suited England, or rather the landlord classes in England, were deemed to be necessarily suited to Ireland, the under-lying assumption being that the conditions of land tenure in both countries were identical. Such an assumption was utterly at variance with facts. In England property in land meant the rights of the rent-receiver who had equipped the land and prepared it for the capital and skill of the tenant. In Ireland property in land, in the mind at least of the vast majority of the population, included rights of the cultivator whose labour had drained the land, reclaimed it and fenced it, and made farm roads and put a dwelling and farm build-ings on it, and given it all the working value it possessed.[*] The English notion of property in land was founded on feudalism : the landlord, under the Crown, was deemed to be exclusive owner of the land for the use of which a tenant bound himself to render certain services or to pay an agreed rent. The old Irish land system was founded on the tribal[†] basis : the people indeed paid tribute to the chief of the tribe, but they were always regarded as co-owners. This notion of partnership in Irish land had been to some extent

[*] Cf. Morley's *Life of Gladstone,* vol. i., p. 688.
[†] Cf. *Phases of Irish History.* MacNeill, pp. 289 and foll.

recognised in practice. For although, in the eye of the law, the landlord everywhere in Ireland was regarded as the sole owner of the land to the exclusion of the tenant, there existed, in fact, in certain parts of the country, a custom which admitted the tenant to a kind of partnership. This custom existed largely in Ulster, and to some extent outside of it. The essence of the " Ulster Custom" was, in the first place, that as the occupying tenant had possessory rights in his farm, a fair rent should be fixed not by competition but by valuation, and exclusively of improvements effected by the tenant; secondly, that the tenant should have the power to dispose of his interest in the holding, or, as it was called, of his goodwill. The law, however, recognised no such customary right. Throughout Ireland generally long-term leases were not granted to tenants, and leases from year to year were not unknown. A tenant who had not a lease was a tenant-at-will. The rent of the tenant-at-will was fixed arbitrarily by the landlord. If a tenant by his own unaided exertions had quadrupled the value of a patch of bog or prairie, the landlord might, without let or hindrance, quadruple the rent; moreover, the landlord might, without assigning cause or granting any compensation, turn a tenant out of the farm which he had drained and equipped, and on which he had erected all the steading.

Such was the system under which the vast majority of the tenant-farmers of Ireland had to live. The condition of the Irish tenantry might be painted in a single touch —they were yearly tenants-at-will.* The population of

* "What is the spectacle presented to us by Ireland? It is that of millions of persons whose only dependence and whose chief occupation is agriculture—for the most part cultivating their lands—that is sinking their past, their present, and their future upon yearly tenancies. What is a yearly tenancy? Why, it is an impossible tenure—a tenure which, if its terms were to be literally interpreted (and its terms were literally interpreted in Ireland) no Christian man would offer, and none but a madman would accept."—Lord Dufferin, quoted in Barry O'Brien's *The Irish Land Question,* p. 222.

Ireland at this time (1881) was about 5,000,000. There were approximately 600,000 agricultural holdings in the country, and, due allowance being made for dual ownership and occupancy, between three and a half and four millions of the people were directly and indirectly dependent on the land. This single fact stamped the land question as a central and vital issue in the Irish politics of the period. A single bad season was sufficient to cause widespread want and even famine; and rural hardships reacted on a great part of the business of the country. Trade in towns languished, debts to traders mounted up, farm rents remained unpaid, evictions followed, discontent and agitation ensued, with disorder and outrage in their train.*

It was with a view to remedying these evils, and especially to removing the inherent injustice of Irish land tenure, or, at least, of abating the acute and intolerable grievances of the occupying tenants, that Gladstone introduced the Land Bill of 1870. " The policy of the Bill," wrote Gladstone to Cardinal Manning, " is to prevent the landlord from using the horrible weapon of undue and unjust eviction, by so framing the handle that it shall cut his hands with the sharp edge of pecuniary damages. The man evicted without any fault and suffering the usual loss by it, will receive whatever the custom of the country gives, and where there is no custom, according to a scale, besides whatever he can claim for permanent buildings or reclamation of land. Wanton eviction will, as I hope, be extinguished by provisions like these. And if they extinguish wanton eviction they will also extinguish those demands for *unjust* augmentations of rent which are only formidable to the occupier because the power of wanton or arbitrary eviction is behind them."†

The Act of 1870 provided (1) that the Ulster Tenant-Right Custom should be converted into law; (2) that the usages

* Cf. *Ireland and the Empire*. T. W. Russell, p. 135.
† Cf. Morley, vol. i., p. 695.

outside Ulster analagous to the Ulster Custom should have the force of law; and (3) that "tenancies from year to year" unprotected by custom should imply the right of receiving

(*a*) "compensation for disturbance" by eviction, and

(*b*) "compensation for improvements" effected by the tenant or by his predecessors in title.

These rights of compensation, like many other benefits of the Act of 1870, were limited by a very zareba of provisos and restrictions, so that ingenious lawyers were easily able to draft leases and other agreements which completely, or almost completely, evaded the provisions of the Act. This is abundantly illustrated by the case of the "Leinster Lease."

The college at Maynooth possessed two holdings under the Duke of Leinster : one a perpetuity on which the college is built, the other a farm—the Laraghbryan Farm, as it was called—which was held from year to year. The college Trustees became tenants of the farm in 1849 in the time of the third Duke; and between him and the college authorities there always existed most friendly and neighbourly relations —the Duke's residence, *Carton*, and the college being situated in convenient proximity at opposite ends of the town of Maynooth.

In 1867 the Duke, wishing to re-arrange the boundaries of his property, purchased from the college some three-and-a-half acres of the perpetuity, which was a fee-farm tenure, and added it to the Laraghbryan farm which, with the addition, amounted to one hundred and thirty-seven acres, Irish. The extension of the farm entailed a revision of the rent, and the Duke wrote to the Bursar of the college, making the proposal that a rent of £4 18s. 0d. should be paid for the three-and-a-half acres, which would bring the rent of the farm—originally £295 2s. 0d.—up to £300 0s. 0d. a year. That will make the rent for the future £300 a year"—these were the Duke's words. The proposal was at once acquiesced in, and everything went smoothly during the Duke's lifetime. He died in 1874.

Sometime after the succession of the fourth Duke to the Leinster estate, the trouble commenced. In June 1877, the agent of the estate wrote to the Bursar of the college to say that the Duke thought that " it was high time for some more rent being paid by the college, and that the Trustees should not object to taking out a new agreement at £3 an acre." In other words, he proposed to raise the rent from £300 to something over £400 a year. The Trustees did not agree to the proposed increase. They represented to the agent and to the Duke that the college had regarded the letter of 1867—in which the rent was fixed *for the future* at £300—as giving complete security against an increase of rent, and they represented further that, viewing the letter of 1867 as giving all the security that any lease could afford, the college had expended a large amount on the permanent improvement of the farm : " farm buildings had been erected, old fences removed, new fences put up, thorough drainage carried out, and valuable manures liberally applied —all at the expense of the college without the contribution of a single shilling from the estate."

The only answer to this representation was a demand made by the agent in the following September for £470 rent —a rent at the rate of £3 10s. 0d. an acre. The agent thus demanded an increase of more than fifty per cent. on a rent which but ten years before had been fixed *for the future*, and regarded as a final settlement.

This new demand was based on a report of the Duke's valuator. In his report the valuator stated that the farm was thoroughly well cultivated, that everything was in first-class order, that it had been drained, that it had excellent fences and that it was in every way well-managed and was by a long way the best farm he had ever been employed to value for the Duke. The valuator, in making his estimate, had acted according to the Duke's instructions,

which were to value the land at " its fair letting value,"
taking no account of who had made the improvements or of
how far the improvements, on which he relied as adding
materially to the actual value of the holding, represented
the property of the Duke or the property of the college.

The Trustees, being anxious to retain the farm, as it was
situated conveniently near the college, endeavoured at first
to induce the Duke to withdraw the demand for an increase
of rent and allow them to continue on the same conditions
of tenure as obtained in the old Duke's time. This he
refused. In the course of further negotiations they intimated their readiness to pay the increased rent of £400.
But they informed the agent that they did so under con-
straint, and because, as they said, "they were entirely at
the mercy of the Duke." At this stage, March 1878, a
serious difficulty first presented itself. The Duke would
not consent to allow the college to retain the farm even at
the increased rent, except on the condition of the Trustees
accepting and signing the " Leinster Lease." As that lease
contained certain objectionable clauses, the Trustees would
not consent to sign it. The most obnoxious of these clauses
was *Clause 18*, the clause by which the tenants were to
agree to contract themselves out of the benefits of the Land
Act of 1870.*

Though refusing to accept the terms of the " Leinster
Lease," the Trustees were willing to take out a lease

---

* Clause 18 read as follows :—" Provided always, and it is
hereby expressly agreed, that the said Lessee, his Executors,
Administrators or Assigns, or any of them, shall not make any
claim for compensation in respect of disturbances or improvements (except improvements made with the written consent of
the Lessor, his Heirs or Assigns), or for compensation in any
other respect, under any of the clauses or provisions of the
Landlord and Tenant (Ireland) Act, 1870, save and except that
the portion of the buildings set out in the Schedule hereto
annexed which has been erected by the Lessee. The annual
value of the said demised Premises (i.e., the Laraghbryan farm)
being under the Acts relating to the Valuation of the rateable
property in Ireland (i.e., Griffith's valuation) the sum of two
hundred and fourteen pounds, sterling."

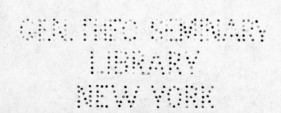

(excluding the peccant clauses) for thirty-one years, and they signified their willingness, if such a lease were granted, to abandon all claims for agricultural improvements. On this offer being refused, the Trustees made a further advance with a view to meeting the Duke's wishes. On October 17, 1878, their secretary wrote to inform the Duke " that the Trustees have the same confidence in the Leinster family as they reposed in the late Duke and that they are willing to accept the offer of the Laraghbryan farm at £3 per Irish acre, as tenants from year to year, in the same way as they held it from year to year under the late Duke *without any lease*." But the Duke was inexorable, and through his agent (February 1879) he informed the Trustees of his determination not to give any *lease* or *agreement* except on the form adopted in the whole of his estate (i.e., the Leinster Lease), " so that he declines any discussion on the subject; but he is willing, in other respects, to consult the convenience and wishes of the Trustees." The agent stated further : " I think that there must be some misapprehension on the part of the Trustees as to the terms of the lease, which was drawn up to meet the provisions of the Land Act of 1870, by two of our present eminent judges . . . and adopted by the tenantry on the estate of over 68,000 acres."

But the Trustees still held out. The Duke's willingness to meet their convenience and wishes in other respects could not induce them to yield. With them it was not so much a question of money as a question of principle. They might yield on the one point, they would not yield on the other. As they were all Catholic bishops, they felt that they would place themselves in a false position before the country if they gave their sanction, by their signature, to what they held to be an inequitable demand. Moreover, they were aware that their signing such a lease would be used as an argument to force defenceless tenants to sign similar instruments. If an ordinary tenant refused to sign, the alternative was eviction, and the consequence starvation. With

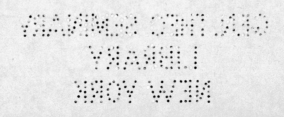

the Trustees the case was different; they were not living by agriculture, and so they might view the alternative with composure. They were quite aware that the lease, which was drawn by eminent lawyers to meet and evade the provisions of the Act of 1870, was a "legal" instrument. But it was none the less inequitable on that account. They knew, too, that the "lease" had been "adopted" over the Duke's estate, but that it was adopted, not because the tenants were satisfied with its provisions, but because in many cases refusal would have meant the workhouse or the emigrant ship. The Trustees stood firm; in due course they received a notice to quit, and were evicted from the farm. On being evicted they claimed and received some compensation for improvements; but they received no compensation for disturbance.

The case of the Laraghbryan farm and the "Leinster Lease" was brought up before the Bessborough Commission. Dr. Walsh represented the dispossessed Trustees. In the course of his examination by the Commissioners, an expression of his opinion on various aspects of the tenant conditions in Ireland was sought and given. On the question of the expediency and justification of state interference with "freedom of contract between landlord and tenant," he pointed out that no such freedom of contract existed, for the tenant was not really free. He possessed, no doubt, the freedom necessary for the performance of a human act, but freedom of bargaining he had none. Owing to the land hunger* in Ireland, tenants seeking land were ready to pay, and eager to promise excessive and exorbitant

* "Why do tenants take the land and offer to pay rent if they are not sure they can fulfil their contracts, and why should the State have to interfere in their bargains? To the first question the simple answer is: they cannot help themselves in what they do. There is a merciless necessity behind them. . . . In Ireland land is life. . . . . In a country like Ireland a land monopoly is fatal to free contract. Where myriad trade industries so compete with land that its occupation is not absolutely a necessity of life, the case is not the same."—*The Irish Land Question.* Barry O'Brien, pp. 107-8.

rents; and occupying tenants, unless protected by the legislature, were completely at the mercy of extortionate landlords. Lord Palmerston had proclaimed that "tenant
right is landlord wrong," but the very reverse was
frequently true. The right conferred on the landlord by
the State enabled him habitually to inflict cruel wrong on
the tenant. The witness pointed out, furthermore, that
ownership of land carried with it certain duties, and that it
was the business of the State to inquire and see that the
landlords discharged their duties as owners. In Ireland,
indeed, it was the right and the duty of the State to go
much further, for in Ireland the land was the monopoly of a
small privileged class, having been transferred by the action
of the State—by conquest, confiscation, plantation—to
landlords comparatively few in number, absentees in many
cases, and strangers as a rule. The landlords with whom
the Commission had to deal were the representatives in title
of those who acquired the land by the action of the State.
Like other monopolies, monopoly in land not only allowed
but demanded interference by the State whenever the
public good required it, for no rights of possession should
prevail against the common weal. He pointed out also
that there was abundant precedent for such intervention,
for it was the policy and practice of the State to intervene
and safeguard the public against monopoly-holders, as in
the case of railways, and by way of illustration he referred
to a speech of Lord Macaulay's regarding London cabs :

In showing that in many, even ordinary, transactions we
are not left to depend on "freedom of contract" he
(Macaulay) gives the example of a cab-driver and his fare.
"Freedom of contract" is an excellent principle where
supply and demand are free also. But sometimes they are
subject to close restrictions. In the supply of cabs for hire,
there is a restriction, imposed under the authority of parliament, for purposes of police. "We do not," says
Macaulay, "suffer everybody who has a horse and cab to
ply for passengers in the streets of London. And this

being so, we do not leave the fare to be determined by the supply and demand. We do not permit a driver to extort a guinea for going half a mile on a rainy day when there is no other vehicle on the stand." Now I am sure Parliament would not listen to a proposal that only the less wealthy classes should have the benefit of this interference with the fare, so that if the driver could identify the hirer as a man known to be well-to-do, with a good balance to his credit at the bankers, he might then extort a guinea if he liked. In other words the sound principle seems to be to look to the nature of the transaction in question and see whether any motive connected with the public good required that the terms of the contract should be regulated by law, and should not be left to be dictated at the discretion of the person who has command of the thing that is to be supplied. In such a case it would seem that the legislation should proceed irrespective of the pecuniary resources of the individual hirer.

Dr. Walsh's view on " freedom of contract" was adopted by the Commission, and is expressed in the report as follows :

We grant that it would be inexpedient to interfere with freedom of contract, between landlord and tenant, if freedom of contract really existed; but freedom of contract, in the case of the majority of Irish tenants, large and small, does not really exist.*

In equally telling fashion Dr. Walsh dealt with the inequitableness of fixing " fair rents" on the basis of tenement value; with the hardships of " town-park" tenants; with the impolicy of debarring lease-holding tenants from the benefits of the Land Acts; with the unfairness of allowing the landlord to pay income-tax on the tenement valuation. This last point he illustrated by the case of the Laraghbryan farm :

In Ireland Griffith's Valuation is, I believe, accepted as the standard or measure of the income-tax that a landlord

---

* *Report of the Royal Commission on the Irish Land Act.*

is called on to pay. In England, the landlord's income is estimated by the amount of rent he actually receives, certain deductions being made for monies laid out on the improvement of the land. But in Ireland any rent he can obtain from the tenants over the amount of Griffith's Valuation is free from income-tax altogether. When we paid £300 a year for the farm, the Duke paid income-tax on only £214 of this [£214 was the tenement valuation or Griffith's Valuation] and it would have been precisely the same if he had got the increased rent of £400 or £470.

The witness made suggestions regarding the emendation of the laws of " entail and settlement," and while expressing approval of the programme of the " three *F's*" (fixity of tenure, fair rent and free sale) he added :

At the same time I consider that without some very extensive legislation in another direction—that of peasant or occupying proprietorship—it will be impossible to make any satisfactory progress towards the settlement of the land question.*

Dr. Walsh's exposure of the " Leinster Lease" did not in any way affect the friendly relations which existed between him and the Duke. On December 28, 1880, he wrote to the Duke to assure him that it was only a sense of public duty which urged him to undertake the painful task of appearing as a witness before the Commission. On the following day the Duke wrote from Carton to reassure Dr. Walsh :

* The following from Morley's *Life of Gladstone* (vol. i., p. 696) is of peculiar interest, as illustrating the foresight of the bishops :—

" In March, 1870, Mr. Gladstone had received from Manning a memorandum of ill-omen from the Irish bishops, setting out the amendments [to the Land Bill] by them thought necessary. This paper included the principles of perpetuity of tenure for the tiller of the soil, and the adjustment of rent by a court. The reader may judge for himself how impossible it would have been even for Mr. Gladstone, in all the plenitude of his power, to persuade either cabinet or parliament to adopt such invasions of prevailing doctrine. For this, ten years more of agitation were required."

I have received your letter of yesterday, and beg to thank you for it; I understand your motives in giving evidence before the Land Commission, and I can assure you that I fully reciprocate the kindly feeling you express towards me personally.

Wishing you all the compliments of the season,

I am,

Your faithful servant,

LEINSTER.

The good relations between the Leinster family and the college continued unbroken.   When distinguished visitors were staying at Carton, it was the Duke's custom to bring them to visit the college, and that practice he kept up till the time of his death.   On November 1, 1883, we find the Duke writing to Dr. Walsh :

Mr. Trevelyan [then Chief Secretary to the Lord Lieutenant] wishes to see the College, and I shall be much obliged if you will allow me to take him to the library, etc., between 11 and 12 to-morrow.*

The Bessborough Commission reported " that (1) Irish tenants were justly entitled to proprietary rights on the grounds of outlay on improvements embodied in and inseparable from the soil, and of custom surviving in spite of legal denials of it; (2) freedom of contract did not exist between landlord and tenant; (3) improvements on and equipments of farms were usually the work of the tenants; (4) raising of rents had absorbed the value of the tenants' improvements; (5) consequently, insecurity and discontent rightly prevailed; and (6) the Land Act of 1870 had completely failed to protect tenants' property in their improvements."

* Mr. Trevelyan wrote to Dr. Walsh from the Chief Secretary's Lodge, on November 3, to thank him for the kind reception given to the visitors, and he added : " We were very much interested by our visit, seldom more by anything I have ever seen.   I am much obliged by your letter [about Lord Macaulay's speeches].   I will keep it carefully until I get back to the ' Speeches '; for I did not bring them here in the books which I have got about me."

The Commission recommended the repeal of former Acts; the simplification of the land laws; fixity of tenure at arbitrated rents; increased facilities for the purchase of their farms by the tenants; and the establishment of local land registries.* It was mainly on this report that Gladstone based the provisions of his great Land Bill of 1881.†

The report of the Commission was presented in March 1881, and on April 7 Gladstone introduced his Bill. The Land Bill of 1881, which is perhaps the greatest of Gladstone's legislative achievements,‡ was a vastly intricate measure. Gladstone himself said it was the most difficult measure he had ever known to come under the detailed consideration of the Cabinet;§ the Bill was so lengthy and complicated that it was commonly said in the House of Commons that there were not more than three men who had mastered it; the three were supposed to be Gladstone, Law (the Irish Attorney-General at the time) and Mr. T. M. Healy. But Dr. Walsh was to be added to their number.‖

When the Bill was printed it was eagerly read and studied in Ireland; but it was so intricate, so cryptic and elusive, that it was almost completely unintelligible to anyone who was not a professional lawyer. On April 12, the Bishop of Limerick, Dr. Butler, writing to Dr. Walsh (to congratulate him on his achievement in smashing a rebutting case made by the Duke of Leinster's agent in reference to the " Leinster Lease"), suggested to him that he " should try his hand at an exposition of the Land Bill." " For," wrote the Bishop, " since the Apocalypse was written, nothing so abstruse has appeared. The meaning, when there is any,

---

* Davitt. *Fall of Feudalism*, p. 322.
† " Mr. Gladstone's Bill omitted many of the most important recommendations of the Commission." *ibid.*
‡ Herbert W. Paul. Art. " Gladstone," in *Dict. of Nat. Biog.,* vol. xxii., p. 733.
§ Morley's *Life of Gladstone,* ii., p. 220.
‖ T. P. O'Connor in *Daily Telegraph,* Ap. 11, 1921.

is so veiled and hidden away that ordinary men cannot
even make a decent guess at it. To make it intelligible to
your fellowmen would be at once a great boon and a great
intellectual achievement that would never be forgotten to
you." Dr. Walsh promised at once to make an effort to
comply with the Bishop's suggestion. Straightway he set
to work with zest and earnestness and in a short time he
had finished his task.

His analysis of the Bill appeared under the title, " *A
Plain Exposition of the Irish Land Bill*, By a Layman."*
The pamphlet, of about one hundred and fifty pages, was
published anonymously. The reason of the anonymity was
given by the writer himself in a preface to one of the later
editions of the pamphlet :

It was published anonymously, for, notwithstanding the
confidence of the author as to its technical accuracy, most
efficiently secured by the kind co-operation of more than
one legal friend, he was not without misgiving as to the
opinion which might be formed of the work as a whole.
For the outline and general plan on which he had
constructed it, he alone was responsible; and he was, of
course, aware that in these respects he had departed widely
from the method usually followed in the explanation of
Acts of Parliament. Thus he felt that the novelty of the
plan on which he had ventured might possibly have the
result of causing the exposition to be regarded as a failure.
In view, then, of what he owed to the position in which he
has the honour to be placed (President of Maynooth), it
was but natural that he should shrink from placing his
name on the title page.

The *Exposition* was orderly, lucid, plain, exhaustive.
In a couple of weeks it ran through two editions. The
pamphlet aroused considerable curiosity as to its authorship,
but it was soon known to be the work of Dr. Walsh; and he
was highly complimented on his achievement by lawyers and
statesmen.

* Layman—*i.e.*, one not a professional lawyer.

Mr. H. C. E. Childers, writing to the author from the War Office, May 17, 1881, said :

Your *Exposition of the Land Bill* seems to me by far the best account of the Bill which has been given, either in print or in speech. Although I have studied the details of the Bill since the first proof was discussed at Cabinet (and there had been twenty different drafts of the Bill before the Cabinet up to that time*) I shall find your pamphlet very useful.

I agree with what you say about disclosing the authorship ; I shall act with prudence, if I am asked any questions on the subject.

Again on July 15, Childers wrote :

I have sent the marked copy of your pamphlet to Mr. Gladstone and he has closely perused it and returned it to me.† I shall study it this evening with care, and I am much obliged to you for it.

Our ultras in the House are behaving incredibly.

Sir Charles Russell, an intimate personal friend, wrote to Dr. Walsh on May 8, 1881 :

I think the *Exposition* in every way admirable. I would suggest a good index, and a marginal note of the sections. I am in doubt somewhat as to the position of the future tenant.‡

While the Bill was before Parliament, Dr. Walsh was in constant touch with the Cabinet. The medium of communication was Childers. Though Walsh had a share in shaping some of the main provisions of the Land Bill, many of his far-reaching suggestions were not adopted by the Cabinet.

The second reading of the Bill began on April 25, and was passed on May 29. The Bill was read the third time in the

* See Barry O'Brien's *Life of Parnell,* vol. i., p. 229.
† The letter contains this interesting postscript : " I hope that there may be some truth in the report which assigns to you, at no remote date, a seat in the Sacred College."
‡ " It is said that the famous *Exposition* of Gladstone's complex and controverted Land Act made that measure clear, amongst others, to the author of it."—*The Tablet,* April 16, 1921.

Commons on July 30, and on August 22 it received the Royal Assent. The Act in its final shape—it had been considerably modified in the House of Lords—was moulded to a large extent on the findings of the Bessborough Commission. It legalised the right of yearly tenants to sell their tenancies at the best available price. It provided for the establishment of a Land Court to which tenants or landlord and tenant acting in common, but not the landlord alone, should have access for the fixing of a fair rent. A limited fixity of tenure was secured to the tenant inasmuch as the judicial rent was unchangeable for fifteen years; during that time the tenant could not be evicted except for breach of contract or non-payment of rent. Nothing was laid down as to what constituted a " fair rent," but what was known as the " Healy Clause" provided that " no rent shall be allowed or payable in respect of improvements made by the tenant or his predecessors."[*]

After the enactment of the Bill, Childers and others urged Dr. Walsh to bring out an exposition of the Act, and to publish it over his own name. Sir Charles Russell especially was most anxious to have this done. Writing to Dr. Walsh from Londesborough Lodge, Scarborough, on August 18, 1881, he says :

Your *Exposition* was admirable of the Bill. I very much wish you would take in hand a brief practical statement in the simplest and least technical way of the *Act*. It would be very useful. Explaining the position of each tenant in classes, and addressing each of the classes in language not to be misunderstood.

[*] Davitt. *Fall of Feudalism,* p. 324.
J. F. Bright, *History of England,* vol. v, p. 14, says that the *Bill* proposed " the establishment, on a somewhat small scale, of peasant proprietorship. In order to afford assistance to occupiers and enable them to obtain possession of their holdings, the Commissioners were to be allowed to advance on satisfactory security, as much as three-fourths of the sum required for purchase; or even directly to purchase estates for the purpose of re-selling to the tenants their respective holdings, if fully satisfied both of the expediency of the step, and that a sufficient number of the tenants on the estate demanded it."

Suggested order :—Arrears; Judicial Rent; Status following, etc.

We shall be here until 1 October. Could you come to us for a few days? I will help to revise your Guide. Do not neglect this opportunity of doing useful work which would be all the more effectual if published under your own name. Pray let me hear. If I don't see you *here* I shall be in Ireland towards the end of September; but I wish you would be our guest for a few days.

On August 28 Russell again wrote importuning Dr. Walsh to undertake the exposition of the Act, and in urging the matter he was supported by Sir Francis (afterwards Baron) Herschell, then the English Solicitor-General, and subsequently Lord High Chancellor of England. Herschell, too, gave his views on how the thing ought to be done :

My idea would be to have the description of the Land Act as short as possible, and told in the simplest manner.

It should deal with the case of present tenants mainly, referring only afterwards to future tenants and the difference in their rights, etc., etc.

Yielding to these urgent requests, Walsh set to work and prepared a pamphlet which he soon published under the title of *A Plain Exposition of the Irish Land Act of 1881.* It was published on September 12, 1881, over his own name. In a short preface he explained the object of the pamphlet and the reason of his putting his name to it.

Although the author is aware that very soon after the publication of the pamphlet (*The Exposition of the Bill*), its authorship was generally ascribed to him, he thinks it right to add that in now departing from the course he originally adopted, and in publishing this new edition under his own name, he is acting solely at the solicitation of those to whose judgment in such a matter he has felt bound to submit his own.

Having done so he feels that he has also placed himself under the necessity of plainly pointing out the scope of the pamphlet and the object which he had in view in writing it.

It is not a political essay. It has no reference to any of

the numerous questions, speculative or practical, which seem at present to attract so large a share of public attention in Ireland. Whether the Land Act, now that it is passed, is to be regarded as a boon or as a national calamity; whether it should be rejected or made use of by the tenant farmers of the country; whether it should be accepted as a final settlement of the Land Question or merely as an instalment, or, indeed, accepted at all; how much of it, or of the good that is in it, is due to English statesmanship and love of justice and how much to the pressure of Irish agitation;* on these, as on all such questions, any expression of opinion in these pages will be sought in vain.

The author has had in view one object only—to set forth in language as free from technicality as the technical nature of the subject would admit, a plain, intelligible, and complete statement of the results of the enactment of the vast and complicated scheme of legislation embodied in the sixty-two sections of this Act.

Whether he has failed or succeeded in this object it is not for him to judge.

The unanimous verdict of those most competent to form a judgment was that it was an eminently successful achievement. Mr. John O'Hagan, who was himself shortly afterwards appointed the Land Judge to administer the Act, wrote on September 16, 1881:

I both thank you and congratulate you on your *Exposition*.

I have as yet been only able to look through it cursorily, but it seems to me most admirably and completely done.

I shall make it my duty to read it through with great care and minuteness.

Lord O'Hagan, the Lord Chancellor of Ireland, gave the pamphlet unstinted praise; so, too, did other prominent

* " There is no use," an Irish Unionist member once said in the House of Commons, " in any Irishman approaching an English minister on Irish questions, unless he comes with the head of a landlord in one hand or the tail of a cow in the other. . . . . We all now know how the Land League triumphed." " I must make one admission," said Gladstone in 1893, " and that is, that without the Land League, the Act of 1881 would not now be on the Statute book."—Barry O'Brien's *Life of Parnell*, vol. i., p. 293.

members of the Bench and Bar in England and in Ireland.
Among these none was more cordial or more unqualified in
his praise than the Right Hon. Edward Gibson, K.C., the
Tory ex-Attorney-General for Ireland, who during the
Liberal administration from 1880 to 1885, was the chief
spokesman of the Opposition on Irish affairs, and the
chief critic of the Land Bill of 1881.   Dr. Walsh and
Gibson had become acquainted during the O'Keeffe trial
when the young professor from Maynooth coached the
King's Counsel in the Canon Law, as they walked by the
seashore at Wicklow.   In 1885 Gibson was raised to the
peerage with the title of Baron Ashbourne; and he was at
three different times Lord Chancellor of Ireland.   His name
is permanently associated with an Act for facilitating the
sale of Irish holdings to tenants, commonly known as the
Ashbourne Act (1885).   For the principle of this and other
subsequent Land Purchase Acts, Dr. Walsh, as will appear,
was in no small measure responsible.

CHAPTER VI

IRISH UNIVERSITY EDUCATION
THE ROYAL UNIVERSITY

AT the time when Dr. Walsh began his administration at
Maynooth, the position of Irish Catholics as regards facilities
for higher education had undergone no substantial change
since the days when he himself had been a student of the
Catholic University. The Queen's University, with the
Queen's Colleges and Dublin University, were still under
the ban of the Church; the Catholic University was without
a charter and without endowment. An attempt had been
made by the Russell Ministry in 1866 to afford the students
of the Catholic University an opportunity of obtaining
degrees, by conferring a new Supplemental Charter on the
Queen's University, empowering it to examine and to confer
degrees on students other than those of the Queen's Colleges.
The plan aroused the hostility of the opponents of
denominational education; its legality was challenged in the
law courts, and an injunction obtained setting aside the
Supplemental Charter as illegal. A scheme of bolder
dimensions, though not without its defects, was put forward
by Gladstone in his University Bill of 1873. Gladstone's
proposal was, in brief, that Dublin University, as distinct
from Trinity College, should be enlarged so as to comprise within it Trinity College, the Catholic University, the
Queen's Colleges at Belfast and Cork, and any other
colleges which should fulfil certain conditions set forth in
the Bill as entitling a college to University status. The Bill
was rejected by a majority of three at the second reading,
and its defeat ousted the Liberal Ministry from office.

The Royal University of Ireland was established by Act of the Imperial Parliament under the Tory Government in 1879. The new scheme in no way affected the status of Trinity College. The Queen's University was dissolved, but the Queen's Colleges retained their status and their endowments. The Royal University, like the Queen's University which it superseded, was in practice a mere examining body; but it was empowered to grant degrees not merely to students of the Queen's Colleges but also to all students who passed its examinations, no matter where they had pursued their studies. It received a grant of £20,000 a year to meet the expenses of administration and to provide " Prizes, Scholarships, and Fellowships" according to a scheme to be drawn up by the Senate. The Senate, which was nominated by the Crown, was also charged with the duty of drawing up regulations for the working of the University. While no direct endowment was provided for the Catholic University, it was understood and arranged that the " Prizes, Scholarships, and Fellowships" should be so allotted as to constitute at least an indirect endowment by giving substantial help to students of the unendowed colleges.

The constitution of the Senate was obviously a vital detail in the scheme. It proved to be its weakest point. The principle followed by the Lord Lieutenant in nominating the members was to give Catholics and Protestants equal representation. The Catholic half of the Senate thus constituted included some of the most prominent advocates of mixed education in the country, among them Dr. Sullivan, President of Queen's College, Cork, and Sir Robert Kane, a former President of the same institution. The Senate included also as first Vice-Chancellor of the University Lord O'Hagan, the first Catholic Lord Chancellor of Ireland. Lord O'Hagan had the hardihood to assert publicly that the Senate, as actually constituted, had been nominated " in an equitable and liberal spirit." " It represented,"

he said, " every religious denomination, every political
section, and every school of thought, and its constitution
was so wise that it defied assault and silenced hostile
criticism." The truth was that the actual constitution
of the Senate was a matter of deep dissatisfaction to
all Catholics except those within the official Government
circle. The bishops had consented to the nomination
of two of their body, but their action was far from being
unanimous; and had the general constitution of the Senate
been known beforehand, their consent would certainly have
been withheld. When the list of senators was published
it was realised that it was too late to take any effective
action. The episcopal representatives were Dr. McCabe,
Archbishop of Dublin, and Dr. Woodlock, Bishop of
Ardagh.

The Senate made certain provisions, more or less effective,
to secure that as little as possible of the annual endowment
of £20,000 should go to the professors or officers, or to the
students of the endowed Queen's Colleges; it also established a system of Fellowships. To each of these Fellowships
an annual salary of £400 was assigned; the duties of a
Fellow were to teach in some college approved by the
Senate, and to take part in conducting the examinations of
the University.

Of the Fellowships, twenty-eight in number, one half was
assigned as the Catholics' share. It was confidently expected
that of these some at least would be allocated to Maynooth,
and that thus an inducement would be given to the
authorities of that college to have their students avail
themselves of the opportunity, then for the first time
afforded them, of obtaining in Ireland degrees recognised by
the State, without having to attend lectures in institutions
condemned by the Church. The junior students at
Maynooth began to be prepared in the courses of the Royal
University (1880), but the expectations regarding Fellowships were never realised.

A scheme was actually drawn up according to which four Fellowships were to be assigned to Maynooth, and the candidates for three of the posts were nominated. These were the Rev. John Healy (afterwards Archbishop of Tuam), the Rev. John Egan (afterwards Bishop of Waterford), and the Rev. Dr. P. J. Tynan (professor at Clonliffe College). For the fourth Fellowship the name of Dr. Walsh was proposed by Archbishop McCabe, but Dr. Walsh declined to be nominated, as he considered that it would not be practicable for him to combine the duty of constant and regular teaching with his office of President of Maynooth. The name of the Rev. M. Murphy, professor at St. Patrick's College, Carlow, was substituted instead.

The scheme was not adopted, owing partly to the unfriendly reception it met with from the staff at Maynooth, but chiefly to " the failure of Dr. McCabe to impress his views on his colleagues of the Senate."*

When the prolonged negotiations regarding the securing of Fellowships for Maynooth had proved fruitless, it was decided by a majority of the Maynooth Trustees that the students of their college should no longer go forward for the examinations of the Royal University. This decision was at once communicated to Dr. Walsh by the episcopal secretary, Dr. Logue, June 10, 1882 :

I have been requested by the bishops to inform you that their Lordships have decided to discontinue the connection between St. Patrick's College, Maynooth, and the Royal University.

The action of the bishops in severing the connection of Maynooth with the Royal University was not in consonance with the views of Archbishop McCabe. He was anxious to continue the connection, and he conjectured that the breakdown of the negotiations regarding the Fellowships had been caused in no small measure by the hostility of the teaching

* Letter of Bishop Gillooly to Dr. Walsh, April 22, 1882.

staff at Maynooth, who demurred to admitting "strangers," as they designated the new Fellows, to their body. Their hostility was attributed particularly to the fact that the "strangers" were to be placed on a more favourable financial footing than themselves. Dr. McCabe was not only disappointed but much annoyed that the scheme for establishing the Fellowships at Maynooth miscarried. Writing to Dr. Walsh the Archbishop gave frank expression to his views, June 12, 1882 :

(Private). You, of course, have heard before this that the bishops decided that the connection between Maynooth and the Royal University is not to be continued. I think that, without breaking the silence which is imposed on us, I may say that I am sorry for this decision. I am more sorry still for the reasons urged on their Lordships to come to this conclusion. The principal argument brought forward from the college was that the connection would injure the discipline of the college, and possibly injure the vocations of some promising students. This may all be true, but we never heard it till there was no chance of getting the four Fellowships. I confess the effect on my mind was not a pleasing one towards my *Alma Mater*.

I will now reconsider the question of closing the Theology classes at Clonliffe, but all this is for yourself alone.

The connection between Maynooth and the Royal University, which was to be discontinued, had consisted merely in the fact that, for a short time after the establishment of the Royal University, the Arts students at Maynooth prepared the courses and presented themselves for the examinations of the Royal University. This line of action had been adopted in accordance with a resolution of the Maynooth Trustees passed in September 1880, requesting " that every effort should be made during the coming year by the professors and superiors of the college to carry out their [the Trustees'] wishes respecting the preparation of the students of the

Philosophy and Rhetoric classes for the Arts Examination
of the Royal University."

A few words may be added in explanation of the
incident referred to in Dr. McCabe's letter, of the
suggested closing of the theology school at Clonliffe.
Holy Cross College, Clonliffe, the diocesan seminary of
Dublin, was founded by Cardinal Cullen in 1859. Almost
from its foundation it had, in addition to classes in
Arts and Philosophy, a theological school where lectures
were given to the students on the usual theological subjects.
The college did successful work; it kept the noiseless tenour
of its way for twenty years till 1880, when the new Archbishop, Dr. McCabe, decided to suppress it as a teaching
centre, and to reduce it practically to the position of a
clerical hostel. The Arts students were to be sent to
attend lectures given by Fellows of the Royal University at
Stephen's Green, and the Archbishop's expressed intention
was to abolish the theology classes, and transfer the
theological students to Maynooth, or to St. Stephen's Green,
if theology was to be taught there. In adopting this course
he was influenced by the advice of Dean Neville and
Dr. Walsh. Dr. McCabe's directions regarding the Arts
students were actually carried out for a while, but the
scheme to abolish the theological school never matured. It
was a proposal in which the superiors and professors at
Clonliffe thought they should not acquiesce, without putting
formally and forcibly before the Archbishop their reasoned
objections to what they considered to be an ill-advised and
unwise scheme.

Accordingly, when Dr. McCabe visited Clonliffe for the
purpose of addressing the students on the proposed new
departure, he was received by the Rector and professors,
who asked to be allowed to put before him a written statement of their views regarding his contemplated changes.
He acceded to the request, listened attentively to the read-

ing of the statement, and then, without addressing the students, he at once left the college, merely remarking to the Rector (Rev. B. Fitzpatrick) : " I am too old now to run my head against a stone wall." For some time after this incident the relations between Dr. McCabe and Clonliffe were somewhat strained. The theological classes, however, were not discontinued. Towards the Rector of Clonliffe, whom he looked on as mainly responsible for the frustration of his plans, and towards the staff, Dr. McCabe manifested some displeasure for a while. But in a comparatively short time he admitted frankly the unwisdom of his project, and during the last years of his life he took many an opportunity of showing his practical and affectionate regard for the college and its staff.

This incident brings into relief and throws an instructive light on Dr. McCabe's character. He was impetuous and easily led, sometimes wrong-headed, not infrequently ill-advised, but always transparently honest and single-minded, and remarkably free from vanity or pettiness and from anything like personal animosity.

Before his election to the See of Dublin, Dr. McCabe had spent his whole life in pastoral work, and was little fitted by education or training to take part in the task of organis-ing or administering a university. Shortly after his appointment to the Senate he became keenly alive to the handicap under which he laboured, and he eagerly looked for an opportunity to resign. He wrote to Dr. Walsh, October 3, 1881 : " If I was sure that a Catholic would take my place at the Senate, I would retire, as I feel out of place in the company we meet there." From a sense of duty, and yielding to the influence of Lord O'Hagan and his friends, Dr. McCabe continued his membership of the Senate. But he continued on the condition that, at the earliest opportunity, he should get the help of an expert

Catholic educationist; and at his suggestion it was arranged that Dr. Walsh should become a member of the Senate. This was in 1883.

The advent of the new member soon produced a certain liveliness and some dissension in the Senate; and the policy he inaugurated speedily brought about a crisis which eventuated in Cardinal McCabe's resignation. In order to understand the policy advocated by Dr. Walsh, it is necessary to explain that, in consequence of the system of examinations adopted by the Royal University, an important change was made in the organisation of the Catholic University by its governing body, the Irish bishops.

The Catholic University—which had neither State endowment nor legal recognition—had up to that time consisted practically of a single college—the college situated in St. Stephen's Green, Dublin. But as in the organisation of the Royal University the Catholic University was not to be in any way recognised as a distinct institution, and as the need of the hour was to establish the injustice done to the Catholics of Ireland by the persistent refusal to them of the endowment for university purposes to which they were, on so many grounds, entitled, the bishops resolved on reorganising the constitution of the Catholic University. It was decided that thenceforth it should comprise all those Catholic colleges which were entitled, by the number of their students and by the standard of their studies, to rank as University colleges. The college which had previously stood alone, as comprising within itself the Catholic University of Ireland, thenceforth became one of a group of associated colleges. Its official designation was accordingly changed. Thenceforth it was known as " University College, Dublin." The Catholic University as reconstituted embraced the following colleges :—University College, Dublin; St. Patrick's College, Maynooth; University College, Blackrock; St. Patrick's College, Carlow; Holy

Cross College, Clonliffe; and the Catholic University School of Medicine, Dublin.*

The new arrangement was made in October 1882. The colleges, while retaining their independent collegiate organisations, were grouped together as parts of an organism to which they naturally belonged. The advantage of this grouping arrangement was that the successes attained at the examinations of the Royal University by the students of the Catholic University would be a set-off against the successes at the same examinations of the other group of students—the students of the Queen's Colleges. For, notwithstanding the dissolution of the Queen's University, the three Queen's Colleges continued, in the public estimation, to form a connected group.

The episcopal scheme of reorganisation did not find favour with the party which controlled the working of the Senate. They had made up their minds that the Catholic University was extinct; the establishment of the Royal University, they considered, had put an end to it. In their view the Catholic University had become simply a college to be " recognised " as such by the Royal University. They adopted the policy, then, of ignoring every other Catholic college except the one in St. Stephen's Green, Dublin. Having done so, they skilfully devised a scheme calculated to create the impression that a substantial endowment had been made available for Catholic University purposes. The Fellowships available for Catholics were to be concentrated in the one " recognised " Catholic college. The income accruing from the Fellowships, £5,600, would in a certain sense constitute an endowment for that callege. This arrangement was at first acquiesced in by the episcopal representatives on the Senate.

When Dr. Walsh joined the Senate he pointed out to his colleagues, Cardinal McCabe and Dr. Woodlock, how

* See in *I. E. Record,* March-June, 1928, *The Catholic University of Ireland,* by Rev. L. McKenna, S.J.

inequitable the existing arrangements were. The endowment of the Catholic college compared most unfavourably with that of the Queen's Colleges. The Catholic institution received about £6,000 from the State funds, the Queen's Colleges about £30,000. Moreover, the Queen's Colleges were aided in preparing for their examinations by State funds—libraries, laboratories, and other educational appliances being provided for them at the public expense—while all such assistance was denied even to the " recognised" Catholic College. Furthermore, he drew attention to the utter unfairness of the policy of the Senate towards the other colleges of the Catholic University. Not only did these colleges not receive any pecuniary aid in preparing their students for the examinations of the Royal University, but the students had to submit themselves for examination to a board of examiners composed of Fellows of the Queen's Colleges and of the "recognised" Catholic College. Thus the examinations of the University, even for the highest honours and most valuable prizes in its gift, were conducted by those who, first of all, had the duty of preparing particular sections of students for examination ; who were then allowed to set the examination papers, setting them, as they must have done, whether consciously or unconsciously, on the lines of their own method of teaching; and who finally proceeded to examine, in a strictly competitive examination, all the students of the University. It is obvious that such a system placed the Catholic colleges of the country, with one exception, at an enormous disadvantage, and that the examinations themselves did not escape the taint of inequality and injustice. For while the students of these colleges received from the University no help whatever in preparing for their examinations, their competitors and rivals were prepared for those very examinations by the examiners themselves. The defect was a defect of principle.

Dr. Walsh proposed that as a first step towards remedying these glaring inequalities a certain number of the

Catholic Fellowships should be allocated to colleges of the Catholic University other than University College, Dublin. He suggested that a beginning should be made with University College, Blackrock.

The Blackrock College, notwithstanding the disadvantages under which it laboured, had done remarkably well at the examinations of the Royal University. Indeed it had in some respects outstripped University College, Dublin, which at the time had nine Fellowships. After the success of Blackrock had made it plain that some of the most efficient work on the Catholic side was being done there, Dr. Walsh, unanimously supported by the Episcopal Educational Committee, advised that in the second appointments of Catholic Fellows a determined effort should be made to secure that the policy of the former appointments should be modified. As two new Catholic Fellows were to be appointed at a meeting of the Senate which was then (January 1884) imminent, it was agreed that it should be proposed at the meeting that one of the Fellowships should be given to a member of the staff of the Blackrock College, the Rev. J. E. Reffé. And as the Jesuit Fathers, who were then in charge of University College, Dublin, were putting forward two members of the Society as candidates, it was suggested that the Superior of the Irish Province should be requested to withdraw one of the Jesuit candidates for the Fellowships.

Notwithstanding this request, which was made through Cardinal McCabe, the candidature was persevered in. The Cardinal, however, believing that, by taking a decided stand in the matter he would be able to prevent an open conflict of the Catholic forces in the Senate, himself proposed the formal resolution for the appointment of Father Reffé, stating expressly that he did so in pursuance of a unanimous recommendation of the Episcopal Committee. It was at once made evident that episcopal wishes were to carry little or no weight in the Senate of the Royal University. A Catholic nobleman, Lord Emly, proposed the appointment of the Jesuit candidate, and after a short discussion the Cardinal's motion was defeated. It obtained only three votes : those of the Cardinal, the Bishop of Ardagh, and Dr. Walsh. Lord Emly's motion was supported by twenty-one members.[*]

It happened that at the meeting of the Senate which rejected Cardinal McCabe's proposal, an award of six prizes, each of £150, was to be made on the report of the University examiners. Two of the successful competitors were Catholics, both students of Blackrock College. The Cardinal made pointed reference to this fact when proposing the appointment of Father Reffé. The reply was that that consideration should not be allowed to influence the Senate ; the Senate, it was added, should be guided by the views of the majority of the Catholic members of the body, and in the opinion of the majority, the interests of Catholic University Education rendered it imperative that their policy, and not the policy of the Cardinal, should be maintained.

This proceeding of the Senate was, naturally, followed by Cardinal McCabe's resignation. Dr. Walsh also resigned. Under great pressure from the Lord Lieutenant, however, the Cardinal consented to withdraw his resignation, without making any stipulation as to the future policy of the Senate. As a matter of fact, the Cardinal never again attended a meeting of the Senate. Dr. Walsh was not asked to reconsider his resignation; he had had it conveyed to the Lord Lieutenant that in the circumstances such a request would be quite useless.

Dr. Walsh was disappointed and indignant that the Cardinal allowed himself to be persuaded into withdrawing his resignation. The policy of resigning if the proposal to appoint Father Reffé were rejected had been expressly agreed to by the Cardinal after careful and

[*] Cf. *Minutes of Meeting of the Royal University Senate,* January 30, 1884, p. 185.

anxious consideration. Dr. Walsh, who had strongly urged
the adoption of that policy, was nettled at the " deplorable
weakness " of the Cardinal. Moreover, he was convinced
that the Cardinal's ingenuousness rendered him unfit to be
leader in a cause in which he had to deal with plausible
Catholic Whigs like Lords O'Hagan and Emly. Rightly or
wrongly, then, Dr. Walsh had definitely made up his mind,
that in matters of education, no less than in questions of
public policy, Dr. McCabe was under the influence, not
to say the domination, of his Whig advisers, lay and
clerical. Consequently, from that time forward he kept
very much away from the Cardinal. He withdrew from the
" University Consultative Council"—a body of Catholic
educationists whom the Cardinal had invited to assist him
—declining to give any further advice, even on questions of
education. Up to the time of the Cardinal's death an
aloofness, almost an estrangement, existed between the two
men. There is no doubt that Dr. Walsh's alienation from
Cardinal McCabe was, in some measure, due to the strong
antipathy he entertained to the Cardinal's political views
and actions. This antipathy was fomented by the influence
of Dr. Croke, Archbishop of Cashel, of whom Dr. Walsh was
a political disciple and an ardent admirer. Between
Dr. Croke and Cardinal McCabe there had long existed a
deep-rooted political antagonism. The Cardinal did not
claim or pretend to understand politics, but his denunciations of agrarian crime were being constantly exploited for
political purposes by the landlord or " Castle" party.

Dr. Croke was a pronounced politician. He, too, had
denounced outrages, had condemned and killed the " No
Rent Manifesto"; but he was a stout defender and a strong
supporter of the Land League and of other popular movements, and in his advocacy of popular views he was forceful
and outspoken. When Dr. McCabe denounced the "Ladies'
Land League," and expressed his alarm about the modesty

of the women of Ireland, who were joining in political turmoil, Dr. Croke wrote a fierce and scathing public denunciation of his action. It is not easy to find in modern ecclesiastical annals a more severe or mordant rebuke administered by a bishop to a brother-prelate. The censure of Dr. McCabe was conveyed in a letter addressed by Dr. Croke to A. M. Sullivan, who himself had just then published a sharp rejoinder to Archbishop McCabe's condemnation of the Ladies' Land League :

ARCHBISHOP CROKE TO A. M. SULLIVAN.

March 17, 1881.

Dear Mr. Sullivan,—I congratulate you on your timely and, under the peculiarly provoking circumstances, very temperate and withal touching letter that appears over your name in this day's *Freeman.*

I adopt unreservedly, the sentiments you have so admirably expressed, and am delighted to find that some one of mark has at last stepped forward from the ranks of the laity to vindicate the character of the good Irish ladies who have become Land Leaguers, and to challenge publicly the monstrous imputations cast upon them by the Archbishop of Dublin.

His Grace will not be allowed in future, I apprehend, to use his lance as freely as he has hitherto done, and to ventilate unquestioned the peculiar political theories which he is known to hold in opposition to the cherished convictions of a great, and indeed overwhelming, majority of the Irish priests and people.

It is a satisfaction, however, to feel that His Grace's political likings and dislikings, though possibly of some importance elsewhere, carry with them very little weight or significance, except with a select few in Ireland.

This ruthless, if eloquent letter, bristling with the writer's *saeva indignatio*, stung the Cardinal to the quick. But generous man that he was, he forebore to utter a word of resentment, nor did he entertain any trace of bitterness towards Dr. Croke, to whom he gave credit for the highest disinterestedness. Indeed, when sometime later the Archbishop of Cashel, in the discharge of his ecclesiastical duty, had occasion to seek a favour from his brother of Dublin, Dr. McCabe acceded so handsomely and so generously to the request that Dr. Croke took a characteristically generous resolution that, come what might, he would never again be provoked to utter in public a word of discourtesy to so high-souled a man. These sentiments are recorded in a letter written by Croke to Walsh, May 26, 1882 :

I can never forget Dr. McCabe's kindness to me who did not deserve it from him. I have sworn eternal friendship to him and shall keep my oath faithfully. He is evidently an honest, honourable, and high-minded man. I am better pleased than anything that events led me to ask a favour of him and that he granted it so promptly and so pleasantly.

Notwithstanding Dr. Croke's feelings of personal esteem for Cardinal McCabe, his disapproval of the Cardinal's political views grew day by day more intense. And while keeping his " oath," as he sat chafing and eating his heart in his palace at Thurles, he allowed his pent-up feelings of indignation at the "Dublin man's execrable politics" to find frank and forcible expression in his private letters to Dr. Walsh. In this way Dr. Croke, unintentionally, yet withal powerfully, contributed to fostering a prejudice against the Cardinal in the mind of Dr. Walsh, and to strengthen the opinion already held by Dr. Walsh that the Cardinal, at least in public affairs, was merely a puppet in the hands of his Whig advisers.

Cardinal McCabe from the time of his appointment as Archbishop, had looked on Dr. Walsh as the foremost and most capable advocate of the cause of Catholic education in Ireland. Accordingly, in 1883, when there was question of appointing Dr. Walsh Archbishop of Sydney, the Cardinal, who judged that his withdrawal from Ireland would be a national loss to education, barred his appointment. This action was entirely in harmony with the views

F

of Dr. Walsh himself, who authorised the Cardinal to convey to the Holy See that he (Dr. Walsh) deprecated the proposal to appoint him to the Australian archbishopric.

Writing to Dr. Walsh about the matter the Cardinal remarked, December 22, 1883 :

I have heard of three names for Sydney—but I have heard of no others—yours, Dr. Moran's and Dr. Murray's. *We* could not afford to lose the President of Maynooth. I know nothing of Dr. Murray's* episcopal life, but with his long experience of Australian life it would seem to me that he would have the best claim. In *confidence* I think the owner of the second name would scarcely suit.

Again he wrote on January 10, 1884 :

I received a letter from Dr. Moran on Tuesday in which he mentioned that Cardinal Simeoni asked him if he had any objection to go to Sydney. I believe he is quite indifferent. He says he fears he is not strong enough. But I dare say the interpretation of it all is that he will accept.

Dr. Moran accepted the Archbishopric of Sydney, and in the following year he was created a Cardinal by Leo XIII.

* Dr. Murray was a Dublin priest who had been appointed Bishop of Maitland.

CHAPTER VII

CARDINAL MCCABE died at his house at Kingstown (Dun Laoghaire) on the morning of Wednesday, February 11, 1885. His death was altogether unexpected. He had been seriously ill for only a few hours before he died, and the announcement of his death in the morning papers caused a sensation in Dublin.

The Cardinal was before all things a faithful ecclesiastic and a man of God. Throughout his life he had been conspicuous for his earnestness and energy, and for the conscientious and scrupulous exactness with which he discharged his priestly and episcopal duties. His single-mindedness and honesty of purpose were questioned by none. Of humble bearing and of great simplicity of character, he was incapable of deception and was remarkable for the fearless candour of his utterances. Austere in manner and stern to view, he was withal easy of approach, meek and kindly. He was deeply religious, and all through life practised a rigorous asceticism. When informed by the priest who attended him in his last illness that it was advisable that he should receive Extreme Unction, the Cardinal remarked that the summons to prepare for death was to him the most welcome announcement he had heard since his appointment to the archbishopric. Though not gifted with great intellectual powers, Cardinal McCabe possessed considerable administrative and literary ability, and a rugged eloquence befitting his frowning countenance.

At the time of his death the Cardinal had not completed his sixty-ninth year. Born in James's Street, Dublin, on February 14, 1816, he was educated in his native city and

at Maynooth.   Ordained in 1839, he served as curate at
Clontarf, and as Administrator at the Pro-Cathedral.   In
1856 he was promoted Parish Priest of St. Nicholas's
Without, Francis Street, and shortly after he was appointed
Vicar-General.   In Francis Street he found ample scope for
his zeal in countering the proselytising agencies of souperism
among the poor of his parish and neighbourhood.   Owing
to a breakdown in health from overwork he was transferred
to the parish of Kingstown in 1865, and in 1877 he was
nominated Bishop-auxiliary to Cardinal Cullen.

The appointment of the auxiliary came about in a curious
way.   When Cardinal Cullen was in Rome in 1877,
Pius IX, noticing that he looked worn and haggard,
suggested that he should get an auxiliary bishop to assist
him in his episcopal duties.   The Pope, while conversing
informally with the Cardinal, asked who was in charge of
the diocese in his absence, and if there was any priest who
was specially helpful to him in the work of diocesan administration.   The Cardinal mentioned that his Vicars-General
took charge in his absence, and that Monsignor McCabe was
particularly helpful.   The conversation then turned to other
topics.

Almost immediately after the Cardinal's departure the
Pope, without further consultation or inquiry, gave directions to the Prefect of Propaganda to prepare a Brief
appointing Monsignor McCabe Bishop-auxiliary to Cardinal
Cullen.   When Monsignor McCabe received the news of his
appointment he wrote to the Cardinal expressing his readiness to assist his Eminence so as to relieve him of the routine
of episcopal work, at the same time expressing his surprise
that the Cardinal had given him no hint of the impending
appointment.   The Cardinal in reply informed him that the
appointment had caused no less surprise to himself, inasmuch as he had neither sought for, nor intended to ask for
his appointment, although, he added, he was glad to have
his assistance.   By the Brief of his appointment Monsignor

McCabe was nominated to the titular See of Gadara, *in partibus infidelium*. He was consecrated Bishop by Cardinal Cullen at Kingstown on the Feast of St. James, July 25, 1877. Always a trusted and devoted servant and friend of Cardinal Cullen's, Dr. McCabe rendered him loyal and whole-hearted service in the administration of the diocese, and in performing the various rites and ceremonies which are proper to the office of a bishop.

On Cardinal Cullen's death, October 24, 1878, Dr. McCabe's name was commended* by the Dublin clergy to the Holy See as worthy to succeed to the archbishopric. In due course he was elected by the Holy Father, and on May 4, 1879, he took possession of his Cathedral. Elevated to the Sacred College in Secret Consistory, March 27, 1882, he received the Cardinal's Hat from the Pope in Public Consistory on March 30, with the title of Santa Sabina.†

Archbishop McCabe's lines were fallen in difficult places. The partial famine of 1879, resulting in industrial and

* The voting at the commendation was :

Dr. McCabe	43
Dr. Moran, Bishop of Ossory	7
Dr. Woodlock, Rector of the Catholic University ...	1

For the information of those who are not acquainted with ecclesiastical procedure it may be well to indicate the method then followed in the appointment to bishoprics in Ireland. The canons of the Cathedral Chapter and the parish priests of the diocese in which the episcopal See had become vacant commended to the Holy See the names of three ecclesiastics whom they deemed worthy and suitable to fill the vacant office. The bishops of the ecclesiastical province, in which the vacancy had occurred, in due time met and drew up a report on the merits and suitability of the candidates commended by the canons and parish priests. Both the choice of the local clergy and the report of the bishops of the province were forwarded to the Holy See immediately after each of these bodies had held its meeting. The election or appointment to the bishopric rested with the Holy See, which was not necessarily limited in its choice to those commended by the local clergy or even to those favourably reported on by the bishops. The local clergy " commended," the provincial bishops " reported on " those commended, the Holy See " elected " or " appointed."

† Cf. *Men of the Time*, 1884, pp. 721-728; *Dublin Diocesan Register*, s. v. McCabe; *D.N.B.*, vol. xxx.; Annals in *Catholic Directory*, 1886.

agricultural depression, the pendulum-swing of coercion and
agrarian outrage, the activities of the " Invincibles," the
machinations of English and Irish political intriguers at
home and at Rome, the neglected condition of education,
secondary and university—these were some of the matters
with which he was called on to deal.

He faced his difficulties with an intrepidity and honesty
of purpose that was beyond cavil.   In educational matters
he relied largely on Dr. Walsh's help and advice.   On
political questions his views were coloured, and his action
was influenced by the opinions and advice of a *coterie* of
Catholic Whigs, who, taking advantage of his inexperience
of public life, and exploiting his scrupulous honesty,
used to harrow his unsuspecting soul by their exaggerated
tales and highly-coloured pictures of agrarian crimes
that were being committed sporadically throughout
the country.   Prominent among these whisperers and evil
counsellors were Lord O'Hagan, the Lord Chancellor of
Ireland, George Errington*, and Lord Emly.   Of Errington's ambiguous position at the Vatican the Cardinal was
probably aware ; but it is almost certain that he went down
to his grave utterly unsuspicious of the machinations of
O'Hagan, and of other schemers of lesser note. O'Hagan
for many years was a secret agent for the British
Government, paid out of the Irish Secret Service money to
further the interests of England.†   It was mainly at the
instigation of such sinister advisers that Dr. McCabe
was induced to denounce not merely the agrarian crimes

---

* Of Errington's Roman Mission in 1883, Cardinal Manning
left sundry notes : " Mr. Errington was in the confidence of the
Government and of Cardinal McCabe.   The Cardinal Secretary,
and, perhaps, the Holy Father, thought that they had got at last
full information about Ireland.   I considered it my duty to
say, ' Mr. Errington represents the English Government, but he
does not represent Ireland.' "—(Leslie's *Life of Manning*, p.
387.)

† Cf. *Life of Sir Charles Dilke,* Gwynn and Tuckwell, vol. i.,
p. 376.

which were then unfortunately being committed here and there in Ireland, but also the legitimate agrarian agitation for justice which was then sweeping the country. Moreover, it should be mentioned that these atrocities were being perpetrated almost entirely outside the diocese of Dublin. His denunciation of the Ladies' Land League drew forth from Dr. Croke the scathing letter of protest and rebuke, which led to unseemly acrimony in the Press. The Phoenix Park murders (May 6, 1882) cast a gloom over Dr. McCabe's whole subsequent life. The murders took place when he was on his homeward journey from Rome, where he had just received the Cardinal's Hat; and his entry into his cathedral city presented a spectacle from which we may easily judge of the feelings with which he was regarded by a large section of the Nationalist members of his flock. He entered Dublin almost by stealth, and was escorted to his house from Westland Row railway station by a body of the Dublin Metropolitan Police, his carriage being preceded and followed by outside cars carrying detectives. His house at one time was the object of attack, the escutcheon at the door being battered and defaced, and his life, it is said,* was once threatened. But none of these things moved him, nor did he count his life dear unto himself. Almost throughout his episcopate he was most unpopular politically with a large section of his people, whom he loved and for whom he would gladly spend himself and be spent. He entertained no bitterness or resentment towards them; he regarded them as misguided members of the household of the Faith, the dupes of cunning and wicked men. His feelings towards them were the feelings of the Good Shepherd for the straying sheep, of the father for the prodigal. When he denounced and smote his—as they seemed to him—wayward, erring children, he did so from the highest and most disinterested motives in the discharge of what he considered a peremptory, sacred duty.

* Cf. *Dictionary of National Biography,* vol. xii, p. 432.

He was altogether unambitious. He neither sought recognition nor coveted honours. He had no desire to become Archbishop. He refused the cardinalate, and was induced to withdraw his refusal only at the urgent and insistent request of his Cathedral Chapter. He was, however, a man of undaunted courage and dogged perseverance. Once he had made up his mind that the duty of his sacred office required him to take a certain line of action, he pursued his course unflinchingly, regardless of the censures of men or of the consequences to himself. In his ecclesiastical administration, as well as in his public life, he endeavoured to tread in the footsteps of his great predecessor, Cardinal Cullen, whom he regarded as a shining example of what a bishop ought to be; and during his own episcopate, whenever any critical difficulty presented itself, he tried to think out how the Cardinal would have viewed the matter, and then he acted accordingly. But he lacked Cullen's intellectual power, his judiciousness, his wariness and distrust of designing counsellors.

The following appreciation of the Cardinal is substantially accurate : " Cardinal McCabe was a man of rugged honesty, not schooled to use well-placed words of glozing courtesy. He sought no honours, but he evaded no responsibility. The curate became a Cardinal, but the man remained the same . . . Let him suspect that any interest, which he believed God to have entrusted to him as pastor, was assailed by active enemies or endangered by mistaken friends, then swift as the sparkle of a gleaming star his whole being was changed. Careless of consequences, incapable of counting odds or costs, he hurled defiance sturdy and uncompromising; he launched lightnings of denunciation fierce and headlong."*

On the death of a bishop the diocesan jurisdiction is vested in the Cathedral Chapter; but as a Chapter, like all other

* Sir George Fottrell.

corporations, is unwieldly and ineffective for executive purposes, the Canon Law ordains that the Chapter shall within a brief period divest itself of its authority and elect a Vicar-Capitular to whom all diocesan jurisdiction passes, and whose duty it is to administer the diocese until the Holy See appoints a new bishop. The election of the Dublin Vicar-Capitular took place accordingly on Friday, February 13, and the Chapter elected Dr. Walsh by a substantial majority.*

On receiving the news of the election, Dr. Croke, Archbishop of Cashel, immediately wrote to Dr. Walsh :

No news ever pleased me more than that which I have just got from Dr. Browne by telegram. Thank God.

Ireland deserves well of the Almighty, and who knows but the day of her triumph has arrived.

I got a long letter from Parnell. I shall not answer till after our interview. Letter is important.

Dr. Walsh sent the following reply dated from Maynooth, February 14 :

A thousand thanks. Awkward as the business is for me, it has one good side to it, at all events. The Pale is out of fashion.

The funeral of Cardinal McCabe took place on Tuesday, February 17, and amongst people in a position to know, the prevailing opinion, even at that time, was that a very large majority of those qualified to vote would commend Dr. Walsh to the Holy See for election to the diocese of Dublin. Even at that early date, however, Dr. Walsh had anxious misgivings about his fitness for the pastoral office, and to Dr. Croke he had confided his doubts on the matter. Croke contemned these scruples, as he called them, and strove in every way to have Dr. Walsh commended by the vote of the diocesan clergy.

On February 18, the *Freeman's Journal*, then the popular

* The voting was :—Dr. Walsh, 12; Dr. Donnelly, 4; Dr. Lee, 3; Monsignor Kennedy, 1.

organ of news in Dublin, contained an account of the
funeral of Cardinal McCabe, and on the following morning,
Thursday, February 19, there was a leading article in the
same journal on the vacant See. The article dealt with the
efforts of certain parties to make the Archbishopric of
Dublin " an appanage of Dublin Castle," and of the scandal
of allowing " George Errington to nominate the new
Archbishop"; and strongly emphasised the desirability of
having in the metropolitan See an Archbishop who would
be in sympathy with popular aspirations. There appeared
also in the *Nation* of the same date an article which was
" really good," and one in *United Ireland* which was " a
model of judiciousness."*

In the same issue of the *Nation* appeared a letter suggest-
ing Dr. Croke's name for the vacant archbishopric. On
February 27, " A Carlow Priest" published a letter on
" Lay and Clerical Union," urging the appointment of an
Archbishop of popular sympathies. The *Tablet*, after a
deliberate silence, published a most complimentary three-
column article (February 28) on the Vicar-Capitular of
Dublin, and in the same vein its Irish correspondent wrote :
" Dr. Walsh, who administers the diocese *sede vacante*,
is the right man in the right place." On March 4, the
Standard announced : " It is reported that Dr. Walsh will
succeed Cardinal McCabe in the archbishopric of Dublin.
Dr. Walsh is a moderate Nationalist."

On March 10, the voting for commendation of names for
the vacant archbishopric took place at the Pro-Cathedral,
Dublin. The result of the voting was :

> Very Rev. Wm. J. Walsh, D.D., President of
> Maynooth, 46 votes.
> Most Rev. Dr. Donnelly, Bishop of Canea, 12 votes.
> Rev. Patrick Tynan, D.D., Secretary to late Car-
> dinal McCabe, 3 votes.
> Most Rev. Dr. Woodlock, Bishop of Ardagh, 2 votes.

* Walsh to Croke, February 21, 1885.

In a special article on the result of the voting the *Freeman's Journal* commented : " Dr. Walsh has received more votes from the diocesan clergy than were ever before cast for an Archbishop of Dublin.   Cardinal Cullen was *dignissimus* in 1852, but he secured only 23 votes; and it is too near our own times to forget the settled feeling of security that the Propaganda and the Holy Father would surely respect the almost unanimous expression of the clergy of the diocese, no matter how great the weight of personal merit and influence on the other side, when they placed the late Cardinal McCabe at the head of the list with 43 votes, But the President of Maynooth has now received 46 votes, the largest number, as we have said, ever cast for an Archbishop of Dublin since the present mode of procedure was prescribed for Ireland in 1829."

The tone, however, of the *Freeman* and of the other Nationalist papers was one of apprehension lest sinister political anti-Irish influence at the Vatican might interfere with Dr. Walsh's selection for the archbishopric.   It was a matter of notoriety that at this time Mr. George Errington* was an active, officious, though not an official, agent of the British Government at the Vatican, and that he would exert all his influence against Dr. Walsh's appointment.

---

* Dilke has left his impressions of the Errington affair : " The British Government now [1881] endeavoured to back up the policy of force by dividing the opposition . . . . Dublin Castle had been seeking to enlist on its side the spiritual power of Rome.   There were two lines of approach of which the first is indicated in a note, under November 22, 1880 :

" Lord Granville (foreign secretary in Gladstone's ministry) was engaged at this time in trying, through Cardinal Newman, to induce the Pope to bully the Irish bishops; but the Irish bishops told the Pope in reply to his remonstrances, that if he adopted a policy of compromise in Italy that was unpopular with the Church, he must leave them alone with Irish affairs.

" The ' policy of compromise ' was not likely to be adopted.

" Far more continuous were the negotiations, with a view to influencing the Irish Church, carried on through Mr. George Errington, a gentleman of an old Roman Catholic family, who had sat since 1874 as a moderate Home Rule member for Co. Longford."—*Life of Sir Charles Dilke,* vol. i., p. 374.

Since the establishment of the Land League, and especially from the time that Dr. Croke and other ecclesiastics had shown publicly their strong sympathies with the suffering Irish tenantry in their agitation for justice, Errington had been constantly representing to the British Foreign Office the importance of undermining the influence of the Archbishop of Cashel at the Vatican, and of securing if possible the help of the Pope in restraining the ardour of Dr. Croke, and in keeping the clergy from supporting or countenancing the popular movement. In December 1880, Errington obtained, at the request of Lord Spencer, who was then Lord Lieutenant of Ireland, " some sort of private commission from Lord Granville. The commission was afterwards made definite."*

Under date October 28, 1881, Sir Charles Dilke wrote in his diary :

I saw Errington who was in Paris on his way to Rome with letters from Lord Granville, based on the request of Spencer and Forster, that he, Errington, should represent the Irish Government at Rome during its great struggle with Parnell, matters in Ireland being too serious to make roundabout dealing through Lord Emly and Cardinal Howard safe; and Errington was to be tried from October until Easter . . .

In the evening of November 10 Gladstone told me that he was bitterly opposed to the notion of re-opening relations with the Papal Court; and there can be no doubt that he assented most unwillingly to the views of Spencer, Forster, and Harcourt in favour of the Errington Mission.

For over four years Errington continued to busy himself at the Vatican, and at the beginning of 1885 his influence against Dr. Croke and Parnell was so acutely felt that the Irish Parliamentary Party thought it advisable to send Michael Davitt to Rome to counteract Errington's mischievous activities. Davitt arrived in Rome in January 1885, and was kindly received in high ecclesiastical quarters. On February 8, 1885, the *Times* Roman correspondent

* *Life of Sir Charles Dilke,* vol. i., p. 375.

remarked that " it would interest Mr. Davitt's friends to hear of the distinction with which he was received in Rome," and the *St. James's Gazette* of the same date betrayed its uneasiness as follows :

It will interest other people besides the elect who call themselves Michael Davitt's friends to hear that the " Mission" of Mr. Errington also appears to have been futile here. The Papal Court was to have been gained over to help us in our Irish troubles, and here is one of the chief movers in these troubles ostentatiously welcomed and patronised by great personages at the Vatican.

Before Davitt started on his Roman mission, he told W. T. Stead* what he would say if asked by the Holy See what the Pope could do for Ireland :

This is the substance of what I would say, in more diplomatic language, of course, if the Holy Father were to deem it worth while to ask my opinion on the matter.

Ireland is to-day the great propagandist of the Catholic Faith. Irish bishops and priests rule the Catholic Church throughout the English-speaking world. Irish emigrants have taken the seeds of the faith into England, Scotland, Wales, America, Canada, South Africa, Australia. This missionary work has never been recognised at the centre of the Christian world. Ireland's enemies have been more than once on the point of poisoning your ear against the most devoted of Catholic nations, simply because you have never commanded *your faithful Irish people to send you an accredited representative to reside in Rome*, and to advise you from time to time regarding Irish political or social movements, and their real bearing on religion and morals.

For want of such an official Irish nuncio there has been twice in recent years a narrow escape of conflict between the whole Irish race and your headship of its national Church. Thoroughly Catholic as the Irish race are, they are equally Nationalist, and will never allow their fidelity to the Catholic faith to be presumed upon with reference to their nationalist cause. A pronounced hostility to Home Rule by your Holiness would strike a bigger blow at the

* Editor of the *Pall Mall Gazette*.

Catholic Church throughout the English-speaking world than did Luther's revolt in Germany. Guard against the possibility of this, therefore, by asking the Irish bishops to send, on behalf of the Irish Catholic race, an accredited representative to reside near Your Person in Rome, and give him the dignity of a Cardinal in compliment to the race which to-day is making the Church truly universal.*

Davitt was in Rome when Cardinal McCabe died, and at once he busied himself about the succession to the vacant See. He wrote to Dr. Croke immediately after the Cardinal's death was announced, to point out the importance of securing as successor an Archbishop who would be in political sympathy with the main body of Irish Catholics. Again, a couple of days later, Davitt wrote to Croke to impress upon him the national importance of the appointment to the Dublin See; and he outlined a plan of securing the votes of the parish priests and canons in favour of one or two priests of known nationalist sentiments. In the meantime, Davitt watched Errington's movements in Rome most closely. Errington, too, was on his mettle, for the very crisis had arrived which Lord Granville maintained to be a justification of the " Mission to the Vatican " :

The appointments to bishoprics both in Ireland and in the colonies were matters in which the good-will of the Pope could make itself felt, and felt effectively, if the Holy Father so chose. Such was the origin of the so-called ' mission' of Mr. Errington.†

Soon after it had become publicly known that by the voice of the Dublin clergy Dr. Walsh had been so strongly commended for the vacant See, attacks upon him and on the Irish Catholic clergy generally began to appear. The Dublin *Evening Mail* published libellous attacks on Dr. Walsh in the form of anonymous letters signed " A Loyal Catholic " and " Another Loyal Catholic." In the first

* *The Pope and the New Era.* By W. T. Stead, pp. 153-4.
† *Life of Lord Granville.* Fitzmaurice, vol. ii., p. 285.

letter he was accused of being a close ally of Parnell's, and it was stated that " it was by his [Dr. Walsh's] sanction the No-Rent Manifesto was published"; and the anonymous assailant invited Dr. Walsh to " deny these accusations if he could." " Another Loyal Catholic" asserted that the President of the College of Maynooth was a dangerous revolutionist, and that " he was not merely cognisant of, but was the instigator of the No-Rent Manifesto ! . . . If he is made Archbishop of Dublin, good-bye to Ireland as a Catholic, moral, Christian country. In two years it will be overrun by unbelievers in faith and in morals."

The *Saturday Review*, April 18, 1885, had a long article on " The Roman Catholic Archbishops of Dublin," which, after stating that " men of all parties are naturally watching with anxiety the appointment of a successor to what is in reality, though not in titular dignity, the highest position in the Roman Catholic, as in the Protestant, hierarchy of Ireland," proceeded as follows :

The Archbishop of Armagh ranks as Primate of All Ireland, but the Archbishop of Dublin holds, from the nature of the case, the most prominent and influential post. The result of the voting of the diocesan clergy is much what might have been expected, though not what any but " Nationalists" could have desired.

The *Tablet*, in reporting the result of the election, was careful to add that " it was more than anticipated by public opinion," and what had been predicted and urged in its own columns . . . Dr. Walsh, who obtained three-fourths of the votes is known as an advanced Nationalist.

It is—or was before the time of Pius IX—usual to appoint the one who headed the list, and it was considered very high-handed procedure to supersede all three, as was done in the case of Cardinal Cullen (for Armagh) and Archbishop Croke (for Cashel) . . . But the Pope is not, as we have said, at all bound to take the *dignissimus*, or indeed any of those selected, and Pius IX would not for a moment have hesitated to treat the Dublin electors, if he felt so disposed for any reason, as he treated the West-minster electors, when he appointed Dr. Manning to the See over the heads of the candidates returned by the

Chapter . . . Leo XIII has always shown himself a scrupulously constitutional ruler—' even though it be to his own hurt '—and it remains to be seen whether his dislike to any semblance of a stretch of arbitrary authority will be counterbalanced by the objection he cannot but very strongly entertain to placing at the head of the Irish Hierarchy a prelate whose influence is sure to be exerted in a direction so entirely adverse to the traditions of his See for many years past. For, it is only fair to acknowledge that in this respect Cardinal Cullen acted on the same principles as Cardinal McCabe, and before Cardinal Cullen came the venerable venerated Archbishop Murray, ' whose praise was in all the Churches,' so to speak. *A Nationalist Archbishop of Dublin would be a no less novel than startling and unwelcome portent* . . .

Archbishop Croke of Cashel, who had not, however, as yet hoisted his colours, was appointed by the late Pope over the heads of all the clerical nominees. The present Pope may, perhaps, see the wisdom of subordinating for once an excellent principle to the demands of a grave emergency, and taking into his own hands the nomination to the primatial See. The legal *Summum ius est summa iniuria* has its application both to Church and State.

After the beginning of April 1885, veiled and oblique attacks on Dr. Walsh began to appear in the *Times*. These attacks were contained in anonymous letters which assailed Irish Catholics, their religion, their priests and bishops. Soon, however, appeared an open libel on Dr. Walsh from the pen of one L. Agar-Ellis—a notorious character at that time. The letter was published in the *Times* of April 9, under the heading " Loyalty of Catholics," and was as follows :—

Sir,—Every loyal Irishman will thank you for publishing a letter signed " An Anglo-Catholic" in the *Times* of April 7. It cannot be too often impressed upon Englishmen that for good the Irish Roman Catholics are powerless. It is a small minority that is in favour of law, and they are not capable of moving the body of their co-religionists in the right direction. It cannot either be too constantly repeated that the bulk of the Roman Catholic clergy in Ireland are merely agents of the Parnellites and Fenians.*

Their common talk is treason and not a word do they ever utter in favour of order. Maynooth is a machine for turning out rebels, and it is on account of this that the present head of the college has been chosen *dignissimus* for the See of Dublin by so overwhelming a majority. A pretty quarrel is in progress now between the moderate Roman Catholics and the Parnellite faction as to who should be appointed by Rome. The Fenians have their partisans in the Curia, and I shall be surprised if they do not carry their man. If they do not, there shall be hundreds of thousands of Parnellites and Fenians insisting on knowing the reason why. In the face of all these squabbles which show how divided the Catholic Church is in Ireland, the Government keeps an official agent† at Rome and the Irish Executive truckles to Roman Catholics in Ireland. The present Viceroy has never gone beyond trying to govern by faction. I dare say the good man fancies he has invented the system. As a matter of fact it has been going on for about 700 years ... If any proof were required of the importance of "Anglo-Catholic's" communications, two letters you print to-day would supply it. "A Roman Catholic Layman" fancies he disposes of his co-religionist, Vatican decrees and all, by quoting Dr. Newman : " It is this blind giving up of private judgment

---

* That the charge of being mere agents of the Parnellites and Fenians was not confined to the Catholic clergy in Ireland but extended also to their brethren abroad, is evident from the words of—as well as of other witnesses—Lord E. Fitzmaurice :—" The Vatican was dependent on the Irish College in Rome, the Principal (in 1881) and some of the members of which were violently nationalist, indeed almost Fenian in sentiment."—(See *Life of Lord Granville,* Introduction.)

The Principal of the College in 1881 was Most Rev. Dr. Kirby, and his two assistants—presumably the Fenians—were Rev. Canon Verdon and Rev. Denis O'Haran. They were anything but violent politicians.

† The historic difficulties in the way of an embassy to the Vatican had been surmounted (in view of the Pope's temporal sovereignty) by the practice of allowing a Secretary of Legation, nominally appointed to the Grand Ducal Court of Tuscany, to reside at Rome, where he was regarded as *de facto* minister to the Vatican, but he was always prepared to assert that, like the Earl of Castlemaine (in 1687) he was there for secular purposes only. Cf. *Life of Lord Granville,* ii., p. 282. *Life of Dilke,* vol. i., p. 374.

which makes the Roman Catholic Church so dangerous to a liberally governed country." As long as men look to a priest in a foreign country to tell them what to do on every important occasion, they must expect to be looked upon shyly by their " thoroughly loyal countrymen." At the risk of shocking " A Roman Catholic Layman," I will present him with a bit of information. Priests and laymen in Ireland with few exceptions care as little for the Pope as I do, and I am much mistaken if this will not be pointedly shown in the next few years.

Be just in your dealings with Roman Catholics, but do not truckle with them.

Mr. L. Agar-Ellis was a man professing some form of Protestantism, who had married a Catholic wife. Before contracting the marriage he had pledged his word in the presence of witnesses not to interfere with the free exercise of her religion by his future wife, and to bring up in his wife's faith any children that might be born of the marriage. Subsequently, availing himself of his legal right, he took the children from their mother's faith, thus publicly repudiating his own word so solemnly given. The standing of such a character in the estimation of honourable men was not high, and when his insolent libel appeared there was no mincing of words in the popular Irish Press. One journal wrote :

The advice of not truckling to Catholics coming from this man, a publicly convicted liar, is refreshing . . . No honourable man would treat an accusation coming from Mr. Agar-Ellis personally with anything but the contempt which a man of his antecedents deserves; but when the charge is published in the *Times* it contains an importance not due to the writer. It is one of a series of letters lately published by the *Times* with a deliberate object—that of discrediting the Rev. Dr. Walsh. The writers no doubt assumed that the President of Maynooth would not condescend to notice these attacks or bring them to book in a court of law. But as public journalists we are bound to expose what we consider to be a foul conspiracy against Dr. Walsh, whose sole offence in reality is the fact that his selection was received with acclamation by all sections of

Irish Catholics, and that he is not the nominee of the English and Castle clique. The idea of suggesting that the man who was selected by the bishops of Ireland as most fitted for the position of President of Maynooth College was a revolutionist whose appointment to the See of Dublin would be destructive of Catholic morality and Christianity, and that it is because he is a revolutionist that he was selected *dignissimus* by the Chapter of Dublin, most of whom are mature and elderly men, of certainly anything but revolutionary tendencies, is so outrageously preposterous as to be likely not to excite anything but a smile in Ireland. But the *Times* circulates amongst people who are ready to believe anything bad of an Irishman, and of any priest, and especially of an Irish priest . . . These letters are political dodges written for the purpose of creating the impression at Rome that the appointment of Dr. Walsh would be impolitic. We trust and believe that they will have the reverse effect. They are outrageous insults to Catholicism —outrageous insults to the whole body of Irish bishops and clergy, outrageous insults to the Irish Catholic people as well as to the President of Maynooth. There is only one way for Rome to answer these insults effectually—by confirmation of the selection.*

When the *Times* and other reputable papers allowed their columns to be used by anonymous and other writers for the purpose of vilifying Irish Catholics, and of making grave charges against Dr. Walsh, and of seeking to cajole or bully the Holy See into appointing a pro-Englishman to the See of Dublin, one may easily imagine how outrageous, during this time, were some of the less reputable journals; for the question of the Dublin appointment was being canvassed ever since the diocesan clergy had made their recommendation to the Holy See. The question had, in fact, become a matter of imperial interest, and was discussed in the columns of newspapers not merely in the British Isles but also in Canada, Australia, India, even at Shanghai, and of course in the United States of America.

* *Freeman's Journal*, April 13, 1885.

After Easter Sunday, which in that year fell on April 5, several of the Irish bishops proceeded to Rome to make their quinquennial visit *ad limina Apostolorum*. The visit had an important bearing on the Dublin appointment. Early in the year the bishops had been requested so to arrange their official visits that all the members of the episcopate should be in Rome at the same time, in order that they might take part with the Prefect of Propaganda in a conference on Irish ecclesiastical affairs. The conference took place at the office of the Congregation of Propaganda, under the presidency of the Prefect, Cardinal Simeoni. Practically all the Irish bishops were in attendance. Bishop Donnelly, too, as *Vescovo Aussiliare di Dublino** was specially summoned by Cardinal Simeoni to the conference.

In the *Nation* of April 25, the following appeared in its Roman notes :

The Archbishopric of Dublin is still the theme of conversation. In the ordinary course of things the Sacred Congregation of Propaganda arranges and classifies the documents which record the votes of parish priests and bishops, submits them to the Committee of prelates and consultors, lays them afterwards before the Cardinals of the Congregation and reports the opinion arrived at to the Pope for the final decision. In this case routine has been dispensed with. The Holy Father has taken charge of all the documents himself; he will consult only the Irish bishops upon the choice to be made, and will then in the exercise of his sovereign power, nominate a pastor to the widowed See of Dublin. The action of the Sovereign Pontiff has given rise to the most contradictory surmises. To some it looks as if Propaganda were hostile to the Dublin majority, and had not the courage of its opinion; while many do not hesitate to say that Leo XIII has been won to the Anglo-Saxon side, and will make an appointment to rejoice the backstairs aristocracy of the Castle. A near future will dispel the nightmare. No one can possibly guess the intention of His Holiness, but we may reasonably

* Bishop Auxiliary of Dublin.

suppose that his known love for his faithful Irish flock will prompt an action in harmony with the momentous interests at stake. No better counsellors, at any rate, could be found than the Irish bishops.

The Irish bishops were in fact consulted by the Pope, with what result will appear later.

The question of the interference by the English Government at the Vatican in the appointment to the Archbishopric of Dublin was raised by Mr. Thomas Sexton, M.P., in the House of Commons in April 1885. The Prime Minister, Mr. Gladstone, in his reply used a cloud of words to convey the assurance that the *Government* was not interfering; but he was careful to leave a loophole for escape from the *exposé* of English intrigue in case the true facts of the situation should at some subsequent time come to light. The Cabinet, he said, had not sought to interfere with His Holiness in deciding the question, nor, so far as he was aware, had individual Ministers. The answer was disingenuous; for it is unquestionable that Gladstone knew of Errington's " mission," and he can scarcely have been unaware that the Foreign Secretary, Earl Granville, was in constant communication with Errington, and that Errington had been urging on Propaganda all the objections that could be made against the appointment of Dr. Walsh.

The month of May came, and still no appointment had been made to Dublin. Errington, dissatisfied with his efforts at Rome, left the Eternal City and came to London, presumably to get more ample powers from Earl Granville; for he had by no means abandoned the hope of preventing Dr. Walsh's appointment. If he could succeed in that he felt that he would have justified the " mission" to the Vatican.

At first Errington had supported Dr. Donnelly's candidature with vigour. Dr. Donnelly had been Auxiliary Bishop to Cardinal McCabe, and was known to have been in the Cardinal's confidence, and in full sympathy with his political views. Bishop Donnelly used, in fact, humorously to describe himself as the " last of the Whigs." It was known that at the beginning of the intrigue Errington and Lord Emly, on behalf of the Government, were negotiating with the Vatican for Bishop Donnelly's appointment; and when the *Vescovo Aussiliare di Dublino* was summoned to Rome shortly before Easter, the " report was circulated in Dublin that the Government had made overtures to the Pope on the basis of mutual concessions—Dr. Donnelly's appointment to be the *quid pro quo* for the granting of a charter and endowment of the Catholic University."*

Soon, however, Bishop Donnelly's prospects began to wane, and the English faction veered about and transferred all its influence to another candidate. The new candidate was the Most Rev. Patrick Francis Moran, Archbishop of Sydney. Dr. Moran, like Dr. Donnelly, was a prelate of dignified bearing and varied accomplishments. He had been all his life a close student of Irish hagiology and of Irish history generally. He was a near kinsman of Cardinal Cullen's, and had for some time acted as his secretary. From 1871 till 1883 he had been Bishop of Ossory. During that time he had not taken any prominent part in political affairs, but was reputed to be a Nationalist, though he had not identified himself with the policy of Dr. Croke. Neither had he expressed any sympathy with Cardinal McCabe's political views. He was known, however, to be a man of strong personality, of fearless character and deep convictions. It will be remembered, too, that when Cardinal McCabe was commended for the Dublin Archbishopric in 1878, Dr. Moran's name had been placed second on the list by the diocesan clergy.

Shortly after the middle of May an incident occurred in connection with the vacancy in the Dublin See which caused

* Walsh to Croke, March 20, 1885.

no little commotion in the House of Commons, and much
indignation throughout Ireland. A letter* written by
Errington to Lord Granville in the library of the House of
Commons, was placed in the hands of Mr. William O'Brien,
who forthwith published it in *United Ireland*. The letter
read :

House of Commons,
Friday, May 15, 1885.

DEAR LORD GRANVILLE,—The Dublin archbishopric being
still undecided, I must continue to keep the Vatican in good
humour about you, and keep up communication with them
generally as much as possible.

I am almost ashamed to trouble you again when you are
so busy, but perhaps on Monday you would allow me to
show you the letter I propose to write.

The premature report about Dr. Moran will cause
increased pressure to be put upon the Pope, and create
many fresh difficulties. The matter must, therefore be
most carefully watched, so that the strong pressure I can
still command may be used at the right moment, and not
too soon or unnecessarily (for too much pressure is quite
as dangerous as too little). To effect this, constant communication with Rome is necessary.

I am, dear Lord Granville,
Faithfully yours,
G. ERRINGTON.

The publication of Errington's letter to Lord Granville
was made the occasion of a debate in the House of
Commons on the whole question of the Government's
interference in Irish ecclesiastical affairs at the Vatican.
The usual denials were made. " The line taken by the
Government in the House of Commons was that
Errington had no formal appointment and that his
communications were not officially dealt with by the
Foreign Office.† In accordance with the traditional policy

* Cf. Barry O'Brien's *Life of Parnell,* vol. ii., p. 27. Both
the date of the letter and the date of its publication as given
by B. O'Brien are incorrect.

† *Life of Dilke*, vol. i., p. 375.

of British statesmen, the Government repudiated all
responsibility, though Lord Granville admitted* that
Errington had a private letter from him, saying that
Errington had the confidence of Forster and of the
Government. This private letter was sent to Errington at
Rome in the Foreign Office's despatch bags. It was said
that Errington got no money, at least no money from the
Foreign Office. Whether sustenance money was forthcoming from any other source is not clear, but it is unlikely
that Spencer and Forster, whose confidence Errington
enjoyed, and at whose request his "mission" was
commended by Granville, would have left him in a worse
financial position than men like Lord O'Hagan, whose
"private" visits to Rome were financed out of the Irish
Secret Service money.†

It cannot be questioned that the Government put forth all
its power at the Vatican to hinder Dr. Walsh's appointment.
Its influence, however, was exercised indirectly and by backstairs methods, and neither the Government, as such, nor
any Cabinet Minister, took a direct share in the intrigue.
Granville directed the campaign; Errington and Lord Emly
were the pawns. Granville, according to Manning, was the

---

* *Life of Granville*, vol. ii., p. 288.

† "On December 24, 1881, Lord O'Hagan passed through
Paris, despatched on a secret mission to Rome about Ireland by
Forster, who was not satisfied with the results up to then of the
Errington mission. . . ."

Of this visit of O'Hagan's no notice was taken in the papers.
"Lord O'Hagan used to go to Rome at *the expense of the Irish
Secret Service money, as a private traveller,* and he used to
carry on negotiations with the Vatican."—*Life of Dilke,* vol. i.,
pp. 375-6.

Dilke was in a position to know, for before entering the
Cabinet in 1882 he represented the Foreign Office in the House
of Commons, being Under-Secretary for Foreign Affairs.

"Lord O'Hagan would take any opportunity which might
arise of making such private and confidential communications
as might be desirable on the above subjects (i.e., on securing
the influence of the Pope in the interest of law and order in
Ireland, and in reference to the appointment to bishoprics, both
in Ireland and in the Colonies)."—*Life of Granville,* vol. ii., p.
286.

only opponent of Walsh in the Cabinet;* and Manning was
in a position to know, for he was kept in constant touch with
the inner workings of the Cabinet by one of its members, his
intimate friend and confidant, Sir Charles Dilke. But there is
no doubt that the British Government in Ireland was resolutely opposed to Dr. Walsh, and was actively fomenting
hostility to him. Both Dilke and Chamberlain were disposed
to think that the apparent neutrality of Earl Spencer may
have been assumed for tactical purposes. So much was the
question of interference with the Dublin appointment a
matter of concern to the Government, that it threatened
to break up the Cabinet.† Dilke and Chamberlain were
strongly opposed to any Government interference, and they
endeavoured to " bring to an end the communications that
were made at Rome *on behalf of the British Government*,
believing that we had no right to interfere in such a matter,
and that there was no ground of opposition to the selection
of Archbishop Walsh." Dilke, even more strongly than
Chamberlain, resented the Government's interference against
Dr. Walsh. On June 27 he addressed to Gladstone a strong
protest :

Since I have been a member of the " Inner Circle," many
decisions of the gravest moment as to Irish affairs have been
taken without reference to the general opinion of the leaders
of the Party. When Mr. Forster induced Lord Granville
to give letters to Mr. Errington, I stated my own view in
favour of the appointment of an official representative of
this country to the Roman Church, if there was work which
must be done between the Government and that Church. I
always protested against the secret arrangement, and the
last straw has been the resistance to Walsh.§

Meanwhile the case was receiving careful consideration at
Rome. The Pope, as the *Nation* reported, had withdrawn

* Leslie, *Life of Manning,* p. 389.
† *Ibid.* p. 390.
‡ Letter of Chamberlain. Oct. 6, 1885, quoted by Leslie.
§ *Life of Dilke,* vol. ii., pp. 149-50.

the business from Propaganda, and taken it into his own hands.   He decided to consult the Irish bishops on the matter, and with a view to securing a more frank and detailed expression of their sentiments he determined to give audience to each separately before seeing them collectively.

Dr. Croke was, of course, among the bishops at Rome, where he received a letter from Cardinal Manning dated May 1, 1885, in which the Cardinal asked for information :

Let me hear of our affairs at Rome, for the newspapers make me anxious, especially about Dublin. And let me know whether I can be of any use. Ireland has never been so represented in Rome as at this moment. And I hope greatly.

On May 5, Croke replied :

There is no news about Dublin, but there are various reports. One is that Dr. Moran will be recalled and appointed to Dublin.   *It is absolutely certain that the Government has made this proposal to the Pope.*   I do not, and cannot believe that it will be accepted by His Holiness.   Dr. Moran is doing well, I hear, where he is, and is wanted there.   Anyhow the setting aside of Dr. Walsh *for anyone* would raise such a storm in Ireland and in the United States that His Holiness should be solemnly warned against doing so.   Your Eminence alone can give such a warning *and I earnestly ask you to do it.*

Manning at once complied with Croke's request, and wrote to the Pope pointing out :

(1) The supreme danger of even *seeming* to be swayed from here (England).
(2) The united wish of the Irish bishops.
(3) The worthiness of the man.*

* In a private communication forwarded (April 26, 1885) to Dilke, Manning states :—" I have thought it best to put in writing what I said on Friday on the subject of the appointment to the See of Dublin. My first and chief anxiety is that the Government shall in no way, either officially or officiously, through Mr. Errington or any other, attempt to influence the election. Already the belief to this effect has been expressed

In their audiences with the Pope, the Irish bishops spoke favourably of Dr. Walsh's qualifications for the See of Dublin, and many of them dwelt strongly on the impolicy of setting him aside for anyone else.   None spoke more strongly in this sense than did the Archbishop of Cashel. Notwithstanding the strong recommendations of the bishops, Dr. Croke feared that their advice would be unheeded, and his anxiety about the appointment was becoming very acute.   His apprehensions were increased by the news which had reached him about the beginning of June, that Dr. Moran had been urgently summoned to Rome by the Prefect of Propaganda.   Cardinal Simeoni had cabled to Dr. Moran : "Venias Romam quamprimum."

in the Irish papers.   Two effects would at once follow.   The archbishop would be ' suspect ' and his influence for good in the sense of the Government would be paralysed.   And next, the influence of Rome, in the direction I desire as much as you, would be dangerously lessened.   So much in general.

"Next, for the three names before the Holy See.   They are all good and safe in every sense.   Any of them may be confided in as holding the opinions and principles of the seven bishops [Irish bishops on their way to Rome] who were here the other day. But there is one of them beyond compare the ablest—namely, Dr. Walsh, President of Maynooth.   He has been tried in governing that vast college, and has been found very able and successful.   He has great weight in Ireland, and, as the bishops unanimously assured me, he would unite the whole episcopate, for they all confide in him.   I have an impression that efforts have been made to represent Dr. Walsh as a Nationalist.   He is no more so than I am, and whether that is excessive or obstructive you will judge.   That you may better know how far my judgment may be taken, I will here add that I had a special and unusual share in the selection and nomination of the late Cardinal Archbishop MacCabe.   And I believe you know me too well to need that I should say more.   I put ' Private ' on this letter, but you may use it as you see fit."

On Tuesday, April 28th, Cardinal Manning again spoke to Dilke about the archbishopric, expressing his great vexation as to Spencer's action through Errington.   Dilke sent a minute to Spencer which he returned, writing with regard to Manning's estimate of Dr. Walsh's moderate opinions : " I wish it may be so.   Responsibility does wonders.   Maynooth is so bad that the Pope is now discussing it with the bishops."   Dilke sent Spencer's minute to Chamberlain, who returned it with a strong minute of his own for Spencer, who again wrote : " H.E. the Cardinal is wrong in his estimate of Dr. Walsh."—(Cf. *Life of Dilke,* vol. ii., p. 131.)

Dr. Croke had left Rome for Ireland before the message to Dr. Moran was despatched. On hearing of Cardinal Simeoni's action he wrote immediately to Manning :

CROKE TO MANNING.

Thurles, June 7th, 1885.

Things look very threatening here. The people cannot be persuaded that the Pope has not entered into some sort of agreement with the Government, the price paid by His Holiness being the setting aside of the popular candidate for the See of Dublin and the appointment of some cold and colourless ecclesiastic. I dread this myself, for, in point of fact, during our last interview with His Holiness, he formally sketched such a plan and declared that " he was not the Pope of Ireland alone, but of the Universal Church." Dangerous indeed it is, if it should turn out that English influence proved to be so potent in the Vatican as to cause His Holiness to discredit one of the foremost ecclesiastics of the day, simply because he happened not to be a *persona grata* to the Government. This is my sober and solemn judgment as to the situation. I write it to your Eminence as the highest and most influential ecclesiastic within the realm, with the hope that you may have it conveyed to the proper quarter.

To this Manning replied at once. Again on June 12, the Cardinal wrote to Croke informing him that no adverse or other decision had yet been reached, that he had already written fully to the Pope in the sense suggested, and assuring him that he might confide on his (Manning's) leaving nothing undone that he could do.

While the question of the vacant archbishopric was still undecided, Dr. Walsh's position was one of great embarrassment. He felt the awkwardness of the situation from the very day of his election to the Vicar-Capitularship. For that election the main responsibility rested on the Dean of the Chapter, Monsignor Walter Lee, V.G. The Dean, however, had the entire approval and cordial co-operation of the other two Vicars-General of the late Cardinal-Archbishop. In choosing Dr. Walsh as Vicar-Capitular they were actuated in the first place by their conviction of the fitness of the man; they were also influenced by their desire of doing honour to Maynooth, the *alma mater* of which they were devoted sons. Besides. they were not unwilling to administer a rebuke to Dr. Donnelly, whose impulsive and somewhat overbearing manner had provoked some resentment; for since his appointment as Auxiliary to Cardinal McCabe, he had initiated a number of innovations which he urged on these elderly men with the zeal of an enthusiast. Moreover, though not one of the three Vicars-General was a politician, they wished to emphasise the fact that the Bishop of Canea, to whom Queen Victoria and the Lord Lieutenant of Ireland had sent messages of deep regret on Cardinal McCabe's death, was not the authorised exponent of the political views of his brethren in the Chapter. Added to these considerations was the further one that the election of Dr. Donnelly as Vicar-Capitular might be interpreted as an act of confidence in his fitness for the archbishopric, and against this they were anxious to guard; for they did not consider that he was endowed with the prudence or circumspection or ability to stand alone on the bridge in the stormy times through which Ireland was then passing. For that post they had marked out Dr. Walsh.

With these sentiments the Archbishop of Cashel was in full sympathy. He was anxious to have the most capable man appointed to the most important and difficult post in the Irish Church; and he was scarcely less anxious that the Archbishop of Dublin should be a man of pronounced Nationalist views, and one who would cordially co-operate with himself in securing redress of the grievances which pressed so heavily on the agrarian community. As Dr. Walsh was the man who combined these qualifications in the highest degree, Croke energetically worked for his appointment. He put his views very plainly before Dr. Walsh in a personal interview in Dublin on February 17. Walsh assented whole-heartedly to the Archbishop's principles; he thoroughly realised the importance of securing the appointment not merely of an able churchman but also of one who would be quite independent of the influence of the party of the Pale. However, he caused Dr. Croke no little surprise and uneasiness when he expressed rather determinedly his own unwillingness to have his name put forward as a champion of the popular party. Dr. Croke deprecated the idea of Walsh's reluctance, but the only assurance he was able to obtain was that Dr. Walsh would co-operate whole-heartedly in supporting a worthy candidate of sound political views. He told Dr. Croke most explicitly that he did not wish to be appointed a diocesan bishop. Walsh must, of course, have been well aware that he possessed many qualities which would fit him for the archbishopric. He was well equipped with the knowledge of theology and canon law so requisite in a bishop. He had shown at Maynooth that he was possessed of rare administrative ability, that he was thoroughly familiar with educational questions, that he was a controversialist who would be able to give an account of the faith that was in him; and he had reason to know that he enjoyed to a remarkable degree the confidence of the Irish bishops. But his life had been spent in academic work, and in college administration. He had had no experience of missionary life, and little inclination for the pastoral duties of a bishop. He disliked and dreaded preaching, and was almost wholly devoid of unction. The pomp and dignity of pontifical functions were uncongenial to his highly-strung nervous temperament and shy disposition. He shrank from the prospect of a daily routine that would engross his attention and take him away from his books and the seclusion of his study. True, indeed, he was by no means devoid of ambition; in a sense it might be said that he coveted distinction, but this he looked to attain in the world of learning or, preferably, in a diplomatic career. Such a career he outlined in his letter to Dr. Croke. In a word, though he was, as he himself knew and confessed, fitted to deal with questions of ecclesiastical policy, and though he was, as was widely known, a priest of irreproachable and even severely restrained life, he had no inclination towards the episcopate. Though he had taken no public part in politics, he was known to be an intimate friend of Dr. Croke's and to share his political views.

During all this time a continual, almost a daily, correspondence passed between Croke and Walsh. At Croke's expressed wish, all his letters to Dr. Walsh dealing with the episode of the Dublin archbishopric were burned when read. And of Walsh's letters written during this time to Croke only a few remain. From these, fortunately, sufficient material can be extracted to form an accurate idea of Dr. Walsh's feelings and of his attitude throughout the crisis.

It may be, perhaps, opportune to mention here an incident of no small importance to a biographer of Dr. Walsh. From the time of Dr. Croke's appointment to the archbishopric of Cashel in 1875, there existed between him and Dr. Walsh an acquaintanceship which quickly grew into friendship. A constant correspondence was carried on between them on all kinds of questions—theological, economic, political. As the matters discussed in the letters were often of more than passing interest, Dr. Croke had early formed the habit of preserving Dr. Walsh's letters for purposes of reference. During his career Dr. Croke had been much in touch with many of the prominent public men of his day—Isaac Butt, Shaw, Parnell, William O'Brien, Davitt, John Dillon, Gladstone, Manning, etc.—and in the course of years he had got together a valuable collection of important letters. When Purcell's *Life of Cardinal Manning* was published in 1895, Dr. Croke read it with the greatest eagerness, but he was so pained at the ruthless fashion in which Purcell dealt with the Cardinal* that he at once determined to make it impossible for anyone ever to have access to his own private papers. And so, one day after reading Manning's Life, he took his collection of private letters, including Dr. Walsh's, and consigned them to the flames. By a lucky chance some few of Walsh's letters escaped destruction, amongst them being about a dozen that were written during the period of the vacancy in the See of Dublin.

But to resume the story of the choice of the Chapter. While giving no sanction to allowing his own name to go forward for the archbishopric, Dr. Walsh discussed with the greatest frankness the course which the diocesan clergy were likely to take in making their commendation to the Holy See. In reply to a letter of Croke's, he sent the following :

WALSH TO CROKE.

Maynooth,
February 21, 1885.

I thought the *Freeman* article a little strong in putting pressure on the priests. Several, I hear, are likely to resent it.

I have been told that of the 64 votes about 40, or possibly 44, will go for me—the rest to Dr. Donnelly, who will be second, and to Tynan, who will be third.

The suggestion of your Grace being voted for in to-day's *Nation* will probably lead to a certain number voting so. I *wish we could transfer the* 40. It is the only way I see out of the difficulty, as far as I am concerned.

Again, on February 27, in a letter marked "Confidential" :

For myself I am fully convinced, now that the people seem generally reconciled to the idea of my leaving the college, that by far the most useful position I could occupy

---

* Croke and Manning were intimate friends. They met for the first time at the Vatican Council in 1869-70, and Manning's affection for Croke was such that he spoke of him as *dimidium animae meae*. Dr. Croke looked upon Manning as the most honest Englishman he had ever known—a man absolutely fair and friendly towards Ireland.

Photo by]   ARCHBISHOP WALSH IN 1885.   [Lafayette, Dublin

for the service of the Irish Church would be that of a representative in Rome.

I take it, as a sort of first principle, that the Irish bishops should have a representative there.

Then the representative should be (1) a person commanding, at least to a fair extent, the confidence of the Irish bishops. He should be (2) a person who would not look on the emoluments of the position except as a means of enabling him to do his work in Rome. He should be (3) have no prospect of promotion to a home mitre to act as a temptation leading him aside from the straight path of advancing the general interests.

Of the three qualifications, I could answer for myself in Nos. 1 & 2. As to No. 3, the fact of my " declaring off" just now would give about the strongest guarantee that it would be possible to conceive.

Think over this.

I am satisfied as to my fitness for *that* position.

Speaking to your Grace as I would *to no one else,* I must say that I am so thoroughly satisfied as to my *unfitness for the place in Dublin* that I have not had two hours unbroken sleep since the election to the Vicar-Capitularship. I twice went to Dublin fully determined to lithograph a letter to the P.P's and Canons which would infallibly save me from getting even one vote on Tuesday week [March 10, the date fixed for the voting].

My sole difficulty in the way of doing this is *the political side of the case.*

I feel that no one was ever placed in such an awkward plight.

Say what you think of the *Roman project.*

Dr. Croke's reply has not survived. It was " burned when read" in accordance with the writer's injunction.* However, there is complete collateral proof that Croke's view about the necessity of having an Irish representative at the Vatican harmonised with Davitt's. Indeed Davitt's idea was a re-echo of Croke's view. In a public speech the Archbishop of Cashel had made reference to this matter, and laid stress on the importance of such a

---

* Letter, *Walsh to Croke,* March 14, 1885.

G

representative being placed in a position of eminence so as to enable him to deal effectively with the activities of wealthy Englishmen and Palesmen who haunted the Vatican.* Neither is there any doubt that Croke made light of Walsh's misgivings about his fitness for the post in Dublin, and that he considered that, for national and other interests, it was most important that Dr. Walsh should be the choice of the Dublin diocesan clergy.

In a letter written from Rome towards the end of February Davitt had suggested to Croke the advisability of getting some priest to organise the Dublin clergy so that a big majority of votes might be recorded in favour of a candidate or candidates of sound nationalist principles. Croke forwarded Davitt's letter to Dr. Walsh, with an intimation that he might make any use of it that he might think fit. When returning Davitt's letter on March 3, 1885, Dr. Walsh commented :

The first suggestion (*re* organising) may be very good in the abstract. But it is impracticable. There is no organising power, or next to none, in Dublin. Then Dublin is a very scattered, straggling sort of diocese; and the city priests form a body very much cut off in sympathy and in every way from those of the country, and the country, like Caesar's Gaul, *divisa est omnis in partes tres*—the northern parishes, those of Wicklow, and of Kildare. Even with the best organiser in the world and plenty of time, organisation would, in the circumstances, be impossible. But, I don't at all like the idea of wire-pulling in such a matter.

After mentioning that in his view it would be more advisable to have *one* nationalist candidate receive a large number of votes than that the votes should be divided among two priests of sound nationality, he went on to say that he had heard that the party of the Pale, headed by Fr. Healy, the famous Parish Priest of Little Bray, were making strenuous efforts on behalf of Dr. Donnelly :

* Cf. Supra, p. 142.

I am indeed exceedingly sorry [he continued] that this political element enters into the case. If I could think that he [Dr. Donnelly] would only keep quiet on such (viz., political) questions, I should certainly vote for him. In every other way he would make an excellent bishop.

Early in March Dr. Walsh had apparently accepted the situation that had developed, and had consented to the Dublin clergy's voting for him if they should so choose, but he was quite prepared for the hostility which he knew would be manifested against his appointment on political grounds; for attacks in the newspapers had already commenced. On March 4 he wrote to Dr. Croke pointing out what an awkward situation would arise for him if, after he had received the overwhelming support of the diocesan clergy, he should be passed over on account of hostile political influence :

The " passing over" in the circumstances would be such a public mark of disapproval from the Holy See that it would make it practically impossible for me to maintain my position here. A college community like ours, where people are so independent, cannot be kept together by force of arms : without strong personal influence to keep the machine together it would smash up very soon.

As the day for the voting drew near, Dr. Walsh, who as a member of the Dublin Chapter was himself entitled to vote, consulted Dr. Croke as to whom he should vote for. He wrote, March 7, 1885 :

It is not easy to see what I should do with my vote on Tuesday. Of course I will take your Grace's advice and keep my mind to myself. At first I assumed that there would be an absolute concentration *for me* and *against me*, as there was last time in Dr. McCabe's case. Then I would, as a matter of course, vote for your Grace, which would put you on the *terna*. Now that the votes not given for me may be more or less scattered, I would not like to do this. Giving a vote to bring a bishop on the list is one thing; to give it merely to throw it away is another. *Omnibus pensatis* I incline to think I ought to vote for Dr. Tynan. I regard him as certainly fit for the post, which in the circumstances is scarcely as much as I could say for Dr. Donnelly. Then it may be of advantage to help Tynan's chance of being on the list in preference to Ardagh* who may run him close. The problem, however is a difficult one.

Dr. Walsh's forecast of the voting was very accurate : Walsh securing 46 votes, Donnelly 12, Tynan 3, the Bishop of Ardagh 2. Dr. Walsh voted for Tynan.

A curious sidelight is thrown on the situation by a remark made by Dr. Walsh in a letter to Croke, March 14 :

The Coadjutor of Clonfert (Dr. Healy) is, it is said, very indignant that the Castle ring did not put him on the list. No doubt they could have done so. They number 5 or 6. But they saw that it was only by going in with Dr. Donnelly's *personal* friends that they could succeed in having anything like a good second.

The free use of Dr. Walsh's name in the public Press, and the attacks which were being made upon him about this time, made him very unhappy, especially as he was debarred by the circumstances of the case from uttering a word of defence.

WALSH TO CROKE.

March 31, 1885.

For myself every day makes me more and more anxious that the whole affair should be dealt with as soon as possible, and that some way may be found of dealing with it, *that will make it unnecessary for me to be disturbed from where I am.*

At the beginning of April Dr. Croke left for Rome. During his stay at Rome he kept Dr. Walsh informed of the trend of events there. He also informed him of Manning's active interposition in trying to baffle the intrigues of Errington and the English Government at the Vatican, and to secure, if possible, Walsh's appointment.

* Dr. Woodlock, Bishop of Ardagh, whose name was then being canvassed, and who in fact received two votes.

From the same source Dr. Walsh learned of Manning's endeavour to dissuade the Government from interfering with the election, and of the practical steps which Dilke and Chamberlain were taking to protest against the Government's support of the Errington intrigue—a proceeding which, as we have seen, threatened to break up the Cabinet.

At this time Dilke, who was President of the Local Government Board and a member of the Cabinet, was acting as Chairman of the " Royal Commission on the Housing of the Working Classes," of which the Prince of Wales and Cardinal Manning were also members. The Commission came to Dublin on Friday, May 22, to take evidence in Ireland. Cardinal Manning did not travel with the Commission. He had been invited by Lord Spencer to be the guest of himself and Lady Spencer at the Viceregal Lodge; but he decided not to come. When Dilke was coming over, Manning recommended him to see Dr. Walsh, and an opportunity of their meeting was afforded by E. Dwyer Gray, who invited Dr. Walsh and Dilke to meet at dinner at his house in Dublin.

In the *Life of Dilke* we read the following extract from Dilke's diary :

May 1885.—On Tuesday evening, May 26, the Commission dined with Gray, and met Dr. Walsh, the new Archbishop : but at Dr. Walsh's wish I had gone to Gray's house half an hour before dinner to see the Archbishop privately, and to be thanked by him for the part I had taken in trying to prevent opposition to the choice.

There is here clearly an error on Dilke's part; his memory must have played him false, for in May Dr. Walsh was not Archbishop, his appointment not having been made till near the end of June. It is true, however, that Dr. Walsh met Dilke and thanked him for his endeavour to prevent the Government from encouraging or countenancing Errington's activities at Rome.

In the interview at Gray's house Dilke spoke freely of Cardinal Manning's great anxiety that the Government should cease its meddling at the Vatican and that Dr. Walsh should be elected. A fortnight later (June 9, 1885) we find Walsh writing " sadly but calmly to Manning" :

The times are indeed troublous. The complications which have arisen have sadly embarrassed me, and deprived me of all freedom of action as to my own position. One thing only is clear : my Presidentship is necessarily at an end; the office is not one that could be held even for a day by anyone on whose career an adverse judgment had been pronounced by the Holy See. Personally I exult at the prospect of getting back to my theological work. But I cannot shut my eyes to the prospect of all that may happen besides.

The suspense was, however, soon to be ended. On June 23, the Pope informed Cardinal Simeoni, Prefect of Propaganda, that he had appointed Dr. Walsh to the Archbishopric of Dublin, and he directed the Cardinal to inform Dr. Walsh at once.

The appointment was published on June 24, 1885. Among the numerous messages of congratulation which Dr. Walsh received, none was more cordial than Dr. Croke's. Dilke, too, was glad of Walsh's election; and towards the end of the month he wrote his congratulations. We read in his diary :

On July 4 I received from Maynooth a letter of thanks from Dr. Walsh for my congratulations on his appointment to the Archbishopric of Dublin, and he expressed the hope that we should meet in Dublin when I came over with Chamberlain.*

On Saturday, June 27, Dr. Walsh, having received an intimation through Dr. Kirby, Rector of the Irish College, that the Pope expressed a wish that he should be consecrated in Rome, at once sought Dr. Croke's advice :

* *Life of Dilke,* ii., p. 154.

Sunday (June 28, 1885).

I will ask your Grace kindly to give me your opinion, not as an element that is to be taken into account in a general consideration of the case by me, but as an indication simply of what I am to do. From your knowledge of Roman ways you are the best judge in the matter. So *I leave the decision altogether in your Grace's hands.*

My personal leaning in the matter would be in favour of acting on the Pope's suggestion. I see several advantages to be gained by following it. But I mention my own view, not at all to influence your Grace's opinion if you lean at all strongly the other way, but only because I think you may wish to know what my own feeling in the matter would be.

Croke at once replied, June 29, 1885, strongly urging on Dr. Walsh the duty of complying with the Holy Father's wish regarding the consecration at Rome. And fearing that Dr. Walsh might be deterred from going to Rome by want of money, Croke enclosed a cheque for £500. Dr. Walsh replied on June 30 :

It is poor thanks for me to say that I cannot find words to thank your Grace for this last great act of your kindness towards me.

Somehow people have had the idea of me that I had some private source of income. As a matter of fact that is not so. . . . My own balance at the bank is not worth talking of. Your Grace's thoughtfulness, then, may, and probably will, be of substantial help to me now. Over and above this, I prize it, as I cannot but regard it as the truest act of friendship I have ever known. Somehow I do not feel half so grateful to your Grace for having done it as for having thought of it as a thing to do.

I only hope that I may be able to thank you in some more substantial way than by these empty words.

On the eve of his departure for his consecration in Rome, Dr. Walsh wrote again to Croke, July 7, 1885 :

I find there is no possibility of my wanting your Grace's cheque. The amount in hands will go quite far enough for all present purposes. So I return the cheque. When I come back from Rome I will have no difficulty in writing to your Grace to say that I want money if I should want it then.

I may as well say now plainly what your Grace may not be unprepared to hear—that before I accept the archbishopric I must clearly put before the Pope my view as to the necessity of an Irish representative having the confidence, etc., etc., and as to my conviction that I am fit for the one position and *unfit for the other*.

Now that the Pope has put down the intrigues of the Vetoists, the Dublin question is a much simpler one than it was.

I take no merit in all this. For all my personal feelings are in favour of the Roman post and against that of the archbishopric of Dublin.

Dr. Croke's reply, written on the following day, July 8, is characteristic—racy, humorous, decisive, extravagant, charming—and runs as follows :

Yours to hand. Cheque all right. Cash always on hands here, in plenty, and at call.

Do not be coquetting at all with the Dublin See. Fit or not fit, you must go ahead now, or we would eat you down to the boots. I now tell you *deliberately* that Dr. Moran was called home to be appointed to Dublin, and that he would have been appointed had we not spoken out so plainly as we did. That has come to me in a way that cannot be doubted. On inquiry in Rome you will find it to be correct.

I saw a letter to-day from Rome in which it was stated that the idea about me is (or was) that I never attend to anything but politics. That's funny, whereas, in reality, I never mind politics at all but spend all my time at my diocesan business. Should you get a chance, especially with the Pope, though I indeed care but little what they think of me, dispel this delusion. Even in politics I am most moderate, and have kept down many a rising wave of trouble.

You will, I am sure, drop me a line, now and then, stating how the cat jumps.

This letter will reach Rome before yourself. I direct it to Irish College.

Postcript.—*Pièces justificatives* of your humble servant, may be opportunely put *into* the Pope when you are speaking of the necessity of having an accredited representative in Rome. Here is an instance of defamation of character, etc., etc.

The *Life of Dilke* (vol. II., pp. 155-6) contains the following entry from Sir Charles's diary, for July 7, 1885 :

I received interesting letters from Dr. Walsh and Sir Frederick Roberts.

Dr. Walsh wrote that in going to Rome he was by no means determined to accept the archbishopric. " I am not Archbishop; acceptance is an essential point, and I have a view of certain matters to set before His Holiness before that stage is reached. I have sent on to Rome a written statement of my views, that the matter may be considered before I arrive there. I am thoroughly convinced that there is another position in which I could be far more useful both for church and country. The archbishopric of Dublin, now that it can be dealt with as a purely ecclesiastical matter, can be very easily provided for."

Dilke's comment on these words of the Archbishop-Elect was : " I suppose that Dr. Walsh wished to be Papal Legate." Walsh wished to be the representative of the Irish Bishops at the Vatican. He had no desire to be Archbishop of Dublin. He shrank from undertaking so onerous an office through dread of the responsibilities attaching to it, and because he was "thoroughly satisfied of his own unfitness for the position."

Dr. Walsh arrived in Rome on Sunday, July 19, and on the same day he was received by Cardinal Simeoni, Cardinal Prefect of Propaganda, to whom he had forwarded a written statement asking him to request the Pope to excuse him from accepting the archbishopric. On the following Wednesday, July 22, he had audience of Leo XIII. In this audience Dr. Walsh expressed to the Pope his apprehension and misgivings at undertaking the pastoral responsibilities of the archbishopric, dwelling on his unacquaintance with missionary work, on his disinclination for pontifical functions, and his unfitness for preaching. But the Pope, like Dr. Croke, waved aside these objections, bade Dr. Walsh undertake his new office with confidence in the Lord, and reminded him that to refuse office when proffered by lawful authority was not " *lo spirito della Chiesa*." The Pope informed him that he thereby appointed him Archbishop of Dublin, and commanded him under obedience to acquiesce in the appointment.

Dr. Walsh was consecrated on Sunday, August 2, 1885, in the Church of St. Agatha dei Goti. Cardinal Moran was the consecrating prelate; the assistant bishops were Dr. Kirby, the Rector of the Irish College, and Dr. Donnelly, Bishop of Clogher. On the following Thursday, Dr. Walsh left for Ireland.

The following three letters to Dr. Croke, written by Dr. Walsh from Rome, are of interest :—

Irish College, Rome,
21st July, 1885.

MY DEAR LORD ARCHBISHOP,—On arriving here on Sunday evening, after I had dined and read my letters, I went over to see Cardinal Simeoni. The interview was substantially *commonplace*, owing in great measure to my great difficulty in understanding him in his *mumbling way of talking in conversation*. However, I made an opportunity of putting in, as a natural digression in the conversation, a short statement of the ecclesiastical affairs in Cashel. Simeoni had introduced the topic fairly by laughing good-humouredly on my telling him that my two travelling companions, Secretary and Chaplain, were outside, and that one was a Rapotensis and the other a Cassiliensis. So he launched out into an exposition of his views upon the speeches in the recent " campaign" [i.e., Dr. Croke's.]

They seem to have given unbounded satisfaction— especially the numerous and emphatic expressions of confidence in the Pope, and exhortations to the people to have full confidence in him. But Simeoni seemed to regard this as a sort of conversion. So I then struck in and said that the newspapers reported only the *political* proceedings of public interest—that the Papal aspect of the case now happened to be closely mixed up with this, but that it was notorious that in the pastoral, as distinct from the purely political, part of your ordinary course, no bishop in Ireland stood up more stoutly for the Pope than your Grace did, and no one did more to lead the people to have confidence in him, just, I added, as there was no diocese in Ireland where there was better or more regular administration as regards priests, nuns, churches, schools, etc., etc.

Just at this time came Kenrick and O'Donnell*; so of course we went off on some tangent.

I have got notice of my audience with the Pope for to-morrow [Wednesday, July 22, 1885] midday. Then I go out to Genazzano for a few days retreat; return on Sunday; see the Consistory, etc., etc., next week: Consecration by Sydney at special desire of the *Pope*, on Sunday, August 2.

I will write again after the audience.

Genazzano,

Confidential.
23rd July, '85,

MY DEAR LORD ARCHBISHOP.—I had my audience [of Pope Leo XIII] yesterday. It lasted three-quarters of an hour. Nothing could be more satisfactory, whether as to substance or as to tone. He spoke most freely about the opposition to my appointment, the stories about my most extreme politics, etc., but he said he had satisfied himself it was *tutto esagerato, tutto falso*. Then he spoke at great length about the appointment being altogether his own act. Even towards the end it was suggested to him to let the case go to Propaganda, but he said, " No; this Archbishop is to be appointed by myself." He told me that Simeoni had come to him with a letter of mine† but that when he heard it was to raise difficulties about accepting the appointment he (the Pope) said he had refused to listen to it. "This," he said, "is a *cosa risoluta*' "; he knew I had not looked for the position [of Archbishop of Dublin] and he put me under obedience to go on without a word of hesitation (*non e lo spirito della chiesa ricusare il lavoro*).

Then he turned on the Errington question—the incorrect

---

* Fr. Kenrick, of Cashel, and the Rev. Patrick O'Donnell, late Cardinal Archbishop of Armagh.

† This is the letter referred to by Dilke. Cf. *Life,* vol. ii., p. 154.

representations made by Errington and others about Irish
political affairs—how he inquired and found out that they
were telling him " *menzogni*." " Then," said he, " I
decided to see Errington no more. I gave directions also
to the Propaganda and to the Secretary of State, and
though, of course, they could not close their doors against
him, he was made to see that he was not wanted to prolong
his stay in Rome."

At this point comes the most satisfactory part of it all.
After talking a little about India, the hierarchy, etc., and
the advantage of his having relations with the English
Government, he said : " I know that the Irish are afraid
that any thing of this sort may be injurious to them, and I
see that their view is reasonable." " Yes, Holy Father,"
said I, " it is quite exposed to great risk of being misrepresented to you"; and I then brought in what your
Grace suggested about yourself, and the idea that you
devote yourself to politics neglecting your pastoral work.
" Well," said the Pope (just as I was about to make a
suggestion about a representative) " I have been thinking
of a plan for some time past; I think it would meet the
difficulty, but I don't know what the Irish bishops may
think of it; I have not mentioned it to anyone, but I said,
' I will ask *Walsh* when I have him here'."

So thereupon he propounded his scheme, consisting in the
establishment of an Irish representative, fully recognised
as such, an ecclesiastic having the confidence of the Holy
See and of the Irish bishops. " We could make him," he
said, " a bishop *in partibus*." Of course I said at once
that this was the very thing we wanted, and that I had a
letter from Cashel two days before suggesting it to me if
the Holy Father would approve of it. " Oh," said he, " it
depends altogether on yourself and the other bishops, so
we may say it is done."

I said " Yes, it only remains to get the individual."
" Well," said he, " I have been thinking of the third who
was on the list sent out by the Dublin priests," i.e. Tynan.

Now (although I did not commit myself to this) I believe
Tynan would do really well, and, taking things as they are,
I don't see how we can get better. The only point to
secure would be that Tynan, or whoever would be here,
should hold his office as an exponent of the bishops' views,
and as an efficient medium of communication with them.
Fortunately at this point the Pope asked me, how is this
plan to be carried out? So I said, " We can arrange it at

the Synod "* (my idea being that we can there draw up a formal petition asking for the appointment of a representative, and putting down as clearly as possible the precise nature of the office, so that the document will be there *in perpetuam rei memoriam* to appeal to, if necessary). He at once assented.

On other topics he spoke very freely also, e.g., on Moran and the suggestion made to appoint him to Dublin, as he was already a bishop of experience, etc., etc. " But no," said he, " Moran has a great mission before him where he is, he has great ideas in his head about the Australian Church, and we must leave him to carry them out," etc., etc.

Putting together what the Pope said and all that I have picked up in Rome, I don't think the project of appointing Sydney went very far. But I hear from Sydney himself that he came over fully believing that he was coming to Dublin; and he made no secret of his surprise when he heard at Naples that he was summoned to Rome to bring back the Hat to his Australian See. It was Simeoni that telegraphed for him, " *Venias Romam quamprimum.*" I think he told me the telegram was sent some day early in June.

As to political affairs at home, the Encyclical is to lay down all sorts of directions. Going in for separation was the only political programme he (the Pope) seemed to object to.

He told me repeatedly that it was the strong recommendation of the Irish bishops [i.e. the Irish bishops who had been summoned to Rome for a conference preparatory to the holding of a Synod] that had most weight with him in my appointment—their confidence in me, and the prospect of their being more united if I were in Dublin than if anyone else were there. " They were," he said, " unanimous—we may call it unanimous."

Finally, when the others came in (i.e. O'Donnell and Kenrick) he spoke mainly of my appointment, and wound up by giving me an admonition to take a good rest after my consecration to recover strength after the heavy work of my double office for the last few months, the long journey, etc., etc. But his idea of resting is staying in Rome for the month of August!

* A Plenary Synod of the Irish bishops was then in contemplation; it did not, however, take place till 1900.

I am to be consecrated by *Sydney*, in the Irish College on Sunday, 2nd August.

No other news.

WALSH TO CROKE.

Irish College, Rome,
6 Aug., 1885.

MY DEAR LORD ARCHBISHOP,—I hope to leave Rome to-day for Ancona. We were to have left yesterday morning, but on the previous day an invitation came from Cardinal Pecci* for a dinner party yesterday. The occasion, of course, was the Consecration, held in his Church of St. Agatha. His Em. of Sydney, who has been quite knocked up for the last few days, could not come; so we had Dublin (Walsh), Clogher (Donnelly), and Lita (Kirby), with our respective " secretaries." The Cardinal gave us a first-rate entertainment, and we (especially Lita) gave him the full worth of it back in information, of the right sort, about Ireland.

When the Cardinal said we could now look forward to getting good measures passed, Lita struck in boldly about the Irish Parliament. This seemed to surprise the old Cardinal; however, I assured him it was a matter now of a very short time " pochi anni" at the outside, etc., etc.

It is plain Lita (Dr. Kirby) has the full confidence of the Vatican; and certainly, according to his lights, he makes good use of his opportunities. To-day he has gone to the Vatican with Clogher who has been kept here without his audience until now.

Lita was (confidentially) sent for last night to bring me the address (autograph) sent by the Belgian bishops giving adhesion to the Pope's letter on the excessive Ultramontanism of some of the Catholic papers.

Fearful weather here. All Rome is complaining of it. It will be an immense relief to get away.

To complete the story of the appointment to the archbishopric of Dublin in 1885, it may be well to refer briefly to Cardinal Moran's interview with Leo XIII, and to the acute disagreement between Gladstone and Dilke in connection with the Errington baronetcy.

* Cardinal Pecci was brother of Leo XIII.

When Dr. Moran arrived at Naples in response to Cardinal Simeoni's summons, he was met by a Papal courier bearing the *biglietto* of his appointment to the Sacred College. On receiving this news Moran was much disappointed, for before leaving Australia he was so fully persuaded that the summons meant his transference to Dublin, that he had actually packed up his books and papers. At the audience which the Pope granted to Dr. Moran immediately after his arrival in Rome, Leo XIII informed him that when summoning him from Sydney His Holiness's intention was to transfer him to the archbishopric of Dublin, and to send Dr. Walsh to Sydney : " *Lei a Dublino e Walsh a Sydney.*" The Pope, however, as he informed Dr. Moran, was led to change his original purpose, because of the strong feeling of the Irish Catholics against the appointment of anyone other than the candidate of their choice, and because he had discovered for himself the lying nature of the anti-Walsh conspiracy. This course was also strongly urged by Cardinal Simeoni, who had become definitely convinced of the propriety of appointing Dr. Walsh to Dublin.*

While the English agents at Rome were being received with growing suspicion at the Vatican, their influence was further lessened by a growing weakness within the Liberal Party itself. Since the spring the Government had been drifting towards a sharp division on its general Irish policy. Spencer, Forster, Harcourt, and the more moderate Liberals advocated the continuance of the Crimes Act of 1882 and the introduction of further coercion. The more advanced Liberals were already converted to a policy of appeasement, and were opposed to any further irritation of Irish feeling. By June the state of the parties brought a general election into the immediate prospect, and the Government difficulties were increased by

* Letter from Cardinal Moran to Rev. B. Fitzpatrick, Sept., 1885.

the necessity of facing an enlarged electorate containing political elements hitherto unexplored. The Ministry fell on June 12, and pending the appointment of a new administration the promoters of the Errington intrigue were too anxiously occupied with the uncertainties of domestic politics to permit their lending active support to the efforts of their emissaries at Rome.*

The outgoing Liberal Government had rewarded Errington by conferring on him a baronetcy. Dilke strongly resented this action, which he considered politically discreditable, and wrote a vigorous protest to Gladstone. Incidentally, he made a complimentary reference to Dr. Walsh :

I feel bound to express my dismay at seeing this day that honours have been conferred on that excellent fellow Errington at a moment when it will be felt by the great majority of people who do not see round corners that he is rewarded for the fight made by him on behalf of the defeated policy of resistance to the selection as Roman Catholic Archbishop of Dublin of *the accomplished gentleman on whom the whole Irish Roman Catholic clergy and people had set their hearts*. I have already described to Lord Granville in your presence what I thought the fatal results of this policy of interference against a unanimous Irish sentiment in the choice of the great Roman Catholic dignitaries in Ireland—a policy which has, in the belief of the thoughtful men of all parties, among whom I may name

* Manning was strongly opposed to diplomatic relations with the Vatican. Dilke, however, did not take the same view. He writes :

" Such perpetual applications have to be made to the Court of Rome, not only (as the public thinks) with regard to Irish affairs, but with regard to Roman Catholic interests in all parts of the world, that I have always been favourable to taking the public into our confidence in the matter and appointing a representative at the Court of Rome. At one time we used to carry on our affairs with the Papal Court through Cardinal Howard, an English Cardinal, but the Pope is so *anxious to obtain official representation* that he throws difficulties in the way of ecclesiastics acting as informal representatives."—*Life of Dilke,* i., p. 376.

privately the new Lord Chancellor of Ireland,* undone the effects of your Land Acts of 1871 and 1881, and made the resistance to the Union stronger and more unanimous than it ever was before. Surely such an intention as that to specially honour Mr. Errington at such a moment might have been named to me when I so strongly expressed before you and Lord Granville my opinion of the policy. Mr. Forster, the initiator of the Errington policy, has returned to the Liberal front bench, and sat next to me there. I fear I must take the opportunity of leaving it, as I do not see how I can fail to express the opinion I hold of the conferring of special honour at such a moment on Mr. Errington.

To this letter Gladstone replied, June 27, 1885 :

I feel that the coincidence of the Walsh appointment with the Errington baronetcy is unfortunate, but I think that the grant of the baronetcy or something in that sense is unavoidable. I regard Gibson's confidential disclosure to you as an absurd exaggeration indulged in for party purposes. The policy, and any ingratitude to an agent of it, are wholly different matters; and your disapproval of the first never conveyed to my mind the idea of speaking to you about the second. You are aware of the immense stress laid by Spencer on the Errington mission, which Granville more traditionally (as I think) supported. For my part, I never did more than acquiesce in it, and I think it highly probable that no such thing will be renewed. As to " diplomatic relations" with the Pope, I am entirely opposed to them.

Dilke, reviewing the whole Errington business, says :

There was never a more discreditable piece of business than the whole of the Errington matter. Errington himself is an excellent fellow, and I have not a word to say against him. It is the Government and not Errington that must be blamed . . . One result of the concealment as to the whole Errington business was that Mr. Gladstone on one occasion (1882) gave an answer in the House of Commons which

* Mr. Edward Gibson, afterwards created Lord Ashbourne. Dr. Walsh was one of the first to congratulate Gibson on his appointment to the Lord Chancellorship. (Cf. *Life of Dilke*, vol. ii., p. 151.) Gibson had been coached in the Canon Law by Dr. Walsh during the O'Keeffe trial.

was untrue, although he did not know that it was untrue, and that on another occasion the same thing happened to Courtney, who as Under-Secretary of State for the Colonies denied that a Roman Catholic question affecting the Colonies (the proposal for a Cathedral at Gibraltar) had been discussed, when Errington himself told me that it had. The Colonial office did not know.*

I was opposed not to diplomatic relations with the Pope, but to the extraordinary anomalies involved in a mission that was no mission.†

* *Life of Dilke,* i., pp. 428-9.

† *Ibid,* ii., p. 151.

CHAPTER VIII

ARCHBISHOP

THE Archbishop of Dublin made his homeward journey from Rome in easy stages, visiting on his way various places of interest on the continent. At the last stage of the continental journey, he made a pilgrimage to the shrine of his sainted predecessor, St. Laurence O'Toole, at Eu in Normandy. There he remained a few days in quiet retreat. He then set out for his diocese, arriving at Kingstown on the afternoon of Friday, September 4, 1885.

His reception at Kingstown was enthusiastic. All along the pier crowds had gathered to greet him, and a peal of welcome went up as the mail-boat bearing the Archbishop approached the jetty. Before coming ashore he was presented with two addresses of welcome, one from the Town Commissioners—a mixed body of Catholics and Protestants—the other from the Catholic and Nationalist inhabitants of Kingstown. At Westland Row he received an ovation. He was met by the Lord Mayor and Corporation of Dublin, wearing their robes of office. They had come in state to receive him and to present to him an address in which they tendered him a civic welcome. The address, which was unanimously presented by the municipal body, expressed the pride of the citizens at the appointment of a native of their city to fill the See of St. Laurence, praised his Grace's mature wisdom, and expressed the hope which they felt was shared by him that peace and unity among her children would mark the onward progress of their native land to the attainment of her just and rightful hope—the restoration of her native legislature.

In the course of his reply the Archbishop said :

A people laying claim to the name and dignity of a nation must prove not merely by words, but still more by the acts of its public men, that it has the self-restraint which, especially in matters where religious feeling comes into play, will guard with the most delicate care against all that could savour of disregard of the sincere convictions of even the smallest minorities amongst its citizens. Among those who took part in your meeting for the preparation of the address were some members of your body whose religious convictions debar them from recognising any duty of spiritual allegiance to a Catholic bishop. And I have no reason to believe that those other non-Catholic members of your body who were absent on that occasion were influenced by any other feeling than that of an unwillingness to mar by the presence of any element of discord, the unanimity of a proceeding to which they were in no way opposed, but in which they did not feel themselves free to take an assenting part.

You assure me that it is a source of pride and gratification to you that a native of the city has been elected to fill the See of St. Laurence. I accept this assurance all the more gratefully that it comes to me from a body which in the conferring of its own highest honours has not allowed itself to be swayed by any narrow consideration of the accident of birth . . . Even in its latest nomination to the Civic Chair, the members of the Council of Dublin have with grateful unanimity selected for the Lord Mayoralty one* to whom Dublin can unfortunately lay no claim.

And now, without needlessly trespassing on your time to disclaim the language of eulogy with which your address has embarrassed me, I hasten to assure you of my full and ardent sympathy with the wishes expressed in its closing words.

With me it is no new theory of to-day or yesterday, but a settled and deeply rooted conviction, that for a remedy of the many grievances for the removal of which the people of this island have so long laboured but with partial success, there is but one effectual course—the restoration to Ireland of that right of which we were deprived now nigh a century ago, by means as shameful as any that the records of national infamy can disclose. With you, then, I rejoice

* T. D. Sullivan, who was the Lord Mayor of Dublin.

that the flag which fell from the dying hand of O'Connell has once more been boldly uplifted, and I pray that it may never again be furled, until the right of Ireland is recognised to have her own laws made upon Irish soil, and by the legally and constitutionally chosen representatives of the Irish people.

As I have expressed freely my personal opinions on the great political question of the day, I must in conclusion add one more word.

Among the Catholics of Dublin there are and will be as there ever have been in the past, differences of opinion in political matters no less strongly marked than those which separate our citizens generally in their religious creeds. I wish then, to proclaim once for all, at the very outset of my episcopal labours, that in every relation of my pastoral office, in the house which is henceforth to be my home, in the Cathedral which will be the chief centre of my episcopal work—in a word, in every scene and sphere of duty, I shall with God's help know no difference between those whose views in public affairs are most thoroughly in sympathy with mine, and those from whose honest opinions my own are most widely divergent, ever bearing in mind that I have been placed here by the Sovereign Pontiff as Archbishop of Dublin, and thus as the pastor and spiritual father, not of any section or class, no matter how numerous or how powerful, but of all our Catholic people.

The induction of the Archbishop into his See took place at the Pro-Cathedral, Marlborough Street, on Monday September 7. After the conclusion of the religious ceremonial, the Archbishop, accompanied by the members of the Corporation and many other public representatives who had assisted at the induction, withdrew to Holy Cross College, Clonliffe, where arrangements had been made for the presentation of an address from the clergy and laity of the diocese. Long before the appointed hour thousands of people had assembled in the grounds of the college, and the platform and the approaches to it were crowded by Members of Parliament and deputations from various public bodies in the city and throughout the diocese, as well as by clergymen in large numbers from all parts of the country.

The address, after making complimentary reference to Dr. Walsh's fitness for his exalted office, proceeded :

We rejoice in a special manner that your appointment has put an end, and we hope for ever, to any attempt to revive discussion on the hateful question of the Veto, on which the bishops, priests, and people of Ireland, with the concurrence of the Sovereign Pontiff, pronounced an emphatic, and, we had hoped, a lasting condemnation nearly seventy years ago.

After detailing a number of grievances which were clamouring for settlement—education, poor-laws, etc.—the address continued : " As a means to remedy these and many other evils we look forward to a thorough reconstruction of the system under which Ireland has been and is still being governed.

" In our efforts to procure the reform of abuses, and to obtain such other measures as the requirements of our country imperatively demand—to be obtained, however, by just and constitutional means—we rely on your Grace's cordial sympathy and encouragement."

In his reply the Archbishop stated that he was keenly alive to the difficulties that lay before him, but he was comforted by thinking that he could count first and before all on the enlightening grace of God, and in the next place on the steadfast co-operation of his priests and people. He promised encouragement and assistance in the removal of religious and national grievances, and expressed a hope that a brighter day was about to dawn upon Ireland.

I will ask you (he concluded) to remember that it is to those who seek first the Kingdom of God and His glory, these other things shall be added. May I not even count on the continuance of the same loving confidence which has been so lavishly showered on me by the people of this diocese since I came among you ? May I not ask you to remember that I shall always rely with confidence on your prayers ? I ask you indeed ever to pray that in the days that are before me, whether in the good providence of God they are to be few or many, I may never betray the trust reposed in me by our Holy Father, Leo XIII; that I may never act in any other spirit than that which inspires the beautiful prayer in the Church's liturgy recited over me on the day of my consecration; and that thus I may ever have the grace to keep in the straight path of duty, never putting forth darkness for light nor light for darkness, never calling evil good nor good evil, and swayed neither to the right hand nor to the left by the fear of human censure or by the foolish and unprofitable desire of human praise.

From the day of Dr. Walsh's arrival at Kingstown till the end of the month of September, he was receiving addresses and making speeches almost daily; and for months hardly a week went by in which he did not receive a deputation. Wherever he went he was hailed as a kind of national hero. His energy was marvellous. In addition to discharging the numerous and onerous duties of adminis-tering his diocese, and carrying on an extensive corres-pondence with prominent ecclesiastics and laymen, he found time to deliver a series of carefully prepared statements regarding the grievances of Irish Catholics, chiefly in matters of education, and other public questions. Of this " most remarkable series of addresses on public questions," a discerning critic, John George McCarthy, wrote, October 5, 1885 :

We have had many addresses of loftier eloquence and many of more rhetorical beauty—but in my experience of public life in Ireland we have had none so wise and calm, so affluent in knowledge and so lucid in style, so outspoken, and yet so absolutely inoffensive.

Among Dr. Walsh's replies one finds here and there references of biographical interest. Replying to an address in which it was said that " born in the capital of Ireland, and drawing your origin from Connaught and Munster, your Grace is truly a representative Irishman," he spoke of his early religious training (September 20, 1885) :

Sunday after Sunday, during the years of my boyhood, I received from the Christian Doctrine Confraternity of my native parish those lessons in the Christian Doctrine, by the standard of which the actions and omissions of my life will one day be weighed when I stand before the Judgment seat of God. If I am here to-day speaking to you as your Bishop, and invested with that authority which has been confided to me by our Holy Father, it is owing, I firmly believe, under the providence of God, to the sound and solid instruction which, thanks to the watchful care of a good mother, I received in my early days in that dear old parish church of SS. Michael and John's.

Speaking in the church of his native parish, January 17, 1886, he said :

I was not indeed baptised within the sacred walls (of the Church of SS. Michael & John's) for in the days of my infancy and childhood, down to the time of the Synod of Thurles, it was a very general usage to administer the Sacrament of Baptism in the houses of the parishioners, as it was then also not unusual to perform there many other religious rites which, in the altered circumstances of the times, we are now enabled to perform, in fuller accordance with the law of the Church's liturgy, within the parish church. It was, however, at the hands of the parish priest, afterwards the venerated Dean O'Connell, and with water taken from the baptismal font of the parish church, that this first great grace was imparted to me. It was within these walls and under the instruction of your edifying parochial Confraternity that I received, I may almost say, my first lessons in the Christian Doctrine.

It was here that I made my first Confession. It was here that I received the Sacrament of Confirmation. Here, too, I was first permitted to minister in the service of the altar, and here I made my first Holy Communion. It was here, in fine, that I first had the happiness of offering up the Holy Sacrifice, for my first Mass was said at that old high altar which has since given place to this new and more suitable one.

Replying to an address from the Dr. Cahill Memorial Committee, September 18, 1885, he said :

The address brings back to me the memory of my school-boy days. How well I now remember how, week after week, especially on Saturdays and on Sunday mornings, a striking object in so many of our city thoroughfares, and in the neighbourhood of our city churches, was the display of those announcements of the weekly letter of Dr. Cahill on some subject of absorbing interest on the religious or political questions of the day.

I say political, but I do not know if he ever dealt with politics as such. I dare say he did not. At all events it is likely that he but rarely did so. But in Ireland the line between religion and politics is a line by no means easy to draw. I have some experience now in critically observing such matters, and I have never known that feat to be accomplished with success. Those, as it seems to me, have made the most signal failures in it, who have usually been loudest in proclaiming that it is a thing of such easy accomplishment, that to do it, and to do it perfectly, is the first duty of us all. To me it seems very plain what it is that really is objected to by those worthy critics of so many of our own prominent ecclesiastics and public men. I am willing to assume that it in no way presents itself in this light to their minds—but what really is objected to by them is the contact of religion with politics of any hue or shape save one; the exception, of course, being made in favour of that which happens to coincide with their own personal views.

In reply to an address, September 11, 1885, he referred to his reluctance to becoming Archbishop :

The office to which I have been appointed by the Sovereign Pontiff is indeed, as you remind me, an office both impor-tant and responsible. It is an office which no man can hope worthily to fill. Conscious of my own special unfitness for it, I was unable to bring myself to accept so weighty a trust until I had recourse, without effect, to every means that seemed likely to prove effective in enabling me to decline the responsibility; until, indeed, it had become with me a question of obedience or disobedience to the formal command laid upon me by the Holy Father.

In the words of paternal tenderness in which His Holiness at length solemnly enjoined upon me the duty of going for-ward in the path in which he, by his own act, had set me, he put before me one by one the many sources of grace, of

light and of strength, on which he bade me rely. Amongst
these, and prominent amongst them, was the feeling of
unbounded trust with which he knew that the clergy and
people of this diocese were prepared to welcome me. His
words have indeed come true.

On the same occasion he made reference to his relations
with Cardinal Cullen, of whom he always spoke in terms of
high appreciation :

Clonliffe, as the chairman [of the Town Commissioners of
Drumcondra, Glasnevin, and Clonliffe] has reminded me, is
the seat of my episcopal seminary—that splendid college upon
which we look with such pride as one of the noblest monuments of the pastoral zeal, and a most cherished portion of
the rich inheritance of religious and educational institutions
handed down to all future Archbishops of Dublin by one of
my immediate predecessors in the See, Cardinal Cullen. It is
indeed specially dear to me, for it is there within the college
church, that in accordance with his dying wishes, are
entombed the remains of that great prelate, its founder,
under whose loving auspices my own ecclesiastical studies
were commenced.

Three days later, September 14, 1885, speaking at
Clonliffe College, the Archbishop again referred to Cardinal
Cullen in terms of eulogy and affection :

I feel most deeply grateful to you for those sentences in
your address in which, with pardonable ingenuity, you trace
out—even though in tracing you exaggerate—the ties that
from the very earliest days of my life as an ecclesiastical
student united me with him of whom you speak so gratefully, so lovingly—our first Irish Cardinal, your founder.
One thing you could not exaggerate—my readiness to place
at his disposal whatever of humble service I had to offer
him, whenever he seemed to think that my aid in any
undertaking in which he was engaged would not be wholly
useless to him.
The Cardinal, as you know, was not demonstrative in his
ways, and it was not until we had lost him that from
conversations with others, whose relations with him I had
ever regarded as having been more intimately confidential
than mine had been, I came to know to how large an extent

I had enjoyed his confidence. It will always be a source, I cannot say of pleasure, but of comfort and consolation to me, to reflect that it was through my recollection of a conversation with him here in your college grounds, that those who had charge of his solemn obsequies were afterwards enabled to give effect to his wishes as to his resting-place in death. For I believe that, with possibly one exception, I was the only person to whom he had confided the expression of his wish that his remains should be laid, as they have been, in the place which, by his otherwise unexplained direction, was so suitably arranged for the purpose in the building of your college church.

The presence of that tomb can never fail to keep before you—and as I now look on this College as part of my home, may I not add that it never can fail to keep before me also—the memory of the virtues of our great pastor, in whose steadfast devotion to duty, untiring energy in the work of the pastoral office, and unfailing care for the poor and the afflicted, we may all of us find, a noble model for the imitation, whether of the bishop, or of the priests, or of the ecclesiastical students who are to be the future clergy of this diocese.

In many of these qualities, while we must labour with all our might, we must indeed be content to follow at an humble distance. But there was one feature, a great and striking and characteristic feature, of his personal character, in which it should not be too difficult for any of us to approach him more closely—in which indeed even the humblest and youngest student in the college may in this respect most naturally hope for the fullest measure of success—that humble and unassuming demeanour, in which, more thoroughly perhaps than in any other way, he reproduced among us for our edification and instruction the spirit of that holy city in which his youth and so many years of his life were passed.

There was another characteristic quality of his which comes prominently before me this evening, finding myself, as I do, for the first time among you, the students of my diocesan seminary. It was the kindly and affectionate interest he always took in the progress towards the sanctuary of every ecclesiastical student who came within reach of his inspiring influence.

To Cardinal McCabe he referred more rarely. Speaking

at the Dominican Convent School, Eccles Street, Dublin, on October 15, 1885, he remarked: "This school was founded by my venerable predecessor the late Cardinal Archbishop of Dublin, not only my predecessor in the Archbishopric, but a kind and true friend of mine; and I owe it surely to his memory and to the kindness that he never failed to show me that I should do what I can to help on the work of those institutions to which he stood in the special relation not only of patron but of founder."

" In your township also," he said to the Commissioners of the Township of Drumcondra, Glasnevin, and Clonliffe, "in Glasnevin, lie the remains of my immediate predecessor, Cardinal McCabe, whose dying wish it was that he should be interred, not within the burial place in his Cathedral, among those whose munificent devotedness to the interests of religion and maintenance of her costly works have established for them a claim to rest in that holy place, but in the graveyard in Glasnevin, and even there, so far as his last wishes could effect it, amongst the poorest of the poor of his flock."

There were, of course, in the replies to the addresses of congratulation numerous expressions of attachment to the Holy See and of devotion to Leo XIII. In commending the people of Killcullen for the sentiments conveyed in their address, the Archbishop said, September 26, 1885: " Of these sentiments the first is that of loyal, earnest, enthusiastic love for our Holy Father, Pope Leo XIII, by whose act—an act that, as I had the privilege of hearing from his own lips, was very specially his own—I am here as your Bishop, and from whose consecrated hands, as a pledge of his affection for me and for all the people of my diocese, I received this cross that I now bear upon my breast."

In one of Archbishop Walsh's first pastoral discourses to the people of his mensal parish, he spoke with grateful appreciation of the happy bond which united his faithful people to their priests, and of the loyalty and affection which had characterised the relations of the clergy of Dublin to their archbishops. He also referred to the ties of mutual confidence which secured the solidarity of the Irish episcopate.

It is a source of consolation to me (he said) as it will always be to me a source of strength, to think that those who have incurred the responsibility of bringing about my appointment to the archbishopric—the members of our venerable chapter, our respected parish priests, the suffragan bishops of this ecclesiastical province, in fine, the bishops of our Irish Church—will, I am sure, bear in mind that they have incurred a heavy responsibility; for they have put on themselves the duty of aiding me now and henceforth by their wise counsels and by their holy prayers.

I pray to God that in the united deliberations of the episcopate, in the united action which it must be from time to time our duty to take in the general interests of Irish Catholicity and of Catholic Ireland, we may ever be animated by that spirit, in which alone we can hope to find the union which is strength . . .

The main work of a bishop, however, lies at home, in the pastoral care of his own diocese and of his own priests and people. The union on which the success of my ministry must chiefly depend is, first, the union of the clergy of the diocese, their union with one another and with me their bishop; and secondly, the union which will bind in indissoluble bonds the members of our faithful flocks with us their pastors and spiritual fathers. This is the spirit in which our religious confraternities carry out their work, performing, as they do, the various spiritual and temporal works of mercy for which they have been established, supplementing in their measure and degree the labours of their pastors in the salvation of souls. The spirit of co-operation and obedience is the spirit which will bring down on the confraternities an abundant blessing.

At the very outset of his episcopate Dr. Walsh was confronted with the problem of how to thwart and undo the work of proselytism among the poorer members of his flock in Dublin. The work of the proselytiser was no new evil. For centuries—from the time of the national apostasy of England from the Catholic Faith—determined efforts had been made, overtly or covertly, to induce the Catholics of Ireland to conform to the " true religion as by law established." For this purpose confiscations, threats, imprisonments, tortures were tried by turns; and when force had failed recourse was had to the more subtle methods of legal bribes and educational systems. The granting of Catholic Emancipation (1829) did not put an end to the evils of proselytism; the proselytiser continued his activities, merely changing his weapons. The new methods were more insidious, though less savage, than the old. Many devices were employed to subvert the faith of Catholic children; but the meanest and most disreputable of all the proselytising methods was " souperism."

The " souper" movement started during the great Irish famine in 1847. Under the guise of a philanthropic movement it was set on foot ostensibly to provide food for the starving people of Ireland—mainly in the province of Connaught—but in reality for the purpose of inducing the poorest of the Catholic people, under pressure of starvation, to abandon their faith. The " soupers" were liberally supplied with funds, contributed by charitable and philanthropic English Protestants. An organisation was developed to direct the campaign, and Dublin was selected as headquarters. The " soupers' " activities, thwarted to a great extent in Connaught, were directed and prosecuted with intensive vigour in and around the city of Dublin.

During the episcopate of Cardinal Cullen and of Cardinal McCabe much had been done to counteract the inroads of proselytism. Cardinal McCabe, during the time that he was Parish Priest of St. Nicholas', Francis Street, had had intimate practical experience of the sad havoc which the proselytiser had wrought among Catholic children who were the innocent victims of their parents' negligence or misfortune, and when he became Archbishop he did much to frustrate the depredations amongst the little ones of his flock. In each of the slum parishes he appointed a priest who was specially enjoined to look after the weaklings to whom proselytising agents were paying attention. Lay co-operators, mainly ladies, formed themselves into "Save the Child" organisations to lend their aid. Numbers of children were saved for the Church, and some provision was made for their housing and education. One such home erected at Stradbally was placed in charge of the Presentation Sisters; but this home was far removed from Dublin, and besides, it was altogether inadequate to meet the needs of the anti-proselytising agencies.

To secure Dr. Walsh's interest in their work, and to further the project of speedily providing in Dublin a commodious Home for rescued Catholic children, the Orphanage Committee of Our Lady of Mount Carmel called on the Archbishop, September 21, 1885. After outlining the work of the society, its origin and development, the spokesman of the Committee proceeded:

In the darkest hour of the last Irish famine a notorious society was organised to carry on the work of proselytism in the sorrow-stricken homes of our starving people. Agents were supplied with gold and sent into the most afflicted districts, decoy-schools were opened for famishing children, and Dublin was selected as the centre of operations and government.

Of this society we must speak plainly. But, at the same time, we do not hesitate to make profession in your Grace's presence of our respect for the conscientious opinions of our Protestant brethren, no matter how and where they worship. We are not here to condemn the zeal, however mistaken, of those who wish to make converts by fair argument and honourable methods. But we must denounce mission agents who degrade religion and dishonour the Christian name by the vile means they employ to fill foul nests and dreary homes in earning their share of mission pelf.

We have had evidence that these mercenaries have bribed the homeless, the sick, the dying; have ensnared,

enticed, or stolen helpless infants; and have detained them
as prisoners by various threats and devices in proselytising
dens.   We know that Catholic children have been removed
from home to home, from town to town, to baffle the
pursuit of parents, and have been kept under restraint not
only in disregard of their own protests, but in defiance of
the application and entreaty of friends and relatives.   We
have had proof that these guileless captives have not only
been compelled to learn and repeat horrid blasphemies
against the Catholic Church and all she holds most sacred,
but have been urged to take part in public insult and dishonour heaped upon the statue of the Blessed Virgin and
upon the hallowed sign of the world's redemption.   We
have had sad experience that such training when completed
strips the soul of every vestige of religion, and prepares the
way to a career of sin and infamy.

The Orphanage with which we are identified was established to rescue Catholic children before perversion.   Ours
was not the work of aggression.   We sought our own; we
claimed our own.   Since our beginning, nine years ago,
four hundred children have been rescued from the snare of
the proselytisers.   It is something done, but not enough.
There are many Catholic children in proselytising schools
who are to-day praying for their deliverance . . .   We trust
that your Grace will use words of warning to check this
horrid traffic in souls; that you will be able to awaken a
sense of shame and justice among fair-minded Protestants,
and move them to condemn and denounce unscrupulous
proselytisers, and that you will teach emphatically those
who need the lesson, that the children of the poorest
beggar ought to be, and must be, safe from assault and
outrage.

The Archbishop in his reply informed the Orphanage
Committee that he had already determined to make a careful examination of the abominable system which they had
exposed and that, on account of the paramount importance
of the matter, he would at once take practical steps to deal
with it.   He expressed his conviction that even the
publication of the Committee's address would not be
without effect in checking to some extent the evil they had
described.   " It is," he said, " all but incredible that a
traffic so disreputable should not long since have been put

down by the responsible authorities of that religious denomination in whose supposed interest its operations seem to be carried on. It is difficult, too, to account for its not having received an effective check from another source. Our Catholic poor in Dublin are indeed patient in their poverty. But the patience even of a long-suffering people has limits which it is not always safe to pass. If the law be powerless, as it seems to be, to protect them in their humble homes from the visits of those insidious emissaries of sin, it would seem to me anything but strange, if they had long since taken the matter into their own hands to protect themselves."

As might be expected the Archbishop was vigorously censured in various quarters, and especially in what had been called the mosquito Protestant Press, for inciting to a breach of the peace.

Dr. Walsh kept the question of proselytism prominently before his mind, and some months after entering on the archbishopric he was able to provide a home in Dublin for rescued Catholic children. This refuge, known as the Sacred Heart Home, Drumcondra, was opened on the Feast of the Sacred Heart, June 1886. The building in which the Home was started had been acquired as a temporary training college for primary teachers while the new St. Patrick's Training College was being built. When the premises became vacant, the Archbishop, who was the landlord, offered it rent free for the purpose of a Rescue Home. The Home was entrusted to the management of a committee of ladies who had been organised by the Rev. M. Waters, S.J., and this committee devoted itself to the work, and has ever since conducted the Home with marked ability and great success.

Founded on June 2, 1886, the Sacred Heart Home was not established as an ordinary orphanage. It was to be a Home for the immediate admission and free support of

Catholic children rescued from proselytising "Birds' Nests." In its reports the Committee constantly put before the charitable public the purposes for which the Home was founded.

It cannot be too often repeated (says the report of 1905) that this is not a proselytising home ; that no Protestant is, or ever can be, admitted within its walls ; that no Protestant child has ever been induced to change its faith through its agency . . . Let it be once more openly declared that the Sacred Heart Home is a refuge for Catholics only—such as children rescued from a Protestant Home, where their faith was being undermined, or else children whose circumstances were such that they were in imminent danger of being taken away to some Home or place where they would be brought up as Protestants.

During the first few years after its establishment hundreds of Catholic children were rescued and received into the Home, or maintained at the expense of the Committee. In 1896 a large addition was built to the Home at a cost of over £4,000. Of this sum Archbishop Walsh provided £1,000. Henceforward the number of children maintained at Drumcondra was more than doubled. Besides the children sheltered within the walls of the Home a considerable number were put out to be nursed at the Committee's expense. In 1913 the Committee of management were fortunate in getting the Sisters of Charity of St. Vincent de Paul to take charge of the work in the Home.

Since the foundation of the Sacred Heart Home the Committee have rescued and provided for almost four thousand Catholic children. At the present time they have to provide for over three hundred children within the Home or boarded out in Catholic families. Their expenditure is over £5,000 a year, and they have no permanent endowment. The work of the Home has made itself manifest in the diminished numbers of the children now attending the Ragged Schools or housed in the "Birds' Nests."

In the autumn of 1886, the same year in which the Sacred Heart Home was opened, Dr. Walsh took steps to provide a Home for working-boys in Dublin. He purchased extensive premises in Abbey Street, in a central position in the city, and here in the month of September was established the Working Boys' Home. The cost of the premises was something over £1,000, and this sum was available from the residue of the estate of Francis Pilsworth, a worthy Dublin Catholic who, after having left large bequests in charity for specified charitable and benevolent institutions, entrusted to the Archbishop's discretion the distribution of a substantial sum—the residue of his estate.

The Archbishop presented the premises free of rent to the Committee. A further sum of £1,000 was needed to repair the premises and to provide the necessary furniture. To devise means to secure this sum a meeting of the citizens was summoned by the Lord Mayor, T. D. Sullivan. At this meeting, which was attended by many Protestants, the Archbishop proposed the principal resolution. The money needed was quickly subscribed, the Archbishop himself subscribing £100.

The Catholic Boys' Home was established mainly for the reception of poor Catholic newsboys and other Catholic lads who eke out a precarious livelihood upon the streets of the city of Dublin. Besides the poor street-boys, who were for the most part orphans or the neglected children of drunken, idle, or dissolute parents, there was another class of boys for whom the Home was intended to be available. This class comprised the considerable number of country lads apprenticed to traders in Dublin. As those young apprentices received very small wages they were greatly in need of cheap food and lodging.

The Home served the double purpose of providing comfortable lodging and wholesome food for those poor lads who were trying to support themselves in casual or ill-paid callings. It was to be conducted mainly on commercial lines, and the committee proposed to " give to each boy, for one penny, a decent, clean, and comfortable bed as a resting-place for the night, and likewise for one penny, a breakfast and supper of wholesome food." The expense of the breakfast, which consisted of cocoa and an adequate portion of bread, was to be met in part by the pennies which the boys contributed. The supper, consisting of good soup and bread, was to be supplied at less than cost price; but the annual deficit from this source did not amount to more than £100. Later a system of penny dinners was introduced.

The Home always received generous support from the citizens of Dublin, and ever since its foundation has been a popular institution with the boys for whose benefit it was established. The Archbishop all through his episcopate was a regular attendant at the public meetings held periodically to solicit funds in aid of the work for which the Home was founded.

CHAPTER IX

LAND PURCHASE AND HOME RULE

THE references to questions of national weal to be
found in many of the congratulatory addresses presented
to the Archbishop on his return from Rome, reflect
the political situation in Ireland at the time. From
the Irish point of view the situation was unusually favourable, and there were not wanting grounds for Archbishop
Walsh's hope that Ireland was on the eve of a brighter
day.

The Gladstone Government, which had held office since
1880, had resigned on the defeat of its Budget proposals,
June 12, 1885. A Conservative administration succeeded,
with Lord Salisbury as Prime Minister and Lord Carnarvon
as Lord Lieutenant of Ireland. Almost immediately the
Government announced " a new departure" in dealing
with Ireland. They dropped the Crime's Act and proceeded to rule the country according to the ordinary laws
of the realm. This policy of conciliation was announced
in the House of Lords on July 6, 1885, by Lord Carnarvon,
who stated in the presence of the Prime Minister that in
making that declaration he " expressed the views and
opinions of his colleagues." The new policy, Lord Salisbury subsequently declared, was the logical outcome of
the Franchise Act of 1884; " for to extend the suffrage
and at the same time to ignore the voice of the people was
impossible." A general election was impending, and the
announcement of the Tory policy for Ireland was naturally
interpreted as a bid by the Conservatives for the Irish
vote.

The Ashbourne Act was a further step towards conciliation. The Bill, which was introduced by Lord Ashbourne,
Lord Chancellor of Ireland in Salisbury's administration,
was an advance on Gladstone's Land Act of 1881. Under
the new Bill, which passed both Houses without serious
opposition, tenants who were able to come to an agreement
with their landlords for the purchase of their holdings
could borrow through the Land Commission the whole of
the purchase money, to be repaid in forty-nine yearly
instalments of four per cent. on the money so advanced;
of this four per cent. annuity two-and-three-quarter per
cent. was to be interest on the money borrowed, and
one-and-one-fourth was to go to a sinking fund for the
liquidation of the loan. A Parliamentary grant of
£5,000,000 was made to the Land Commissioners for the
purposes of the Bill.*

To Dr. Walsh much of the credit was due in connection
with the Land Purchase Act of 1885. It was a lucid statement of his regarding the feasibility of the financial provisions
of the scheme—a statement prepared at Lord Ashbourne's
request—which decided Lords Carnarvon and Ashbourne to
urge on the Cabinet the adoption of the measure. It was
Walsh who first convinced Lord Ashbourne—as he afterwards
informed Chief Baron Palles—that the purchase project was
practicable, and who showed him how, by the establishment
of a sinking fund, a satisfactory scheme could be devised by
which the money to be advanced by the State (for the
purchase of the land of Ireland) could be safely lent
without loss, and practically without risk to the financial
credit of the State.

Two days after Lord Carnarvon's declaration of policy
in the House of Lords, Dr. Walsh had an interview with
him in London. The interview took place at the instance

---

* Michael Davitt, *The Fall of Feudalism in Ireland,* pp.
485-86.

of Dr. Walsh, who had been commissioned to put before the Lord Lieutenant the views of the Irish Episcopal Education Committee. Dr. Walsh wrote to Dr. Croke, July 3, 1885 :

There were also two resolutions [of the Episcopal Education Committee], not to be published, authorising me to put these [resolutions] before Lord Carnarvon, and to use Mr. Parnell and the members of the Irish Parliamentary Party to secure the pressing of the matter at once on the attention of Parliament and the Ministry.

The interview with Lord Carnarvon took place on July 8.* How far Lord Carnarvon took the Archbishop into his confidence has not fully transpired, but he assured him that it was the intention of the Government to apply a radical cure to Irish ills, that he himself was strongly in favour of a policy of complete appeasement, and that if he failed to receive Cabinet support for his schemes he would resign from the Ministry.

Dr. Walsh left London on July 9, 1885, to proceed to Rome for his consecration. From Rome he wrote to Lord Carnarvon a letter of acknowledgment of the Lord Lieutenant's courtesy in the matter of the interview, and of recognition of his desire to meet the constitutional demands of the Irish people. Lord Carnarvon replied, July 26, 1885 :

I cannot refuse myself the satisfaction of thanking you for the frank and kindly expressions of your letter of the 21st, and I hail your Grace's recognition of my desire to meet the constitutional desires of all good and loyal Irishmen. It is, indeed, my most earnest wish not only to do justice to all people and interests in the office which I hold, but to contribute—as far as it may be given me—to bring into friendly and much more friendly relations the nations who have become so unhappily estranged, but who also

* The meeting between Parnell and the Archbishop referred to above took place about the same time.

ought to be so harmoniously united. Nothing can aid more powerfully in this than the frank and friendly spirit in which your Grace has met me.

I may perhaps add that the line of action which we propose to take on the important question of Higher Education is one that will commend itself to you.

Towards the end of July—a couple of days after Lord Carnarvon's letter to Dr. Walsh—occurred the famous interview concerning a " constitution for Ireland," which took place in an empty house in Grosvenor Square, London, between the Lord Lieutenant and Parnell. The conference was held with the privity of Lord Salisbury, and after the interview the Lord Lieutenant gave the Prime Minister a full account of the topics discussed. Besides these private conversations there were public indications that at this time the Conservatives were not averse from entering into some sort of alliance with their old antagonists, the Irish Parliamentary Party. These overtures were continued even after Parnell had declared, August 24, 1885, that the Irish platform at the coming elections was " to consist of one plank only—national independence."

As late as October 7, 1885, Lord Salisbury stated in a speech at Newport that the first principle of his Party was " to extend to Ireland, as far as they could, all the institutions of this country," and he spoke of the advisability of having in Ireland a large central authority " in which the wisdom of several parts of the country would correct the folly and mistakes of one."

The Liberals, on their part, were keenly exercised over their Irish policy. In his election manifesto Gladstone had been studiously vague in his reference to his Party's intention regarding Ireland. "The limit," he declared, " is clear within which any desires of Ireland constitutionally ascertained may, and beyond which they cannot, receive the assent of Parliament. To maintain the supremacy of the Crown, the unity of the Empire, and all the authority of

Parliament necessary for the conservation of this unity, is the first duty of every representative of the people. Subject to this crowning principle every grant to portions of the country of enlarged powers for the management of their own affairs is not a source of danger, but a means of averting it, and is in the nature of a new guarantee of increased cohesion, happiness, and strength." Although the language of the manifesto was vague, its significance was well understood, and in the course of some weeks it became clear that Gladstone was prepared to go a long distance towards conceding what the Irish people were then demanding.

Consequently there was at that time a hope stirring amongst Irish Nationalists that whatever Party secured a majority at the polls, it would be forced by circumstances to grapple with the question of Home Rule.

The general election which took place in December 1885 brought a decisive majority to neither of the great English parties. In the new Parliament, which met early in the new year, the Conservatives with eighty-five Irish Parnellites in momentary alliance, exactly equalled the Liberal strength. Lord Salisbury's Ministry retained a precarious direction of affairs until February 1, when the Government, having been defeated on an amendment, resigned, and the Liberals again took office. Gladstone became Prime Minister for the third time, and in forming his Cabinet he assigned the post of Chief Secretary for Ireland to John Morley. H. C. E. Childers became Home Secretary. As the new Irish Secretary had been a consistent advocate of Colonial Home Rule for Ireland, Morley's appointment was generally construed as an indication of the Government's intention to grant some measure of political autonomy to Ireland. This interpretation was soon justified. The policy announced by the new administration was to submit to Parliament with all possible expedition two Bills for Ireland, a Home Rule Bill and a Land Purchase Bill.

Later, when the Bills were introduced, " Gladstone was careful to explain that the two formed in fact one indissoluble scheme separated only for convenience."

Morley's appointment was hailed with approval in Ireland. Dr. Walsh greeted him with no unstinted welcome. However, as a Bishop, he felt it his duty to couple the greeting with vigorous protest; for at the very time of the new Secretary's appointment there appeared an article most offensive to Catholics, published by him in the *Fortnightly Review*, in which *inter alia* he wrote :

The Church, it has been truly said, has broken with knowledge, has taken her stand with ignorance, and is striving, might and main, even in countries where she has no chance, to use the machinery of popular government to keep back education. The worst enemy of science, *c'est le clericalisme*.

The Archbishop, in a public speech on February 4, while extending a cordial welcome on political grounds to the new Chief Secretary, made a strong public protest "against the language of insult in which he has had the bad taste to assail us. Wise and well-informed as Mr. Morley thinks himself to be, and as in many fields he undoubtedly is, we may surely say of him, and I wish to say it without offence, that on one subject at all events, he has something yet to learn. Mr. Morley is coming to Ireland in very special circumstances. He is not coming to govern us. He comes to lend his help in carrying out the scheme of Mr. Gladstone to set us free, within limits, to govern ourselves. In these circumstances the Chief Secretary ought to be received by us with no unfriendly greeting. In almost any other circumstance the appointment should be protested against by every Irishman who sets store by the preservation of our Christian and Catholic people."

Referring to Dr. Walsh's friendly reception of Morley, Lord Randolph Churchill wrote to Lord Salisbury, March 29, 1886 ;

Ashbourne was commenting last night on the fact that Archbishop Walsh had swallowed John Morley's atheism. "Ah," said Morris, " John Morley spells ' God ' with a small ' g,' but he spells ' *Gladstone*' *with a big ' G,' and that satisfies the Archbishop.*"*

On February 16, 1886, was published a letter written by Gladstone to Lord de Vesci in which, dealing with the wants and wishes of the Irish people, he observed that there were three great Irish questions which demanded the immediate attention of the Government, namely, self-government, the settlement of the land question, and social order. On the following day the Archbishop, on behalf of a representative body of the Irish Catholic bishops, wrote to Gladstone setting forth the views they entertained regarding " the wants and wishes of the Irish people" :

1st. As regards self-government or Home Rule, it is our firm conviction—a conviction based, as we believe, on the fullest, most varied, and at the same time the most reliable information—that it alone can satisfy " the wants and wishes of the Irish people."

2nd. As regards the settlement of the " Land Question," we have no hesitation in stating that, in our opinion, it now imperatively calls for a final solution, and that this cannot be better effected than by some such measure as the purchase by the Government of the landlord interest in the soil, and the reletting of it to the tenant farmers at a figure very considerably below the present judicial rents.

We desire to have it perfectly understood that the Irish people do not aim at the confiscation of any species of property, but only ask for fair play as between man and man, in what has been described as the right to live and thrive in their native land.

3rd. As regards " social order" . . . Every disturbance of social order that has occurred amongst us for years has arisen from a sense of wrong entertained by a large majority of the occupiers of the soil, owing to the remorseless exactions of needy or extravagant landlords.   Even now, the peace of the country is seriously imperilled by the fact that very many landlords have entered on an ill-

* *Life of Lord R. Churchill,* vol. ii., p. 78.

conditioned course of eviction against their unfortunate tenants. We would, therefore, earnestly urge that, pending the final settlement of the Land Question, the power of eviction be suspended in Ireland; at the same time that in the more impoverished districts some provision, in the shape of remunerative labour, be made out of the public purse to support the starving poor in the present, and help them on to better times.

Gladstone introduced his Irish Government Bill on April 8. The Bill as outlined to Parliament provided for the "establishment of a legislature in Ireland to consist of the Queen and an Irish Legislative Body." This legislative body was to have power to deal with all matters subject to certain specified reservations. The matters excepted were no fewer than twenty-five. The Legislative Body was to consist of one chamber with a "first and second order." Ireland's representation in the British House of Commons was to cease when the Irish legislative body came into existence. Provision, however, was made for the temporary attendance at Westminster of a certain quota, on occasions when the interests of Ireland required their presence. A veto on all legislation was to be vested in the Lord Lieutenant. Judges and the Royal Irish Constabulary were, for a time, to continue under Imperial control. Ireland was to contribute to the Imperial Exchequer an annual sum equivalent to one-fifteenth of the total Imperial expenditure.

The discussions in the Cabinet centred mainly on three points : (1) exclusion of the Irish members from Westminster; (2) transfer after a time to the Irish legislature of control of judges and police; (3) a proposal to specify the restrictions on the powers of the Irish Legislative Body rather than to specify the powers which alone would be delegated to that body. The Cabinet was divided on these points, and Chamberlain and Trevelyan resigned from the Ministry on March 26. Parnell, who was consulted confidentially through Morley, was severely critical, and unhesitatingly rejected the financial proposals of the Bill. " It is not at all improbable that if the Bill had gone into Committee, it would have been rejected by the Irish on this department of it."*

While the Irish Bills were being drafted and discussed in the Cabinet, Childers invited Archbishop Walsh to help them with suggestions. From the time that Childers first made Dr. Walsh's acquaintance in 1881, he held a high opinion of his abilities, and was anxious at all times to ascertain his views on Irish questions.

Writing to the Archbishop, whom he had just missed seeing in London, Childers says, October 21, 1885 :

> I should have greatly liked to see you, and to have some conversation with you on Irish affairs . . . I shall not be able to come to Dublin before the General Election [Nov. 1885], but if I do so afterwards, I hope I may be allowed to call on you.

Again he writes, Nov. 4, 1885 :

> I am anxious that we should first see our way clearly as to what is imperial and what is local. When this question has been well threshed out, it will be time to consider how the legislative and administrative bodies [for Ireland] should be constituted. Your letter is a great encouragement to me to persevere. I have already skimmed the pamphlet which you have been good enough to send me, but I shall now study it carefully.

Again, March 18, 1886 :

> I await the further communication which you promised to make to me, and I will place in Mr. Gladstone's hands anything you may send me for him. He is at this moment extremely busy, maturing his plan, which will, I hope, do much to bring about good feeling between Great Britain and Ireland, and endeavouring to conciliate those† whose

* Morley's *Life of Gladstone,* vol. ii., p. 409.
† He referred chiefly to Chamberlain and Trevelyan,

co-operation is so desirable. Should you be in England during the spring, it will give me great pleasure to be of service to you to the best of my power. Your presence here at a certain time might be most valuable.

On April 3, 1886 :

Although you have asked me not to answer your letter, I think you will allow me to say that I have laid before Mr. Gladstone, your enclosure.

On April 8, 1886 :

Mr. Chamberlain's language to myself up to the time of the resignation of Mr. Gladstone's last Government was always most friendly to Ireland and Irishmen. He knew that my own views as to the true policy for Ireland had been the same as they were then (and are now, since 1880).

I am just going to the House to hear the speech* on the success of which hangs the welfare of Great Britain and Ireland for years to come. I think that the conclusions at which the Cabinet have arrived are, on the whole, wise and prudent, reserving (as everyone must) my opinion on one or two points. I trust that this will be the judgment of patriotic Irishmen.

On April 17, 1886 :

Thankful for your note. I don't feel at all easy about the Bill; but the language used by Mr. Gladstone, about representation at Westminster, makes the chances of success somewhat greater. The compromise you suggest as to the number of Irish members being proportional to the Irish contribution, seems very fair; but their exclusion from debates on English and Scotch affairs is practically very difficult to work out. If the Imperial Parliament and the legislature of Great Britain met at different times, and if the Imperial Government and the Government of Great Britain could be more distinct bodies there would be less difficulty. But the 570 members for England and Scotland might be by a small majority Conservative, while the fifty Irish members

* Gladstone's great speech introducing his Home Rule Bill.

might be by a large majority Liberal. Thus there might be a Liberal majority in the Imperial Parliament and a Conservative majority in the legislature of Great Britain. Of what colour would His Majesty's Ministers have to be?

On the other hand, if they always sat together, the Irish members might carry English and Scotch measures which without them might be negatived, and *vice versa.*

Home Rule, to be logically perfect, must be applied to the three kingdoms. Of course we never are logical, and find rough and ready solutions; and I hope we may do so now . . .

It was a great misfortune that the two Bills (the Home Rule Bill and the Land Purchase Bill) had to be separated : and the Land Bill contains proposals affecting both.   Mr. Gladstone's second speech (I mean the one on Friday, April 16) was not so clear as that of Thursday week. His short story on Tuesday was admirable. It was more like one of his admirably put-together speeches of 20 or 25 years ago, terse and lively.

You will be so busy in Holy Week [commencing on the following day] that I hope you will not think of answering this.

Dr. Walsh was even more dissatisfied than Parnell with the financial provisions of the Home Rule Bill. Parnell contended that Ireland's just contribution to Imperial expenditure should not exceed one-twentieth or one-twenty-first part of the total. Dr. Walsh maintained that the just proportion should be one-twenty-fifth or one-twenty-sixth. Parnell did not attach vital importance to the discontinuance of Irish representation at Westminster. Dr. Walsh, while admitting that the withdrawal of the Irish members would be in some respects desirable, rather favoured the continuance of representation in the Imperial Parliament until such time at least as the main restrictions contained in the Bill should be removed. His proposal on this head, which Childers submitted to the Cabinet, was that the number of Irish members to be retained should be proportional to the Irish contribution to imperial expenditure. In making this proposal he was influenced by three main considerations : (1) that the retention of the Irish members would lessen opposition to the Bill; (2) that their presence would safeguard Irish interests in matters of taxation, etc.; and (3) that, incidentally, Catholic interests in Great Britain and throughout the British Empire would benefit thereby. He might have been influenced too in this matter by Cardinal Manning, with whom he was in close and constant communication from the time of his appointment to the See of Dublin until the Cardinal's death. Manning was most anxious for the retention of the Irish members. " Michael Davitt first suggested to me," he wrote to Walsh, February 25, 1886, " the risk of losing 40 or 50 Catholic members from the Imperial Parliament. It is obvious. It is a Catholic and world-wide danger. I hope justice will reign in Ireland without this danger." This was in reply to a letter from Dr. Walsh, written two days previously :

There is a view of the Irish case which I should wish your Eminence to take into consideration, if you have not already done so, as affecting the interests of the Church in England.

It is generally felt, I believe, by English Catholics, that the granting of Home Rule, to whatever extent it may be granted, means to that extent a weakening of the force now available for the protection in Parliament of Catholic interests in England. But there is another side to the question. The Newcastle Election . . . brings it into prominence. Does not the continuance of the present state of affairs involve the presence of a powerful disturbing element in the election contests of very many English boroughs? Besides, supposing the Irish difficulty done away with, would not the Parliamentary vote of English Catholicity become far more available than it now is even when aided by the somewhat irregular help given by the Irish M.P's in the House of Commons? Mr. Morley, for instance, would have had absolutely no chance of election last time but for the Irish vote. In other circumstances that vote could be sent solidly against him.

WALSH TO MANNING.

April 14, 1886.

To me it was a great puzzle why Mr. Gladstone should have attached such importance to the exclusion of the Irish members, and why the opponents of the Bill should have concentrated their fire on what seems so easily alterable a provision.

For my part, I must regard the amendment of the Bill in this respect as an improvement in every way. It takes from us nothing that is given to us in any other part of the scheme. It gives an additional power over and above those otherwise given.

Then for the English Catholics (little as they, as a body, deserve it*) it is a decided advantage, and one of which I should be sorry to see them deprived.

How is it that no one has put forward the claim of the English Catholic body to a set of " guarantees" such as are now to be provided for the Irish Protestants?

The Home Rule Bill was rejected in the House of Commons on June 8 by a majority of 30. The numbers were 343 against 313. The defeat of the Bill was due to a combination of causes : the defection of Lord Hartington and his Whig adherents, the resignation from the Ministry of Chamberlain, who with Bright and those who followed them voted against the measure, and the aggressive hostility of the Conservatives led by Lord Randolph

---

* The English Catholics—at least those of Tory sympathies— were strongly opposed to Home Rule. The *Tablet,* December 26, 1885, had an article headed "Home Rule," in which the arrangement based on the interests of the "predominant partner" and of the Empire was vigorously pressed. " English duties and English obligations have grown with time and clustered thickly around English rule, and may not be abandoned now for the sake of peace and a ' quiet ' life."

Lord Bury wrote in the *Tablet,* March 27, 1886, a strongly anti-Irish article in which in addition to using " vile language regarding the Irish bishops he openly denies the jurisdiction of the Pope in a manifestly spiritual affair." (Walsh to Manning, March 27, 1886.)

Dr. Walsh, after repeated private remonstrances through Manning, and direct protestations to Dr. Vaughan, Bishop of Salford, proprietor of the *Tablet,* at length publicly attacked it, and a sharp correspondence passed between Vaughan and Walsh on the matter.

Churchill and Lord Salisbury.   Churchill visited Belfast,
where on February 22 he delivered an inflammatory and
seditious speech which was described by Lord Salisbury as
" a brilliantly successful effort."   In this speech he told
his Orange audience that if Parliament would " hand over
the loyalists of Ireland to the domination of an assembly
at Dublin, which would be for them a foreign and an alien
assembly . . . then in that dark hour there will not be
wanting to you those of position and influence in England,
who would be willing to cast in their lot with you, and
who, whatever the result, will share your fortune and your
fate. There will not be wanting those who at the exact
moment, when the time is fully come, will address you in
the words of one of our greatest English poets :

> The combat deepens ; on ye brave
> Who rush to glory or the grave.
> Wave, *Ulster*, all thy banners wave,
> And charge with all thy chivalry."

At a later period, in a letter addressed to a Liberal-
Unionist Member of Parliament, he used the famous
jingling phrase : " Ulster will fight and Ulster will be
right."

Lord Salisbury expressed with mordant piquancy his
opposition to the Bill. " Ireland," he said, " is not one
nation but two nations." He would not place confidence
in people who had acquired the habit of using knives and
slugs.   His policy, he said, was that Parliament should
enable the Government of England to govern Ireland, and
should " apply that recipe honestly, consistently, and resolutely for twenty years."   In the same " genial vein" the
sardonic Conservative leader proceeded to say that " if
some great store of imperial treasure were going to be
expended in Ireland, instead of buying out landlords it
would be far more usefully employed in providing for the
emigration of a million Irishmen."*

* Morley's *Life of Gladstone,* ii., p. 417.

Outside of Parliament hostility to Home Rule was fomented and directed by the organisation known as the " Primrose League," and a kindred ancillary society of ladies, the " Primrose Dames," by the " Irish Loyal and Patriotic Union," and by the publication in the *Times* of sensational and lying documents, the authorship of which Michael Davitt afterwards traced to a disreputable journalist named Richard Pigott. This Pigott was the same forger whom Archbishop Walsh was instrumental in unmasking a couple of years later. The leaders of the English Catholic laity, headed by the Duke of Norfolk, were opposed to Gladstone's policy, and they " succeeded in creating the impression in circles hostile to Gladstone and the Irish members that the wishes and the interests of Rome lay in the defeat rather than in the success of the proposed plan of Irish government."

Towards the end of February 1886, the Duke of Norfolk, addressing a meeting of the " Primrose Dames"—" an audience composed (as it was) almost entirely of persons opposed to him in faith and differing from the speaker in sex"—condemned the conduct of the Irish clergy and bishops in supporting Home Rule and the National League, and declared that the action of the bishops had caused him " special grief and *shame*," with much else to the same effect.

On the publication of the Duke's attack on the Catholics of Ireland, Dr. Walsh at once wrote privately to Manning, who was on friendly and intimate terms with the Duke :

February 23, 1886.

Has your Eminence seen the extraordinary speech of the Duke of Norfolk on the Catholics of Ireland? To me it seems one of the most unprovoked attacks upon the people of this country that I have met with for a very long time. His Grace seems to have gone out of his way to drag us in. This is the sort of action that really embitters the relations between the Catholics of the two countries.

Manning wrote in reply, February 25, 1886 :

You will say that the good Duke of Norfolk is old enough to be more guarded in speech. But he is both young and surrounded by those of whom you complain. In public life he has had little experience. In this way I understand what I very much regret. In Ireland he will be regarded as the English laity. It is not so. In the time of my predecessor there was a great breach between English and Irish Catholics. For twenty years I have laboured to heal it. It is unhappily again open. But the English Catholics are few. The mass of our people are Irish and united with Ireland.

The Land Bill which was introduced on April 16 was a gigantic system of purchase. Machinery was to be established by which landowners could sell their property to a specified State authority at twenty years' purchase, to be retailed subsequently to small purchasers. The cost, which was to be met by the issue of a new stock, was calculated at about £120,000,000.

The Bill was furiously attacked. Even the landlords for whose benefit the scheme was brought forward joined in the onslaught. The British tax-payer was alarmed; indeed, " the whole of Great Britain rang with denunciation of a proposal which was represented as asking the labouring and ratepaying classes of England and Scotland to run the risk of being taxed to the tune of one thousand million dollars for the benefit of Irish landlords and Irish farmers."*

Sir James Caird, who, according to the *Times*, was an economist " whose authority upon agricultural questions was universally recognised," wrote to the *Times* an interesting letter against Gladstone's proposal to buy out the Irish landlords, March 20, 1886 :

The land of Ireland is held by two distinct classes of tenants—the small farmers who pay rent from £1 to £20, and the comparatively large farmers who pay rent from

* Davitt's *Fall of Feudalism*, p. 504.

£20 upward. Of the first class there are 538,000 holdings averaging £6 each; of the second class, 120,000 holdings averaging £56 each. The rent payable by the first class is £3,572,000, and by the second class £6,845,000. Five-sixths of the Irish tenants thus pay about one-third of the total rental, and one-sixth pay nearly two-thirds . . . If the present prices of agricultural produce continue, I should fear that from the land held by the large body of poor farmers in Ireland any economical rent has for the present disappeared. A purchase of it, at any price, would, therefore be certain loss. How many years' purchase, even with better prospects, would any sane capitalist give for a nominal rental of three-and-a-half millions, to be collected from five hundred thousand holdings of poor land from tenants averaging £6 each?

The collapse of agricultural values, when capitalised, amounts to many hundred millions, to which must be added losses, probably not less in proportion, in every other branch of business and trade in this kingdom.

A change so great, however brought about, whether by enormous development of foreign production and diminished cost of transport, or by appreciation of gold, or by these united, cannot be met by partial help in favour of a single interest. All interests must be allowed time to settle into what may prove a new condition. But there can be no adequate security at present given by the land of Ireland for such a stupendous advance by the British people. And I trust that the wisdom of Parliament may guard the country from being committed to an engagement which could only end in loss and possibly disaster.

Archbishop Walsh sent to Childers a memorandum on the Land Bill in which, dealing with the proposal that the landlords should receive twenty years' purchase, he laid special stress on the need of having the years' purchase calculated not upon a judicial or " nominal rent but on an effective rent." Deductions should be made from the nominal rent of the expenses of collection, and of the other burdens from which the landlords were to be relieved by being bought out.

The substance of this memorandum was afterwards published in the form of an " interview," August 11, 1886.

To Manning Walsh had written, March 26, 1886 :

As to Mr. Gladstone's project of buying out the landlords, it is no doubt very chivalrous of him to embarrass himself for the sake of a class of people who are bitterly hostile to him and to his projects. They seem quite blind just now.

I have no doubt that, if some reasonable settlement be not made this time, the people will take the Land Question into their own hands and solve it by a general refusal to pay rent. It will be a sad result, coming on us at a time when everything seemed so hopeful for a thoroughly constitutional settlement of all our difficulties.

Cecinit uti vates. Sad and evil days were close at hand which were to witness the spectacle of an exasperated tenantry driven by untoward conditions to adopt the desperate methods of the " Plan of Campaign."

The parliamentary rejection of Gladstone's Home Rule Bill, involving also the failure of his Land Purchase scheme, was not accepted by the Liberal leader as a final defeat of his Irish policy. Hoping that the voice of the electorate would reverse the decision of Parliament, he resolved on an immediate appeal to the constituencies. Parliament was dissolved on June 26, 1886, and the second general election within six months was held. The result was decidedly unfavourable to Gladstone. The Tories, with the schismatic Liberals—78 in number—returned to Parliament 316 members, while the Gladstonians numbered only 191. The Parnellite strength remained practically unchanged at 85. Gladstonians and Parnellites combined were in a minority of 118. Gladstone at once resigned, and Lord Salisbury again undertook the administration, July 20, 1886. Lord Randolph Churchill became Chancellor of the Exchequer, and Sir Michael Hicks-Beach Chief Secretary for Ireland. One of the earliest acts of the new Government was to appoint a Royal Commission, under the presidency of Earl Cowper, to inquire into the conditions of agriculture in Ireland as affected by the marked fall in the prices of produce for the years 1885 and 1886, and to consider the bearing of these conditions on the Land Act of 1881.

Lord Randolph Churchill, who was Leader of the House of Commons, in stating the Government's proposals to the House, outlined its Irish policy :

The Irish question (he said) presented itself in three aspects—Social Order, the Land Question, and Local Government. The Government proposed to treat these questions to a large extent as separate and distinct. The law was to be uncompromisingly maintained. Sir Redvers Buller would be sent forthwith to take all necessary measures. With regard to land, the Government would not encourage any extension of the revision of rent by the direct interposition of the State, but would rather aim at the creation of a general system of single ownership by the influence and leverage of the credit of the State . . . A scheme of Local Government was to be placed before Parliament at the beginning of the following year, February 1887. " The signposts of our policy are equality, similarity and simultaneity of treatment in the development of a genuinely popular system of Government in all the four countries which form the United Kingdom."

Lord Randolph's words that the law was " to be uncompromisingly maintained," were interpreted by the landlords of Ireland as an invitation to " use to the full their legal powers," and as a promise that the Executive would do its best to support them. The number of evictions for nonpayment of rent had considerably increased; for, owing to agricultural and economic depression, the tenants were unable to meet their liabilities incurred under the Land Act of 1881. Yet, the tenants were to get no protection; for the Chancellor's declared policy was that, pending the report of the Cowper Commission, the law was to take its course. When Parnell made a proposal in favour of the evicted tenants (August 24) it was rejected by Parliament. The Liberal-Unionists were even more vigorous than the Tories in their opposition to it, and in their assertions of disbelief in the incapacity of the tenants to pay their rents,

A Tenants' Relief Bill, which Parnell introduced, September 10, 1886, met with a similar fate. This Bill proposed (1) that leaseholders should be admitted to the benefit of the Act of 1881; (2) that power should be given to both landlord and tenant to appeal to the courts for an alteration of judicial rent; and (3) that the court should be authorised to stay eviction when the tenant had paid half the rent.

That there was a real need for staying evictions was beyond doubt. Both Buller, who was acting as a kind of Government agent in Ireland, and Hicks-Beach, felt constrained to use " great pressure" to induce the landlords to refrain from pressing their demands. Yet, as a matter of course, Parnell's Bill was rejected (September 27). Notwithstanding these disappointments, the Irish people had accepted the failure of Gladstone's legislation and the defeat of Parnell's measure with remarkable patience.* By this time the National League† was as strong a power as the Land League had been in 1881. Its resources were increasing, and the auxiliary organisations in America and Australia were progressing in active co-operation. The third Convention of the American League was held at Chicago about the middle of August 1886. In view of the defeat of Home Rule, it was apprehended, and generally expected, that the Irish-American organisation would favour an extreme policy.† These expectations were not realised, owing, in a large degree, to the influence of Michael Davitt, who was present at the Convention. Davitt was aided powerfully by the action of Archbishop Walsh.

---

* Bright. *History of England,* vol. v., p. 100.

† The National League was the Land League in a new guise. It was formed at a conference held in Dublin, October 1882, to evade the suppression of the older organisation (October 1881). Its objects as set forth by Parnell were " national self-government, Land Law reform, extension of the parliamentary and municipal franchise, and the development and encouragement of the labour and industrial interests of Ireland."—Bright, *History,* vol. v., p. 30. Cf. Davitt, pp. 375-7.

‡ Davitt, *Fall of Feudalism in Ireland.*

The Archbishop, at the suggestion of Cardinal Manning, and with Davitt's approval, published two articles in the form of " interviews," August 11 and 16, 1886, in which he dealt with the question of agricultural rent in Ireland, with Irish Land Purchase, and with Home Rule. Writing to Manning, August 13, 1886, Dr. Walsh said : " The ' interview' which is cabled across and appears simultaneously in a leading newspaper in every great city of the United States and in the *Freeman's Journal* here . . . may help the M.P's who have gone over in their work of steadying the Chicago Convention and keeping things within bounds."

The " interview" began by clearing away certain absurd and almost incredible notions that were being entertained regarding the causes of the agricultural crisis in Ireland.

It was grotesque (the Archbishop said) to explain the refusal of Irish farmers to pay their rent, by saying that the question was in a sense a religious one.   Yet it had been gravely asserted that it was all " an unwillingness on the part of the farmers, who were mostly Roman Catholics, to allow so much money to go into the pockets of landlords who were mostly Protestants."   Equally absurd was it to treat the question as if it were a matter merely of politics. Such, however, was the explanation naively given by a lady, the wife of an Irish landlord, who just then had sought financial help from the Archbishop.   " My brother," said she, " is an English landlord, and he is financially embarrassed because his tenants cannot pay their rents owing to the agricultural depression, and my husband is straitened for money because our Irish tenants will not pay because of the political agitators."

The interview then dealt with the actual condition of English and Irish farmers, and with the difference in the tenure of Irish and of English rented land :

As a matter of fact the rents of farmers in England had at that time been lowered enormously, in some cases by so much as 50 per cent. Lord Fitzwilliam gave his Irish tenants a reduction of about 50 per cent.—the same reduction as he had given to his English tenants.   But Lord

Fitzwilliam's example had been followed by no other Irish land-owner. In England, landlords found it impossible to get tenants to take farms or to continue to hold them on any terms. The English tenant had no dread of being over-rented, nor was he afraid of being evicted; while in Ireland evictions for non-payment of rack-rents were witnessed almost daily. If there were any attempt to over-rent an English farmer he simply left the farm, bringing with him all that was his. He had entered on a fully equipped farm, bringing capital and farm implements; he left the farm, leaving behind him neither capital nor implements nor anything that was his. He had in fact just hired the farm which the landlord was expected to keep in good order, just as one might rent a shooting lodge for a season. The Irish tenant could not act in like manner. To him and his fore-fathers for generations the farm had been a fixed and cherished home. Every field, every path of it had for him some association which was part of his existence. Whatever there was in it above the surface of the earth had been put there by the tenant's hand, and, in a word, " this plot is his whole dominion, his world, his all; he is verily a part of it like the ash or the oak that has sprung from its soil. Removal in his case is a tearing up from the roots, where transplantation is death. The Irish tenant is *adscriptus glebae*. He pays rent as long as he is able, sometimes even when he is unable and when he needs must leave other debts unpaid." A crisis, however, might come when even this shift was no longer possible. Such a crisis had over-taken the Irish tenant.

Dealing with Land Purchase, the Archbishop advocated an extension of the Ashbourne Act of 1885 :

That Act embodied a scheme of Land Purchase " which was beyond question the best scheme of Land Purchase that has yet found its way to the Statute Book. Lord Ashbourne gets the credit of all the good in it, and I have no doubt he deserves it all."*

The Ashbourne Act was not flawless. It required to be modified and amended in order to get rid of defects both in its policy and in its machinery. The chief cause, however, of the comparative failure of the Ashbourne Act " was a misunderstanding or misconception as to the proper

* For the extent to which Archbishop Walsh himself deserved " the credit of all the good in it," see *supra,* p. 198.

way of fixing a fair rate of purchase—I mean the number of years' purchase to be given for the land. The Ashbourne Act makes no provision for the price to be paid for the land. That matter was left entirely to the joint discretion of the landlord and the tenant. In determining the price to be paid, discussion centres generally on the question of the number of years' purchase to be paid by the tenant. The real question, however, is not how many years' purchase ought to be paid, but rather what is to be purchased. So many years' purchase—certainly. But purchase of what? The first question to be inquired into is, what is the yearly value of the thing that the landlord has to sell, and that the tenant is about to buy? In estimating the one year's value, which is to be our starting-point, we must, as a matter of course, take a really fair rent of the land, and the fair rent may have varied considerably since the present actual rent was fixed. We must deduct the landlord's part of the poor rate and of the county cess—liabilities which are to be transferred from the selling landlord to the purchasing tenant. We must take into account the burden which the landlord is to be freed from in the matter of agency, also law charges and all other charges incidental to the ownership of the land; for he is getting rid of all these and he has no right to make the tenant pay for relieving him of them. We must consider, too, the improvement accruing to the landlord in the shape of fixed and regular payments, freedom from bad debts, and from the necessity of making casual remissions and deductions of rent. Every one of these things . . . universally recognised as existing, should in the first place be taken into account, and a fair and full allowance out of the existing rent should be made for them. It is only then, when we have thus ascertained what is really the one year's actual value of the property which is to be bought and sold, that the question will arise —how many years' purchase of the actual yearly *value* is to be taken as the fair selling price?

The Archbishop gave an illustration of what he meant. The tenants on a certain little estate came to the landlord and expressed willingness to buy. They offered 14 or at most 15 years' purchase, and stated that they were fully determined to give no more. The landlord refused to sell for less than twenty years' purchase. As the land was held by the landlord as a charitable trust, he could not, without violating his trust, dispose of it except at a fair price. He explained, however, to the tenants that he meant twenty years' purchase of the actual yearly *value*, not of the actual *rent* paid by the tenants. A calculation was made at his suggestion and it transpired that the landlord's proposal of twenty years' purchase of the actual value meant a sum really less than the fifteen years' purchase offered by the tenants. The landlord in the case was the Archbishop himself, and the spokesman for the tenants and their chief purchaser was Mr. Fagan of Dubber, near Finglas in the County of Dublin.

It was on this occasion that the Archbishop first publicly expressed his views on the subject of Land Nationalisation :

No land purchase scheme, no matter how carried out, can be a final settlement of the land question. I am so thoroughly convinced that the form of land tenure, now popularly known as " the nationalisation of the land," is the only system fully consonant with the principles of justice, that I must hesitate in regarding as absolutely final a scheme based upon any other principle. Lord Ashbourne's Act may solve the difficulty as between landlord and tenant. But a much larger question lies behind, a question that sooner or later will press forward for settlement—the question between the tenants and the nation. However, there is so much loose talking and writing on this matter that I think it better to keep clear of it altogether. If I went into it at all, I should do so at considerable length, to guard against possible and probable misconception of my views or misrepresentation of them.* For the present, at all events, land nationalisation is hardly a question of practical politics. Let me say just one thing about it. I am for it, of course, in Michael Davitt's sense as differing from Henry George's. That is to say, keeping clear of all abstract questions, I hold that the nationalisation of land, whenever it is effected in this country, must be effected on

---

* Because of Dr. Walsh's advocating land nationalisation he was charged with being a Communist; and a myopic scribe in the *Saturday Review* failed to discern the difference between a " Walsher " and a " Welsher."

the basis of fair compensation to the owners or actual holders of the land.   Land nationalisation to be brought about, here at least, in any other way is a chimera.

Dr. Walsh's views on Home Rule can be briefly outlined. He regarded Gladstone's scheme as the only sound basis of settlement of the old feud between the peoples of Great Britain and Ireland.   Gladstone's Bill was henceforth to mark the minimum, " the low water mark" of the Irish national demand.   The Bill needed much modification, and the direction in which the necessary improvements were to be sought was indicated in an article in the *Contemporary Review* for June 1886, written by Dr. Dale, a Liberal-Unionist Member of Parliament for Birmingham. Dr. Dale's scheme would be generally described as Federal. It was rather a scheme of " inverted federation."   He took as his starting-point Gladstone's Bill for setting up a statutory Parliament in Dublin, and fixing the extent of its legislative and administrative powers.   He would also set up a corresponding statutory Parliament for Great Britain (or, if deemed preferable, local Parliaments for England, Scotland, and Wales).   The Imperial Parliament would continue to deal with Imperial affairs, and Ireland would continue to be represented in the Imperial Parliament, but not, of course, in the Parliament of Great Britain.   This scheme was not the usual sort of federal scheme, for federation generally was the process by which two or more states previously independent of each other combined for certain purposes into a union, having a central authority created to deal with the common interests of the various States thus bound together.

In a federal scheme (he said) what generally happens is that the various federation bodies transfer portion of their powers to a central body which is called into existence ; the scheme of Mr. Dale is the reverse of this, for it is a setting up of subordinate legislatures by a delegation or devolution of the exercise of a certain portion of the authority which already exists in the supreme Parliament at Westminster, and so it is more correctly described as a scheme of "inverted federation." Such a scheme, I have no doubt, would be accepted loyally by the Irish people. Our national faith has been pledged to it. For my own part, I must say that I was a little surprised at the readiness with which that pledge was given* as regards certain portions† of Mr. Gladstone's Bill. Personally I could not have been a party to the giving of it. But the time for cavilling at such matters has passed. The Irish nation has now, through its Parliamentary representatives, pledged its faith to the honest acceptance of that scheme as a fair and honourable compromise.

The views set out by Dr. Walsh in the two " interviews" led to much correspondence with prominent public men —Gladstone, Manning, Davitt, Archbishop Corrigan of New York, Dr. McGlynn, Archbishop Croke, H. C. E. Childers, Dr. Dale, Wilfred Blunt, and others. With Gladstone in particular he had several exchanges of view on such topics as Home Rule, Land Purchase, and Fair Rent. The following letter, marked " Private," is an interesting example of Gladstonian caution :—

> Hawarden Castle,
> Oct. 30th, '86.

My Dear Lord Archbishop,—. . . I am very sensible of the weight attaching to what your Grace has said, as well as of the importance of the topics themselves.

I will only touch, and that briefly, on the key question, that of Home Rule.

Constant meditation, as I may call it, on the subject, has not led me to contemplate as legitimate or desirable a contraction of the scale on which the Home Rule Bill was framed. Indeed, I incline to think that the pecuniary arrangements to be proposed ought to be considered on a wider historical basis than was possible in the time which was so grudgingly given us for framing the measure. I do not know what would be the result, but it might be favourable in a pecuniary sense to Ireland.

* Parnell's declaration.
† The financial arrangements chiefly.

But looking to the strange position of affairs, I think
questions may arise more complex and formidable than any
that I foresee on the extent of the Bill.

What I am most afraid of is an endeavour to shuffle off
the question on the pretext of procedure—of Land Purchase
—or some other plea equally plausible and equally unsound.
If I am right as to the direction which my fears are taking,
this question cannot be too maturely weighed.

There is another subject which is delicate but which I do
not so much dread. It seems possible that offers may be
made which could not be accepted as final, but which might
be tolerated as intermediate, if they contained substantial
and considerable good. On this point, of some nicety, I
think it likely that Irish opinion would weigh very much
with (what I call) the Liberal Party.

Another letter written by Gladstone on the same subject,
May 25, 1887, is worthy of notice :

I thank your Grace for the interesting communication of
May 21, which greatly commands my sympathy ; and I need
not assure you that I pay close attention to whatever concerns the settlement of the great Irish question, which has
brought about, age notwithstanding, my continuance in
public life.

Pray look to a reference in an article by Dr. Dale on
Home Rule in a forthcoming No. of the *Contemporary
Review* (June 1887), to an opinion of your Grace on a
scheme submitted not long ago.

Dr. Walsh replied to Gladstone, May 30, 1887 :

Dr. Dale's reference to me is quite correct. In an interview I pointed out that Dr. Dale's article in the *Contemporary Review*, June 1886, seemed to me to secure for us all
that your Bill secured, and that it did this on lines that
fell in with the views of most of your leading opponents,
who insisted on identical or practically identical treatment
of the various countries of the United Kingdom ... Very
shortly after the " interview" appeared in the newspapers,
Dr. Dale wrote to me ... Until I heard from him I
had no idea that he was himself a member of the dissentient section* ... In writing to him I said something

* The radical section which under Chamberlain had revolted
from Gladstone.

to the effect that if he represented the dissentient view, I could not comprehend how the dissent had been allowed to pass into schism.

As you have thought Dr. Dale's reference to me of sufficient importance to merit your calling attention to it, let me say as briefly as I can, in a letter written necessarily without a moment's thought beforehand, what view I take of Dr. Dale's plan, as set out in the article of June 1886.

It seems to me to get rid of many difficulties.

1st. It provides for a continued Irish representation in the Councils of the Empire, free from all possibility of corrupt bidding by rival English parties for the Irish vote. I mean that in this plan the Irish vote could not be secured for the keeping in or for the turning out of an English Ministry by the promise of adoption by English party leaders of a certain policy on Irish questions. Ireland could, of course, influence Imperial policy, but the votes would turn on the merits of the Imperial questions at issue.

2nd. It puts an end to the cry of separation.

3rd. It provides for the (necessary) amendment of the new Constitution as regards working arrangements. It is inevitable that in the working of our " legislative body" in Ireland some unforeseen difficulties should crop up. If we looked, as we should look, for the removal of these, English prejudice would be incited against us. " These Irish," it would be said, " are never satisfied." I see a great advantage in a system which would give rise to a common interest in the efficient working of the various " legislative bodies."

4th. It appeals powerfully to English popular opinion, by the practical removal of all obstruction in English legislation by the House of Lords.

5th. It removes the " tribute" difficulty. And so on.

But I should say that if the plan were to be taken up as a basis for an amended Home Rule proposal, it would be unwise to put it forward in its integrity as a plan to be embodied in a Bill. Dr. Dale contemplated (as I understood him) the adoption of your Bill as a first step in the introduction of a uniform system for all the countries concerned (the total number of " legislative bodies" to be created being 2, 3, or 4, as the case might be). Taking your proposal in this way, the Irish representation might well remain as it is until the time—necessarily, as he showed, a very short one—should come for the completion of the work by the creation of the other legislative bodies.

All this, I know, is very crude. But you may find something in it that may be turned to account.

On May 31, 1887, Gladstone replied :

I am very sorry to have given you, unawares, the trouble of writing at length . . .

Some of the lines of my duty in a rather perplexed question are clear, and among them this : it is not for me to stand between Ireland and what she may incline to accept as a definitive settlement (unless it were unjust to Great Britain, of which there is no fear).

Neither do I think that I ought to repel any settlement just and satisfactory to Ireland if Great Britain chooses to embody in it provisions inconvenient to herself, especially should they be such as without breach of compact she can cure hereafter. I have, however, to be on my guard against proposals which (as your Grace observes) tend to impair Irish Home Rule under the name of keeping up Ireland's interest in Imperial affairs; or which may enlarge the field of the question and tie on to it a number of extraneous clogs.

Dr. Dale is, I believe, a very honest as well as a very able man.

On the next day, June 1, 1887, Gladstone again wrote :

I received your Grace's packet* this morning, and I return you the MS. enclosures. Perhaps you have understood Dr. Dale's proposals better than I have. I hope so, for I certainly had not supposed him *now* to make the Bill of 1886 a minimum or starting-point as to concession.

If *Ireland* shall consider a smaller measure or a different measure of Home Rule satisfactory (no injustice at the same time being done to Great Britain or the Empire) I shall wish it all success. But I hope to deal with Ireland as an *integer*, and I would respectfully recommend that those who, like your Grace, have much influence in the formation of . . . Irish opinion, should communicate much together so that we may know authoritatively the general upshot (as we believed ourselves to do last year), so that we may be able to say to ourselves : This, and no less than

---

* The packet contained a copy of Dr. Walsh's " interview," and letters from Dr. Dale and Cardinal Manning dealing with the same matter.

this, is what Ireland wants and is willing to accept. We have then a solid point of departure and can proceed to deal with England.

Dr. Dale's dispositions, I am sure, are good, but I am afraid he represents more of actual mistrust than of contingent support.

MANNING TO WALSH.

August 17, 1886.

It seems to me of much moment that you should distinctly and fully declare yourself. And I have carefully read the two reports of the " interview " in the *Freeman's Journal* with much pleasure. If your Grace and the bishops do not speak out, and first, others will take the lead and the due order will be reversed.

In the last year I have noticed that the bishops are guiding the question. This seems to me vital.

If I rightly understand your meaning, and I think I do, I fully agree in what you have said.

If you can put before the Holy See and the English people such an outline as you have sketched, with the concurrence of the bishops, its success is certain.

There is much bigotry, ignorance, and suspicion here.* But the last two will give way before a definite plan from the united episcopate. It would also unite and guide the clergy and laity of Ireland. Much of the opposition of England springs from not knowing the precise demand. People are always afraid in the dark.

I have read with much satisfaction Michael Davitt's speech† in America. It is the sure way to gain what

---

* Gladstone wrote to Dr. Walsh *privately,* April 6, 1887 : " It unfortunately happens that some leading non-conformist ministers in Ireland are wholly or partially unsound on Home Rule. Alas ! the old *anti-Irish feeling* is not wholly dead amongst them and is lively enough with the Tories. But the body of non-conformists are true as they have so often been, and the strongest Protestants are exempted from the bigotry of Protestantism. Your Grace will easily believe that to me, as a man in his 81st year, it is inexpressibly sad to be engaged in this fierce contention. Considering it as a personal dispensation, I can well discern the hand of God in it. But I do long for the day when poor Ireland shall cease to drink the cup of sorrow."

† A speech at the Chicago Convention in which Davitt advocated the continuance for a further time of constitutional methods.

Ireland needs.   Justice is working widely here if imprudence does not wreck it.

I know what Henry George means by " nationalisation " of the land, but I am not sure of your meaning, unless it be that the Irish people shall re-enter into the possession of their own soil.   The garrison must give way to the nation.

In a letter to Manning, December 28, 1886, Dr. Walsh developed his views on the nationalisation of land :

The *Freeman's Journal* of to-day gives a letter of your Eminence's written to the *Brooklyn Review*, in which you speak of Henry George's views.   This reminds me of a question you put to me some time ago in reference to a statement I made in an " interview," in which I said I was for the nationalisation of land here, but in Michael Davitt's way, not in Henry George's.   Your Eminence asked me what was Davitt's view.   The appearance of your letter to-day reminds me that I have not yet answered the question.

The difference between the two is (or was) that George, taking it as a fundamental principle that there can be no *private* property in land, would transfer the land from the present owners to the State, *giving them no compensation*, but Davitt, while relying on many considerations to show that the present owners (in Ireland, remember) have claim but to a small share in the property, fully recognises that property of theirs, *and would make compensation to them for it*.

The difference is manifestly one of fundamental principle. As regards George's views, I must say that since I read his book *Progress and Poverty*, several years ago, I have felt convinced that the nationalisation of the land will infallibly be a point of practical politics before very long.   The sooner it is carried out, the less revolutionary the measure will be as regards respect for the rights of the present private owners.

In the *Social Problems* I don't think George explicitly denies the right of private property in land.   Nothing could be more explicit than his denial of it in *Progress and Poverty*.   *Progress and Poverty*, at least in those chapters that deal with the nationalisation question, is a singularly interesting as well as ably written book. . I wish your Eminence could make out time to read it, or to read so much of it.   It is very plain, very painfully so indeed,

that the Archbishop of New York, whose pastoral condemns
it so strongly, cannot have read it all.

In the *Social Problems* George advocates the imposition
of a land tax, so as (either at once, or gradually) to absorb
all the rent, and in this way to make the rent available for
the general purposes of the State.

This plainly contemplates a transfer without compensation, practically a confiscation. Is not this going very far?
I put this question in reference to the justice of the transaction. As to the political economy of it, I am not in a
position to form any opinion upon it, as I know nothing of
political economy.

But I understand that it is a maxim of that science that
taxation should not be thrown exclusively on any one kind
of property, but should be fairly distributed over all. If
this be so, the way in which he puts his plan forward in the
later book seems open to serious objection.

In the *Progress and Poverty* he refers, no doubt, to the
old land tax in England, and shows how the State would
be independent of all other taxation, if that were paid
now. But this is introduced merely as an illustration of
the results of carrying out his principle.

I would put the matter thus : Let us suppose the ownership of all the land in the country transferred to the State,
then the land is rented by the tenants from the State, which
thus receives, not a land *tax*, but simply the value of its
property—which it holds for the nation, but which, as a
practical means of turning that property into money, it has
so rented out to a certain number of individuals, the landowners or farmers.

This being so, the rest of the community, *and with them
the landowners, are free of taxation*. No taxes need be
paid at all. The State is rich enough to do its work out of
the proceeds of its own property. Indeed, as is evident,
millions would remain over for expenditure on purposes of
public or general utility.

In Dublin our Corporation is the owner of a certain
amount of house-property. The house-holders pay rent to the
Corporation. *This is not a tax*. Let us suppose that the
Corporation owned the houses of one half of Dublin. They
would then have, out of their house rents, more than enough
to bear all the municipal charges. The inhabitants of those
houses could not complain that all the city taxation was
thrown upon them. There would be no city taxes at all.
Nor could they claim that their house rents should be

reduced so that no balance should remain over for general expenditure. They should pay the full value of the property they held from the city, leaving for the benefit of the city whatever balance might remain over and above. They, of course, would share in the benefits of that expen - diture, in common with their fellow citizens.

Now in the " nationalisation" scheme the position of the landowners—*all the landowners*—would correspond with that of the householders of Corporation houses in my illustration. They could not complain that no one else was called upon to pay anything into the public treasury ; for no one else would hold any property from the public. Those who hold any should pay for what they held, and pay for it at its full value.

Whatever advantage is in this way of putting the case is lost when it is put on the ground of " taxation."

But I cannot see that the absorption of the rent in the form of a land tax is free from the objections (on the score of injustice) to the simple transfer of the ownership from the private owners to the State.

At this time, towards the end of 1886, the Archbishop of New York, Dr. Corrigan, had felt it to be his duty to rebuke and censure a priest of his diocese, Rev. Dr. McGlynn, for certain views published by him concerning Henry George's teaching in reference to the right of private ownership in land. Archbishop Corrigan's action aroused much criticism and evoked strong comment from Dr. McGlynn's friends. Amongst the most outspoken of Dr. McGlynn's sympathisers was Michael Davitt, who was in the United States at the time. The excitement over the McGlynn incident was prolonged into the following year, and when Davitt returned to Ireland Dr. McGlynn's supporters wrote to him urging him to see Manning and Walsh with a view to securing their aid in obtaining an impartial hearing of his case by the Holy See, to which the matter had been referred by Dr. Corrigan. Davitt wrote to Walsh, November 4, 1887 :

I enclose the documents which I have been asked to bring under your Grace's notice. To the statements from the Rev. Dr. Burstell I add some facts which are not included in his letter to Dr. Moore, but which are necessary to a full presentation of Dr. McGlynn's case. These facts were gathered by me from interviews with representative priests and laymen during my recent visit to New York.

I do not like *writing* the other facts, about which I even felt a reluctance to talk with your Grace to-day; but they will come out, I fear, before very long if Dr. McGlynn's friends among the priesthood in New York are compelled by Archbishop Corrigan's persecution of them (for their refusal to sign the circular calling for Dr. McGlynn's punishment) to strike back in self-defence.

I have no hesitation in saying that if all that was told to me by *venerable and most exemplary priests* in New York is ever published to the American world, it will give a setback to the Catholic Church in the United States.

These priests and many influential Catholic laymen with whom I had interviews in New York appeal to your Grace and Cardinal Manning to avert this calamity by bringing pressure to bear upon Rome to grant Dr. McGlynn a patient hearing and to curb the high-handed proceedings of Archbishop Corrigan.

A letter written by Dr. Walsh to Manning shows that Dr. McGlynn's case had been engaging their attention for a long time :—

WALSH TO MANNING.

January 7, 1887.

I enclose Dr. Corrigan's letter. What he mentions about Dr. McGlynn's case is very sad.

I cannot at all agree with what the Archbishop says about H. George's use of language. The extracts quoted by His Grace are quite sufficient to show, what indeed is quite manifest to anyone who has read *Progress and Poverty*, that George is a writer of singular definiteness and clearness.

The mistake made by the Archbishop in his Pastoral was in ascribing to George the doctrine denying the right of property, as if George held that no ownership (in anything) could exist. I do not think it possible that anyone who had read *Progress and Poverty* could have made such a mistake, or, as regards the reasoning of the case, could have failed to see the irrelevancy of the arguments on which His Grace relies.

But I wrote at such length on all this matter in my last letter to your Eminence, I must say no more about it now. I send your Eminence a copy of this day's *Freeman's Journal* that you may see in it a letter of mine written to the *Daily News* in reference to a recent telegram from the Roman correspondent. The *article* on the letter was written by one of our priests here to whom I usually commit such things. I took the liberty of indicating the outlines of the reference to be made in the articles to your Eminence.

The following letter of Michael Davitt's, one of a number written by him to Archbishop Walsh on the matter of the "interviews" of August 1886, deserves to be quoted in full :—

I am ashamed to have put your Grace to the trouble of copying the document relating to the proposals made by Mr. Parnell in 1880. I could have done without it until it had answered the purpose for which it was required. I am contemplating a History of the Land League sometime, and it is for this purpose I am anxious to preserve the evidence of what was generously proposed by *Land Leaguers* in the way of compensation to the landlords almost at the commencement of the movement.

I think you have acted with your usual courageous prudence in not withdrawing your proposal (to invite landlords and tenants to a Round-Table Conference with a view to the settlement of the Land Question). The temptation to do so in protest against the Mitchelstown butchery* must have been very strong; but for the reason given in your Grace's letter, it is well you did not. Your proposed R.T. Conference has attracted unusual attention—in Rome as well as in England—and while it may possibly not lead to big results it will show the world that you are anxious *another* opportunity should be given to the landlords to make terms with the Irish people. I confess I was in a mood similar to that which prompted your Grace's proposal a year or so ago. But seeing the vindictive way in which

---

* At Mitchelstown the police fired on farmers (assembled to hold a meeting of protest against ruthless eviction), killing three and wounding several. With this incident is connected the notorious telegram : " Don't hesitate to shoot," sent from Dublin Castle to a southern magistrate. Cf. Davitt, *Fall of Feudalism,* p. 525.

evictions were being carried out, and noting with satisfaction the rejection of Mr. Gladstone's Land Purchase scheme by the democracy of Great Britain, I have become convinced that the Irish landlords are reserved by fate for a punishment which will be all the more heavy because of their own brutal obstinacy. For the crime of this horrible system they cannot be held morally responsible, but for what they have done themselves and are still doing against our poor people I have been forced to steel my heart against them, and I find myself in a mood of exultation now at their approaching ruin.

I read with pleasure and profit the recent reprint of your Grace's " interview" with Mr. Gill*—I was in America at the time it was originally published—and have noted your remarks upon the point about the number of years' purchase. In warning tenants from time to time about the purchase schemes and Bills of the past few years, I have repeatedly pointed out to them how they would be swindled if they allowed themselves to be persuaded to buy, not alone the *net* rent of the landlord but his cost of collection, share of poor rate, etc. But it is impossible to make some of our people think before they are made to see the consequences of their want of thought. Hence, in Kerry, Mayo and Donegal, landlords have succeeded (with Ashbourne's Act) in getting twenty to thirty years' purchase of the judicial rental for their interest. Fr. Sheehy has congratulated tenants whom he had induced to purchase at seventeen years of the judicial rent. In fact there is no point in connection with the present phase of the Land Question upon which *priests* and people need more instruction than upon that which your Grace has laid such emphasis in the interview referred to.

It will be interesting to see what lines the landlords will take at to-morrow's conference. I am almost tempted to confess I would be glad to find both wisdom and prudence absent from their councils. They are a God-forsaken crew, and the word and meaning of justice would be mockeries if punishment were not to overtake them for what they have done in Ireland during the last ten years.

I thank your Grace for your very kind letter.

---

* *Vide supra,* pp. 217 and foll. The " interviews " of August 11 and 16, 1886.

CHAPTER X

" THE PLAN OF CAMPAIGN "

In the year 1886 the Irish farmers were passing through a critical time. Agricultural trade was undergoing a period of severe depression; rents were in all cases high, and in many cases exorbitant; and tenants were called on to meet liabilities for rent out of proportion to the productive value of their holdings. During the previous five years many of them, availing themselves of the Land Act of 1881, had entered the Land Courts to have judicial rents fixed for their holdings. These rents were, as a rule, considerably lower than the exactions previously made at the pleasure of rapacious landlords. But many of the farmers, owing to legal restrictions and a variety of circumstances, were debarred from seeking relief in the Land Courts, and, as a consequence, had to continue to endure the burden of excessive rents. Besides, even the judicial rents—fixed on a generous scale in more prosperous times*—were fast becoming intolerable on account of the steady deterioration in the value of farm produce.

In the spring of the year Sir James Caird, an expert on agricultural questions, had drawn attention† to the collapse of agricultural values, and even Mr. Joseph Chamberlain admitted in the House of Commons, August 1886, the inequity of the judicial rents in the altered and straitened circumstances. " We have to deal," he said, " with a crisis which is apparently imminent, with the general

---

* The Cowper Commission reported, 1887, that 176,000 of the judicial rents fixed during the years 1881-87, were too high. Cf. Davitt, *Fall of Feudalism*, pp. 325-6.
† Letter to the *Times*, March 20, 1886.

inability to pay rents, with the numerous evictions and consequent suffering, and with great danger to social order. I do not think that anyone will deny that there has been a great fall in the price of almost all the chief produce of Ireland since the judicial rents were fixed.   That fall may be variously estimated, but I should put it myself at twenty or thirty per cent.   Now, if the judicial rents were fixed upon the basis of the former prices, and at that time they were fair, then they must necessarily be unfair now.   I do not admit for a moment that there is any sanctity about judicial or any other rents.   If rents cannot be paid and leave a fair subsistence to the tenant, no doubt the landlord must bear the loss."*

It was to meet this situation, admirably summed up by Chamberlain, that Parnell had introduced his Tenants' Relief Bill.†   This measure, however, which would have averted a storm of trouble and suffering to come, was rejected, September 27, 1886; and as the actual policy of the Government was a rigid enforcement of the law enabling the landlord to distrain or evict for non-payment of rent, the situation among the occupiers of the land steadily worsened and soon became desperate.   In this extremity recourse was had to a drastic remedy; this was popularly known as the " Plan of Campaign."

The Plan of Campaign was launched on October 23, 1886, by Timothy Harrington in consultation with John Dillon and William O'Brien.   Parnell was not consulted and seems never to have approved of the Plan.   The chief proposals of Harrington's plan were : The tenants of an estate where no voluntary abatement of rent was offered by the landlord were to wait on him in deputation and ask for

---

* *Parliamentary Debates,* August, 1886.

† Parnell's Bill proposed (1) the prevention of evictions in cases of the tenants' *bona fide* inability to pay rent, (2) revision of the judicial rents, and (3) the admission of leaseholders (hitherto excluded) to the benefits of the Act of 1881. Chamberlain voted against the Bill.

one, on reasoned grounds. If this were refused the tenants were then to resolve not to pay any rent until the landlord would agree to a reduction commensurate with the prevailing depression. They were to pay into a " campaign fund" on the estate the reduced rent offered to and refused by the landlord—to be given to him should he, under this pressure, consent to grant the abatement asked for, or to be used, as far as necessary, in the fight which might follow if he should resort to legal proceedings and eviction.*

The plan was put into operation on over a hundred estates. The tenants formed estate combinations, paid the " plan rent" into the hands of a committee, and awaited results. In no fewer than sixty instances the landlords gave way and settled on the " plan" terms, which averaged less than twenty-five per cent. of an abatement. On twenty-four estates a brief struggle took place, but the landlords came to terms on a similar average of reductions. In the case of seventeen estates where the landlords, including Lord Clanricarde, stood out against the tenants' demand, an average concession of thirty per cent. abatement would have procured a similar peaceful settlement. Evictions followed instead of agreements, with the result that hundreds of thousands of pounds were lost by landlords and tenants, and by the State; and much misery and turmoil and some bloodshed ensued.†

* Cf. *Fall of Feudalism in Ireland,* pp. 516-17.

† Davitt has left on record the following :—" In one—and that the most striking—instance of the ' Plan of Campaign ' contests, the leaders did, in my opinion, commit a big blunder. The Tipperary fight was a great mistake. On one important point it violated even the principles of the Plan itself. The scheme of combination very wisely laid down the rule that ' Holders of town parks who are shopkeepers have a strong claim to exemption (from joining the combination) for a judgment against them may be ruin.' Just so. It is both bad tactics in a fight of the kind, and a lamentable want of sound knowledge of human nature also, to ask a man to run the risk of losing a business worth £5,000 on account of an agricultural rent of £20 or £30. Some of the Tipperary shopkeepers were called upon to sacrifice sums equal to this, and herein is where the

Three months after the " Plan" was started the Cowper Commission, which the Tory Government itself had set up, issued its report, February 1887. The Report stated *inter alia* :

The fall in the price of produce of all kinds, and in all parts of the country, has much impaired the ability of the farmers to pay the full rent, and this, following on a previous restriction of credit by the bankers and other lenders of money, as well as by the shopkeepers, has very greatly increased their financial difficulties.

The Land Commissioners, recognising this depression, began towards the end of 1885 to reduce the rents then being judicially fixed by from ten to fourteen per cent. below the scale of reduction in the four previous years, and they have since continued to act on this principle.

The sudden fall in prices during the last two years was intensified in its effect by a gradual deterioration which had been going on in the quality and produce of the soil, both tillage and grass, during a series of years of low temperature and much rain, especially in 1886, the worst year of the century. During this period much of the tenants' capital had disappeared. The cost of cultivation, compared with that of an earlier period, had also greatly increased.*

The Plan of Campaign was condemned by the *Times* and by the Tory Press generally, as a criminal conspiracy to repudiate legal contracts; as a system of robbery, organised by disaffected tenants against loyal landlords. The *Times* special correspondent wrote of the " abhorrence" with which the " Plan" was viewed by " all honest men" in Ireland ;

blunder of breaking away from the written advice of the plan itself came in.

"Smith Barry's (the landlord's) policy of retaliation in helping to frustrate what otherwise promised to be an amicable settlement on the Ponsonby estate brought upon himself the weight and cost of the Tipperary struggle; but his opponents gave themselves very badly away, when they put their own weakest wing—the shopkeepers—forward, to turn the flank of their strongest antagonist. It was magnificent, no doubt, and called forth a few splendid exhibitions of self-sacrifice, and enthusiasm galore, but it was very bad ' war ' all the same."—*Fall of Feudalism in Ireland,* pp. 521-22.

* *Cowper Report.* Nos. 16, 17 and 18.

and he added that even the more reputable elements among the Nationalist Party condemned the " Plan."

Archbishop Walsh followed with close and anxious attention the steps which were being taken in defence of the Irish tenants. He had, of course, no responsibility for the adoption of the " Plan." Indeed he had privately conveyed to Harrington his apprehensions regarding its moral justifiableness. For weeks after the " Campaign" was launched he made no public pronouncement on the matter, and his first public utterance regarding the Plan was given in an " interview" published in the *Pall Mall Gazette*, December 2, 1886 :

INTERVIEWER : What have you to say about the famous Plan of Campaign ? Does not such a scandalous outrage on the principles of common honesty scandalise you, the official chief of the Christian Church in Ireland ?

ARCHBISHOP : Well, I confess that at first I was a little startled at it. I was not only startled but grieved. I had never yet had cause to express my dissent from the programme of the present national movement. I speak of the dissent that it would have been my duty as an Irish bishop to express, if that programme, as it came under my observation in this diocese, contained anything that I should regard as contravening justice or morality. Notwithstanding all my sympathy with the movement, the adoption in this diocese of any unjust or immoral means for the furtherance of its object would, of course, put upon me the painful duty of publishing an episcopal condemnation of it. We Catholics cannot act on the principle—rather fashionable, I am sorry to say, nowadays—that " the end justifies the means." So, apprehending that the Plan of Campaign might at any moment be brought into requisition in this diocese of Dublin, I was grieved to think, as I did think for the moment, that it might perhaps prove inconsistent with my duty as Bishop of the diocese to abstain from a condemnation of it. But when I looked into the matter carefully, as of course it was my duty to do, my anxiety was relieved. On closer inspection the difficulties which at first embarrassed me practically disappeared.

The great difficulty, indeed I may say almost the only one, was that the Plan of Campaign leaves it practically to

the judgment of the tenants—that is to say, to the judgment
of one of the parties to the contract of tenancy—to fix the
terms on which that contract is to continue in force. That,
no doubt, in the abstract, seems at first sight a formidable
difficulty; but we must look at the other side of the question.
If the tenant is to be viewed merely as one of the two parties
to the rent contract, in what other light are we to view the
landlord? He, too, is only one of the contracting parties,
and he has had the fixing of the terms of the contract long
enough. Is it quite clear that the tenants are to be blamed
if they claim to have their turn now?

Q. But does not that argument ignore the fact that the
tenants are setting aside contracts already in existence?

A. In the view of the case I am now contemplating,
practically no. The old contracts, even those that have
taken the form of "statutory" tenancies under the Land
Act of 1881, with judicial rents, are not at present " in
possession," to use a technical phrase. " In possession," I
should explain, is a term familiar to churchmen and possibly
also to lawyers, which implies that the agreement or contract being valid and " in possession" has nine points of the
law on its side; and that therefore the *onus probandi* is
thrown on the other side.

Q. Do you maintain that there are practically no contracts of tenancy now valid and binding in Ireland?

A. I would not put it exactly in that way. This is how
I would state my view of the case. It is admitted on all
hands that practically all over Ireland, reductions, and large
reductions, are to be made in the rents, even in the judicial
rents. The question is as to the amount of these reductions.
Whatever inconvenience there may be in having that great
question decided by the tenants, I must maintain that there
is just the same inconvenience—indeed, I see in one way a
much greater inconvenience—in having it decided by the
landlords. The landlord, like the tenant, is now merely
" one of the contracting parties"—neither more nor less.

This is, of course, a bad, a deplorable state of things. It
is a disgrace to the legislature of the country that things
should be left in this state of disorganisation, but surely we
are not to blame for it. Within the past six or seven months
two proposals had been made by the friends of the Irish
tenants, the adoption of either of which by Parliament
would have saved us, or rather I should say, would have
saved the Government of the country from the responsibility
of the present deplorable state of affairs. I refer to Mr.

Gladstone's Land Purchase Bill and to Mr. Parnell's proposal for the relief of the tenants. Both of these proposed to take this whole question of the present fair value of the land out of the hands of the landlords on the one side, and of the tenants on the other, putting it altogether into the hands of the constituted judicial tribunal of the country.

Having referred to the folly of the landlords in rejecting Gladstone's Land Purchase scheme, and to the unwisdom of Parliament in rejecting Parnell's proposal for placing the fixing of the " fair rent" in the hands of a judicial body, the Archbishop continued :

There must be some means found of deciding this question of the value of the land. It is purely and simply a question of value. The landlords cannot now lay claim to any exclusive right to decide it. Some of them, I know, do set up this claim ! but the claim is monstrous. Mr. Gladstone and Mr. Parnell each proposed an appeal to the legal decision of the courts. Their proposals were rejected. The matter is now thrown into the hands of the tenants themselves, and those who were responsible for the rejection must bear the responsibility for the result.

INTERVIEWER : But ought not a tenant who wished for a change in the existing condition of the rent contract, to begin by giving up the holding which he has hitherto held on those terms which he now repudiates as unfair and impossible ?

ARCHBISHOP : That, for a time, was one of my chief difficulties, but recent land legislation has cut the ground from under every objection of the sort. Until 1870 the laws of this country recognised but one ownership in the soil ; that, as a matter of course, was the ownership of the landlord. While that state of affairs continued, a tenant in thus holding out for a reduction of rent should undoubtedly have been regarded as keeping possession of that which was the property of another. But the case is now entirely altered by the Land Acts of 1870 and 1881.   For now, beyond all question, the system of land tenure in Ireland is a system of *dual ownership*. It is no longer a system of landlord ownership exclusively. The tenant now is recognised by law as having his ownership as well. This fact is recognised even by the present Tory Government, who have proclaimed their intention of getting rid of dual ownership—of buying out the landlords.   That is to say, the Government has adopted

Michael Davitt's policy of " abolition of landlordism in Ireland."

Q. But how does this bear on your remark in reference to the tenants' surrender or non-surrender of their holdings ?

A. What I wished to say was this—that while the tenant had no legal ownership in the land, he was holding on to what was unquestionably the legal property of the landlord, and of the landlord only. But now that the property of the tenant in his holding has received full legal recognition—for its existence, at all events, is recognised as fully as the existence of the property of the landlord —a tenant forcibly ejected from possession is ejected from possession of the landlord's property, no doubt, but he is ejected also from the possession of *that which is his own*. The existence then of our present system of land tenure in Ireland has put this question of the rent-fixing on a very special footing. It can no longer be safely left in the hands of either landlord or tenant. The maintenance of social order requires that it should be dealt with by some authority independent of both. Every effort has been made by the tenants and their friends to have it so dealt with. All these efforts have, so far, failed. They have failed through the influence of the landlord class. And the strength of the tenants' position now is that they merely dispute the exclusive right of the landlord as a rent-fixer. They simply say that if the landlord has his position they have theirs. Our Imperial legislature in its wisdom seems to leave the matter to be fought out between both parties, and so the tenants say that they will stand upon their rights; that, in other words, they will not now give up at the landlord's bidding that which the law has fully recognised as being their own property. All this may represent a state of things not far removed from social disorganisation, but it is a state of things the full responsibility of which must be thrown on those who are responsible for the rejection of Mr. Gladstone's Land Purchase Bill.

INTERVIEWER : There is some apprehension that there will be much danger of outrage increasing if a policy of repression is adopted.

ARCHBISHOP : God forbid ! But I do not like to enter into the question, as I am responsible only for my own diocese. Thank God we have, so far, been very free from agrarian crime. I have remarked that in every address of welcome presented to me by the people of the rural portions of my diocese on the occasion of my first visiting them,

crimes and outrages were strongly denounced. I have
always taken advantage of the opportunity thus afforded
me to speak out pretty strongly on the subject. And I have
remarked on every occasion with singular pleasure that when
speaking thus, addressing crowded gatherings of people, no
words that I spoke were more loudly or more cordially
applauded than those in which I spoke in condemnation of
crime and outrage; and I have every confidence I shall
never have to speak otherwise of the people of this diocese.

The Archbishop's " interview" in the *Pall Mall Gazette*
caused a sensation. It was reproduced and canvassed and
criticised in the leading newspapers of the United Kingdom.
The *Times*, the *Morning Post*, and most of the organs of
Unionist opinion were roused to fury. The *Tablet* wrote,
December 4, 1886 :

His Grace has answered the questions put to him by the
representative of the *Pall Mall Gazette* with the utmost
frankness and directness, and we make little doubt but that
this " interview" will long be famous in the history of
journalism. The Archbishop's bold and unequivocal defence
of the action of the tenants in the present crisis is well
calculated to cause a sensation in this country; but for all
that, if any man can see his way to accept his Grace's facts,
he must not hesitate at the conclusion. What we have got
to do first is to rid our minds of all notions of the tenures
of England. The State has recognised a dual property in
the soil of Ireland. Recent legislation has made the word
" owner" in relation to Irish land a word of equivocal meaning. The fields of Ireland belong neither to the landlord nor
the tenant, but to both. The tenant is lord of the land he
tills, subject to the payment of a certain money tribute
known as " fair rent." Judicial tribunals have been busy
for years all over the land fixing these money tributes. It is
asserted that since these legal rents were settled there has
been a heavy, unforeseen, and permanent fall of prices all
over Ireland, so that the sum which two years ago represented a fair rent represents a rent unjust and impossible
to-day. Is, then, the landlord taking advantage of the
seasons to make profit out of his neighbour's extremity, and
to be free, not only to do what he can to exact an unjust and
extortionate tribute, but also to go further and by resorting
to eviction, to invade the property of another, and possess

himself also of the tenant's lawful share of the ownership of
the farm? Clearly then, as we pointed out when Mr. Parnell's Bill was under discussion, the facts are the only things
which can possibly be in issue. Upon the question of
principle there is no room for dispute. For it is obviously
idle to urge, as many are doing, that the judicial rents were
fixed for a term of years. The question is not one of contract
at all, but of *status*. The judicial rents were not contract
rents arrived at by the haggling of the market and agreed
to be paid. They were fixed by an outside power, and as
representing, not what the tenant thought he could afford
to pay, but what it was equitable that he, with his part
ownership, should pay. The rents were fixed as fair rents
—have they ceased to be fair? That is the question. If
the fall of prices in Ireland has been so heavy and so unforeseen, and at the same time so permanent in its character as
to make the recently fixed judicial rents no longer equitable,
the tenants are entitled to a readjustment. The legislature,
by declining to intervene, has practically decided against
the tenants' claim and in favour of the landlords. To
advise the tenants, therefore, to disregard the decision of
the legislature and treat it as ill-informed, and to act on
their own judgment and knowledge, is the tremendous
responsibility which the leaders of the National League have
accepted.

The following week, December 11, 1886, the *Tablet* had
an article on "The Policy of the National League" in
which it purported to "judge the whole conduct of the
League in the campaign on which they have embarked."
After setting out again that if the allegation that the judicial
rents were no longer fair, and if a fall in prices heavy,
unforeseen, and permanent, could be proved to have taken
place, the tenants would be entitled in all equity and justice
to a re-adjustment of their rents, the article continued :—

But the matter has already been brought before the right
tribunal, the legislature of the land, and the decision is in
favour of the existing settlement.* Let the leaders of the
League be ever so convinced of the truth of their statements

* The "right tribunal" soon reversed its judgment, *vide
supra* p. 236.

and the equity of their claim, and the question will remain
—are they justified in counselling the tenants of Ireland to
take the law into their own hands? See how the case
stands. The tenants upon any given estate think the change
in the economic conditions of the country entitled them to
a reduction of—say—thirty per cent. They have called
upon Parliament to ratify and sanction that claim, and
Parliament has refused. The tenants, then, acting on the
advice of the League combine together and make offer of
the rent reduced by the thirty per cent. If the landlord
refuses to accept, and in full quittance, the reduced rent
which the tenants, judging their own case, think equitable,
the tenants pay him nothing at all but straightway hand
the amount of the reduced rent over to two trustees to be
spent for the general purposes of the campaign. We have
certainly no wish to resort to the feeble device of damning a
cause with an epithet, but we have no choice but to say that
such doctrines amount to the doctrines of anarchy and
revolution. We are quite prepared that such words are
not final, for there are times when the sacred duty of
obedience may have to give way to the still more sacred
duty of rebellion. It is for the advisers of the League to
say whether such a time has come now.

Having referred to the fact that the action of the tenants
is not allowed to be isolated and independent, but that the
League required combination and concerted action, and that
tenants who wished to pay the unreduced rents were
inhibited from doing so, and thus from paying their just
debts, the article continued :

What we want our readers to feel is that the teaching of
the League, whether they realise it or not, is revolution,
and what we want the leaders of the League to do is to tell
us whether they have any better grounds for the propagation
of this most demoralising doctrine that the people are free
to defy the legislature, to judge their own cause, and to be a
law unto themselves, than the *fall in the agricultural prices
in a single year*.* We take it then, that the policy of the
League, whether moral or immoral, is a policy of anarchy.

* The findings of the Cowper Commission were widely divergent from the *Tablet's* statement. Cf. *supra,* p. 236.

It tells the people that they may disregard the law of the land and decide the cause, in which they themselves are suitors, at their own discretion. And we say without hesitation that we believe such doctrines are not to be justified merely by proof that the fall in prices has been adverse to the tenants, making judicial rents no longer fair, and eating into the value of the tenants' share of his farm. On the other hand we fully recognise that there may be a necessity overriding all law of the kind to justify the preaching of this bloodless rebellion—but the burden of the proof lies heavy with the defenders of the League.

The *Times* continued its attacks on the Plan of Campaign, and urged the Chief Secretary to give no heed to Archbishop Walsh's views. The *Pall Mall Gazette* wrote in opposition to the *Times*, December 17, 1886 :

The Archbishop of Dublin had an interview yesterday afternoon at the Castle with the Chief Secretary. We are glad to hear it. Even if you are going in for an inflexible system of " thorough " it is desirable to know your facts; and foremost among the facts of the situation with which Ministers have to deal is the close union at this stage—as in preceding ones—of the Nationalist movement between the Church and the people. Sir M. Hicks-Beach is wiser than his counsellors in the *Times*, who shut their ears to such obvious sources of information as the deliberate utterances of the Archbishop of Dublin, and still have the courage to speak of Mr. Dillon's " Plan of Campaign" as the offspring only of the " brute instincts" of " all that is base and sordid in the human breast."

The *Times* is inventing a new moral code of its own for application to Ireland. Sir M. Hicks-Beach has explained that the Government is on the side of mercy; the *Times* denounces such pitiable poltroonery. The Government is for bringing pressure to bear on harsh landlords " to follow the example of their more generous fellows"; the *Times* deplores such miserable clemency and shrieks for the full pound of flesh. And the effrontery of it all is that it exhorts the Government to the policy of Shylock in the name of a " nation which has not ceased to prize integrity." Evil will not become good, however, simply because Shylock is installed as God in Printing House Square.

Amongst those who publicly expressed dissent from Archbishop Walsh's views on the morality of the Plan of Campaign were some of his episcopal brethren, notably Dr. O'Dwyer of Limerick and Dr. Healy, Coadjutor to the Bishop of Clonfert.

Dr. Croke made no public statement. He publicly approved the plan, however, but on grounds quite different from Dr. Walsh's. Indeed it was said by an ultra-Tory scribe that the difference in the attitude of the two Archbishops towards the plan was that each was in cordial sympathy with the immoral organisation, but the other more so; that it was a moot point, however, whether Dublin dissented from Cashel regarding the expediency of the maiming of cattle, especially the " curtailment" of cows.

The two Archbishops were assailed in the Press and arraigned in Parliament. To every thrust Dr. Walsh returned a riposte; but Dr. Croke maintained his silence. To his " Dublin brother,"* however, the Archbishop of Cashel explained his views in a private letter, December 19, 1886 :

I returned a while ago from Fethard and found yours before me. There was no enclosure.

The arrest of Dillon and O'Brien is serious, but it brings matters to a head, which, I think, is not undesirable.

There certainly is, as you say, no law compelling a tenant to " surrender his tenancy"; but there is, it seems to me, a *law*(?) that obliges him not to hand over the landlord's money (it must be his, or else it would not be offered to him) to a third party who has no claim to it; who may never give it to the rightful owner; and who declares, moreover, that he will not only strive to induce other tenants to do likewise, but will actually spend all or a portion of said landlord's money, in a campaign against him. If I owe a landlord £10 and I cannot, or will not, pay him more than £8 and offer him that sum which he refuses, believing (wrongly or otherwise) that I am able to pay the full amount, can I as an honest man recognising the existence

* The " Dublin brother " was the formula by which Dr. Croke usually spoke of Dr. Walsh.

of British law in Ireland, not only hand over to Jack or
Harry the £8 aforesaid to be employed as above, but also
go round to twenty other tenants, each owing him £10
also, and, telling them what I had done, induce or intimidate
them to do in like manner?   I do not see how you can
justify this " Plan of Campaign" if you admit that there is a
lawful Government here, and that that lawful Government
has declared the above conduct illegal and immoral.   Now
the Government, i.e., the legislature, has actually declared
it to be so; and when asked to oblige the landlords to accept
—say the £8 out of £10—they not only refused to intervene,
but distinctly stated that there were no grounds for doing so,
and that they would therefore assist the landlords as usual
in squeezing the full £10 out of their tenants.   For me the
answer to this is very easy.   The so-called law, as expounded
by Irish judges and enforced by British bayonets, is simply
no law at all inasmuch as it is for the benefit of the few to
the grave and obvious detriment of the many, and inasmuch, moréover, as it is upheld as the law by an alien legislature for purposes other than and antagonistic to the peace,
prosperity, and social progress of the whole Irish nation.

These are my sentiments.   They have always been so.   I
do not mean of course to make them public.   But if forced
to do it, I should not hesitate to do so.

Archbishop Croke's views were reflected in a letter which
appeared in the *Tablet*, December 25, 1886, written by the
Rev. Arthur Ryan of Thurles, although it does not appear
that the Archbishop had direct responsibility for the
opinions set forth, or for the language in which they were
expressed.   Fr. Ryan wrote :

In your recent article on the " Policy of the National
League," you have called upon Irish Nationalists to say
whether the time for " the sacred duty of rebellion" has
come, or, in other words, whether the action taken (by the
League) is moral or immoral . . .   I venture to answer as
follows :—
Ever since the Union the best and most honourable of
Irishmen have looked on rebellion as a " sacred duty,"
providing there were a reasonable chance of success.   It was
the absence of this reasonable chance of making rebellion
successful that alone bound wise and brave Irishmen

conscientiously to oppose armed resistance to the Government of this country. It has never occurred to me to consider acquiescence to the Government of England as a moral obligation or as other than a dire necessity. I would fearlessly ask any English gentleman, even Catholic first and English after, would he, were he in my place, think otherwise? I ask him, would he who has applauded the valour of his countrymen in Egypt, in Ashantee, in Zululand—would he have scruples about fighting for his own nationality, for what he believed to be the sacred right of his own country—the right of freedom from foreign misgovernment, and from the constant anarchy and misery resulting therefrom? My conviction is that Englishmen, as I know and honour them, would never have borne what we have borne. But we have borne it simply and solely because we could not help it. We have sorrowfully bowed to might, but we have never acknowledged it to be right. We have never, thank God, lied to our oppressors by saying we feel loyal to them. And when we have condemned the rebels whose heroism and whose self-sacrifice we have loved and wept over, we condemned in them, not their want of loyalty but their want of prudence. We thought it wrong to plunge the country into the horrors of war with no hope of success. But in common with humanity we have rejected what O'Connell led himself to say if not to think, that the liberty of our country is not worth our blood if blood could win it.

If, then, the legislature in London, having declined to protect the homes and property of the tenants of Ireland, and the Government having, despite soft words, threatened brute force and imprisonment—its time-worn plan of campaign against us—if under these circumstances we find that our new plan in self-defence is likely to succeed, why should we care whether it be an act of rebellion or not? Its chance of success is, indeed, all we look to. Rebellion with the chance of being successful rebellion against tyrannous misgovernment is, the wide world over, a sacred duty. Englishmen blessed it in their own case—in the case of every nation except Ireland. Irishmen bless it, and Irish priests and Irish bishops bless it, and declare it to be high and unassailable morality—a holy war in the cause of the poor and oppressed, a struggle for hearths and homes. Rebels we are, almost to a man, against the injustice and misgovernment —the hollow mockery we see and touch on every side, but which our pious critics cannot or will not recognise. True, we have been up to this " inopportunists" in the matter of rebellion; but now our opportunity has come, and we give our glad " God-speed" to what promises to be, at long last, a successful Plan of Campaign.   Whether or not that plan be constitutional may be an interesting question of politics; but it is no question of morals.

At the beginning of March 1887, Hicks-Beach was replaced in the Chief Secretaryship by Mr. Arthur Balfour, who very shortly after introduced legislation on the very lines proposed in vain by Parnell in the previous September.   This Bill authorised the Irish Land Commission :

(1) To revise the judicial rents that had been fixed from 1881 to 1886, and

(2) to admit the exempted leaseholders to the benefits of the Gladstonian Land Acts.

Had this been done six months earlier there would have been no Plan of Campaign.   But being six months too late, it became necessary, " in accord with English ideas, to accompany the ameliorating Bill with a corresponding measure of repression."   No provision was made in Mr. Balfour's Bill for staying evictions in any circumstances. " There was, in fact, to be a further provision for closure on debates in the House of Commons, and a maximum of coercion for Ireland."   A perpetual Coercion Bill was made to signalise the year of Queen Victoria's Jubilee.   Mr. Balfour devised a comprehensive policy of " legal aggression" to defeat the Plan of Campaign, a policy which led to the " Mitchelstown Massacre" of September 1887, when three men were killed by the armed constabulary who fired on a crowd estimated at between five and ten thousand persons who had assembled to hold a public meeting of protest against the Government's coercive measures.

CHAPTER XI

ANXIOUS DAYS

THE Duke of Norfolk was warmly applauded, as we have seen, when (February 1886), addressing a meeting of the Dames of the Primrose League, he declared that the conduct of the Irish bishops and priests, in supporting Home Rule and the National League, had caused him special grief and shame. The Earl of Ashburnham, a Liberal peer and a Catholic, protested in the *Tablet* (March 20, 1886) against the Duke's language as " unworthy of the speaker, inappropriate to his audience, unnecessary for his purpose, and unjust towards his subject."

Viscount Bury, also a Catholic peer, in replying in the same paper (March 27, 1886) to Lord Ashburnham, took occasion to advance the charge that the action of the Irish bishops and clergy in supporting Home Rule was " political and withal treasonable."

Their action (he wrote) is not religious. The Catholic bishops teach rebellion . . . Rebellion is punishable by the law of the land. Why is it not enforced by the proper officers of the law ? The political *dicta* of the Irish bishops are *ultra vires* as regards their ecclesiastical functions. Englishmen must see that it will be better for them to defend themselves by the might of their own laws and the strength of their own right hands without calling on foreign powers for aid. It is difficult to see why (as some had been urging) the Vatican should interfere. We all agree, as a matter of law and history, with the Protestant Prayer Book which tells us that " no foreign potentate hath, or ought to have, any jurisdiction within these realms"; so far as I know the Pope does not claim any . . . The matter is not one of faith or discipline, and the Pope, if he took a side unasked would do a thing very unusual among foreign powers. His action would justly be resented as an interference with the domestic economy of another nation.

Lord Bury spoke also of the " brutal terrorism of the Land League"; condemned Gladstone's parleying with " Parnell, Davitt, O'Donovan Rossa, and the bloodstained mandatories of the Land League"; and advanced the view that Gladstone's plans " are supported by paid agitators, by the gold of the American dynamiters, and by the whole riff-raff of the socialistic enemies of England. Without the aid of that gold, and of those cruel and reckless hounds, the so-called demand for Home Rule would die. It is kept up by hireling agitators alone; and the concession even of the outrageous demands now formulated will not satiate their rapacity. Be not misled by the idea that this is a religious dispute. They know better in Ireland. The line of cleavage is not religious."

The *Saturday Review* and its Tory congeners were even more violent than Lord Bury in their criminations, of which no small share was levelled at the head of Archbishop Walsh. The Archbishop addressed a private letter of remonstrance to Dr. Herbert Vaughan, the proprietor of the *Tablet*, in which he protested against Viscount Bury's most offensive and lying, and even heretical article in that paper. Dr. Vaughan replied :

We live in a plague of lies, and you, as being so very active and prominent, are the most violently attacked. There is one thing which I do not know how to answer, and I should be very grateful for an answer that would satisfy my own mind. The question is asked—Why do not the bishops speak out more plainly and also frequently against crime ? The reproach of being " *dumb dogs*" dates from the beginning of time, and human nature often deserves the reproach when silence is pleasanter than speech. I should have thought that the pursuance of O'Connell's plan of continually denouncing the man who commits a crime as the enemy of his country would have told well in every way. I know that if the bishops were loud on the side of virtue and order—I mean if they denounced evil—they would stand better on this side of the water. There must therefore be some strong reason which renders the contrary policy the more desirable one. I should much like to understand it.

A number of influential Catholics who shared the views of the *Tablet* and the Norfolk faction dissented from Lord Bury's opinion as to the expediency of a direct appeal to Rome to check the Irish bishops and restrain them from actively aiding the National League and the Nationalist Party. The leader of this group was the Earl of Denbigh, who urged the establishing of diplomatic relations between England and the Vatican as the most likely and effective means of securing the intervention of the Pope on their side. He believed that with the establishment of diplomatic relations the Vatican could be made an instrument for furthering the interests of England generally, and especially for curbing disloyal Irish Catholics and Irish bishops. Speaking at the annual dinner of the Rugby Conservative Association (November 1886) Lord Denbigh reminded his audience that with the defeat of the Liberals and the advent of the Conservatives to power, confidence had been restored abroad, and he thought that it would afford his hearers great satisfaction to learn the effect already produced on one great potentate, who although he was not often spoken of in England, was coming to be more thought of by the people; he meant the Pope. His Holiness, in conversation with him (Lord Denbigh), said that he had the greatest opinion of England, and that he should always respect her laws and constitution because he saw that she was just, and because she was just she was strong; and Catholics under her rule had greater liberty and freedom than they had in any other part of the world. "For that," said the Pope, "I thank her and respect her, and I am so penetrated with that feeling that I wish to help her to the best of my power wherever my influence may extend. I can not only help her in Ireland, but I can help her in India; but I must know what you are doing. I have no means of knowing what England is doing, nor what the English Government wishes. I have no representative at the English Court, nor is there any English representative at the Vatican. If there were I should know what to do, but until I have one it is impossible for me to act."

He (Lord Denbigh) thought such information would cause his political friends to consider whether they had not made a mistake in ignoring the good offices of the Pope—especially when one of the wisest men in Europe, Prince Bismarck, had sought his aid. Bismarck found he had put his foot into a hole, but wanted to draw it out. He accordingly sent an agent to the Pope, and he was now reconciled, and had extricated himself from his difficulties. Lord Denbigh thought that a similar expedient was very likely the key to the whole question with regard to Ireland. He was at Rome that winter and had frequent interviews with the Pope, and found that His Holiness was ignorant of what was going on in Ireland. He had no means of knowing except through the Irish themselves, and consequently he knew nothing about boycotting and outrage in Ireland. There was no doubt the Pope had a world-wide power, and he could help them in a way no one else could help them, and he (Lord Denbigh) wanted the Government to consider whether something ought not to be done to remedy the state of things in Ireland.

Archbishop Walsh, in a public speech delivered in Dublin, on November 14, 1886, made pointed reference to Lord Denbigh's pronouncement :

The union of faith and patriotism here in Ireland is due in great measure to the unswerving loyalty with which the Irish people clung to the centre of Catholicity—the Holy See of Rome. That fidelity you have preserved without a rupture or a flaw, despite those enemies of our nation, if not of our faith, who have not scrupled, sometimes by bold unblushing statements, sometimes by the cunning of a crafty insinuation, to sow in your minds the seeds of suspicion, and

hus to sap your love of and confidence in the Holy See.
n speaking to you thus I have especially in mind a speech
r statement delivered not many days ago by a certain
prominent English nobleman, one of our own faith. In it
he managed to convey, though he did not dare openly to
assert, that the influence of the Holy See could now be
ecured for the advancement of English interests in Ireland
cries of " never"). I am glad to hear that confident cry,
or, believe me, it can never be secured for any effort to
rush out the constitutional movement in which you are
ngaged for the restoration of our native legislature. The
nobleman to whom I refer seems to have conveyed to his
hearers that the feeling of the Holy See is adverse to this
national movement, and that the influence, if not the
authority of the Sovereign Pontiff may soon be exercised, at
he suggestion of an English ministry, to withdraw from all
urther expression of sympathy with that movement myself
nd other prominent ecclesiastics.

The Holy See does not condescend to contradict such
ctions, but it is well that I should not let them pass without
otice.

Some weeks later, January 5, 1887, the *Daily News*
ublished from its Roman correspondent a statement made
n the authority of an " eminent English member of the
Roman Catholic Church" that the Pope had written to the
Archbishops of Cashel and Dublin not to support Mr. Par-
ell, but his injunctions were disregarded." The Archbishop
rote to the *Daily News* : " The statement thus made is in
he most unqualified sense of the words an absolutely
nfounded falsehood."

During the early months of 1887 rumours were being
onstantly bruited concerning the re-establishment of
iplomatic relations between England and the Vatican, the
ostility of the Holy See to Irish Home Rule, and mysterious
issions from the Pope to the Archbishops of Cashel and
ublin, rebuking them for their action in identifying them-
lves with the Home Rule Party. Numbers of Catholics,
pecially in England, had come to believe that Home Rule
r Ireland would be inimical to the interests of the Catholic

Church in Great Britain, and that consequently all good
Catholics were bound to oppose it. Such views had been
freely put forward by Catholic Tory candidates at the
parliamentary elections held after the defeat of Home Rule.
The *Tablet* was in some degree responsible for insinuating
these views; at least this was the belief of Archbishop Walsh,
and with a view to neutralising the influence of the *Tablet*
he had published in the *Pall Mall Gazette* (April 4, 1887) an
interview in which he dealt with the question of the opposition of English Catholics to the political aspirations of the
Irish people.

ARCHBISHOP WALSH : Great allowance must be for
the Catholic body in England who are so systematically kept
in the dark as to many facts of the utmost importance
bearing upon our present Irish movement.

QUESTION : Do you mean to say that the *Tablet*, the
organ of the Catholics in England, actually deprives its
readers of the benefit of such information as your Grace
now refers to ?

A. : Yes. Its policy on this point is one of most deliberate
misrepresentation, effected by means of wholesale suppression of the truth. I regard the *Tablet* as in this way
responsible for practically all the soreness of feeling that
now exists to so large an extent between the Catholics of
the two countries. I do not condemn the action of the
English Catholics as a body. They see on the very front
page of the *Tablet* as it comes to them a quotation from a
letter written years ago by Pius IX to the editor of the
Tablet, approving of the lines taken by that paper and
exhorting and encouraging him to persevere in it. I ought
to mention that the words addressed to the *Tablet* by
Pius IX—*Dum vobis gratulamur animos etiam addimus ut
in inceptis vestris constanter maneatis*—had no reference
whatever to the politics of the paper ; they referred simply
and solely to its action on a purely ecclesiastical matter.
People of confused habits of thought may have come to the
conclusion that the *Tablet* is a sort of semi-official organ of
the Holy See. This bubble would very speedily burst if the
Tablet had the honesty to put its readers in possession, for
instance, of the articles which form so prominent a feature
of the editorial columns of the *Moniteur de Rome*. The

Moniteur is not an organ of the Vatican—but it is a newspaper in which the Holy Father is known to take a strong personal interest. The *Moniteur* is in strong sympathy with our Irish cause. It has endorsed the Home Rule policy. It has condemned most emphatically Lord Salisbury's coercion policy. The *Moniteur* as an influential organ of opinion in the highest ecclesiastical circles in Rome is ignored by the editorial management of the *Tablet*. Thus a gross deception is practised upon those readers who are simple-minded enough to regard the *Tablet* as a newspaper conducted on Catholic principles, and therefore fairly and fully representative of Catholic views.

Q. : Is it your Grace's view that the Roman feeling, if I may use the expression, is rather favourable than otherwise to the cause of Home Rule? It has been most circumstantially stated that the very contrary is the fact, and that your Grace has been made aware of this by certain communications from the Holy See itself?

A. : In all the statements which you refer to, there is not one particle of truth. When, some time ago, I contradicted the statement to this effect which was published in the *Daily News*, a certain Roman correspondent reiterated the statement saying that the statement referred to " came to me, not from His Holiness personally, but from Cardinal Simeoni or from some other high official." The fact, of course, is, that there was no such communication.

Q. : It has been stated, too, that certain instructions were sent to your Grace for the guidance of the Irish clergy as regards their interference in political matters.

A. : Yes. And it has been furthermore stated that those " instructions," although they were intended to be communicated to the clergy, had been suppressed by me. The statement is untrue and wholly groundless. The case of Ireland is thoroughly understood, and therefore thoroughly safe, in Rome.

In what I have been saying about the *Tablet*, I have been animated by no personal feeling. The *Tablet* has indeed treated me with every consideration that courtesy and kindly feeling could suggest.

Q. : What about the establishing of diplomatic relations between England and the Vatican?

A. : I do not propose to discuss that matter in detail, but I am able to state with the very highest authority that, if any such relations should be established, such a step will not be taken at all events during the pontificate of Leo XIII without provision of the most effective kind being made to safeguard the interests of Ireland from any English interference at the Holy See.

The *Pall Mall*, when publishing the " interview," stated editorially that their representative in Ireland was assured by the Archbishop of Cashel that his views were identical with those of Dr. Walsh.

Dr. Croke wrote to Dr. Walsh on the day that the interview was published, April 4, 1887 : " The ' interview' is excellent. It will do a great deal of good." And he added, with gleesome satisfaction : "The *Tablet* gets its tea anyhow." Dr. Logue, the recently appointed Coadjutor to the Archbishop of Armagh, wrote, April 12, 1887 : " I am delighted to find your Grace administering to the *Tablet* a castigation which it richly deserves."

The *Tablet* in its issue of April 9, 1887, replied to Dr. Walsh's onslaught. After stating that if the words applied to the *Tablet* by the Archbishop had been used by a layman, a publicist, or a politician, " we should have known how to deal with him, and certainly our reply would have been very simple and very straight," and having recounted how, notwithstanding its own hostility to Gladstone's Home Rule Bill, it had invited leading Catholic supporters and opponents of the Bill to express their views in its pages, the *Tablet* gave its readers its estimate of the *Moniteur de Rome* :

We know that it is a journal that usually has very trustworthy information upon Catholic and local matters. We are also aware that at intervals the views shared by the very active and patriotic colony of Irishmen in Rome have found expression in its columns. About the last thing that would have occurred to us would be to have regarded these somewhat crude compositions as due directly or indirectly to the inspiration of the Holy See.

Immediately on the publication of the *Tablet* article which was telegraphed to Dublin, the Archbishop replied

April 8, 1887. He repeated the charge of misrepresentation by suppression of truth, and even widened his former statement by adding the charge of " misrepresentation made by statement of that which is not true." "The *Tablet* says that I have ' told' the ' tale' that it has tried to stifle and gag every opponent . . . I made no such statement. I neither said nor implied anything like what it conveys. I must now charge the *Tablet* with an attempt to bring me into disrepute with English readers by telling of me a ' tale' that is simply not true."

The Archbishop went on to heap contumely on the *Tablet* for its " imbecile pleading in defence which is out of place in any article addressed to readers of ordinary intelligence, prefaced though it may be by the appeal *ad misericordiam* that ' we will meet this accusation with what defence we may.' The *Tablet*, a Tory anti-Home Rule organ, sailing under the figurehead of an extract from a Papal letter, and persistently assailing Home Rule so as to imply that it may be at variance with Catholic interests, is charged with keeping back certain important facts . . . Its defence is that neither the *Weekly Register* nor the *Nation* is any better. Is the *Tablet* serious? Does it mean to say that either the *Nation* or the *Weekly Register* may be fairly charged with dishonest concealment of facts tending to advance Home Rule?"

The proprietor of the *Tablet*, Dr. Herbert Vaughan, Bishop of Salford, wrote to Dr. Walsh, Easter Sunday, April 10, 1887 :

I have read your Grace's words—may I say savage words —in this week's *Tablet*.

I cannot but think it a little unkind of you not to have called my attention to the articles of the *Moniteur*, to which you attach so much importance. You had so frequently— and so kindly—in the past told me of matters which you thought it important to print in the *Tablet*, and I had always so gladly tried to meet your wishes that I am unable to account for the change. I do not attach so much importance to the *Moniteur* as your Grace does. But it is a pity if we cannot differ on matters of opinion without the danger of being considered dishonest.

I should only be too glad to get a fair statement of views or facts which you think should be put before the Catholics of England, and if you write such a statement yourself it shall have every prominence.

What I now say I have always felt. These debatable questions should be heard on both sides.

However, let me end by wishing you all *gaudia paschalia.*

CARDINAL MANNING TO ARCHBISHOP WALSH.

April 5, 1887.

I read the report in the *Pall Mall* with great interest. You have, I believe, rightly estimated the feelings of the English people. They have been blinded and misled by a false tradition; but now for fifty years they have seen and known, and grown familiar with and fearless of, the Catholic Church, and they have so much in common with the people of Ireland that they are in good-will towards it.

What I add is for you and the Archbishop of Cashel.

On Sunday [Palm Sunday, April 3] I wrote to the Holy Father, and I translated the chief parts of Sir Redvers Buller's evidence [before the Cowper Commission]. Moreover, I said that half the Irish bishops had been invited to Rome, but that the other half, including the Archbishops of Cashel and Dublin, remained to be invited, and that the Irish people, as once before, would feel great confidence in such a representation of their State.

WALSH TO MANNING.

April 12, 1887.

From information that has come to me from Rome I can assure your Eminence that misrepresentation is strongly in the ascendant there. More than this I am bound in the circumstances not to mention to *anyone*. Even this I can only mention in the strictest confidence.

MANNING TO WALSH.

April 13, 1887.

You will have seen Reuter's telegram about the Irish bishops (being invited to Rome). What does it all mean If anything! I hope you will go again; if not, we shall all be misrepresented. But so it must be.

Again, on the following day, April 14, 1887, Manning wrote :

Does the misrepresentation affect Ireland? The Bishop of Richmond in a letter just received tells me that the *Moniteur* published my letter (on Ireland) without opposition or animus. But it must displease some people. I am all the more anxious that the remaining number of the Irish bishops should go to Rome. It is the only sure way to exclude officious persons.

About the same time the Earl of Ashburnham wrote to Dr. Walsh :

I write on behalf of a number of English Catholics favourable to the Irish national cause, to consult you as to the advisability of our taking some steps to counteract certain efforts which we believe to have been made at Rome to persuade the Sovereign Pontiff that English Catholic opinion is unanimously on the other side.

Dr. Kirby, Rector of the Irish College, Rome, wrote to Dr. Walsh, May 7, 1887 :

I related to Cardinal Simeoni the advanced state in which you had succeeded in putting the Training Schools question, commencing with Sir. M. Hicks-Beach. This was most grateful news to His Eminence.

Let us hope that Divine Providence will guide your Grace and the other prelates in the remaining steps which the interests of education require to be made. I do not think you need fear anything from English influence here in thwarting your exertions in that direction, or giving Lord Salisbury any pretext for any retrograde move on his part, supposing him to have ever had any intentions on the subject.

On Ascension Thursday, May 19, 1887, the *Daily Chronicle* published from its Roman correspondent a statement to the effect that a Memoir on the Irish question, entitled " Ireland as it is," " has just been drawn up by the Irish College in Rome ; that the Memoir goes straight against the Parnellite Party, and hails with joy the passing of the

Crimes Act. In the Memoir, the connection is clearly traced between Parnellism and crime, and the Holy Father is informed from a source of unquestioned and unquestionable sympathy with the cause of constitutional freedom in Ireland, that the present national movement deserves the reprobation of every honest and law-abiding man." The correspondent informed his employers in London that he had seen an actual copy of the document.

Dr. Walsh immediately (May 19, 1887) wrote to the Rector of the Irish College drawing attention to the statement, and asking for information. Dr. Kirby replied by telegram. It so chanced that the telegram arrived on the morning of Monday, May 23, when Dr. Walsh was about to visit Carlow to make a public statement there. He availed himself of the occasion to expose the calumny by reading for his hearers the telegram handed in at Rome at 10 a.m., May 23, 1887. It read as follows :—"The Memoir attributed by *Daily Chronicle* to Irish College is entirely and absolutely false.—Archbishop Kirby." Archbishop Walsh added that although it was his invariable custom to take no notice of any statement, however slanderous, which affected only himself personally, he felt it incumbent upon him to expose the falsehoods to which he was then referring, " inasmuch as their unchecked circulation might give success to the unprincipled tactics of those opponents of your cause, who seek by means of them to drag down our Holy Father the Sovereign Pontiff from his exalted office, irreverently exhibiting him in the rôle of a political partisan by insinuating, nay, by openly stating that your peaceful, constitutional political organisation has fallen under the condemnation of the Holy See."

Reuter's Roman agent also published a formal denial of the statement attributing the authorship of the Memoir to the Irish College.

On the same day (May 23, 1887) Dr. Kirby wrote to Dr. Walsh :—

I am sure you have before now (7 p.m.) received my telegram of this morning declaring the statement of the *Daily Chronicle* a falsehood. Concocters of absurd fables should not put forward such nonsense which, they could not but see if they reflected for a moment, would drag on them the shame of immediate exposure. For the rest, we should not much disquiet ourselves about such things, but after doing our own part rely on the protecting hand of Divine Providence on our humblest efforts for His cause, and say with confidence : " *Libera me, Domine, a labiis iniquis et a verbo mendacii.*"

Towards the end of May, 1887, an English Tory Member of Parliament, speaking to an audience of political sympathisers, told them that although the official voice of the Catholic Church in Ireland—the voice of the bishops— was on the side of lawlessness (that is, of the National League), a number of Irish Catholic laymen were banding themselves together " to free their Church from this stigma," by making a public protest against the attitude of the hierarchy on the national question. " Lord Emly," he said, " formerly a member of Mr. Gladstone's Government, and the poet, theologian, philosopher and politician, Aubrey de Vere, are taking action in this matter."

The action of the Irish Catholic laymen mentioned came about in this manner. The English Catholic Tories, headed by the Duke of Norfolk, having failed to move the Vatican to proceed against the Irish bishops, decided to approach Cardinal Newman to get his signature to a memorial of protest to the Holy See. Newman refused to allow his name to be used in the manner suggested. The memorialists also asked for the co-operation of the English Catholic bishops. But they were informed that an English memorial on the proceedings of the Irish bishops would not be well received at Rome; that such a memorial would come with better grace from Irishmen. It was then that the Emlys and the De Veres were drawn into the movement.

Throughout all this intriguing, Cardinal Manning showed

himself an invaluable friend to the Archbishops of Dublin and Cashel, and to Ireland. Dr. Walsh wrote privately to a journalist friend on April 4, 1887 : " Don't fail to pay a strong tribute to Cardinal Manning. We never can make him a suitable return for what he has done, and is doing, to help on the Irish cause."

From the beginning of Dr. Walsh's episcopate the relations between himself and Manning were based on terms of mutual confidence and great frankness. The Cardinal had outlined his attitude towards the Irish Question in a letter dated December 28, 1885 :

I feel that your Grace's position in Ireland, and, I may say, my own in England, make it to be of no light moment that you and I should be open to one another. With this motive I will say at once that I know of no one who desires to subordinate the Irish movement to English education.

I know of two bishops who have advised us to unite with the Irish members with the view of co-operation. The one is the Bishop of Meath (Dr. Nulty); the other is the Bishop of Nottingham (Dr. Bagshawe). The latter made this proposal in the summer of last year. I opposed it, and am of opinion that the Catholic Church cannot unite itself with any party.

The Holy See refuses all political alliances, holding itself absolutely independent. And so ought every episcopate to maintain itself independent of all parties as such. For this reason, at Easter last I proposed the appointment of a Committee of Bishops, at the first meeting of which we had the pleasure and help of your presence. For this reason I was thankful to hear you say that the episcopate of Ireland had appointed a committee of twelve to communicate, as they saw fit, with the Irish members. It seems to me that we are acting on the same lines.

And you may rely on me for refusing to subordinate the Irish movement to any English question, as I believe you would refuse to subordinate the Irish movement to your own Education. I know that I labour under the "*peccatum originis*," but if you can trust me, and you seem to say so, let us lay aside all mistrust, for if you and I are of one mind we may better serve Ireland and the Church than if we were doubtful of each other.

As to the newspapers, I read with indignation only less than yours the language of most of them.

And I know how I stand almost alone in my judgment about Ireland among the old Catholic families. It was so in O'Connell's time; it will be so till this question is passed away. But if this divides us it weakens us; and if we should be weakened the faith and souls will suffer both with you and with us.

I am glad you have written to the Bishop of Salford (Dr. Herbert Vaughan), for I suppose your words in some degree include the *Tablet*.

Let me ask you always to let me know what you find amiss in it. I will always do, as I have always done, my best to correct it.

I have written, my dear Lord, *aperto corde*—for I have no hidden thoughts.

Manning wrote to Walsh, May 8, 1887 :

I should like to hear more of the anxiety you had about Rome. You will see perhaps some action of a handful of English Catholics. Don't notice it. They, both in numbers and influence, are powerless.

And again, June 1, 1887 :

I hope you and Monsignor Kirby are active in Rome, for there are mischief-makers abroad. Have you seen a paper in English and Italian which has come to me from Rome ?

Our handful of English Catholics are also busy here. It is the hour and power of darkness just now.

WALSH TO MANNING.

June 2, 1887.

I can well understand your Eminence's anxiety. As for me, I am not taking action of any kind in reference to the present unhappy proceedings in Rome. If, as there seems but too much reason to fear, the Holy Father is in imminent danger of being led into a grave mistake, I must take care to keep myself clear of all share in the terrible responsibility that will be incurred by all who may have a share in the transaction.

So far I have not been consulted in any way. If I were to offer advice or express an opinion, unsolicited, I might afterwards have to reproach myself that the cause had suffered from the unskilfulness of its advocate. If my advice or opinion were asked, I should do my best, and thus should feel that I was clear of all responsibility in the matter. I could not feel that freedom from responsibility if I had volunteered my advice.

I cannot indeed believe that the Holy Father will act without some previous reference to us in Ireland. I have it from his own lips that he knows he was deceived before.

If my opinion is asked, I will at once reply requesting permission to confer with the other Archbishops and with the newly-appointed coadjutor to the Primate (Dr. Logue). I can answer for it that we may be counted upon to act in solid unity. Even if a bad mistake be made, I have no fear as to any substantial harm of a permanent kind coming from it. Things, please God, will right themselves, as tney did after the Parnell Circular*. I have seen the famous " Memoir" (Ireland as it is).

WALSH TO MANNING.

June 3, 1887.

My letter [referred to in an enclosure sent to the Cardinal] was an ordinary one thanking Dr. Kirby for having enabled me to contradict the *Daily Chronicle* statement about the Irish College.

---

* The following is the text of the Instruction prohibiting clerics from contributing to the Parnell Testimonial Fund. The Instruction was sent to each of the Irish bishops, May 11, 1883 :

" Quidquid sit de persona Parnellii eiusque consiliis, exploratum tamen est plures ex illius asseclis eam agendi rationem in multis casibus adhibuisse quae plane abhorret ab iis quae Summus Pontifex in suis ad Cardinalem Archiepiscopum Dublinensem literis enunciavit, quaeque in instructionibus huius S. Congregationis ab Hiberniae Episcopis in nuperrimo Dublinensi conventu unanimiter receptis continentur. Enimvero iuxta haec praescripta *fas est Hibernos fortunae suae afflictae levationem quaerere, fas est pro iure suo contendere*. Servandum tamen semper divinum illud praeceptum, *quaeri primum oportere regnum Dei et iustitiam eius; turpe autem esse causam quamvis iustam tueri non iuste*. Porro Cleri *totius et maxime Episcoporum est incitatos multitudinis animos temperare et ad iustitiam necessariamque in omnibus rebus moderationem tempestivis hortationibus revocare, ne vehementiori cupiditate ducti emolumenta rerum fallacibus iudiciis videant, aut spem publicae felicitatis in dedecore flagitiorum ponant*.

" Hinc sequitur nemini clericorum licere ab his regulis deflectere, nec iis motibus, qui prudentiae et studio placandorum animorum minime conveniunt sese immiscere, aut illis provehendis dare operam. Haud certe vetitum est pecunias ad conditionem Hibernorum levandam conferre; verumtamen ex

In reply, Manning wrote, June 4, 1887 :—

Both your letters have given me a sensible relief. The *Times* to-day contradicts the rumours that the Duke of Norfolk has been treating with the Pope about Diplomatic Relations. So far, well; but there are others at work. The Duke wrote to me some time ago and said : " The Pope sees that your views and mine about Ireland do not agree, and I am sorry to say that he trusts yours rather than mine."

Monsignor Kirby is right—we shall save the faith in Ireland and in England as the Apostles spread it in the world, without the world and against the world. Any contact with the world would leave a stain and paralyse our strength. The more the bishops of Ireland vindicate the law of God against English and Irish wrong-doers, the stronger we shall be.

I hope the Archbishop of Cashel will hold his hand on Michael Davitt.

Dr. Kirby to Archbishop Walsh, June 17, 1887 :

Yesterday I had the honour of an audience with His Holiness, and I took with me the famous document

praedictis mandatis Apostolicis eae collectae omnino reprobandae sunt quae proclamantur ad cupiditates populi inflammandas, ut iis facile homines abuti queant ad turbulenta consilia contra leges ineunda. Potissimum vero ab iis abstinendum, cum haud obscure patet exinde odia excitari, convicia in viros spectatos congeri, neque crimina ac caedes quibus flagitiosi homines sese polluerunt ullimode reprobari; maxime sicubi asseratur mensuram veri in patriam amoris ex conlata vel denegata pecunia aestimari, quo fit ut quadam veluti vi ac metu adigi ad haec homines videantur.

" Quibus positis compertum Amplitudini tuae esse debet, eam pecuniae collectam quae *Parnell Testimonial Fund* audit, ab hac Sacra Congregatione non posse probari, nec proinde ecclesiasticis viris, maxime vero Episcopis licere eam ullo modo commendare vel promovere.

" Interea precor Deum uti Amplitudinem tuam diutissime sospitet.

" Datum Romae ex Aed. S.C. de Propda. Fide, die 11 Maii, 1883.

" JOANNES CARD. SIMEONI,
Praefectus.
" D. ARCHIEP. TYREN.
Secretarius.

" Emo ac Rmo Dno Cardinali McCabe,
   Archiepiscopo Dublinensi."

(D 700)   K 2

("Ireland as it is") against the Irish movement, with some written observations of mine to confute, as well as I could, its false statements. Of what I had written I gave a verbal summary, which His Holiness was pleased to listen to with much attention. I also brought to him your most useful collection of the charges made by the judges at the late Assizes, with a brief analysis showing that of 39 judicial charges thirty-two proved the favourable state of the respective districts whilst only seven were of a contrary nature. His Holiness showed a great interest in all the case.

He spoke to me about the Queen's Jubilee, and said, notwithstanding the present hostile attitude of the English Ministry towards Ireland, it would be becoming if something were done in Ireland complimentary to the *Queen personally* on the occasion, as she represented the principle of authority which comes from God, and "as she is a woman." It would look well, he said, making such an act of respect as a personal act of respect towards herself, prescinding from all political considerations. But His Holiness did *not* give these observations any form of *command*, nor did he charge me to communicate them so to your Grace. But if your Grace and even our good friend of Cashel would see your way to do anything in that line, as of your own accord, I think it would be most useful and would make our cause stronger, as indicative of that generous spirit of Christian forgiveness and charity which has always happily animated the Irish Catholic heart. A few words, spoken or written, showing the Catholic spirit of charity which dictated the act, would probably be appreciated by our people so proverbially Catholic and generous. But your Grace doubtless understands these things better than I do.

I think you should write to Propaganda often during these times. They receive "whole files" of accusations against us, and not a word scarcely coming to them directly from the episcopal body in our defence. Collective letters from the episcopacy at periodical occasions do not, I think, produce the desired effect, as they are not followed up by private, frequent, confidential communications. Here the authorities are most anxious to receive information favourable to us. So write often and confidentially, and make Cashel and Tuam and Dr. Logue do the same. *Se la campana non suona, nessuno andrà alla Messa.*

As the year 1886 was drawing to a close, political excitement ran high in Ireland. The "Plan of Campaign" was being operated with determination. Counter-operations of eviction were carried out on a widespread scale. Public men and leading Members of Parliament were arrested and tried before carefully packed juries. The law officers of the Crown conducted many of these prosecutions; but the director-in-chief of the packing of juries was Mr. Serjeant O'Brien. The services of this gentleman were richly and rapidly rewarded. He was promoted Solicitor-General, Attorney-General, and finally Lord Chief Justice of Ireland. Later he was created a baronet, and ultimately a peer of the United Kingdom, taking the euphonious title of Baron of Kilfenora in the County of Clare. But throughout all his promotions and changes of title he was popularly though not affectionately known as "Peter the Packer"—a nickname which he had earned for himself by his systematic and artful methods of packing juries. William O'Brien, speaking almost prophetically, once said of his notorious namesake that by the discreditable legal practices of his earlier years "Lord O'Brien of Kilfenora has earned for himself a title more enduring than his peerage."

The first glaring instance of jury-packing under the new Government occurred at the Sligo Assizes, December 1886. Amongst the prisoners to be tried were certain persons charged with complicity in resisting evictions which had taken place at Woodford, Co. Galway, in the previous August. In preparing the jury panel the law had been flagrantly violated, but the presiding judge, Chief Baron Palles, stated that the law allowed him no discretion as to the panel. He added, however, that if he had any discretion he would quash the panel, owing to the irregularities that had been proved. The Chief Baron made no concealment of his decided opinion that to proceed with the trials with such a panel would result in a miscarriage of justice. Yet, in the face of all this, Serjeant O'Brien persisted in prosecuting the trials. Archbishop Walsh, speaking publicly of the Sligo jury-packing said, December 6, 1886 :

The Catholics in Sligo outnumber the Protestants by nine to one, yet the Protestants are in an actual majority on the panel. The irregularity in the panel was proved in court. It was admitted by the sub-sheriff, the responsible officer. It was proclaimed from the Bench by the judge. It was presented as their finding by the " triers." Yet the panel has not been quashed, the Assizes are to proceed, and the prisoners are to be tried by jurors selected out of a panel which has not been prepared in accordance with any Act in the Statute-book. Such is the anomalous state of the law which is powerless to check the ill-advised persistence of the Crown in the Sligo persecutions. The hands of the judge were practically tied though he has stated that " the panel returned is a different panel from the one that would have been returned if the law had been complied with." The Crown, and the Crown alone, that is to say, the Government, can interfere with effect. On the Government, then, must be the responsibility of all the bitterness of feeling that must come of the continuance of those judicial proceedings now poisoned at their very source.

For his reference to the Sligo jury-packing, the *Dublin Daily Express* clamoured that proceedings should be instituted against the Archbishop for contempt of court. He was, however, unperturbed.

The comment of the *Tablet* on the jury-packing methods was very apposite : " It is attempts to administer the law in this fashion which makes the Irish people regard law as usually equivalent to injustice, and Crown prosecutors as persecutors and oppressors."

A couple of months after the Sligo Assizes, John Dillon and other leading Nationalists were put on their trial at Green Street, Dublin, charged with resisting the law. Again a packed jury was empanelled to try the "traversers" —the accused—whose plea in defence was a denial of the facts alleged by the Crown. Catholics who were entitled to be on the jury panel had been systematically and shamelessly excluded. Serjeant Peter O'Brien, however, found his task of securing a conviction by hook or by crook facilitated by the compliance of the judge—one Judge Boyd—of whose legal attainments the least disparaging thing to be said is that they did not compare favourably with those of Chief Baron Palles. About the middle of February 1887 a Defence Fund for the " traversers" was opened by the editor of the *Freeman's Journal*, Ed. D. Gray. The list of subscribers was headed by Archbishop Walsh, who took advantage of the occasion to make a further protest against the methods of Serjeant O'Brien.

I should gladly co-operate (he wrote) in any way in my power in an effort to secure, if it were possible, a fair trial for the traversers. But in the present instance a fair trial is impossible. The first essential element of fairness—a fairly empanelled jury is wanting. The jury before which John Dillon and his fellow-traversers are arraigned in Green Street has not been fairly empanelled. It has been most unfairly packed.

And as this most recent instance of jury-packing has been effected by the wholesale exclusion of Catholic jurors of the County Dublin, I send this subscription to the fund, not merely as a mark of sympathy with the traversers, but as a protest, which, as Archbishop of Dublin, I feel it my duty to make against the gross insult that has thus been inflicted on many upright, conscientious members of my flock.*

But Dr. Walsh's protest was a mild remonstrance compared with a fierce indictment of the responsible Government by Dr. Croke which appeared in the issue of the *Freeman* of the following day. The Archbishop of Cashel wrote :

I enclose £10 towards the Defence Fund. But when is this style of business going to cease? I opposed the " No Rent Manifesto" six years ago, because, apart from other reasons, I thought it was inopportune, and not likely to be generally acted on. Had a manifesto against paying taxes been issued at the time I should certainly have supported

* *Freeman's Journal,* February 16, 1887.

it *on principle*. I am in precisely the same frame of mind just now.

Our line of action, as a people, appears to me to be in this respect both suicidal and inconsistent. We pay taxes to a Government that uses them, not for the public good and in accordance with the declared wishes of the taxpayers, but in direct and deliberate opposition to them. We thus supply a stick to beat ourselves. We put a whip into the hands of men who use it to lash and lacerate us. This is suicidal.

In the presence of the actual state of things in Ireland just now, it is inconsistent besides. We run the " Plan of Campaign" against bad landlords, and stop what we call their rent; and we make no move whatever against the Government that pays " horse, foot, and dragoons " for protecting them and enforcing their outrageous exactions. Our money goes to fee and feed a gang of needy and voracious lawyers; to purchase bludgeons for policemen, to be used in smashing the skulls of our people; and generally for the support of a foreign garrison, or native slaves, who hate and despise everything Irish and every genuine Irishman.

The policeman is pampered and paid, the patriot is persecuted. Our enforced taxes go to sustain the one—we must further freely tax ourselves to defend the other. How long, I ask, is this to be tolerated?

The tone and tenor of the letter aroused a storm of wrath among the enemies of the Nationalist Party, who construed its terms as a deliberate incitement to revolutionary action; and it caused no small apprehension to the friends of the Archbishop, who feared for the effect it might produce at Rome. In England it created a furore. The *Saturday Review* and other prints worked themselves into paroxysms of fury. The English colony at Rome denounced him to the Vatican, Cardinal Howard, the Duke of Norfolk's kinsman, being particularly clamant in his " petitionary vehemence" that the Holy See should administer a public rebuke to the Archbishop of Cashel. By the ecclesiastical authorities at Rome, the Archbishop's action was regarded with extreme displeasure, as compromising the Holy See and the Irish hierarchy in a policy of violence; and the Tory faction confidently looked for a public reprimand for the unruly prelate. None, however, came.

The Rector of the Irish College at Rome, Dr. Kirby, Archbishop of Ephesus, wrote anxiously to Dr. Walsh, March 2, 1887 :

The authorities are intensely grieved and displeased at the letter recently written by Dr. Croke recommending or suggesting the non-payment of taxes. The impression produced by it here is exceedingly bitter, as such things, they seem to fear, coming from an archbishop, embarrass and compromise in some way the Catholic Hierarchy and the Holy See itself. I think it would be most useful if your Grace wrote a good letter to Cardinal Simeoni giving him an account of the state of things in Ireland and stating what you think may be proper and opportune regarding the letter of Dr. Croke, as I fear our good English friends may be tempted to press forward their own views on the subject.

The present moment seems critical both in Ireland and here with regard to our Irish affairs. But we must not despond. By prayer and patience and the prudent use of the legitimate means in our power, we may hope for better times.

I sincerely trust and pray that our Divine Lord and His Blessed Mother will firmly sustain your Grace, so as always to do the right thing and say the right thing—the *verbum sanum et irreprehensibile, ut ii qui ex adverso sunt nihil habeant malum dicere de nobis.*

During these anxious days the two Archbishops had in Dr. Kirby a friend of mark and influence. Archbishop Kirby had known Leo XIII from the days when they had both studied theology together at Rome. When Leo became Pope, he promoted Dr. Kirby to a titular bishopric, the See of Lita *in partibus infidelium,* and later on to the Archbishopric of Ephesus, one of the most highly prized of the titular archbishoprics. Dr. Kirby had spent nearly all of his life in Rome, engaged in the administration of the Irish College, where he had been Rector since Dr. Cullen's promotion to the archbishopric of Armagh in 1850. For more than forty years before his death he had not been to Ireland. He enjoyed to a remarkable degree the friendship and confidence of Pope Leo, to whom, and to the Holy See, he was devotedly attached.

Dr. Kirby was then (1887) a very old man; *trisaeclisenex*, he was the survivor of three generations of men. Towards Dr. Walsh the old man's attitude was uniformly friendly; towards Dr. Croke his tone and attitude were fatherly. For Dr. Kirby had had much to do with the moulding of Thomas Croke's character when, as a student of the Irish college in the early forties of the nineteenth century, Croke brought credit to his Alma Mater, and won the unstinted encomiums of the celebrated Father Passaglia* who presented him to Gregory XVI, commending him to the Pope as his favourite and most brilliant disciple.

Immediately after Dr. Croke's letter of February 17 had appeared in the *Freeman's Journal*, Dr. Kirby wrote to him in terms of mild remonstrance, deprecating his impetuosity, counselling prudence and circumspection, and enforcing his admonitions with passages of Scripture, of which he had an apt and ready command. It was the last time that " Ephesus" adopted that tone in writing to the Archbishop of Cashel. The gentle admonition of his kindly old friend had no other effect than to irritate the overwrought feelings of Dr. Croke, whom we find writing to Archbishop Walsh, March 9, 1887 :

I had a letter from Ephesus of a most dolorous, and indeed, offensive kind. He wrote to me as if I were still a student in the Irish College, Rome. But I retorted in a style that must, I'm sure, have astonished him.

The fact of the matter is that Archbishop Croke was at the time in indifferent health, and the attacks made upon him in England and at Rome were causing him considerable

---

* Fr. Carlo Passaglia (1812-67) was a famous professor of theology at the Gregorian University, Rome.

annoyance. To Dr. Walsh he had written, February 23, 1887 :

I am to be before " the House," it appears, to-morrow. The Killybegs man* has a question down for that day anent my letter to the *Freeman* of some days past.

I am getting a dreadful mauling about it in the English papers. Next *Saturday Review* will hit hard. And, of course, in due time, my Roman friends will interrogate me. 'Tis hard to know what to do. Perhaps the best thing to do is to do nothing but wait upon events.

CROKE TO WALSH.

February 27, 1887 :

I have got and read your pastoral letter. It is very good. One would imagine you were at such things all your life. As regards the Education Question in all its branches, it is almost exhaustive. It is a trifle too long, but, having regard to the weight and variety of the topics treated, it could hardly be much shorter.

I am suffering dreadfully, and have been for some time, from headache and sleeplessness. In fact, I am quite beaten up ; and the uncertainties of the moment are not calculated to soothe or strengthen me.

For both Archbishops these were anxious days. They were saddened and depressed by the hardships of their people. They were attacked and maligned in the Press at home and in England, and hostile influences were working against them at Rome. Dr. Kirby at this time was insistent in his advice to Dr. Walsh that he should write constantly to the Cardinal Prefect of Propaganda, stating his views on Irish affairs. This, however, Dr. Walsh was loth to do. He was determined to await official invitation from the Holy See before he directly intimated his views ; he was convinced that his opinions would carry greater weight if withheld until they were asked for. Meantime his views were conveyed indirectly to the Vatican by Dr. Kirby. Cardinal

---

* A famous Orange member of Parliament—William Johnston, of Ballykilbegs.

Manning also was always ready to communicate with the
Vatican at his suggestion.

For a fortnight the Archbishop of Cashel made no reply to
the sharp criticisms that were levelled against him. He
then addressed a public letter to the editor of the *Freeman's
Journal*, explanatory of his position (Monday, March 7,
1887) :

I am tempted by certain editorial remarks that appeared
in last Saturday's *Nation* (March 5) in reference to a letter
written by me and published in the *Freeman* about a fortnight ago (February 17), when sending a subscription to the
Dillon Defence Fund, to trouble you with a few lines of
explanation concerning the letter in question.

It has given rise to a good deal of talk. It has been
misunderstood by some, and wilfully misrepresented by
others. The *Nation* says that I " have been charged with
suggesting an alternative policy to the one at present achiev-
ing such success, and that the policy I propose is utterly
impracticable."

I was quite unprepared, I confess, for this interpretation
of my words, and must not allow it to pass unnoticed. I
proposed nothing. I simply expressed my individual
opinion, which I had a perfect right to do, as to the relative
value and reasonableness of a no-tax manifesto, if issued,
compared with a no-rent manifesto. That is all I said so far.
I added, it is true, that a Government expending the public
money in collecting rack-rents is far more to be blamed than
the landlords who impose them, and that it was hard to
bear with and impossible to justify such a course.

But it never entered into my head to recommend a
general uprising against the payment of taxes, however I
may deplore the use to which the present Government has
been converting them, or to suggest a policy in any way
adverse to the one so successfully pursued by the Irish
Parliamentary Party.

Of that policy I am one of the staunchest and most
strenuous supporters. I trust to constitutional agitation
alone, and have so trusted this many a long day for the
restoration of our national rights. *As we are circumstanced*,
no one, I believe, but a fool or a knave, could put his trust
in any other line of action. Not being either, as I may
venture to presume, I have not openly recommended or

covertly hinted at an alternative course ; and cannot conceive how any fair-minded person could gather from the terms of my impugned letter that I had the most distant idea of doing so.

On the same day Walsh wrote to Manning, March 9, 1887 :

Yesterday evening I sent to your Eminence a copy of the *Freeman's Journal* containing an important letter from Cashel. Would it be well for you to follow up your former letter to the Holy Father by another now, stating that the Archbishop, finding that such a construction was put upon his words, had written in the most explicit way disavowing the project of suggesting a strike against taxes, and unequivocally declaring himself in favour of constitutional means of action and of constitutional means only ?

Lord Denbigh is in Dublin. A friend of his called here yesterday to know at what time I was likely to be at home, as Lord D. wished to find me here when he calls. It is, of course, well that I should see him.

From Rome Dr. Kirby wrote to Dr. Walsh, March 18, 1887 :

We had a *triduum* in preparation for the Feast of our National Apostle, St. Patrick . . . I had an audience of His Holiness one of the days of the Triduum. He spoke to me about the affairs of Ireland. I gave him my poor views, which I confirmed by reading in Italian what your Grace wrote to me on the subject. His Holiness is much grieved that he cannot read English. At the end of the audience he told me to see Cardinal Simeoni, and to explain to him what I had mentioned to himself. I had gone to the audience with much anxiety, knowing of the bitter and galling impression which the letter of our friend of Cashel of the month of February had produced on the minds of the authorities here—an impression which the second letter of March 7, helped to assuage but by no means could wholly efface. I explained to Cardinal Simeoni the state of our case at some length, I hope with some favourable or at least some less unfavourable impression being left on his mind.

I trust and humbly pray that God may preserve your Grace, in your difficult and delicate position, from the danger of giving any pretext to our enemies to implicate you in the meshes of law proceedings.

Write now and again to Cardinal Simeoni and give him an account of current matters. His Eminence and the other authorities at Propaganda are anxiously waiting for the report or statement regarding the Education Question, which, as they say, your Grace has promised them. They have your able statement on that subject in general in your Lenten Pastoral, but they want the one which you are to send for themselves, and in which they wish you to speak on the matter freely and in confidence. They are the more anxious to have this, as others of contrary views have written to them, and are, perhaps, still writing. But they will not reply to the latter till they hear from your Grace.

Viva la fede dell' Irlanda, di Pietro, e di Patrizio !

On June 3, 1887, Reuter's Agency at Rome announced that the Pope had appointed Cardinal Rampolla to succeed Cardinal Luigi Jacobini as Pontifical Secretary of State, and that His Holiness had appointed a special delegation to bear the Papal congratulations to Queen Victoria on the occasion of her Jubilee, which was to be celebrated on June 21. Cardinal Rampolla's appointment synchronised with the vigorous prosecution of negotiations for establishing diplomatic relations between England and the Vatican. The Duke of Norfolk was Lord Salisbury's "officious" representative in these negotiations.

A few days later the Roman correspondent of the *Temps* announced that with reference to the Duke of Norfolk's negotiations at Rome for the appointment of an official representative at the Papal Court, the Vatican would have no compromise; there should be either a representative on the same footing as those of Germany and other countries, or nothing. The negotiations might therefore be considered at an end.

The *Temps* view, however, was not shared by Dr. Kirby, who wrote to Archbishop Walsh, June 18, 1887 :

His Holiness told me that he is considering the entire Irish question. So I think it would be most advisable if the bishops kept the Holy See well informed with their views well corroborated by proofs.

The re-establishment of diplomatic relations between the English Government and Rome seems most likely. If it takes place God may draw great good out of it even for our country, if we all do our duty to God and His Holy Church. For, *Si Deus pro nobis, quis contra nos*? Indeed it may be that the Pope in his own quiet way may induce the Government to secure as much or even more for Ireland than the 86 Irish members were able to obtain, and perhaps on a more safe and durable basis. I am *a priori* most unfavourable to the establishment of such relations. But if God, in the ways of His adorable providence, so dispose ... The present Pontiff seems to have a special mission from God to governments and sovereigns, and great victories for the Church and the salvation of souls may, and let us trust will, be the happy result.

On the same day on which Kirby expressed his opinion as to the progress of the Norfolk negotiations, his Excellency Monsignor Ruffo-Scilla, special envoy of the Pope for the Queen's Jubilee, arrived in London. He was met by the Duke of Norfolk, the Marquis of Ripon, and other Catholic noblemen. A week later it was publicly announced that the Queen had received a magnificent Jubilee Gift from the Pope—a copy in mosaic of Raphael's famous representation of Poetry.

The presence of the Papal envoy in England occasioned some anxiety in Ireland where it was feared that the mission had a significance prejudicial to Irish interests. These speculations soon came to an end, and a new phase of the Irish question was opened by the announcement that the Pope had appointed a special commission to visit, inquire into, and report upon the actual conditions of affairs in Ireland. The purpose and scope of the mission and the events which directly led up to it are recorded to some extent in contemporary correspondence.

Dr. Kirby to Archbishop Walsh, June 20, 1887 (Telegram) :

Authorities wish you to write full information.

—EPHESUS.

On the same day Dr. Kirby wrote :

I had a long conversation at Propaganda with the Under-Secretary, Signor Gualdi—the Prefect and Secretary being engaged in Congregation. Dr. Gualdi repeated what I had already known, that the authorities at Propaganda and of the Holy See generally are most anxious to receive information from the bishops, not only in their collective capacity but also as individual prelates. So your Grace ought not to have any hesitation or scruple on the subject. You may be sure that your letters will be always welcome.

Your Grace is already aware that two ecclesiastics are going to Ireland from Rome. It is as yet a secret. One—Archbishop Persico, and the other—Sig. Gualdi above alluded to. The motive of their being sent, as the latter has informed me is, that the Holy Father wished to remove from the minds of the Irish prelates any apprehensions that his envoy to compliment the Queen on her jubilee had anything whatever to do with Irish ecclesiastical matters (his information on which he wishes to receive from the proper source of information, the Irish prelates themselves). On that account he has deputed the two above-named ecclesiastics to go to Ireland directly as a proof of this his intention.

This will afford the bishops an occasion of making known to the envoys the true state of their respective localities, and of making them see with their own eyes the true state of the country and the religious feeling of the people, and the consequent falsehood of the calumnious reports continually spread against our country. Their communications with your Grace will be of immense utility even for further occasions.

Tell our friend in Cashel and your other episcopal friends that the cordial reception which they will give to these worthy ecclesiastics, and the information they will afford them, will, D.V., be productive of great good for Ireland.

They will leave Rome for Ireland during the course of the present week.

Since writing the above I have received a courteous invitation to attend a demonstration at the English Embassy for the Queen's Jubilee, to which I sent a reply (of refusal). Enclosed is a verbatim copy of my reply.

Last week the Rector of the Scotch College got up a *Te Deum* in his church in connection with the Queen's Jubilee. As it was merely a religious act in a Catholic Church to return Thanks to God, I went to the function. Afterwards the same Rector invited me to dinner on St. Margaret's Day. Having ascertained that he intended to propose the Queen's health at it, I sent him an apology. Now comes this invitation from the Embassy. So you see we have got ourselves into the meshes of diplomacy. What harm if some good come of it for our poor country and for the conversion of some of these Saxons.

KIRBY TO WALSH.

June 24, 1887.

The two envoys left last night for Ireland. You may soon expect them. Their mission is a new proof of the mind of His Holiness not to credit information received or forced on him through English channels. He must have it through reliable and unsuspected mediums—from the fathers and pastors of his Irish children. So we have reason to hope that what the envoys will see and hear will produce so much good as to strengthen, were it possible, the sacred union which has ever existed between the children of St. Patrick and the Chair of Peter.

KIRBY TO WALSH.

June 27, 1887.

Yours of date 21st received this morning just as I was starting for an audience of Cardinal Rampolla, Secretary of State, to which he himself had invited me.

He told me that he called me by order of His Holiness who wished me to know the spirit and terms of the Commission confided to Monsignor Persico in Ireland. He had them all written—a copy of that given to him. He read them for me from beginning to end.

The instructions stated that this mission was intended to be one of sympathy and deference to the Irish episcopacy in the troubles and afflictions in which their country was at present placed. The Cardinal called my attention to the words "*simpatia e deferenza*" as a proof of the spirit which impelled His Holiness to send this message of paternal affection to his Irish children through their sacred pastors. Monsignor Persico's mission will also enable him to ascertain from the bishops the actual state of things in their respective dioceses, and to hear their opinion on the different subjects which at present most concern the good of religion and the country, such as education, etc.

I am sure that, with the divine aid, Monsignor Persico's

visit and his own testimony to the feeling of confidence that exists throughout the country towards the Holy See, notwithstanding the persistent efforts of our enemies to render it suspect, will have most beneficial effects for the future of the country.   In fact, to increase the feeling of full confidence of his Irish children towards the Head of the Church is the main scope of the mission, as your Grace will easily understand from your interviews with Monsignor Persico, who is accompanied, as I mentioned before, by Dr. Gualdi.

I gave the Secretary of State three copies of your *Monita*, which arrived most opportunely—one for the Holy Father, another for himself and his office, and the other for his other office, that of *Affari Ecclesiastici*.   The others I will distribute to Cardinal Simeoni, and in other influential quarters.

Drop me a line after your first interview with Monsignor Persico, and give me your views and feelings thereon.

For the rest, my dear Lord, let us not fear anything. When we act with a pure intention for God's glory, and keep, as ever, well united with the Rock of Peter, we may smile at all the howling of our enemies throughout the world.

MANNING TO WALSH.

June 25, 1887.

You may like to know that Monsignor Persico and Don Enrico Gualdi are intimately known to me.   The latter was for fifteen years a priest in this diocese, and knows English well; thoroughly good and decent.

Monsignor Persico I have known for thirty-six years.   He is a Capuchin.   He was Bishop of British India; then in the United States.   He knows English well.   Thirty-six years ago he translated a book of mine which was printed at Propaganda.   He knows the English-speaking world, and I am much mistaken if his heart is not with the poor.

It all now depends upon his relations and his contacts in Ireland.   He will be (I take for granted that he will be) in immediate contact with you and the bishops.   Let him be kept in Ireland till he has seen with his own eyes the Glenbeighs and the Bodykes.*   This is the best set-off to Fr. Bellamy's pamphlet, and certain whisperers.

The selection of these two implies impartiality and a desire to know the truth.

---

* Glenbeigh in Kerry and Bodyke in Clare, where cruel evictions were being carried out.

If they come to London you may trust me to give them an outline of inquiry.

The resolution of the bishops is a strong and temperate document.

I am unable to think that some of the Irish members have helped Ireland lately in the House of Commons.

WALSH TO MANNING.

June 25, 1887.

As yet no official announcement has come, but I had yesterday a letter from Dr. Kirby to whom Mgr. Gualdi had explained the proposal of the Holy Father in sending this mission to us. It is quite in accord with the view which H.H. put so plainly to me when I was in Rome for my consecration. He knows that our only difficulty here in Ireland in reference to the re-establishing of diplomatic relations is that we should in that case be placed at the mercy of a possibly unscrupulous, and probably hostile, English representative in Rome. His view, then, as I have already told your Eminence, is that the Irish bishops should have an officially recognised representative of their own, with the recognised function of checking all statements made about us or affecting our interests.

Well, His Holiness, having now sent an envoy to England, sees that some distrust may spring up at our side of the water. He meets this by sending us an envoy to get from the Irish bishops, as the most trustworthy sources of information, the true state of things in Ireland. Monsignor Persico, as is most important, is to see as much as possible with his own eyes.

What an exposure it will be of the tactics that some have been employing against us! Coming to a country that is represented as being on the verge of anarchy and civil war, he will find himself amongst the most peaceful people in the world.

I sent to Propaganda a paper which I had compiled (a copy of which I enclose) giving the statements of the judges in their charges at the last Assizes as to the presence or absence of crime in the country. That paper has had a good effect.

I have since had translated into Italian a speech made by Mr. Harrington as chief of the organising committee of the National League in Dublin. Your Eminence may have noticed some public references of mine to the strong check which the Central League keeps on the branches throughout the country. This is an instance in point. Michael Davitt made a very imprudent speech at Bodyke, claiming his freedom to advocate any policy he liked, even within the ranks of the National organisation, in the absence of some guidance in the present crisis from the leader, Mr. Parnell. Harrington's speech introduces a most effective passage from a recent speech of Parnell's. Next day a letter came to me from South Africa, the publication of which gave me a natural opportunity of referring to the incident. My letter, with Harrington's speech introducing Parnell's words, are now in the hands of Propaganda in an Italian translation. I put to the little pamphlet the title, in inverted commas, " *L'Irlanda nella sua condizione attuale.*" My letter contains also a reference to Fr. Bellamy's calumnious pamphlet.

Your Eminence will be glad to hear that my view is accepted as to sending out from here full information on Irish affairs. I have always said I would not do it as a volunteer but I should be most happy to do so if it came to me officially that I was expected to do so. I had an opportunity of saying this again in writing the week before last. I told Dr. Kirby (who is acting as my agent) that our annual episcopal meeting was to be held on the following Wednesday (June 22), and that there was full time to communicate with me by telegraph, as I should wish, if the thing was to be done at all, that it should be done openly and above board, for which reason I should wish to speak of it at the meeting. The telegram came at once; and since then I have had a letter telling me that Monsignor Jacobini (the Secretary of Propaganda) is to see the Holy Father and then write to me an official letter. Thus, thank God, we seem to be making our ground good.

I find, however, that there is an uneasy feeling in reference to Monsignor Persico's visit.* I can only make known in a quiet way, hoping that it will spread, all that I know about the object of the mission.

As regards the action of our members—some of them—in Parliament, it seems to me unintelligible. I suppose you refer to their prolonging the discussion on the Coercion Bill. While that Bill is before the House, the Liberal-Unionists must back up the Government, and again, the Government are free of all responsibility in reference to general legisla-

* Dr. Croke had written to Walsh : *Persicos odi*, thus anticipating Fr. Healy's use of *Hor. Od.*, 1, 38.

tion, which in its progress through the House could hardly fail to exercise a disintegrating influence. I have thought this from the beginning. A strong protest should have been made, and the Bill should have been allowed to go through as it stood.

I understand that Mr. Parnell, whose illness put him completely out of working order, is of the same opinion.

What a long letter I have written.

MANNING TO WALSH.

June 27, 1887.

Your letter of this morning is a real relief to me. I was full of fear about Propaganda and Rome. They are so easily misled; and, inculpably, so unable to understand the state of Ireland. What you have done is of vital effect; I thank God for it.

When Monsignor Persico comes, let him have the report of Lord Cowper's Commission to take back to Rome.

What you say about Michael Davitt, I felt. But I can be surprised at nothing. If I had been at Bodyke I should have been far worse.

You have the Irish people in your hands, and everything, to my eyes, is towards a just and peaceful settlement. The change in this country towards Ireland is very extensive; I hope there is some change in Ireland towards us.

The visit of the envoy* here has no bearing on Ireland. You will do me real service and kindness in keeping me well informed. I sent the testimony of the judges to the Holy Father three weeks ago.

On June 27 Reuter's Agency telegraphed from Rome that " in consequence of the representations made by Cardinal Manning and Archbishop Walsh of Dublin upon the inexpediency of an intervention of the Vatican in Irish political affairs at the present moment, and the bad impression it would produce, the Pope to-day ordered the suspension of the mission to Ireland with which Monsignor Persico and Fr. Gualdi were to have been entrusted." Immediately on the publication of this telegram, Dr. Walsh

* Mgr. Ruffo-Scilla—Special envoy from the Pope to Queen Victoria on the occasion of her jubilee.

wrote a public letter in which he characterised the report as untrue, June 27, 1887 :

> I have made no such remonstrance. The statement that the " mission" has been abandoned or postponed in consequence, or partly in consequence, of a remonstrance from me is absolutely unfounded. Knowing something of the nature of the " mission" projected by the Sovereign Pontiff, and of the object which it is intended to accomplish, no thought could be farther from my mind than to offer any remonstrance on this subject.

On the same day Cardinal Manning wrote a vigorous denial in the *Times*, June 27, 1887 :

> In your leading article of this morning you express your regret that the mission of Monsignor Persico has been revoked " at the instance apparently of Cardinal Manning and Archbishop Walsh," adding, "the active promoters of Separatist intrigues are hardly the persons who should have a determining voice in the Councils of the Church."
>
> On this I have two remarks to make :
>
> 1. The word " apparently" will not clear the *Times* of the grave responsibility of sending all over the world a statement which is false. A contradiction in the name of Archbishop Walsh and in my own is to be found in the *St. James Gazette*, and in the *Pall Mall Gazette* of this evening.
>
> 2. My other remark is of a graver kind. You describe Archbishop Walsh and myself as " active promoters of Separatist intrigues." No gloss or evasion can explain this away ; for you fix the meaning of the terms by describing us as having " a determining voice in the Councils of the Church." This can apply to no layman, and the Archbishop of Dublin and myself are the text of this comment.
>
> I gladly unite myself with the Archbishop of Dublin. He is but slightly known in England, except in the descriptions of those who are fanning the flames of animosity between England and Ireland. I am known in England, both to the Ministers of the Crown and the leaders of the Opposition. I leave to them, who well know my mind, to answer for me ; and I who know the mind of the Archbishop of Dublin answer for him. We are neither intriguers nor Separatists.
>
> If, sir, I have written with unusual warmth I will confess

to you that I hold resentment to be sometimes a duty. And this is such a time, when your words touch our highest responsibility and inflame more and more the heated contentions between the two peoples whom justice and truth still bind in peace and unity.

The *St. James Gazette* had the following note, June 28, 1887 :

It is now stated that the Pope has reconsidered his determination [to cancel the mission of Mgr. Persico] and has ordered the envoys to proceed. We shall be sorry if there turns out to be at least an element of truth in the earlier report. The Pope has nothing to do with " Irish political affairs." But if His Holiness will see to it that his bishops and priests in that country do not place organised crime and the violation of the law under the blessing of the Church, for that we shall thank him indeed.

The *Times* (June 29, 1887) dealt with Cardinal Manning's letter editorially. After stating that later information showed that the mission of Mgr. Persico was not to be abandoned, and that the second change of view at the Papal-Court was attributed to the intervention of Monsignor Ruffo Scilla, the Papal Envoy sent to London for the Queen's Jubilee, the *Times* continued :

Cardinal Manning, accepting the reference " active promoters of Separatist intrigues" as applying to Archbishop Walsh and himself, answers for both : " We are neither intriguers nor Separatists." We are constrained to differ from Cardinal Manning on this point. Archbishop Walsh is a good deal better known in England than Cardinal Manning would have us believe; he is known, not by the invectives of his enemies, but by his own spoken and written words. He is, in the very strict sense of the word, a Separatist. He is working for the establishment of an independent Irish Parliament and Executive. In pursuing that policy he has identified the Irish Roman Catholic clergy with the cause of the National League, he has given his public approval to the Plan of Campaign, and his conduct has tended during the last eleven months to embarrass the Government and paralyse the enforcement of the law in Ireland. This is a course which Archbishop Walsh may be legally entitled to pursue, but it is in our judgment rightly described as a Separatist intrigue.

WALSH TO MANNING.

June 30, 1887.

I thank your Eminence for your letter. Few knew how thoroughly you had been with us through this trying time.

I have just come in from a long and hard day's work, and can only write these few words, if I am to catch the post. You will, of course, have observed that you have driven the *Times* to confess that what it means by Separation is Home Rule in the shape of a legislative body.

CROKE TO WALSH.

June 30, 1887.

Nothing could be more opportune, or more satisfactory than Cardinal Manning's letter to the *Times*. It identifies the Cardinal *publicly* with the Irish cause and with yourself.

KIRBY TO WALSH.

June 30, 1887.

This morning I had audience of His Holiness, and I showed him your beautiful Pastoral on his Jubilee. When he saw it was in English he expressed, as usual, his disappointment at not being able to read it. And I had to explain to him its scope and tenor.

At the end of the audience he told me to go to the Secretary of State (Cardinal Rampolla) as he had something to communicate to me on the part of His Holiness, who was too hurried then to mention the matter in detail to me. I went accordingly to His Eminence who kept me a good while. He said that the son of the Prince of Wales was about to visit Ireland very soon—Prince Victor. He said that it was the wish of His Holiness that your Grace should show him the usual acts of courtesy due to the members of reigning royal families, as, he added, to fail therein might be prejudicial to the country, and in the eyes of Europe might be considered as not creditable to the dignitaries of the Irish Church. He spoke a good deal on the subject, all tending towards the same point—to show that we ought not to mix up the question of our general rights, which are strong on their own merits, with the received usages of *personal* courtesy to the members of the reigning sovereign family—that not lacking in such courtesy will render our cause and ourselves more strong and respected.

So he charged me to write at once to your Grace in this sense, adding, that you would kindly try to interest the other bishops through whose places the prince would be known to pass, to mention to them confidentially the wish of His Holiness on the subject.

I replied that I would at once fulfil his Eminence's commission, adding as my own personal feeling that from what I know of your Grace, I am sure you would only be too happy to carry out the wishes of the Head of the Church on this and every other point to which His Holiness attached importance. *Ecco tutta la mia comissione* !

Drop me a line in reply, as they will be most anxious on the subject.

The Archbishop complied with the Secretary of State's suggestion that he should communicate to his episcopal brethren His Holiness's wishes regarding the reception to be accorded to the royal visitor. But he informed Rampolla that he himself could take no notice whatever of the prince's visit, adding at the same time a reasoned account of his unwillingness to accede to the Pope's request.

CHAPTER XII

His Excellency Monsignor Ignatius Persico, Papal Envoy to Ireland, arrived in Dublin on July 7, 1887. As the date of his coming had not been publicly announced, his arrival was unnoticed, and immediately, together with his secretary, Fr. Gualdi, he took up residence as the guest of Archbishop Walsh. He was described officially as Archbishop of Damietta, Commissary Apostolic appointed by the Pope to enquire into and report to the Holy See on the actual condition of affairs in Ireland.

Monsignor Persico was at that time a man of mature years and wide experience. He was homely in appearance, of medium height and portly build, grey-headed and grey-bearded. He possessed no distinction of gait or mien; his manner was affable, the expression of his features intelligent and kindly, and his dark piercing eyes betokened the trained and cautious observer.

A Neapolitan by birth, he had as a boy entered the Capuchin Order. After completing his studies for the priesthood at Rome, he was ordained at the age of twenty-three, and almost immediately was sent to India, where for a time he acted as chaplain to the British troops. In India he founded and directed a college at Darjeeling, and after the Goa schism he gave evidence before a Parliamentary Committee in London, where he was examined regarding certain claims made by the Catholics under British rule in India for whom he obtained several concessions, including Government patronage for the Catholic schools. Subsequently he was consecrated coadjutor Bishop of Bombay, and was in India during the Sepoy Mutiny, 1857, when his vicariate was ravaged and he himself beleaguered in the fortress of Agra for over six months. At the termination of the mutiny he came to Europe and to England, where he collected large sums to repair the losses sustained by the Indian Catholic missions during the troubles. In 1859 he was again in London on a mission in connection with Catholic interests. A few years later he was sent by the Prefect of Propaganda at Rome to the United States to administer the diocese of Charleston, and to assist in the pacification of the people, then much excited with the War of Secession. He was present at the plenary Synod of Baltimore after which he was appointed, on the recommendation of the American prelates, to the bishopric of Savannah, where after his return from the Vatican Council of 1870, he laid the foundation of a cathedral. Failing health compelled him to resign the See of Savannah in 1873. Soon after he was sent by Propaganda to Canada on a mission concerning Laval University. On returning to Rome he was dispatched to Malabar, where he acquitted himself with distinction in dealing with the Syro-Chaldean schism. The success which attended that mission was rewarded by his being recalled to Italy, and at the suggestion of Cardinal Franchi, Prefect of Propaganda, he was appointed administrator of the dioceses of Aquin, Pontecorvo, and Lorro, and Apostolic Visitor to the Chinese College at Malta. On his return to Rome he was appointed by Leo XIII Consulting Prelate to the Propaganda, and, at the time of his visit to Ireland, he was titular Archbishop of Damietta, a See of which Leo XIII himself was titular Archbishop when he was Envoy in Belgium.

Monsignor Persico was thus a man of wide experience, much travelled in many parts of Europe and America; and besides his acquaintance with India, he knew something of Tartary, Tibet, and Afghanistan. He had been in Ireland too before this occasion, having visited Dublin in Cardinal

Cullen's time. As might naturally be expected, his linguistic accomplishments were very varied.

The Rev. Monsignor Enrico Gualdi, who accompanied Monsignor Persico as his companion and secretary, was a man of distinctly Italian appearance. He spoke English fluently, having been for years engaged in missionary work in London. At the time of his visit to Ireland he was one of the *minutanti* or assistant secretaries at Propaganda.

WALSH TO MANNING.

July 8, 1887.

The " Mission" has arrived.

It has been most industriously circulated that Monsignor Persico was to stay with his religious brethren and not with the bishops. It will rather disturb the minds of certain friends of ours to find that I am to have the honour of his staying with me while he is in Dublin. The Mission is to the bishops. The Holy Father is naturally troubled at the representations so freely made to him about the state of things here. He has given us the best possible means of letting him know the truth.

Both our visitors are loud in praise of your Eminence's letter (to the *Times*). The " Separatist" cry is one that evidently had told in Rome.

My view of the case is that I should put before our visitors in fullest detail an exposition of the present state of Ireland under the following heads :—

1st.—The political movement; not revolutionary, but thoroughly constitutional in its aim and in its means. This is to be shown (*a*) from the nature of our demand, viewed in itself; (*b*) from the fact that we have Mr. Gladstone, Lord Spencer, Sir G. Trevelyan, etc., with us.

2nd.—The land movement; not communistic, etc., but a just and reasonable demand to save the people from eviction, so long as they pay a really *fair* rent (reference to Cowper Commission).

3rd.—Comparative freedom of Ireland from crime (judge's charges, etc.).

4th.—All that is satisfactory in the preceding, the result mainly of guidance of the movement by the bishops and priests (contrast with time when Fenianism was the only line of action in Ireland designated as " Nationalism"),

I know you will be good enough to send me any suggestions that occur to you.

To this letter the Cardinal at once replied :

MANNING TO WALSH.

July 10, 1887.

Your letter was very acceptable, and I thank you much for it.

The heads you have drawn up contain everything; and in working them out much will arise.

1.—I hope Monsignor Persico will go to Glenbeigh and Bodyke, and see with his own eyes the people and the ruins.

2.—I will send certain information about Kerry where he can examine with the bishop and the parish priests.

3.—No doubt the " Separatist" outcry has had its effect in Rome.

4.—And also the charge that the bishops have not spoken out strongly enough, or often enough against outrages and atrocities. Under this head let me know whether there is any case in which moonlighters have abused wives or daughters. I ask this because a friend of Home Rule has been led to believe it. If I could refute it much good would be done.

5.—Also the apparent solidarity of the bishops and the Irish members, and of these with Chicago, is always used here and in Rome.

6.—I hope that Mgr. Persico will go and see the next eviction with his own eyes. " *Summum jus summa injuria.*" By English law a man for forging a shilling was hanged, a woman was burnt—as late as 1776. A theft of 5s. in a shop was capital—hanging. All these executions were *legal*. But they all cried to Heaven. I hope Mgr. Persico will master this distinction well.

You will do me great service by keeping me informed.

Dr. Croke was keenly exercised over the purpose of Mgr. Persico's mission :

CROKE TO WALSH.

July 9, 1887.

I have no fancy for Persico and Co. But still, of course, I shall do all I can to make their mission a success.

I have nothing to add to your programme. Only I think

it essential that this Envoy would tell us precisely, and in every point, what are the charges made against the movement, the men connected with the movement, and the results of the movement. Let us hear all, *once for all*! We are able to smash it up. How do they (P. & Co.) intend to proceed? How are they going to get the knowledge that they seek? Will they go round to the bishops or what?

Write me all the news.

Dr. Walsh in reply gave an outline of the statement he intended to put before Mgr. Persico—Home Rule, Land, and Education—and asked for suggestions.

CROKE TO WALSH.

July 15, 1887.

There does not appear to me to be any difficulty whatever about Home Rule, Land, or Education, any more than about the religious condition of the country and our devotion to the Holy See.

I.—*Home Rule.*—We do not ask for any system of Home Rule that would trench on " the supremacy of the Crown," or on " the unity of the Empire." And as for " Separation" from England, I would oppose it by all means in my power, preferring vastly the English connection to a French or American one. In one word, we all think *separation* impossible, and even if possible, I for one would oppose it. I never heard one rational man, no matter how advanced, going in for separation. On that head there is no room for doubt.

II.—*Land.*—The land question admits of just as little doubt. We are prepared to pay *fair* rents; but will never consent to pay more. What are fair rents? Rents compatible with the support, clothing, and education of the tillers of the soil, according to the standard of England, Scotland and other countries, and in proportion to the price of agricultural produce and the annual yield of same. Let these things be fixed by an *impartial* tribunal—not by landlord or tenant.

III.—*Education.*—In Education we want " *equality*."

A week after Monsignor Persico's arrival in Ireland, July 12, 1887, the *Times* published from its Roman correspondent a report that

. . . the Papal mission was to have visited Ireland under orders to avoid all relations of a compromising kind with partisans on either side of the Irish dispute, and especially to abstain from identifying itself with Cardinal Manning or Archbishop Walsh. On learning this the Cardinal informed the Vatican that if it came under such conditions it would be boycotted and perhaps insulted. The action of Monsignor Persico in taking up his residence with Archbishop Walsh is certainly a singular method of getting impartial views on the Irish difficulty. But the Envoy is too able a person to be permanently misled by any such bias, and before leaving Ireland he will probably find opportunities to hear the other side.

This second report of interference by Cardinal Manning the Cardinal denied publicly in the *Times*. " So far as I know," he wrote, " there is neither a word nor a shadow of truth in the statement of your correspondent."

WALSH TO MANNING.

July 12, 1887.

Your Eminence's letter is, I need not say, most valuable. As regards Glenbeigh, etc., I will press the matter on Monsignor Persico. But, of course, much will depend on the local authorities of each place. I have picked out a few instances of the most absolutely baseless statements, made in the most fully circumstantial way, about myself. I shall use these by way of caution. They fully bear out my view that no weight whatever is to be attached to any statements made against anyone who is in sympathy with the tenants by those who are on the landlord side.

As for denunciation of outrages, I have a statement made out.

My only opportunity for uttering a word of denunciation was in replies to addresses received in country places; these addresses always contained a passage denouncing outrages; I could then speak out on the subject, as on such occasions I never failed to do.

This and other questions about the imprudent action of priests are strictly *local* questions. My advice to Mgr. Persico will be to deal with them as such, and to note carefully where any need for dealing with them exists.

In this diocese, for instance, but one case came under my notice of a priest's using unbecoming language. The case occurred during the election contests of 1885. All I had to complain of was a rude personal reference to the family history of a prominent Catholic gentleman. Next morning after the incident was reported, the priest in question had a letter from me putting an absolute restriction upon him against taking any further part in political affairs, either by writing or speaking in public. I have repeatedly told him that I have full confidence in him as a priest for his strictly religious work. I have even shown my confidence in him in a way that is well understood. But as he has shown that he is wanting in prudence, I have felt myself bound to keep him safe.

Mgr. Persico sees everyone who cares to call on him.

Dr. Walsh complied with Manning's request to be kept informed of the course of events in Ireland at this time.

WALSH TO MANNING.

July 20, 1887.

I send two numbers of the *Freeman's Journal* from which your Eminence will see that just now I have not idle times.* It is most important to bring out the fact that the demands of our people are most fully within the lines of justice, as laid down by the public courts. Until I went to work on the returns I had no idea how the case stood. The National League officials at first feared I had made some slip in the figures. But every figure has been checked over and over again.

The final percentage (of reduction) which I describe, for popular purposes, as " practically 24 per cent.", is in reality 24·69, i.e., nearer to 25. But I thought it better to keep on the lower figure. What we have now to struggle for is that, if the [land] question is to be dealt with, as apparently it is, the line drawn shall not be an arbitrary one.

* These papers contained two long letters, dated July 16, and 19, dealing with the current percentages of reduction of rents in the Land Courts. The letters were replete with figures and schedules adduced by the Archbishop in support of his statements. The Archbishop's statements were assailed and his figures challenged, but unsuccessfully. In fact, as he mentions in his letter to Cardinal Manning, he rather understated his case.

The practical purpose of the letters was to urge on the Government the advisability of suspending evictions, pending the settlement of the Land Question which then seemed imminent.

Our people want justice : they appeal to the recorded and published decisions of the courts, and they claim access to the courts, that their cases may be dealt with in like manner to those in which reductions have been granted. But as usual, I fear that the Government will spoil their concessions by petty and indefensible restrictions. However, this may be all the better in the end : their own supporters may not stand by them very enthusiastically if any strong opposition is shown to them on any point.

MANNING TO WALSH.

July 21, 1887.

The *Freeman* has not yet reached me.

Lord Salisbury seems to have made certain concessions, but as yet we have not got certain knowledge.

Will Mgr. Persico see the Lord Lieutenant before he leaves Dublin ? I see the two sides of the question for you—but Mgr. Persico is a stranger to all local conditions and embarrassments. He represents the Holy See and is neutral beyond question.

The Government here are making it a test of his impartiality, and so, I hear, is Sir Redvers Buller, who is certainly no adversary. My own opinion is that it would be an act of simple courtesy due to the representative of the Crown, if he were to write his name in the book, or even to see Lord Londonderry. It would also stop the mouths which complain of his being under your roof. Where else could he be ?

This is confidential, and no one knows of my writing it.

Monsignor Persico did in fact call on the Lord Lieutenant and on Sir Redvers Buller.*

---

* Buller, whose military exploits in South Africa were to bring him into prominence at the beginning of the Boer War, had been appointed Under-Secretary to the Lord Lieutenant of Ireland by the Tories in 1886. He supplanted Sir William Hamilton, who by his Liberal and Home Rule sympathies had made himself obnoxious to the Tories. Buller also soon showed himself too sympathetic, and he likewise had to make way for another. He resigned at the beginning of September, 1887.

Buller was probably the only official connected with Irish Government from whom Archbishop Walsh accepted hospitality. It came about in this way. Buller, who well knew the Archbishop officially and had heard that he was pleasant in social intercourse and perhaps the best conversationalist in Ireland, was anxious to have Dr. Walsh dine with him. The

During the first couple of weeks after his arrival in Ireland, Monsignor Persico visited a number of religious and other Catholic institutions in Dublin in company with Dr. Walsh. The Archbishop also accompanied him when paying a visit of courtesy to the Lord Lieutenant. His first public statement was made on Sunday, July 17, at Greystones, Co. Wicklow, whither he had accompanied the Archbishop, who blessed and opened for public worship a church dedicated to St. Killian.* He (Mgr. Persico) spoke generalities.　He

Archbishop, however, had made it an invariable rule not to accept invitations to the social functions of anyone officially connected with the Irish Government.　Buller got over this difficulty in a rather ingenious way. He sent Father Healy to inform the Archbishop that he was no longer Under-Secretary, as he had resigned the post; that his resignation had been accepted, but the fact was not to be made public for some days. The Archbishop in the circumstances accepted the invitation and dined with Buller on Thursday, September 22, at the Under-Secretary's Lodge in the Phoenix Park.　It was a small party, and the evening was very pleasant.　Among those present were : Dr. Mahaffy, Provost of Trinity College, and the Chief Justice Peter O'Brien.

One incident amused Dr. Walsh considerably.　The conversation turned on the character and worth of the evidence of expert witnesses at legal trials.　Mahaffy regarded them all as unconscionable more or less.　Peter O'Brien expressed surprise and horror that reputable engineers, medical men, and even ecclesiastical experts should be found ready to swear to positively contradictory views about a plain matter of fact.　The Archbishop twitted Peter on this unexpected manifestation of scrupulosity, quoting at him from the *Fortunes of Nigel* King James's assertion : " Every liege subject is bound to speak the whole truth to the King, but there is nae reciprocity of obligation . . . . O Geordie, Jingling Geordie, it was grand to hear Baby Charles laying down the guilt of dissimulation, and Steenie lecturing on the turpitude of intemperance."

Father Healy took the obvious and charitable view that even the most upright and honourable men might conscientiously differ on questions of fact.　But Sir Redvers put an end to all the finicky talk by the bluff remark : " Why, the poor devils must live "—a remark which evoked general laughter.

* This little church is the only church in Ireland, perhaps, towards the building of which one of the crowned heads of Europe has contributed.　The Empress Elizabeth of Austria, on learning that the church was to be dedicated to St. Killian, sent a substantial donation towards its erection.　She herself was born in Wurzburg, the city of which Killian, the great Irish saint and Apostle of Germany, is the patron.

said that since he came to Dublin he had been much edified by the manifestations which he had witnessed of the faith and piety of the Irish Catholics. He had known and loved the Irish for over forty years. The Pope also loved Ireland, and the coming of the Papal mission was intended as a manifestation of his Holiness's affection for his Irish children.

On July 26, 1887, Monsignor Persico left Dublin and proceeded to " explore the interior of Ireland." His first visit was to Limerick, where he was the guest of Lord Emly at Tervoe. He then visited Armagh and Dundalk, and interviewed the Primate and his coadjutor, Dr. Logue, and the other bishops of the province of Armagh. On August 22 he visited Tuam, and on the 29th Cashel, where he was received by Dr. Croke.

His Excellency made a favourable impression on Dr. Croke, who wrote to Walsh, September 2, 1887 :

The Envoy has come and gone. He is a nice man, and, I think, friendly in a high degree. So, indeed, is Gualdi. We received them warmly and, of course, respectfully here. We made no displays, following your example, either in demonstration or address. We parted last evening on the best of terms.

Meantime Dr. Kirby wrote regarding the state of feeling at Rome :

KIRBY TO WALSH.

July 26, 1887.

We arrived here (Tivoli, at the Villa of the Irish College) on Saturday.

I saw His Holiness and Cardinals Simeoni and Rampolla before leaving Rome. All feel greatly anxious about Ireland. But the observations were general. His Holiness told me that he wished Monsignor Persico not to be in a hurry to leave Ireland, in order to be able to know well the condition of the country, and the state of religion, etc., in the several localities. From what the newspapers say, the impression made on him (Monsignor Persico) seems to be most favourable to us, and I am sure he reports accordingly.

Your Grace's letter, directed to obtain a Bill of protection for the tenants from being evicted till the passing of the Land Law, will, please God, do good. It seems to have had a useful influence in the late discussions in Parliament.

I was delighted to see the account of the Peter's Pence collection in Dublin. *Viva la fede dell' Irlanda.*

KIRBY TO WALSH.

August 16, 1887.

I have come in from Tivoli for the Pope's Feast (of St. Joachim, August 16). .

I saw Cardinal Simeoni. I also communicated to him that the Australian Government had awarded 600,000 acres for whatever Catholic Congregation will devote itself to the civilising of the natives in the new vicariate of Kimberly.

The Pope held his levee this morning. All the cardinals, bishops, prelates, and other ecclesiastics and lay dignitaries attended. The conversation touched on several religious subjects, many of which showed the progress of Catholicity in different countries. As an additional proof of this, Cardinal Simeoni mentioned the above fact regarding Australia, and mentioned my name as his latest informant. This brought me on my legs and I detailed the circumstances briefly. His Holiness asked me was the above gift of land made by the English Government. I replied in the negative —that it was the gift of the Colonial Government; because, I added, Australia divided into several territories has a separate Parliament of its own for each—a fact which accounts for the marvellous progress of the country in arts, commerce, etc. "And this, Holy Father, is what Ireland demands for itself—the right to make its own laws, retaining its subjection to the English Crown*, but with its own Parliament."

All the cardinals listened, with the other dignitaries present, and not one uttered a word of contradiction or dissatisfaction at what I said. After the meeting one of them said to me : "It was well for you that Cardinal Howard was not present, as he would have jumped up *con fuoco* to assail you."

I know your Grace will be glad to get this piece of news, which, I hope, will not get into the newspapers, as this might hurt my usefulness on future occasions.

---

* This condition was expressly accepted by Parnell in 1886,

Monsignor Persico reports favourably. I hope your Grace continues to write often to Cardinal Simeoni. Let not Monsignor Persico's reports prevent you. He will have his say, but you can have yours also.

MANNING TO WALSH.

October 4, 1887.

In the enclosed, which I ask your Grace to forward, I have advised Mgr. Persico to invite the four Archbishops to meet him as his last act in Ireland.

I hope I have done rightly. I should like to know your impression of his work.

WALSH TO MANNING.

Dublin, October 4, 1887.

I have sent on your Eminence's letter to Mgr. Persico. He is in Wexford. He has now only two dioceses to visit— Ferns, where he is, and Meath—before returning to Dublin. I expect him back here before this day week. This time he stays with the Capuchins. He intends to stay in Dublin for ten days or a fortnight, during which, I suppose, we shall have many talks over the whole situation. The landlords will make a dead set on him, I am sure. But I have given him a test question for any landlord who comes to him to talk of the dishonesty of Irish tenants : *Have any of your own tenants submitted the question of the fairness or the unfairness of your rents to the decision of the Court? And what was the result?* For 99 out of every 100 landlords in Ireland, the only answer would be a confession that the decision went against them . . .

Until Mgr. Persico returns to Dublin, I cannot say what views he has formed. But from scraps of evidence that have come to hand, I feel very confident that his views are favourable. Every effort will be made to discredit him in Rome. He must, therefore, act with great prudence and caution.

Monsignor Persico's visits to the various Irish bishops lasted till October 24, when he returned to Dublin. Here he took up his residence with his religious brethren the Capuchin Fathers at Church Street. The chief reason for his going to reside there was that he wished to have one

of the Fathers act as his secretary; for by this time
Fr. Gualdi had returned to Rome, where he died in
the course of a couple of weeks. The departure of
Fr. Gualdi gave rise to public comments unfavourable to
the Envoy. It was freely stated that Fr. Gualdi had been
recalled at Mgr. Persico's request; and that the humiliation
of that recall had broken Fr. Gualdi's heart. Persico,
however, always maintained that the departure of
Fr. Gualdi was a cause of deep regret to him personally,
and that his loss seriously hampered him in his work in
Ireland, and that Fr. Gualdi's departure was due solely to
failing health, on which account he had sought and obtained
permission to return to Rome.

Monsignor Persico remained about a month with the
Capuchin Fathers at Church Street. During that time he
was busy interviewing various public men, receiving
addresses from the Dublin Corporation, from the Dublin
clergy, etc. On the Feast of St. Laurence, Patron of the
Diocese of Dublin, he preached at the Pro-Cathedral, laying
special emphasis on the great benefits which St. Laurence
secured for the Irish people by his vigilant care for the
interests of religion, and by his tactful dealing with King
Henry II. On the same day he was entertained at Clonliffe
College, where the Archbishop had invited a distinguished
company to meet him, including many of the Irish bishops.
Shortly after this, November 20, 1887, the Envoy left
Dublin to return no more. He proceeded to Cork and went
to reside with the Capuchin Fathers at Rochestown.

From Cork Persico wrote to Archbishop Walsh, November
23, 1887 :

I have received your Grace's letter conveying the mourn-
ful news of good Father Gualdi's death. I must confess
that, though half prepared for it, the news has terribly
affected me. He was indeed a good priest and an able
official, and the Propaganda has lost one of its best officers.
My own health is more or less the same. Your Grace need

not write a memorandum on Home Rule or on the Land
Question [which questions he had previously informed the
Archbishop he understood]. A memorandum on the
Education Question will be sufficient.

PERSICO TO WALSH.

November 29, 1887.

I am interested to hear that your Grace has reached page
40 of the Memorandum on Education. It will be a volume
in folio. This is not surprising. You can write so easily.

PERSICO TO WALSH.

November 30, 1887.

The moment I receive your Memorandum on Education
I shall insert it in my report.

On December 5 the newspapers announced that Archbishop Walsh had left Dublin, and that he would be absent
for some weeks.

PERSICO TO WALSH.

December 5, 1887.

There must be some misunderstanding about your
Memorandum on the Education Question which I have not
yet received. As I told you, I had been charged to ask
the opinion of every bishop—which I did. Though I
remember very well the substance of your Grace's views, I
should like to have your opinion in your own words. In the
Report I have to send to Rome, I must write a special
chapter on the Education Question.

So your Grace is in Italy by the time this letter reaches
you, and I am in the interior of Ireland !

Dr. Walsh had, in fact, just left Ireland and was on his
way to Rome for the celebration of the Pope's Jubilee, and
Mgr. Persico feared that the Memorandum had been
forgotten. But it was not so, for on December 17, the
Envoy wrote acknowledging receipt of it :

I have just received your Grace's Memorandum* on the Education Question—in fact Dr. Murphy† has kindly sent me six copies of it. I need not say with what deep interest I shall peruse and study it, and I beg to return your Grace my best thanks for it.

The Papal Envoy's longing to return to Italy (hinted at in his letter of December 5 to Archbishop Walsh) was accentuated by the rumours and reports which had begun to be published about him in the newspapers. *United Ireland* announced, in its issue of December 15, 1887, that in Unionist circles in London the report was current that the Government had succeeded in securing the support of Mgr. Persico and a few of the Irish bishops for the policy of coercion. " In consideration for this service the statement is that the Government have undertaken (1) to endow richly a Catholic University in Ireland, and (2) to receive an Envoy from His Holiness, and to send an ambassador to the Vatican."

On the next day, Friday, December 16, the *Pall Mall Gazette* enlarged on the report published in *United Ireland* :

The Government wish to checkmate Home Rule by Rome Rule. They have determined to strike up an alliance with the Pope of Rome. It has for some time been an open secret that Lord Salisbury contemplates some such concordat with the Vatican, and in this he was strongly encouraged by the Duke of Norfolk.

When Father Gualdi died and Monsignor Persico, leaving the healthy atmosphere of the archiespiscopal residence at Dublin, had made his way southward to the diocese of Limerick, the shattered hopes of the Unionists began again

---

* The " Memorandum on the Irish Education Question " is a printed statement, covering 79 large folio pages, divided into three sections : Section I. (pp. 1—49) deals with Primary Education ; Section II. (pp. 50—55) with Intermediate Education ; and Section III (pp. 55—79) with University Education. The Memorandum, which is dated December 3, 1887, is a valuable historical sketch of the Irish Education Question—lucid, accurate and well documented.

† The Archbishop's secretary.

to revive. The Bishop of Limerick (Dr. O'Dwyer), like the
Coadjutor Bishop of Clonfert (Dr. Healy), and one or two
other prelates who could be named "Landlord Bishops,"
regards the national agitation with undisguised dislike. At
the same time the word was given in Tory circles that the
Papal Envoy had to be taken in hand, and that every effort
should be made to nobble his Excellency by profuse hospitality and the most deferential treatment.

Monsignor Persico was given the hint that the Castle
intended locking up the priests who took part in the meetings
of the suppressed branches of the National League, but that
if his Excellency put the screw on the priests through their
bishops the Government would gladly refrain from taking so
extreme a step. Willingly or otherwise, Mgr. Persico seems
to have fallen into the trap. The way the thing is done is
very simple. The Monsignor gives the hint to the bishop.
The bishop nothing loth—for the game is tried on in dioceses
where the bishop can be relied on by the Castle—despatches
private and confidential communications to the clergy warning them of what is in store for them.

Delighted with the success of this manoeuvre the Govern-
ment have now further undertaken to endow a Catholic
University in Ireland for the benefit and the welfare of Irish
Catholics.

In the midst of the commotion caused in Ireland by the
discovery of the extent to which the astute intriguer of the
Castle* had been able to use the Papal Envoy as a coercionist
catspaw, Archbishop Walsh has been suddenly summoned to
Rome by the Pope.†

The publication of the reports in *United Ireland* and the
Pall Mall Gazette, and their re-publication in the *Freeman's
Journal*, gave great pain to Monsignor Persico, and called
forth an indignant and trenchant letter of repudiation from

---

* Mr. A. J. Balfour, then Chief Secretary for Ireland.

† Archbishop Walsh had not been *summoned* to Rome. He
had left Ireland on December 5, *en route* for Rome, but his visit
was not undertaken in response to any summons. It was undertaken as a pilgrimage and was to be merely a visit of courtesy,
loyalty and devotion to the Holy See on the occasion of Leo's
Jubilee.

As will appear Dr. Walsh's visit was, at the instance of
Pope Leo, prolonged over months.

Bishop O'Dwyer,* December 19, 1887.   Monsignor Persico
remained silent, though much obloquy was spoken and
written about him.   His uneasiness and anguish are,
however, apparent in the private letters which he wrote at
this time.

PERSICO TO MANNING.†

Capuchin Convent, Cork.
December 21, 1887.

Out of the great respect I entertain for your Eminence, I
write to tell you *that as far as I am concerned* there is not
a word of truth in all that has been lately published in the
Pall Mall Gazette and other newspapers about my league
with the Government, either in Ireland, or much less in
England.   My intercourse with the bishops has been
straightforward and loyal, and nothing underhand has
passed between me and them.   I have strictly confined
myself to the object of my mission—to observe, to study,
to know—and in due time to make my Report.   Beyond
this I have done nothing, and I even safely defy anyone to
prove the contrary.   Your Eminence will understand that I
must remain silent before these attacks, but I have been
deeply pained at the language of some newspapers in
Ireland, specially two articles in the *Freeman* on the 17th
and 19th inst.   I am afraid that the enemies of Ireland will
take advantage of that.   Of course there are things to

---

* After denying in burning words that he was either an
" intriguer," a " Unionist," or a " Landlord Bishop," Dr.
O'Dwyer declared that he considered " boycotting " to be
irreligious and the Plan of Campaign to be " unjust," and
that in the last resource its only sanction is " violent resistance
to the law . . . ." and he added that " the guidance of the
agitation was not only politically stupid but morally wrong."

† Of the letters written by Persico to Manning those of December
21 (1887), January 6, January 11, February 20, May 9, May
19 (1888), have already been published.   They appeared
in the *United Irishman* of April 23, 1907, of which the late
Arthur Griffith was the editor.   The present writer asked Arthur
Griffith, shortly before his death, how he had come by these
letters.   Griffith said that the letters were unquestionably
genuine, and that he had obtained them from a very reputable
journalist, whom he named, and who was then in South Africa.
Griffith even volunteered to communicate with this journalist,
and to put the present writer in touch with him, but before an
answer could have come Arthur Griffith had died.   (August 12,
1922)

be corrected and certain *inconvenients* to be removed; and when I have the honour of seeing Y.E. I will freely mention them to you. But I may even now tell Y.E. that in submitting my *subordinato parere* to my superiors I have said that whatever is deemed necessary or useful for Ireland must be done *with and through the bishops*; that any other mode of acting or a different procedure may have deplorable consequences.

On the following day the Envoy wrote to Walsh :

I beg to acknowledge your note of the 16th wherein your Grace apprehends the danger that the educational question may be settled with the English Government in view of diplomatic relations that would be established between the Holy See and England, and that they may be effected independently of the bishops.

As to the probability or rather the possibility of diplomatic relations between the Pope and England, I have nothing to say, as I am a perfect stranger to all these things.

But as to the settling of the education question, that is a thing which I cannot believe : and if the *Tablet*, or other British papers say it, I say that they only give expression to their own wishes, and not that they have a real foundation for asserting it. I repeat I cannot, nor do I, believe this to be possible. For on what basis could the Court of Rome have entered into this settlement, not having as yet received my report on the Education Question? And yet the Holy Father was desirous to ascertain and to know the views of the bishops in the matter. And in pursuance of such commands I asked every bishop, beginning from your Grace, to give his opinion. Again, I have not received any *intimation whatever* on this special subject, so I shall be really surprised if anything be done without the necessary elements. As your Grace will soon be in Rome* it will not be difficult for you to know something about it.

Again, it is utterly false that I have been in league with some of the bishops to serve the Government, etc. My intercourse with the bishops has ever been straightforward and loyal, and nothing underhand has ever taken place with any of them. In a word, everything that has been published is false and calumnious and I repudiate it most emphatically.

* The Archbishop was on his way to Rome.

Your Grace well knows that I have strictly confined myself to the mission I have received, and that I have tried to execute it most guardedly and impartially.

PERSICO TO WALSH.

Christmas Day, 1887.

No doubt your Grace must have seen the publications made in the *Freeman's Journal* for the last eight or ten days and how my name has been dragged along, etc. Now, in justice to myself, and also in justice to the Bishop of Limerick, I deem it proper to let you know, *privately* and *confidentially*, the following particulars :—

At a dinner given by Mr. Moran of Lucan, at which your Grace was also present, we met a Major or Captain Turner, R.M., if I mistake not, of Ennis. I was simply introduced to him, but he talked a good deal with poor Fr. Gualdi, and told him that he would write to him now and then. In fact, from time to time he sent Fr. Gualdi either complaints or copies of reports against the action taken by priests, etc. The only reply that was ever given him was that we had received his communication and taken cognisance of it. I need not say that since my arrival in Ireland I received hundreds and hundreds of such communications in different shapes—to which the same reply has been invariably given.

Your Grace also remembers that a few days after my arrival in Cork, I begged of the Bishop of Limerick to pay me a visit, and I wrote to your Grace to say that he had come and I also informed you of the result of my conversation with him.* Now, it so happened either the day before or the morning of the day that Dr. O'Dwyer called on me I had received a communication from this Major Turner, in which he complained against three or four priests of the Killaloe diocese, adding that he had written several times to the Bishop without any effect; that he should be sorry to send summonses against priests, and would be glad if the

---

* Persico to Walsh, November 26, 1887.
" I hasten to reply to your Grace's letter marked *confidential*. I have already made the personal communication you allude to. After my arrival here I invited the person to come and see me, which he promptly did on Wednesday last. The interview was, I am happy to say, most satisfactory, and I have reason to believe, conclusive. I shall, however, take another opportunity either by letter, or by another personal interview in order to still more warn that person. Your Grace has done very well to give me due information."

Bishop took matters into his own hands, etc. I had thought of sending that same communication to the Bishop, Dr. Ryan, but availed myself of Dr. O'Dwyer's visit to beg of him to give it to the Bishop. Dr. O'Dwyer promised to do so, adding that if the Bishop, Dr. Ryan, was unwell he would either give the letter or speak to the Vicar-General, who, he said, was a friend of his. I did not hear anything more about it, nor have I heard a word either from Dr. O'Dwyer or from anyone else on the subject. Yet, reading the articles of the *Pall Mall Gazette*, and the way in which they insist on the same thing, it strikes me that either the Vicar-General must have acted imprudently, or the priests who were warned resented it, and so, what was done for good and with a good intention has been misinterpreted and given an odious sense altogether.

This, my dear Lord Archbishop, is the fact whereupon may have been built all those imputations against me and the Bishop of Limerick—that I have been cajoled by the Government, and become their agent, and commenced my operations in one diocese through Dr. O'Dwyer, etc., etc.

PERSICO TO WALSH.

December 28, 1887.

I have duly received the registered letter of the 20th inst., which your Grace sent me from San Remo. It contains a cutting from the *Scotsman* newspaper, which proves what your Grace says about the fabrication (so to say) of news, etc. This, of course, is an instance of what we find every day in newspapers. You may depend on it that I shall not fail to make this known at the proper quarters. Fr. Gualdi communicated to me the fact of Cardinal Cullen's alleged condemnation of Home Rule and other things which your Grace had told him.*

* The story of Cardinal Cullen's views regarding Home Rule is interesting. During the agitation against Gladstone's Home Rule Bill (1886), the names of Cardinal Cullen and Cardinal McCabe (as well-known opponents of Home Rule) were frequently used at public meetings in England and Ireland. The Duke of Norfolk quoted Cardinal Cullen's views on more than one public occasion. How flimsy was the pretext for invoking Cardinal Cullen's name in this connection will appear from the following letter of Archbishop Walsh, written to the Dublin *Evening Mail,* September 15, 1887.

After having complained that the *Mail* had attributed to himself certain views and expressions which he had not used—which

Regarding the publications that have recently taken place,
I do not think that we ought to take any notice of them.
For, if we begin to contradict, we ought to do so every day;
as every day you find something either in Unionist or
Nationalist papers which we ought to contradict or rectify.
In my humble opinion the most effectual way of dealing
with certain publications is either not to admit them (that
is republishing them) or to treat them with the utmost
contempt.   Discussions ought always to be avoided on
certain subjects.

expressions were quoted by the *Mail* in inverted commas—the
Archbishop continued : " I have more than once had occasion to
complain of the use of inverted commas ascribing to me words
which were neither spoken nor written by me. The *Evening
Mail* has more than once used them, but, I am sure, in perfect
good faith. But the practice of employing what is generally
recognised as an assurance of actual and accurate quotation,
when it is employed in reference to a person individually named,
is a practice of a very objectionable kind. It is unfortunately
becoming a practice by no means uncommon.

" Let me give one instance which just occurs to me. Not very
long ago, a fly-leaf published, and, no doubt, very widely circulated, by the Irish Loyal and Patriotic Union was sent to me
by an English friend. It is headed : ' Cardinal Cullen and
Home Rule.' Then follows, in *inverted commas* from first to
last, a very strong denunciation of Home Rule, thus most
formally ascribed to the Cardinal, as if it was a transcript from
something written, or a verbatim report of something spoken by
his Eminence.

" Now, I have traced this pretended quotation to its source,
and I find it, in its first appearance *in an anonymous letter* in
the *Tablet* newspaper, where it is given as the *writer's recollection* of a conversation which he says he had with Cardinal
Cullen many years ago !

" To make the matter more blameworthy, the number of the
Tablet in which the letter appears is mentioned on the fly-leaf
as the source from which the quotation is made. How few of
those into whose hands the thousands of copies of that fly-leaf undoubtedly in circulation have come, are likely to search through
the back numbers of the *Tablet* and there to discover for themselves that the whole fabric rests upon the recollections of an
anonymous correspondent ! But the author of the fly-leaf, as
his reference to the *Tablet* shows beyond question, well knew
that this was its sole foundation."

As a matter of fact, Archbishop Walsh had written privately
to Houston—the Secretary of the I.L.P.U.—protesting against
the unfair and misleading use of the alleged views of Cardinal
Cullen concerning Home Rule. This Houston is the same who
a little later on (1888—9) figured so prominently in connection
with the *Times*—Pigott forgeries regarding " Parnellism and
Crime."

As you will now be at the Irish College (Rome), I write direct.

Your Grace can now know things much better than I can here.

PERSICO TO MANNING.

Epiphany Day, January 6, 1888.

I have read and re-read your Eminence's letter with an ever increasing interest and sincere satisfaction, for I find therein the confirmation of my deeply settled convictions on the subject of Diplomatic Relations. Your Eminence may remember that from my early youth I have been engaged in examining the subject of Concordats between secular governments and the Holy See. My studies in that subject commenced on the question of the Portuguese pretended right of patronage in East India. From that time I became persuaded that in all these transactions the Holy See has not gained much—on the contrary the Church lost a great deal, especially in the choice of bishops and in points connected with ecclesiastical jurisprudence and discipline. If so with the old Catholic countries, what must we say of England and of Ireland? Their condition and their status is something *sui generis*, and quite exceptional. The history, the succeeding events, and a thousand other circumstances must be taken into consideration; and hence, people ought to stop before running to the conclusion that Diplomatic Relations may be advantageous and useful in England and Ireland. I agree fully with your Eminence that " the true *nunciatura* for England and Ireland is the episcopate." If the bishops do not know the state of the country they are not fit to be bishops. If they do, what more can *una persona ufficiosa o ufficiale* do for the Holy See?

And again, I fully understand what your Eminence adds, " the English people tolerate the Catholic Church as a spiritual body. The first sign of a political action on the part of the Government would rekindle all the old fears, suspicions, and hostility." And it is also a great pity that English Catholics do not understand all this! I am sure that His Holiness understands it well, but I share your fears that those about him may harass him with the fickle and vain glory that would accrue to the Holy See by having an accredited representative from England also. I may assure your Eminence, of course *in a most confidential way*, that even in my humble position I do not fail to represent my views to the Holy See. Above all, I have informed the Secretary of State of the way in which such a thing would be felt in Ireland.

As far as my mission is concerned, I must say that my instructions are to keep aloof from the English Government; and I may assure your Eminence that I was happy to receive such instructions, and have been *most careful* in observing them. I hope that when in England I may have the opportunity of seeing your Eminence. I recommend myself to your Eminence's prayers, as I am tried by the continuous attacks of the newspapers, and therefore I need great patience.

The rumours noised in Ireland of diplomatic intrigue on the part of Monsignor Persico were re-echoed in Rome. These rumours were brought to the notice of the Envoy by Dr. Walsh, who had misgivings as to his being free from responsibility in the matter of Fr. Gualdi's recall. The purport of the Archbishop's communication may be judged from Persico's reply :

PERSICO TO WALSH.

January 12, 1888.

On my return from a pleasant visit to Thurles* I have found your Grace's letter (written from Rome) of the 7th inst., with a slip from the *Irish Times* about Father Gualdi's recall, etc. I had already read the same thing in the *Freeman's Journal* and had written to you on the subject. I must, however, thank your Grace very much for your

* Croke to Walsh, January 12, 1888 :
　　　　　　" THE PALACE,
　　　　　　　　" Thurles, Thursday, 12th Jan.
" As I told you in my last, the Mgr. arrived here, with Donato, on Monday last, and has just left for Cork. He remains in Cork till Tuesday next, and then leaves for Torquay, *via* Bristol, ' for the benefit of his health.' He is to remain there for about a month, when he will return to Dublin ! Such is his programme. During his stay here I had several exhaustive interviews with him in reference to the situation generally. If he is to be believed he is ' *ipsis Hibernis Hibernior.*' He *is* the friend of Ireland, and has always been, and he never wrote a line to Rome, and never will, not favourable to all her legitimate

consideration on this and other occasions in sending me current reports about my mission.

The people who are said to have got hold of Fr. Gualdi's papers were quite welcome to publish them; as I mentioned in my last, Father Gualdi had written more than once, on account of his health, and towards the end *most urgently*, to be allowed to return to Italy. The idea of his having been recalled is the offspring either of malice or ignorance, as Fr. Gualdi's letters *must be at the Propaganda*; and hence all that is said about his recall, disgrace, etc., etc., is nothing but calumny and falsehood.

As to myself, I must tell your Grace plainly that I have made up my mind not to say one word, either to correct or contradict any statement that may be published about me. I am now the representative of the Holy See, so that everything that has public reference to my mission must be taken up by the Holy See and not by myself. I shall be in a position to speak for myself, but for the present I must be silent, and rest satisfied with the will of God and my own conscience.

WALSH TO MANNING.

Naples, January 22, 1888.

I did not care to write to your Eminence, until I had some definite news, satisfactory or unsatisfactory, as it might be, to send you. Rumours have been in circulation by the dozen—all of the most unpleasant character. But, as your Eminence knows, there is nothing in all this to disturb me. The only rumour that seemed to give solid ground for uneasiness was one about Fr. Gualdi. It was, and is, very generally believed. I thought it right to let Mgr. Persico know of it, as it made use of his name. He writes as if there was nothing in it. But any reference to his having contradicted it only sets people's heads and shoulders wagging in the way recognised as a very emphatic indication of incredulity. The story is that the Monsignor made up his

aspirations including Home Rule. The rumours that come from Rome are, according to him, the merest tittle tattle, such as was going on in the Eternal City during the Vatican Council, and such as is sure to go on whenever large gatherings of English people are in Rome. He positively denies the Gualdi incident, and expresses the greatest regard for him, and deepest regret at his lamented disappearance. He denounces the English Catholics most vehemently for their hostility to Ireland, and their shameless and flagrant ingratitude for the blessings of freedom won for them by Irishmen. ' Nominatim ' he is death on Salford,"

mind that Fr. Gualdi's strong feeling of sympathy with the Irish cause was an element to be got rid of from the "mission"—and so represented to the Vatican the advisability of recalling the obnoxious individual—Fr. Gualdi's known delicacy and also his known wishes to be taken out of an unpleasant position being taken into account as sufficient ground to put before the public for what was done. It is even said that representations were made as to the advisability of removing him from the office of Irish *minutante** at Propaganda.   On all hands one is assured here that the poor man died simply from the effects of the communications made to him on his return to Rome. Notwithstanding the contradiction to which I have referred, I must continue to believe what has been so circumstantially stated to me, especially in one quarter in Rome.   It leaves no doubt in my mind that Fr. Gualdi (R.I.P.) regarded himself as being " in disgrace" and took it very heavily to heart.   Of course, it is possible that he may have been the subject merely of a delusion on the matter.   As one most important part of the story was told to me, it included the statement of a series of incidents which, at all events, as they occurred, were only known to Fr. Gualdi, to Mgr. Persico, and to myself !

The Pope now thinks he can settle the Irish question. 1 am to play some important part in the transaction. The details are reserved for some conference or conferences to which I am to be called after February 1.   All this may mean something particular.   But, unless I can see my way very clearly into what the Holy See means it will, of course, be my duty to tell them of the serious risk that is run by mixing up the Holy See in so uncertain a transaction.   If H.H. is prepared, in communicating with the Ministry, to put forward as an essential basis of settlement the two unchangeable requirements of Home Rule, and a thoroughly satisfactory reform of our land system, all may be well.   These points are essential.

No influence could, I apprehend, move our people to abandon either the one or the other.   If things are to enter upon a course in which the Holy See may be able to figure as claiming an influence to secure the abandonment of either, we must see that the Holy Father is sufficiently forewarned to have himself to bear the full responsibility of any disaster that may follow.

* Under-Secretary who dealt with Irish affairs.

While Monsignor Persico was the object of hostile criticism from various quarters, Dr. Walsh did not escape attention. His prominent participation in public affairs led certain onlookers, both friendly and hostile, in Ireland to think and to say that it was not possible for him to combine the adequate discharge of his pastoral duties with his almost incessant activities in regard to political and public questions generally.   Such was the opinion of some of the Archbishop's episcopal brethren, as we learn from Mgr. Persico's letters.   Complaints were made to the envoy of Dr. Walsh's interference in politics, and it was represented to him that the Archbishop of Dublin ought to be directed to confine his activities to matters purely ecclesiastical.   Similar complaints and representations were made at Rome, but apparently without much effect. A hint of those things may be discerned in a characteristically gentle and sympathetic letter written to Dr. Walsh about this time by his kindly old friend Dr. Kirby.

KIRBY TO WALSH.

(Undated).

I think your Grace is right in standing out for full justice and equality, not half or three-quarters, but full fair play. And with God's help you will gain it, especially by the great weapon of prayer, which you so often and so happily inculcate in your public discourses, thereby making our fine Catholic people, whilst they do their own part, rest all their hopes of victory on the blessing of God.   " *Equus paratur ad bellum, Deus autem victoriam tribuit.*" ("*Veni, vidi sed Deus vicit,*" said John Sobieski in his letter to Innocent XI, after defeating the Turks at Vienna).

I must now implore of your Grace to look to your own personal care. I do not mean a spiritual care, as you can well teach me by your own practice that "*qui sibi nequam est cui alii bonus erit*"—but I mean in not overpowering yourself with too much mental and corporal labour. Indeed I have been written to from Ireland by mutual friends on this subject.   So you must divide the work; make others do their share, and do not attempt more than you can fairly and without pressure compass, reserving to yourself full time for your private spiritual refreshment, without which all our exterior discourses would be without life or efficacy, as St. Bernard took care to remind Pope Eugene III in his book *De Consideratione*. But this will be impossible if your Grace overpower yourself with too much labour which would oppress you both mentally and physically. *Est modus in rebus*, etc., and as the Roman adage has it, *Chi troppo abbraccia poco stringe*.

For the rest, my dear Lord, fear nothing. Continue your confidence in our Blessed Mother, and as your primary care is to promote her honour and the faith and glory of her Divine Son, you will experience her maternal care in everything, "*Ipsa tenente non corrues, ipsa duce pervenies.*"

Do not forget to pray for this *povero vecchio*, who is always yours affectionately,—T. Kirby.

On Persico the reports regarding Dr. Walsh's lack of pastoral spirit made a deeper impression :

While on this point [he writes in the course of a letter to Manning, February 12, 1888] I must confide to your Eminence my impression about the Archbishop of Dublin. He has most eminent qualities and can do an immensity of good, not only in his own diocese, but for the whole of Ireland. I would like to see him a little more spiritual and more attached to his *pastoral* duties. I am in hopes that he will do so in time, for he is young, and has only been a professor all his life. To your Eminence also I must *confide* that this is the opinion of many bishops in Ireland. My intercourse with all the bishops has been of a most friendly character, and so it has been with the Archbishop of Dublin. He has written to me constantly, except for the last month. On his arrival in Rome he heard (as he himself wrote to me) many things about me. Among others, that I had caused Fr. Gualdi's recall and similar things, and from the tenor of his letter I could see that he had doubts about me. I must confess to your Eminence that the good soul, Father Gualdi, was himself very desirous to return to Rome as soon as possible, and I saw the letters that he wrote to the Propaganda for it. In fact he obtained leave to return in consequence of *his own request*. And, going to Rome, I know that he was received, as he himself wrote to me, with kindness and consideration.

I must add that, as far as I am concerned, I was very glad to have him as my companion, and I have invariably entertained for him respect and esteem. The Archbishop of Dublin does not know Rome with regard to rumours and reports. Your Eminence knows it well. Often a word from a writer or under-writer of a Sacred Congregation is given as a fact, and goes round Rome. Again, at the evening conversazioni, comments are freely made from unknown sources or from personal feelings, and these comments are given out as certain facts the next morning. I am sure your Eminence remembers well what was going on in Rome during the Vatican Council !

I am also afraid that the Archbishop of Dublin and the majority of the clergy of Ireland take me for a man *ligio al governo inglese*. They are generally mistaken in this. Providence so disposed things that even from my early youth I should have become acquainted with the sad history of Ireland. That history made so deep an impression upon me that even then I became convinced of the fact that Ireland had been the most tried and persecuted nation on the face of the earth ; while England the most cruel and cold-blooded towards poor Ireland. I may safely assure your Eminence that I am a great friend of Ireland, and with all my heart I wish Ireland happiness and prosperity.

I had not forgotten to tell your Eminence that there is another point about which I have given my *negative* opinion in my reports, and that is against the appointment of a permanent Apostolic Delegate for Ireland. Such a thing would not only humble her, but wound the feelings of both clergy and people.

That Manning in reply took pains to express his disagreement with Monsignor Persico's impression of the Archbishop of Dublin is evident from a further letter from the Envoy, February 29, 1888 :

I have just had the pleasure of receiving your Eminence's letter of yesterday, for which I am very grateful.

With reference to the person alluded to in my last (Archbishop Walsh), I beg to assure your Eminence that I fully agree with you as to the character and aptitude, nay, I acknowledge his eminent qualities. If I opened my mind to your Eminence upon one thing only, I did it from my wish for the greater good. But we must take into considera-

tion his being taken from college life and other circumstances.   Above all, I am decidedly of Y.E's opinion that
it would be a great disaster if the confidence of His Holinesss
in him should be shaken.   On this point I may also assure
Y.E. that, as *far as I am concerned*, I have shown the
necessity of *hearing and acting in concert* with him about
everything.   And,   writing   to   Cardinals Simeoni and
Rampolla, I have *insisted on their showing and placing in
him great confidence.*

CHAPTER XIII

CONDEMNATION OF THE PLAN OF CAMPAIGN

ARCHBISHOP WALSH left Dublin on the morning of December 5, 1887, *en route* for Rome, where he was to assist, together with other members of the Irish Hierarchy, at the celebrations in honour of Leo XIII's sacerdotal Jubilee. About the same time, an Irish National Pilgrimage of over three hundred members set out for the Eternal City to present their congratulations to the Holy Father. On the morning of Dr. Walsh's departure the newspapers contained the announcement of the death of the Archbishop of Armagh, Dr. McGettigan. Dr. McGettigan was succeeded by his coadjutor, Dr. Logue, who immediately became Archbishop of the See, and Primate of All Ireland.

Dr. Walsh went directly to Milan, where he rested for a couple of days, occupying his leisure in writing a pastoral letter on the Pope's Jubilee. This letter was read in the churches of the diocese of Dublin on Sunday, December 18. He reached the Eternal City on Thursday, December 29. On the following day he introduced to the Pope the Irish deputation which had come to congratulate His Holiness. The Pope received the Archbishop with such marked cordiality as to call forth comments from certain English newspapers. On the same day the Archbishop was present at a banquet in honour of the Pope given by Cardinal Simeoni. On New Year's Day, Dr. Kirby gave a dinner at the Irish College in honour of Dr. Walsh.

On the Feast of the Epiphany, Archbishop Walsh presided at a meeting at the Church of S. Maria in Posterula, at which

317

arrangements were made for the laying of the foundation stone of an Irish National Church in Rome. It was arranged that the ceremony should take place on February 1, the Feast of St. Brigid. By special deputation of Cardinal Parocchi, Vicar-General of His Holiness, the stone was to be blessed by the Archbishop of Dublin.

On January 7 Archbishop Walsh and the other Irish bishops had audience of Leo XIII. After the audience Dr. Walsh received an intimation from the Secretary of State, Cardinal Rampolla, that the Pope wished to have a consultation with him and others about Irish affairs, and that a conference was to be fixed for some day early in February. The Archbishop of Tuam and the Bishops of Galway and Elphin left Rome immediately to return to Ireland. Dr. Walsh spent the interval at Naples.

He was in Rome again on February 1, when the Pope received at the Vatican the members of the Irish National Pilgrimage. On this occasion the Archbishop read two addresses to His Holiness—one from the Irish bishops, the other from the clergy and faithful of the diocese of Dublin. He also presented the Pope with the sum of £4,000—the Jubilee offering of his flock in Dublin.

The Pope, speaking in Latin, replied to the two addresses. He thanked the pilgrims for their presence and for their expressions of devotion to his person and loyalty to the Holy See. From the very beginning of his pontificate, he said, he had taken the greatest interest in Ireland. The Irish people might confidently trust in his continued good-will towards them. He wished to see Ireland peaceful and prosperous, and Monsignor Persico's mission was a proof of his good-will. The letter of instruction which he had sent to the Archbishop of Dublin (Cardinal McCabe) some few years before, laid down safe and right rules of action to be followed by the Irish people in their political struggles. Religion and justice were necessary to the public welfare. In Germany his (the Pope's) action and counsels had happily resulted in peace.

Why should not similar happy results for Ireland, with God's help, be obtained by like methods? The Pope also expressed his fullest trust in the wisdom of the Irish bishops and in the uprightness of the Irish people.

This speech was interpreted as an advice to Irishmen to try to come to an agreement with England, and also as an expression of the hope cherished by His Holiness that he might be able to render assistance in bringing the Irish national question to a satisfactory and timely settlement.

The Roman correspondent of the *Times* telegraphed, Sunday, February 5, 1888 :

The Pope has not sanctioned the publication by the Catholic journals of the address read to His Holiness by Archbishop Walsh on the occasion of the recent visit of the Irish pilgrims to the Vatican, because it was couched in terms not sufficiently measured. A résumé of the Pope's address in reply has also been transmitted from Rome to the news agencies. From this résumé the modifications in the version transmitted by the Irish themselves are expunged.

There was no truth in the statement that " modifications" had been introduced because the address was " couched in terms not sufficiently measured."

Dr. Walsh had written to Dr. Croke from Naples towards the end of January 1888, giving him an account of the Pope's reception of the Irish bishops. Dr. Croke replied at once :

CROKE TO WALSH.

Thurles, January 28, 1888.

I have got your welcome and interesting letter from Naples, and write you a line in reply.

The Pope, of course, is well disposed, but I think he over-estimates his influence greatly, if he suppose for a moment that he can settle the Irish question in a manner satisfactory to the Irish people. But, still, we must not put any obstacles in his way, so that his experiment may be tried under favourable circumstances.

Your programme is all right. We simply want to manage

our own affairs, stock, lock, and barrel. We are satisfied to live for evermore under the sceptre of England's king or queen, yielding all due obedience to the same, provided that Ireland's administration be in the hands of the sons and friends of the Irish people.

Voila tout! We have a right to that, and we are bent on that. With anything short of that we will not be satisfied. Any compromise of that right we will not accept. When that right is conceded, all other things will, in due course, come to us.

I am afraid, though, that His Holiness either misunderstands our needs, or miscalculates his own ability to supply them. As things go, the Tory Government appears to be greatly shaken. It has not left us a vestige of liberty. Every day reveals some fresh excess of despotism. When it will end nobody can tell. 'Tis hard to bear it; but any uprising against it would be worse than a crime.

The special interview between Archbishop Walsh and Pope Leo XIII took place on Monday, February 13, 1888. The Pope was accompanied by his Secretary of State, Cardinal Rampolla, and with Dr. Walsh came the Bishop of Cork, Dr. O'Callaghan. The latter was present chiefly that he might act as interpreter if the occasion should arise. The discussion was carried on in Italian, and Dr. O'Callaghan, who had resided in Rome for several years, spoke the language with ease and fluency. Dr. Walsh knew Italian well and followed and took part in the discussions without difficulty, but through want of opportunity and practice he lacked the facility and readiness of idiomatic expression which comes only by use.

For nearly two hours the whole Irish situation was reviewed and discussed. The Education Question was quickly disposed of, for both the Pope and the Cardinal-Secretary declared that they fully understood that question after they had read and studied Dr. Walsh's " Memorandum on Irish Education." The next topic discussed was the question of Home Rule. On this matter the Pope expressed his great anxiety lest the cause of

Catholicity in England should suffer serious injury by the
withdrawal of the Irish members from the Imperial Parliament. Dr. Walsh assured His Holiness that the cessation
of Irish representation was not an essential part of a Home
Rule settlement; that, in fact, he himself rather favoured
the continuance of Irish representation at Westminster
—until such time, at least, as certain outstanding questions
affecting the two countries were settled. He pointed out,
however, that withdrawal of Irish representation would not
be an unmixed evil, even in regard to questions affecting
education and Catholic interests generally in England,
inasmuch as Irish Catholics, in English boroughs especially,
not unfrequently supported Liberal candidates of Irish
sympathies, who on religious grounds were entirely
objectionable; as an instance of this he referred to the action
of the Irish at Newcastle by whose vote the agnostic,
Morley, had been returned to Parliament at the head of the
poll. Cardinal Rampolla then raised the question of
" separation." Rampolla had been much impressed by
the arguments of English representatives at Rome, who
had insisted that Home Rule meant separation of Ireland
from England; and the Cardinal expressed the view that it
would be unreasonable to expect England to agree to a
measure which would inevitably lead to the disruption of
the British Empire. The Archbishop replied that he was a
staunch Home Ruler, but not a separatist; neither was
Cardinal Manning, nor the Archbishop of Cashel. They,
like himself, were Home Rulers, but all three of them had
publicly disapproved of separation. So, too, Parnell, speaking for the whole constitutional party in Ireland, had
declared against separation.*

* Some months later, June 23, 1888, appeared Parnell's famous
letter to Cecil Rhodes, in which he wrote :—
" You have correctly judged the exclusion of the Irish
members from Westminster to have been a defect in the Home
Rule measure of 1886, and further, that this proposed exclusion
may have given some colour to the accusation so freely made

M

In confirmation of his statement regarding separation the Archbishop referred to a public letter written by him some months previously to a Scotch Liberal-Unionist who had asked for an assurance that Home Rule did not involve separation. The Archbishop went further and reminded Cardinal Rampolla that the Irish members were elected to Parliament to obtain for the Irish people their just political rights, and that these members were perfectly within their rights in pressing for Home Rule or even for complete separation or independence, although the achievement of this purpose might possibly entail hardships on the Catholics of England.

In the course of the discussion Rampolla appealed to Bishop O'Callaghan for confirmation of a report that Cardinal Zigliara, one of the Cardinals of the Congregation of Propaganda, considered Home Rule to be but a stepping-stone to separation. "Yes," said Dr. O'Callaghan, "Cardinal Zigliara considers that Home Rule endangers the unity of the British Empire, or, as the Cardinal expressed it, *est contra principium unitatis*." "How, then," said the Archbishop, "does the German Empire hold together, seeing that it embraces four kingdoms, together with over twenty archduchies and duchies and principalities, all more

---

against the Bill—that it had a separatist tendency. I say this while strongly asserting and believing that the measure itself was accepted by the Irish people without any afterthought of the kind, and with an earnest desire to work it out with the same spirit in which it was offered. . . .

"My own views upon the points and probabilities of the future, and the bearing of this subject (of the retention of the Irish members at Westminster) upon the question of Imperial Federation—my own feeling upon the measure is that if Mr. Gladstone includes in his next Home Rule measure provisions of such retention, we should cheerfully concur with them, and accept them with good-will and good faith, with the intention of taking our share in the Imperial partnership. I believe also that in the event stated this will be the case, and that the Irish people will cheerfully accept the duties and responsibilities assigned to them, and will justly value the position given to them in the Imperial system."

or less autonomous?"   Whereupon Leo remarked to Rampolla : " *Ecco un nuovo aspetto !*"

At the end of an hour's animated discussion the Pope declared that he understood clearly the bearings of the Home Rule question.   He then invited the Archbishop to address himself to the question of Irish land.   For over half an hour Dr. Walsh spoke without interruption on this complicated subject, explaining the system of land tenure in Ireland, the hardships and injustice of evictions, the constitution and scope of the land courts established by the State, and other kindred matters.   The Pope then put several questions to the Archbishop with the view of clarifying his own ideas.   During this part of the conference Cardinal Rampolla and Dr. O'Callaghan remained practically silent.   At the end of almost two hours Pope Leo declared that he had a definite and clear notion regarding Education and Home Rule, but that as the Land Question was so complicated he would ask Dr. Walsh to prepare a Memorandum, like his Memorandum on Education, in which he would set forth the case in its historical and practical bearings.   The Archbishop readily undertook to comply with the Holy Father's request.   Thus the conference concluded, and after a few minutes' conversation on topics of general interest the audience came to an end.

On Sunday, February 19, 1888, Dr. Walsh, writing from Rome, sent to Dr. Croke a detailed account of the discussions which had taken place at the audience with the Pope. An outline of the discussion is also contained in a letter written by Dr. Walsh some weeks later to Cardinal Manning.

WALSH TO MANNING.

Rome, April 2, 1888.

The Holy Father undoubtedly has a strong conviction that he can get something very substantial done for us in Ireland.   So he asked the Bishop of Cork and myself to go to him one day, and to tell him fully how the whole case stands. It was marvellous to see how he entered into everything. One would think that outside the shores of Ireland there was nothing in the world that he took the smallest interest in. We were with him for nearly two hours, and his sole anxiety at the end seemed to be to learn whether there was anything else we wished him to understand. At the end he charged us to draw up a *relatio* on the whole question of the land. Home Rule he understands fully and needs no information about.

As for Education, we could hardly get him to notice the question at all. He sees very clearly that it is not, as he said, *la questione attuale*.

In dealing with the Land question I went mainly on the subject of arrears; the reference to the Scotch crofters' case evidently roused his indignation as to the way in which Ireland is treated. Fortunately I was able to show him a number of the *Illustrated London News*, with a picture of the crofters fighting the military. " Ah !" said he, " *una vera insurrezione !*" I said, " Yes, Holy Father, and that answers your question why this Arrears Bill was passed for the Scotch crofters and why no such Bill is passed for us ; our people are too quiet, and if things are allowed to go on much longer in this way, we shall have *una vera insurrezione* in Ireland, too."

Now, coming to the *relatio*, I decided on writing a historical statement giving all the prominent incidents, including the various Bills and Acts of Parliament for the last thirty or forty years. This seems to me to be the best way of showing that the people want nothing but common justice, and that the great obstacle in the way of their getting it has been, and is, the Tory Party.

CROKE TO WALSH.

London, February 23, 1888.

Yours of Sunday (February 19) reached me here this morning. It afforded me the greatest pleasure as far as regards the audience.

'Tis an ease to us to know that the Pope is all right. I hope he will keep so. But our friends on the other side will be active. His position is a difficult one, he hears so many conflicting stories. Still, one would imagine that the Irish bishops ought to be the best judges of the situation, and on Irish affairs the most reliable advisers of the Pope.

I shall be very anxious to hear that you are well. I can easily understand how you are so knocked up. Such tension as yours must be terrible. But your success will have a soothing effect.

Fail not to let me know when you are coming here. Anyhow drop me a line on receipt.

CROKE TO WALSH.

Thurles, March 25, 1888.

I have been daily expecting to hear from you, and very likely you were similarly looking out for a line from me.

Let me tell you my story. A band came here, as usual, on St. Patrick's Day to serenade the "Great Man," and after having played well and long in front of the Palazzo I took them out to the Ursulines to cheer the good nuns with their music. There, too, they played a good while. At last they stopped. Refreshments were produced in the shape of wine and lemonade. The non-teetotallers took the wine and the teetotallers tackled the lighter beverage. One bottle of this latter was so refractory that the cork could not be got out, and, as no corkscrew was at hand, I had recourse to the usual means in such difficult cases and struck the bottle against the wall and, of course, close up to the latter. Well, my dear, the bottle, not being *used* to such treatment, burst into pieces in my hand and carried away the greater part of the fleshy portion of my thumb. It was a dreadful wound. Fortunately the Dr. (Laffan) was at hand, and I got him to fix up the thumb as well as he could, and so the member remains even unto this day. It gave me a deal of pain and trouble for a couple of days, and left me sleepless for a couple of nights; but to-day, thank God, I find it somewhat better, and in a fair way to become useful again. Such is my story. From it you may infer I was not in a condition to write much to friend or foe of late, and indeed I make an effort to epistolise you just now, the pen being located between my index finger and its next-door neighbour. I have been hard set to dress myself. I am unshaved, more than usually ugly, as are indeed most males who wear a short shaggy and greyish beard. My peregrinations are confined to my own demesne, but inquisitive folk, lay and clerical, make occasional raids on my premises, and carry afterwards to the outer world the assurance of my existence, anyhow.

Dr. O'Callaghan of Cork called here yesterday, and in a very disjointed way, partly in Italian and partly in English, gave a sketch of the Roman campaign and of your hard work. I could never go to such lengths to satisfy Roman authorities as regards Ireland.

Immediately after the conference with the Pope and Cardinal Rampolla, Dr. Walsh set himself to prepare the Memorandum on the Irish Land Question. The Memorandum was drawn up at the Augustinian convent at Genazzano. On the invitation of the Augustinian Fathers the Archbishop retired to their convent of S. Pio, where Prior Glynn made arrangements to secure that he might work without interruption. Here for three or four weeks he toiled with unflagging energy. His daily routine during these weeks is described by the Rev. Dr. John Condon, O.S.A., who, then a student, was appointed by the Prior to see to the Archbishop's comfort and to serve his Mass.

At 6.10 each morning the Archbishop was in the convent oratory ready to say Mass. He had already shaved—it was his invariable practice throughout his life never to leave his room in the morning with this duty unperformed—and by that time also he had finished the recitation of Matins and Lauds. After Mass he made his thanksgiving and then recited the Small Hours of the Divine Office. At seven he and Mr. Condon took their coffee together. The Archbishop then went at once to his room and worked without a break until he joined the little community at the midday meal. An hour was devoted to dinner and a walk in the cloister. He wrote again from one till half past five, when, in company with Mr. Condon, he took a short walk and paid a visit to one of the neighbouring churches. Three-quarters of an hour was devoted to supper and conversation, and at half past seven the Archbishop retired to his room to continue his labours till about midnight.

He wrote the Memorandum almost without books—which is surprising in view of the fact that the printed work bristles with references. These references he had sent to him from Ireland while the work was in progress. He thought the most effective method to follow was to treat the question historically, and as he proceeded with his task it soon became evident that a rather elaborate statement would be necessary in order to set forth clearly the principles and historical development of a system of land tenure with which the Pope and Rampolla were quite unacquainted. He worked hard, and in the course of some weeks he had his work well forward. He wrote in English, and two translators* were kept busily engaged in turning the statement into Italian. The Archbishop revised their work, and carefully corrected all the sheets as they came from the Press. At Easter, April 1, 1888, he had got ahead of his printers, and for a few days he interrupted his work, the "*lavoro*," as the Pope called it, in order to compile an "*opuscolo*" in which he set out a summary refutation of a mischievous and misleading pamphlet which was being circulated in Rome at that time.

To Manning Dr. Walsh wrote, April 2, 1888 :

At a critical moment my translators, for I had two of them at work, failed me. I was then driven to the expedient of making up the enclosed *opuscolo* which was in the Holy Father's hands last Wednesday (March 28). I do not expect to have the *relatio*—the fuller composition— ready for about a fortnight.

The pamphlet I refer to in the *opuscolo* is just what I describe. It is one of the I.L.P.U. publications which has been widely circulated here in Rome, and it has done great harm. One would think from reading it that everything possible has been done for the Irish tenants. But, as this is brought out by downright lying, the pamphlet gives a good opportunity for reply.

---

* The work of translation was done mainly by Fr. (afterwards Cardinal) Martinelli, who was a guest in the convent at the time.

In the fuller *relatio* I refer frequently to these misrepresentations, taking them up individually as occasion arises.*

The completed "*relatio*" or "*lavoro*" was entitled *La Questione Agraria Irlandese*. It was a volume of "pp. 313 et xvi.", beautifully printed in folio, with large margins. The book was divided into sixteen chapters, with an introduction in which the position and claims of the tenants and the principles of Irish land tenure were compendiously set out—references being given in the margins to the pages of the body of the work where the questions were fully treated. The body of the work (pp. 1-283) contained sixteen chapters divided into sections, each section being liberally supplied with marginal notes indicating the subject-matter dealt with and the pages in which further information might be obtained. There were also several pages of figures and schedules. At the end of the work there were five short appendices (pp. 285-313) containing certain important documents printed in full. The whole was printed in Italian. *La Questione Agraria Irlandese* is not only a valuable historical document, but also a monument of work well done under great pressure in difficult circumstances.

Just within the fortnight mentioned in his letter (of April 2) to Manning, the final sheets of the "*lavoro*" were passing through the Press, and Dr. Walsh was beginning to heave a sigh of relief that in a few days it would be in the possession of the Pope. But before the work reached the hands of the Pope Dr. Walsh read the startling and almost incredible report which was published in the *Times* of April 19, 1888 —that the Holy See had condemned the Plan of Campaign ! The *Times* of the following day contained a definite and

---

* Manning to Walsh, London, April 5, 1888 :—

" The ' opuscolo ' I have read with great interest. It is clear and firm. The Holy Father has already detailed knowledge to supply its brevity. I will carefully keep the ' operazione ' for you—as a pledge of my seeing you, when you return.

" I hope you are well, and up to your work."

detailed statement of the contents of a document of condemnation which, it was said, was to be published forthwith. Dr. Walsh was at first inclined to give no credence to these reports, but soon it was evident that they were well-founded, and all doubt was removed when he received, on April 23, 1888, an official letter from Cardinal Simeoni, accompanied by a Reply or Decree of the Congregation of the Holy Office formally condemning the Plan of Campaign and Boycotting.

Cardinal Simeoni's letter with the Reply of the Congregation—which was addressed to each of the Irish bishops—ran as follows :—

Illme ac Rme Domine.
Ex. Suprema S. Romanae et Universalis Inquisitionis Congregatione editae sunt literae, sub die 20 vertentis mensis Aprilis, ad singulos Hiberniae Archiepiscopos et Episcopos transmittendae.

Earumdem literarum exemplar ad Amplitudinem Tuam heic inclusum transmitto ; meoque officio functus precor Deum ut te quam diutissime servet ac sospitet.

Romae ex Aed. S.C. de Propaganda Fide,
die 23 Aprilis, 1888,
A.T.,
Addictissimus uti Frater,
JOANNES CARD. SIMEONI, *Praefectus*,
D. Archiep. Tyren. Sec.

Illme ac Rme Domine,
Saepenumero Apostolica Sedes populo Hibernensi quem praecipua benevolentia semper prosequuta est, cum eius res postulare videbantur, opportuna monita et consilia praebuit, quibus iura sua defendere aut vindicare salva justitia et incolumi publica quiete posset. Nunc vero SSmus D.N. Leo XIII. veritus, ne in eo belli genere, quod apud populum illum in controversias inter locatores et conductores fundorum sive praediorum inductum est, quodque audit *The Plan of Campaign* et in ea interdictionis forma quae ob easdem controversias *Boycotting* nuncupatur, genuinus justitiae et caritatis sensus in eo pervertatur, mandavit Supremae Congregationi S.R. et U. Inquisitionis ut rem serio ac

diligenti examini subiiceret. Itaque Emis Patribus Card.
contra haereticam pravitatem una mecum Generalibus
Inquisitoribus, propositum fuit dubium : *Utrum liceat in
controversiis inter locatores et conductores fundorum seu
praediorum in Hibernia uti mediis vulgo appellatis the Plan
of Campaign et the Boycotting*—et ab Emis Patribus re
diu ac macture perpensa unanimi suffragio responsum fuit :
Negative.

Quam profecto responsionem SSmus Pater feria IV die
18 huius mensis probavit et confirmavit.

Huius iudicii quanta sit aequitas facile quisque perspiciet,
si animadvertat locationis pensionem quae mutua consensione statuta sit, privato unius conductoris arbitrio imminui,
salva consensionis fide, non posse ; praesertim cum certa
tribunalia huiusmodi controversiis dirimendis statuta sint
quae pensiones justo majores intra aequitatis limites cohi-
beant et moderentur, habita etiam ratione sterilitatis vel
calamitatum quae incidere potuerint. Neque fas putandum,
ut a conductoribus extorqueatur pensio et apud ignotos
deponatur, locatore posthabito. Denique a naturali justitia
et christiana caritate est omnino alienum, ut nova quadam
persecutione et interdictione saeviatur sive in eos qui
contenti earum pensionum, de quibus cum dominus praediorum convenerant, eas potius solvere parati sunt ; sive in
eos qui vacuos fundos, utentes iure suo conducunt.

Quare erit Ampl. Tuae prudenter quidem sed efficaciter
de hac re tum ecclesiasticos viros, tum fideles monere
eosque exhortari, ut dum levamen afflictae suae fortunae
quaerunt, christianam caritatem servent et justitiae fines
non transiliant. Mihi interim gratum est fausta omnia Ampl.
Tuae a Domino adprecari.

A.T.

Romae die 20 Aprilis, 1888,

Addictissimus in Domino,

R. CARD. MONACO.

[Translation.]

MY LORD—A letter was issued by the Supreme Congregation
of the Holy Roman and Universal Inquisition on the 20th
of the present month of April for transmission to the
Archbishops and Bishops of Ireland.

Herewith I send your Lordship a copy of this letter, and

having discharged this duty and wishing you every blessing, I remain yours devotedly,

JOHN CARD. SIMEONI, *Prefect*,

D. Archbishop of Tyre,

Secretary.

S. Congregation of the Propaganda,
   Rome,
    April 23, 1888.

Reply of the Holy Office.

MY LORD,—Whenever the affairs of their country seemed to require it, the Apostolic See has frequently addressed to the Irish people—towards whom it has always shown special affection—seasonable words of warning and counsel with the object of enabling them to defend or to assert their rights without prejudice to justice or to public tranquillity. At the present moment our Holy Father, Pope Leo XIII, fearing lest right notions of justice and charity should be perverted amongst that people in consequence of that mode of warfare called the *Plan of Campaign,* which has been employed in that country in disputes between letters and holders of lands or farms, as also in consequence of a form of proscription in connection with the same contests known as *Boycotting,* commissioned the Supreme Congregation of the Holy Roman and Universal Inquisition to make the matter the subject of grave and careful examination. Accordingly the following question was submitted to the Most Eminent Fathers who share with me the office of General Inquisitors against heretical error, etc., viz. : In disputes between letters and holders of farms or lands in Ireland, is it lawful to have recourse to those means known as the *Plan of Campaign* and *Boycotting ?*—and their Eminences, having long and maturely weighed the matter, unanimously replied : *In the negative.*

Our Holy Father confirmed and approved this reply on Wednesday the 18th of the present month.

How equitable this decision is any one will see who reflects that a rent fixed by mutual consent cannot, without violation of contract, be reduced at the arbitrary will of the tenant alone. This the more, since for the settling of such disputes courts have been established which, allowance being made even for failure of crops or disasters which may have occurred, reduce excessive rents and bring them within the limits of equity.

Again, it cannot be held to be lawful that rent should be
extorted from tenants and deposited with unknown persons,
no account being taken of the landlord.

Finally, it is altogether foreign to natural justice and to
Christian charity that a new form of persecution and of
proscription should ruthlessly be put in force against persons
who are satisfied with and are prepared to pay the rent
agreed on with their landlord; or against persons who in the
exercise of their right take vacant farms.

Your Lordship will therefore—prudently but effectively—
admonish the clergy and people in reference to this matter,
and exhort them to observe Christian charity, and not to
overstep the bounds of justice whilst seeking relief from
the evils which afflict them.

Your devoted servant in the Lord,

Rome, 20th April, 1888.   R. CARD. MONACO.

The publication of the Decree* of the Holy Office and
Cardinal Monaco's letter caused great satisfaction in Tory
circles and corresponding disappointment amongst Irish
Nationalists. By the former the Decree was hailed as an
authoritative condemnation of the Irish National movement,
more particularly of the National League and its methods of
Boycotting and Plan of Campaign. The Decree gave rise to
much misleading and inaccurate writing in the newspapers
—both Irish and English—and some ill-advised statements
regarding it were made by politicians and public men. The
situation thus created was a very awkward one, especially
for the Irish bishops and for the Irish Nationalist Party.
For Dr. Walsh the situation was not only awkward but very
painful. For weeks he had been labouring, in compliance
with the Pope's express wish, in preparing an exposition of
the Irish Land Question—including a full statement on the

---

* In the Press, the document issued by the Holy Office was
styled, not incorrectly, *Reply, Rescript, Decree.* In canonical
usage the word *Decree* has various senses. In Jure . . . *decretum*
praesertim dicebatur id quod statuebatur, deliberatione prae-
missa, vel causa sive quaestione cognita . . . . Hodie omnia
acta SS. Congregationum aut Officiorum S. Sedis dicuntur
Decreta. Rescriptum est responsum principis, Ordinarii, etc., ad
alicuius consultationem *in scriptis* datum. (FERRARIS s. vv.

Plan of Campaign and Boycotting—and just when the task was completed came the blow which he had hoped to avert.

When the Decree of the Holy Office was published in the newspapers, Dr. Walsh wrote to Dr. Croke advising that it should be quietly accepted, and that as far as possible, all public discussions, especially in the newspapers, should be avoided. He pointed out that such discussions would almost inevitably lead to grave inconveniences, and possibly to wild and inaccurate utterances. Like Cardinal Manning, he feared lest something might be said which would transgress the limits of faith or morals. Unfortunately, however, the Archbishop's prudent counsel was unheeded; indeed, before his letter reached Ireland the discussions had begun. Severe strictures were made regarding the fact that the contents of the document addressed to the Irish bishops had been communicated to newspapers like the *Times*, or at least allowed to appear in its columns long before the document itself had come into the hands of the Irish bishops to whom it was addressed.

Much also was spoken and written at the time both in England and Ireland, concerning the interpretation and application of the Decree. On the one side it was contended that the Decree had little or no practical bearing on the facts of the situation then actually existing in Ireland. Those who put forward this view were met by their opponents with the cry of Jansenism.

With the view of appraising the action of certain public bodies in Ireland with regard to the Decree, as well as of understanding some comments which Dr. Walsh felt it his duty to make regarding their action, it will be necessary to give here an outline of the manner in which the Decree was analysed and criticised.

In the first place the coldness of Cardinal Simeoni's official communication was noted. It was commonly believed that he by no means welcomed Cardinal Rampolla's interference in Irish affairs. Rampolla, it was said, in his eagerness to hasten on the settlement of the question of diplomatic relations with England, had thrust himself in between the Irish bishops and the Cardinal-Prefect of Propaganda.

In the next place it was remarked that the question dealt with in the Reply or Decree of the Holy Office and in Cardinal Monaco's letter was a question of morals. It was not a political question. Indeed, the Congregation of the Holy Office had nothing to do with political questions. As the question was one of morals, no Catholic could say that it was not within the competence of the supreme ecclesiastical authority—and on the question of morals the Holy Office was practically the supreme authority, the Pope himself being Prefect of the Sacred Congregation—to discuss and decide it. The Congregation had considered and decided the question, as it was undoubtedly competent to do.

In an elaborate article in the *Freeman's Journal* (May 1, 1888), evidently written by a theologian, the purport and scope of the Decree were analysed :

The purport of the reply of the Holy Office is plain. The Plan of Campaign is described as a certain composite thing made up of contract-breaking by private authority accompanied by intimidation and extortion, although the Courts of Law are accessible and available to procure just remedies. Such is the Plan of Campaign which was condemned. If all or any of these constituent elements were absent from a combination of tenants, such a combination ought not to be called the Plan of Campaign condemned by the Holy Office. If, in the same way, Boycotting is a refusal of intercourse in which charity is violated—and this is the boycotting condemned by the Sacred Congregation—no Catholic could question the decision of the Sacred Congregation.

Moreover [it was noted] the Decree did not condemn the Plan of Campaign or Boycotting in general. The Decree contained three things :

1.—A question submitted to the Congregation by the Pope, viz. : " Is it lawful to use the Plan of Campaign in controversies between *locatores* and *conductores* of farms in Ireland ?"

2.—The answer to that question, viz., that " it is not lawful to use the Plan of Campaign in the controversies between *locatores* and *conductores* of farms in Ireland."

3.—The Pope's approbation of that answer and decision of the Sacred Congregation.

The Plan of Campaign was not condemned—there was no question put about it. The use of the Plan of Campaign was not condemned ; there was no question about it. Its use in one particular case was condemned—its use namely in the case of controversies between *locatores* and *conductores* of farms in Ireland. To condemn the use of a thing in a particular case was not to condemn the use of it in every case. The Church, for example, condemned the reading of the Scriptures in the versions habitually circulated by the Protestant Societies. The Irish bishops condemend the use of the Scriptures in certain cases, for instance, as a school book in " National" schools, but neither the Church nor the Irish Bishops ever condemned Scripture or the use of Scripture. As far, then, as the Decree went (it was argued) it might be lawful to use the Plan of Campaign and Boycotting in every controversy except in controversies between *locatores* and *conductores* of farms in Ireland. Furthermore, it was averred that in order to understand the exact force of the reply of the Holy Office, it was necessary to bear in mind the assumptions of fact, in reference to the Plan of Campaign, as they were set out in the Decree. These assumptions were :

1.—That the fixing of existing rents on the estates to which the Plan of Campaign was applied, was a matter of free contract (*mutua consensione statuta*).

2.—That the Land Courts were open to the tenants who adopted that Plan (*cum certa tribunalia huiusmodi contro- versiis dirimendis statuta sint*), " or at least, for the phraseology seems somewhat ambiguous, that they are now open."

3.—That the reductions of rent made by the Land Courts were what equity demanded (*pensiones, justo maiores, intra equitatis limites cohibent et moderantur*).

4.—That the rents deposited with the estate trustees in the cases in which the Plan was put into operation were " extorted" from the tenants, and that these trustees were unknown persons (*ut a conductoribus extorqueatur pensio et apud ignotos deponatur*).

5.—That under the Plan of Campaign the interest of the landlord was not sufficiently consulted (*locatore posthabito*).

6.—That the relation existing between the contending parties in agrarian disputes in Ireland was the ordinary relation of landlord and tenant, and not rather that of joint-owners; the landlord was referred to as " the owner of the farms" (*dominus praediorum*), and spoken of as "letting" or " hiring out" (*locator*) those farms to the tenant (*conductor*); in other words, it was assumed that the contract in question was that technically known as *locatio-conductio*.

Whether those assumptions (of fact) were correct or not was a question of fact; whether or not the Plan of Campaign were lawful *in the cases in which those assumptions of fact were realised* was a question of theology, and upon this latter question alone the Sacred Congregation had pronounced its definitive judgment.

Similarly (the writer argued) the condemnation of " Boycotting" was based on the assumptions of fact :

1.—That it was carried to merciless extremes (*saeviebatur*); and

2.—That is was employed either (*a*) against those who were content with the rents fixed by mutual consent between themselves and their landlords, and who were willing to pay those rents; or (*b*) against those who took vacant farms which they were within their rights in taking (*in eos qui contenti earum pensionum de quibus cum dominis praediorum convenerant, eas potius solvere parati sunt, sive in eos qui vacuos fundos, utentes iure suo, conducunt*).

An important question then to be determined was whether the controversies between landlords and tenants in Ireland were controversies between *locatores* and *conductores*. Was the relation between landlord and tenant in Ireland that of *locator* and *conductor*? If the contract was *locatio-conductio*, then according to the terms of the Decree it was unlawful to use the Plan of Campaign or Boycotting against such landlords; but if there were landlords and tenants in Ireland who were not *locatores* and *conductores*, the condemnation of the Holy Office did not apply to them.

A vital matter was to understand clearly the meaning of the words *locatores* and *conductores* and of the contract *locatio-conductio*.

The words *locator* and *conductor*, it was pointed out, were technical words used in theology and Canon Law. " A *locator* is one who lets; but not everyone who lets is a *locator*, but only he who has absolute and complete right to the thing he lets, and to everything that appertains to it. The *conductor* is a hirer, but is not everyone who hires. He is one who has no antecedent right whatever to the thing that he takes or hires or to anything that appertains to it. A man hires a horse to plough his land; the man who gives the horse is a *locator*; the man who hires the horse is a *conductor*. A man employs a painter to paint his house, or a stone-mason to build a wall; the employer is the *conductor*, and the painter or mason is the *locator*. A man builds a house in a street and lets it out to a tenant; he is the letter or landlord or *locator*, the tenant is the *conductor*." The essence, then, of the contract *locatio-conductio* seemed to be that the locator had complete rights of property in what he let, and that the conductor had no antecedent right at all to what he hired. The man who hired the horse had no right whatever to the horse; the man who gave the horse was complete owner of the horse. The servant who engaged with a master for specified wages, before he entered into his contract, was complete owner of his services, and the master had no right to them whatever. The man who built the house in a street and let it had complete rights over the house, and the man who took it had none at all in the house. The contract "locatio-conductio" was thus seen to be one in which the locator had complete rights of property in what he let, and the conductor had no rights of property in what he took.

But in the vast majority of cases of landlord and tenant in Ireland, the landlord had not complete rights of property in the farm which he let, and the tenant had a just right to a considerable share in the value of the farm of which he was tenant. The tenant's right was indisputable. It was recognised by the law of the land. The ownership of the farm was a joint ownership, a *condominium*. The contract, therefore, in those cases was not *locatio-conductio*, but a contract technically known as *emphyteusis*. It was contended, then, that if the Sacred Congregation had meant to refer to such contracts, it would presumably not have employed the words *locatores-conductores*, but would have use the available recognised terms for such contracts. The words *dominus emphyteuseos-emphyteuta* were the recognised technical terms.

But, it was contended, furthermore—" grant for the sake of argument that the Holy Office believed

that landlords and tenants in Ireland are included
under the terms *locatores* and *conductores*; grant that the
Holy Office intended to include them under these words;
grant even that it tried to include them under the words,
yet if the words themselves do not include landlords and
tenants as commonly found in Ireland, such tenants are
not included under them."

The views just set forth seem to have been in substance
the views of Dr. Croke.

Dr. Walsh had written to Dr. Croke from Rome, Sunday,
April 29, 1888, giving an account of the history of the
issuing of the Decree, and on receiving the letter the
Archbishop of Cashel replied :

CROKE TO WALSH.

May 2, 1888.

Your letter of the 29 ult. just to hand was an immense
relief to me. I could not account for your silence.

I got your telegram in due course. Dillon called to see
me on Saturday morning, 28th. He is quite cool over the
matter. We understood each other fully, and the course
determined on was to agree with Inquisitors in condemning
Plan and Boycotting when they were, or are, attended with
the conditions referred to in the so-called " Decree." I
have written to the *Freeman* every day since " Decree "
appeared putting forward that line of defence. You will
have seen, before this reaches you, the admirable *exposé* on
the whole affair that appeared in yesterday's *Freeman*,
presumably from the pen of Dr. McGrath of Clonliffe. It is
quite clear and conclusive. If I have a warrant in my
possession for the arrest of a man with red hair, heavy
beard, no teeth, black eyes, protruding stomach, a lame leg,
and six feet high, and if I arrest a man in whose person
all the above qualities are wanting, I surely should liberate
the supposed culprit on seeing my mistake, and make an
apology to him besides. *Sat verbum.*

I had a letter this morning from Cardinal Manning. He
says he has written to you for information. We all want
that. He says, *inter alia*, " I always thought the Plan
legally untenable but morally just." I wrote to Dr. Logue
yesterday, *half* recommending and *half* suggesting a general
meeting of the bishops. But I see great difficulties in that

course. So I wired him this morning not to summon it, and I added that you do not appear to be favourable to it.

As regards the feeling through the country all that can be said is that no public notice has been taken of the decree at all yet. The people don't seem to mind it. Everything goes on as usual. The *Freeman*, at my suggestion, is taking up campaign cases through the country and means to give reliable statistics to show that " contracts" were not free, that " courts" (impartial) were not accessible in numerous cases (if at all), and that money was paid into the " war chest" most freely by the campaigning tenants, and not " extracted" from them. So also of boycotting.

I met the priests here at conference, yesterday; we talked over " *decree*." I issued no instructions, except, of course, to discourage hasty and irreverent language addressed to the Holy See, and to condemn the Plan and Boycotting when the " *decree*" *applies*. Have you seen the Pope since " decree" was issued? If so, what did he say? When did you get official intimation of existence of " decree"? Did you present your report? What are you at? Why don't you come home? What is the good in wasting and worrying yourself over this matter any longer? How is your health? What does Ephesus say or think? Will write again as soon as I hear from Dr. Logue. Thumb still sore and useless. Still I write a deal. O'Brien in the dock daily. Dillon preparing for same. Write immediately and in detail. Give some facts instructive or interesting in the case. Weather boisterous and wet. God bless you.

After these remarks, needlessly long perhaps, on the discussion in the Irish Press regarding the exact bearing of the meaning of the Decree condemning the Plan of Campaign and Boycotting, the account of Dr. Walsh's activities at Rome may now be continued.

The text of the reply of the Holy Office and of Cardinal Monaco's letter, with a translation, was published in the *Freeman's Journal* on Monday, April 30, 1888. On the same day Cardinal Manning wrote to Dr. Walsh :

Pray without delay let me know the history of the Decree. Had you any knowledge of it ?

Had Mgr. Persico ?

1. While it stands all must submit.

2. But the reasons may be analysed and laid before the Holy Office.

Mgr. Jacobini of Propaganda and Cardinal Schaffino would probably advise best.

I am glad you are well, and I am glad you are in Rome.

To this Dr. Walsh replied at once.

WALSH TO MANNING.

Rome, May 3, 1888.

I have really nothing to add to what your Eminence has seen in the papers. The condemnation of Boycotting does not seem to be objected to by anyone. As for the Plan of Campaign, it is obvious that some most misleading statements regarding its nature were set forth in the case dealt with by the Holy Office. The three reasons set forth in the Decree are unassailable as statements of truths. They are equally satisfactory, no doubt, as reasons applying to the case that was in hand. But manifestly they have no bearing upon what we know as the Plan of Campaign in Ireland.

If the Holy Father had waited for another week when my information would have been in his hands the Decree could not have been issued in its present form. But then I should have felt some responsibility in the matter. As things stand, I am quite clear.

Now that the Decree has been issued, I see great advantages in what has been done. The Holy Father, in clearing away from our cause those things that were, honestly or dishonestly, put forward by our adversaries, as reasons for leaving our case undealt with, has done us, I think, an enormous service. He meant all this, and if he is able now to carry out the rest of his programme his jubilee year may yet bring us a long way forward in the direction of a satisfactory settlement of our difficulties.

Feeling as I do upon the whole question I should be sorry to see any move for an interpretation or explaining away of the Decree. We should leave things as they are.

Thus our case is an immensely strong one. If, however, nothing is done for us, and the people are left without help to face another winter, we must give them a free hand.

MANNING TO WALSH.

May 6, 1888.

Your letter reached me late last night and gave me much relief. Our papers have been full of folly, and I could not tell what might be passing.

It is strange—nothing surprises me—that you were not consulted, and that no one verified the reasons alleged for the decisions as to rents.

Boycotting, I said some years ago, begins in horse-play but may end in bloodshed.

The Plan of Campaign is a true reflex of the whole Irish question. " Legal right and Moral wrong." " *Summum ius summa injuria.*" I have written these words long ago, you know to whom (Leo XIII).

For the moment worldly influence has prevailed. My daily fear is that some word or act may exceed the limit of faith and morals. At first I wished that this decision had been sent in private to all your bishops as private direction.

But then I saw that you might have been embarrassed and the brunt would have fallen on you. Now it comes over your heads from the highest source, and you are all shattered, and have the pastoral and painful office of guiding and guarding your people in submission.

But I hope that the Plan of Campaign will be explained and understood as an abnormal but moral equity. Parliament has recognised this in the arrears of the Crofters of Scotland. Try to convince Cardinal Monaco and Cardinal Mazzella. The former is very acute, the latter knows the Irish and the English outer world. If you can gain them and Monsignor Jacobini of Propaganda, they will guide the rest.

One thing more. Do not let pain, or uprightness of heart, or any self-renouncement lead you to offer to leave your post of duty, difficulty, and danger. God has chosen you to fill it, and to stand there till you die.*

On May 5 Dr. Walsh wrote from Rome to Mr. Timothy Harrington, Secretary of the National League. The letter was marked " confidential," and ran as follows :—

* It was announced in the newspapers at the time that Dr. Walsh had tendered his resignation of the See of Dublin, and it was rumoured in Rome that the resignation would be accepted, and that Dr. Walsh would be made a Cardinal in Curia.

I mark this letter " confidential" in the sense that it is not to be published, and that its contents should not in any way be used as coming from me.

I write for your own guidance, as I think there will be a meeting of the League on Tuesday; and I am, of course, anxious that nothing should be said or done to give a handle to its enemies.

I have practically no doubt of the following :—

1st.—That for some time past a very complex machine has been at work to obtain a condemnation of the Home Rule movement if possible, *but at all events of the League*. This, if successful, would of course make it necesary for ecclesiastics at once to withdraw from all connection with it.

2nd.—That the points dealt with in the Decree, Plan of Campaign and Boycotting, were taken up by the opponents of the movement with the view of obtaining a condemnation not of these things only, but of the League itself.

3rd.—That the clear limitation of the Decree—to say nothing of the general words of encouragement—has been a source of bad disappointment to the originators of the intrigue.

4th.—That the Pope saw through the whole affair from the beginning, and took the very best way of counter-mining the plans of the intriguers. He simply referred a case stated to the Holy Office, which in the discharge of its duty examined that case and decided it.

5th.—That the chief hope of the intriguers now rests on the chance that the League may commit itself by some imprudent action which will bring it under the condemnation of the Holy See.

6th.—That the business of the hour is to take every possible precaution on this point. Not only should the Central League keep its hands clear, but it should act, as it has always acted, in condemning the excesses of any local branches that may be guilty of them.

All this being so, you may ask what I think should be done on Tuesday.

I should make the following suggestions :—

1st.—Pass a resolution declaring that any political organisation would be out of place in a Catholic country such as Ireland, which would fail to receive not only with respect, but with profound submission, the teaching of the Holy See on a point of morals.

2nd.—Pass another resolution saying that in the present

case as *questions have been raised as to the precise meaning and extent of the Decree*, you await whatever instructions may be issued regarding it *by the bishops*.

3rd.—And a third, that you impress earnestly upon all who have the success of the National movement at heart the necessity of abstaining from anything in discussions, whether oral or written, that could be construed by the enemies of the movement as a questioning of the authority of the Holy See on matters of faith and morals.

I am strongly of opinion that, as a matter of *politics* or *tactics*, an opportunity should be taken just now to drop the Plan of Campaign as quietly as possible.

It did splendid work for the tenants. But there is no doubt it led recently to much embarrassment. Mr. Parnell never liked it. Of course the same must be said of Gladstone and the other Liberal leaders who have given such splendid help for the last year or two.

As regards its justification from a moral point of view, a great deal could be said about the Plan in abstract, which could not be said of it in actual operation.

At all events, waiving the theology of the matter, and looking at it as an affair of *practical politics*, I can see no room for doubt in the matter.

Not only the Government, but the " Unionist" people generally, would find themselves in a most serious difficulty —in fact, I don't see how they could justify any further inaction—if the excuses on which they have so long been relying were suddenly cut away from them.

I take it for granted that Mr. Parnell would in no way incur the responsibility of advising the continuance of the means in question, in face of the new state of things that has arisen; and this being so I don't see how the responsibility is to be incurred.

I write, I need not say, altogether from myself; and also altogether to yourself, merely that you may make your own use of the ideas that occur to me.

P.S.—Of course I include any two or three confidential persons you may think it necessary to consult.

I did not answer telegram as I am as yet unable to say when I can reach home. I hope to leave Rome in a few days. But I really must take a good rest before facing my work at home.

There must be no notice taken of my arrival in Ireland.

On May 7, in response to urgent requests from many quarters in Ireland, Dr. Walsh gave public expression of his views on the nature and implications of the Decree. In the course of a lengthy letter addressed to the editor of the *Freeman's Journal* he wrote :

It is well to have three things most distinctly understood in Ireland : first, that a most determined effort has been made, or rather that for a considerable time past a series of such efforts has been made, to bring under the unfavourable judgment of the Holy See the Irish Nationalist Movement, or at least the Irish National League; secondly, that the tactics relied upon for the accomplishment of this design were skilfully chosen, and consisted, in fact, in an effort to identify the League, and the movement generally, with methods of action which undoubtedly had in many instances been used in the furtherance of the work of the League in particular localities; and thirdly, that the persistent efforts thus made for months, and, as regards one point, for years, have ended in the most absolute and signal failure as regards the only object that was really aimed at or substantially cared for, by their originators.

The methods of action in question, that is to say, the Plan of Campaign and Boycotting—involving, as they do, many grave questions of morality—were submitted by the Holy Father himself to a tribunal where they were to be considered on their own merits, and without any reference whatever to political considerations, with which, in fact, that tribunal has nothing whatever to do. The decision come to, after prolonged deliberation, was an adverse one; and at once, not perhaps unnaturally in the circumstances, the conclusion was rashly drawn in certain quarters that the National League, if not indeed the National Movement in Ireland, was thereby condemned.

This pleasing delusion, however, had soon to be abandoned. But since then no effort has been spared by the discomfited intriguers to make it appear that the Nationalist organisation has somehow or another fallen under a ban; that the step already taken by the Holy See is indeed only the first of a series of such steps which will be taken, no doubt deliberately, but with the utmost determination; that the formal condemnation of the National League is thus a matter of time; and that, as a natural consequence all good

Catholics who are to be found among its members will take the first opportunity of severing their connection with it.

Now, for all this there is not a particle of foundation. The decision of the Holy See, which has already been published in your columns, is clear and definite in its terms. It is a decision on a question, not of politics, but of morals. As such it will be received by our Catholic people as every decision which has ever yet been pronounced by the Holy See in reference to either faith or morals has been received by them. If doubts or controversies should arise as to its meaning or extent, these will speedily be solved by the bishops of Ireland, or, if it should be necessary, by the Holy See itself. But the question of morality being thus decided, the operation of the recent action of the Holy See is at an end.

The Irish people, whether at home or abroad, will, I trust, accept my assurance that neither the Nationalist Movement nor the National League is in the smallest degree injuriously affected by the recent decree.

Beyond this I do not wish to go. As no one would be justified in supposing that the Irish cause is even indirectly censured by the recent act of the Holy See, so neither should we be justified in asserting that the Holy See was influenced in it by a desire to hasten on the triumph of our great constitutional movement. *But that this will be the necessary result of what has taken place, I, for my part, have not a shadow of doubt.*

A new responsibility, in fact, which it would seem impossible much longer to evade, now lies upon English statesmen. The Irish cause will henceforth stand before the Empire and before the world as one that will have to be dealt with on its merits. Discussions about it can no longer have a tendency to drift away into side-issues as to the real or alleged obstacles which imprudence or want of skill may have placed in the path of statesmen sincerely anxious to take it in hands with a view to its satisfactory settlement.

Is it too much to hope that there may be found in Parliament a body of independent opinion sufficiently strong to make it a matter of necessity that the Irish question, at least in its more urgent aspects, should now be taken in hand without delay? Not many years have elapsed since a great constitutional struggle was happily terminated in Parliament by the business-like and simple expedient of dealing with it in a private and friendly conference between the leaders of the two great political parties whose interests it vitally concerned. Why could not something of the kind be now done for Ireland?

If the work of pacification is to proceed with any prospect of success, the speedy removal of the more pressing difficulties of the land question must undoubtedly be regarded as a matter of absolute necessity. Oppressive evictions should forthwith be rendered impossible. A simple method should be adopted of fixing speedily, and upon some equitable principle, the rent to be paid upon each holding in Ireland for whatever interval must still elapse before the final settlement of the Irish Land Question can be effected by the enactment of a really comprehensive measure.

To anyone who has given practical thought to the subject it must be manifest that there is a way, well worth at least the careful consideration of statesmen, by which all this could be accomplished.

Would it be possible to find a time when statesmen could take the work in hand with better grace, or with more hopeful prospects of success?

When the reply of the Holy Office was published Monsignor Persico was in England, where he awaited official permission to terminate his mission and return to Rome. Since the middle of January he had been residing at Teignmouth, Devon, having retired there for the benefit of his health, which had been for some time indifferent and unequal to the cold and damp of the Irish winter. It was generally assumed that Persico was responsible, by the reports he had submitted to Rome, for the condemnation of the Plan of Campaign and of Boycotting; and, as a consequence, from every side abuse and blame were hurled at his head. The fact, however, seems to be that the action of the Roman Congregation came as a complete surprise to the Envoy, and that his first intimation of it was a copy of the Decree which he received when the decision of the Holy Office was communicated to the Irish bishops by Cardinal Simeoni. Popular opinion, however, assumed that the Envoy was responsible for the action of the Holy Office— that he had played the Irish bishops and people false, and had secretly and basely lent himself to the political designs of Mr. Balfour and Lord Salisbury to crush the Irish Nationalist movement. On April 28, 1888, a statement by Michael Davitt on the Decree of the Holy Office published in the *Pall Mall Gazette* ended thus :

But what a comment on the boasting of Mr. Balfour that he had conquered the League in Ireland. Here we have the people solicited to help the forces of coercion in Ireland to put down Boycotting and defeat the Plan of Campaign; while Monsignor Persico, a once intimate friend of Mr. Patrick Forde of the *Irish World*, has been a welcome aide-de-camp to Lord Salisbury in the contest against the Irish movement.

Monsignor Persico felt his position keenly. The letters whch he wrote at the time express surprise, disappointment, and extreme pain. In the course of a letter to Manning, May 9, he wrote :—

I speak of my return to Italy, as I do not see what I could do in Ireland since the publication of the Decree of the Holy Office, seeing especially that all attribute to me the said Decree, and hence I am now considered the greatest enemy of Ireland. Of this I have daily proofs, not only from public utterances, but from letters and messages which I would be ashamed of particularising to your Eminence. In England I do not see what I could do, and so the best thing the Holy See can do is to recall me to Rome. You are a Cardinal of the Holy Church, and one I deeply esteem and respect, hence I feel that I can speak as I would before the whole Church, and before God Himself. Now, it is known to Y.E. that I did not expect at all the said Decree, and I was never so much surprised in my life as when I received the circular from the Propaganda on the morning of the 28th ultimo. And fancy, I received the *bare* circular, as I suppose every Irish bishop did, without a letter or a word of instruction or explanation. And what is more unaccountable to me, only the day before, I had received a letter from the Secretary for the Extraordinary Ecclesiastical Affairs, telling me that nothing had been done about Irish affairs, and that my reports and other letters were still *nel casetto dell Emo Rampolla* ! And yet the whole world thinks and says that the Holy Office has acted on my report and that the Decree is based on the same ! Not only all the the Roman correspondents, but all the newspapers *avec le Tablet en tête* proclaim and report the same thing ! Hence I must incur and bear the whole odium of the act with all the disagreeable and painful circumstances. I may freely assure Y.E. that my report and all my letters have been written with a most friendly feeling to Ireland; and I need not say that I have been most impartial in all my doings, and in every respect excluding every acceptance of person. The condition of Ireland and all its wants I have exposed most fully, and if I had to touch on certain points I did so in the spirit of charity, making allowance for circumstances, and even when I thought it my duty to allude to inconvenients (*sic*), I proposed discreet and prudential remedies.

Oh, I wish that my reports and all my letters had been studied and seriously considered, and that action had been taken from the same. Above all, I had proposed, and insisted upon it, that whatever was necessary to be done, it might be done with and through the bishops. As I already mentioned to Y.E., I made a special proposal of having in Rome the four archbishops, with a bishop from every province, and in their presence hold a fair discussion about everything. And the conclusions and resolutions thus taken ought to have formed a matter for the coming Synod. In a word, my desire was that the bishops should have ample opportunity to explain or defend every controversial point; and so acting on full conviction of their duty, their action might have been firm and united. I know not whether the Archbishop of Dublin has been heard or been given an opportunity of explaining things. Upon this also I wrote most urgent letters both to Cardinal Rampolla and Cardinal Simeoni, showing the necessity that the said Archbishop should be fully heard and consulted on everything, as he was not only competent but deserved confidence and consideration. I am afraid, however, that the Archbishop also thinks me adverse to the Irish cause, as he must have heard a great deal in Rome about it. I know of old how people talk in Rome; the officials shuffle and speak at random, whereas the writers and underwriters speak most freely, and as knowing everything about affairs and persons. Therefore I must not wonder if the Archbishop of Dublin and other Irish bishops are now inbibed (*sic*) with such ideas. The only thing I can say is : *Dominus est qui judicat me.*

I must confess to your Eminence that all this creates a feeling of sadness, not only for the interests of the Church, but for personal considerations also. In my old age I must be hunted (*sic*) by the thought of being considered and handed down as the enemy of a race which I have ever cherished and loved, and still cherish and love. I need not say, that in all that is published about instructions received by me from Rome, there is no foundation whatever. I have received neither instructions nor explanations, and I am in *perfect* ignorance of what they mean or intend to do. The only letter I received from Card. Rampolla some time ago was to the effect to remain in England until further orders. Beyond this I know nothing. And now I must bring this to a close, having taken too much time from your serious occupations. As I said, the day after to-morrow morning I leave for Parkminster, Partridge Green, Sussex. And imploring from your charity a prayer, I beg to subscribe myself,

IGN. PERSICO, *Archbishop of Damietta*.

Again, May 9, 1888, he wrote :

I would not have the slightest objection to make the following declaration before the whole world, viz., that I had no idea that anything had been done about Irish affairs, much less thought that some questions had been deferred to the H.O.; and the first knowledge I had of the Decree was on the morning of the 28th of April, when I received the *bare* circular sent me by the Propaganda. I must add that had I known of such a thing I would have felt it my duty to make proper representations to the Holy See.*

On Monday, May 14, 1888, a meeting of the Catholic members of the Irish Parliamentary Party, summoned by the Lord Mayor of Dublin, Mr. Thomas Sexton, M.P., on a requisition presented to him by sixty-six members of the Party, was held at the Mansion House, Dublin, to consider

---

* Persico was recalled to Rome soon after the publication of the Decree of the Holy Office. After some time he was appointed Secretary for Oriental Affairs at Propaganda, and later on, General-Secretary of the same Congregation. At the Consistory of January, 1893, he was created a Cardinal, and subsequently he became Prefect of the Sacred Congregation of Indulgences. Dr. Walsh visited him in 1895, shortly before Persico's death.

the reply of the Holy Office and its effects upon the Nationalist movement. After a prefatory statement deprecating the attempts made by unscrupulous enemies of the Holy See and of the Irish people to employ the circular of the Holy Office as a political weapon to prejudice the Irish cause and to create estrangement between the Irish people and their spiritual guides, and declaring the sense of obligation which bound the Irish Catholic representatives to the Holy See and to the Irish people, the meeting adopted a series of resolutions which may be summarised as follows :—

1.—That the allegations of fact set forth in the circular of the Holy Office were unfounded, and would never have been promulgated had they been tested by reference to the prelates of Ireland and the elected representatives of the people.

2.—The status of Irish farmers was not—as the circular assumed—that of mere tenants-at-will; not only in equity but in law the dominant interest in agricultural holdings in Ireland belonged to the tenants.

3.—It was a cause of deep regret that the Holy Office was silent as to the source of the evils and disorders which afflicted the Irish people, namely, the perversion of natural justice by a system of calumny, coercion, and extortion.

4.—This silence of the Holy Office was the more to be deplored, because it enabled the enemies both of religion and of the national cause to misuse the name of the Holy See by an assumption of its hostility to the political claims of Ireland, and might be of untoward consequence at a time when popular patience had been strained to the point of exasperation by persistent misgovernment.

5.—The demand of the Irish people for agrarian reform and political liberty was necessary and just, and conducted by modes of action and methods of organisation that were legal and constitutional; to organisation and agitation the Irish people owed whatever they had won of civil or religious freedom, and the force of the nationalist movement would continue to be exerted until it should have achieved success.

6.—As Catholics the Irish representatives acknowledged unreservedly the spiritual jurisdiction of the Holy See, but they could recognise no right in the Holy See to interfere in their political affairs,

On Wednesday, May 23rd, the *Freeman's Journal* announced that the Archbishop of Dublin had a farewell audience of the Pope preparatory to his departure for Ireland. The audience was a most gracious one, and the Archbishop spoke of it as gratifying and satisfactory. Three days later he left Rome. The *Times* correspondent telegraphed on the following day, Sunday, May 27, 1888 :

Archbishop Walsh left Rome last night. He had a final audience of the Pope in which His Holiness assured him that he had no intention of taking part in political matters. But I understand that the Pope also convinced His Grace that the Decree will have to be obeyed by all good Catholics, so that the Archbishop is fully persuaded that no course remains for them except conformity. While the Vatican will not make conformity needlessly difficult, it will not modify the Decree in the least, or release the bishops from their obligations in the case, and indeed I hear that in high quarters displeasure has been expressed that they have not before this published the Decree. In high ecclesiastical circles it is felt that the bishops have committed a serious error in neglecting to publish it before the politicans had taken it up, and this is said to be the feeling of Archbishop Walsh himself. He has expressed his determination to endeavour to stop the meetings on the subject and bring about submission and tranquillity.

How accurately the *Times* correspondent was informed may be judged from a telegram which the Archbishop had addressed to the Lord Mayor of Dublin on the evening of the audience, and from a letter to Archbishop Logue written on the day of his departure from the city. The Lord Mayor, at the request of several burgesses, had convened a meeting of the municipal representatives to consider, and —if approved—to adopt the resolution of the members of the Parliamentary Party relative to the circular of the Holy Office. At the commencement of the meeting, which was held on Thursday, May 24, the Lord Mayor, Mr. Thomas Sexton, M.P., read the message telegraphed by Archbishop Walsh from Rome the previous evening. It ran :

It may be useful to assure the Municipal Council of Dublin, in my name, that all apprehensions of political interference of the Holy See in Irish affairs are absolutely groundless. The cause of Ireland has nothing to fear from Leo XIII. Accept my most distinct assurances on this point. Protest by all means in the strongest terms against the action of those hostile journals which insult the Holy See by representing the Sovereign Pontiff as a political partisan. But at the same time make it clear that as Irishmen and Catholics you are not to be misled by any such device of the enemies either of the nationality or of the Catholic faith of Ireland.

The telegram was well-timed and proved effectual in calming excited feelings and in restoring confidence in the friendliness of the Holy See towards Ireland.

WALSH TO LOGUE.

Rome, May 26, 1888.

My DEAR LORD PRIMATE,—I telegraphed yesterday evening as the result of a good deal of consultation at the Vatican.

At first it seemed as if matters might be allowed to stand until the ordinary meeting [of the bishops] at the end of the month. But from the tone taken by some of the speakers through the country it is considered that great harm may be done if the field is left in possession of the lay element much longer.

I had a very long audience on Wednesday last (May 23), when I had from the Holy Father most distinct statements to the following effect (1) That he wishes the Decree to be communicated at once to the clergy for their guidance; (2) That he regrets that this was not done before now; (3) That the reasons stated in Cardinal Monaco La Valetta's letter are in no way to be taken as limiting the sense of the Decree; the Decree is the official act of the Holy Office, confirmed by the Pope; the statement of reasons is the act merely of the individual Cardinal who wrote the letter to Propaganda; (4) That it is important that the people should be *at once* instructed that the Decree is a decision in *morals* and is not a *political* interference.

This, I think, exhausts my official commission. But I may add from myself, as the result of all I have had the opportunity of learning here, that *collective* action on the fourth point would seem to be desirable; without this it would be difficult to secure the unity of action which is so important. Also : there seems to be no idea entertained here of any formal *promulgation* by reading the Decree in the churches. Each bishop is to take the course he deems most prudent in this matter. I shall probably write a letter to each parish priest, marking it private, suggesting that he should explain the state of the case personally to the local political leaders, if he finds that any cases of the condemned practices exist in his parish. Where no cases exist, I think it better to let matters alone. According to the official reports, Boycotting is fast dying out; Parnell's advice will probably relieve us of all trouble as regards the Plan of Campaign.

I am authorised to give the strongest assurances that the Pope is most friendly as regards our whole popular programme, and anxious to help our people in any way that may be in his power. He trusts that the bishops will leave nothing undone to remove the impression that has been created that he has in any way been influenced by political considerations in the condemnation. As he views the matter, he has removed obstacles out of our way.

I fear all this is very disjointed. But I have to write hurriedly to catch the post.

The archbishops and bishops of Ireland met on Wednesday, May 30, at Clonliffe College. Dublin. The following resolutions were unanimously adopted and ordered to be published :—

1. In obedience to the commands of the Holy See, and in willing discharge of the duty thus placed upon us, we desire to put on public record that the recent Decree of the Holy Office, addressed to the Irish Hierarchy, was intended to affect the domain of morals alone, and in no way to interfere with politics, as such, in this country.

2. Even this day we have had from our Holy Father the Pope direct and unequivocal assurances of his deep and paternal interest in the temporal welfare of our country, and that, so far from intending by this Decree to injure our national movement, it was the hope and purpose of His Holiness to remove those things which he judged might, in

the long run, be obstacles to its advancement and ultimate success.

3. With these facts thus clearly before us, apart altogether from his other numerous titles to our filial affection and respect, we must warn our people against the use of any hasty or irreverent language with reference to the Sovereign Pontiff or to any of the Sacred Congregations through which he usually issues his Decrees to the faithful.

4. While expressing our deep and lasting gratitude to the leaders of the national movement for the signal services they have rendered to religion and country, we deem it our duty, at the same time, to remind them and our flocks, as we most emphatically do, that the Roman Pontiff has an inalienable and divine right to speak with authority on all questions appertaining to faith and morals.

Dr. Walsh commenced his homeward journey on Saturday, May 26. Fatigued by his heavy labours in Rome, and by the anxieties and worries through which he had passed, he combined with the journey a holiday rest. He first travelled to Pisa, where he remained for a couple of days. On Thursday, May 31, the Feast of Corpus Christi, he said Mass in the crypt of Milan Cathedral. Sunday, June 3, was spent at Einsiedeln, and the following Sunday found him at Freiburg in Baden. A week later he had reached London, where, on Sunday, June 17, he had a long conference with Cardinal Manning. He had also two further conversations with the Cardinal before he departed from London.

In London he gave two interviews to the Press—one to a correspondent of the *Freeman's Journal*, the other to a representative of the *Star* newspaper. In the former interview the Archbishop dealt with the Decree of the Holy Office, which had been the subject of so much comment in the public Press. The *Tablet*, in a leading article on the Decree, had stated (May 5, 1888) :

The Holy Office, without care for consequences, has simply affirmed that Boycotting and the Plan of Campaign are unlawful and sinful . . .

The Holy Office has examined with minute care the recorded proceedings of the [National] League. It has had the advantage of the presence of the Archbishop of Dublin in Rome for months together. Monsignor Persico, the special agent of the Holy Father, has been for months on the spot studying the question on the ground. And the result is that the Inquisition pronounces both the Plan of Campaign and Boycotting to be unlawful . . .

There will be some spluttering perhaps, some angry discontent on the part of the leaders of the League at finding methods which have successfully transferred the property of the landlords to the tenants on so many estates now called by their right name, and declared to be as dishonest and immoral as the Bishop of Limerick said they were months ago.

. . . The chapter about the Pope being bribed, etc., may be dismissed, for nobody believes it. It is a graver sign when we find the *Freeman's Journal* setting itself to whittle away the meaning of the condemnation, or rather to patronise it as excellent in its way, and probably applicable to some of the remoter planets. Our contemporary is too deeply committed to the practices now declared to be immoral to find it altogether easy at once to submit, and so eagerly catches at the reasons which Cardinal Monaco gives, as justifying the decision, and then asserts that they assume a set of conditions which have no place in Ireland. If our contemporary is right, there is one of two things—either it suggests that the Holy See is trifling, is talking in the air, and affirming propositions which no man denies, or else that in applying its condemnation to Ireland the Holy See is absolutely ignorant of even the elementary facts of the question with which it has undertaken to deal.

In the following week (May 12, 1888) the *Tablet* had an article on " The Binding Force of the Papal Decree," in which it was stated that " until the [Irish] bishops have spoken it is natural that amid the conflicting voices, men, especially those outside the Church, should look to these columns [of the *Tablet*] for an authoritative interpretation of the disputed Decree." Having set out what it conceived to be the bearing and binding force of the Decree, and having adverted to the distinction drawn in the *Freeman's Journal* between *ius* and *factum*, the *Tablet* continued :

The attempt to evade the force of the Papal Decree by distinguishing between *ius* and *factum* as regards the matter of the Decree is nothing new. The Jansenists had recourse to this distinction in order to avoid having to submit to the Bull *Unigenitus* . . .

The Jansenists by their distinction between *ius* and *factum* attacked the infallible *magisterium* of the Holy See. The Decree against Boycotting is not a Dogmatical Decree, and those who oppose it do not attack the infallibility of the Pope. But it is a judicial act, an exercise of the judicial authority of the Holy See, which extends not only to the exposition of the law, but to the questions of fact such as whether the actions of certain individuals are or are not contrary to the divine law.

In the interview with the representative of the *Freeman's Journal*, which was published on June 22, Dr. Walsh explained at length the nature of the Decree :

Q. : What is the exact bearing of the Decree of the Holy Office ?

A. : The Decree is a decision strictly and exclusively on a question of morals. The question put to the Congregation by the Holy Father regarded those methods known as the Plan of Campaign and Boycotting ; the point to be considered was the lawfulness, the moral lawfulness of those methods of action in the agrarian struggle described in the question. The decision was in the negative, that is to say, that those methods of action cannot be lawfully employed.

Q. : But has the matter a political aspect also ?

A. : Yes. A most important political aspect. But that aspect does not and cannot alter the essential character of the question itself. Every question as to whether a particular action, or line of action, is morally right or morally wrong is a question of morals, and as such it comes within the sphere of the authority of the Church. The action or line of action in question, if considered from a worldly point of view, may be political, or social, or medical, or legal. But the question whether that action or line of action is or is not in accordance with the principles of morality, that is to say, with the natural law, is not a question of political, or of social, or of medical, or of legal science. It is essentially and exclusively a question of morals. As a question of morals it is to be dealt with by that tribunal which is competent to deal with it on moral grounds.

Persons who are not Catholics have to examine such questions conscientiously for themselves, each man according to the lights of his own private judgment as to what is right or wrong. In matters not decided by the authority of the Church, Catholics are left free to do the same. But when such a question is decided by that authority, mere private judgment is called upon to give way.

The matter may be illustrated from law or medicine. Take the case of surgery, for example. There are certain cases in which the health of a patient might be restored, or in which the life of a patient might be saved, by the adoption of some line of treatment the moral lawfulness of which is, let us say, open to difference of opinion. There are, in fact, some operations in surgery which many conscientious surgeons abstain from performing, but which others, many of them no less conscientious, perform without scruple or hesitation. Suppose that the question of the moral lawfulness or unlawfulness of such an operation was formally adjudicated upon by the Church, and that the decision was to the effect that the operation is unlawful, that decision would not in any way call in question the advantages of the operation, considered merely from a surgical point of view. The Church has no jurisdiction, and consequently she makes no claim, to deal with matters under that aspect. But she has jurisdiction, and in well-known cases she has exercised it, in considering whether the operation in question, however advantageous it may be from a worldly point of view, is or is not in accordance with the moral law. Her decision, given on that question, is in no possible sense an invasion of the realms of surgery. She stands strictly upon her own ground as the divinely constituted guardian and interpreter of the moral law.

What I have said in reference to the surgical case applies in the same way to politics—that is to say, when there is a question of the moral lawfulness of an action which is productive, it may be, of enormous advantage in politics, the question of moral lawfulness stands altogether apart from the question of political utility. Those questions belong to different spheres. Politicians may deal with one, the Church deals with the other. The Church has no more to do with the political advantage or disadvantage of a given line of action, than the constituencies or the Houses of Parliament have to do with its morality. She deals with the

moral aspect of the case, and with that only. Of course
her decision may be set at naught, either by those who
repudiate her authority, or by those who, without formally
repudiating it, disregard it. The Church can only declare
what is the law. She cannot always hinder men from
breaking it.

In the recent decison of the Holy Office there is no new
law made by the Church or by the Pope. The Church is
competent to make laws in certain matters. Those
laws are binding upon all her children. She forbids us, for
instance, to eat meat on Fridays. She obliges us to fast in
Lent. It is her authority, and her authority alone, that
has established the feasts of Easter and of Christmas, and all
the festivals of the Christian year. It is her law, and her
law only, that has made the difference that exists between
Sundays and the other days of the week. But the recent
Decree is in no sense an exercise of the legislative authority
of the Church. She has simply given us—but she has given
it with authority—an interpretation, an exposition, of the
natural law. Over that law she has no control, that is to
say, she cannot add to it or take from it, or change it in any
way. She is bound by it; the Pope himself is bound by it
as much as you or I. It is her duty, it is the duty of the
Holy Father, to point out from time to time, as occasion
may require, how that unchangeable law bears upon
particular cases that arise. In the discharge of that duty
the Holy See has issued the recent Decree.

Adverting to the *Tablet*'s " authoritative" interpretation
of the Decree, the Archbishop observed :

No Irish Catholic believed the *Tablet* in its statement that
anything published in it on the Decree was in any way
authoritative. The statement of the *Tablet* seems to have
been made with the view of imposing upon non-Catholics
rather than upon Catholics. To a certain extent the harm
was taken out of the *Tablet*'s statement by certain expressions that occur in the same article. These made it plain
enough that the writer of the so-called " authoritative"
exposition of the Decree is some person who does not
know what an " authoritative" exposition means. The
Roman correspondent of the *Times*, having quoted
the exposition word for word from the *Tablet*, added,
" I happen to know that the article in the *Tablet*
is an authoritative utterance." The correspondent

naturally thought that a Catholic journalist would not make such a statement if it were untrue. He accepted it as a true statement. But it happens not to be true. If he were a Catholic he might have seen this at a glance. I was in Rome when the *Times* article appeared, and I put myself in a position to give an unqualified contradiction to the statement. I am in a position to contradict the statement absolutely, and this contradiction may be taken as really " authoritative." The claim of the *Tablet* was a most audacious one. If the *Tablet* had been singled out in the way implied by the statement, the Irish people would be justified in protesting in the most vehement way against such a mode of dealing with Irish ecclesiastical affairs. They have undoubtedly been sorely tried in many ways in connection with the recent Decree. Some newspapers especially have acted throughout as if their main inspiring motive was the diabolical one of striving to drive our people into schism. Pretended friends have acted in this way quite as shamelessly as avowed enemies. Sneering and gibing at people is not exactly the way to lead them to obedience to ecclesiastical authority in a matter where obedience must seem to them to involve an almost heroic sacrifice of present temporal good. I trust, however, that all will come right in time.

It was unfortunate that so many things occurred to complicate the situation and to fill the minds of our people with suspicion; yet I cannot but think that, taking the matter in its merely personal aspect, our people ought to have shown more confidence in the Holy Father. Some things that have occurred in Ireland since the publication of the Decree have caused him great pain.

Apart altogether from the question of authority, he feels that he has been treated with mistrust. He feels and knows that he did not deserve this from Ireland.

It has been said that in the resolutions of the Irish Members of Parliament there was nothing but a protest against the interference of the Holy See in the political affairs of Ireland. But what is meant by protesting against this imaginary danger of his interfering with our political affairs ?

These protests I cannot regard as consistent with the feelings that ought to exist in Ireland towards the Holy See, and, I will add, most especially towards his present Holiness.

If he were to interfere at all it would be to help us. As Sovereign Pontiff he would willingly use his political influence, if he had any, for the protection of our people, a people who have always been so devoted to the Holy See. But this would be the interference of a friendly advocate. Authority to interfere he has none. The fear, then, of his interfering in our political affairs in any hostile or unfriendly sense is a mere phantom. It has come to our people as a wicked suggestion of those who are as hostile to the faith as they are to the nationality of Ireland.

On the evening of the day on which the Archbishop granted the interview to the representative of the *Freeman's Journal* in London (Thursday, June 21, 1888), a second interview was given by him to a representative of the *Star*. The interview published in the *Star* dealt with Cardinal Monaco La Valetta's letter regarding the Decree of the Holy Office, and with the question of evictions of tenant farmers in Ireland. The portion of the interview dealing with the Holy Office, important though it was in itself, was merely subsidiary to the Archbishop's main purpose, which was obviously to gain wide publicity for his views regarding the imperative need of suspending evictions. And as the question of the Decree of the Holy Office was sure to get great prominence in the paper, Dr. Walsh hoped in this way to bring under the notice of the Ministers and other prominent public men in London the pressing and vital question of evictions.

On the Thursday evening the London streets were placarded with the announcement, " Archbishop Walsh on Boycotting."

Q. : In view of various statements which have been made it is hard to know what the Decree is, if it is not a sweeping condemnation of the Irish Land Movement in every shape and form.

A. : You may take it on my authority that there is no such condemnation. I cannot deny that statements such as you have quoted are to be found in the letter that accompanies the Decree. But the Decree itself, approved as it is by the Pope, is one thing : the letter of Cardinal Monaco is another.

There has been much foolish writing upon this subject in some of the newspapers. The Decree itself, as a decision in morals, is binding upon the consciences of Catholics. As to Cardinal Monaco's letter, it is to be treated, of course, with respect; but it has no binding force whatever. It was not intended, and indeed, it could not have been intended to have any.

Dealing with the statement in the letter regarding freedom of contract between landlord and tenant, the Archbishop remarked that, as a rule, freedom of contract was unknown between landlord and tenant in Ireland, and he quoted from the report of the Bessborough Commission of 1881 :

When the rent is raised the tenants must, as a rule, submit . . . Not to come to terms with his landlord means for him (the tenant) to leave his home, to leave his employment, to forfeit the inheritance of his fathers . . . It is no matter to him of the chaffering of the market, but almost of life and death. The farmer bargains with his landlord under sentence of losing his living if the bargain goes off.

" You take my life when you take the means by which I live."

We grant that it would be inexpedient to interfere with freedom of contract between landlord and tenant, *if freedom of contract really existed.* But freedom of contract *in the case of the majority of Irish tenants, large and small, does not really exist.*

Having dealt with the question of the " impartial tribunals" for fixing rents, and with the question of arrears, the Archbishop put forward a strong and earnest plea for the staying of evictions pending a general settlement of the Irish Land question.

Leaving London the same evening, Dr. Walsh arrived in Ireland on Friday, June 22. He had taken care that no announcement of his home-coming should appear in the newspapers, and his arrival was almost unnoticed. On landing at Kingstown he was met by Dr. Croke, who accompanied him to his house; and on the following day the two Archbishops drove to Maynooth. On Sunday morning he officiated at the annual ordination ceremony at the college, and conferred the priesthood on over sixty students. During the whole of the week following he was engaged at Maynooth in various meetings with his episcopal brethren, and on Saturday evening (June 30) accompanied by an old friend, Dr. Duggan, Bishop of Clonfert, he returned to Dublin to resume the ordinary routine of his pastoral work.

His Cathedral Chapter entertained him at dinner on Wednesday, July 4, and presented him with an address of welcome to which he returned a lengthy reply. *Inter alia* he said :

The Holy Father was no less anxious to learn the truth about Ireland than I was to make the freest use of the occasion which he so graciously extended to me of putting before him in the fullest detail the true character of the claims and aspirations of the Irish people. . . .

He has grasped them in all their bearings, and, while we must remember that in matters purely of politics it is not for him to interfere, it is well for us to know, as it is my privilege to be authorised to make it known to the people of Ireland, that in every legitimate effort for the attainment of that for which they strive, our people may count on his fullest sympathy.

Some incidents of our recent history have brought pain to the heart of the Holy Father. He was much grieved at the thought of the injustice which seemed to be done to him by some whose words appeared to indicate a want of confidence in the sincerity and earnestness of his desire for the welfare of our people. Of all this I had, before leaving Rome, an assurance from his own lips. I have in my hands to-day an assurance of it, in more enduring form, in a letter to the Irish bishops.

The letter of the Pope thus alluded to, together with a pastoral letter from the Archbishop, was read in all the churches of the diocese of Dublin on Sunday, July 15, 1888 :

To Our Venerable Brethren the Bishops of Ireland.
Leo the Thirteenth, Pope.

Venerable Brethren,—Health and Apostolic Benediction.
From this supreme dignity of the Apostolic office We have
frequently directed Our solicitude and Our thoughts to your
Catholic people ; and Our feelings have been more than once
recorded in published documents from which all may learn
clearly what are Our dispositions towards Ireland. They are
sufficiently attested by the provisions which, under Our direction, the Sacred Congregation of Propaganda made in former
years respecting Ireland, and also by the letters which, on
more than one occasion, We addressed to Our venerable
brother, Cardinal McCabe, Archbishop of Dublin. Once
again they have been attested by the address which We
recently delivered to a not inconsiderable number of
Catholics belonging to your nation, from whom We received,
not only congratulations and heartfelt wishes for Our
preservation, but also expressions of gratitude on account
of Our benevolent dispositions, clearly discerned by them,
towards the Irish people. Furthermore, within these last
few months, when it was resolved to build a church in this
city in honour of St. Patrick, the great Apostle of the Irish,
We most warmly encouraged the undertaking and We shall
substantially aid it within the limit of Our resources.

Now, this Our paternal affection remaining, as it does,
unaltered, We cannot disguise that tidings which have
recently come to Us from Ireland have deeply grieved and
pained Us. We have learned that an untoward excitement
has suddenly arisen because the Sacred Congregation, whose
office it is to vindicate the authority of the Church against
those who resist it, has decreed that those methods of warfare known as Boycotting and the Plan of Campaign, which
had begun to be employed by many, may not lawfully be
used. And, what is more to be deplored, there are not a
few who have come forward and summoned the people to
excited meetings where inconsiderate and dangerous
opinions are set in circulation, the authority of the Decree
not being spared. For not only is the real scope of this
Decree grievously perverted by means of forced interpreta-
tions, but, furthermore, it is even denied that obedience is
due to the Decree, as if it were not the true and proper
office of the Church to decide what is right and what is
wrong in human actions.

Such manner of acting is but little in harmony with the profession of the Christian religion, which assuredly brings in its train the virtues of moderation, respect, and obedience to legitimate authority. Besides, in a good cause, it is not fitting to seem in some sense to imitate those who in the pursuit of a lawful end seek to attain it by disorderly effort.

Such line of action, too, is the more painful to Us, inasmuch as We had carefully inquired into the case so that We might obtain full and reliable knowledge of the state of your affairs, and of the causes of popular discontent. Our sources of information are trustworthy; We investigated the matter in personal interview with yourselves; further, last year We sent to you as legate a man of tried prudence and discretion, with the commission to use the greatest diligence in ascertaining the truth, and to make a faithful report to Us. For this very act of watchful care the thanks of the Irish people have been publicly given to Us. Can it, therefore, be asserted without rashness that We have given judgment in a case with which We were not sufficiently acquainted—the more so as We have condemned things which fair-minded men, not mixed up in your struggle and thus bringing a calmer judgment to the consideration of the case, unite in condemning?

There is also a suspicion not less unjust to Us, namely, that the cause of Ireland appeals but feebly to Us, and that the present condition of her people gives Us little care. Now, on the contrary, we yield to no one in the intensity of Our feeling for the condition of the Irish people, and We have no more earnest desire than to see them at length in the enjoyment of that peace and prosperity which they have so well deserved. We have never opposed their struggling for a better state of things, but can it be regarded as admissible that in the carrying on of that struggle a way should be thrown open which might lead to evil deeds? Rather, indeed, for the very reason that, under the influence of passion and political partisanship, things lawful and unlawful are to be found mingled in the same cause, it has been Our constant effort to mark off what was right from what was wrong, and to withhold Catholics from everything not sanctioned by the Christian rule of morals.

On this account We gave the Irish people timely counsels to be mindful of their obligations as Catholics, and to take part in nothing at variance with natural right or forbidden by the divine law. Hence the recent Decree ought not to have come upon them unexpectedly; all the more as you yourselves, Venerable Brethren, assembled in Dublin in the year 1881, bade the clergy and people to beware of everything contrary to public order or charity—such as refusing to discharge just obligations; preventing others from discharging theirs; inflicting injury on anyone either in person or property; violently resisting the law or those engaged in the discharge of public duties; joining in secret societies; and the like. These injunctions, most just in themselves, and given most seasonably, were praised and approved by Us.

Nevertheless, as the people were being carried away by ever-increasing vehemence in the pursuit of the objects of their desires, and as there were not wanting those who daily fanned the flame, We perceived that something more definite was needed than the general precepts of justice and charity which We had previously given. Our duty forbade Us to suffer that so many Catholics, whose salvation must be Our first care, should pursue a hazardous and unsafe course leading rather to disorder than to the relief of distress.

Let matters, then, be viewed in their true light, and let Ireland read in this Decree Our love for herself and Our desire to promote the prosperity she hopes for; since nothing is so harmful to a cause, however just, as recourse to violence and injustice in its defence.

These instructions which We address to you, Venerable Brethren, you will convey to the Irish people. We feel confident that, united in due conformity of views and of purpose, and sustained not only by your own but also by Our authority, you will accomplish much; and chiefly this, that the true estimate of things shall not continue to be obscured by passion, and most especially that those who have urged on the people to excitement may come to regret the rashness with which they have acted. Since there are so many who seem to seek out means of escaping from even the plainest obligations, take all necessary steps that no room be left for doubt as to the force of this Decree. Let it be understood by all that the entire method of action whose employment We have forbidden is forbidden as altogether unlawful.

Let your people seek to advance their lawful interests by lawful means, and most especially, as is becoming in Christians, without prejudice to justice or to obedience to the Apostolic See, virtues in which Ireland has in all times found comfort and strength.

In the meantime, Venerable Brethren, as a pledge of heavenly favours, and in testimony of Our affection, We most lovingly in the Lord bestow on you and on the clergy and people of Ireland the Apostolic Benediction.

Given at St. Peter's, Rome, the 24th day of June, in the year 1888, the eleventh year of Our pontificate.

When sending out the papal encyclical to his priests the Archbishop addressed to them the following letter :

VERY REVEREND AND DEAR FATHER,—You will receive with this a translation of an important letter of our Holy Father the Pope, sent by His Holiness as an encyclical letter to the bishops of Ireland.

His Holiness, as you will observe, has addressed this letter to us with the view, in the first place, of removing a painful misconception which seems to have arisen in the minds of some in connection with the recent Decree of the Holy Office. To those who have not personal knowledge of the warmth and depth of the paternal affection of our Holy Father for the Irish Church and for its faithful children, it may, indeed, seem strange that the Sovereign Pontiff, the successor of the Prince of the Apostles, the Vicar upon earth of Our Lord Himself, should condescend to address us as His Holiness has done in this most memorable letter. For in it he seeks, as it were, to justify himself in our eyes, explaining to us with patient care the true bearing of the recent Decree, and protesting with most earnest emphasis against that reproach which has so deeply wounded his paternal heart, that he is wanting in sympathy with the people of Ireland in their present trials.

In words of no ordinary impressiveness the Holy Father now assures us of the depth and fulness of that sympathy. "There is a suspicion," says His Holiness, "which is unjust to Us, namely, that the cause of Ireland appeals but feebly to Us, and that the present condition of her people gives Us little care. Now, on the contrary, We yield to no one in the intensity of our feelings for the condition of the Irish people and We have no more earnest desire than to see them at length in the enjoyment of that peace and prosperity which they have so well deserved."

Is there any Irish Catholic to whom those solemn word

will fail to bring the fullest assurance? Assuredly, there is not one whom they will not most fully satisfy that, no matter what pain may have been brought to the heart of our Holy Father by those occurrences, to some of which he alludes in his letter, they have in no way lessened the sincerity of his love for Ireland, the earnestness of his desire to see her sufferings at an end, or the fulness of his sympathy with every effort, provided only that it be made within the limits marked by the law of God itself, for the improvement of the temporal condition of her people, and for their advancement in the paths of prosperity and peace.

From some expressions in the letter of His Holiness you will also observe that it was written before he could have known, as he now knows, that the excited discussions to which he refers in it have come to an end. In the circumstances it can scarcely be necessary that I should make further reference to them. The agitation of which they were the leading incidents took place during my absence in Rome. It had fully come to an end before my return to Ireland. Its close was brought about by the prudent action of our Irish bishops at their meeting held in Dublin some six weeks ago. The statement of Catholic truth embodied in the resolutions adopted by the bishops on that occasion was at once received with unhesitating loyalty by our Catholic people. The confusion of thought, then, that for a time had seemed to stand in the way of the prompt and practical recognition of the authority of the Holy See in matters of morals as well as in matters of faith, was at once cleared away.

Those days of painful doubt and misgiving, as they seemed even to us who were away from Ireland—days of torturing anxiety as they must have been to those who lived through them at home—have now passed away. Let us thank God for it, and let us pray that they have passed over. The hasty words that in the confusion and excitement of the moment may have been uttered even by men who would willingly lay down their lives in defence of the Catholic faith and the Holy See, are now forgotten. Or rather they are now looked back upon with feelings of deep and lasting regret that even in a time of agonising excitement any word should have been spoken in Catholic Ireland which could be regarded, or represented even by the bitterest of our enemies, as open to the construction that it called in question one particle of the divinely-established authority of the Successor of St. Peter to teach the Church of Christ.

Looking away, then, from the troubles past, let us take the words which His Holiness now addresses to us as words of hope and promise for the future. Differences of view in reference to our public affairs there may, and must be, amongst the Catholics of a diocese such as this. But amongst us there is surely no one who will hesitate to join in the wishes so earnestly expressed in this letter of our Holy Father, that the present pitiful condition of our country may speedily come to an end; that peace may once more be established amongst us; and that the dawn may not long be delayed of that era of prosperity to which Ireland may justly look forward as the reward, well and nobly earned, of her centuries of suffering and of fidelity to the faith.

But these blessings it would manifestly be idle to hope for except as the fruits of wise and beneficent legislation, based upon the principle of even-handed justice to all classes and sections of our people, and putting an end to the disastrous collision of conflicting interests, of which the present state of unrest in Ireland is the deplorable result.

Within the last few days some ground for hope would seem to have arisen that, although the present session of Parliament is now all but ended, it may yet be possible for the legislature before the close of the present year to put its hand to the work and to make at all events some substantial provision for the more urgent needs of the hour. That this hope may be fulfilled, and that our people may thus be enabled to wait in patience and security the more comprehensive and permanent measures of the coming year, should be the object of the fervent prayers of every lover of justice, of charity, and of peace.

Let us unite in earnest supplication to the Giver of all good gifts that these blessings may be granted to us, and that through them peace and prosperity may be restored to our beloved country. And that our prayers may be rendered efficacious, let us present them through the hands of her whom in every necessity we may confidently invoke as the Help of Christians and the Comforter of the Afflicted.

Dublin, July 13, 1888.

On Monday, July 16, 1888, the Archbishop received at Clonliffe College an address of welcome and congratulation from the Municipal Council of Dublin. In his reply he referred to the time of painful anxiety which followed the publication of the Decree of the Holy Office :

Men's minds were strangely troubled. It seemed almost to be the opinion of some that all the ancient moorings of our Irish Catholicity had been disturbed, and that our nation was in danger of drifting away upon those shoals where other nations, once as Catholic as ours, thank God, still is, had made shipwreck, if not of the faith, at all events of that hearty loyalty to the Holy See, the loss of which the faith of no Catholic nation could long survive. It is only since my return to Ireland that I have been able to realise the painful intensity of the crisis through which our people had, thank God, safely passed.

Referring to the resolutions of the Irish Parliamentary Party, which the Dublin Municipal Council was invited to adopt at the meeting held on May 24, the Archbishop said :

As to these resolutions, let me say that they have, at least in my opinion, been grievously misrepresented and misunderstood. I wish, indeed, I could think that the misrepresentation was in all cases the result of misunderstanding.

As to the resolutions (of the Irish Members) which you endorsed, while of course I cannot say that as regards their form and phraseology they were such as I should myself have drawn up, they undoubtedly seemed to me to set forth, so far as their substance was concerned, what I cannot but regard as an honest and accurate statement of the case of the Irish tenants, and not only of that case as it stands in itself, but also of the view really taken of it by the Holy See. I do not now, of course, speak of the expressions, many of them hasty and unguarded, which were issued at some of the meetings throughout the country. Looking at these resolutions what do we find the sum and substance of them to be ? I take it to be this. They are made up mainly of three protests. They protest, in the first place, against the action of those who, endeavouring to twist the Decree of the Holy Office to political purposes, seek to create misunderstanding and estrangement between the Irish people and their spiritual guides, and to increase the dangers which threaten the liberties, and even the very existence of the Irish people. With the sentiments thus expressed in that resolution I am fully in agreement, and I cordially and unreservedly approve and endorse it.

Secondly the Irish members formally assert the right of Irish Catholics, and of the people of Ireland, to manage their own political affairs, and to do so free of all external control. This portion of the resolution has been represented as if it put forward, on the part of the Irish people, a claim that in politics the end justifies the means, and that the political liberties of the nation, or the material interests of its people, could legitimately be advanced by any means that seemed to serve this purpose, utterly regardless of the consideration whether the means in question were or were not in accordance with the law of God. No such preposterous doctrine, I take it upon myself to say, was ever laid down by anyone who could establish the faintest shadow of a claim to speak for the Irish people.

Thirdly the resolution seems to contemplate a possible or probable danger of some political interference of the Holy See in the affairs of Ireland. There is no such danger. On this matter I can give you an authoritative assurance.

With a reference to the letter of the Pope which had been read in the churches of Dublin on the previous day, the Archbishop brought to an end his reply to the address of welcome from the Dublin Corporation.

CHAPTER XIV

DIOCESAN WORK

To describe in detail Archbishop Walsh's purely ecclesiastical activities would be to record the history of the diocese of Dublin for a period of nearly forty years. Such is not the purpose of this biography. Some account, however, ought to be given of the ordinary routine of his episcopal work, and of the manner in which he discharged his ecclesiastical duties.

Dr. Walsh resided habitually in his diocese. With the exception of the five months that he was detained at Rome in 1888, he was never absent from Dublin for any extended period during the course of his long episcopate. Every autumn he took a holiday of some weeks, generally on the continent—in France, Belgium, Spain, Italy, Austria, or Germany. The work of administering his diocese was, of course, his chief care, and necessarily occupied much of his time. In dealing with questions affecting his clergy and people he was assisted by a diocesan council whose advice he sought in all matters of importance. It was his custom never to appoint to any parochial charge without consultation with his council. Even minor ecclesiastical appointments were always made in council. The council met generally on Tuesdays, and more frequently as occasion arose.

The Archbishop always presided at these meetings. Endowed with a judicial temperament, he was painstaking, orderly, and expeditious in the despatch of business. The clergy generally acknowledged him to be a just and considerate ruler; they recognised his spirit of impartiality and fair dealing, and they felt confident that, if any complaint were made against the humblest priest, no disciplinary action would be taken unless the delinquency were flagrant, or until the accused had an opportunity of being heard. He discountenanced *susurrones* and paid no attention to anonymous complaints, and it was his practice not even to read through anonymous letters denouncing his priests, lest the very reading of them might leave in his mind some trace of prejudice.

Only once during his whole episcopate did he feel bound formally to impose the penalty of suspension on any of his priests. He had, of course, from time to time, to take stern disciplinary action with regard to some of the clergy, for although inclined to leniency he was unflinching in inflicting chastisement when he felt it his duty to do so. He experienced but little trouble at any time from his priests, and in any action for the enforcement of discipline he knew that he could always confidently count on the support and hearty co-operation of the general body of the clergy. He had a good grasp of business methods, and he was admittedly a capable administrator and a vigilant guardian of the interests of religion.

It was sometimes said in criticism of his method of dealing with his priests, that he relied too much on the opinions of his counsellors, and allowed himself to be guided almost entirely by their advice. But such criticisms, if they ever reached him, moved him not. His policy in this matter was fully deliberate, for as he realised that his official position, his studious habits, and especially his personal temperament, kept him very much aloof, he felt that in estimating the character and appraising the merits of his priests he ought generally to rely on the judgment of his official advisers whose knowledge of the clergy was more intimate and likely to be more accurate than his own. He was always constitutional in dealing with his clergy; he greatly disliked interfering with their legitimate freedom, and he was adverse to introducing disciplinary regulations that might unduly hamper them. He was personally acquainted with all his priests, and when making his official visitation he always made it a point to meet and converse with the local priests, and especially with those who had been recently ordained.

A visitation was held and Confirmation administered in every parish of the diocese at least once in every three years. In some of the more populous parishes Confirmation was administered every year. Although throughout his epis-copate he had the aid of an auxiliary bishop, Dr. Walsh himself generally managed to confirm the children in all country parishes, and very frequently too, in the other parishes of the diocese. It was his invariable custom on these occasions to examine the children in the catechism, and to address them from the pulpit in homely, simple language, and he used always conclude his address by administering to the children confirmed a pledge against intoxicating drinks, to be binding on them till they reached the age of twenty-one. Except on these occasions, Dr. Walsh scarcely ever preached. He had a mistaken notion that he was unfitted for that most important work. Inability to preach was, it will be remembered, one of the reasons he urged on Leo XIII against his being appointed bishop. Indeed, on the few occasions on which he preached a formal discourse from the pulpit he was embarrassingly ill at ease, and his nervousness was painfully evident.

The reader will not be surprised to learn that Sunday was generally a busy day with the Archbishop. After celebrating Mass in the morning and presiding when possible at High Mass at the Pro-Cathedral, he very frequently spent the Sunday afternoons in attending religious functions such as the laying of foundation-stones or the formal opening of churches and schools, and in presiding at meetings to appeal for funds in aid of works of religion or charity. In the carefully prepared addresses which he delivered at these meetings he was constantly setting forth the Catholic ideal and stimulating and instructing his people on important questions of Catholic discipline; and as these addresses were always fully reported in the Dublin Press, his utterances were brought to the notice of the whole Irish people. It was mainly owing to the ability of these pronouncements and the publicity which they commanded that the Archbishop came to be recognised throughout Ireland as the watchful guardian, the able advocate and the dauntless champion of the Church's cause. His own people always rallied round him at these meetings. They had confidence in him; they were proud of him; his appeal to them never failed, and he knew—as he often said—that he could always confidently count on " the unending flow of Dublin Catholic charity." It was owing to the never-failing generosity of the charitably disposed members of his flock that he was enabled to contribute, often week after week, not only hundreds but thousands of pounds to Catholic charities. The extent of the labours undertaken in connection with the building, enlarging, and repairing of churches, chapels, schools, colleges, hospitals, and other charitable institutions was a most notable feature of Dr. Walsh's pastoral activities.*

It used to be said that very few bishops conferred the

* A notice of some of the new churches erected, and of existing churches which had been transformed or enlarged in the diocese of Dublin from 1885 to 1916, will be found in *The Builder,* January, 1917. In the archives at Archbishop's House there is preserved an accurate account of the sums contributed by Dr. Walsh towards the building, enlargement and equipment of churches, schools and charitable institutions generally. His chaplain, who also acted as *économe,* had constantly to keep a restraining hand on his chief, lest his bounty should issue in insolvency. The Archbishop, however, never gave a promise of financial aid, which, through the generosity of his people, he was unable to redeem. At the outset of Dr. Walsh's episcopal career, Dr. Croke counselled him to be generous in giving to charities of all kinds : " Give constantly, give lavishly, munificently. Promise even when you have nothing in hands. You have the confidence of the country, and Dublin and Ireland will never see you short."

Sacrament of Order more frequently, or ordained a greater number of priests than Dr. Walsh. Outside the general ordinations which were held in Ember Week and on the other ordination days prescribed by the liturgy, he held special ordinations whenever occasion required; and besides the annual general ordinations at Maynooth, at which he nearly always officiated, he conferred Orders every year at the Jesuit theological College at Milltown Park, and whenever possible at All Hallows College also. So that thousands of priests received ordination at his hands.

He performed the sacred rites of the church with dignity and with great precision, and his powers of physical endurance during long ceremonies was remarkable. Hardly ever was he known to complain of weariness after a long function. Once, however, he admitted being nearly exhausted. It was on the occasion of the consecration of over a hundred altar-stones, at a time when he was a septuagenarian. The ceremony began at 7 a.m., and lasted till one o'clock in the afternoon, when it ended with the celebration of Mass. The Archbishop was on his feet for the greater part of the time, during which he had to make numerous incensations and unctions and signs of the cross, accompanied by the recital of various prayers and formulae.

It was a common criticism among clergy and laity alike, that the Archbishop was unapproachable. It used to be said that it was easier to gain audience of the Pope than of Dr. Walsh. In this criticism there was some truth. After he had been a couple of years in the archbishopric he found that a great deal of his time was taken up with unnecessary or useless interviews. The majority of those who called on him were, he found, bent on securing financial aid, or were seeking his help and influence in matters in which he could not or would not interfere. Half-an-hour was often spent in listening to the details of a request which he soon saw he could not grant. Financial help he was always ready to

give according to his means to deserving cases of distress
or misfortune.   To meet such cases he put aside each
month a substantial sum to be distributed by his chaplain
after careful inquiry into the circumstances of each case.
It was a rule for the guidance of the chaplain that even in
these cases no assistance was to be given unless the appli-
cant was recommended by the local clergy.   Besides helping individual cases of urgent need, the Archbishop every
year contributed large sums from charitable funds at his
disposal to be distributed to the deserving poor through the
Society of St. Vincent de Paul and other charitable
organisations.   The adoption of the system of getting the
chaplain to deal through the local clergy with applications
for financial aid reduced by at least one-half the number of
the Archbishop's visitors.   In order to deal with the other
class of cases—that of persons seeking for favours or for
his influence in securing appointments, the Archbishop
required all those asking for interviews to state in general
the nature of their business and whether the matter concerning which the interview was sought was one that required his
personal attention.   It was, of course, very often found
that the matter was one in which the Archbishop would
not interfere or could not grant the favour sought.   In
course of time the number of applicants requesting the
Archbishop's intervention greatly diminished, especially
when it became known that he had made it a rule not to
forward any recommendation to government or public
authorities, or to make any request on behalf of seekers
for office or positions of trust.   In these cases his refusal
to take action which might, perhaps, compromise his
independence, left not infrequently a sense of grievance
among disappointed petitioners.

The ecclesiastical reader especially will readily apprehend
how large a portion of the Archbishop's time had to be
devoted to purely episcopal and diocesan work when he

recalls that in the diocese of Dublin there are between six hundred and seven hundred priests, more than half of whom belong to the secular clergy; that amongst the regular clergy are Augustinians, Carmelites (Calced and Discalced) Capuchins, Dominicans, Franciscans, Holy Ghost Fathers, Jesuits, Marists, Oblates of Mary Immaculate, Passionists, Redemptorists, and Vincentians; that besides the large number of Christian Brothers who are engaged mainly in teaching, there are Carmelite Brothers, Hospi-taller Brothers of the Order of St. John of God, De La Salle Brothers, Presentation Brothers; that in addition to the Orders and Congregations of men there are over one hundred separate houses of religious women, and that the nuns and sisters in these establishments number 2,500.

His correspondence on ecclesiastical affairs was naturally extensive. It was his invariable custom to open and read all letters addressed to him,* and the number of letters he himself wrote was very considerable. He wrote a neat, flowing, legible hand, and he rarely had recourse to the use of the typewriter. Periodically he sorted and classified the letters received from correspondents, destroying such as seemed to be useless or of merely passing interest, but notwithstanding the fact that the process of weeding out was gone through again and again, he left in the archives of Archbishop's House some forty thousand letters deal-ing with ecclesiastical matters exclusively.

He took a lifelong interest in endeavouring to promote the worthy rendering of the ecclesiastical chant, and in further-ance of that end he edited a handbook for the use of the clergy in which the prayers and chants of the Exequial Office

---

* There is no foundation in fact for Mr. Serjeant Sullivan's sur-mise about a letter addressed by him to the Archbishop on December 22, 1919. Regarding this letter the Serjeant remarks : " No response was made to the message. I am now convinced that the Archbishop was not allowed to hear of it. In his household and among his staff were spies. Much was written and spoken in his name of which he knew nothing." (*Old Ireland,* p. 263. Thornton, Butterworth, London, 1927.)

were carefully set out. It was chiefly Dr. Walsh's well-known concern to secure the worthy rendering of ecclesiastical chant and to provide fitting music in the churches that induced Edward Martyn of Tillyra to found the Palestrina choir at the Dublin Pro-Cathedral, and to place in trust a substantial sum towards its endowment.

In addition to the duties proper to the administration of his own diocese, Dr. Walsh had from time to time to undertake certain tasks which concerned the general ecclesiastical affairs of the country. He was, for example, chiefly responsible for the editing of the Statutes of the Irish Plenary Synod of 1900, and in connection with that work, he compiled a valuable appendix to the Synod in two volumes in which there was brought together a very useful collection of papal and other documents. Another work of national importance which he undertook, at the request of the Irish bishops, was to prepare and present to the Holy See the case for the introduction of the cause of the Irish Martyrs. The preparation of the case involved an inquiry into the facts concerning the lives and deaths of the various servants of God reputed to have been put to death for the faith in Ireland during the religious persecutions under Elizabeth, James I, Cromwell, and Charles I. This inquiry extended over several years, and entailed a great amount of labour. The investigation was conducted in strict accordance with the directions of the Sacred Congregation of Rites. All witnesses had to give their evidence under oath in the presence of the Archbishop or his deputy. During the years that the inquiry was continued, sessions were ordinarily held two or three times a week, and at the great majority of these sessions, which generally lasted about three hours, the Archbishop himself presided.*

It was sometimes asked how a bishop so much occupied

---

* *Studies,* vol. x. (1921), pp. 178 ff. and 527 ff.

with ecclesiastical work could find time to devote attention to the various public matters in which Dr. Walsh took an active part. The reason of this was that he was very methodical and punctual, and scrupulously economical of his time. Hardly ever was he known to have been late for an appointment. It was chiefly owing to these habits of punctuality and orderliness that he was able to crowd a great deal of work into his ordinary day.

Now and then it happened that much time and pains were spent in schemes that proved abortive, or about which the public heard little. Such a project was the compilation of a catechism of christian doctrine. Dr. Walsh always took a deep interest in the teaching of the catechism in the primary schools. Shortly after his appointment as Archbishop, he took steps to reorganise the system of religious inspection and examination in the schools, and appointed two priests whose duty it was periodically to visit the schools and hold in each an examination in christian doctrine. With the advice of a committee he drew up a programme in which was set out the matter of instruction and examination in the various classes, and the examiners were directed to prepare a detailed report of the results of the examinations, to be presented annually to the Archbishop. This report was printed and a copy sent to each of the managers of the schools. The scheme worked well, and contributed much to the raising of the standard of religious knowledge among the children.

After some years' experience of examining the children presented to him for Confirmation, the Archbishop became convinced of the need for the revision of the catechism. The catechism in current use in the schools throughout the diocese was that known as " Butler's Catechism" or the " Maynooth Catechism." This catechism had been drawn up in 1775 by Dr. James Butler,* Archbishop of Cashel.

* During the eighteenth century three archbishops of the name of Butler successively occupied the See of Cashel. These were

Butler's Catechism, in various editions and with some slight modifications, continued to be used throughout Ireland for a century. At the Plenary Synod of the Irish Church held at Maynooth in 1875, the question of revising the catechism was brought forward for consideration; but nothing effective was done by the Synod. An edition of Butler's Catechism, much modified and in some respects improved, was, however, published about 1882. This catechism was described on its title page as the " Catechism ordered by the National Synod of Maynooth, and approved by the Cardinal, the Archbishops, and Bishops of Ireland for general use throughout the Irish Church." Hence it became commonly known as the " Maynooth Catechism." The Maynooth Catechism was not by any means satisfactory. It was much longer and more complicated than the original " Butler's", owing mainly to the fact that in many of the answers a self-contained statement embodying the words of the question was substituted for a word or phrase. For example :

Q. : Who made the World ?
A. : God (*Butler's Catechism*).

was replaced by

Q. : Who made the World ?
A. : God made the World. (*Maynooth Cutechism*).

With a view to securing a satisfactory revision of the catechism the Archbishop appointed a committee of priests, secular and regular. For their guidance he set out certain suggestions :

(1) One of the chief features of the work to be done should

(1) Christopher Butler, grand-nephew of the Duke of Ormond, Archbishop of Cashel, 1712—1757; (2) James Butler, coadjutor to the former, 1750, Archbishop, 1757—1774; (3) James Butler, coadjutor to his namesake, 1773, Archbishop, 1774—1791.
Another Dr. Butler, John Butler, was Bishop of Cork, 1763—1787, when he resigned his See and abandoned the Catholic faith. He was the notorious Lord Dunboyne. It was James not John Butler who compiled the catechism.

be the introduction of short reading lessons, one to be appended to each chapter of the catechism. Those reading lessons should treat, in somewhat fuller form, of the matter dealt with in the questions and answers of the chapter.

The insertion of such lessons would make it possible to omit, without loss, many questions, the answers to which now impose a heavy burden on the memory of the children. In this way room would be made for the insertion of several matters of importance at present not to be found in the catechism.

In each chapter the answers should comprise only such matter as it is really of importance should be formally committed to memory; everything requisite, or useful, by way of further information, or of illustration, might find a place in the appended lesson.

If these lessons are written with care and skill, and in a style attractive as well as simple, the children will soon have learned them by heart, from the mere fact of repeatedly reading them, and without any formal effort at committing them to memory.

The additional matter dealt with in the lessons could be made a subject of examination, at all events in the more advanced classes. The advantage of adding an examination of this kind to the examination on the mere questions and answers of the catechism is obvious.

(2) Our present catechism seems to be defective in its omission of many matters that plainly are of practical importance in the fulfilment of ordinary Catholic duty.

Moreover, the matters of this description which are dealt with in the catechism, are dealt with much more in their mere doctrinal bearing than as matters of practice.

Almost any practice or observance of religion that may be mentioned will illustrate one or other of these defects. Take for example : The Feasts of the Church (such as Corpus Christi, the Assumption of the Blessed Virgin, the Feast of All Saints, etc.) ; Solemn Ceremonies of the Church (such as the Exposition and Benediction of the Blessed Sacrament) ; Devotions (such as the Devotion of the Sacred Heart, the Rosary, the Stations of the Cross, etc) ; and Pious Practices (such as the use of Scapulars and the use of Holy Water).

Again, the absence of all instruction as to the virtue of " Temperance" seems a somewhat serious omission,

As a result of it our people are left exposed to the damaging influence of unauthorised teaching, a great deal of which is far from being in harmony with Catholic doctrine.

(3) Our catechism also seems open to objection on the score of the prominence occasionally given in it to the controversial element, as distinct from the positive exposition of Catholic truth—in other words, the object sometimes seems to be to insist rather upon what a thing is not than upon what it is.

(4) Sometimes difficulties arise from the questions and answers being so planned as to require the children in repeating the answer to move upon the lines of some scientific classification.

In cases where matters are needlessly complicated by such an arrangement, it ought to be possible to retain all the advantages of the scientific classification without putting the formal enunciation of the classification as a task upon the children. To force this upon them has, so far as I can see, no other effect than to put an additional, and sometimes peculiarly unwieldly burden upon their memories.

(5) It will be found in some instances that there is room for improvement in the direction of a more rigorous accuracy of expression. Take for instance the following :—

Q. : What are the principal Mysteries of Religion ?

A. : The principal Mysteries of Religion are : The Unity and Trinity of God, the Incarnation, Death, and Resurrection of our Saviour—which are most necessary to be known and believed.

Q. : What do you mean by Mysteries of Religion ?

A. : The Mysteries of Religion are revealed truths which we cannot comprehend.

It may be asked :

(a) Are the mysteries here enumerated the 'principal' mysteries of religion in the sense of being " most necessary to be known and believed" ?

(b) Are the five doctrines mentioned mysteries in the sense of being revealed truths which we cannot comprehend ?

Obviously three of these truths—the Unity of God, the Death and Resurrection of our Saviour—are not mysteries at all in the strict theological sense defined in the catechism.

Another example of want of strict accuracy is the following :—

> *Q.* : Where was Christ's body while His soul was in Limbo?
>
> *A.* : When Christ's soul was in Limbo His body was in the sepulchre or grave.

This plainly conveys the idea that our Lord's soul did not descend into Limbo—it may possibly even suggest the error that His soul remained united with His body—until the body had been taken down from the Cross and was laid in the tomb.

A third example of inaccuracy is the wide extension, so misleading, given in the catechism regarding the obligations of Christian charity :

> *Q.* : How does a person sin against the love of his neighbour?
>
> *A.* : A person sins against the love of his neighbour *by not assisting him when able in his spiritual and corporal necessities.*

(6) In some answers in the catechism words are used of needlessly difficult length.

Even where fairly easy words are at present used, it might be well to replace them by still easier words, by the easiest indeed that can be found.

(7) Some of the answers in the catechism are inconveniently long.

This fault may arise from the unnecessary grouping into one answer of matter that might equally well be dealt with in two or more distinct answers.

(8) There is sometimes needless complexity in the structure of an answer.

Each answer should, as far as possible, be put in the form of a direct simple statement, free from qualifying or other clauses that might hinder children of the duller class from taking in a clear view of the meaning of the answer as a whole.

(9) Closely connected with the point dealt with in the preceding suggestion (8) is the difficulty that has arisen from the change made in the catechism some years ago, by introducing the words of the question into the corresponding answers.

This change has added enormously to the difficulty of learning Butler's Catechism, partly from additional length, but much more from the additional intricacy which it has necessarily introduced into the answers. The change has the advantage of having each answer in the form of a distinct statement or sentence, so that the answer, as it is committed to memory by the child, may be a definite intelligible statement of some Catholic truth.

In most cases this can conveniently be brought about by repeating in the answer the words of the question. But then, both question and answer should, in the original composition of the catechism, have been so framed as to allow of all this being done without producing, as the result of the fusion, an answer of embarrassing length, or of complicated structure. The questions and answers in Butler's Catechism were not so framed. It is from this, then, and not from the mere fact of the answers being thrown into the form of sentences, that the serious difficulty complained of in the case of the " Maynooth" Catechism has arisen.

(10) Needless difficulty is, sometimes created by the recurrence of almost identical forms of expression, or of almost identical arrangement of words or phrases, in different questions.

(11) A similar, but still more embarrassing difficulty, is caused when the defect mentioned in the last suggestion occurs in the answers.

(12) The question of the order best suited to a catechism is one that will not arise, unless, in the progress of the work of revision, it should be found by the committee that something more than a mere revision of our present catechism is advisable.

As a matter of fact, after the committee had been at work for some time it was decided that not a mere revision but a reconstruction of the catechism was advisable.

After two years labour the committee had completed the first draft of what was in great measure a new catechism. The work of revising this new catechism was continued for nearly two years more, and at the end of 1895 the work was completed. The outcome of the committee's labours was three booklets :

(1) *Catechism of Christian Doctrine for Primary Schools.*
(2) *Elementary Catechism of Christian Doctrine.*
(3) *Lessons on the Catechism, being a short Summary of Christian Doctrine for the Use of Schools.*

Photo by]   ARCHBISHOP WALSH IN 1910.   [*Lawrence Dublin*

The plan of the whole is clearly set out in the Introduction to the *Lessons*, which is as follows :—

Our chief business here on earth is to know God, to love Him, and to serve Him, that we may be happy with Him for ever in Heaven. To this end we must believe what God has taught, we must do what God has commanded, and we must use the means of salvation which God has given to us. The catechism is the book in which we first learn how we are to fulfil these duties.

Hence the catechism may be divided into three parts. In the first part we learn chiefly what we have to believe. It teaches us the principal truths of the Christian religion which are contained, in a short form, in the Apostle's Creed.

In the second part we learn chiefly what we have to do and what we have to avoid. It deals with the Commandments of God and of the Church, with the virtues of faith, hope, and charity, and with sin and the passions.

In the third part, we learn what are the chief means given to us by God, to enable us to serve Him here on earth, and to gain the happiness of Heaven hereafter. It treats of Grace, Prayer, and the Sacraments.

The closing pages of the catechism bring before us the end of the world. They tell us of the four last things which we should always remember, that is, Death, Judgment, Heaven and Hell; also of the resurrection of the body on the Last Day, the General Judgment, and Life Everlasting.

The *Catechism* contained forty-two chapters, and the *Elementary Catechism* eighteen. The *Lessons on the Catechism* contained fifty-four lessons, besides the Introduction. All three booklets were printed, and a copy of each was sent for criticism to every priest in the diocese and to many bishops. Each copy was numbered, and directions were given that within a specified time the copy was to be returned to the Archbishop with such observations and suggestions as might occur to the readers. Some useful criticisms and suggestions were received, and these were classified with a view to a final revision.

Meanwhile arrangements were being made for the holding of a Plenary Synod of the Irish Church, and with a view to

having the question of introducing a uniform catechism
into all the Irish dioceses considered by the Synod, the
work on the Dublin Catechism was suspended.

The question of the catechism was not dealt with at the
Synod of 1900 any more than at the Synod of 1875.   On
learning of the intention of Pope Pius X to issue a
catechism for general use throughout the Church, Dr.
Walsh abandoned the idea of publishing the catechism on
which he and his committee had spent so much time.   The
catechism, though printed, was never published, and
Butler's Catechism is still used in the diocese of Dublin and
throughout Ireland commonly.   The *Lessons on the
Catechism* has been published by the Catholic Truth Society
of Ireland.

CHAPTER XV

THE PIGOTT FORGERIES

In the year 1885 a society which called itself the Irish Loyal and Patriotic Union was established in Dublin. The object of the society was to counteract and defeat the movement for Irish Home Rule, and the plan adopted to that end was to bring discredit on Parnell and his Party by showing that the leaders of the Home Rule movement were intimately associated with crime and lawlessness and unfit to be entrusted with the responsibility of government. Some of the activities of the I.L.P.U. have already been noticed in connection with the anti-Nationalist propaganda which was carried on during the stormy days of the Plan of Campaign. The secretary of the I.L.P.U. organisation was an energetic young journalist named Edward Caulfield Houston.

Houston quickly enlisted the services of Richard Pigott in the effort to disgrace Parnell and destroy the Nationalist Party. Pigott was a Dublin journalist of shady character. He began his career as an office-boy in the offices of the *Nation*; later he became commercial manager of the *Irishman* newspaper. The *Irishman* was not a financial success, and in 1865 it was acquired by Pigott for a nominal figure from its proprietor, P. J. Smyth. Shortly before that time the Fenian organ, the *Irish People*, had been suppressed, and the new proprietor of the *Irishman* cleverly availed himself of an opening to increase the circulation of his paper. He affected Fenian sympathies, and the circulation of the paper soon reached fifty thousand a week. For a time Pigott lived in considerable affluence; his paper was reputed to bring him in an income of about £2,000 a year; this was substantially augmented by sums of money which he extracted from various persons, and from politicians of different parties by means of systematic blackmail. His prosperity, however, did not long survive. By the time that the Land League was founded in 1879 he was practically bankrupt in money and influence. "The circulation of the *Irishman* had gone down almost to zero, and Pigott's character and reputation had followed suit. All Dublin knew of his scheming, borrowing, and blackmailing practices. His credit, pecuniary and political, was gone, and it was only a question of a short time until his papers would disappear too."*

Pigott's first contribution to the work of the Loyal Irish and Patriotic Union was a pamphlet called *Parnellism Unmasked*, which was published anonymously by the I.L.P.U. in September 1885. Later on in the same year Houston commissioned Pigott to search for documentary evidence "connecting the Parnellite movement with the crime prevalent in the country." While engaged on this congenial work the needy journalist was to receive a guinea a day together with hotel and travelling expenses. Pigott set out on his quest at once, and in a short time he had visited Paris, New York, and Lausanne. In the course of a couple of months he informed Houston that he had come upon letters and other documents directly connecting Parnell and his associates with murderers, and identifying the Nationalist organisation with the policy of assassination. The incriminatory documents were in the possession of certain persons in Paris who had shown them to Pigott and allowed him to make copies of them. The copies Pigott showed to Houston, but the originals were kept in a black bag by the "unknown persons" whose names were not to be disclosed. These

* Davitt. *Fall of Feudalism,* p. 566.

men guarded the letters carefully, and would not hand them over except in circumstances of the greatest secrecy and on the receipt of a substantial sum of money. Such was Pigott's story.

After some time Houston decided to procure the letters. He crossed to Paris, July 1886, and in an upper room at a hotel in that city he received the contents of the black bag from Pigott, paying him £500 for the unknown persons—" the men downstairs"—who had brought the letters, and £105 for himself.

Houston, after consultation with his employers and some prominent political sympathisers decided to offer the letters for sale to the *Times*. The editor and manager of the *Times* at first refused to treat with Houston, and the letters were offered in other quarters. It is said, too, that they were loaned to a person who took them to Rome and submitted them to the authorities at Propaganda.* Finally after much negotiation the letters were accepted and purchased by the *Times* for £2,530. The letters were forgeries fabricated by Pigott. Before, however, the fraud was established, the letters had served the political purposes of the *Times*.

In the beginning of the year 1887, there were indications that the Unionist Government was determined on introducing repressive legislation to cope with Parnell and the Irish National movement. With a view to preparing the way for the enactment of coercive measures by the Government, the *Times* published a series of articles on " Parnellism and Crime," in which it charged that " the Land League chiefs based their movement on a scheme of assassination carefully calculated and coolly applied." The articles on " Parnellism and Crime" began to appear on March 7, 1887, and were continued at intervals for months. On March 22, Mr. Arthur Balfour, the Chief Secretary to the

* Davitt. *Fall of Feudalism in Ireland,* p. 574.

Lord Lieutenant of Ireland, gave notice in the House of Commons of his Coercion Bill. The division on the second reading of the Bill was to take place in the House of Commons on April 18. On the morning of the 18th, there appeared in the *Times* what purported to be a letter written by Parnell to Patrick Egan in 1882. The letter, which was dated some days after the assassination of Lord Frederick Cavendish and Burke, Under-Secretary to the Lord Lieutenant, in Phoenix Park, Dublin, was reproduced in facsimile, and read as follows :

DEAR SIR, 15/5/82.

I am not surprised at your friend's anger, but he and you should know that to denounce the murders was the only course open to us. To do that promptly was plainly our best policy.

But you can tell him and all concerned that though I regret the accident of Lord F. Cavendish's death, I cannot refuse to admit that Burke got no more than his deserts.

You are at liberty to show him this, and others whom you can trust also, but let not my address be known. He can write to the House of Commons.

Yours very truly,

CHAS. S. PARNELL.

On the evening of the publication of the facsimile letter it was repudiated and denounced as a forgery by Parnell in the House of Commons. The repudiation, however, was received with incredulity by many within and without the House. The comments of the Unionist Press generally were to the effect that if Parnell wished to vindicate his character, the proper course for him to follow was to challenge the *Times* in an action for libel before an English jury. This course his friends dissuaded Parnell from taking.

After an interval of several months, legal proceedings were taken against the *Times* by a former member of the Nationalist Party—F. H. O'Donnell—who felt that he was libelled by certain statements made by the *Times* in its articles on " Parnellism and Crime." The case of *O'Donnell*

v. *Walter* (manager of the *Times*) was tried in July 1888, and a verdict for the defendant was returned on the ground that there was nothing in the articles which was a libel on O'Donnell. In the conduct of the case, however, the Counsel for the *Times* reproduced and commented upon all the " Parnellism and Crime" articles, and brought forward other *facsimile* letters, more damning even than the first. He declared on behalf of his clients that the *Times* would retract nothing.

After this declaration, and the challenge implied in the submission of the counsel that, if the *Times* statements were false no grosser libels ever were written, Parnell decided to take action. On July 6, 1888, the day after the verdict was given against O'Donnell, Parnell, in the House of Commons, formally denied the authenticity of the letters, and asked for the appointment of a select committee of the House to inquire into the matter. This request was at first refused, but subsequently the House agreed to grant an inquiry which should be entrusted to a Commission of Judges to be appointed by Act of Parliament. The Commission, however, was not merely to inquire into the question of the letters, but into ten years of Irish history.

The great assize, presided over by three judges, began its sitting on October 22, 1888, and on November 22, 1889, it held its one hundred and twenty-eighth and last public session. The Commission was in fact what its President, Sir James Hannen, styled it—"a Great Inquisition." Before the three grand inquisitors was arraigned the whole Irish movement of which Parnell had been leader since 1879 —Political Leaders, the Land League, the National League, and all the Press activity of the Nationalist papers. Four hundred and fifty witnesses were examined in close upon one hundred thousand questions. It was a trial without a jury, and a political trial too; the cause of the trial a half-successful revolution, with the tribunal and its defined juris-diction constituted by the political adversaries of the Party impeached. Although the allegations contained in the letters to the *Times* were the central and paramount charges against Parnell, the Commission had been sitting for four months of continuous inquiry before Pigott was put in the witness-box. The English Attorney-General, who was leading counsel for the *Times*, had induced the court to relegate this vital part of the investigation to the very last stage of the accusers' case. " Thus every possible allegation arising out of ten years of political agitation, excitement, and semi-revolution in Ireland could be piled up against the accused and be reported during four months in the daily Press of Great Britain."* When Pigott was at length produced, he blew the gaff upon the *Times*, and with his disappearance and suicide the proceedings of the tribunal should have come to an end. Sir Charles Russell, Parnell's counsel, however, decided to put forward the rebutting case. Parnell was the first witness called by Sir Charles. He began his evidence on April 30 and concluded on May 8, 1889. His evidence is recorded in the *Report of the Special Commission Act, 1888*, vol. VII., pp. 1 to 370. Archbishop Walsh, who was the witness called next after Parnell appeared before the Commission on May 8 and 9, and his evidence may be read in the *Report of the Commission*, vol. VII., p. 379 to 402. His examination had reference mainly to his views on the working of the National League, and on boycotting and exclusive dealing. It is not necessary to refer to this evidence in detail. It was concerned chiefly with what one of the *Times* counsel afterwards described as " the metaphysical side of the agrarian question."

Dr. Walsh, however, played a decisive part in resisting the widespread and deeply-planned assault on the leaders and character of the Irish National movement. In two different ways he rendered effective assistance to Parnell and his associates. In the first place he supplied Sir Charles Russell with letters which established Pigott's complicity in the " Parnellism and Crime" articles, and led to his confession that he had forged the *facsimile* letter of April, 1887. In the second place, Dr. Walsh, by deciphering an important despatch which had fallen into the hands of the Nationalists, enabled them to counter a dangerous move against them which was being conducted by the *Times* in the United States.

The Archbishop seems never to have met Pigott, but for many years he had been receiving letters from him. These were mostly begging appeals. Dr. Walsh had given him some slight financial help from time to time, but when on inquiry he had ascertained that Pigott was not only an impoverished journalist but also a discredited and dangerous adventurer, he ceased to heed his appeals. On March 4, three days before the publication of the first of the articles on " Parnellism and Crime," Pigott wrote to the Archbishop :

> Anderton's Hotel, Fleet Street,
> London,
> March 4, 1887.

MY LORD,—The importance of the matter about which I write will doubtless excuse this intrusion on your Grace's attention. Briefly I wish to say that I have been aware of the details of certain proceedings that are in preparation with the object of destroying the influence of the Parnellite Party in Parliament.

I cannot enter more fully into the details than to state that the proceedings referred to consist in the publication of certain statements purporting to prove the complicity of Mr. Parnell himself and some of his supporters with murders and outrages in Ireland, to be followed in all probability by the institution of criminal proceedings against these parties by the Government.

Your Grace may be assured that I speak with full knowledge, and am in a position to prove, beyond all doubt and question, the truth of what I say. And I will further assure your Grace that I am also able to point out how the designs may be successfully combated and finally defeated. I assure your Grace that I have no other motive except to respectfully suggest that your Grace would communicate the substance of what I state to some one or other of the parties concerned, on, however, the specific understanding that my name will be kept secret, to whom I could furnish details, exhibit proofs, and suggest how the coming blow could be effectively met.

For reasons which no doubt your Grace will have no difficulty in discovering, I could not apply to any of the parties direct, and that is why I venture to ask your Grace's interference.

At the same time I know that in adopting this course I run the risk of incurring your Grace's displeasure : but perhaps the deep interest which your Grace is known to take in the preservation of the integrity of the Party that is so seriously threatened will plead my excuse. Moreover, I am forced to beg your Grace's assistance from the strong conviction in my mind founded on what I have learned of the evidence relied on, which is *prima facie* serious, that the proceedings, unless met in the way I suggest, will succeed in their object.

In any case, however, I trust your Grace will regard this letter as private and confidential, except in so far as it may be used or referred to in furtherance of the motive with which it is sent.

I shall probably leave here for Paris to-morrow evening, but should your Grace think of replying I would await receipt of your letter on receiving a word by wire from your Grace to that effect in the course of the day, to-morrow, Saturday.

I remain, your Grace's obedient servant,
RICHARD PIGOTT.

P.S.—I need hardly add that did I consider the parties really guilty of the things charged against them I should not dream of suggesting that your Grace should take part in an effort to shield them ; I only wish to impress on your Grace that the evidence is apparently convincing, and would probably be sufficient to secure conviction if submitted to an English jury.

On the following day Pigott again wrote to the Archbishop informing him that he would continue to be in London for some days, adding :

In any case I would respectfully beg of your Grace to favour me with a line of acknowledgment of the receipt of the letter, and an assurance that your Grace will treat it as private and confidential.

Again, March 7, 1887, Pigott wrote :

I was somewhat disappointed at not having a line from your Grace, as I ventured to expect I might have been so far honoured. I can assure your Grace that I had no other motive in writing, save to avert, if possible, a great danger to people with whom your Grace is known to be in strong sympathy. At the same time should your Grace not desire to interfere in the matter, or should you consider that they would refuse me a hearing, I am well content, after having acquitted myself of what I conceived to be my duty in the circumstances.

I will not further trouble your Grace save to again beg that you will not allow my name to transpire, seeing that to do so would interfere injuriously with my prospects, without any compensating advantage to anyone.

I make the request all the more confidently because I have no part in what is being done to the prejudice of the Parnellite Party, though I was enabled to become acquainted with all the details.

The Archbishop replied to Pigott's letters, writing from Dublin on March 9, 1887 :

Your first and second letters reached me in due course in London. On my arrival here last night I found your third awaiting me. I have had no time for letter-writing in that short interval.

As regards the matter on which you write, I certainly should not be inclined in any way to interfere. And I see quite clearly that any offer of interference on your part would be ascribed to unworthy motives.

It is well that all such " evidence" as you have heard of should be brought out into the light of day. No honest cause has anything to fear from the publication of the truth. And as for the publication of falsehood, it can do no harm except to the falsehood and its author.

I have now had such abundant experience of how shamefully lies of the most circumstantial character can be told of persons regarded as sympathisers with the Nationalist cause, that I attach no weight whatever to any statement adverse to that cause or to its leaders or advocates, until I have an opportunity of judging of the statement for myself.

It is unnecessary for me to add that I shall respect your wishes as conveyed to me in your marking your letters " Private."

Sir Charles Russell explained to the Commission that the letter just quoted was the draft of the Archbishop's reply, and he added : " I ought to explain—these letters have not been sent to the solicitors (Mr. Parnell's solicitors) but have been sent to me direct. And I ought to say to your Lordships also that they were not sent by the Archbishop to me until in the public Press it was announced that there had been a reference by this gentleman to the fact of this correspondence."

Pigott's reply written from Paris was as follows :—

Hotel St. Petersburg,
March 12, 1887.

My Lord,—I am much honoured by your Grace's reply to my letters. I have no doubt at all that your Grace is right in what you say with reference to the subject of them. My motive was that the evidence I heard of, which is both documentary and personal, would produce a bad effect if published, seeing that it is an artful admixture of what I believe to be true with what I expect to be false; and that it might be forestalled and rendered harmless by publicly exposing the discreditable means by which it was obtained, and by which further testimony is being sought on which to found a criminal prosecution. Moreover, I thought that such a course would forearm the parties concerned with the knowledge of what precisely they would be charged with, so that they might be prepared to meet it.

However, your Grace puts the matter in so clear a light that I now perceive I was quite astray in my calculation as to the effect of the coming publication and prosecution, and it remains but for me to repeat my apologies to your Grace for having troubled you, and my grateful thanks for your Grace's reply.

Pigott once more wrote to the Archbishop, May 1, 1887. The letter was written from Paris :

I trust your Grace will pardon me for briefly recurring to the subject of our correspondence of a short time ago. If your Grace will allow me I will make a communication to your Grace direct, which I am sure will be found useful now to the gentlemen referred to in my letters.

Your Grace would be free to use the information I would give in any way that would not indicate that I was the informant, or give any clue to such a supposition, but I would make it a condition that my name should not be mentioned to anyone, at all events without previous consultation with me. If your Grace will favour the writer with a reply as soon as convenient, addressed to me at Anderton's Hotel, Fleet Street, London, I will attend to it promptly.

The Archbishop's reply, dated from Dublin, May 3, 1887, was as follows :

So long as there was a question of interfering in any way to prevent the publication of statements such as you described to me in a former letter, I felt that it would not be right for me to move in the matter at all. I stated to you, as you may remember, the considerations that led me to that conclusion.

Now, however, as I understand your letter, you are anxious to make a statement that may be of use to the victims of fraud and slander in refuting the slander and in exposing the fraud.

I cannot, of course, take the responsibility of refusing to receive such a statement from you. Indeed, it is so plainly a matter of duty, of Christian duty, for any one to make such a statement who is in a position to do so, that I cannot but regard it as a matter of duty with me, as a minister of religion and as a bishop, to afford you every facility for communicating with me as you propose.

As you request it, you may, of course, rely with the most absolute confidence that I shall not, without your express consent, make use of any information that you may think it right to give me, in any way that would indicate that you were my informant or that would give any clue to such a supposition.

Pigott replied, London, May 5, 1887 :

I am favoured by your Grace's letter of yesterday, which is entirely satisfactory.

As it is possible that I may be home on Saturday (May 7) I consider that it would be more satisfactory for my purpose to wait till then in order that I may communicate what I have to say to your Grace personally, should I be favoured with an interview. If I should be detained longer than I anticipate, however, I will write the statement to your Grace to-morrow (Friday, May 6), so that you will receive it on Saturday morning.

The statement was sent on the Friday, and on the following day, May 7, the Archbishop wrote to Pigott :

I have read your letter very carefully, and I think it better to return it to you at once. Letters preserved here, even amongst the most confidential papers, must eventually fall into other hands, and I daresay you would wish to guard yourself against any danger of your letting your letter be read by anyone but myself.

As regards the main purpose of your writing, I must say that I cannot see how what you have written could be of any use to Mr. Parnell or others in enabling them to expose the fraud or to bring the author of it to justice.

That their political opponents have employed a number of agents to hunt up " evidence " is what everyone takes for granted. That agents so employed did not work without substantial remuneration is equally to be taken for granted. It is also manifest that in such a proceeding there is offered a very substantial temptation to manufacture " evidence." The *Times*, I am sure, would be willing to admit all this; but it would add that the real question is : Has the evidence been manufactured or is it genuine?

From your former letters I assumed that you had some knowledge which you could communicate, either as to the author of some fraud or as to the fact that means had been employed to procure " evidence " avowedly of a fraudulent character.

Anything short of this is, in my opinion, absolutely useless, whether as regards the stopping of further publications, if it be desirable that they should be stopped, or as regards the exposure of fraud in any publications that have as yet taken place.

I can have no desire to learn the name of the gentleman who is at the bottom of this transaction. I assume he regards his action as justified by the political exigencies of his Party. It would be a mere gratification of curiosity if you were to tell me, as you offer to do, who he is. And in the circumstances I could not but regard your telling it to me in any other light than as an unjustifiable breach of confidence.

Pigott on receiving the above letter wrote again to the Archbishop, and on May 12 the Archbishop sent him the following reply :

I enclose, as you request, your last two letters. I do not see how I could think of interfering in the way you suggest. I do not know Mr. Parnell at all intimately, but from what little I do know of him I should be very slow to undertake to put before him, as you suggest, a proposal that he should do anything with a view of preventing a continuance of the publication, or of securing a withdrawal of those already published, or an apology for them. As regards the famous *facsimile* letter, no withdrawal would be worth looking for which did not candidly avow that the letter was a forgery, and secure the handing over of the forger to the hands of justice. If those responsible for the publication cannot do this they are not worth while treating with. If they can do it and yet decline to do it, except on certain conditions to be imposed on Mr. Parnell, they are plainly persons with whom neither he nor any other gentleman could afford to treat.

This, at least, is my conjecture, as to the way in which Mr. Parnell would view the matter, if anyone were to communicate with him about it.

I need not repeat my assurance that I fully accept your unqualified disclaimer as to your having anything to do with the publications.

As regards a personal interview, I should say that your calling here might just now be regarded by those who might become aware of it as an indication that you had something to communicate in reference to recent events. You probably would not wish to have this thought of you.

Pigott appeared as a witness at the Parnell Commission on February 20, 1889. His cross-examination began on the following day, when the production of the Archbishop's correspondence with Pigott caused quite a sensation in court, for "not even to Parnell had Russell confided the fact that Dr. Walsh had sent him these proofs of Pigott's intimate knowledge of the Houston plot, and the line of examination which they disclosed was as great a surprise to us all as it was a thunderbolt in the camp of the forger and his backers. The production of these letters knocked Pigott to pieces."*

In his cross-examination of Pigott, Russell made the most skilful and effective use of the forger's correspondence with the Archbishop. Sir Charles began by asking Pigott to write certain words including the word " hesitency"—so mis-spelled in a letter written by Pigott to Patrick Ford. And after a few further questions, he came to the correspondence with the Archbishop.

The following account, copied from the pages of a diarist who was present in court,† gives a good idea of the scene :

And now for his correspondence with the Archbishop. Pigott changed colour. Yes; he had written to the Archbishop, but that was under " the seal of the confessional" —an assurance which Sir Charles received with a sceptical little laugh. What was the correspondence about? I asked his advice. About what? Was it not respecting "incriminatory matter" about Mr. Parnell and others? Pigott pondered for a minute or two. Yes, it was. And the matter included the letters? Yes—after another long pause. Here the court was wrought to the highest pitch of curiosity. And this particular letter to the Archbishop was dated 4th of March, 1887, three days before the series of the *Times* articles called " Parnellism and Crime" began? Yes. And so, then, Pigott was aware on the 4th of March that the *Times* would or might print the incriminatory " letters"? No, he was not. What! was he not aware that Houston had all those letters in his possession ready to produce them, to the damage of Mr. Parnell and his associates? Again a

* Davitt. *Fall of Feudalism in Ireland,* pp. 577—578.

† *Diary of the Parnell Commission.* By John McDonald, pp. 154—157.

long pause, after which Pigott admitted that—he "supposed" he was.   Then Sir Charles Russell began to read from the Pigott letter (marked private and confidential) to Dr. Walsh.   Did Pigott remember the passage in which he said that proceedings were imminent which would destroy Mr. Parnell's influence in Parliament?   "What were these proceedings?"   "Can't say."   Sir Charles stared at him. " I don't know, really," pleaded Pigott in a half-audible voice.   "Was it the letters?"   "Can't say; I thought it was the forthcoming articles."   "What, have you not just said that you knew nothing about the articles forthcoming in the *Times*?"   Pigott held his peace.   " I suppose I was mistaken," he said at last.

Sir Charles proceeded with his reading. Did Pigott say in his letters to Dr. Walsh that Mr. Parnell would be accused of having " participated" in crime, and that " criminal proceedings" might follow?   " I won't swear," said Pigott after some reflection.   Then Pigott admitted that if the letters were genuine they would prove Mr. Parnell's complicity in crime. And did not Pigott write to the Archbishop that he (Pigott) was in a position to prove all he said, and to " show how the designs of Mr. Parnell's opponents could be successfully combated, and finally defeated?" Yes. But how could Pigott do that if the letters were not forgeries? At this question Pigott came to a dead stop. He was utterly confused. He stammered; he declared that he could not have had the letters in mind; that the whole thing had passed out of his recollection.

Sir Charles pressed his question. If the letters were genuine, what means would Pigott have of saving Mr. Parnell and his associates?   " I can't think."   " Oh, yes; you must try."   " I can't think."   " You must think." " Had you any qualms of conscience? All this happened only a short time ago. No qualms? Then try and remember?"   " I can't. I really can't give any explanation."

Sir Charles went on with his reading. Had Pigott not asked Dr. Walsh to introduce him to some one to whom he could show how the " blow" might be avoided?   Pigott could not remember. Nor could he think what he meant by the blow. " My memory is a perfect blank." Well, did he say in a P.S. to his letter to Dr. Walsh that, had he considered the accused really guilty he would not have troubled the Archbishop; and that he was sure, if they were tried in an *English* court they would be convicted?

The question was followed by a murmur of astonishment all over the court. Pigott hesitated, wrinkled his forehead, stammered, and at last declared that he must have had in his mind some other charges "more serious" than the letters, and that, in fact, he did not consider the letters to be so "serious" as to justify the language of the postscript. A minute or two before Pigott declared that if the letters were genuine, they were sufficient to bring the charge of complicity in crime home to Mr. Parnell and his associates.

But what were these other terrible secrets? Pigott could not tell. Surely the letters were serious enough, said Sir Charles; they had at any rate cost two thousand pounds. "Yes, they had," Pigott replied. "I say the Archbishop has deceived me," said Pigott, moving restlessly, "I thought he had returned me all my letters." Then he said he did not believe the Archbishop had ever sent him any reply. "Is not that the Bishop's writing?" retorted Sir Charles. "It appears to be." "And if this other secret of yours was locked up in your bosom, where could the danger to Mr. Parnell be?" Pigott could not tell. All he could say was that when he wrote to Dr. Walsh he must have had something in his mind "more serious" than the letters. But as to who told him this other secret, or what it was, or where he learned it, or how—Pigott's mind was a blank. "Hermetically sealed up in your bosom?" "No, it has flown out of my bosom." In the roar of laughter which followed, the day's proceedings came to an end.

On the following morning, February 22, Sir Charles continued his cross-examination of Pigott. Putting a letter into Pigott's hand Sir Charles asked "Is that your handwriting?" Pigott stuck in his eyeglass and looked long and curiously at the paper. "Yes," he said. This letter was Pigott's answer to the Archbishop's reply. In it Pigott said that he had only thought the impending accusations against Mr. Parnell might be forestalled by his (Pigott's) showing the accused the disgraceful means by which the documentary and personal evidence against them had been procured; at any rate, it would be useful to Mr. Parnell and his friends to know beforehand the charges which were to be laid against them.

"What have you to say to that?" asked Sir Charles Russell, after he had read Pigott's letter. Pigott wanted to explain, and he "explained" that having as a matter of fact procured the letters and given them to Houston, and knowing their compromising character, he began to grow

alarmed at the prospect of their disclosure—although
it had been agreed he should never be called upon to
give evidence with respect to them. He further explained
that when he first received them he was given to understand
that they never would be published. So, under the circumstances, he wished to leave the country, and he wanted
Dr. Walsh to introduce him to Parnell, who might, perhaps,
be prevailed upon to help him with money in return for the
information he could give him as to the source of the
letters.

" And so it follows" said Sir Charles, " that since last
night you have removed from your bosom the idea that
your letter to Dr. Walsh had reference to some fearful
secret not yet disclosed?" " I shall say at once,"
answered Pigott, " that what I wrote to Dr. Walsh was
entirely unfounded. I only wrote as strongly as possible
in order to make him interfere." Then Pigott had
deliberately written "lies"? "No," he had only written
" exaggerations." These communications with Dr. Walsh
were followed by two " statements" from Pigott. These
statements do not appear to have furnished Dr. Walsh
with any additional information, for in returning them to
Pigott the Archbishop wrote that he could not see how
anything contained in them would help Mr. Parnell " to
expose the forger or bring the forger to justice," and that
any help which would fall short of that would be useless.

Poor Pigott was, so to speak, falling to pieces. He was
rapidly losing what little presence of mind he had. Before
Sir Charles Russell reached the end of the Dr. Walsh
portion of the case, he convicted poor Pigott of three or
four gross lies at least. Thus, it appeared, from one of the
Archbishop's replies to Pigott, that Pigott had assured him
that " he had neither hand, act, nor part" in the publication
of the alleged Parnell and Egan letters in the *Times*. And
this, in spite of Pigott's own story of his journeys to Paris,
and the discovery of the miraculous black bag ! Pigott
repeated the same disclaimer in equally strong language,
in another letter to his Grace. " And the disclaimer was
not true?" exclaimed Sir Charles Russell, looking at his
witness curiously. " N-no," muttered Pigott.

Once more, in one of these letters and despairing communications of his to the Archbishop, Pigott had said that he
did not believe the alleged Parnell letters published in the
Times were genuine. The buyer of the contents of the
black bag doubting the worth of his purchase !

Finally, Sir Charles asked him about the most interesting and famous of the *Times* letters, that particularly known as the *facsimile* letter, apologising for condemnation of the Phoenix Park murders. Of this famous letter, Pigott wrote to the Archbishop : " I am not the fabricator of the published letter, as has been publicly circulated; and I defy anyone to prove that I had anything to do with it. It is another instance of one having to suffer for the sins of others." And denying that he had anything to do with the notorious *facsimile* letter, Pigott merely repeated his falsehoods.

It was fortunate for the vindication of Parnell that the Archbishop had preserved Pigott's letters and copies of his replies to him.

The unfortunate Pigott made a formal confession, signed in the presence of witnesses, on February 23, 1889, in which he stated that " the circumstances connected with the obtaining of the letters, as I gave in evidence, are not true. No one save myself was connected with the transaction. I told Mr. Houston that I had discovered the letters in Paris, but I grieve to have to confess that I simply fabricated them."

The second matter in which Archbishop Walsh gave important help to the Nationalist Party during the time of the Parnell Commission is recorded by Davitt, though he does not mention the Archbishop's name.

During the proceedings before the Parnell Commission, Soames, the *Times* solicitor, sent agents to various British, Irish, and American cities to hunt up witnesses and information. These agents were supplied with secret codes by means of which they communicated with their employer. The code messages not infrequently fell into the hands of Parnell's friends. In this way, says Davitt, " we were enabled to read, almost as soon as Mr. Soames, all his code dispatches from the United States and Canada. We easily deciphered these messages, and in this way learned what his agents were doing, all about their plans, and whom they wished to enlist in the battalion of testimony for the purpose of the *Times*."

One cipher message to Mr. Soames from Colorado gave our experts in reading cryptic cables much trouble. It was not " built" upon any scientific or systematic plan, and was on that account unintelligible to us. It looked formidable, and coming from where we knew the *Times* agents to have been engaged in hunting up Land League organisers, it was tantalising not to know as much as Mr. Soames did about this particular private despatch. It obstinately refused, however, to divulge the secrets represented by words, figures, and hieroglyphics, and we had to cable agents in New York and Chicago to keep an eye on Colorado. Fortunately, a distinguished Irishman, a learned embodiment of all the sciences, arrived in London at this time, and the puzzle from the Colorado Springs was submitted to him in the despairing hope that, as he was an authority on almost everything, he might unravel its hidden story. He succeeded after a whole night's labour, and the startling statement which it unfolded gave us a bad quarter of an hour the following morning.

The "distinguished Irishman" was Archbishop Walsh. The manuscript in which he deciphered the message lies before me as I write, and the story of the negotiations between the *Times* agent and a rancher at Colorado Springs is told by Michael Davitt.*

* *Fall of Feudalism in Ireland,* pp. 551—560.

CHAPTER XVI

THE PARNELL CRISIS

THE Report of the Parnell Commission was published in February 1890. In the previous December a petition for divorce had been filed by Captain William O'Shea against his wife on the grounds of her misconduct : the co-respondent in the case was Parnell. Very soon after the divorce proceedings were first mentioned in the public Press, Michael Davitt had an interview with Parnell, in which Parnell spoke to him as follows :—" Davitt, I want you to go back to Ireland to tell our friends that I am going to get out of this without the slightest stain on my name or reputation."* Davitt fully believed, and thought that Parnell intended him to believe by those words, that he was entirely innocent of the charge made against him. Davitt immediately went and told Morley so. He also crossed over to Ireland and told Archbishop Walsh. " Mr. Morley was delighted," writes Davitt, " and so was Archbishop Walsh—intensely relieved Archbishop Walsh was. I told these and others of my friends that I had never known Parnell to lie to me; and that until the charge should be proved at his trial, I would believe implicitly in his innocence."

When the petition for divorce came to be tried in London on November 15, 1890, the action was undefended, and a Decree *Nisi* was granted to O'Shea on Monday, November 17.

On the following day, November 18, a meeting of the National League was held in Dublin. A resolution of

* The *Labour World*, Nov. 20, 1890.

confidence in Parnell was passed, and the meeting declared its determination to stand by him, notwithstanding the result of the divorce proceedings. A similar course was followed at a largely attended meeting of Irish Nationalists held on Thursday, November 20, at the Leinster Hall, Dublin.

Meantime certain Nonconformists in England had raised their voices in protest against Gladstone's continuing to associate his Party with Parnell, after the decision in the divorce court. Davitt also, November 20, pronounced against the retention of Parnell as leader, on moral as well as on political grounds, and he severely censured the Irish bishops and priests for not having publicly condemned Parnell :

They should have spoken out, because, poor as Ireland has been, and trampled upon as she has been in the past, she has at her moral banker's probably greater credit than any other nation. In other words, Ireland has always been remarkable for her regard for chastity and virtue, and especially for the sacred rights of the domestic hearth. Well, now, notwithstanding Mr. Parnell's outrage upon his friend, and his being proved guilty of acting the part of a dishonourable man and thereby tarnishing the movement of which he has been a leader, there has not been an expression of opinion from a single bishop or priest in Ireland; and their neglect of their duty to speak out in the name of Ireland puts them, I am sorry to say, in rather a bad light before the Irish people throughout the world. It has been left to the Nonconformists in England to speak out in plain language about this crime of Mr. Parnell's. However, it is perhaps not too late. Something may be said by Archbishop Croke or Archbishop Walsh before next Monday. But many of us expected that last week we should have had a pronouncement from some of these quarters which would have told the world that although Mr. Parnell is a Protestant, and this woman is a Protestant, nevertheless, as Mr. Parnell is our leader, we are morally concerned in his acts; and all the more so, that as a Catholic people we are jealous of the moral reputation of our race.

On the same day (November 20) Davitt wrote privately to Dr. Walsh :

Why cannot Parnell retire for this session ?   Is he going to force himself and his paramour upon Ireland at the expense of Home Rule ?

Four days only remain for us to make choice between Parnell and Ireland.   If he appears next Tuesday at the opening of Parliament as the *newly-elected leader* of the Irish people, good-bye for this generation to Home Rule and God help Ireland.

The Archbishop replied to Davitt by return of post, November 21, 1890 :

A particular course is publicly urged on the country with the greatest vehemence, so that those who differ from the view so taken have to choose between effacing themselves and causing a split.

I can, I think, see a way in which a perfect political loyalty to Parnell could have been reconciled with the other requirements of the case.   But that way has not been taken. Perhaps I ought to be glad that the whole affair has been so managed as to leave me and the episcopal body as a whole no voice in the consideration of it in principle or in detail.   We stand clear of the responsibility that has been so rashly undertaken by others.

On November 19, 1890, Manning wrote to Walsh :

This O'Shea case is a supreme disaster.   My hope is that Mr. Parnell will say : " I will serve Ireland with redoubled devotion ; but I will not bring on you any of the censures which will fall on me.   Let three or five of you be elected as a permanent direction of your political action in the House, in close communication with the leaders of the present opposition.   Mr. Sexton, Healy, and Justin McCarthy, Mr. Dillon and O'Brien could not without risk be left out."

I have a strong feeling, I will even say an instinct, that this is higher than all political expediency.   I have been urged here to speak on the subject, but have refused.   You may depend on my silence.

If we keep morally right no harm will come to Ireland.

Later on the same day, Manning again wrote :

I cannot let a day pass without writing again. Since this
morning I have found that the judgment here of the most
vital friends of Ireland is that if the leadership of the Irish
members is to remain unchanged, the bishops, priests, and
people of Ireland will be seriously affected in the judgment
of all English friends, or the chief of them. Already this
has been shown by the Nonconformists, and it is certain of
a great part of Mr. Gladstone's supporters.

Moreover, I am sure of the judgment and feeling of Rome.
What I wrote this morning I most strongly repeat as my
conviction and hope. And I know that it is the mind of
some of the most forward of the Irish politicians here.

Apart from all this, if ten years ago the bishops and priests
had spoken and acted together, the movement would not
have fallen into the hands of laymen. There is now both in
Ireland and in Rome the opportunity of your regaining the
lead and direction.

Croke, to whom Walsh sent Manning's letter, communicated to Walsh his views on the situation, November 22,
1890 :

I do not go so far as Cardinal Manning, who seems to
think that Parnell's holding on to the leadership means
ruin. But I believe that by doing so he will do serious
damage to the cause. Besides, if he had an atom of shame
left in his composition, or if he were capable at all of
grasping the situation, even from a personal point of view,
he could not fail to see that retirement, on Tuesday morning last, would have created sympathy for him on all sides,
and caused a strong flow of the tide in his favour.

I have flung him away from me for ever. His bust,
which for some time has held a prominent place in my hall,
I kicked out yesterday. And as for the " Party" generally,
I go with you entirely in thinking that they make small,
or no account, of the bishops and priests now, as independent agents, and only value them as money gatherers and
useful auxiliaries in the agitation. This I have noticed
for a considerable time past; and I believe we shall have
to let them see and feel, unmistakably, that without us,
they would be simply nowhere and nobodies.

The main point at issue now is a difficult, as it is a
delicate one. Its difficulty is greatly enhanced by the
action of the Press and of the Irish Parliamentary Party.
Had silence been observed up to this, something might

have been done to facilitate, or to bring about a reasonable compromise, such as abstention from the House of Parnell for a month or so, or for all the present session. But now, really, I fear things must be allowed to take the direction given them by the Irish members—come what may. I see no practical way out of the difficulty. Davitt, though substantially right, was, as usual, precipitate.

It is fortunate for me that I had left Rome before this sad catastrophe had occurred. The Pope would surely " have at me" about it; for he had a personal dislike, somehow, to Parnell, and was not pleased with me for having constantly defended him.

On Sunday, November 23, Dr. Walsh saw Dr. Joseph Kenny, M.P., a close personal friend and devoted adherent of Parnell's, and strongly urged that Parnell should retire, and that in the meantime the Party should concentrate on the question of the Evicted Tenants. On the next day, November 24, he wrote to Kenny a private letter intended to be shown to Parnell, in which, after emphasising his views as to the advisability of concentrating on the question of the Evicted Tenants, he continued :

Anything beyond this, it is, I am satisfied, hopeless to look for unless the leader by a bold manly act now adds one more to the many claims he has established upon the country. The question now really is this, whether we are to have things go on unchanged or to have Home Rule in our time. Both cannot be combined.

All that has been done by the members up to this is excellent. It puts an end for ever to the stories of disunion. But *above all*, it makes it easy now for him (Parnell) to do the right thing.

The English canon is a strange one. I cannot say that I understand it in all its details. But wrong and inconsistent as it is in some respects it is right in others. And the English people most manifestly have a claim upon us just now.

Everything will depend on what to-morrow may bring.

On the morrow, Tuesday, November 24, the Irish Parliamentary Party were to meet to elect a sessional chairman.

On the evening of the 24th Gladstone wrote to Morley the famous letter in which he stated that he had arrived at the conclusion :

That notwithstanding the splendid services rendered by Mr. Parnell to his country, his continuance at the present moment in the leadership would be productive of consequences disastrous in the highest degree to the cause of Ireland. I think I may be warranted in asking you so far to expand the conclusion I have given above, as to add that the continuance I speak of would not only place many hearty and effective friends of the Irish cause in a position of great embarrassment, but would render my retention of the leadership of the Liberal Party, based as it has been mainly upon the presentation of the Irish cause, almost a nullity.*

Gladstone communicated fully his views about Parnell's retention of the leadership to Justin McCarthy, whom he asked to see Parnell, and to bring these views to his notice before the Irish Parliamentary Party met on the following day to elect their sessional chairman. " This expansion of my views I begged Mr. McCarthy to regard as confidential, and not intended for his colleagues generally, if he found that Mr. Parnell contemplated spontaneous action (in resigning); but I also begged that he would make known to the Irish Party at their meeting to-morrow afternoon that such was my conclusion, if he should find that Mr. Parnell had not in contemplation any step of the nature indicated."†

McCarthy saw Parnell on the following day, November 25, before the meeting of the Irish Party, and communicated to him Gladstone's message. Parnell was obdurate and determined to stand to his guns.‡ The meet-

---

* Morley's *Life of Gladstone* (Bk. x., chap. v., sec. iv.).
† *Ibid.,* loc. cit.
‡ *Recollections* by Viscount Morley, vol. i., p. 262. (Macmillan & Co., London, 1917.)

ing of the Irish Party took place. McCarthy, who was present, made no reference to Gladstone's message. Why he refrained from doing so has never been explained. Parnell was unanimously elected chairman. After the election Gladstone's letter to Morley was given to the Press, and its publication caused consternation in the Irish Party.

When Gladstone's letter to Morley was published, a number of members of the Irish Party requisitioned that a meeting of the Party should be summoned for the following day, November 26. On the morning of the 26th, William M. Murphy, M.P., telegraphed to Archbishop Walsh :

Most serious situation here. Gladstone's message to McCarthy not conveyed to meeting yesterday which acted in ignorance of its existence. Meeting called to-day two o'clock on requisition of about twenty members. [Parnell] determined to hold on, and no one here strong enough to avert catastrophe. If you think your interference called for you might wire Sexton. In any case kindly send me wire, which, if desired, I shall regard as strictly private.

To this an immediate telegraphic reply was sent by the Archbishop :

Dr. Kenny knows my view by private letter. It is unchangeable. Manifestly members hold no mandate from the country to wreck the national movement. Take time. There never was a case more clearly requiring calm and full deliberation.

The Archbishop also telegraphed to Kenny : " Have you shown him my letter ?"—and received a reply, dated November 26 (4.15 p.m.) : " Have not yet done so, but shall do so this evening."

Mr. Murphy wrote to the Archbishop the same evening :

I received your telegram just as our meeting adjourned from 3.30 to 5 p.m., and I wired you then that the feeling was overwhelmingly in favour of Mr. Parnell's retirement. The most passionate appeals were made to him by his oldest followers, but he had set his teeth and declared that he would not stir unless the Party voted him out of the leadership. He used the adjournment to arrange to get a motion proposed to adjourn the debate until Monday next to give time to communicate with America (with Dillon and O'Brien) and, as it would look badly to rush the decision, this was agreed to. Parnell had more support at the adjourned meeting to-day than I expected, but there was clearly a majority against him. He made no attempt to show on what grounds he took his obstinate stand.

From all I can learn here, there is no doubt that even with Gladstone at their head, the Liberals could not get a majority at the general election which the Tories will precipitate if Parnell is retained, and that being so Gladstone's retirement is a certainty, with the result of wrecking our cause for this wretched woman.

The interval between this and Monday will be used by Parnell to strengthen his hands, and we should get some support from home in this crisis.

I arrived here with the expectation that we could get along with him, but I had no idea of the situation until last night.

Your views were not communicated to the meeting, and as in my telegram I said your reply would be treated as private, I did not take the responsibility of making them known, as Dr. Kenny had your letter.

Meanwhile the keenest public interest was manifested regarding the attitude which the Irish bishops and clergy would adopt towards the retention of Parnell as leader. Davitt had, as we have seen, publicly blamed Dr. Walsh and Dr. Croke for their silence, and had strongly urged them to repudiate Parnell on moral grounds. The first public statement made by an Irish bishop concerning the crisis was made by Dr. Walsh. The statement was contained in an answer to the editor of the *Irish Catholic*, communicated to the Press on November 28 :

The matter on which you have written to me is, in my opinion, altogether too grave to enable me, an individual bishop, to feel warranted in making any public statement of my opinion in reference to it, until I have had the opportunity of consultation with my episcopal brethren.

The Irish Parliamentary Party will, I understand, meet next Monday [December 1] to decide upon the action to be taken by it in the lamentable crisis with which it is confronted.

It is easy to conceive that the decision then come to by our parliamentary representatives may have the effect of opening up a new phase of the Irish national movement and that the situation resulting from the decision may be one that will put upon the bishops of Ireland collectively as well as individually a very grave duty—the duty of considering whether, or how far it will be in our power to continue in future to place in the Irish Parliamentary Party that confidence which, as a body, we felt justified in placing in it in the past.

The letter ended with this paragraph :

For the last few days certain events of not very remote occurrence have been prominently before my mind. With remembrance of these before me, I am, I confess, unable as yet to feel absolutely convinced that we are even now in a position to form a final judgment in the case out of which the present unhappy crisis has arisen. In this way I may be illogical. But it is better to be illogical than to run the risk of being uncharitable or unjust.

The " events of not very remote occurrence," had reference to the case of the Pigott forgeries. When the first of these forged letters appeared in the *Times*, Parnell publicly protested his innocence. Though he did not choose to defend his character by a process in the courts, he vindicated his honour, however, by publicly pledging his word that he stood absolutely free of the infamy with which he was charged. So long as Parnell had not spoken about the findings of the divorce court, the Archbishop was apparently not without hope that the trusted political leader would be able to clear himself of the charge of misconduct alleged against him. The ground of that hope was the assurance which Parnell had given to Davitt that he would get out of the divorce proceedings without a stain on his name or reputation.

On November 28, Walsh wrote also to Manning :

I see by the *Irish Times* that my telegram is becoming
public property. I am glad of this. The M.P. (Wm. M.
Murphy) who had telegraphed to me for an expression of
opinion said that *if I desired it*, he would regard my
communication as strictly private. I put no reservation on
him in my telegram. Yet he treated it as private and did
not communicate it to the meeting. Now, however, it
must become public. As it contains a reference to my
private letter to Dr. Kenny (urging Parnell's temporary
retirement) that, I daresay, will have to be made public
also.

All this will be of use. It will show that the Irish Church
is not silent at this great crisis. When the storm blows
over a little, all will see that the line of private communication of view was much more likely to be effective than that
of public declarations. I am convinced that some, at all
events, of the public declarations have done more harm
than good.

When at length Parnell did issue a public statement,
Saturday, November 29, it contained no reference to the
incident of the divorce. The statement was in form a
manifesto addressed to the people of Ireland, in which,
with great skill and effect, he launched an attack on Gladstone. It was the opinion of Lord Randolph Churchill,
expressed in a letter written December 3, 1890, that
Parnell's manifesto was " a masterpiece. It lifted the
issue between Mr. Gladstone and himself from the small
ground of divorce up to the large ground of a great
political question."*

Immediately on the publication of the manifesto, Archbishops Walsh and Croke decided to state publicly their
attitude towards retaining Parnell in the leadership. It
was agreed that Croke should address a public telegram to
Justin McCarthy and that Walsh should communicate his
views in the form of an interview with a representative
of the Central News.

* *Life of Randolph Churchill,* vol. ii., pp. 437-38.

Dr. Croke's telegram, dated Saturday, November 29, stated his views clearly :

All sorry for Parnell; but still, in God's name, let him retire quietly and with good grace from the leadership.

If he does so the Irish Party will be kept together, our honourable alliance with Gladstonian Liberals maintained, success at general election assured, Home Rule certain.

But if he does not retire, alliance will be dissolved, election lost, Irish Party seriously damaged, if not wholly broken up, Home Rule indefinitely postponed, coercion perpetuated, evicted tenants hopelessly crushed, and the public conscience outraged. Manifesto flat and otherwise discreditable.

Dr. Walsh, in the interview published through the Central News, referred " to the assurance which Parnell had given to Davitt that his reputation would be unsullied by the divorce proceedings, and to the fact that Parnell's continued silence seemed to shatter that assurance." He went on to say that " if the Irish leader would not, or could not, give a public assurance that his honour was still unsullied, the Party that takes him or retains him as its leader can no longer count on the support of the bishops of Ireland. In speaking as I have spoken, I confine myself almost exclusively to the moral aspect of the case.* If Mr. Parnell can set himself right, I raise no question as to the probable political results of yesterday's political manifesto. That is a political matter and I leave it to be dealt with by those who are the accredited representatives of the Irish people in the political affairs of the country. But . . . I cannot but look upon the issuing of that document (the manifesto) as an act of political suicide. It will bring disaster upon Ireland unless those whose duty it is to guard her interests are now faithful to their trust."

* Clearly Mr. St. John Ervine is inaccurate in stating that " Dr. Walsh, the Archbishop of Dublin, suggested that Parnell might temporarily retire, *not on moral grounds, but on grounds of expediency.*" Cf. *Parnell*, St. John Ervine, p. 275. (Ernest Benn, London, 1925.)

On the same day Dr. Walsh sent to William M. Murphy, M.P., the following telegram :—

Strong telegram from Archbishop of Cashel to Vice-Chairman urging Parnell's retirement. See it at once. See also detailed interview of mine Central News to-morrow's papers. Standing Committee of bishops meet on Wednesday [December 3] to consider our position, if present leader retained. We have been slow to act, trusting the Party will act manfully. Our considerate silence and reserve are being dishonestly misrepresented.

Besides the public expression of the views published through the Central News on November 30, Dr. Walsh, on the same day also conveyed his opinion of the situation in a personal letter to Mr. T. M. Healy :—

I have often recalled what you said to me some years ago, that but for my strongly expressed opinion as to the necessity of maintaining the unity of the Parliamentary Party unbroken you would not have given way to Mr. Parnell, as you did, in the crisis of the unhappy Galway election case in 1886.

I have had it in my mind for the last few days that I ought to write to you to say that my opinion expressed in 1886 had no reference to one leader more than another.

I take it that we are on the eve of a great change, which will apply to the discipline of the Party the severest test that we can conceive it possible the Party could be subjected to.

The leadership, I take it, is practically vacant. If there was any doubt, or room for doubt, on that point up to this, there will, I trust, be none to-morrow.

Mr. Parnell, I should say, is bound, like the rest of you, by the pledge to abide in parliamentary matters by the voice of the Party.

You may take it from me that the support of the Irish bishops will be given *to the Party*, and to its duly constituted *leader* or *leaders* as the case may be. We know in this matter no distinction between individuals, so long as they are not disqualified for a part in public life.

This letter may be of use to you in coming to a right decision. Make any use you wish of it, short of publishing it in the papers.

On the day that Croke's telegram and Walsh's interview were published in the papers [Monday, December 1], the adjourned meeting of the Irish Party took place in London. The proceedings in Committee Room 15, as is well known, were protracted, bitter, saddening.

Mr. T. M. Healy wrote from the meeting to Dr. Walsh, December 1, 1890 :

I delayed acknowledging your Grace's letter till five minutes before post hour, in the hope that some decision would be come to. I thank you very much for the communication made to me by your Grace, which was most serviceable. As I write (in the midst of the meeting) it looks as if an adjournment till to-morrow would be secured by Mr. Parnell's friends, as their talking power is great, and it is only fair that everyone should have a chance of putting his views on record.

In my life I never spent so awful a time, and I am harassed body and soul.

I do pray that all will turn out best for Ireland. When I return I will try and obtain from your Grace a few moments interview to explain matters.

On Wednesday, December 3, the Standing Committee of the Irish bishops assembled in Dublin to consider the unhappy situation which had arisen. The meeting was summoned by Dr. Walsh at the urgent request of some of the bishops. The Primate, Dr. Logue, was absent in Rome making his visit *ad limina*; he was accompanied by Dr. O'Doherty, Bishop of Derry, and Dr. O'Donnell, Bishop of Raphoe.

From the bishops' meeting a telegram, signed by the chairman, Dr. Walsh, was sent to Justin McCarthy :—

Important you and members should know bishops issue unqualified pronouncement. Mr. Parnell unfit for leadership, first of all on moral grounds, social and personal discredit as result of divorce court proceedings, also in view of inevitable disruption, with defeat at elections, wreck of Home Rule hopes, and sacrifice of tenants' interests.

The following address was unanimously adopted and ordered to be communicated to the Press for publication. The Standing Committee (consisting of the four Archbishops, four Bishops representing the provinces, and two episcopal secretaries) deemed it their duty to communicate with their absent brethren of the episcopacy, and received the adhesion of most of them. Three, however, declined to sign the address. These were Dr. O'Dwyer, Bishop of Limerick, Dr. Higgins, Bishop of Kerry, and Dr. Healy, Coadjutor to the Bishop of Clonfert. None of these three prelates was a supporter of Parnell.

ADDRESS OF THE STANDING COMMITTEE OF THE ARCHBISHOPS AND BISHOPS OF IRELAND TO THE CLERGY AND LAITY OF THEIR FLOCK

The bishops of Ireland can no longer keep silent in presence of the all-engrossing question which agitates not Ireland and England alone but every spot where Irishmen have found a home. That question is—who is to be in future the leader of the Irish people, or, rather, who is not to be their leader?

Without hesitation or doubt, and in the plainest terms, we give it as our unanimous judgment that, whoever else is to fill that highly responsible post, Mr. Parnell decidedly is not.

As pastors of this Catholic nation, we do not base this, our judgment and solemn declaration, on political grounds, but simply and solely on the facts and circumstances revealed in the London Divorce Court.

After the verdict given in that court we cannot regard Mr. Parnell in any other light than as a man convicted of one of the gravest offences known to religion and society, aggravated, as it is in his case, by almost every circumstance that could possibly attach to it, so as to give it a scandalous pre-eminence in guilt and shame. Surely Catholic Ireland, so eminently conspicuous for its virtue and the purity of its social life, will not accept as its leader a man thus dishonoured, and wholly unworthy of Christian confidence.

Furthermore, as Irishmen devoted to our country, eager for its elevation, and earnestly intent on securing for it the benefits of domestic legislation, we cannot but be influenced by the conviction that the continuance of Mr. Parnell as leader of even a section of the Irish Party must have the effect of disorganising our ranks and ranging in hostile camps the hitherto united forces of our country.

Confronted with the prospect of contingencies so disastrous, we see nothing but inevitable defeat at the approaching general elections, and, as a result, Home Rule indefinitely postponed, coercion perpetuated, the hands of the evictor strengthened, and the tenants already evicted left without the shadow of a hope of being ever restored to their homes.

The meeting in Committee Room 15 which began on Monday, December 1, was protracted throughout the week. Although the majority was opposed to Parnell, there seemed a possibility of a compromise, and in view of that possibility Dr. Walsh wrote to Wm. M. Murphy on Friday, December 5 :

I do not feel much confidence in the present position of affairs. You may rely upon it that the country is rising rapidly in opposition to the continuance of Mr. Parnell's leadership of the Party. Any compromise, or result of any kind that will leave that point without a satisfactory settlement will end in hopeless disunion in the country and consequent disaster . . .

Why not think and act boldly? The Party, I fear, will otherwise be led into some morass.

Show this letter to Sexton, Healy, and any one or two others you think desirable.

Murphy replied, December 6 (4.30 p.m.) :

Your letter received to-day which I have used as suggested. Our party of 44 are solid for no more compromises.

After a stormy discussion, Justin McCarthy rose at 6 p.m. (December 6) and said that it was idle to continue the proceedings any longer, and that he and his friends had resolved to retire from the room. Then McCarthy, accompanied by forty-four members, withdrew, leaving Parnell with twenty-six supporters in the room. The split in the Party was complete.

After the split it was charged against Dr. Walsh that he had adopted a halting attitude towards the retention of Parnell in the leadership, that he had suggested his retirement on political and not on moral grounds, and that he and the other bishops had given no indication of hostility to Parnell until Gladstone had written his ill-advised letter to Morley.

It is true that the Archbishop did not *publicly* advocate the retirement of Parnell before the meeting of the Parliamentary Party which took place on November 25. He did, however, endeavour privately to procure Parnell's retirement. This course he urged strongly in the private conversations which he had with Dr. Kenny, one of Parnell's most trusted Parliamentary colleagues, and in the letter written to Kenny (November 24) which he intended that Kenny should show to Parnell. Moreover, we have his own testimony contained in his letter of November 28 to Manning that he had adopted the line of private communication because he was persuaded that this course " was much more likely to be effective than that of public declarations." His action was prompted by considerations both moral and political. In his interview of November 30 he stated that " the Party that takes him or retains him as its leader can no longer count upon the support of the bishops of Ireland," and that " in speaking as I have spoken I confine myself almost exclusively to the *moral* aspect of the case."

The statement that Archbishop Walsh's opposition to retaining Parnell as leader was due to Gladstone's letter to Morley is unsustainable in view of the chronological order of events above narrated. Besides, when such a statement was made by Parnell it was at once challenged by Dr. Walsh. Speaking at a public meeting at Limerick on January 11, 1891, Parnell said :

The bishops said that it is all a question of morality. I say it is not a question of morality. If it had been a question of morality, these estimable men would have interfered at once. They waited for a whole fortnight before they expressed their opinion; they waited until Gladstone had expressed his opinion before they expressed theirs; and I declare . . . that it is not open to the Irish bishops to claim that they interfered on the question of morality because they were too late. No, it was a question of politics.

The Archbishop at once replied to Parnell in a public letter, January 12, 1891:

In reference to Mr. Parnell's statement I wish merely to say that Mr. Parnell, I am satisfied, would not have spoken in this way if he had been informed, as I think he ought to have been informed, and as I had hitherto supposed he had been informed, as to certain matters that occurred in the early stages of the present unhappy deadlock in Irish affairs.

For myself, for instance, the time has come for me to mention that previous even to Mr. Parnell's re-election to the Chairmanship of the Parliamentary Party, I expressed myself very plainly on the subject of his leadership in a letter which I thought it my duty then to write to a prominent member of the Party (Dr. Kenny), a gentleman whom I knew to be one of Mr. Parnell's most devoted supporters.

In that letter I spoke of Mr. Parnell's continued leadership in the circumstances of the case as identified with disaster to the Irish cause. In the plainest terms I stated my conviction that Mr. Parnell's duty was clear, that he was called upon, by a manly act of self-sacrifice, to add one more to the many claims that he had established upon the gratitude of our country.

This letter to which I have now for the first time made public reference was written, as I have said, before Mr. Parnell's re-election to the Chairmanship of the Party. It was written, consequently, before Mr. Gladstone had given any intimation of his view of the case.

I have no reason to think that, even if my letter had been shown to Mr. Parnell, it would have influenced to any very noticeable extent his action in reference to the leadership. But I have to regret that it was not shown to him. If it had been, he would not, I am confident, have relied on the argument ascribed to him in the reports of his speech at Limerick yesterday, in sustainment of his view that the question involved in the present controversy as to his leadership is not a question of morality.

I need hardly add that my letter had reference only to the supposition of Mr. Parnell's being unable to clear himself of the stain attached to him by the unrebutted and even uncontradicted evidence that had been brought against him in the divorce court.

The charge that the bishops' action in opposing Parnell sprang not from a love of morality but from political motives, made in a more offensive form by T. Harrington, M.P. at the same meeting in Limerick, elicited from Archbishop Croke a characteristically vigorous rejoinder, January 12, 1891 :

Talking of Morals and Morality, Mr. Harrington is represented as having said :

" They were told by high authority (the Irish bishops) that this was a moral question. The question they (Mr. Harrington & Co.) had to consider was, whether this cry (including the declaration of the Irish hierarchy) that was raised was an honest cry, whether the opposition to Mr. Parnell's leadership sprang not from a love of morality but from an innate love of whiggery in the hearts of the men who were proclaiming themselves Nationalists to-day."

It is not easy for me to convey to the public with common patience or in measured language what I think and feel about the studied insult thus offered to the august body to which I have the high honour to belong, and to myself as well, by that peerless politician Mr. Timothy Harrington.

I am a Nationalist, as is well known, of over forty years' standing. During that period I have taken a prominent part, and, as I trust, not an inglorious part in every movement that had for its object to elevate the Irish people and root them to their native sod. A Young Ireland and hillside man with Mitchel and Meagher, I was a Land Leaguer with Gavan Duffy, and a Home Ruler with Parnell. My record as an Irishman is before my country, and until the political purist, Mr. Timothy Harrington, dared to asperse me on a public platform, at least by implication, no one, even *amongst my enemies,* had ventured to charge me with an innate love of whiggery, or to insinuate that I had raised or was a party to a cry, in the justice and propriety of which I did not believe.

No, I have never found it necessary to simulate patriotism, nor have I trafficked in it for emolument. My purse and influence have been always at the public service. I have incurred the displeasure of those for whose good opinion I should, if needed, lay down my life, rather than check the onward career of the man whom I am now reluctantly compelled to denounce, or the progress of the cause with which his name has hitherto been honourably associated.

As for my venerable brethren in the Irish hierarchy, they are well able to defend themselves if they choose to do so. Possibly, however, more prudent than I am, or possessed of a larger stock of patience, they may suffer the silly though offensive references of Mr. Timothy Harrington to pass, if not unnoticed, at least unheeded and unrebuked.

Throughout the crisis which eventuated in the Parnell split, Walsh and Manning were in constant (almost daily) communication. The Cardinal wrote, November 29 :

Mr. Parnell's manifesto makes it more advisable and even necessary that you should speak. And if the bishops and clergy speak, the guidance of everything in principle will return into your hands. The late leadership had become a domination.

The bishops and clergy of America are with you, and will support your appeal to Catholic Ireland throughout the world. This is the best answer to Mr. Parnell's imputation of dependence upon England and upon English parties. Ireland has the popular sympathy and support of the English people who are of no party and have suffered under both parties.

This is a supreme moment to convince Rome that you do not put politics before faith and morals.

Do not be too anxious. The power is in your hands, but the people of Ireland need guidance and support . . .

December 1, 1890 :

Your declaration in the papers to-day gives me great joy. Catholic Ireland will now speak with one voice—and I hope (as I wrote yesterday to the Pope) " *il resultato della*

*presente crise deplorabile sara la subordinazione della
politica alla fede ed alla morale.''*

The bishops and clergy will resume their old lead of the
people. The manifesto shows where you would have
been . . .

December 2, 1890 :

The persistence of Mr. Parnell as shown yesterday makes
it doubly necessary that the bishops should speak with one,
and that no uncertain voice, to-morrow.

Delay was prudent, for if you had spoken and the Irish
members in London and America had opposed you, Ireland
would have been sorely tried and divided. As it is, the
people are, or the " sanior pars" will certainly be, guided
by you.

December 4, 1890 :

You have indeed fulfilled my hope of a supreme voice.
If you do not object I should be glad that the enclosed
[letter congratulating the Irish bishops on their address]
should appear in the Irish papers and in ours.

The publication of Manning's letter, however, was at first
deferred and finally abandoned for the reason given by Dr.
Walsh in a letter to the Cardinal, December 14th :

I have been waiting from day to day to see whether it
would be judicious to publish your Eminence's letter. As
yet at all events it would not, I think, have been right to
publish it. Some of the Tory papers here started the cry
last week that your Eminence acting through Arthur
O'Connor, was the real author of the revolt of the Party
against Parnell ! This is brought in to prop up the cry that
the real issue is between the English and the Irish leaders,
between Gladstone and Parnell. So far I am satisfied that
the more carefully we keep ourselves to the arguments on
the *Irish* side of the case the better.

As Manning's letter has never yet seen the light, it may
fittingly be transcribed here :

December 4, 1890.

To His Grace, the Archbishop of Dublin.

MY DEAR LORD ARCHBISHOP,—I have this morning read
with full assent the declaration of the archbishops and
bishops of Ireland on the deplorable events which are now
upon us. It is a document worthy of Ireland, and of your
people of whom, in all these years of trial, I have never
ceased to say that they are the most profoundly Christian
and the most energetically Catholic people on the face of
the earth. The voice of the bishops has not faltered and
the conscience and heart of the Irish people in all the world
will answer to it.

For a time, some, who from natural love to Ireland shrink
from the great sacrifice they are called on to make, may
hesitate. But they will see that if politics govern the lower
instincts of men, faith and morals govern all wise and
prosperous politics; and that no nation can prosper where
faith and morals do not reign supreme.

Ireland by its fidelity has outlived all that politics can do
against it, and by that same Christian and Catholic fidelity
of its pastors and people, it will win all the rights it has so
long striven by suffering to attain.

During the early stages of the Parnell crisis feeling ran
very high in Ireland. This was especially the case in
Dublin where Parnell's followers were both numerous and
vocal. The Archbishop was the object of much vigorous
criticism. He lost his popularity, but this did not trouble
him much : to Manning he wrote : " It will be of use to
some of us to find ourselves, for once, on a really unpopular
side." He was not, however, by any means reduced to
silence, although he was hampered considerably by the fact
that the *Freeman's Journal* had sided with Parnell and
was no longer ready to publish his communications uncen-
sored.

Up to that time the *Freeman's Journal* had always been
at the Archbishop's service, and its columns were the
ordinary medium of his numerous public communications.
On the defection of the *Freeman* the Archbishop availed
first of the pages of the *Irish Catholic*, but as it was but a

weekly publication, he encouraged and aided the issuing of a little daily called the *Insuppressible*, and later of a more substantial paper styled *The National Press*. Besides the letters dealing with the different phases of Parnellism addressed by the Archbishop to the *Times* and other English newspapers, interviews given by him on the same matters were published through various news agencies.

The questions dealt with in these utterances concerned various charges made by Parnell and his followers against Dr. Walsh and the bishops. It was said that the bishops' condemnation of Parnell was prompted, not by moral but by political considerations; that their condemnation, such as it was, was the outcome of English political interference; that the bishops were jealous of Parnell's undisputed authority with the Irish people, which they regarded as an intolerable check to their own political ambitions; that the bishops made the divorce case a pretext for ridding the country of a Protestant leader, who had always shown himself intolerant of clerical dictation and impatient even of clerical interference in civil affairs.

Fortunately there is no need in these pages to record the many unpleasant and painful political discussions in which the Archbishop deemed it his duty to take part throughout the Parnell split. Two incidents, however, ought not to be passed over in silence. The one occurred on the occasion of Parnell's marriage, the other on the occasion of his death.

Parnell's marriage with Mrs. O'Shea took place before a civil registrar at Steyning in June 1891. The announcement of the marriage caused considerable embarrassment to one section of his followers. Another section boldly proclaimed that the marriage ceremony had set everything right, that Parnell had made the *amende* to society and full reparation to Mrs. O'Shea. These applauders of Parnell's action were vigorously denounced by Archbishop Walsh. In a public letter (August 5, 1891) he reminded them " that adultery is a grievous and shameful sin; that the guilt of it, so far from being washed away, is but deepened and blackened when sinners, instead of turning from their evil way, deliberately enter into a public compact to continue their sinful career.

" This in plain language is the nature of the compact entered into in the registry office at Steyning by Mr. Parnell and his partner in guilt."

It may be remarked here that the *Freeman's Journal* took occasion of Parnell's marriage to withdraw its support from him, and very many of his followers who up to that time had implicitly believed him innocent of the charge of adultery, were disillusioned and fell away from him.

Parnell died, quite unexpectedly, on October 6, 1891. On the occasion of his death a leading article dealing with his career which was published in the *Irish Catholic* gave great offence, and met with widespread condemnation. In the United States the condemnation was levelled against Archbishop Walsh to whom—erroneously, if not maliciously —the authorship of the article was attributed. This unfounded story was sent to America by the correspondent of the *Chicago Herald*, who cabled from London on October 7 :

The Dublin *Catholic*, an official organ of the Catholic hierarchy will print to-morrow a leader written by Archbishop Walsh which is sure to create a sensation, and to meet with some expression of dissent. The prelate boldly follows Parnell into the grave with the denunciation of the Church. He says : " Mr. Parnell's death is one of those events which remind the world of God. So far as is known Mr. Parnell died unrepentant of his offence against God and against his country. He died plotting fresh discord, while the champion or the tool of faction steeped in traitorism to the very lips. By the grave now open charity can scarcely find a place, etc., etc."

In commenting on the *Irish Catholic* article, the *Chicago Herald* remarked :

The bitter denunciation of Parnell by Archbishop Walsh breathes a spirit of vindictiveness that ill becomes any minister of religion.   In tone and temper it betrays a personal hate that is amazing.   It breathes a spirit as rancorous as any that the world ever noted in times of greatest religious intolerance, and the assertion that charity can find no place at the open grave is as inhuman and as indecent as it is impious and shocking.

Archbishop Walsh was fiercely denounced in New York, Chicago, and other American cities for his " unpatriotic, un-Christianlike, and shocking tirade." And he received from America many letters of denunciation and abuse.

As a matter of fact the Archbishop had nothing to do with the article published in the *Irish Catholic*. On learning of the libellous attack on him by the *Chicago Herald*, he at once publicly denied all responsibility for the peccant article.   He also put the matter into the hands of his lawyers, and wrote to a legal friend in the U.S.A. informing him that the statements contained in the *Herald* article, so far as they regarded him, were absolutely without a particle of foundation.

The sole foundation [he wrote] for the *Herald's* article would seem to be that a day or two after Mr. Parnell's death an article which I have heard was written in a strongly denunciatory spirit was published in a weekly newspaper, the *Irish Catholic*.

The *Irish Catholic* is published in Dublin, but with the management of it, or with its articles, I have no more to do than you have.   It may be useful, moreover, for you to know that, as a matter of fact, I was away from Ireland at the time of Mr. Parnell's death, and so far from having written or inspired the article, I never even heard of it until several days after my return to Ireland.   If the American law affords any protection to those whose reputation is assailed by the publishing of libels in which there is not a particle of truth, this plainly is a case for taking action.

This disclaimer was accepted, and many apologies were tendered to the Archbishop.

CHAPTER XVII

ECONOMICS AND LAW

THE death of Parnell was soon followed by that of Cardinal Manning. The Cardinal died in January 1892, and was succeeded in the archbishopric of Westminster by Dr. Herbert Vaughan. Towards the end of the same year it was announced that Dr. Vaughan was to be raised to the Cardinalate, and it was rumoured that an Irish Cardinal was to be created at the same time. Dr. Walsh was commonly mentioned as the most likely of the Irish bishops to receive this signal honour. His two immediate predecessors in the See of Dublin had been members of the Sacred College, his diocese was the most important in Ireland, and he himself was at the time the most prominent among the Irish bishops. His political activities, however, were viewed with disapproval in influential quarters, and had evoked strong hostility towards him in England and at Rome. Shortly before this time, Lord Salisbury, the Prime Minister of England, had publicly charged the Archbishop with defying the Pope's authority,* and his association with the Plan of Campaign had in certain influential ecclesiastical circles attached suspicion to his name.

At the same time the Pope was well disposed towards the Archbishop. Leo XIII had always treated him with much personal kindness; he appreciated his talents and admired his energy and versatility. His Holiness was strongly influenced in his favour by Cardinal Manning, who had repeatedly written to the Holy Father to defend Walsh

* See Appendix B.

430

against "whisperers." Had Manning been then alive, he would undoubtedly have urged Dr. Walsh's advancement to the Purple. A letter written (November 28, 1892) by Dr. O'Dwyer, Bishop of Limerick, to Dr. Walsh's auxiliary, Bishop Donnelly, shows how the affair of the Cardinalate stood at the time.

I hear that the Pope stated recently that he will create an Irish Cardinal at the next Consistory. But who it is to be he did not say. Persico (who it was then announced was to be created Cardinal) is all right, and I am extremely glad of it. And his promotion is, I think, an evidence that Armagh and not Dublin will represent us. In many personal gifts your man would be better, but for the substantial interests of religion I have no doubt of the greater safety and reliability of the other.

The Bishop of Limerick's views regarding the greater safety and reliability of Dr. Logue were shared by Archbishop Vaughan, Cardinal-Elect, whose advice the Pope had sought on the matter. That advice was strongly adverse to Dr. Walsh, and in favour of Dr. Logue. Dr. Vaughan himself more than once told a venerable Prelate who is still living that it was his opportune intervention which had decided Leo not to create Dr. Walsh Cardinal.

Dr. O'Dwyer exercised influence against Dr. Walsh's admission to the Sacred College. His opposition, as appears from contemporary correspondence was not generous.* Indeed, Dr. O'Dwyer was *saevus ambobus Achilles*. Writing to Bishop Donnelly about this time he says :

I know from a reliable source that the question of the Hat has been under consideration, and that up to a recent

---

* A different account of the affair was given by Dr. O'Dwyer to the Bishop of Killaloe. He told Dr. Fogarty that he was in Rome about the time that the question of creating an Irish Cardinal was first mooted. Before having audience of the Pope, the bishop had an interview with Monsignor Persico, who then occupied the important post of Secretary at Propaganda. Persico informed Dr. O'Dwyer that Leo was then

date the merits of the two [Walsh and Logue] were being weighed, and no decision had been come to. My information would point to Armagh as the most likely. I sincerely hope it is true. You remember O'Connell's remark about the caubeen in the window—" If it did not let in the light at least it kept out the cold."

The news of Dr. Logue's appointment was published about the middle of December, 1892, and he received the Red Hat in the following month of January.

BIMETALLISM.

While the question of the Cardinalate was being discussed (December 1892), Dr. Walsh's name came prominently into public notice in connection with a question of political economy. The question of the currency was then receiving attention from statesmen and economists in Europe and throughout the world generally. The awakening of interest in the currency question was due mainly to the fact that at that time and for some years previously there was a steady fall in the value of silver. One result of this depreciation of silver was that countries whose standard unit of value was silver were adversely affected in their dealings with countries in which the standard unit was gold. Gold was the standard in England, silver in India. The gold price of the silver rupee—the standard Indian coin—had fallen in the course of a very few years from two shillings of English gold to less than one shilling and four pence. The consequence of this decline in the value of their money was to increase the burden of foreign obligations in gold on the people of India.

anxiously considering the Irish appointment, and was sure to ask the bishop's advice on the matter, and he (Persico) urged him to oppose Dr. Walsh, and to support Dr. Logue vigorously. At the audience the Pope almost immediately introduced the question of the prospective Irish Cardinal. His Holiness, who was evidently very favourably disposed towards Dr. Walsh, asked the bishop to say frankly, which of the two—Logue or Walsh—ought to be appointed. Dr. O'Dwyer, however, respectfully declined to express his preference.

One remedy suggested to meet such hardships arising out of the fluctuations in the value of money was to replace the single standard unit of value—whether that unit were gold or silver—by a double standard, to substitute bimetallism for monometallism. The bimetallists proposed to make gold and silver legal tender to unlimited amounts. And in order to render their proposal feasible they required that a relation should be fixed by law between the two metals; that, for instance, one ounce of fine gold should bear to one ounce of fine silver a ratio of sixteen or fifteen-and-a-half to one. Various means were suggested for securing a fixed ratio between the two metals, but all bimetallists were agreed that fixity could be most effectively secured by international agreement.

The most prominent advocate of bimetallism in Great Britain at that time was Mr. Arthur Balfour, and owing to his advocacy and to the support of many distinguished economists and politicians the matter attracted much public attention in England. In Ireland, little or no interest was manifested in the question of the currency. It was looked upon as a purely academic matter, which could have no practical bearing on anything directly connected with Irish affairs. Archbishop Walsh was the first to arouse the attention of the public to the important practical bearing of the British system of currency on the interests of Irish farmers.

In November of the year 1892 it happened that the Archbishop, at the request of John Morley, gave evidence before the Evicted Tenants' Commission—a commission set up by the Liberal Government to inquire into the case of the Irish Tenant Farmers who had been evicted from their holdings. In the course of his evidence Dr. Walsh expressed his entire approval of the course followed by certain tenants who, after having urged on their landlord a demand for a reduction of 30 per cent. in the rents, rejected an offer made by the landlord, the effect of which

would have been to secure for them a reduction of 36 per
cent. In the case of the 30 per cent. reduction, however,
the rent was to be determined for one year only; in the
other case, the tenants were asked to bind themselves to
pay a fixed rent for a number of years, inasmuch as their
acceptance of the landlord's offer would involve their
becoming tenant purchasers under a Land Purchase
Act, and so placing themselves under an obligation to pay
a fixed amount to the Government for a period of forty-
nine years. The Archbishop explained to the Commission
that he considered that it would be unwise, and it might
prove ruinous, for the tenants to pledge themselves to pay
a fixed sum for so long a period. The reason why he took
that view was, he said, because, owing to the state of
affairs in the world of money at that time, the difficulty
of paying any fixed amount (of money) was increasing
from year to year. That difficulty, he pointed out, was
due to the fact that gold—the standard unit of value in
the British Isles—was appreciating and seemed likely to
continue to appreciate. Bearing this consideration in
mind, the Archbishop was of the opinion that a tenant who
might very reasonably engage to pay a fixed rent for a
year or two, would act very imprudently in binding himself to pay the same rent for a long period of years. For,
he said, if gold continued to appreciate it could easily
happen that a rent which remained nominally the same
might, in the course of some years, be really very much
higher than when the tenant undertook the obligation.

It did not lie within the scope of the Commission to deal
with the difficulty of long-term payments, or to consider
the means by which that difficulty might be remedied.
The Archbishop, however, deeming it important to bring
the matter under public notice, published a lengthy
statement in the form of an interview in which he set forth
his opinions regarding the unwisdom of Irish farmers
entering into long term engagements to pay fixed rents

to landlords or to the Government, unless some effective
means were found of safeguarding them from the hardships likely to result from a probable rise in the value of
gold. These hardships, he pointed out, could be prevented
only by the stabilisation of the currency, and stabilisation
could, in his view, be most effectively secured by abandoning gold as the sole standard unit of value and substituting
for it a bimetallic standard.

The " interview," which was published in the *Freeman's
Journal*, November 28, 1892, was really a statement of the
case for bimetallism as opposed to monometallism. It was
an exposition clear, simple, popular, but at the same time
accurate, of the meaning of both these systems. It set
forth persuasively the advantages which might be expected
to accrue from the adoption of bimetallism as the most
likely means of stabilising the currency; and it showed how
important stabilisation was for the Irish farmers—many
of whom were bound by lease or otherwise to pay fixed
sums for a number of years.

Dr. Walsh's "interview" attracted widespread attention.
Mr. Henry Chaplin, who shortly before then had been
Minister for Agriculture in the Conservative Ministry, speaking at the National Agricultural Conference in London,
December 7, 1892, referred to the "interview" in words of
striking eulogy, and expressed the hope that the views as set
forth by the Archbishop might be embodied in a pamphlet and
distributed broadcast among the agriculturists of England.
A similar request for the re-publication of the " interview"
in pamphlet form was addressed to the Archbishop by a
number of the delegates assembled at the International
Monetary Congress, which was being held at Brussels.
That Congress was attended by representatives of twenty
governments or states, and some of the delegates, especially
those who favoured bimetallism, made a joint request for
the re-publication of the " interview." The General

Secretary of the Bimetallic League of Great Britain wrote to the Archbishop from Brussels, December 1, 1892 :

I cannot adequately convey to you the gratitude of the bimetallist delegates assembled here, for the great service which you have rendered to the cause of humanity by the public pronouncement in favour of International Bimetallism contained in Monday's *Freeman's Journal.* A number of copies of that journal arrived here to-day, and they have been read with the greatest interest by many of the delegates —bimetallist and monometallist.

I trust your Grace will forgive me taking the liberty of saying that while I have not heard of any of the latter being able to lay a finger upon a single flaw in any of the statements or arguments in the " interview," the bimetallists here, and they embrace some of the ablest in the world, are moved to the deepest admiration at the complete grasp of the question which is evidenced throughout the whole four columns of the *Freeman.* I am asked by some of the delegates of England, India, the United States, Holland, and Spain, to ask your Grace's permission to publish the "interview" as a pamphlet, and if you desired to supplement it in any way (we have nothing whatever to suggest) it might be done in a preface.

On hearing from the Archbishop that he intended to re-publish the " interview," enlarged and altered, the same correspondent wrote, December 23, 1892 :

May I take the liberty of saying that I half regret your intention of altering the " interview." It is so admirable and so clear that, to adapt the quotation,

> " One touch the more, one trace the less,
>   Might half impair its natural grace
>   And rob it of its plainness."

We feel, however, that it will be quite right in whatever form it leaves your Grace's hands.

The " interview " was referred to in terms of praise and quoted by writers in various financial journals. Mr. Moreton Frewen, who referred to it appreciatively in an article on Silver in the *Fortnightly Review* (January 1893) wrote privately to Dr. Walsh :

I have during the past ten years resided for the most part in America. Since 1875 I have carefully watched the development of this currency crisis now upon us, and the conviction with me has gained ground steadily, that all effort and every industry is under a ban because of this novel and legislated contraction of the world's currency.

And, while I yield to no one in my admiration of the federal principle of government—a principle to which I have always believed the Home Rule effort would guide us, yet I am so convinced that constitutional reforms of this nature are worse than useless unless, as you pointed out to your interviewer recently, this cataclysm of all prices is arrested, and the plague stayed.

I believe it is in your Grace's power to further this international movement more effectually than any one man, excepting perhaps President-elect Cleveland or Mr. Gladstone. The latter I regard as now too old to learn; neither is he willing to let his Party learn. But your Grace could reinforce the reform movement most powerfully, and I attach to your sanction and action an influence both at Westminster and Washington second to none.

That Dr. Walsh's views on economics did attract notice at Washington appears from a letter written to him from New York by Patrick Ford, December 13, 1892 :

I was in Washington yesterday and had a long interview with President Harrison. The conversation was chiefly on political and economical subjects, including the Monetary question. You perhaps know that this is the greatest silver-producing country in the world, and naturally we are much interested in the question of bimetallism. Referring to this the President said, " I am greatly pleased to see that Archbishop Walsh has come out in favour of bimetallism. I certainly think with him that its adoption would be of material benefit to Ireland."

Your name had not been spoken of in our talk before the President introduced it. He alluded to you as a statesman and patriot whom he greatly admired.

The " interview" was published in pamphlet form at the beginning of 1893, the title of the pamphlet being, *Bimetallism and Monometallism: What they are and how they*

bear upon the Irish Land Question. The pamphlet
contained over one hundred pages. The edition was
quickly disposed of, and a reprint called for. A second
and enlarged edition was published in June 1893, and a
third edition quickly followed. The pamphlet was translated into French and German. It was quoted in the German
Reichstag by Count Herbert Bismarck, the champion
of the agricultural interest in the Fatherland, in support of
a motion in favour of bimetallism. In the United States
the pamphlet was widely read, and for years it continued
to be circulated in America as an able statement of the
case for currency reform.

During the election campaign for the Presidency of the
U.S.A. in 1896, the money question was one of the great
issues. The Democratic Party favoured currency reform
and the free coinage of silver. They insisted that silver
should receive at the hands of the Government the same
treatment as gold, at a ratio of sixteen to one, and this independently of any international agreement. They advocated
the adoption of bimetallism by the United States, even
though monometallism should continue to be the currency of
other countries. The Republicans were opposed to any
change from the gold standard except by international
agreement. The Republicans were dubbed " Gold-bugs,"
although McKinley in accepting the nomination of his Party
had declared in favour of bimetallism on the basis of international agreement, or at least of concurrent international
action.

Dr. Walsh's pamphlet on bimetallism was distributed
broadcast in the interest of the Democratic candidate. It
was quoted extensively as an authoritative work on the
currency question, and permission to reprint the pamphlet
in the U.S.A. was sought by printers and publishers in
Philadelphia, Boston, Columbus (Ohio), and elsewhere.
The pamphlet had such influence with certain sections of
the American public that the President of the " Democratic

Honest Money League" of New York wrote to the Archbishop, October 6, 1896 :

> Your work (on Bimetallism) has been extensively circulated in this country by the party espousing the " Free and Unlimited Coinage of Silver at a Ratio of Sixteen to One." Its use as an authority on the subject of free coinage and violation of contracts has resulted in placing, it is said, 85 per cent. of the Catholic clergy of the United States in opposition to what we term " honest money" and in allying them with the party of repudiation and national dishonour, which with their great influence with the people of Catholic faith, is very effective.   This cannot but work disadvantageously to Catholic interests in America.

Many efforts were made to induce Dr. Walsh to issue a statement on the currency question, to be used for political propaganda during the election campaign in the U.S.A. Amongst those who tried to secure Dr. Walsh's intervention was W. H. Frenfell, M.P. for Salisbury, Vice-President of the Bimetallic League of Great Britain, who wrote, October 17, 1896 :

> I have just received a telegram from Chicago saying that the Roman Catholic vote is of the greatest importance in the present Presidential Election, and asking if I could possibly get from your Grace a pronouncement similar to that made by Prince Bismarck in favour of the United States taking the initiative in establishing Bimetallism independently of other countries as being the speediest and surest method of eventually securing the co-operation of other countries . . .   If you can see your way to address to me a letter on the silver question, it will be immediately cabled to New York, and will not fail to have great weight in the United States.

Dr. Walsh, however, did not consider it right for him to intervene personally in the election campaign in the United States, especially as Archbishop Ireland and other well-known American ecclesiastics were prominent supporters of the Republican candidate.   Though urgent and repeated requests from America were addressed to him to join issue with Archbishop Ireland and the " Gold-bugs," he declined to be drawn into a discussion on American politics. The Democratic candidate, W. J. Bryan, was defeated at the election. With the Republicans in office the gold standard was maintained, and excitement regarding the currency question quickly abated in America. As for the Archbishop, his active participation in discussions on currency reform ceased as soon as he perceived that there was no likelihood of a change being introduced into the British system, but he continued to take a deep interest in the question, and to the end he adhered to his opinion in favour of bimetallism.

When Mr. Bryan, some time after his defeat at the presidential election in the United States, visited Ireland, he called on the Archbishop to pay his respects.

LAW OF CHARITIES

The study of law had always had a special attraction for Dr. Walsh. During the years when he was reading and teaching theology he made a systematic study of the Canon Law, and he was particularly interested in tracing the influence of the Canon Law on the Common Law of England. While he was still at Maynooth he had been collecting materials for a comprehensive work dealing with this matter, and had sketched for himself the outlines of the plan he was to follow. But owing to preoccupation in the business of administration he was able to make but little progress with the work. He did not, however, abandon the project, hoping that he would, at some time, find leisure to carry out his scheme.

His interest in the subject of the law was evinced by articles which he published from time to time, chiefly in the pages of the *Irish Ecclesiastical Record*. In 1885 he

began a series of articles in the *Record* on " The Law of
Charitable Bequests in Ireland," but his appointment to
the archbishopric interrupted the work after the publication
of three short papers. After an interval of ten years he
found time to take up the subject again, and each of the
twelve numbers of the *Record* throughout the year 1895
contained an article written by him on " The Law in its
Relation to Religious Interests."

His purpose in writing these papers was to set forth in
outline a general view of those sections of the law of Great
Britain and Ireland in which the law comes into contact
with religious interests. In the early papers he dealt with
the legal position of Charitable Bequests—explaining the
technical sense of the word " charity" in English law, the
legal position of bequests which are in the legal sense
" charitable," the notable privileges accorded by law to
such bequests, and the legal drawbacks to which they are
occasionally subject.

Then followed papers dealing with bequests for Masses,
which are of peculiar interest. An outline of his treatment
of the legal history of that question may be worth reproduc-
ing here. The legal position of such bequests differed
notably in Ireland and in England. In Ireland, from the
time that the rigour of the penal code began to be relaxed,
bequests for Masses were in certain circumstances held to be
valid by the Irish courts. In England it was not so. Even
after the passing of the Catholic Relief Act of 1829, bequests
for Masses were held by the English courts to be void.
This continued to be the practice of those courts down to a
very recent date.

The question of the validity of a bequest for Masses was
first raised in Ireland, since the days of the open persecution
of Catholicity, in the year 1823, in the case of *The
Commissioners of Charitable Donations and Bequests* v.
Walsh. The judgment in that case, delivered by Lord

Manners,* Lord Chancellor of Ireland, upheld the validity of the bequests for Masses; and that decision has been uniformly followed by the Irish judges ever since.

A further question regarding bequests for Masses was raised for the first time in the Irish courts in 1875. Can bequests for Masses in Ireland be considered not only to be valid, but also *charitable* in the legal sense of the word?

The question was one of great practical importance. In the first place, such bequests, if charitable, would come within the general exemption of Charitable Bequests in Ireland from legacy duty. But, besides this, there was at issue the more important question of validity. Bequests for Masses are, from the nature of the case, not unlikely to be made in the form of perpetuities. But if so made they cannot be upheld as valid unless they are charitable. The case submitted to the Irish Court of Exchequer in 1875, *Attorney-General* v. *Delaney*, was one in which a testatrix left several bequests, one of which was " to the Right Rev. Dr. Delaney, Roman Catholic Bishop of Cork, £100 to have 400 Masses offered up for the repose of the soul of my brother Timothy and myself."

The court decided that the bequests for Masses in the case were not charitable on the grounds that the celebration of the Masses for the repose of the souls of the testatrix and her deceased brother did not tend to the benefit of the public. Chief Baron Palles in delivering his judgment in the case laid it down that " a gift for a religious or any other purpose to be charitable must, to some extent at least, be in the nature of a general public use. It must be of such a nature that the court can determine that its

---

* Lord Manners was Lord Chancellor of Ireland from 1807 to 1827. He was not, it would seem, a great lawyer, but he was in an exceptional degree dignified and courteous as a judge.

O'Connell declared that he was " a bad judge, but the most sensible looking man talking nonsense he ever saw."—(Cf. *D.N.B.*, vol. xii., p. 945.)

execution shall confer *a benefit on the public*, or upon some section of the public." He argued :

Thus the question of the charitable nature of the bequests in hand resolves itself into this : Does the celebration of the Masses for the repose of the soul of the testatrix and of her deceased brother tend (and in such a way that the court can judicially ascertain and declare that it tends) to the benefit of the public ?

To some it may appear unnecessary to say more than that it does not, but I prefer expressing in detail the reasons for which I have arrived at this conclusion.

The case is not affected by the direction of the testatrix that the Masses should be offered for the repose of the souls of her brother Timothy and herself. The Sacrifice is offered . . . either with or without a particular memorial for the deceased person specified. If it be celebrated under such circumstances as to be charitable if offered without any particular memorial, the addition of the memorial cannot deprive it of its otherwise charitable character . . .

In the present case there is not on the face of the will— nor indeed at all—an obligation that the Masses shall be said in any public congregation in Ireland—or in public at all.

If the will had prescribed that those Masses should be celebrated in public in a specified public church or chapel in Ireland, it would, I confess, appear to me that the bequests would be charitable, as gifts for the public celebration of an act of religious worship which tends to the edification of the public congregation.

Although Baron Palles in the hypothetical case just mentioned had expressed his opinion that a bequest for Masses would be charitable if the will prescribed that these Masses should be celebrated in public in a specified church or chapel, yet, when such a case came before Vice-Chancellor Chatterton in 1880, that judge decided that the bequest was not charitable, notwithstanding the fact that, according to the terms of the will, *the Masses were to be cele-brated in Ireland in a church open for public worship at the time of such celebration.* That judgment was binding on all courts of co-ordinate jurisdiction, and for seventeen years all cases regarding bequests for Masses were declared not to be charitable, even though the will directed that the Masses should be said in public.

In the year 1897 a case came before the Irish Court of Appeal in reference to three legacies of £50 each, which a testator had directed to " be applied for Masses for the repose of my soul and my wife's soul, same to be celebrated publicly" in three Catholic churches in Dublin which were specified. After a hearing of the case (*Attorney-General* v. *Hall*) in the Court of Appeal, the Court unanimously over-ruled the decision of 1880, and decided that the bequests for Masses to be celebrated publicly in Ireland were *charitable*.

While the case was being argued before the Court of Appeal, reference was made to the previous case of *Commissioners of Charitable Donations and Bequests* v. *Walsh* (1823), and it was contended that the decision in that case was inconsistent with the law as expounded by Chief Baron Palles in the case *Attorney-General* v. *Delaney* (1875). It happened that Dr. Walsh in one of his papers published in the *Irish Ecclesiastical Record* (1895) had carefully analysed the judgments in both cases, and pointed out that there was no inconsistency.   Referring to Dr. Walsh's paper, Lord Justice Barry, in giving his judgment that bequests for Masses to be celebrated in public were charitable, said :

He agreed that the suggestion of the Lord Chief Baron in *Attorney-General* v. *Delaney* was sound, and that the fact, as is the case, that the Masses were to be celebrated in public in the manner referred to made this bequest chari-table as well as pious. He concurred in the suggestion he found in a very remarkable paper written on the subject-matter in which they were engaged, by an eminent ecclesiastic (the Most Rev. Dr. Walsh) who, he would venture to say, from a perusal of that paper, had in his adoption of the more sacred calling lost to the science of jurisprudence one of the most acute of equity-lawyers.

Nine years more were to elapse before the Irish Court of Appeal was called upon to reverse the decision of 1875 which declared a bequest for the celebration of Masses not to be charitable because the will had not provided that the Masses should be said in public. The opportunity came in 1906 in the case of *O'Hanlon* v. *Logue*. In deciding that case the court disaffirmed Palles's judgment of 1875, and declared the law to be that a gift, simply for the celebrating of Masses in Ireland, is a valid charitable gift, irrespective of the mode of their celebration. Baron Palles in 1906 opted to sit in the Court of Appeal in order that he might have an opportunity of disaffirming the judgment which he had given in *Delaney's* case thirty-one years before.

In England, as has been stated, the state of the law regarding bequests for Masses was different. Down to the year 1919 bequests for Masses in England were held by the courts to be void. The action of those courts was based upon the judicial interpretation of a statute of Edward VI, passed in 1547, and known as the Statute of Chantries* or the Statute of Superstitious Uses.† That statute did not, of course, apply to Ireland, and no statute analogous

---

* The word " chantry " is used in two different but closely related senses :

1.—The name is given to a foundation providing for the maintenance of a trust, usually out of lands, for the saying or chanting of Masses for the repose of the soul either of the founder or of some other person.

2.—The name is given also to the particular chapel or other place set apart for the religious service thus provided for. In the Cathedral of Winchester, for example, there are preserved to the present day, with the greatest care as regards their material structures, several noble chantries, including those of William of Edington, William of Wykeham and Cardinal Beaufort—three Bishops who occupied in succession the See of Winchester, and also, though not in immediate succession, the office of Lord Chancellor of England.

† *Superstitious uses.* In the legal sense the expression " superstitious uses " is practically synonymous with " forbidden religious trusts," or trusts for the " propagation or rites of a religion not tolerated by law."

In a restricted sense of the expression, " superstitious uses " are uses or trusts for Masses for the dead, or for prayers for the dead.

to it was ever enacted by the Irish legislature. The statute of Edward VI dealt with certain endowments, existing at the time of its enactment, for the maintenance of Masses for the souls of persons deceased. Its preamble recites that certain endowments of this kind were amongst the chief means by which was maintained " the doctrine and vain opinion" elsewhere described in the preamble as the " superstition 'of Purgatory and Masses satisfactory . . . to them which be departed." This is followed by the further recital, that all property devoted to such purposes ought to be applied to the founding of schools or other such charitable uses, and that for this purpose it should be entrusted to the King. Then comes the enacting portion of the Statute. It simply vests in the King all existing endowments of the class to which the statute refers. There is no formal prohibition of such endowments for the future; there is no enactment that such endowments established in the future should be transferred to the King; the statute deals solely with endowments already in existence. It did not make belief in any doctrine or in the performance of any religious ceremony an offence. It did not make any gift for the celebration of Masses, or any ceremony for the repose of deceased persons, illegal or void. It recognised them as valid, but enabled the King in the specific instances mentioned, but in no others, to capture the subject matter of each gift and employ it for purposes other than, and different from, those for which it was originally given. Every section of the Act, except one (38) dealt with the past. Section 38 alone dealt with the future. That section of the Act enabled those to whom gifts were made for the performance of ceremonies for the repose of souls to omit, with impunity, to fulfil the duties for the discharge of which they were given.

Yet purely retrospective as it is in form, the statute of Edward VI influenced the subsequent action of the English courts in their dealing with the class of endowments to which it refers. For mainly with this statute as a foundation was constructed the legal doctrine of the invalidity of gifts for superstitious uses.

" A superstitious use may be defined generally to be one which has for its object the propagation, or the rites, of a religion not tolerated by law." (1) Previous to the time of Edward VI, Masses for the dead were not illegal at Common Law, but, on the contrary, dispositions of property to be devoted to procuring Masses to be said or sung were recognised by Common Law and by Statute. (2) At the date of the passing of the Act of Chantries, no Act, or provision having the force of an Act, had made Masses illegal. (3) That Act (1 Ed. VI, cap. 14) did not itself make Masses illegal, or provide that property might not thereafter be given for the purpose of procuring that Masses might be said or sung. It merely confiscated property then held for such similar purposes. (4) It was only when the Acts of Uniformity of 1549 made Catholicity no longer a tolerated religion that Masses became illegal as a result of those Acts. From 1581 to 1791, the saying or singing of Masses was a penal offence, and no court could enforce uses or trusts intended to be devoted to such uses. Although by the Relief Act of 1791, Catholics, on taking a prescribed oath of allegiance, were permitted to conduct and be present at their religious services, although they were entitled to believe in the existence of Purgatory, as they had always done, and were also entitled to have the ordinary Masses said for the repose of the souls of the dead, yet no relief was given regarding *Bequests for Masses*. On the contrary, in the 17th section of the Act (31 Geo. III, cap. 32) it is expressly provided that " all uses, trusts, and dispositions, whether of real or personal property," which previous to the passing of that Act had been deemed " superstitious or unlawful" should continue to be so deemed and taken. This state of the law continued unchanged, at all events down to the passing of the Catholic

Relief Act.   On the passing of that measure—the Catholic
Emancipation Act of 1829—an important question arose.
The invalidity of bequests for Catholic purposes came
in solely as a matter of necessary legal inference from the
policy of the law towards the Catholic religion.   It might
well seem that, on the formal reversal of that policy as
attested by the Act of Catholic Emancipation, the illegality
would, as a matter of no less necessary inference, disappear.
As, however, some doubt on this matter existed in the minds
of lawyers of repute, the legislature passed the Roman
Catholic Charities Act of 1832.   By this Act, Catholics in
Great Britain, " in respect of their schools, places of
religious worship, education, and charitable purposes . . .
and the property held therewith, and the persons employed
in and about the same" were made subject to the same laws
as Protestant Dissenters.*

* " The Toleration Act," passed in 1688, granted toleration
to Protestant Dissenters only. By that Act Protestant Dissenters
were set free from disability, and their religious, educational and other charitable trusts thenceforward stood upon
the same footing as trusts for similar purposes connected
with the established religion. " Popish recusants " were
rigorously excluded from all share in the protection which the
Toleration Act afforded. Unitarians and Jews were also excluded. A Unitarian Relief Act was passed in 1813, but even
then nothing was done for the Relief of English Catholics. The
Catholic Relief Act, 1829, and the Roman Catholic Charities
Act of 1832 granted partial toleration to Catholics. Toleration
was granted to Jews by the Religious Disabilities Act of 1846.

Christianity is no longer part of the law of England. " At
the time of the Revolution of 1688, the law relating to religion
may be summed up by saying that there was a common law
principle that Christianity was part of the law of the land, and
there were a number of statutes which may be called Acts
of Intolerance, enforcing conformity with the established religion, and enforcing heavy penalties for the exercise of any
other form of religion."—(Tyssen, *The Law of Charitable
Bequests*, p. 100.)

It would be a mistake to suppose that at the present day
" Christianity is part of the law of the land." Lord Coleridge,
in 1883, laid down the rule : If the decencies of controversy are
observed, even the fundamentals of religion may be attacked
without a person being guilty of blasphemous libel. Lord
Coleridge's rule was approved by the decision of the House of
Lords in 1917 in *Bowman* v. *Secular Society*.

The Roman Catholic Charities Act of 1882 did not, however, remove all doubt about the validity of bequests for Masses in Great Britain. Indeed, in the year 1835, three years after the passing of that Act, a case (*West* v. *Shuttleworth*) was brought before the courts in England, in which a testatrix had bequeathed to certain chapels and to certain priests named, specified sums of money for Masses for the repose of her own soul and that of her deceased husband. It was held by Sir C. Pepys (then Master of the Rolls, and known as Lord Cottenham when later on he became Lord Chancellor) that the bequest for Masses was void. The judge held that bequests for prayers and Masses for the repose of the souls were " within the Superstitious Uses intended to be suppressed by the Statute of Edward VI"; that they were not within the relieving words of the Act of 1832, and that consequently they were void. Sir C. Pepys was under no misapprehension as to the enactment of Edward VI, but he said that by the preamble it was generally regarded that all such uses were superstitious and consequently void :

The legacies in question, therefore, are not within the terms of the Statute of Edward VI. But the statute *has been considered as establishing the illegality of certain gifts*, and amongst others the giving of legacies to priests to pray for the soul of the donor has in many cases (collected in Duke, p. 466) been decided to be within the superstitious uses *intended to be suppressed* by the Statute.

As a matter of fact the cases quoted in Duke's* " Charitable Uses" are, all of them, cases relating to the

---

* The work referred to by Sir C. Pepys was originally published in 1676, but his reference was to an edition which, though of much later date than the original work, was published in 1805, over a quarter of a century before the enactment of the Act of 1832. The edition of 1805 was entitled : *The Laws of Charitable Uses as laid down and digested by George Duke, Esq., in 1676 . . . . the whole continued to the present time, enlightened by an Abridgment of all the Adjudged Cases.* By Richard Whalley Bridgman, Esq. London, 1805.

special application of the section in Edward VI which
forfeited *the then existing* gifts in favour of the Crown.
They are of no assistance for the purpose of showing that it
was intended by that statute to declare all such uses superstitious and void.

The decision in the case *West* v. *Shuttleworth*, based, as
it undoubtedly was, on a misinterpretation of the law, was
destined to rule all cases regarding the validity of bequests
for Masses in England for eighty-four years to come.

Writing in 1895 on the law regarding bequests for Masses
in England as expounded by Sir C. Pepys, Archbishop
Walsh remarked : " It is somewhat strange that a point of
such importance has never yet been brought up for final
decision in the English Appeal Court, and if necessary in
the House of Lords." Proceeding to examine the matter
critically, he pointed out that, since the legislature by the
Act of 1832 legalised the endowment of a church and an
altar for Catholics, it legalised by necessary inference an
endowment for Masses. For the Mass was fundamental in
the belief of Catholics, and without it church and altar
would be alike meaningless and useless.

Twenty-four years after these words were written the
question of the validity of bequests for Masses came up for
final decision in a case which came before the House of Lords
in 1919, and the decision of the supreme tribunal then given
declared the bequests for Masses to be valid. The relevant
facts of the case, *Keane* v. *Bourne*, were these : One
Edward Egan, an Irishman domiciled in England, died in
London in 1916. He had made a will appointing James
Keane and another executors, and the will contained,
amongst others, the following bequests :

To the Cathedral (subsequently determined to be Westminster Cathedral) for Masses, £200.

To the Jesuit Fathers, Farm Street, £200 (and the residue
of the Estate) for Masses.

The executor, James Keane, caused an originating

summons to be issued in the Chancery Division with a view of ascertaining *inter alia* whether the several gifts for Masses were valid. The judge, in the Chancery Division, declared that the bequests for Masses to Cardinal Bourne as representing the authorities of Westminster Cathedral, and to the Jesuit Fathers of Farm Street, were void. In delivering his judgment the judge, Mr. Justice Eve, said : " I do not think it is open to me to express an opinion of my own upon the very forcible and able arguments which have been addressed to me in support of these bequests. The decided cases are really too strong, and the law in the matter has been settled now and for well nigh a century past. Under these circumstances, if it is to be altered, it must be effected by the House of Lords."

When the case came before the Court of Appeal, that court, apparently without going into the merits of the case, simply affirmed the order of the Chancery judge, and the way was clear for appeal to the House of Lords to have the law correctly ascertained and defined.

The case was argued in the House of Lords in April 1919, and on June 3 the court gave its decision. The Lord Chancellor, Lord Birkenhead, delivering his judgment, began with these words : " This is a difficult and extremely important case. Your Lordships cannot, in my view, escape the duty, anxious as it undoubtedly is, of overruling decisions which have been treated as binding for generations." And Lord Atkinson in the course of his judgment said :

I think it is too late in the day to hold in this country that a religious ceremony believed by the millions of the Roman Catholics of Christendom to be a solemn and sacred Sacrament is merely a superstitious rite. I should be myself prepared, if it were needed, to hold that if not *Adams* v. *Lambert* (decided in 1602), certainly all the cases which have followed it and purport to be based upon it down to the year 1832, were wrongly decided. For the purpose of the present case, that, I think, is scarcely necessary, because, in my opinion, the statute of that year changed fundamentally the entire situation—the whole outlook and underlying principle of the law in reference to the Roman Catholic religion.

I am clearly of opinion that all relevant cases decided from this new point of departure to the present time were wrongly decided, and that the bequests—the subject of controversy in the present case—were not void on the sole grounds that they were gifts for superstitious uses.

From the very commencement of the legal proceedings in reference to the Egan Bequests, Dr. Walsh took the keenest interest in the case. With a view to awakening and stimulating a like interest in others, and especially in the hope that the interest would be such as to secure that the question at issue would be brought for decision to the House of Lords, the Archbishop wrote articles in the *Irish Ecclesiastical Record* dealing with the history of the question, and discussing the anomalous position of the law in Great Britain in reference to bequests for Masses. While purporting to be mainly expository of the strange state of the law, the articles contained some acute criticism on the reasoning of the judges in some of the leading cases to which reference was made. The articles—entitled " Superstitious Uses"—appeared in the July, August, and November numbers of the *Record*, 1918.

These papers were carefully read, and even quoted by the learned counsel who argued the case in the House of Lords. The counsel in the case was the Hon. F. Russell, K.C., a son of Dr. Walsh's old friend, the distinguished Lord Chief Justice of England, Lord Russell of Killowen.

Dr. Walsh had made the Canon Law of the Church in its relation to the civil Law of Charity the subject of close and constant study. For over twenty years he laboured, with intermittent intervals, in compiling materials for an exhaustive treatise on the subject, and actually completed the work. The results of these labours, however, were

fated never to see the light; for, although he wrote and
re-wrote the treatise, and even went so far as to have the
greater part of it printed, he was never quite satisfied with
it. A relentless critic of anything written by his own hand,
he was unwilling that a work of reference which he felt to
be imperfect and possibly inaccurate should be associated,
even posthumously, with his name, and before his death
he gave directions to his executors for the destruction of
all the materials he had collected.

CHAPTER XVIII

DENOMINATIONAL EDUCATION

AMONGST the many matters in which Dr. Walsh took an active interest and a leading part, the question of education held a foremost place. For nearly half a century he applied himself to advocating and advancing the claims of Irish Catholics for equality with their fellow-citizens in the matter of education. During his lifetime much was done to remove Catholic disabilities and to remedy their educational grievances. Equality was his watchword. While he never demanded privilege for Catholics, in education or in any other matter, he abated no jot of their just claims to absolute equality. Constantly and persistently he urged those claims. A demand for equality might seem a reasonable and even a mild programme, especially when one considers that the population of Ireland was predominantly Catholic. Yet, strange as it may seem, that modest demand was regarded, not uncommonly, as an insolent aggression. To understand this mentality of Irish Protestant ascendancy, it will help considerably to have before one an outline of the dealings of the Protestant Parliaments of Ireland and England with Irish Catholics in the matter of education.

Until near the end of the eighteenth century a Catholic had no legal status in Ireland. The highest legal authorities had laid it down from the Bench " that the law does not suppose any such person to exist as an Irish Roman Catholic."* At a time when at least three-fourths of the people were Catholics, a Catholic could not sit in Parliament, he did not enjoy the elective franchise, he was

* Scully. *On the Penal Laws,* p. 344.

excluded from the professions, he might not carry arms. In a word, Catholics were deprived of all civil life, and were recognised by the law " only for repression and punishment."*

It was the object of the Irish penal code not only to proscribe Catholics but also to unfit them permanently for civil life. One object of the penal laws, says Lecky,† was " to reduce the Catholics to a condition of the most extreme and brutal ignorance. The penal legislation on the subject of Catholic education may be briefly described —it amounted simply to universal, unqualified, and unlimited proscription. The Catholic was excluded from the university. He was not permitted to be the guardian of a child. It was made penal for him to keep a school, to act as usher or private tutor, or to send his children to be educated abroad ; and a reward of ten pounds was offered for the discovery of a Popish schoolmaster." In 1733, it is true, the Charter Schools were established for the benefit of Catholics ; but these schools—which were supported by public funds—were avowedly intended, by bringing up the young as Protestants, to extirpate the religion of their parents. The alternative offered by law to the Catholics was either absolute and compulsory ignorance or education directly subversive of their faith.

The Charter Schools originated by Marsh, Protestant Bishop of Clogher, and afterwards (1733) adopted by Boulter, the Protestant Primate, were established "to rescue the souls of thousands of poor children from the dangers of Popish superstition and idolatry, and their bodies from the miseries of idleness and beggary." The managers of the Charter Schools proposed to Catholic parents, to take their half-starving children between the ages of six and ten, to feed and clothe them, and to give them not only free education but an industrial training, to apprentice the boys, and

---

* Lecky. *Ireland in the Eighteenth Century,* vol. i., p. 148.
† *Ibid.* vol. i., p. 148.

provide the girls with places. The indispensable condition was that the children should be educated as Protestants. The children admitted to the schools were carefully removed from their Catholic parents, were forbidden to hold any communication with them, and were apprenticed only to Protestants. Large annual grants of public money were given to these schools, which continued to be supported by the Irish Parliament till the Union; and after the Union the English Parliament spent large sums on them till, literally, they died of physical and moral rottenness. They were denounced by Howard in his *State of Prisons*, as dens of lies and deception on the part of those who controlled them; and as dens of mental and religious ignorance and of moral and physical filth on the part of the the unfortunate children who were decoyed or forced into them. After a sweeping condemnation of them by a commission of inquiry, even the Government could endure them no longer.* It must then be borne in mind that the only elementary schools which Catholic children might, by law, attend, were these proselytising establishments, supported by public funds, for the ruin of their faith; that there were no state secondary schools to which Catholics might have access; and that the one Irish university—the university of Trinity College, Dublin—was an anti-Catholic establishment, founded by Elizabeth to serve as a stronghold of Protestantism in Ireland. Neither should it be forgotten that throughout the greater part of the eighteenth century determined and constant efforts were made to apply rigorously the provisions of the educational penal code. The schoolmaster was constantly being hunted, fined, imprisoned, transported. Moreover, one must not lose sight of the fact that when, towards the end of the eighteenth century, some measure of toleration was

---

* Cf. O'Riordan. *Catholicity and Progress in Ireland.* Lecky. *Ireland in the Eighteenth Century,* Vol. i., c. 2. Barry O'Brien. *Fifty Years of Concessions to Ireland.*

granted to the Catholic religion, and some financial aid afforded out of the public funds for the higher education of Catholic ecclesiastics, the new century found Ireland entirely unprovided with any system of public elementary education which could be conscientiously availed of by Catholics.

While the attempts to wean the Irish children from their faith, through the medium of the Charter Schools and similar institutions, were proving a decided failure, provision for elementary education was a crying need. In 1811 a new society was formed, called "A Society for Promoting the Education of the Poor in Ireland," subsequently and better known as " The Kildare Street Society." Unlike its predecessors, this society disclaimed any proselytising intentions; its schools were to be open to Catholic and Protestant alike, and no attempt was to be made to interfere with the religious belief of the children. The scheme was immediately recognised and assisted by Parliament, which voted a grant, soon raised to £30,000 a year, and the schools rapidly multiplied. For a time the Kildare Street Society successfully masqueraded in a guise of liberality; but it soon betrayed its complicity in the sins of its predecessors. By 1820 its proselytising activities had become notorious, and popular feeling was aroused against it. It finally collapsed along with other outworn institutions before the storm of the Emancipation movement.

To replace the discredited Kildare Street Society, Parliament, in 1831, adopted the system of primary education known as the system of National Education, which, with modifications, is still in operation in Ireland. The author of the new system was Mr. Stanley, then Chief Secretary for Ireland. Its avowed objects were :

(1) The education of the poorer classes in Ireland;

(2) The prevention in State schools of the proselytism which had vitiated the previous systems; and

(3) The establishment of a system of " mixed

education," in which Catholics and Protestants would be brought up together in the same school.

" Combined secular and separate religious instruction" was the principle on which the system was based; literary and moral instruction was to be given in common to Catholic and Protestant children for four days of the week, and one or two days in the week were to be set apart for religious instruction. The scheme was financed by the appropriation of the annual sum of £30,000 granted to the Kildare Street Society; and its administration was committed to a new board, the members of which were designated " Commissioners of National Education in Ireland." This body, which was to be representative of both Catholics and Protestants,* was entrusted with the supreme control of the system; the only restriction imposed was that even the " suspicion of proselytism" was to be excluded.

Stanley's scheme was hailed, and has since been regarded by not a few, as a triumph of statesmanship. Of its author's honourable purpose there can be no doubt. An adequate system of primary education that guaranteed against even the suspicion of perversion† was a welcome novelty to Irish Catholics.

But its fundamental principle of mixed instruction, involving the divorce of religious from secular teaching, was opposed to the Catholic ideal and did violence to Catholic

---

* Stanley had emphasised the necessity of having the Board fairly constituted. Yet out of seven members of the original Board, only two were Catholics. These were Dr. Murray, Archbishop of Dublin; and a Government official named Blake.

† Dr. Whately, Protestant Archbishop of Dublin, one of the most prominent members of the original Board, regarded the system as a promising instrument of proselytism. " The education," he wrote, " which is being supplied by the National Board is gradually undermining the vast fabric of the Irish Roman Church "; and again, " I believe, as I said the other day, that if we give up (the National system) we give up the only hope of weaning the Irish from the abuses of Popery. But I cannot venture openly to express this opinion,"

feelings. In practice the maintenance of the " mixed or undenominational principle was secured by a rigid code of regulations that were strictly enforced." In the actual working of the scheme it was found more convenient to allot a certain time each day for religious instruction, instead of the complete day or two days each week originally contemplated. In each school the actual work in progress had to be declared by a chart displayed in a prominent position and indicating " Religious Instruction" or " Secular Instruction" as the case might be. While the chart indicating " Religious Instruction" was exhibited, religious instruction was permissible, religious emblems might be displayed and suitable acts of piety performed by the children. But apart from the time so assigned and indicated, religion in any form was a thing proscribed. While " Secular Instruction" was indicated no reference to any religious subject was allowed, no religious practices might be performed, no religious objects displayed to view. Where religious images, such as a crucifix, or a statue or picture of the Blessed Virgin, were provided out of private funds, these religious objects had to be hidden away from sight in a box or cupboard during " Secular Instruction," as if they were the emblems of some disgraceful superstition, and unfit for the light of day.

Besides the National Schools there existed in many districts throughout Ireland voluntary schools—maintained by voluntary local effort, Catholic or Protestant. The Catholic voluntary schools were for the most part those conducted by the Christian Brothers; the Protestant ones were chiefly those of " The Church Education Society." These schools were conducted on thoroughly denominational lines; not being subject to the National Education Board, they were independent of its restrictions. But they were denied State aid or State recognition of any kind. It should be explained that, besides these voluntary schools, there was a large and increasing number of the National

Schools which were denominational in every respect except the rules to which they were obliged to conform. The popular demand for denominational education expressed itself in the erection, wherever possible, of separate schools by the different denominations. By 1880, no less than 51½ per cent. of the National Schools, attended by 570,000 children, were purely denominational in management, teaching-staff and attendance. Yet in these schools, where the question of perversion could in no way arise, the absurd anomaly was maintained of stringently enforcing the vexatious rules of mixed education. Where the attendance was actually mixed, there was, admittedly, justification for this policy; but in the majority of cases the policy of the Board was indefensible.

The advent of Dr. Cullen to the See of Dublin was the signal for an intensified campaign against the policy of the National Education Board. In 1853 he succeeded in having Whateley's *Evidences of Christianity*—a book to which Catholics took serious exception—removed from the school text-books. In 1860 the membership of the Board was increased to twenty, half of whom were Catholics. But the essential Catholic demand for denominational liberty in denominational schools was obstinately and successfully resisted by a group of educational doctrinaires who regarded the system of mixed education as a method so excellent in principle that it ought to be enforced in theory even where it had no justification in fact. Year after year the bishops continued to press the Catholic claims, and at length the Government, yielding to pressure, issued a Royal Commission of Inquiry (January 1868). The Commission, which was presided over by Lord Powis, strongly recommended the concession of the bishops' demand for the removal of all religious restrictions in schools of unmixed attendance. The report of the Commission was issued in 1870, but nothing was done to give effect to its recommendations during the episcopate of Cardinal Cullen or of his successor Cardinal McCabe, although the adoption of its recommendations was year after year urged upon the National Education Board.

The Catholic grievance against the policy of the National Board was aggravated by the maintenance of a class of schools under special regulations and privileged conditions. These " Model Schools," as they were called, were designed as part of a general scheme for the training of primary teachers, and unlike the ordinary National Schools, which were under local management, they were under the direct management of the Board. The first of these institutions was opened at Merrion Street, Dublin, in 1833, and in the following year a few masters were called up from the country for a short course of training. Five years later a large establishment was opened at Marlborough Street, Dublin, known as the Central Model School, for boys, girls, and infants, and the Merrion Street School was closed. In 1843 the Commissioners of National Education received extensive discretionary powers for the establishment of schools " such and as many as they should think proper" throughout Ireland, and the Model Schools rapidly multiplied. By 1866, besides the central institution in Marlborough Street, there were two auxiliary Model Schools in Dublin, and twenty-six others throughout the country. Everywhere, except in the Presbyterian districts of Ulster, the establishment of these schools met with violent local opposition, until, in 1866, after a strong protest by the Irish bishops, the Government intervened to prevent their further extension.

The Model Schools, pampered to the last degree by the Board, and enjoying almost unlimited resources for their development, vaunted a superior standard of educational efficiency calculated to be a successful inducement to Catholic parents. But notwithstanding their alleged superiority, popular opposition to them continued. The number of Catholic children who attended them was in every case either nought or negligible.

In the official rules and regulations of the Model Schools, their objects were set forth as being :

(1) To promote united education ;

(2) To exhibit to the surrounding schools the most improved methods of literary and scientific teaching ; and

(3) To educate young persons for the office of teacher.

The Powis Report, already referred to, pronounced the Model Schools a failure on all three heads : the first cbject was undesirable in principle and had been in nowise promoted ; while as regards their teaching and training they were inadequate and inefficient. The whole system was severely condemned. The schools were declared to be unsatisfactory in their organisation, administration, teaching and examination methods ; they were " displeasing to all sects but one" —the Presbyterians of Ulster ; and were attended chiefly by the children of the middle-class Protestants ; finally, the Report asserted, " they ought to be given up." Fourteen years later (1884) the Model Schools were described by Lord Randolph Churchill as being " about the greatest imposture that could be kept up in Ireland." " The House of Commons," he said,—" particularly the English portion of it—has always been under the impression that there is a system of mixed education in Ireland, and those Model Schools are very often pointed to as a part of the great success of mixed education in Ireland. But the fact is that mixed education does not exist in that country. The education there is thoroughly denominational." He asked was it worth the while of the House of Commons to spend large sums every year for the sake of maintaining what was really nothing more nor less than an imposture.

Yet the imposture, which had involved a capital outlay

of about £500,000, continued to be maintained at an annual cost of about £30,000.

The principle of undenominationalism which characterised the teaching afforded in the schools of the National Board was also applied in the training colleges established by the Board for preparing teachers, male and female, for their profession. Although one of the purposes for which the Model Schools were established was the training of teachers, the supply from that source was almost negligible. In practice, therefore, those candidates who sought training as primary teachers had to pass through the Board's Central Training College at Marlborough Street, Dublin. This College, which was under the direct management of the Board, was conducted on the "mixed" system. Not only was the teaching in the college undenominational, but the approved lodgings or hostels in which the students in training had to reside were conducted on the "mixed" system. In the domestic life of these hostels there was no recognition of religion, and no provision was made for its practice or teaching.

The Catholic bishops had from the first denounced the godless system of the Central Training College, and constantly warned Catholics against the danger of entering it. The teachers as a body heeded the bishops' warning, with the result that a large proportion of the teachers employed in the National Schools throughout Ireland was untrained. The bishops had meanwhile been pressing for the establishment of denominational training colleges, and had even expressed their willingness to erect such colleges, provided that they received the recognition of the Board.

In 1866 the number of untrained teachers employed in the National schools was no less than 4,369, and in that year Chichester Fortescue, the Irish Secretary in Earl Russell's Whig administration, deemed it his duty to write to the Board of National Education to call attention to the deplorable state of things brought about by its short-sighted policy.

The official system of training, he informed the Board, had proved altogether inadequate, and owing to the hostility it had evoked, especially from the Catholic body, the Government were not prepared to extend the system further. He suggested the establishment and recognition by the Board of a system of denominational training colleges, under local management, and the reform of the Central Training establishment, so as to allow teachers to lodge out of the official boarding houses. The Board expressed its willingness to adopt the Minister's suggestion, but a month later the Russell Ministry was defeated and Fortescue ceased to be Chief Secretary.

The Powis Commission in 1870 recommended that " the claim for denominational training should be conceded.'' The Commission reported strongly in favour of reform on the lines indicated by Fortescue, recommending that denominational training colleges should be recognised, under certain specified conditions, and that the National Education Board should be empowered to contribute three-fourths of the annual cost of maintaining these colleges; furthermore, that all training colleges, denominational or otherwise, should be treated on terms of absolute equality. The Commission declared, moreover, that the Central Training College was unsatisfactory in its working, that the period spent in training—about six months—was too short, and that there was no satisfactory test of the work done in the college.

For thirteen years nothing was done to give effect to these recommendations of the Powis Commission. It was not till 1883 that action was taken. In that year Mr. George Trevelyan, the Irish Chief Secretary in Gladstone's Ministry, addressed an official letter to the Board of National Education, requiring immediate reform in the system of training primary teachers as a matter " of absolute urgency.'' By this time the number of untrained teachers had increased to 7,067 or 66 per cent. of all the teachers working under the Board. The vast majority of the untrained teachers were Catholics who on conscientious ground had refrained from entering the Marlborough Street College. Of the total number of Catholic teachers in the country only 27 per cent. were trained. To remedy this state of affairs the Chief Secretary announced that the Government " were prepared to encourage and facilitate the establishment in Ireland of training colleges under local management, by authorising the Board to make grants towards their maintenance." He recommended the adoption in its entirety of the training system in operation in England. The Commissioners of National Education signified their willingness to adopt the English system— *mutatis mutandis.*

Almost immediately the necessary preliminary steps were taken to provide two Catholic training colleges near Dublin, one for male and the other for female teachers. About the same time a Protestant college was also opened. For the Catholic colleges no existing buildings were available. The Protestant college, which was started in Kildare Place, was able to begin its work in buildings originally erected almost exclusively at the public expense out of grants formerly administered by the Kildare Street Society.

The treatment of the Catholic training colleges, as regards provision for buildings, compared very unfavourably with the treatment of the denominational training colleges in England, on the one hand, and that of the Board's undenominational training college at Marlborough Street, on the other. The Board's training college had been built, equipped, and entirely supported out of public funds from the beginning. The training colleges in England were almost all denominational*, and all English training colleges, whether denominational or undenominational, were dealt with by the State

---

* According to the *Report of the Committee of the Council on Education for the Year* 1888—9 there were then 44 training colleges in England and Wales. Of these 41 were denominational.

on a basis of absolute equality. Though these colleges were established by private endeavour, the State had, in every case, made liberal grants for their building and equipment. The Irish Catholic training colleges, on the contrary, had to be built and equipped altogether from private resources. The college for women teachers in Dublin was built at the expense of a religious community, the Sisters of Mercy. The building of the training college for male teachers at Drumcondra, Dublin, was made possible only by Cardinal McCabe's giving security for a loan of £8,000 to purchase a site, and by his advancing a sum of £14,500 out of certain diocesan funds entrusted to him for educational purposes. When the college was built, it is true, the Board of Works advanced to the manager a loan of £10,075; but for the balance of £4,425 and the other private monies borrowed to provide suitable equipment, no public loan could be obtained. This loan of £10,075 had to be repaid to the Board of Works in thirty-five half yearly instalments (of £252) covering principal and interest. When therefore the Irish Catholic training colleges started on their career, they were hampered by charges for rent and interest and repayment of borrowed capital. In this respect they presented an unfavourable contrast to the English colleges and, needless to add, to the undenominational college at Marlborough Street.

A further unfair differentiation against the Catholic training colleges arose in connection with the contribution for maintenance which they received from the State. The colleges relied for support on a fund called the " Credit Fund." The method of payment by means of the " Credit Fund" was borrowed from the system in operation in England. According to that system the colleges were supported by the State to the extent of *three-fourths of their annual expenditure*, within a maximum limit fixed at £50 for each male student and £35 for each female student in training. In practice the " Credit Fund" was an account opened by the education authority in favour of the various training colleges. In this account each college was credited with £50 or £35 for each student trained, in whose case certain conditions had been fulfilled, namely, that the student (1) had been a year in training in the college, (2) had passed the required examinations, and (3) had given two years' satisfactory service as a National Teacher. From the fund thus established, the yearly grants were made to each college, subject to the conditions mentioned. Although rent and interest were recognised as legitimate items of expenditure chargeable on the " Credit Fund," the repayment of a loan was not so regarded and had to be met from private resources.

The condition of the Catholic training colleges, consequently, contrasted most unfavourably in two respects with that of the official undenominational college. In that college all liabilities—for building, equipment, the entire maintenance of students—had been met from public funds, while the denominational colleges entered on their work burdened by the loans raised for building and equipment; and secondly, even after they began to function, they were to receive from the State, not the entire amount spent on maintenance, but only three-fourths.

It is easy to see how unfair was the system under which colleges handicapped as were the Catholic colleges had to compete with the " vast official ' mixed' establishment at Marlborough Street, all the expenses of which, to the last penny, were defrayed by the State." Moreover, it is apparent how great a danger to Catholic interests arose from the discrimination made by the State in favour of the " mixed" college. For, while on the one hand, teachers in the official training college were supported entirely free of charge, in the Catholic colleges, owing to the fact that only 75 per cent. of the charge of maintenance was borne by the State, substantial fees were necessary; and in not a few cases, Catholic teachers who were unable to meet these charges were forced by circumstances either to enter the Marlborough Street college or to remain untrained. In this way a tempting bribe was offered to Catholic teachers to ignore the advice of their spiritual guides and to submit to the mixed system of training.

Such was the condition of primary education in Ireland when Dr. Walsh succeeded to the archbishopric of Dublin in 1885. For over half a century a tedious and sustained struggle for the removal of the many hardships endured by Catholics in the matter of education had been maintained by the Irish bishops with disappointing results. The new Archbishop lost no time in taking up the cause of education. and under his leadership the case for Catholic relief in the matter of education was presented with skill and persistent vigour and intrepidity. At the very outset of his episcopal career he announced his programme. "I will avail myself," he said, " of every legitimate opportunity of pressing forward our demand for the removal of our grievances in this important question, and what is more, I intend to go on doing so until the very last of these grievances is removed." He was true to his promise. He never relaxed his efforts to secure the just rights of Irish Catholics. On questions of education he spoke with authority, both as an expert and as the accredited spokesman of the bishops and Catholics generally, and soon the education question was accepted for what the Archbishop declared it to be—" one of the great public questions of the day."

Speaking at St. Vincent's College, Castleknock (September 9, 1885), he dealt with the question of Irish education in all its departments. With regard to the subject of primary education, he directed his attention chiefly to exposing the radically objectionable principle on which the " National " system was based.

What we object to (he said) in the present Government system of primary, or, as they are so strangely called, " National" Schools, is this—that State aid is persistently withheld from every primary school in the country which is not conducted on the principle of an absolute separation of religious from secular instruction—a principle inflexibly carried out, so far as the authority of the Education Commissioners is effective in carrying out the fundamental principle of their system, even in the minutest details of the management of their schools.

This principle, which might indeed be accepted within certain limits in cases where the children attending the schools were of different religions, is regarded as so thoroughly fundamental and essential in the system of the so-called National Board that it is carried out with undiminished rigour in every possible case, whether any such difference of religion exists among the children attending the school or not. The school may be a purely Protestant school in a purely Protestant district, taught by a Protestant master, and attended exclusively by Protestant children; or it may be a Catholic school in a purely Catholic district, taught by a Catholic master, and attended exclusively by Catholic children. But in both cases the facts of the case must give way to mere possibilities and theories and fictions.

In the one case, every element of Protestant religious influence must be rigorously excluded during the chief part of the working school hours of the day. Of this it is not, of course, for us to complain, if those whom it directly concerns are content to submit to the arrangement. What we do complain of, and what we most strenuously protest against, is this, that in the other case—the case of the Catholic schools—every element of Catholic religious influence is rigorously excluded, as rigorously as if it embodied the teaching of some anti-Christian and immoral sect.

Such is the system which has been so long and so persistently maintained in our midst, and against the principle of this system—the principle namely of " combined secular and separate religious instruction," we take our first and fundamental objection, as Catholics.

Between this system and the system of this college conducted by the Vincentian Fathers here at Castleknock, there is an essential difference. The fundamental principle on which your education is conducted here is that secular and religious education must ever go hand in hand.

Neither is the system of the " National" Board the system of the Board of Intermediate Education. For, as the records of the Intermediate Board prove, your college is in working relation with the Intermediate Board. You have taken a high place among the most successful competitors at its examinations; and it is manifest that if the radical difference of which I speak did not exist between the two systems, your great Catholic college could have no more to do with the one system than with the other.

Now, though the distinction between these two systems is obvious, yet the very basis of our protest against the so-called National system is not understood even by the administrators of the system themselves, and it is not understood because they have failed to grasp the true nature of the very system which they administer.

In proof of his statement the Archbishop referred to a pronouncement made some time previously by Lord O'Hagan, a Catholic of position and intelligence—a man who was connected with the working of Irish education in all its branches, being a Commissioner of National Education, a Commissioner of Intermediate Education, and a member of the Senate of the Royal University.

Speaking at Salford of our system of National Education he (Lord O'Hagan) dwelt with satisfaction on the principle of combined secular and separate religious instruction which I have described as its fundamental principle. He spoke of that principle as one that in the early days of the system had to struggle against a fierce opposition. And he then went on to speak of it in words to which we surely cannot assent; for he spoke of it as a principle that had outlived all opposition, inasmuch as it was a principle now universally accepted throughout Ireland—accepted even by the leading ecclesiastics of the country—in the Intermediate system and in the system of the Royal University, in the governing body of which were to be found not only some prominent Catholic priests, but even some of the Catholic bishops of Ireland.

You, however, surely know the case too well not to know that, grave as are the defects of both the Intermediate system and the system embodied in the organisation of the Royal University, neither one nor the other of these systems labours, at all events, under a defect so grave as that which vitiates the system of the National Board. The divorce of secular from religious instruction is in no way to be found in either of them. It is their business merely to test secular results. And they do their work on that broad plain principle. But whether that secular knowledge has been imparted in a school where religious influences have to be put out of sight except at certain fixed hours, or whether it has been imparted in a school in which, like this College of St. Vincent, religion is free, as occasion may arise, to make itself felt at any hour of the day—with this question neither the Intermediate Education Board, nor the Senate of the Royal University in any way interferes.

Let the Board of National Education, then, if they approve so highly of the principle which underlies the present Intermediate and University systems of the country, use their influence to have their own system remodelled so as to be based on it.

Two months after the Castleknock speech, Dr. Walsh visited St. Patrick's Training College, Drumcondra (September 29, 1885). The visit afforded him an appropriate occasion to give publicity to his views on the unjust differentiation made against the denominational training colleges by the National Education Board. An address of congratulation on his appointment as Archbishop from the superiors, professors and students of the college, after referring to the inequality of treatment received by the college as compared with similar institutions in Ireland, continued :

Your Grace's long experience in educational matters, joined with your marvellous energy and steadfast devotion to everything calculated to raise the condition of our people, gives every reason to hope that at no distant date our just claims shall be fully acknowledged, and that our Catholic training colleges shall be placed in a position in no way inferior to other training colleges in Ireland.

In his reply the Archbishop dealt at length with the whole question of the training system :

I notice with satisfaction (he said) the acknowledgment which you make of the advantage which has come to you from the act of the Commissioners of National Education,

by which my venerated predecessor was enabled to establish this college for the training of the Catholic masters of
the schools under their control. I am glad you have made
acknowledgment of what has been done by the Commissioners. It has resulted for you in the establishment of a
most efficient and, as we now see, a most successful system
of training; and it has put you in a position not merely to
work with greater success in the schools to be committed
to your care, but also to claim a share in the substantial
advantages enjoyed, under the regulations of the Commissioners, by trained teachers and by trained teachers only.

I observe, too, with pleasure, that you mention in your
address the great public gain which has been secured by the
recognition of denominational training colleges such as this.
For, as you point out, the recognition of the principle of
denominational training has marked the opening of a new
era. To use your own words, " the foundation of this
establishment represents a decided advance" towards what
you, as dutiful Catholics, describe as " the realisation of the
grand and only true ideal of education, namely that which
is based upon religion, and which resolutely refuses to be
dissociated from religion, or deprived of its influence, even
for a single hour, during the ordinary routine of daily life."

I am glad, too, that you have had the courage to go a step
farther and to say that, notwithstanding the great and most
substantial instalment of justice which we have thus gained,
the end has not yet been reached. Your college has not been
placed " on a footing of equality with similar institutions
in our own country." You refer, of course, to the undenominational training college.

I wish now to state plainly my attitude towards this
college in which we are to-day assembled. I have come to
the conclusion that, in my office of Archbishop, I am bound
to make a stand against the perpetuation of the system of
inequality and injustice of which this college—in its material
building, in its daily work, and in its relations towards you,
its students—is a standing memorial. While doing, as I
hope to do, everything in my power, within the sphere of
my duties as Bishop of the diocese, to advance the interests
of this college, I can have no part in its official management.
The Commissioners of National Education are anxious that
I should accept the managership of this college; but I
cannot consent to descend from the platform of equality on
which I have taken my stand, by accepting from the
Commissioners any official charge, so long as they decline

to recognise the necessity of undoing the injustice with which we are at present treated—that is to say, so long as they refuse to put this college on a footing of absolute equality with that official establishment of theirs which has so long been maintained in open defiance of the Catholic sentiment of this Catholic city and of the Catholic nation of which it is the capital.

I am not the man to say that in this, or in any other matter of public policy, we should not make the most of whatever advantages may be offered to us. I do not say, for example, that we should close our doors and say to the Board of Education, " take back your grant." What I do say is, that the time has come—for me, at all events—to say to these authorities : " So far as I am concerned, it will be necessary for you to administer your system for your-selves. It is a system based on manifest injustice. Do not ask the Archbishop of Dublin—whose duty as an Irish bishop it is to press forward, by every constitutional means within his reach, the demand for justice and equal dealing for his people—to help you in the fruitless effort in which you have been engaged for so many years, to force on the people of this Catholic nation a system which we repro-bate." . . . For, remember, our demand for denominational training colleges was resisted by those responsible for the government of this country until resistance had reached its utmost limit. They were beaten and could hold out no longer. Yet we who won the day compromised by allowing ourselves to be drawn into helping out of their difficulties the defenders of the broken-down and dilapidated system of " combined secular and separate religious instruction." And what did we receive in return for our considerateness ? Simply this absolutely indefensible system of denominational training colleges in which, by an enormous strain upon some funds available for educational purposes in this diocese of Dublin, the splendid building in which we are now assembled has been raised—a standing memorial of the folly of submitting to injustice.

As I have here publicly declared that in my carefully matured opinion a most serious mistake was made by accepting for this college a grant on terms so manifestly unjust because so manifestly short of the terms on which the expenses of the undenominational college are borne by the public treasury, I ought to add that it is by no means impossible that, in the circumstances in which the grant was offered, I myself should have acted as did Cardinal McCabe . . .

Underlying what I have been saying there are these three statements First, that the demand for the establishment of denominational colleges was withstood for years, that it was, in fact, withstood till things had come to such a pass that those responsible for the government of the country were forced to recognise the impossibility of withstanding it any longer.　Secondly, that it was the action of the Catholic bishops of Ireland, in setting their faces against the attendance of Catholic schoolmasters at the official training college, that thus forced upon the Government the necessity of dealing with the question.　Protestants of all denominations were satisfied with the system of united training pursued in the central establishment in Dublin, and in the district Model Training Schools.　And thirdly, that when the victory had been won, the National Education Board was helped out of the difficulty in which its policy had placed it, by the acceptance of this inequitable system under which this college had been established . . .

The Commissioners of National Education must at length learn the lesson that what we want is justice and equality, and that we shall not allow ourselves to be put off with one iota less.　The system of training colleges, as it exists at present, though described by the Commissioners in their official reports as having reached a " satisfactory issue," is in reality indefensibly unequal and unjust.　The injustice began with the very laying of the foundation stone of this splendid building in which we are assembled.　The official training college in Marlborough Street was built and paid for out of the pockets of the taxpayers of the country.　This college of ours had to be built, every stone of it, out of our own resources.　Loans, no doubt, may now be obtained under certain conditions and on easy terms for the building of such a college.　But every penny of the loan must, of course, be paid back.　This is the first, and in itself an all-sufficient proof that the arrangement is not " satisfactory"—that it is a system radically inequitable and unjust.

I do not, of course, claim that an indefinite number of denominational training colleges should be built up and down through the country, and that the expense of building them should be borne by the public taxpayer.　But I do say that this institution of ours, now that the need for its existence has been admitted, and that its success as a working institution has been so splendidly proved to the satisfaction of the Commissioners of Education themselves, must be regarded by us as a standing monument of injustice until every penny that has been expended in its erection has been paid back to us, and set free for other educational purposes.

Secondly, and I suppose as a consequence of the first great fundamental injustice, comes another. Every expense connected with the maintenance and repair of the Marlborough Street College is borne by the public treasury. No such regulation exists here.

Thirdly, as to the expenses of maintenance and training of the students, expenses for which in this college provision is to a certain extent made, we have another inequality to complain of. For while every penny of lawful expenditure disbursed in the Marlborough Street institution is paid by the Treasury, the maximum sum that can here be received by those responsible for the maintenance and work of this college is 75 per cent. of the expenditure, or fifteen shillings in the pound. According to the Commissioners' regulations, while the college in Marlborough Street is " entirely supported from public funds," the grant to this college of ours " must not exceed 75 per cent. of the certified expenditure" . . .

Fourthly, teachers coming to the undenominational college receive " their actual travelling expenses to and from Dublin," and other incidental expenses. No provision whatever is made for the payment of the travelling and other expenses of students coming up to attend our Catholic Training College.

Fifthly, I find another special privilege conferred on the teachers in training in the official establishment. In addition to having their board and lodgings provided for them " absolutely free of cost during the period of training," they furthermore receive an allowance of one shilling a week as pocket money. All this is part of an arrangement, officially spoken of as bringing this question of the training colleges to a " satisfactory issue." Who can blame you for appealing to me in protest against the continuance of this inequality? Well, a system constructed as this is shall never find one of its administrators in me.

Passing over in silence a number of lesser inequalities, I take, sixthly and finally, that which is, perhaps, the most serious inequality of all, although from the nature of the case, this inequality has not yet come practically to be felt. It is this. In the official college the payments are made out of the public purse as regularly as the expenditure of the establishment is incurred; and they are made to the full amount of that expenditure; but in this college of ours even the limited contribution of fifteen shillings in the pound is paid only under conditions of the most extreme vexatiousness. Here is the rule drawn up for us :

> " Grants are placed to the credit of the (denominational) college . . . for every master, who having been trained in such college during two years, shall have been continuously engaged as a National Teacher subsequently to his training, and shall during such years have been favourably reported on by the Inspector."

Now, remembering that no such limitation—indeed no limitation of any kind—is imposed in the case of the Commissioners' own college, observe how the concession even of the poor provision made for our college is weighed down by every one of the limitations contained in the cumbersome regulations which I have quoted.

For, without going into detail, I may mention that the provision regards the creation of a fund known as the "Credit Fund," out of which the limited payment even of fifteen shillings in the pound, will have to be made to us, and by the narrow limits of which even the payment of fifteen shillings in the pound will have to be still further curtailed.

Now, observe what the limitations are. First, no contribution whatever will be made to this " Credit Fund," unless the teacher has passed successfully through the various examinations of the college. No such limitation, as far as I can discover, is put even upon the full payments of twenty shillings in the pound that are made to the official college. We are hampered by a regulation which makes no allowance whatever for cases, such as in the nature of things must come from time to time, cases of failure, from whatever cause, to pass the examination, cases of illness, cases even of death.

Moreover, the embarrassing pressure of this most unreasonable condition goes on, not merely during the two years of your college training, but for two years after its close. For the grant will not be made in any case until then. And even then it will not be made if, from whatever cause, the teacher has not actually been engaged for two continuous years, and in fact continuously engaged for these two years, in the work of a National teacher. In our case, then, no allowance whatever is made for an inability springing from no matter what cause, to fulfil this condition. It may be inability to obtain employment in a school; it may be illness; it may be death. But no matter what it be, no account is to be taken of it in the administration of this marvellously perverse system, a system which has nevertheless been paraded before the public and before Parliament, as bringing this question of our teachers' training to a " satisfactory issue."

Now, I do not wish to speak with disrespect of any of those regulations to which I have referred. They come to us as the emanation of long years of official experience. But I do protest against the hardship of imposing them exclusively on us, that is to say, on the denominational training colleges. Let them be extended to the Marlborough Street college. This at least we claim—that the question has not been brought to a " satisfactory issue," unless we have one set of rules, and one set only, applicable in their integrity to training colleges of whatever sort, undenominational or denominational, Catholic or Protestant. When that result, the only " issue" which the Catholics of Ireland can regard as " satisfactory," has been reached, then, but not till then, the Commissioners of National Education will find in me a willing fellow-worker with them in the good cause of the education of our people.

In an address delivered at the Christian Brothers' Schools at Richmond Street, Dublin (September 1885), he made a vigorous onslaught on the conditions that excluded the Christian Brothers from the public grants for primary education :

I need hardly explain to you (he continued in the course of a lengthy address) that the educational work of this country, so far as it is recognised and in any way aided by the State, falls naturally under three distinct heads ... There is, first the department of primary, or as it is so sadly miscalled, " National" education, in which the first elements of literary and scientific knowledge are conveyed. There is then the Intermediate system, in which the education commenced in the primary schools is supposed to be brought fairly to completion within certain lines. And crowning all there is what is called a " University" organisation; I decline to give it the designation on my own responsibility, for, as I view it and its operations, the system which it has constituted and which it controls is, in almost every essential element, unworthy of that honoured name. Now it is one of the strangest anomalies of all this strangely anomalous system of education, that it is in only two out of the three departments or sections which I have mentioned that a school or college conducted on the principle of this school of yours—that is to say, on the denominational principle—can find recognition either for itself or for its pupils. Stranger still, and indeed most unhappily, the one department of the three which declines to recognise any such school or its work is precisely that one department in which the frank and full recognition of the denominational principle is of the most vital importance. Or, to put the matter in another way, the one department in which the maintenance of the non-denominational principle is insisted upon is precisely that one department in which that principle is most signally out of place. In the Intermediate system ... and also in the so-called university system of the Royal University, it matters not whether the school or college from which the student comes up for examination is secularist, Protestant, or Catholic. The test applied to all is the one plain test of examination.

But when we come to the system of primary education, the case is at once reversed. A school such as this of the Christian Brothers is inexorably shut out, and so, of course, are its pupils, from all share in the public endowments, from all recognition by the so-called National Board. For that Board will recognise but one class of schools, that is to say, the schools which are conducted on the " mixed" or undenominational principle. With inflexible rigour it exacts that in all the schools with which it has anything to do, religion, and religious topics, and religious things, shall be dealt with in the way that it has itself prescribed. In these schools, indeed, religion is not altogether ignored, but it is, so to speak, relegated to a corner; the existence of God or of the Church that He has founded is not indeed denied, but they are subjects not to be spoken of within certain prescribed limits of time; and the emblems of religion, even the sacred symbol of redemption itself, though they are not exactly excluded as belonging to an idolatrous rite, are admitted to the school on such humiliating terms that, if they are placed there as a portion of the permanent furnishing of the room, they must be enclosed in a sort of box, the contents of which may not be exposed to view except at a certain half-hour or hour of the day.

The question had been raised as to the wisdom of the policy adopted by the Christian Brothers, whose work lay mainly in the department of primary education, in allowing their pupils to go forward for the examinations of the Intermediate Board. Without passing any judgment on that question, he went on to show that, whatever might be the case, the responsibility was not to be fixed on the Christian Brothers :

Established mainly but by no means exclusively for primary as distinguished from intermediate education, they have for years—from the day of their foundation to the present day—been persistently ignored by those who, under the authority of the State, are administering the system of primary education in this country. Is it not natural, then, that the Christian Brothers, knowing the excellence of their work, should look for recognition of it somewhere? Is it not natural that they should come forward and wish to submit their work to those public standards by which alone the excellence of the schools and the work done within them can be known in this country? Surely it is not their fault, when the doors of the primary system are closed against them, that they should come forward and claim a share in the advantages of that higher system known as the Intermediate. When I speak of the Christian Brothers' schools as excluded from recognition by the State, I speak, of course, of such recognition as is to be obtained by a school without exacting from it the surrender of the fundamental principles of the system on which it exists. And thus in the case of these schools of yours, in speaking of them as excluded from recognition, I mean, of course, that the price at which alone such recognition could be obtained—and no doubt at this price it would be gladly accorded—would be the sacrifice of their fundamental and inalienable principle of denominational, Catholic education. That price, I need hardly say to you, is one that with my consent never shall be paid.

The impression created by these and similar addresses is

recorded in the Press of the time. and in the Archbishop's correspondence. A few days after the Castleknock speech Thomas Arnold wrote :

> 2 Bradmon Road, Oxford,
> 13th September, 1885.

I see that you have already begun to notify your views as to the injustice with which the Catholics are treated in the matter of education, and I hope that the laity will stand by you as they ought.

How tricky, untrustworthy, and thoroughly unfriendly (in spite of fair words) the Government really is, was well shown the other day, when without any debate or trouble of any kind, they increased the small grant to Aberystwith College to £4,000 a year, while all that the Irish members could say or do was powerless to induce them to place a sum for a Catholic college on the estimates. It is only by standing shoulder to shoulder and making their mass tell that Irish Catholics will ever get anything out of either Whigs or Tories.

A Protestant clergyman, an Inspector of Schools, wrote, November 15, 1886 :

J. W. TRISTAM TO ARCHBISHOP WALSH.

> The Rectory,
> Santry, Co. Dublin.

I trust you will permit me to say that I have read with much appreciation almost every published speech of your Grace on the subject of primary education in Ireland, and I have been profoundly impressed by the clearness and justice of the views you have expressed.

My seven years experience as inspector convinces me that if the National system is to be really effectual it must give up the harassing, gratuitous, and dishonest restrictions, which are too often imposed on the imparting of religious knowledge.

The system at present seems to be conducted on no intelligible principle—its rules and practices are more or less in antagonism.

I am quite sure that in the assertion of the predominance of the religious element, the Churches are—or ought to be— at one, but I fear that in my own Church our energy is dissipated in the discussion of minor questions rather than in the assertion of vital principles. I have only to say that so far as my official position shall permit me, I shall be glad to recognise and respect your Grace's truthfulness of perception on this question.

At an early stage Dr. Walsh entertained suspicions of the possibility of a move by skilful statesmen to turn the Irish education question to political purposes prejudicial to the Irish national cause; and he anticipated such a contingency by a clear and frank declaration of his attitude—and that of his brother bishops—towards the education question in relation to the wider question of Home Rule. In a public address,* October 1886, he declared his suspicions and defined his position :

It may perhaps occur to some politician, perhaps even to some statesman of the political party now in power† that a splendid chance has presented itself to them for the further-ance of that which they at all events will not cavil at my describing as the cardinal feature of their policy.

"The Archbishop of Dublin," they may say, "has come forward to treat with us, or at all events is willing to do so, on this question of education. He is not much in the habit of speaking merely on his own account. In dealing with him, then, we may feel pretty secure that we are dealing with the bishops of the country. So far these bishops have been pretty outspoken supporters of that which is known as the Nationalist or Home Rule cause. Let us buy them off. We Tories are in a position to settle this question on religious lines. Our hands are not tied by the secularist principles of any large section of our followers in England. Now, as we view the case, it is the control of the education of the country that the priests and bishops are really look-ing for when they talk of a native legislature in College Green. Let us go, then, for a split in the Irish ranks . . . We can offer them (the bishops) nothing for themselves, but we can offer them, and they will accept it, a fairly satisfactory settlement of that question which, from the

---

* At the Christian Brothers' Schools, Richmond Street, Dublin.
† Lord Salisbury's Ministry was in office.

(D 700)   R

very nature of their sacred office, is of all public questions their main concern—the question of education. When this question is settled to their satisfaction, they will change sides, or at all events, they will fall out of those ranks to which their presence now gives courage and cohesion. In this defection they will bring with them many a waverer. Mutual distrust, suspicions, and demoralisation will speedily set in, and there will remain for us but the easy task for scattering in confusion the broken remnants of a once mighty organisation."

Now, the very foundation of all this superstructure of fancy, if indeed it has formed, as I dare say it may have formed, part of the projected plans of some political party or of some enterprising politician, is undermined by one fatal flaw . . . For of all unprofitable speculations, the most unprofitable are those which deal with the probable consequences of events that are themselves impossible. And what I wish to say upon the matter is simply this, speaking, as I feel myself most fully authorised to speak, on behalf of my brethren in the episcopacy of Ireland, though from the very nature of the case without any formal commission or instruction on the point, but speaking, as I am in a position to speak, from the most intimate knowledge of their sentiments and convictions, I feel that the time has come to make a plain and public declaration that never with our consent shall this question of education, or any other such question, form the matter of any corrupt bargain, or of any bargain at all, between any section of the Irish people, laity or clergy, priests or bishops, and any English party, whether in office or in opposition, whether led by the aged statesman who has earned for himself the gratitude of Irishmen, or by the young and intrepid leader of the Party now in power.

How accurately Dr. Walsh had gauged the aims of the Party in power will be evident from a private letter* written

---

* Lord Randolph Churchill to Lord Justice FitzGibbon :
" *Private.*

" 2 Connaught Place, W.,
" October 14, 1885.

" It is to the bishops entirely to whom I look in future to turn, to mitigate or to postpone the Home Rule onslaught. Let us only be enabled to occupy a year with the Education question. By that time, I am certain, Parnell's party will have become

by its " young and intrepid leader" to Lord Justice
FitzGibbon exactly a year before. At the time Dr. Walsh
made the declaration quoted, Lord Salisbury's Government
was in office; Lord Randolph Churchill was one of the
foremost members of the Cabinet and Parliamentary Leader
of the House of Commons. From the time that Lord
Randolph had first attained ministerial rank (June 1885)
he had much busied himself about a settlement of the
Irish education question, and especially of the University
question. In this he was actuated, no doubt, partly
by a genuine desire to remove the clamant injustice
suffered by the Catholics of Ireland, but partly also by a
desire to further the political interests of his Party, and use
the settlement of the education question to weaken or destroy
the movement for Home Rule. For, although Dr. Walsh
had declared that the settlement even of the university
question was of minor consequence in comparison with
" another question of far more tremendous importance,"
Lord Randolph was sanguine enough to hope that by dealing
with the Irish education question in a manner satisfactory
to the Irish bishops, he would detach them from their
support of the Parnellite Party, then sturdily clamouring
for the establishment of an Irish Parliament.

seriously disintegrated. Personal jealousies, Government influences, Davitt and Fenian intrigues will be at work on the
devoted band of eighty; and the bishops, who in their hearts
hate Parnell, and don't care a scrap for Home Rule, having
safely acquired control of Irish education, will, according to
my calculation, complete the rout.

" This is my policy, and I know that it is sound and good,
and the only possible Tory policy. It hinges on acquiring the
confidence and friendship of the bishops; but if you go in for
their mortal foes the Jesuits on the one hand, and their mortal
foes the anti-clerical Nationalists on the other, for the purpose
of humiliating and beating back Archbishop Walsh and his
colleagues, this policy will be shattered. . . . . My own opinion
is that if you approach the Archbishop through proper channels,
if you deal in friendly remonstrances and in attractive assurances . . . . the tremendous force of the Catholic Church will
gradually come over to the side of the Tory party."—Cf. *Lord
Randolph Churchill*. Churchill, vol. ii., p. 4.

The policy which to Lord Randolph seemed " sound and good" had, within the period mentioned in his letter to FitzGibbon, made little headway towards enlisting the Irish bishops on the side of the Tory Party.   The attitude of the bishops as defined by Dr. Walsh, was consistently maintained by them throughout a long political struggle that was not without its temptations.   During the years of the Home Rule movement, there is no doubt that at various times a satisfactory settlement of the Irish education question would gladly have been conceded by the Tories as the price of the bishops' abandoning the Nationalist Party.   For, while the Tories had frequently proclaimed their readiness to solve the education question by a settlement on denominational lines, they were pledged at the same time to maintain the Act of Union.   On the other hand, the Liberals, whose policy was Home Rule for Ireland, were —especially the Nonconformist wing—openly hostile to denominational education.   Lord Randolph was led to hope that the education question could be used successfully to sever the bishops from the anti-denominational Liberals and the Home Rule cause.

Dr. Walsh never wavered in his attitude towards the two great questions of Education and Home Rule; for him, not for a moment should any other question—even the education question—be allowed to prejudice the question of Home Rule.   This he made plain in his letters to Cardinal Manning, who was fully in agreement with his policy on both questions, as well as in his public pronouncements. In a letter written to Gladstone in 1889, he frankly stated his attitude towards the Tory Government with regard to its educational policy.

WALSH TO GLADSTONE.

October 20, 1889.

. . . I see a clear gain in having the Education question disposed of by the Tories, to whatever extent they are prepared to legislate on denominational lines. Until this has been done, there will always be a set of otherwise well-meaning people, not numerous perhaps, but not without influence, who will lean more or less to the side of keeping the Tories in office, or of bringing them into office, in the hope of getting the Education question settled. If we had from the Tories all that the Tories are inclined to give, there would be an end of this.

From June 1885 to August 1892, with the exception of the short term of Liberal administration, February to July 1886, the Tories were in office, with Lord Salisbury as Prime Minister. The presence of Sir Michael Hicks-Beach and Lord Randolph Churchill in the Cabinet in 1885, and again in 1886, seemed to augur well for an early settlement of the educational question; for both of these statesmen had repeatedly expressed their willingness to meet the educational demands of the Catholics of Ireland, and Hicks-Beach was in large measure responsible for the denominational freedom accorded under the Intermediate (Ireland) Act of 1878. In 1886 Hicks-Beach became Chief Secretary for Ireland; Churchill was appointed Chancellor of the Exchequer; and Dr. Walsh looked with some confidence for the fulfilment of the promises that had been made. " I look," he said, " as I think I have a right to look, to the Government now in office for the redemption of the pledges they have given. I look especially to the statesman who has taken on himself the responsible task of administering the affairs of this country as Chief Secretary to the Lord Lieutenant. I look to him, and I think that speaking publicly here to-day, having distributed these prizes to the successful pupils of this school, it is due to Sir Michael Hicks-Beach that I should take this opportunity of expressing a recognition of what he has done for us; for he is one of the main authors of that educational reform which has enabled the boys of this school to come forward for examination and submit for judgment the results of the

education they have received from the Christian Brothers."*
Of Lord Randolph he said : " He perhaps more than any
other member of the present ministry, is pledged to do us
justice in more than one department or section of this vast
and wide-spreading field of legislative work."†

The year 1886 passed without any progress being made
towards a solution of the problem. In December Churchill
resigned from the cabinet, and in the March of the following
year, 1887, Hicks-Beach had ceased to be Irish Secretary‡
The retirement of Churchill and Hicks-Beach from the
Ministry was a decided set-back to the hopes of an early
settlement of the Irish Education question.

The years 1887 and 1888 were too much occupied with
the great questions of Land and Home Rule to admit of
any effective action being taken with regard to Irish
Education. Gladstone's Ministry of February–July 1886
had lasted just long enough for the defeat of his great twin
schemes of Land Purchase and Home Rule. When the
Tories succeeded, July 1886, they were for the next few
years engaged in a grim and bitter struggle with the Irish
tenantry. Dr. Walsh, while he played a prominent part in
the agrarian struggle, did not allow the education question
to be forgotten. His Lenten Pastoral of 1887 was devoted
entirely to the subject; it was a lengthy and detailed statement covering the whole field of Irish education. The same
year he prepared a " Memorandum on the Irish Education
Question"—a printed document in which was set forth a
rather full exposition of the Irish Education question. The
object of the " Memorandum" he tells himself : " I
prepared the Memorandum chiefly at the request of some
Members of Parliament, who were desirous to take an

* Address at Richmond Street Schools, October, 1886.
† Address at St. Joseph's Asylum for the Blind, October, 1886.
‡ He was succeeded by Mr. Arthur Balfour. Hicks-Beach was
again in the ministry as President of the Board of Trade in
October, 1888.

effective part in bringing our grievances under the notice
of the House of Commons, but who did not consider themselves sufficiently acquainted with the details of the
Education question to be able to speak upon it with effect,
in the absence of such fuller information as I might be able
to place in their hands."*

The Memorandum was distributed privately to the Irish
Members of Parliament, as well as to the leaders of both
the English parties in the House of Commons. From
several English and Scotch members, too, came requests for
copies of the work. The Memorandum, which abounded
with facts and statistics, gave a detailed historical account
of the whole question from the beginning of the century,
laid bare the existing inequalities and injustice, and set
forth the Catholic demand. The whole question of primary
education, the Archbishop maintained, could be satis-
factorily settled by adopting the recommendations of the
Powis Commission, which had been published seventeen
years before, and had since then lain buried in a blue-book.

The Memorandum proved invaluable to the Irish Parliamentary representatives in their subsequent efforts for
remedial legislation. The number of copies available for
distribution was insufficient to meet the numerous requests
which poured in from various public men.   Three years
later to meet these requests, he revised the Memorandum,
and, with large additions, had it reprinted and published
under the title, *A Statement of the Chief Grievances of
Irish Catholics in the Matter of Education.*

Meanwhile, Churchill, no longer in the Cabinet, collabor-
ated with his friend FitzGibbon in an abortive scheme to
solve the Irish Education question by means of a private
Bill. The views of Archbishop Walsh were to be a decisive
factor in determining the final draft of the measure.

* *Statement of Grievances.*   (Introduction.)   Gill & Son,
Dublin. 1890.

LORD RANDOLPH CHURCHILL TO LORD JUSTICE FITZGIBBON.

2 Connaught Place, W.,
November 21, 1887.

This should be the Plan of Campaign. Assume that you are a benevolent despot with unlimited power for carrying out your own sweet will in respect of a legal solution of the education question.

1. Draw your Bill as *per* documents forwarded to me.

2. Ascertain from Walsh how far the draft meets with his concurrence and would secure his support; or what modifications or extensions would be necessary to that end. And, further, whether, if you and he are agreed, he and his Party would desire that I should submit the matter to the House of Commons.

I have a better chance, I think, of carrying a Bill than the Government; for, although I have not the Government command of the time of the House, I can put very considerable pressure upon them to give me facilities, and it would be much easier for the Irish to support a private member than to accept anything whatever at the hands of a Coercion Government. Moreover, I feel confident of Liberal-Unionist support, and, being very friendly with John Morley, I feel pretty sure of his benevolent neutrality —probably of his assistance also.

I will assent to, and assume Parliamentary responsibility for, any scheme which you and the Archbishop can agree upon. I do not think there is any difficulty as to the position of a private member proposing a grant of public money for certain purposes. The transfer of the expenditure on Model schools to other purposes is certainly within the power of a private member.

When you have got your scheme drafted, and feel sure of your Archbishop, then I will get hold of Beach and approach the Government. I cannot move until I get a a Draft Bill.

For strategic purposes, leave alone Erasmus Smith, Incorporated Society, Irish Society, and London Companies; so that, if I am troubled by factious opposition from those interests, I may threaten reprisals by moving to appropriate radically their resources.

Would you approve of making your Bill very comprehensive and in three parts ?

(1) Elementary (see your paragraph, p. 18 of your report).

(2) Intermediate (see following paragraph).

(3) University (i.e., the creation of a Catholic University out of the existing Royal University, endowed by the monies now paid to the Queen's Colleges, and as a subsidiary measure a " Stincomalee" at Belfast).

A large Bill often moves through the House by its own momentum with greater ease than a small one, and the prospect of abolition of the Model Schools and the godless colleges, would, I think, be a lure which the Catholic clergy and laity would greedily swallow.

Your great organising mind could easily arrange a Bill of this dimension, and many circumstances lead me to think that the moment is very propitious for the launching of such a scheme.

2 Connaught Place, W.,
February 6, 1888.

I think the education matter had better wait until you are able to come over to London and we can thrash it out together in conversation. Walsh's absence is decisive against doing anything yet. Perhaps H.M.G. contemplates moving on their own account. Do not say anything to them to give them the idea that you and I contemplate moving.

2 Connaught Place, W.,
July 14, 1888.

I wish very much we could meet the Archbishop's views. It is a great pity that Irish education should be complicated and embarrassed by other political questions. Next year, if all is well, we must make a great effort to get forward. I hope to be in Ireland at the end of August or beginning of September; and, if so, perhaps I may have the great advantage of personally ascertaining the Archbishop's opinions.

If I can only attain full agreement with him I do not anticipate any difficulty with the Cabinet. The present moment is most propitious for action. Later on we may become again involved in the chaotic and whirling conflict of Home Rule, and education will be indefinitely postponed.

The Education question was actively taken up by the Irish bishops early in 1889. At a meeting of the Standing Committee of the episcopal body, held at Archbishop's House, Dublin, on March 21, a series of resolutions was drawn up, covering the whole ground of the Catholic grievances. These resolutions, which had been drafted by Dr. Walsh, were adopted at a subsequent general meeting of the bishops (July 1889), and ordered to be communicated to the Parliamentary leaders of both the Government and the Opposition. The Irish Parliamentary Party were formally requested to press the matter in the House of Commons.

ARCHBISHOP WALSH TO PARNELL.

4 Rutland Square,
July 8, 1889.

At a general meeting of our episcopal body held at Maynooth on the 27th ult., the resolutions on the Education question, previously, as you are aware, drawn up by our Standing Committee were adopted by the assembled bishops.

I have been deputed to communicate with you upon the subject, requesting you at your earliest convenience to put a question in reference to it to the representative of the ministry in the House of Commons.

The resolutions, as you are aware, were forwarded some time ago to the leaders of the ministry, and to those of the opposition as well, in both Houses of Parliament.

I would ask you, then, on the part of the bishops, kindly to ask in the House of Commons whether the attention of the Prime Minister has been directed to the claim in the *matter of University Education* put forward in these resolutions, and whether it is the intention of the Ministry to adopt the necessary measures for the removal of the grievances complained of.

I am also deputed to convey to you the request of the bishops that, in the event of the reply not being satisfactory, you would press this matter on the attention of the ministry and of the House of Commons by every means at the disposal of the Irish Parliamentary Party.

The question was raised in the House of Commons by Parnell on July 15, 1889. The Irish leader asked the First Lord of the Treasury (Mr. W. H. Smith) " whether the attention of the Prime Minister and Her Majesty's Government had been drawn to the claim, in the matter of Irish University Education, put forward in resolutions adopted by the Standing Committee of the Catholic Bishops of Ireland . . . and whether it was the intention of Her Majesty's Government to adopt the measures necessary for the removal of the grievances complained of in those resolutions." Mr. A. J. Balfour, then Chief Secretary for Ireland, replied for the First Lord of the Treasury. " The resolutions," he said, " deal with many questions and cover the whole field of education in Ireland. Without giving specific answers to the various points alluded to in them, I may say that some of them—notably higher education—have long been under the consideration of the Government, and in respect of these we hope to be able to make proposals to the House." The whole question of Irish education, in all its branches, was dealt with towards the close of the same session, " in a speech of singular power," by Mr. Thomas Sexton, M.P., Lord Mayor of Dublin. Of Mr. Sexton's able conduct of the debate Mr. T. D. Sullivan wrote to Dr. Walsh a few days later, August 30, 1889 :

Our Lord Mayor's admirable statement of the case in Parliament was a thing that every friend of our educational cause may well be proud of ; but it is not too much to say that his task was greatly facilitated by the admirable volume of materials which you supplied to him and to other Members of Parliament, and for a copy of which I have to thank you.

Primary education was not included in the programme which the Government hoped to bring before the House in the following session. The immediate attention of the Government was to be directed to the University question,

The question of denominational teaching in the primary schools was again raised by Mr. Sexton in 1892, when an Irish Education Bill—a Government measure to enforce compulsory attendance in primary schools—was passing through Parliament. While the Bill was before the House of Commons, Dr. Walsh, publicly in the Press and privately in correspondence with the Irish members of Parliament, urged that a favourable opportunity then presented itself for securing the removal of the restrictions on denominational teaching. He advocated the adoption in the rules of the National Education Board of a " conscience clause" which could be accepted without breach of principle by the denominational schools. His proposal was that " certain scheduled schools . . . should be regulated by the Conscience Clause which has already received the sanction of Parliament, in the seventh section of the Irish Intermediate Act of 1878."

The section of the Act referred to provided " that no pupil . . . is permitted to remain in attendance during the time of any religious instruction which the parents or guardians of such pupil shall not have sanctioned; and that the time for giving such religious instruction is so fixed that no pupil not remaining is excluded directly or indirectly from the advantages of the secular education given in the school." This was analogous to the conscience clause which had solved the denominational problem in England; its adoption for Ireland would open the State grants to the Christian Brothers' Schools.

In Parliament Mr. Sexton pressed the adoption of the conscience clause on the Government. In a remarkably able speech he urged on the Government that they should admit the Christian Brothers under a regulation considered sufficient for the primary schools of England and Scotland, or else acknowledge that their system would break down in failure and disgrace. The adoption of the conscience clause offered a clear way out of a perplexing situation.

The minister in charge of the Bill, Chief Secretary Jackson,* agreed to the proposal and undertook to recommend it to the Commissioners of National Education. At the same time, he said he had no power to compel them to adopt it.

He understood (he said) that in view of the altered conditions, the Christian Brothers were quite willing to accept the conscience clause, and that being so, he asked the honourable member (Mr. Sexton) had not the time arrived when the Commissioners of National Education should consider the advisability of embodying in their regulations some provisions by which the Christian Brothers' schools would come under the operation of the grants. He had no power to compel the Commissioners, but he did think after the reasonable appeal of the member for West Belfast (Mr. Sexton) that the Commissioners for National Education should consider the question and by the adoption of some rule bring these schools into line with regard to religious instruction.

That the Board would accept the Chief Secretary's recommendation was regarded generally as a foregone conclusion. Jackson's acceptance of Mr. Sexton's proposal was hailed as a triumph for denominational education. The victory was accredited to Dr. Walsh, who was recognised as the prime mover in the enterprise, and immediately he became the recipient of much public attention both by the way of congratulation and attack. The fact that Mr. Sexton's action in Parliament and his able conduct of the debate were inspired and guided by the Archbishop, drew from one reputable Protestant newspaper† the following comment :

Archbishop Walsh has beaten the Irish Secretary. In his anxiety to pass his Irish Education Bill this session, Mr. Jackson has yielded completely. The Christian Brothers are to have their share of the public money on the

* Jackson succeeded Mr. A. J. Balfour as Chief Secretary for Ireland in February, 1892.

† *The Western Morning News.* Plymouth.

condition of a conscience clause. If that clause was drafted
with the same stringency as in the English Education Act,
and if its operation were likely to be watched with the same
jealous vigilance, we could have no objection to the concession. But the practical outcome of the change will be a
further endowment of Romanism. Archbishop Walsh is
now the uncrowned king of Ireland, and, except in
personal character, the succession will not be for the better.
Parnell was anti-English. Dr. Walsh is equally anti-
English, and he is also for Rome.

Congratulation and resentment alike were premature.
About a month after the debate in the House of Commons,
and before the National Education Board had considered
Jackson's proposals, the Tories were defeated in Parliament. A Liberal ministry came again into office (August
15, 1892) and John Morley came to Ireland for the second
time as Secretary to the Lord Lieutenant. The attitude of
the new Secretary towards the proposed educational reform
was awaited with eager interest and much speculation.

The National Education Board met on October 25. The
discussion of Jackson's proposals was the special business
of the meeting. A resolution was proposed by Chief Baron
Palles, one of the most influential Catholic members of the
Board, to the effect that the rules of the Board should be
altered in accordance with the suggestion of Mr. Jackson.
The motion, with a slight amendment made by the proposer
himself, was carried by the substantial majority of eleven
to three. The new regulations thus adopted required for
validity the approval of the Lord Lieutenant. This, of
course, depended on the advice of the Chief Secretary, and
while Morley's action was eagerly awaited, no serious
apprehension was entertained that he would override the
decision of the Board. It seemed as if, at last, the period of
denominational restrictions had reached its closing hours,
and a new era of denominational liberty was about to open.

The decision of the National Education Board to abandon
what a contemporary Protestant journal described as " the

old and tried system of non-denominational education"
evoked numerous protests from non-Catholic bodies
throughout Ireland, notably from Protestant diocesan
synods and from the Presbyterian assemblies. At the same
time T. W. Russell, the standard-bearer of the Ulster
Presbyterians, conducted a hostile and bitter campaign
against the new regulations, and all the force of the
Nonconformist influence and prejudice was brought to bear
on the Chief Secretary. In some of the many discussions
which appeared in the Press, it was suggested that the new
rules furnished the Protestant schools with a grievance, and
Dr. Walsh's name was freely mentioned in connection with
this. These criticisms, however, he effectively disposed of
by publishing a letter in the Press in which he repudiated
the suggestions made, and contended that Protestants had
no reasonable grounds of objection to the Board's decision.
The letter, which was published on November 3, 1892,
concluded :

My principles are these :
(1) Maintain the existing restrictions in so far as they
are required for the protection of the rights of conscience.
(2) Do away with them in so far as they may not be
required.
(3) Deal with absolute equality with all classes of schools,
Catholic or Protestant.
These are not my principles only. They are the principles
of the Catholics of Ireland. They are principles of equality,
of justice, and of respect for the rights of conscience. By
these principles we are prepared to stand or fall.

About the same time T. W. Russell wrote :

Mr. John Morley is now face to face with a difficulty that
will give him more than one anxious hour. He has to
decide whether he will sanction a new rule, the effect of
which is to upset the fundamental principle of the National
System and hand over the schools to Archbishop Walsh and
the priests. Mr. Morley may well, as he really does, curse
his fate, for of all men he is the last who ought to have

been called upon to carry such a burden.　But Archbishop Walsh is inexorable.

Archbishop Walsh had reason to hope that the Chief Secretary, notwithstanding his deep-rooted secularism, would find no great difficulty in accepting the new rule; for, at an earlier period, when the Tories were in office, Morley had hinted to Dr. Walsh his sympathy with Ireland's demand for denominational education.

JOHN MORLEY TO ARCHBISHOP WALSH.

June 20, 1889.

Many years ago I wrote something to the effect that though I was strong for the undenominational system in England (where we have not got it) I did not see why we should force it on a country like Ireland.　I have not considered the matter of late years, but I suspect that I should be nearer to you than you suppose.

Lord Randolph Churchill, I believe, is on the same side.

The Archbishop, in the circumstances, was justified in sounding " a note of legitimate triumph" at the advent of " a truly memorable week in the progress of the great work of the education of the people of Ireland."*

A fortnight later both the opponents and the champions of denominationalism learned with astonishment that, on the advice of the Chief Secretary, the Lord Lieutenant was not prepared to sanction the regulations lately passed by the National Education Board.　Astonishing, too, was the reason which the Chief Secretary alleged for turning down the decision of the Board—that the new rules were " not carried with so near an approach to unanimity as their character would seem to imply.†　The unreasonableness or dishonesty of Morley in submitting this as a justification for his veto may be judged from the minutes of the meeting of the Board at which the rules were adopted.　Adverse

* Address at Christian Brothers' Schools, Francis Street, Dublin.
† Letter to Commissioners of National Education.

amendments to Baron Palles's resolution were rejected successively by ten votes to five (two not voting), eleven to six (one non-voter), and twelve to five; while the motion was finally carried by eleven votes to five; a further proposal which would weaken the force of the letter communicating the resolution to the Chief Secretary, was rejected by thirteen votes to three. The truth of the matter seems to be, that Morley, despite his earlier protestations, was not only a secularist but a bigoted one, and had yielded to the clamour of his Nonconformist supporters.

Morley's action, altogether unexpected, was keenly and bitterly felt by the Irish Catholics, who had begun to congratulate themselves on coming to the end of a tedious struggle to secure their just rights. Dr. Walsh did not conceal his disappointment and chagrin. But at all events the incident brought into clear relief where responsibility for the injustice really lay. The National Education Board, so long the peccant factor, had at last shifted from itself the blame in the matter. Speaking at the Christian Brothers' Schools, Richmond Street, early in the following year (1893), Dr. Walsh gave expression to his disappointment that the Liberals at a critical moment were found wanting. "Responsibility," he said, "must henceforth lie at the door of the present ministry, by whose veto the honourable effort of the National Education Board . . . has, for the time at all events, been rendered of no avail." He shrank from believing that the check put upon the action of the Board was meant to be more than a temporary one. But however that might be, the responsibility lay with the Liberal ministry.

While Morley refused to accept the recommendations of the National Education Board, he, at the same time, expressed his recognition of " the importance of enabling as many primary schools as possible to share, at the earliest opportunity, in the public grants for educational purposes."* A second attempt by the Board to carry through the reform outlined by Jackson met with a fate similar to the first. A committee was appointed by the Board to prepare a plan by which the proposed alterations in the rules of the Board might be made acceptable to the minority who had opposed the resolutions of Baron Palles. The committee, with a single dissentient, agreed upon a plan. A new set of rules, embodying the denominational principle, was submitted to the Board, and adopted by a majority of twelve to seven. Again Morley refused, on the same grounds as in the first instance, to approve of the Board's decision.

For nearly three years Morley dallied with the question without meeting it squarely. No progress had been made towards a solution of the difficulty by 1895, when Archbishop Walsh, with the approval of his episcopal brethren, accepted Morley's nomination to a seat on the National Education Board. Shortly afterwards the question was again taken up by the Chief Secretary. The compulsory Education Act of 1892, which applied to 118 scheduled places, was threatened with a breakdown, as the southern municipal corporations would have nothing to do with the Act while the claims of the Christian Brothers' schools were ignored. To meet this difficulty Morley asked the Board to devise a plan by which the rules of the Board should be modified so as to admit the Christian Brothers.

This time the Board made its proposals in general terms. Morley, however, refused to consider the proposals or refer them to Parliament until they had been submitted to him in detail. The Board agreed; a new set of proposals was drawn up and adopted by a majority of twelve votes to four. These proposals, which were based on the recommendations of the Powis Commission, were, in effect, to omit those rules of the National Education Board which

* Letter to Commissioners of National Education, January 27, 1893.

placed a difficulty in the way of combining religious with secular teaching. For the third time Morley rejected the recommendations of the Board, this time on new grounds : first, that the scheme as presented by the Commissioners was applicable to the schools already controlled by the Board; and, secondly, that he could not agree to " compulsory exclusion from schools of one denomination of all children belonging to another denomination." The Board reluctantly gave way on the first point, and agreed to limit the new regulations to schools in the 118 places contemplated in the Education Act of 1892 ; on the second point, however, they refused to give way. At length, tired of Morley's repeated hedging on the subject, the Commissioners invited the Chief Secretary to bring forward his own proposals. These duly arrived. According to the scheme now proposed by Morley, the new rules of the Board were to be limited in their operation to the denominational schools in the 118 places specified ; but the denominational schools thus recognised should be open to children of every denomination. This was virtually a rejection of the whole scheme of reform. The first part could only be accepted with extreme reluctance ; the second was impossible. Neither the Board nor the Chief Secretary would yield ; and accordingly the Board rejected the proposals *in toto* and went back to the principles it had adopted when it accepted Baron Palles's resolution three years previously. Thus came to an end what promised to be a successful effort to remove a long-standing grievance and source of contention. Morley's secularism and the Nonconformist prejudice successfully barred the way to an act of statesmanship that would have put a satisfactory end to a dispute of sixty years.

Dr. Walsh's disappointment naturally was keen. He felt that as a member of the Board, nominated by Morley, his own position was compromised, and he decided to resign. But owing to pressure from brother bishops and from some of his most influential colleagues on the Board, and in view of the impending defeat of the Liberal Government, he decided to withhold his resignation.

He continued to be a Commissioner of National Education down to the early years of the new century. During that period he was the most prominent and one of the most active members of the Board, contributing substantially to almost every improvement effected in the National Education system during those years. Among the matters in which he exercised an effective influence was the improvement of the position of the National teachers, of whom he was the friend and champion. Throughout a time when primary teachers were poorly paid and had but little guarantee of security of office, he was unremitting in his efforts to protect them against the danger of arbitrary dismissal and to secure adequate remuneration for their services. The gratitude of the teachers for his sympathy and support in promoting their interests is acknowledged in the contemporary Press and in private letters to the Archbishop.

As a builder of schools the Archbishop's achievements were remarkable. Within the bounds of his own extensive diocese, scores of well-equipped school buildings erected under his patronage and supported by his moral and financial aid, are monuments of his practical interest in primary education. So great was his concern for providing suitable school accommodation for the children of the Catholic poor, that he declared publicly that though the erection of a cathedral for his diocese was gravely needed, he would never concentrate his attention on that important undertaking until every parish of his diocese was adequately equipped with primary schools. His efforts for the abolition of mixed education were never relaxed, and though many of the anomalies and annoyances incidental to the (National) system were removed in the course of time, he was never able to have the denominational principle officially recognised in the schools. When on more than one occasion his hopes

seemed almost on the point of realisation, they were sacrificed
to the exigencies of Party prejudice and political expediency.

In one sector of the struggle for equality with regard to
primary education he had the satisfaction of attaining his
objective. During Mr. A. J. Balfour's tenure of office as
Chief Secretary (March 1887 to February 1892) the
Archbishop vigorously pressed forward the claims of the
Catholic training colleges to equality of financial treatment
with the Government's official college. In 1890 the
question of the training colleges was raised in Parliament
at his instigation, by Mr. Sexton, and the Chief Secretary
announced (August 1890) that he had at last conceived a
plan for settling the question of the training colleges on a
basis of " absolute equality of treatment" both in respect of
permanent and current charges. Full details, he said,
would be given during the autumn session of Parliament
or early in the following year (1891).

The plan which Mr. Balfour had in view was outlined in
a letter, dated November 25, 1890, addressed by him to the
Commissioners of National Education. It proved to be
quite satisfactory. All the training colleges of Ireland,
Catholic and Protestant, denominational and undenominational, were to be placed on a footing of absolute equality
as regards the financial assistance afforded by the State.
Each college was to be paid annually from the treasury a
certain fixed sum for each student in training. In addition,
provision was to be made for further payments to be allowed
to the colleges, by way of bonus, for each of their students
who, after leaving college, fulfilled certain conditions of
satisfactory work as a teacher in a National School. With
regard to the burdens which pressed upon the denominational colleges as a result of initial expenditure, these
liabilities were to be removed, and the college authorities
reimbursed for the monies which they had to expend on
building and equipment.

Dr. Walsh was greatly pleased that the claim for equality so persistently advocated by him, was at last recognised, and that full, if tardy, justice was to be done to the Catholic training colleges. In the October of 1891, on the occasion of laying the foundation stone of a new wing to St. Patrick's Training College, Drumcondra, the Archbishop paid a warm tribute to the Chief Secretary's achievement. " The final stage of this prolonged struggle," he said, " was inaugurated by an official letter addressed last November (1890) to the Commissioners of National Education by the present Chief Secretary, Mr. Balfour. This is the first opportunity I have had of making public reference to that letter, and of the policy to which it gives expression. Speaking then on this occasion, I feel bound to say, as I am happy to be able to say without qualification or reserve, that the plan of reform sketched out in Mr. Balfour's letter, or fully covered by the principles laid down in it, is not merely a satisfactory plan, but that it is, so far as my experience goes, the first instance of remedial action taken by an English minister for the removal of an Irish educational grievance, not by a measure of mere compromise hedged in by irritating restrictions and limitations, but by a plain unqualified endorsement of the entire case made out by those on whom the grievance had pressed."

On the same occasion the President of the College* expressed on behalf of the college authorities their sense of indebtedness to the Archbishop for his persistent and successful championship of their rights :

As this report is addressed to your Grace, I am not as free to speak as I otherwise should be. This, however, I cannot refrain from saying—that the changes already made, or about to be made, in favour of denominational training colleges, are due primarily and principally to the action of your Grace, and to the masterly and exhaustive statements

* Rev. Fr. Byrne, C.M,

made by you from time to time in asserting our just claim to educational equality.

To Mr. Thomas Sexton, too, the President of the College paid a well-merited tribute :

I may also be permitted to add that the efforts of your Grace were ably seconded by the members of the Irish Party in the House of Commons. It is always invidious to select one out of many for special praise, but I think I shall run no risk of giving offence, if I say that to Mr. Sexton the training colleges of Ireland are under special obligations, for the unremitting solicitude with which he used his great Parliamentary powers on their part during the late session.

The acknowledgment of Mr. Sexton's services was warmly endorsed by the Archbishop :

I am glad (he said) that Father Byrne has put on record in his report a recognition of the obligation under which everyone who is interested in the success and prosperity of the denominational training colleges of Ireland stands indebted to the chief parliamentary exponent of our claims—Mr. Thomas Sexton. Mr. Sexton's memorable speech in the House of Commons in the August of the year before last made it simply impossible that our claim to equality could be set aside, or, indeed, that its practical recognition could long be withheld.

The financial benefits accruing to the Catholic training colleges as a result of Mr. Balfour's settlement had a sequel of practical interest to the administrators of the diocese of Dublin. The new financial independence of St. Patrick's College made possible the repayment to the diocesan authorities of the substantial sums that were due to the diocesan funds, from the time that Cardinal McCabe had come to the assistance of the college in 1883. The moneys then advanced by the Cardinal were drawn from diocesan funds earmarked for educational purposes.

The repayment of the diocesan money lent by Cardinal

McCabe to St. Patrick's Training College released certain other diocesan funds not impressed with an educational trust. The funds thus released, which were available for general diocesan purposes, the Archbishop was now free to devote to a project he had long been considering and had actually begun. This was the building of a suitable archiepiscopal residence for himself and his successors. The stately building at Drumcondra known as " Archbishop's House"—a spacious and fitting residence for the Archbishops of Dublin—provided with offices for the efficient carrying out of the work of diocesan administration, and with archives for the storing and preservation of important ecclesiastical documents and records, was thus built for the benefit of the diocese out of moneys set free for diocesan use, by the repayment of the loan advanced by Cardinal McCabe and later recouped from the Imperial treasury, mainly through Dr. Walsh's efforts.

Dr. Walsh was a pioneer in promoting and fostering the work of industrial education in Ireland—a department that up to his day had found neither place nor recognition in the National system of primary education. At an early period of his episcopate he declared in a public address* that with one necessary exception the greatest of all the many defects of the National system for the education of the poor in Ireland, was the absence from it of any provision for technical or industrial training :

Let us hope (he said) that the great question will now at length be looked at in all its aspects. It is not a question of politics. It has nothing to do with politics. It is a question simply of selecting the best method of imparting a given amount of information which all parties substantially are agreed it is desirable should be imparted, and of selecting the best method of developing and training those faculties by which such information may be obtained.

* At St. Joseph's Blind Asylum, Drumcondra, Dublin, October, 1886.

There is no reason why it should not be taken in hand and successfully dealt with by one of the two great parties in the State, successfully, that is to say, with that moderate measure of success which alone can be looked for in the treatment of an essentially Irish question, when it is taken in hand to be dealt with by a foreign legislature.

It is a sad commentary on the working of the system under which this country has now been governed for so many years, that in our department of primary education —a department maintained, I may say, regardless of public expense, for its cost to the treasury is now not very far short of a million a year—no place, or practically no place has yet been found for a system of industrial training for our industrial classes. I feel, indeed, that in one sense I am mis-stating the case when I say that no place has been found for it. Industrial training is indeed to be found amongst us, but where? Well, it is to be found, for example, here. Here and in other kindred institutions for the training of the afflicted poor. It is to be found, too, in our industrial Schools, for the children whom I may in general terms describe as neglected or abandoned by their parents. It is to be found in our reformatory schools for the children of the criminal classes. It is not of these departments that I complain. What I complain of is that it finds no place in that most costly system of State education which is kept up in this country for the education of the children of the workingman, and the honest and virtuous poor.

To provide centres for a system of industrial training he suggested a practical plan :

Why should we not try to turn to useful account the Model Schools of Ireland? There are, I believe, thirty-two of them, practically one in every county. What are they at present? They are simply intermediate schools maintained at a cost of over £30,000 a year out of the public purse, and, as was remarked by Lord Randolph Churchill, " for the benefit of a small section of the population, who can very well afford to pay for their own schooling." Now, my suggestion in rough outline is this. Let those Model Schools, as schools of intermediate education for the rich and well-to-do, be simply closed. Speaking at all events for the artisans and for the poorer working classes of the citizens of Dublin, I venture to say that the adoption of such a measure will be hailed as a most welcome boon, always, of course, on the understanding that these schools are to be closed in their present form in order to substitute for them a real centre of industrial and technical education. Let us then set about the establishment of a well-organised system of industrial training, having its centre here in Dublin, having local centres in the district model schools throughout the various counties of Ireland, and exerting its influence to the fullest possible practical extent in every National School throughout the land.

I ask only to have the question taken in hands as a question, not of politics which it is not, but of education which it is. I ask to have our educational system, in all its branches, recognised and dealt with as denominational. I ask for the introduction of an industrial system, so far at all events as regards our primary schools. I am satisfied that on the two general principles thus laid down it is possible, and even easy, to construct an educational system that will be regarded as satisfactory by the members of every Party, of every class, and of every creed in Ireland.

But, speaking especially of the industrial aspect of the question, I ask to have it dealt with, bearing in mind that we have to provide for the education of a population the great bulk of whom must live by the labour of their hands, and that while the children of that population have a right to be provided with all the literary education that can possibly be useful to them, an education that is purely literary, and in no sense industrial, is not only useless but positively unfits them for the work of their lives.

A few days after the above address was delivered the following resolution was adopted by the Irish Industrial League :

That the grateful acknowledgments of the League are due, and are hereby tendered, to the Most Rev. Dr. Walsh, Archbishop of Dublin, for his bold pronouncement at Drumcondra on last Sunday on the industrial question, which we believe is the base and groundwork of all future action to promote the industrial resources of Ireland.

The proposer of the resolution expressed his opinion that

the Archbishop had struck the keynote of the whole future of the Irish industrial movement.

A month later he expounded in more detail his views on the question of industrial training in the primary schools.*

This system (of National Education) is wanting in two requirements essential to every system having a claim to be regarded as a system of National education for the people of Ireland . . . One of these requirements is, of course, the freedom of religious teaching; the other is the training, not of the intellectual faculties, but of the "eyes," the "hands," the "fingers" as well, their training in industrial work, such training as will serve to prepare the schoolboy for that which is to be his work in life.

In this I do not mean that the schools of Ireland should undertake the teaching of trades—though even that is done, and done successfully, in our Industrial Schools—but that they should be so organised as to put our schoolboys in a fair way of preparation for learning their trades when their schooldays are over, by training them—their arms, their hands, their fingers—in the handling and use of tools, and by developing those faculties of observation which rarely can in after life be trained to the full extent of which they are capable, if the foundations of the work be not laid, and solidly laid, from the earliest years.

As illustration of the point of these remarks, he adduced " the painful efforts that are made by children when they are at the very beginning of their musical training"—an example suggested by the Archbishop's interest in music :

It is only now (he concluded) that men of high authority in educational work in this country seem to have grasped the obvious truth that what is necessary for the making of a skilled musician, of a skilled performer on a musical instrument, is no less necessary for the formation of the mason, the carpenter, the turner—in a word for the formation of a good workman in any of those branches of labour that are known as skilled.

The movement to promote an organised system of indus-

* Address at Schools of the Sisters of Mercy, Goldenbridge, November, 1886.

trial training in the primary schools necessarily took a secondary—though important—place in Dr. Walsh's programme of educational reform. The struggle for denominational liberty in the schools, together with the other matters that occupied the first crowded decade of his episcopate, left him little time or opportunity to press his views on the subject of industrial education, important as he regarded it. After the breakdown of the effort to remove the undenominational grievance in 1895, he again turned his attention to " the second great defect" of the National system. Early in 1896, as a Commissioner of National Education, he brought forward the subject at a meeting of the National Education Board. He proposed a resolution, which was passed unanimously, urging the introduction into the system of National education of an organised and comprehensive scheme of manual instruction. The Board expressed its recognition of the existence of a widespread feeling that, in the system of primary education as then administered, too much prominence was given to the merely literary instruction of the children, to their instruction in book-knowledge, and in matters in no way directly related to the work that lay before them in the world.* A memorandum to this effect was drawn up, and a deputation, headed by Dr. Walsh, was appointed by the Board to press on the Lord Lieutenant (Earl Cadogan) the appointment of a commission of inquiry, with a view to introducing the changes that were felt to be necessary in their educational system. The result of these efforts was the setting-up of a Vice-Regal Commission on Manual and Practical Instruction in January 1897. Dr. Walsh was one of the most prominent members of the Commission. Lord Monteagle remarked that it might justly have been called the " Archbishop Walsh Commission." The report of the commission was issued on June 25, 1898. Although it did

* *Report of Commission on Manual and Practical Instruction.* (June 25, 1898.) Appendix A.

not embrace reforms on the extensive scale advocated by Dr. Walsh, its recommendations are to a large extent the basis of whatever progress has since been made in the direction of introducing a system of manual training into the work of the National schools.

In the matter of secondary education, Dr. Walsh's active interest had borne practical fruit long before his elevation to the episcopate. His organisation of the Catholic secondary teachers at the foundation of the Intermediate system (1878) was followed by such marked success in the work of the Catholic schools that, in 1885, the Government admitted that an unanswerable case had been made out for the equitableness of the Catholic demand for a redistribution of the Irish School Endowments. Up to that time public endowments were the monopoly of the non-Catholic schools. To remedy this anomaly an Act of Parliament— the Educational Endowments (Ireland) Act—was passed in August 1885.

The history of this Act is a curious illustration of the haphazard way in which legislation is sometimes made. The Gladstone administration had introduced a Government measure, May 12, 1885, to deal with the question of Irish educational endowments. The Bill had been practically abandoned by its authors before the fall of the ministry in the following month. The Tory " Ministry of Caretakers" which succeeded to office took up the question. Lord Randolph Churchill, prompted thereto by his friend Lord Justice FitzGibbon, succeeded in having the measure taken up by the Government and pushed rapidly forward. The new Bill drafted by the Irish Attorney-General with the co-operation of FitzGibbon, was hurried through its Parliamentary stages almost without discussion, and was enacted on the day on which the session closed, August 14, 1885.

The Act provided that a Commission should be appointed

to carry out the intentions of Parliament. The Commission contemplated in the original Bill was to be a commission of three. In the subsequent Bill, however, the number of commissioners was increased to five. FitzGibbon, who was a Protestant, became chairman, and with him were associated two other Protestants, leaving the Catholics in a minority of two. The composition of the Commission violated even the principle of the half-and-half system, which was then supposed to be the standard of fairness towards Catholics. That system, i.e., half Catholic and half Protestant, fell very far short of the claim set forth by the Catholic bishops in July 1885, " that on commissions or other public bodies appointed for educational purposes we claim as a matter of justice that the Catholic body should have a *representation proportionate to their numbers*, and that the Catholic representatives should be persons enjoying the confidence of the Catholic body."

The five Commissioners nominated by the Government were : Lord Justice FitzGibbon, Lord Justice Naish, Professor Anthony Traill of Trinity College, the Rev. J. B. Dougherty of the Magee (Presbyterian) College, and the Rev. Gerald Molloy, Rector of the Catholic University of Ireland. Of the two Catholics, Naish and Molloy, Naish belonged to the " official circle," and Molloy, though possessing the confidence of the bishops in matters of education, was regarded by Dr. Croke as " an unmitigated Whig, and a jump Jim-Crow man in politics."[*]

Dr. Walsh vigorously protested against the constitution of the commission. " Three of the five commissioners are to be non-Catholics, and we, the Catholics of Ireland, we, the representatives of the interests of the vast majority of the successful Intermediate schools of the country, are to be in a minority of two. Is this equality ? Is this fair play ? I am told, indeed, that a fair provision has been made

* Letter to Archbishop Walsh, January 11, 1886.

for our protection in the appointment of two of the five members of the commission with special powers. They are called Judicial Commissioners. One of these is a Catholic and one a Protestant; and the provision on which we are told to rely is that the Catholic commissioner can effectually protect our interests, inasmuch as he has the power of veto. He can put an end to any scheme of redistribution of these endowments of which he does not approve. So far, no doubt, the scheme looks fair. But then we must remember that if the Catholic commissioner can veto the Protestant scheme, the latter can veto the Catholic scheme, and if the Catholic scheme is vetoed the endowment remains with the Protestants. The whole arrangement reminds me of the theory devised by some ancient philosophers who were puzzled by the old problem of how to account for the existence of evil in this world, created by a God of infinite goodness. They devised the theory that the world was not the work of one Supreme Being but of two—one a Being infinitely good and powerful, the author of all good; the other no less powerful, the author of all evil. This theory, however, explained nothing, for the scheme would not work. The author of good, if infinitely powerful, would as a matter of course put an end to all evil work of his rival; and the author of evil, if infinitely powerful, would put an end to all that was done on the other side. The result, then, of all this complication would be absolute nothingness. So it was necessary to amend the theory, and the amendment suggested by a so-called philosopher was this : that matters could be made right all round by a sort of compact entered into between the two great powers, each of them making the best of a bad case and agreeing to keep his own power in the background while the other did a certain amount of work. And thus, it was hoped, a fair mixture of good and evil might be produced.

" The conclusion I wish you to draw from my parable is obvious. If any scheme of redistribution of endowments

is to emanate from the new commission, it must be the
result of compromise between the two chief representatives
of Catholic and Protestant interests, each meeting the other
half way. Is this then the outcome of all the promises to
do justice to the Catholic schools of Ireland? Our present
Government (Lord Salisbury's) is indeed lavish of promises
and of fair words. Something more than promises is
needed to do us justice. Those who think that we will
submit to such a settlement of our claims are likely soon
to have a rude awakening from their pleasant dreams."

This condemnation by the Archbishop was followed up
some weeks later by a joint protest of the Irish Hierarchy,
October 7, 1885. The bishops called on the Government
to reconsider the constitution of the Endowments Commission so as to give Catholics their due proportion of
representation thereon, and declared their opinion that if
no action were taken to give effect to their protest the
Catholic Commissioners should resign at once. The
question of urging the Catholic members to resign soon came
up for practical consideration. Archbishop Walsh, who
was acting chairman of the episcopal body, on learning
that, owing to the need of special legislation, no action
could then be taken to modify the constitution of the
Commission, immediately took steps to ascertain from each
of the bishops whether he considered that the Catholics,
or at least Dr. Molloy, should forthwith resign. The more
prominent members of the episcopal body recommended
this course. Archbishop Croke wrote, October 29, 1885:

Dr. Carr (the episcopal secretary) puts me two questions,
and bids me send an answer at once to your Grace. I do
so.

Q. 1.—Should Dr. Molloy remain in office till the opening of Parliament will give the Government an opportunity
of declaring their intentions with regard to the resolution
of the bishops asking for a due representation of Catholics
on the Endowed Schools Commission?

I think not.

Q. 2.—What should be done by the Catholic schools in the matter of supplying information to the Commissioners ? *No information should be given.*

Reasons for the first answer : Because if Molloy were to remain *until* the Government, present or future, would give effect to the bishops' resolutions, he would remain in office for years, as I do not think that the *present* Government will ever be in a position to alter the actual state of things as regards the constitution of the Commission ; nor will the Gladstone Government, which is certain to succeed it, make any move in the matter for many a long day, if at all.

So, now or never, with Molloy.

Hoc posito, i.e., assuming that Dr. Molloy retires, then of course the Commission must be thought somewhat less favourable than it is at present, and consequently not to be sustained, or recognised, as it would be, if the information sought for were supplied.

Your Grace will perceive that I take no account at all of the words in the first question, viz., " will give the government an opportunity of declaring," etc., because, let them declare as they like, they will not have time, or power, to *give effect* to the bishops' resolutions.

Dr. Croke's view of the advisability of Molloy's immediate resignation was shared by the more prominent bishops, by the Archbishop of Tuam, by Dr. Gillooly of Elphin, and Dr. Logue of Raphoe. Owing, however, to the strong persuasion of Lord Carnarvon, who informed Dr. Walsh that he would leave the cabinet if justice were not to be done to Ireland, more especially in matters of education, Molloy's resignation was deferred.

As a matter of fact Dr. Molloy served on the Commission. During the nine years which followed the passing of the Endowed Schools Act, the endowments and management of some 1,350 primary schools and of more than 100 intermediate and collegiate institutions were reorganised under its operations.*

The Archbishop himself gave evidence before the

* Cf. *Lord Randolph Churchill*, i. pp. 434—436.

Endowed Schools Commission, August 16, 1886.   The
case in which he intervened concerned the endowment of
the old Borough School at Swords. As the Swords case is a
good illustration of the hardships which the Commission
was set up to redress, it is worth while giving an outline
of the facts of this case.

With the approval and concurrence of the Archbishop,
and to a considerable extent at his suggestion, a satisfactory scheme of redistribution of the Swords endowment
was proposed by the Commissioners.   The scheme proposed was that the endowment, instead of being devoted
as it had been up to that time, to the maintenance of the
" old Borough School" only, should thenceforth be divided
between the two schools of the town, one of which was
under Catholic and the other under Protestant management.
The division was to be a proportional one, in the proportion
of the number of pupils in *bona fide* attendance at each
school. These numbers were at the time in the proportion
of about six or seven Catholics to one Protestant.   The
proposal, which on the surface seemed equitable and
reasonable, was vigorously attacked by the Protestant Press
as being "confiscatory." "The governors of the Protestant
or old Borough School," it was said, " are henceforth to
receive but a fractional proportion of the endowments
which were *left by Protestants for Protestant purposes.*"

Availing of the opportunity which this ill-informed
criticism afforded him, the Archbishop, on August 18, 1886,
wrote a public letter in which he set forth a plain and
convincing statement of the case :

What, in reality, are the facts of the case ?   Is there
question here of an endowment left by *Protestants for
Protestant purposes,* and now to be employed mainly for
the maintenance of a school for the Catholic children of the
place ? Nothing of the kind.

The existing endowment consists of a sum of about
£24,000 producing an annual income of about £720. This
is the fund, which, by the common consent of the

Protestant and of the Catholic inhabitants respectively, it is now proposed to divide between the two bodies. It was granted to the Borough as compensation for the loss of its Parliamentary representation consequent on the legislative Union between Great Britain and Ireland in 1800. There is no question as to public fact; the endowment is unquestionably a public endowment from the State. Nor was the endowment given " for Protestant purposes." It was given for the general benefit of all the inhabitants of the Borough. " As Swords was not a close Borough," report the Endowed Schools (Ireland) Commissioners of 1858, " the compensation money consequent on its abolition was given for the benefit of the inhabitants at large." I do not, indeed, wonder that the Swords Borough School endowment has come in recent years to be regarded as an endowment of Protestant origin, and established for Protestant purposes. For until now, so far as regards the portion of it allotted for school purposes, it was in its application purely Protestant. So far back as 1853 the Catholic children had ceased to attend the school in consequence of the repeated refusal of the governors to discontinue the use of the Sacred Scriptures in the authorised or Protestant version, as a school book. In 1855 the Royal Commissioners reported that the endowment had been grossly mismanaged. " It appears to us," they said, " that a charity like the Swords Borough School, the benefits of which are intended to be conferred without religious distinction, ought not to be entrusted to the administration of an exclusive Board." The report of the subsequent Commission of 1880 was altogether in the same spirit.

It is only now that practical action has been taken to remove this long-standing grievance. By the unanimous desire of the inhabitants, the fund is to be divided into two portions. The proposal of the Protestant inhabitants was —not, perhaps, an unnatural one from their point of view— in favour of an equal division. At the Catholic side it was considered that the division should be a strictly proportionate one. This view has been adopted by the Commissioners.

My main object in attending at the public inquiry held yesterday, August 16, 1886, was to secure the maintenance of the principles thus laid down. At the same time I wished to secure that an efficient provision should be made for the interests of the small Protestant minority, numbering as it does, but one-sixth or one-seventh of the school-going population of the place. For it was put forward, and in my opinion most reasonably put forward, that a bare proportionate division of the fund would not, in such a case as this, provide this minority with the means of maintaining a school at all. Their numbers being below the numbers required by the Board of National Education for the payment of class salaries to a teacher, no sufficient means could be obtained from the Board. The Protestants of Swords would then be obliged either to close their schools or to submit to the disadvantage of a " mixed" school, in which boys and girls would receive their education in common, with but one teacher. My suggestion, which I understand is to be embodied in the revised scheme, was to the effect that the governors of the school of the minority should be rescued from their helpless condition by being provided out of the general endowment with a sufficient sum each year to pay the salaries of a fully qualified master and mistress, thus securing for them the means of obtaining the services of even a " first-class" master and a " first-class" mistress, if, in their opinion, those services were required for the efficient maintenance of their schools.

The arrangement thus suggested does not seem calculated to " leave a sense of wrong in the minds of the Protestant people of the district."

The Archbishop effectually silenced the critics. His letter showed that not only had his proposal been just to the Protestant minority in Swords, but that he had heaped coals of fire upon their heads. It was a signal instance of " how a plain tale put down" the champion of fictions, gross, open, palpable. The Dublin *Daily Express*, which had been blatantly denouncing the inequity of the proposed scheme for the redistribution of the Swords endowment, at once changed its tone. " We willingly accept," wrote the *Express*, " the correction of Archbishop Walsh as to the Swords school, and acknowledge the fair and even generous spirit which prompted him to offer terms higher than strict regard for numerical proportion would warrant, while generally holding strong views as to the claims of the Roman Catholics to practically the bulk of the endowments,

His Grace's explanation will, we trust, go far to remove any feeling of soreness which may remain, and lead to an amicable settlement—which will be final."*

* Anent the Swords Borough School case, the following letter has some interest. It was written by Dr. Kirby, Rector of the Irish College, Rome, to Dr. Walsh, May 7, 1887 :—

"I had an interview with Cardinal Simeoni, to whom I related the gratifying fact of your victory gained over Protestant monopoly at Swords. He listened with deep attention to the entire statement of the case, and expressed himself greatly pleased thereat, and especially at the most gratifying result so favourable to Catholic interests in the parish of Swords. The word 'Swords,' which I had to translate for him into *Spade,* or *Locus Gladiorum* amused him a good deal.

CHAPTER XIX

DEATH OF DR. CROKE

THE years following the political split caused by Parnell's downfall brought pain and sorrow to many an Irishman, and to none more than to Dr. Croke. The personal attacks made on him by former political friends, the accusations of Whiggery levelled against him provoked his anger; but that was only for a passing hour. What grieved and depressed him was the spectacle of the broken and divided national forces, and the squabbles and bitter recriminations of men whose self-denying devotion had once made them a powerful force when united in loyal comradeship. He watched with interest, though not with hope, the various efforts made from time to time to bring the warring sections of the Irish Parliamentary Party into some kind of working union. By the end of 1894 he contemplated retiring altogether from public affairs. On January 25, 1895, he wrote to Dr. Walsh :

William O'Brien wrote me an urgent letter in furtherance of Justin McCarthy's appeal for funds, and in reply I plainly told him that although a couple of years ago I would lay down my life for the " cause," I am not now disposed to give a copper in support of it. However, possibly that is not my last word on this matter ... I have repeatedly told those gentlemen that I would not subscribe any more until they managed to cease vilifying each other. On the whole I am greatly perplexed, and can come to no definite conclusion for a day or two.

But I suppose if you subscribe I shall have to do the same. *Nous verrons*, I am sick of the whole business.

Poor Ephesus has gone to Heaven, R.I.P.

Dr. Croke did subscribe after much hesitation. On February 11, he wrote again to Dr. Walsh :

I have come out of my shell at last by writing a fairly short letter on Justin's appeal, and forwarding a sum of £20 to the fund.

I never thought I could be tempted to do it; but if you and I kept back, and if the collection collapsed in consequence, we would get and deserve a fair share of abuse. So I stepped out. I cannot say that I am pleased with what I have written. I am no good when I go against the grain.

You *must* come out now.

Dr. Walsh did *come out*, and when sending his subscription to the Party fund he referred to the fact that in a recent parliamentary vote regarding political amnesty all sections of Irish Nationalists had been united, and he expressed the hope that means would speedily be found to effect a permanent union of the divided forces. Dr. Croke was not hopeful about reunion.

CROKE TO WALSH.

February 16, 1895.

You turned the amnesty debate episode to good account, but considering the lads we have to deal with I do not think your suggestion will have any practical result.

Neither political Party in Parliament has any fancy for amalgamation with its opponents. So I think that, apart altogether from the personal antagonisms that exist between the mass and the Redmondites neither Party would go in for unity. Hence you cannot hope for any such united action as *chanced* to be exhibited on the amnesty question.

All the same, your letter was seasonable, and the suggestion offered in it was sound.

The appeal for funds cannot be a success. The country is notoriously and indeed shamefully apathetic. There is no desire for Home Rule. The present Parliamentary Party is perfectly played out. The " bounding brothers" are no longer a power in the country. Clerics have apparently buttoned up their breeches pockets, and mean to keep their coin for other purposes than the support of politicians.

So 'tis foolish for the "likes" of me, anyhow—an aged, if not infirm party—to be disposing of cash except for charity, or bothering myself about anything except the "one thing necessary."

About this time the state of Archbishop Croke's health was unsatisfactory. He was suffering much from insomnia and depression.

CROKE TO WALSH.

March 14, 1895.

I do not feel at all well . . . I want you to get me released from the obligation of making my *visitatio ad limina* this year. When you are in Rome settle that with Cardinal Ledochowski. I am nearly seventy-two years of age, and so do not feel equal to the trip to the Eternal City.

In the summer of 1895 the jubilee of Dr. Croke's episcopal consecration was celebrated with great ceremony at Thurles, and the Archbishop himself was apparently in good spirits during those days, but he soon lost his buoyancy and suffered much from insomnia. At the end of the year, December 31, 1895, we find the following letter written to Dr. Walsh :—

Health and benediction. We hear you are well. We know that a blade of the grass of idleness is not suffered to grow under your feet; that your hands are full; that your pen is ready and pungent as ever; your logic trenchant, and your bountifulness beyond dispute. But we regret to say that specimens of your caligraphy have been rarely seen within this castle of late, and that so far as we are concerned, the art of writing might as well never have been introduced into the palace at Drumcondra. Still ancient usages have to be kept up, and New Year's greetings accordingly given.

In the following year Archbishop Croke made up his mind definitely to retire from public life. He spoke and wrote much to Dr. Walsh in this sense at that time. On November 8, 1896, he wrote :

Archbishop Croke.

As for me generally " the shutters are up" never to be taken down. I am done with Irish affairs in Church and State. I have played my last card. Going on 74 years of age I should have something else to think of besides Irish politics. Charity begins at home.

Thenceforth he lived very much at home, rarely absenting himself from Thurles, and only when urgent ecclesiastical duties called him elsewhere.

" I find it hard," he writes, " to go from home—a clear proof that old age is sitting heavily on me. But I must strive to overcome myself in this particular as in others."

And later, at the end of 1897, he writes :

I am leading the life of a recluse. I read a good deal, and there is little else for me to do. Am getting corpulent owing to want of exercise. How did you get on with Dr. Carr? I suppose he is easily managed—not so easily, however, I dare say, as a certain other archiepiscopal friend who pays occasional visits—growing less frequent unfortunately, to the great house at Drumcondra.

At the end of 1899, he writes :

I have been practically confined to my room since July last. I have been out of Thurles but once since then, nor am I likely to be soon. Various ailments—notably insomnia.

In 1900 Dr. Croke petitioned the Pope to grant him a coadjutor, and was much pleased to find that his request met at once with a favourable reception. He hoped, he told his priests, to receive as coadjutor, someone who would be at one and the same time the prop of his declining years and a worthy representative of that ancient metropolitan see.

The appointment of Rev. Thomas Fennelly as coadjutor gave him entire satisfaction.

Dr. Croke died in 1902, and was buried in the mortuary chapel of his cathedral at Thurles. His last letter written to Dr. Walsh very shortly before his death is pathetically brief : " Am holding on. Pray for me. God bless you."

The death of Dr. Croke deprived Dr. Walsh of the episcopal colleague with whom he had lived for years on terms of the most intimate friendship, and to whom especially he was accustomed to look for advice in his difficulties. Besides the personal exchange of views on the occasion of Dr. Croke's periodical visits to Dublin, when he always stayed at Archbishop's House, there was kept up between the two prelates a regular correspondence on questions of all kinds, private and public, ecclesiastical and secular. Dr. Walsh's letters have been destroyed, but many of Croke's have fortunately been preserved. These letters are entirely intimate and informal, reflecting clearly the mood of the writer, charming in their vividness and frankness and occasionally in their piquancy. Dr. Croke was a delightful letter-writer. His style is clear and vigorous, and the man as revealed in his letters, stands out as a staunch friend, loyal and dependable, a sincere lover of his country, and an intrepid champion of her rights; mostly light-hearted, with the brightness and buoyancy of an overgrown boy—at times, however, chafing fretfully against injustice, or again in angry mood bursting out into trenchant fierce invective.

Croke had a varied career. Born in 1824 at Castlecor, near Mallow in the County of Cork, he was the son of a Catholic father and a Protestant mother. The father died young, and the mother, who lived to a ripe old age, remained a Protestant until four years before her death. Three of her sons became priests, and two of her daughters nuns. Thomas William Croke received his early education at the Endowed School, Charleville, where he distinguished himself more in the playing-field and at the boxing-club than in the class-room. He was a student at the Irish College, Paris, from 1840 till 1844, when, owing to alleged insubordination which he however denied, and for which he declined to apologise, he had to leave the college. He then entered the monastery of La Trappe with the intention of becoming a monk, but a brief stay convinced him of his unfitness for the monastic life. Leaving La Trappe he trudged friendless and penniless through various parts of France in search of employment, and at length succeeded in securing an appointment as teacher of English literature at Menin in Flanders. After a year's stay at Menin he determined to complete his ecclesiastical studies. Partly on foot, he made his way to Rome, where he was admitted to the Irish College by Dr. Paul Cullen, who was then Rector of the college. Croke was then a young man of twenty-one, of fine physique, tall and broad-shouldered, and of outstanding ability.

He gained great distinction as a student of theology, and at his examination for the degree of Doctor in Divinity he received the encomiums of the famous professors—Passaglia and Perrone. Ordained priest in May 1847, he left Rome in the October following and returned to Ireland. For a while he taught theology at Carlow and at Paris. William O'Brien in his *Recollections* mentions that Croke, whom he knew intimately, took part in the fighting at the barricades in Paris in 1848. The following year found Croke again in Ireland engaged in missionary work in his native diocese of Cloyne. He was appointed by Newman to the professorship of Ecclesiastical History in the Catholic University at Dublin. From 1858-65 he was President of St. Colman's College, Fermoy—a position which he vacated to become Parish Priest of Doneraile. In 1869-70 he accompanied Dr. William Delaney, Bishop of Cork, to the Vatican Council as his theologian. In Rome he met Manning with whom he formed a friendship which became life-long.

During the Council Croke, on the recommendation of Cardinal Cullen, was appointed Bishop of Auckland in New Zealand, and was consecrated by Cullen in Rome in 1870, and so was enabled to take part as Bishop in the deliberations of the Council. From 1870-75 he administered his diocese of Auckland with conspicuous success, to which his business capacity largely contributed. He cleared off the debt on the cathedral, secured the church property which was in danger of being lost owing to faulty titles, and organised the diocese generally.

In 1875 he returned to Ireland, and through Cardinal Cullen's influence, was appointed Archbishop of Cashel. Shortly after taking possession of the metropolitan see of Munster he preached a remarkable sermon at the Pro-Cathedral, Dublin, on the occasion of the centenary of O'Connell's birth.

From the time that he became Archbishop he was a prominent figure in Irish affairs, and especially from 1879, when famine threatened the Irish farmers with extinction. From that time till he retired, he was in the very forefront of public life in Ireland.

Dr. Croke's withdrawal from public life had a notable effect on Dr. Walsh's connection with politics. He never again took the same active interest in questions unconnected with educational or religious interests. For some years he continued to subscribe to the Irish Parliamentary fund, but though he always remained a convinced nationalist and Home Ruler, he never quite approved of the methods adopted by the Party, and from time to time he criticised them sharply.

He supported the Gaelic League from the time of its foundation, and gave it financial and moral aid at a time when it was looked at askance by politicians. He helped Father O'Growney in preparing and publishing his *Lessons in Irish*. Douglas Hyde, Seán Mac Enri, Pádraic Pearse, and many other workers in the cause of the Irish language revival received from him substantial help and encouragement. Eoin MacNeill stated publicly in 1905 that anything which he had been able to do in promoting the study of Irish was in great measure due to the public and private

solicitude of the Archbishop. Dr. Walsh joined with
MacNeill, Hyde, Pearse, and others in founding the Leinster
Irish Training College to teach the Irish language to all-
comers, and to train the teachers in the best methods of
teaching the language. He attended the formal opening of
the college in 1906 and delivered an interesting address;
and to the end of his life he took an active interest in
its work.

CHAPTER XX

WHILE Dr. Walsh was contending for denominational liberty in the National Schools, he was at the same time conducting a campaign that centred round the cognate question of University Education. Here too, as in the case of primary education, his task was a formidable one, beset with political complications and fraught with many disappointments. Before he was called to the archbishopric of Dublin, Dr. Walsh had had practical experience of the unequal conditions under which Irish Catholics were forced to seek higher education. As a member of the Senate of the Royal University, he had made constant efforts to remove or diminish—so far as the constitution of the university allowed—the hardships to which the Catholic University Colleges were compelled to submit, until in 1884 he resigned from the senate in protest against the inequitable distribution of the University Fellowships.

At no time did the Irish bishops regard the Royal University as anything approaching a satisfactory settlement of the Catholic claims. It was at best a system accepted unwillingly and under protest, to be availed of until such time as the Government could be persuaded or pressed into granting to Irish Catholics facilities for university education on terms of equality with their non-Catholic countrymen. Of such small merit did Dr. Walsh consider the Royal University that he was loth to accord to it the designation of " University," holding it to be " in almost every essential element unworthy of that

honoured name." It was in fact universally regarded at
the time of its foundation as nothing more than " a
temporary expedient the working of which should of
necessity lead up, sooner or later, to the distinct recognition
and endowment of one or more Catholic colleges."* For
some years after its institution in 1880, parliamentary or
public action of any kind with regard to education did not
come within the sphere of practical politics; in the extreme
urgency of the Land Question all other Irish matters were
relegated to the background, and so, in 1885, when Dr.
Walsh became Archbishop, the University Question was
dormant. When the need for a Catholic University was
urged on Parnell in 1885, he (Parnell) asked " if there were
any great need for it."†

A few weeks after Dr. Walsh's elevation to the episcopate
the trend of political affairs in England gave promise of an
Irish educational settlement. After a regime of coercion,
Gladstone's Government fell on June 24, 1885. The Tories
succeeded to office with Lord Salisbury as Prime Minister,
and Sir Michael Hicks-Beach, who had already given earnest
of his sympathy with the educational claims of the Irish
Catholics, became Chancellor of the Exchequer. Conciliation was announced as the Irish policy of the new
Government, and the Ashbourne Act (July 1885) relieved
for the time the pressure of agrarian grievances.

The question of higher education in Ireland was raised
in the House of Commons with little delay. On July 24,
1885, during the discussion on the Civil Service estimates,
Justin McCarthy moved the omission of the annual votes
in aid of the Queen's Colleges. The contribution of the
Chancellor of the Exchequer to the debate that followed
raised high hopes that the claims of Irish Catholics in the
matter of University education would meet with adequate
recognition at an early period.

* *Statement of Grievances,* p. 265.
† Cf. *Life of Parnell.* Barry O'Brien, vol. ii., p. 65.

I must own (he said)* that I have always felt, and still feel, a very deep interest in the matter. Hon. Gentlemen on both sides of the House have referred to my action with regard to Irish Education in so kind a spirit that I think I ought to make some observations on the subject.

I would wish to say, in the first place, that this is not a question which ought to be approached with the idea of concession or conciliation. I should wish to approach it —and I think we would all wish to approach it—with the sole desire of endeavouring to spread as far as possible what I believe to be the great blessing of university education in Ireland, among all persons, whatever their creed, and, so far as possible, whatever their class, if duly qualified to receive it. This is the spirit in which I have always endeavoured to regard the question.

Having dealt with various aspects of the working of the Royal University system, Sir Michael Hicks-Beach concluded his speech in similar strain.

The Hon. Member for Londonderry† (he said) has expressed the hope that we will not depart from the old lines on which the whole question has been dealt with. But what are they?

The lines on which it has been dealt with successfully are those of the Intermediate Education Act of 1878 and of the (Royal University) Act of 1879, whereby it was decided that the State should pay for the results of secular education wherever given, and however obtained, quite irrespective of the circumstances whether they were gained by private tuition, in a denominational college, or in a mixed college.

Now these are the principles the Government ought to maintain . . .

We shall continue to regard this question on the principle I have laid down, with the hope and the wish to do something to make university education more general and more widespread in Ireland; and if it should be our lot to hold office next session, to make some proposals which may deal in a satisfactory way with this most important matter.

About the same time Gerald FitzGibbon, a trusted

* Hansard. Vol. 300, p. 326.
† Mr., afterwards Sir Charles, Lewis.

friend of Lord Randolph Churchill, began to make approaches to Dr. Walsh, whose opinions on educational matters, always influential, were now, since his call to the episcopate, regarded as authoritative, and whose approval was considered to be essential to the success of any scheme of settlement that might be proposed by the Government. The new Lord Lieutenant—Lord Carnarvon —also opened negotiations with Dr. Walsh, whom he informed in an interview, July 1885, that it was the intention of the Government to introduce far-reaching legislation to deal with Irish grievances. How far Lord Carnarvon gave Dr. Walsh his confidence has not transpired, but he assured him that he was determined to apply a radical cure to Irish ills, and that if he failed to obtain cabinet support for his scheme he would resign from the ministry. In the interview Lord Carnarvon spoke of a proposal that a grant in aid should be made forthwith to University College, Dublin, and asked Dr. Walsh whether such a project would meet with the approval of the Irish bishops. Dr. Walsh answered that he could not express an authoritative opinion on the matter, as it had not come in any way before the episcopal body.*

Later in the same month Lord Carnarvon wrote to the Archbishop :

I may perhaps add that the line of action we propose to take in Parliament on the important question of higher education is one that will commend itself to you.

Within a fortnight of his induction to his episcopal See, Dr. Walsh gave public expression to his views on university education for Irish Catholics. The occasion was the presentation of an address to him by the university students of Blackrock College, September 14, 1885. In his reply to the students' address, after referring to his action

* Letter of Dr. Walsh to Fr. Delaney, October 9, 1885.

In resigning from the Senate of the Royal University, he
continued :

Taking, then, but a few of the more salient points that
spring up for consideration on this, the first opportunity
that has presented itself to me of opening out my mind on
the subject, I will, with your permission, say a word or
two in reference to some aspects of the university system,
which is now provided for us, that is to say, the Royal
University; first, as to what I consider the main defects of
the scheme as it was constructed in outline by Parliament;
secondly, as to what I consider the main defects of its
actual structure, as it has been filled up in detail by the
Senate, to whom so much of its organisation was committed
by the legislature; and thirdly, as to the policy which, as it
seems to me, we should pursue in seeking for the replacing
of it by a more satisfactory organisation, or, if you will,
for the re-organisation of the present institution on such
lines as will set it free from the more serious defects to
which I refer.

First, then, as to the fundamental constitution of the
Royal University, as it was set up by Act of Parliament,
the first defect—the most formidable, and, if the word be
not too strong, the fatal defect—of the structure is that it
has been built upon a wrong principle—a principle radically
different from the principle laid down as fundamental by
Mr. Gladstone in one of his greatest speeches. That
principle, so lucidly set forth in the speech in which he
unfolded the nature of his well-meant, but in many
respects sadly defective, Irish University Bill of 1873, was
this, that if the university arrangements of Ireland were
to be remodelled, so as to admit Catholics and their colleges
to the advantages of a university system, the university to
the advantages of which they should be admitted ought
not to be a new university, " hobbling and lagging" as he
expressed it, " behind the University of Dublin."

The very starting-point of Mr. Gladstone's proposed
reform was that the Catholics should be admitted to the
advantages of the University of Dublin, in which, in fact,
he would have included the whole university organisation
of the country. And, as he showed by thus including it,
so far would he have been from introducing any violent
change into the constitution of that ancient university, that
he would, in fact, have been but giving effect to one of the

fundamental principles of its constitution. For Trinity College, Dublin, had been founded, not as practically constituting a university, which it now does, but as the *Mater Universitatis*, meaning thereby, to quote Mr. Gladstone's own words, " that from the college a university was to spring up," as it soon sprang up in fact—a university of which other colleges were to appear from time to time.

I am not now expressing any opinion on the merits of another conceivable project—the project of a distinct Catholic University, independent of every non-Catholic institution, and in this position of independence, chartered and endowed by the State. Such a scheme may have, and probably would have, its advantages. Whether they could be such as to outweigh what seems to me its obvious disadvantages is not a question on which it is now necessary to expend a word. For I am speaking not of the theoretic, or of the possible, but of the actually existing state of things, in which, as I need not explain to you, our Catholic colleges have not been re-organised as constituting a distinct university organisation, but in which, as far as we have been introduced into the university organisation at all, we are introduced into it in connection with the colleges of that " hobbling and lagging" university; while we are excluded from all share in the advantage of becoming an integral part of that which Mr. Gladstone described as the " ancient," " historic," " national," university of the country.

We may well concur in the sentiment expressed by Mr. Gladstone in the course of the same speech that no such plan as that to which we have thus been forced for a time to submit, could be regarded as going to the root of the matter, or as characterised by that comprehensiveness and solidity which are essential elements of any scheme that is to afford promise of giving peace, or of offering finality, even in that limited sense of the term in which it is applicable to human affairs . . .

But in contemplating the amalgamation of all our University Colleges—all that are worthy of the name—into the compact union of a National University, let me not be misunderstood. That union, if it is to be effected, as I believe it ultimately will be, must be effected in a way that shall be in no respect unworthy of the venerable institution which now stands in a so unnaturally isolated condition. Among the advantages resulting from this scheme of amalgamated University Colleges would be the elimination from our present so-called university of much that is out of place in it, and which, to the advantage of both University and Intermediate education, would be fixed in its own natural sphere in the intermediate school. Moreover, if, as an essential principle of such a scheme, it were insisted on, as it ought to be, that the same standard of scholarship and the same amount of academic training, which are now certified by a Degree of Dublin University, should be essential conditions of obtaining a university Degree in the National University of Ireland, it is not from the colleges which form our present Catholic University organisation that any objection to such a proposal need be feared.

Then, over and above the fundamental defect of the present system of grouping our university students, there is another to which I would draw attention. Besides being cut off from the venerable traditions of the ancient University of Dublin, and forced into a companionship of which we Catholics have reason most bitterly to complain, the terms of the working partnership thus forced upon us are terms of the most unjust and glaring inequality.

A body of students, such as the students of your college, and of many other Catholic colleges, for whose preparation for examination not one particle of aid is provided by the Royal University, when they present themselves in the examination halls of the university in competition for its prizes and honours, are disheartened by the reflection that their struggle is to be, not with students prepared on equal terms with themselves, but with those who, as a Presbyterian Professor of the Magee College, Derry, has well expressed it, " are aided in preparing for their examination by State funds—libraries, laboratories, and other educational appliances being provided for them at the public expense, while all such assistance is denied to the students of denominational colleges." And yet it is proclaimed to the world, and on the highest official authority, that you are no longer subject to " any disadvantage" in competing for the rewards that crown success in the university—to say nothing of the substantial prize endowments established and maintained from year to year by the State as collegiate prizes exclusively for the benefit of the non-Catholic colleges . . .

But it is a matter for satisfaction that now at length a promise to sweep away this indefensible inequality has been made by a responsible minister of the day—a minister to whom we are under more than one substantial obligation in this very matter of higher education—a former Chief Secretary of Ireland,* the present Chancellor of the Exchequer, Sir Michael Hicks-Beach. And it is especially gratifying to note the form in which that promise has been made. The question, we are assured, is not to be approached in any spirit of merely making a concession to appease the clamour of a discontented people. It is to be dealt with on its merits, not with the idea of making any unworthy compromise, but " with the sole idea and desire of endeavouring to spread, as far as possible, the great blessings of university education in Ireland, among all persons, whatever their creed, and, as far as possible, whatever their class, if duly qualified."

So far, then, for the defects inherent in our present university arrangements, as set up by Act of Parliament. I shall now endeavour, but much more briefly, to point out what seems to me their most glaring defects, when we view them as now in operation, filled up in detail as they have been by the University Senate.

Of these, indeed, it is enough for me here to mention one. It is a defect which stands out in painful prominence; for it stands at the very threshold of the examination halls of the Royal University, making plain to all who enter, that the examinations about to be conducted there are tainted with the dishonouring mark of inequality and thus of injustice.

You know of what it is that I thus speak. It is the principle which has unfortunately been adopted as a fundamental principle by those responsible for the organisation and management of the Royal University examinations. The principle is that the examinations of the University, even for the highest honours and richest prizes in its gift, are to be conducted by those who have first had the duty of preparing a certain section of the students for the examination in question; who are then allowed to set the examination papers, setting them as they do, and as they must do, whether consciously or unconsciously, on the lines of their own method of teaching; and who then proceed to examine on the questions that have thus been set, to examine in a strictly competitive examination, all the students of the university—students of whom one section has had the enormous advantage that I have

* Hicks-Beach had been Chief Secretary for Ireland from February 1874, to March 1878.

described, while the others, of whom you are among the foremost representatives, are obliged to struggle through with those fearful odds against you, that while you have had from the university no help whatever in your preparation for the examinations, your competitors and rivals have been prepared for those very examinations by the examiners themselves . . .

Coming to the third and concluding topic as to which I wish to suggest for your consideration a point that seems to me of much practical importance, what advice do I give as to the line of policy now to be pursued in our seeking for the just and final settlement of this question for which we have been kept waiting for so many years ?

Are we to go to work, for instance, by putting into shape definite and detailed, whether in the form of a Parliamentary Bill or otherwise, the outline of some scheme which we should be disposed to accept as a satisfactory settlement of our long-standing claim ? So far as my advice can be supposed to have any weight with those who are engaged in the public discussion of the question, I would most earnestly entreat of them to think of nothing of the kind.

Let us take a lesson from what has already been accomplished with regard to another question, and, in one sense, a question of more vital importance—that of our land tenure in Ireland. So long as our public men kept up the demand for a just settlement of that question in the shape of definite proposals and especially of Parliamentary Bills, nothing or next to nothing was accomplished . . .

Then a new policy was tried, and you know with what results. The starting-point was the sound advice of the leader of the new movement—that no further proposals were thus to be presented as embodying the tenants' claims. It was the business, he said, of those members of Parliament and others who had charge of the tenants' interests to make it plain to the legislature and to the responsible Government of the country that an intolerable evil existed, and that for its removal certain principles were essential; but as to the precise mode of applying those principles in detail, and especially of presenting them in the form of a legislative project, that was the business exclusively of the responsible Government of the country.

Is it not a good policy, then, for us who are deeply concerned in the fair settlement of this question of university education, to adopt a similar course? We make no proposals as to one form of arrangement or another. We content ourselves with pointing out the existing inequality —an inequality that no man now undertakes to justify, and for the removal of which we labour. We ask for its removal in whatever way those responsible for the Government of the country deem it most consistent with the principles of sound statesmanship to remove it. But removed the inequality must be, absolutely and unreservedly, so as not to leave a trace behind.

Our demand is a simple one. Let us put it forward in its simplicity, and it must be irresistible; for it is a demand for nothing more than justice and equality and fair dealing. Asking for nothing more, is it unreasonable for us to declare that we shall be satisfied with nothing less, and that so long as this claim remains unsatisfied, so long must the struggle last, for it can only end with the day, whether we live to see it or not, when it can no longer be said with truth of any Irish Catholic that he is placed under any shadow of disadvantage before the law because of his conscientious respect for the commands or for even the counsels of his Church.

The Archbishop's speech was interpreted as the inauguration of a new struggle along bolder lines than had hitherto been attempted. For making the university question a live issue Dr. Walsh was sharply taken to task by the Irish Tory and Protestant Press. The Dublin *Evening Mail* wrote, September 16, 1885 :

We hope that the Irish University question is not going to be galvanised into activity again. Everybody except Dr. Walsh is sick of it. The coming Parliament will have much more important matters to attend to, and so will the Government, whatever be the Government that is then in power. There is no class of the Irish community that desires to make any fundamental change in the present university system. The Protestants are quite satisfied with Trinity College . . . The Roman Catholic population contribute something like six hundred " entrances" every year to the Royal, a sufficient proof, one would say, of the popularity of that university with the denomination for which it was mainly and primarily intended . . . What Dr. Walsh wants is that Trinity should be deprived of her university powers and reduced to the position of a college of a remodelled and probably rechristened Royal University. Obliged to work in partnership with a number of other colleges, most of them Roman Catholics, and in subordination to a university of which Dr. Walsh would be a most important factor, the college now known as Trinity would lose every distinctive trait which endears it to the Protestants of Ireland . . . The Royal University will do very well in its handsome quarters in Earlsfort Terrace, and Trinity College need not be ejected from the buildings of which it has made such good use. It will be time enough to throw sheep's eyes at them when the Archbishop gets his Parnellite Parliament in College Green. When that goal is reached Trinity College and many other good things besides will have to go by the board.

The fair and promising words of Hicks-Beach were followed by no practical measures on the part of the Government. The failure of the Tories to obtain sufficient support at the general elections of December 1885, determined Lord Salisbury to abandon his conciliatory policy and to govern Ireland by coercion. At the end of the year Lord Carnarvon resigned; he was pledged to remedial measures, and had little confidence in coercion. His resignation shelved for the time all practical schemes of educational reform. By February, before Lord Salisbury's ministry had an opportunity to proceed with its new policy, the Liberals were again in office, supported by the Irish members. About this time the Irish Parliamentary Party was revolving plans for parliamentary action with regard to the university question.

JOHN DILLON TO ARCHBISHOP WALSH.

March 8, 1886.

A committee has been appointed by the Irish Party to communicate with the bishops—to lay before them the various ways in which the question of University Education can be raised, and to learn from them in what way they would desire to have it raised. I have been requested by the committee to write to ask you to whom the committee ought to address these formal communications. I shall feel greatly obliged if you will let me have a line on this subject. We shall, of course, treat your letter as private and confidential.

MESSRS. DILLON AND CLANCY* TO IRISH EPISCOPAL
COMMITTEE.

March 18, 1886.

We have the honour to acquaint your Lordships, for the information of yourselves and the other Catholic bishops of Ireland, that the Irish Parliamentary Party have appointed a committee to confer with your Lordships' committee as to the nature and provisions of the University Education Bill of which Mr. Richard Lawlor has given notice, or as to any other steps the bishops may suggest as a desirable expedient for advancing the settlement of the University Question. The members of the committee of the Irish Party are Messrs. Parnell, Sexton, Dillon, William O'Brien, Justin McCarthy, Dr. J. E. Kenny, and Sir Thomas Esmonde.

The second reading of Mr. Richard Lawlor's Bill, as your Lordships will possibly have noted, is fixed for June. Though that date is a comparatively distant one, the interval will probably be found not too long for the consideration that needs to be given both by the bishops and by the Irish Party to the principles and details of what will necessarily be a complicated measure. We are, therefore, requested by the committee of the Party to inform the bishops, through your Lordships, of the fact of its appointment and of the object it has in view, that the bishops may as soon as possible take such steps in the matter as they may deem expedient.

It should be explained to your Lordships that no Bill has yet been drafted and that the drafting will depend upon the course and result of the communications that may take place between the bishops and our committee.

Your Lordships will be aware that there is no prospect of passing any Bill this year. The utmost result that is to be hoped for from the second reading of a Bill in June is a favourable declaration of policy. Should the prelates prefer that action be taken at an earlier date, the Party can raise a full debate on the estimates for the Queen's Colleges, or probably in a still more effective manner by

* Secretaries of Irish Party Committee.

securing a day for a direct resolution on the subject; and on this point also the committee invite an expression of opinion from your Lordships.

June found Parliament hanging on the fate of Home Rule. Gladstone's defeat and his failure at the general election which followed brought his short-lived administration to an end. The Salisbury ministry which succeeded, July 22, 1886, were speedily faced with a new agrarian crisis in Ireland; for the next few years the Tories measured coercion against the Plan of Campaign, and once more the university question had to be dropped, during a struggle of more vast dimensions and more vital consequences.

When the excitement of the Plan of Campaign had subsided, Dr. Walsh was again in a position to re-open the Catholic campaign for equality in the matter of university education. The episcopal resolutions of March and June 1889* were inspired and drafted by the Archbishop, who also officially communicated the request of the bishops to the Irish Parliamentary Party to take action in the House of Commons. The section of these resolutions which dealt with university education ran as follows :—

The Episcopal Committee renew the oft-repeated protest of the Catholic bishops, clergy, and people of Ireland against the unfair and oppressive system of higher education, established and maintained in Ireland by State endowments in the interest of non-Catholics, and to the grave social detriment of Catholics.

Catholics demand equality in university, as well as in intermediate and primary education, with their non-Catholic fellow-subjects, so far as those systems are sustained and endowed by the State. They demand that their educational grievances, which have extended over three hundred years, and which have been a constant, ever-growing source of bitter discontent, be at length redressed; and they appeal to all sections of Parliament, without distinction of political parties, to legislate

* Cf. *supra*, p. 490.

promptly and in a just and generous spirit in this all-important matter.

The committee abstain from formulating the university system which would best satisfy their demands and wishes; they will merely observe that these would be satisfied substantially (*a*) by the establishment, in an exclusively Catholic, or in a common university, of one or more colleges conducted on purely Catholic principles, and at the same time fully participating in all the privileges and emoluments enjoyed by other colleges of whatsoever denomination or character; (*b*) by admitting students of such Catholic colleges equally with the students of non-Catholic colleges to university honours, prizes, and other advantages; (*c*) by securing to Catholics in the senate or other supreme university council an adequate number of representatives enjoying the confidence of the Catholic body.

In Dr. Walsh's letter commending the resolutions to the Irish Parliamentary Party, special reference was made to the subject of university education. Corresponding emphasis was laid on the same point in the question put by Parnell in the House of Commons a week later, July 15, 1889, and in Mr. Balfour's reply. Mr. Balfour declared that of the various claims embodied in the resolutions, the question of higher education in particular had long been under the consideration of the Government, and that the ministry hoped to be able to make proposals to the House.

The Parliamentary session was drawing to a close and the promised proposals seemed to have been forgotten by the Government, when the question of Irish education was again raised by Mr. Sexton, August 28, 1889. Mr. Balfour's reply on this occasion was a virtual acceptance of the principles laid down by Dr. Walsh :

I repeat (he said) in the House what I have said outside the House, that in my opinion something ought to be done to give university education to the Roman Catholics in Ireland.

I regret—I do not deny that I regret—that the Roman Catholic clergy in Ireland have felt it their duty to discourage men of their religion from taking full advantage of the Queen's Colleges in Galway or Cork, or of Trinity College in Dublin. But regrets are vain things. The Roman Catholic Hierarchy have thought it their duty to adopt this policy, and we have to take the facts as we find them.

The experiment of undenominational higher education in Ireland has now been tried sufficiently long to make it, I am afraid, perfectly clear that nothing Parliament has hitherto done to promote that object will really meet the wants and wishes of the Catholic population of the country.

That being so, we have no alternative but to try and devise some new scheme by which the wants of the Catholic population shall be met.

This would not be the proper time for me to suggest even in outline the main lines of what such a scheme should be, but we ought to make some attempt, if possible, to carry out a scheme of the kind I have indicated.*

Pressed by Parnell as to whether he proposed to embody his proposals in a Bill during the following session, or what other steps he proposed to take in the matter, Mr. Balfour replied :

With regard to the question put to me by the Hon. member for Cork, I have to say there is no possibility of dealing with this question of university education except under a Bill. Of course, I cannot give any pledge at this moment as to the exact order in which the various questions will be dealt with by the Government next session.†

* Hansard's *Report*. The *Times* report of Mr. Balfour's speech was as follows : " He (Mr. Balfour) saw no alternative but to devise some scheme by which the wants of the Catholic population should be met, other than those which had been tried up to the present. They ought to make some attempt to carry out a scheme of higher education *which would satisfy all the legitimate aspirations of the Roman Catholic population on that point.* That they should take such a course he entertained no doubt."—*The Times,* August 29, 1889.

The *Times'* report is confirmed by the independent reports of *Freeman's Journal, Daily Express,* and the *Irish Times,* all of August 29, 1889.

† Report is taken from *Freeman's Journal* of August 29, 1889. Hansard omits the reference to next session, but it is to be found in the independent reports of the *Freeman* and the *Irish Times.*

The pronouncement of the Chief Secretary was generally interpreted as a definite pledge to meet the Catholic claims in a University Bill to be introduced in the following session of Parliament. T. D. Sullivan wrote enthusiastically to Dr. Walsh, August 30, 1889 :

Allow me to congratulate you on the victorious close of a long struggle for Catholic rights in the matter of higher education in Ireland. In that struggle I can remember many phases. Of course I know that only the principle has been conceded by the Irish Secretary, and that the details of a measure for the establishment and endowment of an Irish Catholic University have yet to be shaped, considered, and settled; but in this case the principle is almost everything.

Unless I am much mistaken, this announcement on the part of the Government will bring on a good deal of political trouble. The English Home Rule ranks will be divided over it, and there may be a row in the Tory camp. The English Nonconformists and Radicals are almost to a man secularists in educational matters, and after what happened on the Royal Grants question, the arising of a new cause of difference between them and us may, I fear, impair to some degree their sympathy with us on the Home Rule question. We shall soon know more on these points.

The programme announced by Mr. Balfour came as a complete surprise to all outside the ministerial circle, and immediately a jangle of discordant voices was raised in angry criticism. For several days it continued to be the chief topic discussed in the newspapers; and speculations were rife and varied as to its political consequences. Some predicted that it would break up the Liberal Party; some that it would smash the Liberal-Home Rule alliance; others that it would break up the Tory Party. The old rumours that were bruited during the Persico mission were revived. It was suggested that the latest Ministerial departure was not a spontaneous action, but the result of protracted negotiations between the Government and " some of the most exalted members of the Roman

Catholic Hierarchy."* Michael Davitt loudly protested against " the abandonment of the ' single-plank' position of Home Rule for a mess of Catholic University pottage" —" a concession to the rescript policy of Rome."

In the *Pall Mall Gazette* W. T. Stead wrote :

The Pope does not give anything for nothing any more than Prince Bismarck, and it has been well understood that the price of the Rescript (condemning the Plan of Campaign) was to be the formal recognition of the denominational principle in Irish education. That price, it would seem from Mr. Balfour's statement yesterday, ministers are going to pay to the last farthing.

While these rumours and fears found a place in the columns of the Press, and perturbed the political parties, Dr. Walsh, who had left Ireland at the beginning of September, was spending a quiet holiday on the continent. On his return, early in October, he exchanged views on the new situation with Gladstone, who stated his opinions with unusual frankness.

GLADSTONE TO WALSH.

Hawarden Castle,
Private.   October 19, 1889.

I have just received your letter and I shall be very happy to make myself acquainted with your argument.

It appears to me plain that an anti-Home Rule government *ought* to endeavour to give at Westminster what might be reasonably expected by the Roman Catholic body from a Parliament in Dublin.

But I think you will feel that another question arises when the Liberals, and especially the Presbyterians and Nonconformists are asked, by their votes, to reverse a policy which, with respect to universities and colleges, they have been pursuing steadily for half a century.

It seems to me, however, I frankly own, that for practical purposes the question has gone back into the clouds, from whence Mr. Balfour drew, or pretended to draw, it down.

* Central News telegram.

I think he launched it to divide the Liberals. The reception of it by some newspapers appeared to give him hopes of success. He seems to have remained in his " fool's paradise " until he found that his candidates were inconveniently pressed by the electors. He then produced the explanation which your Grace and your colleagues have doubtless read.

I have great doubts whether we shall ever in Parliament have it upon us as a practical proposition.

For my part I have never given a public or private pledge to repent(?) what I said in 1858. My desire has been, as I have told Mr. Parnell, to do what is fair on the one hand by the British Liberals, and on the other by the Irish, especially by their bishops, who must principally feel the difficulty.

Mr. C. Williams (Liberation Society) came here immediately after the scene in the House of Commons; and I thought him reasonable. I advised him to limit Nonconformist action, if he could, to this, *that they would not vote in the British Parliament for endowing a denominational university or college out of British funds.*

My own personal opinion is that a scheme of the kind cannot be carried, and that it is better left to the Dublin Parliament. I have not, however, said this publicly.

I feel pretty confident that the movement on behalf of Ireland runs no risk of being broken up.

Even if the Government were disposed to make a sacrifice in order to remove this grievance, I doubt whether they could do it in 1890.

In the following month (November 7, 1889) Dr. Walsh formally opened the academic session (1889-90) of the Medical School of the Catholic University. The address which he delivered on the occasion, in its eloquence, intensity, and cogency of argument, was perhaps the most remarkable of his pronouncements on the Irish University Question, and won applause even from the most vehement opponents of the cause he advocated. Concluding a lengthy speech, after referring to the unrealised hopes which Sir Michael Hicks-Beach had raised by his statement in the House of Commons four years before, the Archbishop declared :

That was in 1885. We are now in 1889. Recently some new promise has been made—there is some confusion about the precise terms—as to something that is to be done in 1890, or possibly in some other future year. I cannot see what there is in it more definite, or more encouraging as to the hopes of its fulfilment, than there was in the promise given in 1885 by Sir Michael Hicks-Beach. The minister has been in office for the greater part of the time since then. Yet nothing whatever has been done. He was not only in office—he was Chief Secretary for Ireland. I am bound, indeed, in justice to him, to add, that if he had been Chief Secretary until now, his promise would, I feel convinced, have long since been fulfilled. But, taking facts as they are, I find that promise still unfulfilled, confronting me in solemn warning not again to be so easily misled. It is not for me to say whether the new promise that has recently been made is likely to be as lightly treated, or to be as unfruitful in results as the old one has been. It seems to me of much greater moment that I should add some words as to another point.

Reflecting on this university question a few days ago I somehow came to think of the words of that solemn pledge that has come down to us from the early days of the English monarchy, in the Great Charter of English freedom : " to no man shall we deny, to no man shall we delay, to no man shall we sell, justice." In the matter of university education, justice, as we know, was long denied to the Catholics of Ireland. Then came the period when the justice of our claims seemed indeed to be admitted, but still the practical recognition of them was delayed.

In these failures to do justice we had no part. They occurred in spite of us. We could but press our claim. We could not enforce it. But as to the third part of that solemn pledge, it depends upon ourselves to secure that it at all events shall not be broken. Justice was long denied us. It has long been delayed. But, take my assurance, it shall never be sold. It takes two to make a bargain. I do not indeed wish to insult the ministry of the day by ascribing to them the foolish project which has been ascribed to them by some. Insinuations have been made upon this subject. It is humiliating to have to speak of such things, but as these insinuations have been made— and they have been made from quarters from which such things should not have come—it is forced upon me to notice them. I do not attribute to the ministry the folly

SEALS OF THE NATIONAL UNIVERSITY OF IRELAND.

From Drawings by R. M. Butler, F.R.I.A.I., F.R.I.B.A.

of supposing that, by any concession of justice they could make to us, they could hope to detach the influence and the sympathy of the Irish episcopacy from that side on our great public questions, on which that influence and that sympathy have up to this been unitedly and steadfastly exercised. I do not believe that they can have entertained a thought of it. But, however this may be—speaking now not only for myself, but, as I know I am justified in speaking, also for my brethren of the episcopacy of Ireland—I give you this assurance, that whilst we claim justice, we shall never stoop to purchase it, and least of all could we even harbour the thought of purchasing it at the sacrifice, or even at the risk, of the rights of the Irish tenants or of the Irish nation.

Those who heard Dr. Walsh had but one opinion as to the ability of his address on this occasion. By the Press, both Catholic and Protestant, it was acknowledged to be a masterly and convincing presentation of the Catholic case. " It was," wrote one Nationalist journal, "a perfectly exhaustive statement of the case and claims of Irish Catholics in the matter of university education, and surpassed anything that had been said on the subject even by his Grace himself." The speech lasted two hours, during which, with an array of facts and illuminating statistics, with an accumulation of arguments skilfully arranged, with unaffected courtesy to persons whose actions and policy he assailed, and with an intensity of feeling which he rarely betrayed, the speaker reviewed the whole field of Irish university education, laid bare the injustice of the system of ascendancy and intolerance, and laid definitely to rest the " sedulously insinuated rumours" of a secret understanding between the Irish episcopate and the Tory Government.

Even the Dublin *Evening Mail*, which four years before, had vigorously resented his having " galvanised" the Irish university question into action again, confessed itself convinced by Dr. Walsh's latest pronouncement :

The Archbishop's arguments on this subject are con-

(D 700)   T

clusive (it wrote). The Archbishop, we think, is perfectly triumphant in his assault on mixed education . . .

There seems no resource left but a Catholic University, pure and simple, with such Catholic colleges as may be required to prepare its examinees.

And the *Freeman's Journal* wrote triumphantly :

This explicit assurance (by Archbishop Walsh) gives the quietus, administers the *coup-de-grâce*, to the sedulously insinuated story that an arrangement was entered into between the Irish episcopacy and the British Government. They would not. The Archbishop of Dublin has dissipated some misty and malicious mis-statements; in his day he has burst some bubbles from Pigottism and Balfourism. But never has he done a more splendid service than the twofold achievement of winning a confession from the *Mail* that his case for absolute Catholic equality in education on the Catholics' own lines is unanswerable, and of settling and securing the national confidence, in his impassioned assurance that himself and the other prelates of the Irish bench would cut off their right hands before they would abate one jot of the national claim to national rights for any concession or consideration in the matter of education or any other matter that minister could proffer or majority could ratify. We commend the clear and brave words of the Archbishop of Dublin to both the English political Parties. If the Conservative Party had hopes, those hopes are blasted; if the Liberal Party had fears, those fears are banished.

While Dr. Walsh effectually restored the confidence of national opinion in Ireland that the new university policy of the Government would in no way be allowed to prejudice Home Rule, Mr. Balfour's declaration had involved the Tories in no small embarrassment. From the very beginning it was met by a storm of hostile criticism, and its author, mindful no doubt of the consequences of Gladstone's unsuccessful University Bill of 1873, which had brought about the downfall of what was described as "one of the most powerful ministries of modern times," was greatly puzzled to find a graceful way out of a difficult and delicate situation. The opposition blew from many quarters, but most strongly from Scotland, where the Presbyterians were openly and bitterly hostile to the policy which the Government proposed to adopt. In the midst of this excitement Mr. Balfour was entertained at a banquet by the Unionists of Partick, a suburban district of Glasgow, on December 2, 1889, and he availed of the opportunity to explain his views on Irish university education, in such a manner as to placate opposition, and at the same time escape the charge of yielding or inconsistency. He was prepared, he said, to do justice to Ireland, but not at the risk of offending public opinion in England, Scotland, or Ireland :

I am clearly of opinion (he said) that upon this question of higher Catholic education in Ireland, it is absolutely impossible that anything could be done except with general consent.

There are three conditions which I lay down as being absolutely necessary to be fulfilled before anything effective can be done in the direction which my predecessors indicated, and in which I have attempted to follow them.

The first condition is, that what we propose to those desiring higher education in Ireland should be cordially accepted by them as a solution of their difficulties. The second condition is, that the proposal of measures of that description in Parliament should not be used by any Party in Parliament as a means of inflicting a political blow upon their adversaries. And the third condition is, that the general opinion of Englishmen, of Scotchmen, and of Irishmen, should all concur in desiring that this particular boon should be granted to the Roman Catholic population of Ireland. And unless these conditions are fulfilled, I, for one, would never counsel my colleagues to embark in so difficult and so arduous an enterprise as that of dealing with the education question.

Mr. Balfour went on to define his general attitude to the question of Irish university education, and the lines of settlement he proposed to follow if the conditions he had named should be fulfilled :

It is not our business to inquire how far the undoubtedly conscientious objections of the Roman Catholic population to use the means of education at their disposal are wise or unwise. That is not our business. What we have to do is to consider what we can do consistently with our conscience to meet their wants.

My own view is that we cannot with public advantage found a Roman Catholic University, and I think so because I am of opinion that it would be fatal to the cause of higher education in Ireland, if the Catholics and Protestants were not brought into competition in obtaining the degrees and honours of university training. If you do not bring them into competition, you might find that either the Protestant or the Catholic standard was lowered to meet the temporary interests of their clients, and the cause of good education would suffer.

The second thing, I think, we cannot give, is any State endowment of theological teaching . . .

The third condition which I think ought to be laid down before any college of the kind I suggest is founded, is that there should be what I believe is called in other departments a conscience clause, or, at all events, some provision by which any man attending the college, who did not share the religious tenets of the governing body, should not be compelled to attend either theological lectures or theological services.

But subject to these three conditions, my opinion is that we ought to give them a well-equipped college—a college well equipped for all modern purposes of higher education.

The Partick speech definitely, in Gladstone's phrase, sent the whole question back up into the clouds. The proposed line of reform was acceptable enough to Irish Catholics; but the scheme was made dependent on three antecedent conditions, one of which—a consensus of English, Scotch, and Irish opinion—was manifestly impossible. Speaking three days later, at Blackrock College, Dr. Walsh commented :

The fulfilment of the condition here stated is manifestly a matter of absolute impossibility. I say nothing of its obvious unreasonableness. I do not even care to raise the question whether any such extraordinary condition was ever before attached to an official announcement of an important measure of reform. Since the veteran leader of the English Liberal Party first put his hand to the work of setting our local concerns in Ireland free from the vexatious trammels imposed upon them by the need of looking to an Imperial Parliament for every measure of reform, I have met with nothing more clearly conclusive than this statement of Mr. Balfour's is of the hopelessness of the position taken up by those who still believe that such a Parliament can be regarded as an effective machine for working out and administering a system of good government for Ireland.

Nine years passed before an English statesman again attempted to grapple with a problem that had proved to have so disconcerting an effect on British politics. The Government in which Mr. Balfour was Chief Secretary for Ireland survived until August 1892, and during the remainder of its term of office, the Irish university question as a ministerial concern was left severely alone. After two successive Liberal ministries had come and gone, Lord Salisbury was once more (June 1895) at the head of a Tory administration, which was destined to hold office for an unusually long period. When the question was again taken up with a view to legislative action, it was a Liberal Member of Parliament who took the initiative. This was Mr. R. B. Haldane, who towards the end of 1898 essayed to succeed in an undertaking where so many statesmen had previously failed or were found wanting.

JOHN DILLON TO ARCHBISHOP WALSH.

October 2, 1898.

Mr. Haldane—whose name you will remember I mentioned to you—wrote to me that he is coming to Ireland on the 9th of October—next Sunday. He proposes to spend a week in Ireland making inquiries in connection with the university question, and is anxious to see you as soon as possible—if possible first of all. He is furnished with letters of introduction to some people, and is undoubtedly in the confidence—so far as the university question is concerned —of very important people on both sides of the House of

Commons. I have, of course, not felt authorised to make any statement to him on your behalf, but I have undertaken to communicate with you and ask whether you will be pleased to give him an interview . . .

Haldane will arrive at the Shelbourne Hotel on Sunday morning the 9th of October. It occurred to me that you might like to see him before the meeting of the bishops.

MR. R. B. HALDANE TO ARCHBISHOP WALSH.

Shelbourne Hotel, Dublin.

October 9, 1898.

Mr. Dillon informs me that he has put before your Grace some particulars of the circumstances under which I have come over to Ireland to obtain information about the university question. If it would be agreeable to you to receive me for a brief interview I would be grateful, and I will then explain more fully what appears to me to be the position, and ask you for such guidance as you can give me.

At an interview which took place at the Archbishop's House on October 14, and in subsequent conversations, the Archbishop and Mr. Haldane discussed the terms of a settlement and methods of procedure. Mr. Haldane also, before his departure from Ireland, elicited the views of Cardinal Logue, and also of influential Irish Presbyterians from whom opposition might be anticipated. On his return to England he exercised himself with considerable success in canvassing the support of prominent Liberal and Tory Members of Parliament; amongst others whose aid he enlisted were Sir Michael Hicks-Beach and Sir Edward Grey. He also secured the services of a number of leading newspapers, both Tory and Liberal, to educate public opinion for the reception of a new Irish University Bill which he drafted along with Mr. Balfour, and a copy of which he forwarded to Dr. Walsh. When there was evidence of sufficient support in Parliament and in the constituencies, Mr. Haldane was to introduce the Bill, and Mr. Balfour, the First Lord of the Treasury, was to allow the time of the House of Commons for its discussion.

MR. R. B. HALDANE TO ARCHBISHOP WALSH.

January 3, 1899.

Here is the situation so far as this side of the water is concerned. You may assume (1) that the Government as a whole would probably cordially approve of the Bill, and (2) that a majority of the Houses of Parliament would pass it. The difficulty is that the Government as a whole shrinks from the consequences of directly or indirectly (e.g. by giving Government time for debate) fathering the measure. Their fear is of constituencies here, and even Mr. Balfour, who would, if he were permitted, take the risk of the controversy, says this is serious. These constituencies object to the endowment and even the establishment of a Roman Catholic University. But Mr. Balfour thinks that if you in Ireland were to agree on a measure such as we have framed, embodying as it does the result of my conversations in Ireland, not only with you but with influential Presbyterian leaders, it would help us here to educate opinion and get rid of much opposition. If to this were added a pretty solid Irish agreement and demand, it would assist enormously.

After cautious deliberation, Mr. Balfour, who was keenly concerned for the success of the scheme, ventured to sound public opinion by an open declaration in favour of it. The declaration took the form of a letter to a constituent in Manchester, written on January 23, 1899. Having reviewed the conditions of university education in Ireland, he stated what he considered the most feasible plan for a settlement of the Catholic demand.

The plan which seems best to solve the university problem, both for the Presbyterians and other Protestants in the north, and for the Irish Roman Catholics generally, and which does so without revolutionising Trinity College, or violating any accepted legislative principle, is to establish by a single Act two new teaching universities—one in Dublin and another in Belfast—on precisely similar lines, and differing in no particular except the names of the gentlemen first appointed to serve on their respective governing bodies. As the university in Belfast would absorb the existing Queen's College, the governing body of the new institution should be so constructed as to continue the tradition of the old. As the Dublin University is designed to attract those Roman Catholics who now hold aloof from university life altogether, its governing body as first constituted should no doubt be in the main of their own way of thinking, but both universities would be rigidly subject to the Test Acts. All Scholarships and Fellowships paid out of public funds would be open to competition irrespective of creed. No public endowment would be given to chairs in Theology, Philosophy, or Modern History. Professors would have a right to appeal against unjust dismissal, and the number of clergy on the governing body would be strictly limited. A university so constituted, would, I believe, meet the needs of Roman Catholics, but it would not be a Roman Catholic University.

Mr. Balfour's manifesto was favourably received by the London Press, with the exception of the *Morning Post*, but public opinion in the doubtful constituencies did not respond. Mr. Haldane's subsequent letters to Dr. Walsh are full of pessimism as to the outcome of his efforts. On February 2 he wrote :

The angry tide is rising here, and it will take a strong man to breast it. I have not seen Mr. B. since his Manchester declaration, but hope to do so shortly. If his colleagues have courage, this business can be put through, but the question is whether they will have. We have gone out of our way on our side to make the path as clear as possible for them, though we shall not be able to hold in an extreme Nonconformist wing. Anyhow I am certain that Balfour is deeply in earnest.

Again on February 7, 1899 :

The current is running strongly adverse at this moment. The old spirit of intolerance is abroad. The other members of the cabinet are timid. The only chance at this moment would be if the bishops were to give a cordial and complete acceptance to the limited proposals of the Bill. Your Grace will appreciate what I mean when I say that the propositions as to finance are not mine. Details on the other points I should have hope of being able to adjust over here, but as to finance I have but little.

UNIVERSITY COLLEGE, DUBLIN.

I feel the difficulty the bishops are in. If I were sure that we could rely on the Bill being passed this session, I would urge that it should be accepted. But I cannot honestly say that, as things look at this moment, I feel at all sure of this. The forces of Protestant intolerance have not, as I hoped they would, abated. If the bishops accept, they will run a certain amount of risk of tying their hands which they may well be indisposed to run. Possibly our wisest course is to rest content with what has been gained in Mr. Balfour's letter for the moment, and to seek to do no more than to obtain the assent of the House of Commons to a resolution affirming the principles laid down in the letter about which the bishops raise no question. I have not, however, seen Mr. Balfour for several days. I am conjecturing what will be his feeling. If I do not add anything to his letter within the next two days, your Grace will be right in assuming that he concurs. I cannot doubt that real progress has been made with the question. The educational influence of the discussion will be considerable. The cause of Home Rule has at least been helped.

When the anti-Catholic agitation abates, the effect of Mr. Balfour's appeal should be even greater than it has been. Our work has not been thrown away, whether or not it bears immediate legislative fruit.

The " angry tide" submerged Mr. Haldane's well-meant effort, and the Irish university question was again subordinated to intolerant sectarianism and political expediency.

In 1901 (July 1) a Royal Commission on Irish Education was appointed. The Commission was " to inquire into the present condition of the higher, general, and technical education available in Ireland outside Trinity College." The views of the Catholic bishops were ably presented before the Commission by the Bishop of Limerick, Dr. O'Dwyer.

Dr. Walsh was invited, but declined, to give evidence before the Commission. His abstention was due chiefly to the fact that owing to the ruling of Lord Robertson, the Chairman of the Commission, witnesses were to be debarred from recommending as a settlement of the university question, the setting up of a second college along with

T 2

Trinity College in the University of Dublin. One witness, Chief Baron Palles, did manage, however, to give expression to views of this kind.

In declining the Commissioners' invitation the Archbishop wrote, April 25, 1902 :

It would be impossible for me to add to the force of the evidence given at the opening of the Commission by the Bishop of Limerick, with whose views, in so far as he had an opportunity of expressing them, I am in full concurrence. In saying this it is right for me to add that on one important aspect of the case, upon which the Bishop of Limerick had not an opportunity of expressing his views, and which, as I gather from the published evidence, is not to be taken account of in the Report of the Commission, the Lord Chief Baron has said everything that I should wish to say.

Although Dr. Walsh did not give evidence before Lord Robertson's Commission, his views on many aspects of the questions dealt with were brought to the knowledge of the Commissioners in the printed statements contained in his book, *The Irish University Question*,* and in other statements published by him from time to time in various journals.

The Robertson Commission presented its final report on February 28, 1903. The Commissioners recommended that the Royal University should be reconstituted by being converted into a teaching university ; that the reconstituted Royal University should be a Federal University with constituent colleges ; that the constituent colleges should be four in number—the Queen's Colleges of Belfast, Cork, and Galway, and a new college for Roman Catholics to be established in Dublin. The new college was to be provided with buildings and equipped and endowed on a scale demanded by a university college of the first rank, which was intended to draw its students from all parts of Ireland.

Some time after the publication of the report of the

* Published in 1897. Dublin. Browne & Nolan, Ltd,

Robertson Commission, the Irish Chief Secretary, George Wyndham, took in hand the preparation of a University Bill. The scheme contemplated by Wyndham was the setting up in Dublin of a college for Catholics adequately equipped and endowed. There were to be no religious tests for admission to the college, no official recognition of Catholic ecclesiastics on its governing body, and no visitatorial powers granted to the Catholic bishops. The college was to be Catholic merely in the sense in which Trinity College was Protestant. The new establishment, however, was not to be a college of the Royal University reconstituted, as the Robertson Commission recommended, but a constituent college of the University of Dublin on a footing of equality with Trinity College.

Towards the end of the year 1903 a private conference regarding the Wyndham university scheme took place between Mr. Wyndham and Sir Antony MacDonnell on the one side and Dr. Walsh and Dr. Healy, representing the bishops, on the other. The main principles of the project were approved by the episcopal representatives, and a memorandum, to be submitted confidentially to the episcopal body, was prepared by Sir Antony.

At the beginning of the following year (January 1, 1904) Lord Dunraven published a letter in the Press in which he outlined a proposal for the settlement of the university question.

After dealing with the urgency of the question and giving reasons why the proposals of the Robertson Commission had not proved acceptable to any considerable section of Irish public opinion, Lord Dunraven went on to say :

The only real solution of this vexed question will be found in an arrangement which will combine the highest attainable measure of academic efficiency with perfect equality of treatment for all sections of the community.

This ideal might, as it seems to me, be realised by the establishment within the University of Dublin of two additional colleges—the Queen's Belfast, and a King's

College to be established in Dublin—which colleges, like Trinity, should be well equipped financially and should be autonomous and residential, with governing bodies selected exclusively on academical grounds. Within these broad outlines room could be found for a working arrangement with colleges established in other parts of the country.

At the end of his letter Lord Dunraven said :

The Roman Catholic claims will not, as I fully believe, be found on examination to be the bugbear they seem to some ill-informed people. There is no question of a Catholic University, or of the proscription of any kind of learning, or of a college exclusively for Roman Catholics, or of a college to every post and emolument of which a Protestant may not aspire, just as a Roman Catholic may aspire to posts and emoluments in Trinity College or the Queen's College, Belfast. But it seems to me only fair, subject to these safeguards, that my Roman Catholic fellow-countrymen should be given the educational facilities they desire.

After the publication of Lord Dunraven's scheme, Archbishop Walsh was again consulted by Mr. Wyndham as to whether the scheme would satisfy him and would be likely to satisfy the requirements of the episcopal body. The Archbishop's views were known to be not unfavourable to the plan, and shortly after, he was in a position to inform the Chief Secretary that in the bishops' opinion " the university question could be settled on this basis."

Very soon, however, the Archbishop came to realise that Mr. Wyndham, owing possibly to circumstances outside his control, was not at all likely to tackle the Irish university question with determination, and in a letter written to John Redmond, enclosing a subscription to the Irish Parliamentary Fund, he gave public expression, for the first time, to his growing distrust of the efficacy of parliamentary methods, January 13, 1904 :

To be quite candid in the matter, I have to say that of late I have found myself almost driven to abandon the little which still remains to me of faith in the efficacy of parliamentary action as a means of getting redress of our grievances in this country.

About a month later he enlarged on the same theme in a letter written to Sir Christopher Nixon, who at that time contemplated entering Parliament.

Dr. Walsh wrote to Sir C. Nixon, February 29, 1904 :

Since I wrote those words (the words addressed to John Redmond) nothing has occurred to change the view to which I then gave expression.

Action other than parliamentary in any violent or unconstitutional form, I am, of course, debarred from recommending to our people. But there is an alternative form of procedure which I am at present seriously considering, as to the advisability of putting it forward on my own responsibility, possibly in connection with the coming election in Dublin.

I need not go into details, but I may say that my views are of a character that makes it impossible for me to commit myself to approval of the candidature of anyone who is desirous of keeping up the present mode of putting forward the Catholic and national claims of the people of Ireland.

The principle of the Dunraven settlement of the Irish university question was viewed with favour not only by the bishops, but also by many prominent laymen and by Catholic educational bodies. It was commonly believed at the time, and by many it was confidently expected, that the Government had adopted and was bent on enacting the Dunraven scheme. Nothing, however, was done by the Unionists in the two years during which they still continued to direct public affairs.

The beginning of 1906 found a Liberal Government in office, and under pressure from the Irish Parliamentary Party a new Royal Commission was appointed to consider the university question. This Commission, presided over by Sir Edward Fry, was to inquire into the state of Trinity College, Dublin, and the University of Dublin, and to report upon the place which that College and University held as organs of higher education in Ireland, and the steps proper to be taken to increase their usefulness to the country. The Commission, which was appointed on June 5, 1906, presented its report on January 12, 1907.

The Commissioners (with one dissentient, and that one a Catholic Fellow of Trinity College) recommended that a new college acceptable to Roman Catholics should be set up in Dublin. The majority of the Commissioners recommended that the new college should become a constituent college of the University of Dublin; that the university should be remodelled so as to comprise within it five colleges—Trinity College, a college acceptable to Catholics, and the three Queen's Colleges. Three of the Commissioners recommended that the new college, together with the three Queen's Colleges, should be made the constituent colleges of the Royal University, reconstructed so as to become a teaching university.*

While the Fry Commission was still sitting, the Chief Secretary for Ireland, James Bryce, was engaged in conversations regarding education with Archbishop Walsh, and had come to agree with the Archbishop's view that the only equitable settlement of the university question would be the setting up within the University of Dublin of a second college acceptable to Catholics in the sense in which Trinity was acceptable to Protestants.

Shortly after the Commission presented its report Bryce made an important announcement in Parliament, almost the last speech he delivered before relinquishing the parliamentary for a diplomatic career. In his speech Bryce reviewed the recommendations of the Royal Commission. He laid special emphasis on the majority report which recommended the inclusion of all the Irish university colleges, including Trinity College, Dublin, in a single National University. "Such a university," he said,

* *Report*, pp. 32—37.

" would indeed be federal, and federation is a note of weakness; but since in any case some federation of the scattered Queen's Colleges could not be avoided, this was no fatal objection."

The signatories of the majority report were opposed to the establishment of two teaching universities in Dublin, and to the federation of the rest of Ireland against Trinity College. They believed that it would be possible under the scheme to preserve the essentials of college autonomy and college atmosphere. Bryce adopted and recommended to Parliament the scheme set forth in the majority report.

Here (he said) was a document pointing to the establishment of a single university for all Ireland, which should combine Catholic, Anglican and Presbyterian colleges. To the opponents of denominational education in English elementary schools such a solution of the thorny problem of higher education in Ireland naturally commended itself. There were to be no religious tests. The university was to provide teaching in non-controversial subjects, the colleges in subjects into which religious controversies entered. In all controversial subjects there were to be alternative graduation classes. Any class or any subject was to be open to any student. The teaching was to be supervised by the colleges, the enlarged university to be governed by a senate partly nominated by the Crown and partly elected by the university teachers and by the whole body of the graduates. The weaker colleges, like Galway, were to be affiliated. No payment from public funds was to be made for theological teaching, but it should be open to any college, out of its own resources, to establish any theological faculty it chose. "This," he concluded, "is our policy. Our belief is that our policy is likely to receive the support of the Liberal Party in Parliament, because it conforms to the principles they hold to—education without sectarianism —and to their desire to do everything in their power compatible with these principles to meet the wishes of the Irish people . . . I, personally, believe it is the only scheme politically possible under the conditions; and I can hold out no hope that any other will be proposed by the present Government."

This was precipitate . . . Bryce, however, was naturally

impatient to clinch the work on which he had set his heart; and to welcome recommendations consonant with his own enlightened (but undenominational) views as to what Ireland should desire in the matter of university education, and for which he had secured the support of the Roman Catholic Hierarchy and of the General Assembly of the Presbyterian Church.

His rapidity of action did not escape adverse comment. Mr. Balfour was prompted to observe that he had " nailed his flag to another man's mast, and then sailed for America." And Mr. Birrell, his successor, having to explain to the House of Commons that he had quite a different plan for university education in Ireland, suggested that in painting his picture Bryce " had omitted to leave a few clouds on the horizon."*

The man who succeeded in bringing about a settlement of the university question was Mr. Augustine Birrell. Mr. Birrell, who succeeded Bryce as Chief Secretary about the middle of 1907, lost no time in tackling the question. He got into communication with those interested in the matter in Ireland—amongst whom, of course, was Archbishop Walsh. Convinced that it would not be possible to carry Bryce's scheme in the teeth of the opposition of Trinity College, Mr. Birrell fell back upon the plan, adumbrated by Mr. Balfour in 1899, of setting up two new universities in Ireland, one to meet the needs of the Catholics, the other for the Presbyterians.

By the end of the year the Chief Secretary had got ready a printed memorandum or skeleton Bill relating to the university project. When sending the memorandum to the Archbishop, Mr. Birrell dwelt on the many difficulties which beset his path (December 31, 1907). Amongst these difficulties was the fact that "unhappily nobody in England really cares a straw about the University question in Ireland except a fanatic crowd who, stirred by the neo-Catholicism of the Church of England, see Popery writ large over the whole subject."

* *Life of Lord Bryce.* Fisher, vol. i., pp. 352—3.

The Archbishop's views on the scheme were set out in a long letter to Mr. Birrell on January 6, 1908 :

As to the scheme (he wrote) I think it, as I have already said to you, a good scheme, better than the " Robertson" scheme, and better than any other kind of scheme that I can think of, excepting, of course, one that would give us equality with T.C.D. in point of university status, v.g., a second college scheme in the University of Dublin, or a scheme such as Mr. Bryce's, open though his scheme would be to the charge of being a " sprawling" university. But supposing that as regards *status* in the world of learning we have to submit to our fate as representatives of a conquered and subject race, our next look out is, are we to have equality *in anything* in the scheme ? This depends most of all on the amount of money we are to get. I take T.C.D. Are we to get as much as it has from public sources ? Or I take T.C.D. and Belfast. Are we to get as much as these two Protestant colleges and universities will get ? If so we have equality in one substantial point. If not, not.

During the time that the scheme was being incubated and embodied in a Bill, Mr. Birrell was in constant communication with Dr. Walsh, and many of the Archbishop's suggestions were adopted by the Chief Secretary. The Bill was presented in Parliament on March 31, 1908. From that date until its enactment four months later (August 1, 1908) the Chief Secretary not only sought and obtained from the Archbishop constant and valuable help, but he also made the Archbishop the depository of his apprehensions and worries—of his triumphs and failures in strategy and diplomacy. When the Bill passed through Committee, Mr. Birrell wrote to inform the Archbishop, July 8, 1908 :

At last we are through Committee. My illustrious predecessor, the Bishop of Hippo, was a saint and a doctor, but the honours of *martyrdom* have, I think, been reserved for his unworthy namesake. I never heard greater nonsense talked in all my life.

After the Bill had passed the Committee stage, two

matters especially roused much hostility—the proposal to affiliate Maynooth, and the providing of a site for a chapel within the universities and colleges. On both questions the Archbishop helped considerably to tide over the difficulties.

While assisting the Chief Secretary in his difficult task of piloting the University Bill the Archbishop left no doubt on Mr. Birrell's mind about his views regarding the inadequacy of the measure as an equitable solution. The same idea was impressed by the Archbishop on John Redmond, Mr. T. M. Healy, and other members of Parliament. This view was entirely endorsed by Mr. Healy, as appears from a letter written by him to the Archbishop, June 8, 1908 :

The Bill is nobody's ideal, but if we are true to ourselves in the next few years, as the Tories have given Ireland nearly everything Toryism can surrender in other directions, it follows that whenever a new Tory ministry is seeking sops for the Irish, it must find outlet for its concessions *via* educational avenues. Hence the vital necessity of getting a start made somehow, and breaking ground freed from the Queen's College condemnations, by a fresh statute which in a few years will be budded and grafted on with better fruiting stock by new governments.

By the Irish Universities Act 1908 (8 Edw. VII. c. 38) the Royal University was dissolved and two new universities set up in its place—one with its seat at Belfast, the other with its seat at Dublin. In neither university were there to be any religious tests. The annual grant of £20,000 payable to the Royal University was to be divided equally between the two new bodies. The university at Belfast, to be called the Queen's University, was to consist of the old Queen's College, the endowment of which was raised to £18,000 a year. The new university at Dublin, to be styled the National University of Ireland, was to be a federal body embracing the old Queen's Colleges of Cork and Galway, and a new metropolitan college in Dublin itself. The colleges, to be known as University College, Dublin,

University College, Cork, and University College, Galway, were to receive annual endowments of £32,000, £20,000 and £12,000 respectively. In addition to the annual endowments, there was provided for acquiring lands and sites a sum of £60,000 for Belfast, £14,000 for Cork, and £6,000 for Galway, and for the new college and university buildings at Dublin a sum of £150,000. No portion of the grants nor any public endowment might be applied for providing a church or chapel or religious worship or theological teaching or study.

The Act was to come into force on an appointed day within two years after the passing of the measure. To set up the new establishments, two bodies of Commissioners were appointed by statute, and to these bodies was entrusted the duty of drafting the statutes and appointing the staff of the universities and colleges. The Dublin Commission consisted of ten members named in the Act, and the Belfast Commission consisted of seven. A joint Commission to be chosen by the two bodies was to deal with the division of the property of the Royal University, and any other matters of common interest.

The chairman of the Dublin Commission was Chief Baron Palles; Archbishop Walsh was one of its most prominent members. The Commission began its work in October, 1908, and one of its first acts was the appointment of a secretary. The Archbishop was fortunate in securing for this important post the services of Mr. Robert Donovan. The labour entailed on the Commissioners, and especially on the chairman, the Archbishop and the secretary, was enormous. By November 1909, University College, Dublin, was able to begin the work of teaching. It had a staff appointed by the Commission and a body of about five hundred students.

The Statutory Commission brought its labours to an end on July 31, 1911. In the meantime the Senate of the National University, a body nominated in the Universities

Act, had been brought together, and on December 18, 1908, had unanimously elected the Archbishop as its first Chancellor. It was only with reluctance that he accepted that honourable office. But as it was a gracious act on the part of the Senate, and was tendered to the Archbishop as an acknowledgment of the leading part which he had long taken in directing the campaign for university education and conducting it to a successful issue, he felt that he ought not to refuse the proffered honour. He continued to be Chancellor of the National University till his death in 1921.

The time and labour and pains he devoted to the work of the University Commission were enormous. Not only did he give up long hours for several days in the week to the sittings of the Commission, but frequently he had conferences at his house, sometimes lasting till a late hour at night, with the secretary or with the legal draftsman. He revelled in this work, and his energy and endurance and legal acumen often caused surprise, and at times despair, to the draftsmen, D. F. Brown, K.C., and Mr. James A. Murnaghan, B.L. (now Mr. Justice Murnaghan). His interest in the work of the National University and its constituent colleges continued to the end of his life, and a signal proof of his practical concern for the welfare of University College, Dublin, was the presentation which he made to the college of the valuable legal library of Baron Palles which he purchased for the college after the Chief Baron's death in 1918.

Before his death the Archbishop had the satisfaction of seeing the National University securely established and successfully engaged in the work of imparting higher education suited to Ireland's needs, and in sympathy with Irish ideals, to a body of over two thousand students.

In 1920 University College, Dublin, had over 1,800 students attending lectures in its halls, and it afforded the Archbishop much pleasure to be able to congratulate the college on having, by that time, outstripped Trinity College in the number of its students. He visited the college from time to time, and he availed of more than one opportunity of publicly congratulating the college on having the good fortune to possess in its chief executive officer, Dr. Denis J. Coffey, a most capable, devoted and self-denying president.

Two things which Dr. Walsh had striven to secure for the National University, and especially for University College, Dublin, he did not live to see attained. These were an adequate equipment for the " teaching of science, and the provision of suitable residential quarters for the students." He had pressed both these matters on Mr. Birrell's attention while the Universities Bill was passing through Parliament. He urged him to transfer to University College, Dublin, the buildings and equipment of the Dublin College of Science; but though the Chief Secretary was entirely sympathetic, he feared, as he informed the Archbishop, that such a suggestion would cause Trinity College " to prick up her ears," and add new difficulties to a situation already sufficiently complicated.

The College of Science has since been transferred to University College, Dublin, but nothing so far has been done by the State to make the colleges of the National University residential.

CHAPTER XXI

LAST YEARS

THE large amount of extra labour thrown on the Archbishop
by the work of the Statutory Commission on the National
University had a serious effect on his health, and led to a
nervous breakdown. When towards the end of 1911 he was
again able to use his pen, he immediately became involved
in a public controversy.

The controversy was occasioned by the efforts
of certain newspapers to create a political scare in
Ireland and in England on the publication of a
certain papal decree. The decree, issued *motu proprio*
by Pope Pius X, October 9, 1911, and from its first words
known as *Quantavis diligentia*, dealt with the haling of
clerics before lay tribunals. A Dublin Protestant newspaper printed December 21, 1911, a translation of the
decree under a series of sensational headlines representing it
as " A Thunderbolt from Rome," and describing the
issuing of it as " A New Papal Aggression." By editorial
comments, by speeches at public meetings, and by letters
of correspondents published in some of the Dublin papers,
the Irish public was informed that by the papal decree it
was forbidden under penalty of excommunication to compel
the attendance of ecclesiastics in the public courts. No
Catholic judge, it was said, no Catholic magistrate, no
Catholic member of the police force could discharge the duty
that he was sworn to discharge, if his discharge of it should
involve the bringing of a Catholic priest into court in any
case, even as a witness; moreover, that no Catholic member
of the community if libelled by a priest could seek redress

in a court of law, no shopkeeper from whom a priest had obtained goods on credit and refused to pay for them could seek to recover his money by process of law, without, as one of the newspapers expressed it, " automatically " incurring the penalty of excommunication.

To allay the uneasiness which was created in the minds of some Catholics by the publication of these sensational statements, the Archbishop published a letter in the Press, December 30, 1911, in which he assured his people that the issuing of the papal decree had effected no change in the condition of affairs, civil or religious, in Ireland; that the statements of alarmists in the Press and on the platform regarding the effect of the decree were simply untrue; and that, notwithstanding the publication of the decree, Irish Catholics might continue without qualm to follow their accustomed methods of seeking legal redress. In a word, he assured the Catholics of Dublin, addressing them as their Bishop, that, in the absence of any decision of the Holy See to the contrary, they might continue to discharge their duties and to vindicate their rights without regard to the decree.

The Archbishop explained that he was enabled to give that comforting reassurance, because, to anybody familiar with the principles of the Canon Law and with the history of ecclesiastical jurisprudence in Ireland, it was quite evident from the reading of the decree that the provisions of the *Quantavis diligentia* did not apply to Ireland. The Archbishop further pointed out that Ireland was exempted from the decree by reason of a recognised legitimate custom, and he explained the effect of such custom on canonical enactments.

The scaremongers were not satisfied with the Archbishop's assurance. The editor of the Dublin *Daily Express* stated (January 18, 1912) with offensive rudeness that " not only does the *Quantavis diligentia* apply to Ireland, but Archbishop Walsh is perfectly aware of the fact." Other critics

expressed dissatisfaction because the Archbishop's assurance was not authoritative, inasmuch as he did not profess
to give an " official" interpretation of the decree; and his
appeal to legitimate custom as an exempting cause from the
effect of a law was declared to be an attempt to bolster up a
bad case by an appeal to unintelligible intricacies of the
Canon Law.   Even the *Times* newspaper published the
egregious statement of its Dublin correspondent that
" Archbishop Walsh insists once more that the lay intelligence, however highly trained, cannot hope to grapple with
the intricacies of the Canon Law."   Of course the Archbishop made no such statement. What he did insist on in
the course of the controversy was that in order to interpret
correctly any legal document the interpreter ought to be
conversant with the principles of the legal system in question, and that a lawyer unacquainted with the principles of
Canon Law, no matter how profound might be his knowledge
of other legal systems, would most likely be misled, if in
interpreting a canonical document he relied on the rules and
principles of his own system exclusively.

The Archbishop pointed out that the *Quantavis diligentia*
which dealt with the violation of the *privilegium fori*—the
old immunity of the clergy from the jurisdiction of the
secular courts—was to be read in connection with an earlier
pontifical Constitution, *Apostolicae Sedis*, issued in 1869;
that the decree of 1911 had reference to clause 7* (*Cogentes*)
of the Constitution of 1869, in which Catholics are declared
to incur excommunication if they oblige lay judges to bring
ecclesiastics before secular tribunals contrary to the provisions of the Canon Law (*praeter canonicas dispositiones*);
that whether the " *motu proprio*" was to be regarded as an
authoritative interpretation of the clause *Cogentes*, or as an
independent enactment supplementing the Constitution of

---

* " Cogentes sive directe sive indirecte iudices laicos ad tra-
hendum ad suum tribunal personas ecclesiasticas praeter
canonicas dispositiones."

1869, the new decree introduced no change into the existing state of affairs in Ireland. For, as he proceeded to explain, a general ecclesiastical law according to recognised canonical principles does not bind (*a*) in any place expressly excluded from the operation of the law by the terms of the law itself, or (*b*) in any place excluded by agreement or concordat between the Holy See and the head of the State, or (*c*) in any place where a duly constituted custom prevails against the law.

Ireland was excluded from the operation of the *Quantavis diligentia* (in the sense expounded in the Protestant Press) by reason of the existence of a duly recognised canonical custom. The only form in which the excommunication regarding the violation of the " *privilegium fori*" had effect in Ireland concerned the impleading of ecclesiatics by ecclesiastics in the civil courts. No such excommunication extended to laymen who brought ecclesiastics before the courts. Laymen by so doing did not act " contrary to the provisions of the Canon Law." They were guilty of no canonical offence. It was to the offence of bringing ecclesiastics before the courts " contrary to the provisions of the Canon Law" that the clause *cogentes* attached the penalty of excommunication. But there being no canonical offence in the discharge of their duty by Catholic judges, magistrates, policemen, and the Catholic laity in general, there was in their case no offence to which an ecclesiastical penalty could be attached, and so, no ecclesiastical penalty incurred.

One of the most persistent of the Archbishop's critics at this time was Mr. J. H. Campbell, K.C., now Lord Glenavy. Mr. Campbell told audiences which he addressed at Dublin and Ballymena during the scare regarding the *Quantavis diligentia* that Canon Law had been a special study of his, and

that the effect of the papal decree was to prevent any public official from bringing into a court of justice, criminal or civil, any ecclesiastic of the Roman Catholic Church; that in construing the decree he could give Archbishop Walsh some help as well as Cardinal Logue, as for many years he had been engaged in the profession of the law, and during that time it had been his duty to study and interpret Acts of Parliament, and he thought that he knew what the English language meant.

On these words of Mr. Campbell's the Archbishop remarked :

There stands revealed the whole secret of Mr. Campbell's breakdown over the papal decree. He looked upon it simply as a piece of "language" and he set about construing it just as he would construe an Act of Parliament—thus overlooking the essential point that there were applicable to the decree certain important principles of Canon Law—principles that are in no way applicable to Acts of the British Parliament, but that have to be applied in the interpretation of papal decrees, if those who undertake to interpret them are to keep clear of error.

The controversy, which was unduly prolonged—mainly owing to the Archbishop's provoking his critics to make floundering statements regarding the Canon Law—had the effect of putting an end to the scare which had been started for the purpose of fanning the flame of political prejudice.

The end of 1912 found Dr. Walsh again prostrated by ill-health. For months he was unable even to write, and his physicians feared that the nervous affection (something in the nature of creeping paralysis) from which he suffered would soon incapacitate him. But a visit to Marienbad in the following year restored him almost completely. He was unable, however, owing to the uncertainty of his health, to consecrate Dr. Mannix, who was appointed coadjutor to the Archbishop of Melbourne. Although he completely recovered the use of his hand, and was able to write almost as well as ever, he was thenceforth physically enfeebled and subject to intermittent attacks of serious illness until his death.

During the later years of his life Dr. Walsh but rarely intervened in public affairs or took part in the discussion of public questions, although he followed the various phases of the struggle for Irish self-government with interest and with alert concern.

He was in favour of the acceptance of the Government of Ireland Bill 1912, though he greatly disliked the restrictions in the Bill by which so many important services were reserved to the British Government and Parliament, and he entirely disapproved of the statement in which John Redmond, as spokesman of Irish National feeling, declared that he was satisfied to accept the Bill " as a full and complete settlement of Ireland's claim." He also considered that Redmond's speech in Parliament on the declaration of war in 1914 was short-sighted and very impolitic. He viewed with great misgiving the negotiations in 1914 for the temporary exclusion of portion of Ireland from the operation of the Government of Ireland Act. The World War produced in a short time a profound change of political outlook in Ireland, especially among the younger generation, who appeared to have grown tired of the long-standing Parliamentary Party. Parliamentary methods were assailed, and Pearse and his associates envisaged a situation which would call for a resort to arms.

After the outbreak of Easter 1916 Dr. Walsh showed marked favour to the cause of Sinn Féin, and helped the Sinn Féin Party in its opposition to the Redmondites whom he had ceased to trust. He viewed with undisguised uneasiness the efforts made by the Redmondite Party to effect a settlement of the Irish Question before the conclusion of the War, and he regarded the case of a united Ireland as irretrievably abandoned when, on June 23, 1916, a convention of the Nationalists of Northern Ireland carried, in St. Mary's Hall, Belfast, a resolution of partition under threat of the resignation of John Redmond and John Dillon. He regretted that Redmond and Dillon were not then defeated and forced to resign. So serious did he consider the risk involved in any proposal recognising partition even of a temporary character that in 1917 he broke the self-imposed silence of years. He gave great offence to the Irish Parliamentary Party and provoked much obloquy from the Party's supporters by a letter which he published on the eve of a parliamentary election in Co. Longford. In the letter he stated, May 8, 1917 :

The question may perhaps be asked why a number of us Irish bishops, Catholic and Protestant, have thought it worth our while to sign a protest against the partitioning of Ireland. Has not that miserable policy, condemned as it has been by the all but unanimous voice of Nationalist Ireland, been removed, months ago, from the sphere of practical politics ?

Nothing of the kind. Anyone who thinks that partition, whether in its naked deformity or under the transparent mask of " county option" does not hold a leading place in the practical politics of to-day is simply living in a fool's paradise.

In a characteristic postscript he added :

I think it a duty to write this, although from information that has just reached me, I am fairly satisfied that the mischief has been already done, and that the country is practically sold.

He had been informed of the suggestion,[*] transmitted to the Government by Redmond, to summon a Convention of Irishmen to settle their differences between themselves ; he had also been informed that the Irish Party were prepared if they won the Longford election—and they were confident of victory[†]—to accept partition without further consultation of the electorate, to take over the administration of such portion of the country as might be transferred to them, and to utilise for consolidating their position such

[*] Cf. *The History of Ireland*. Stephen Gwynn, p. 517.
[†] *Freeman's Journal*, May 8, 1917.

time as would elapse before they should be compelled to seek the opinion of the country on the termination of the war. The Archbishop's letter had the effect of returning the Sinn Féin candidate who was elected by a small majority.

Dr. Walsh declined to allow his name to be submitted for membership of the Convention, which was convened by the Government and presided over by Sir Horace Plunkett.

In 1918 he took an active part along with his episcopal brethren in opposing conscription for Ireland, and in recommending resistance to that measure " by whatever means should seem most efficacious." The defeat of conscription, in which all sections of Irish Nationalists had a share, was put down to the credit of Sinn Féin, and when a general election on an extended franchise was held in December 1918 the victory of the Sinn Féin Party at the polls was overwhelming. Dr. Walsh recorded his vote for the Sinn Féin candidate—it was the only occasion during his episcopal life when he voted at a parliamentary election.

Out of one hundred and five Irish members returned at the elections, seventy-three were pledged against attending the Parliament at Westminster, and had declared for the Irish Republic proclaimed by Pearse in 1916. In pursuance of the policy long advocated by Griffith, the elected members assembled at Dublin and proceeded to act as a legislature. This assembly styled itself Dáil Éireann, and its members took an oath of allegiance to Saorstát na hÉireann, January 21, 1919. In the following April, when Mr. De Valera was elected President of the Sinn Féin organisation, he declared that Dáil Éireann's attitude as representing Ireland was " that of the Belgian Government towards the German army of occupation," and that the Sinn Féin organisation was to act as " a sort of civil army to carry out the decisions of Dáil Éireann's cabinet."* An appeal for funds was issued by the Dáil to Irishmen at home and abroad,

* Gwynn, op. cit., pp. 519—22.

Ireland was asked to contribute a quarter of a million pounds.

In September 1919 the Government proclaimed Dáil Éireann as a dangerous organisation, and ordered Sinn Féin to be suppressed. Forthwith stringent measures were taken to prevent contributions reaching the treasury of the Dáil. The condition of affairs in Ireland at this time is depicted in a letter addressed by Dr. Walsh to Cardinal O'Connell, Archbishop of Boston, November 10, 1919 :

I wish to contribute a hundred guineas to the Irish National Fund inaugurated under the auspices of the elected body known as Dáil Éireann, our Irish Parliament. I cannot but think that, as far as people of Irish race are concerned, their knowledge of the fact that I have subscribed to the fund would be of at least as much help as any money subscription of mine could be.

But as matters now stand in Ireland none of our newspapers dare publish the fact that I had subscribed. We are living under martial law, and amongst the numerous devices to which our present Government has had recourse in its foolish attempts to crush the national spirit of our people is the issuing of sundry military orders. In one of these they have given notice to the editors, or managers, of our popular newspapers of the fate that awaits any newspaper venturing to publish the names of contributors to the fund, or the amounts contributed.

I, of course, am well aware of the deep personal interest that your Eminence takes in our Irish national affairs, and of the powerful help that you have given to our people in their effort to secure their rightful control of the government of their own country. I trust that your Eminence will not consider it a misplaced confidence on my part that I feel assured of your willingness to come to my aid by helping me to make known in America the fact of my subscription to the Dáil Éireann Fund.

Freedom of the Press, the right to public meeting, the right of personal liberty, the right of trial by jury, no longer exist in this country except in so far as they can exist subject to the absolutely uncontrolled discretion of some military ruler technically designated the " competent military authority."

All this has had its natural effect—the driving of dis-affection underground, with the no less natural result that disaffection driven underground finds an outlet in crime. The "competent military authority" does not seem to realise that there is no possible remedy for this lamentable state of things, so long as the source of all the evil, the present system of military rule, is maintained.

Cardinal O'Connell had Dr. Walsh's letter published throughout the United States. The Cardinal wrote to the Archbishop, December 8, 1919 :

Your Grace's contribution to the cause of Ireland and your message to all our people here were enthusiastically welcomed. and both are bound to do great good.

One of the crimes in which disaffection found an outlet at this time was an attempt made on the life of the Lord Lieutenant, Lord French, in the neighbourhood of Dublin, December 19, 1919. On the following day Dr. Walsh addressed to his clergy a letter of condemnation in which he stated that the attempted assassination of the Viceroy called for " the melancholy protest of every Irishman who loves his country, and hopes to see the present rule of coercive government in Ireland brought to a final close." " Surely," he added, " there is no one in Ireland so ignorant of the moral law as not to know that murder, both in itself and in its consequences, is one of the most appalling crimes in the whole catalogue of guilt. Surely there is no criminal in Ireland who does not know that this is the only light in which the crime of murder, or attempted murder, can be viewed by the faithful members of any Christian Church throughout the world."

He asked the clergy to remind their faithful people of the words of our Divine Lord : *Seek ye therefore first the kingdom of God and his justice, and all these things shall be added unto you.*

Adverting to his long experience of the futility of mere

denunciation as an effective deterrent to crime, the Archbishop mentioned a consideration to be urged on political rather than on religious grounds, but which he thought it well to refer to in view of the deplorable situation :

Is there any rational man (he asked) capable of deluding himself into the belief that such a method of seeking redress for the misgovernment of this country is likely to help the efforts of the righteous men who are working earnestly for the purpose of re-establishing in our own country the reign of liberty and justice ?

Early in the following year (1920) Bishop Donnelly died, and soon after the Archbishop petitioned the Holy See to grant him a new auxiliary bishop. His request was granted, and on his recommendation the Pope assigned to him as auxiliary the Rev. Edward J. Byrne, who was appointed titular Bishop of Spigaz. On October 28, 1920, the Archbishop consecrated Dr. Byrne at the Pro-Cathedral. This was the last great ecclesiastical function at which he officiated.

During the autumn and winter Dr. Walsh had interviews with some of the prominent men who were endeavouring to bring the representatives of Sinn Féin into direct communication with Lloyd George's Government. Amongst these was the Archbishop of Perth, Dr. Clune, whose mediation the British Prime Minister had secured.

At the end of March 1921 the condition of Dr. Walsh's health had become so serious that he had to be removed to a nursing home with the view of securing relief by a surgical operation. His condition, however, was found to be hopeless, and he died on the morning of April 9, 1921. He was buried at Glasnevin where a graceful monument erected to his memory by the clergy of Dublin marks his grave.

An appreciation of the Archbishop contributed by the

present writer to an Irish periodical* shortly after Dr. Walsh's death is here appended.

By the death of William J. Walsh, Archbishop of Dublin, a familiar figure has been removed from the life of the Irish metropolis. His appearance was well-known in the Dublin streets—the brisk, tripping step of the days of his early episcopate; the stooping gait and tottering pace of his later years; the silk hat slightly tilted backwards on the massive head, the strong face; the intelligent eyes—all were familiar.

Though small of stature, he had a well-knit frame, and was blessed with a healthy and vigorous constitution. He was not athletic, and although he used to ride in his younger days, he was but a poor horseman. It is well known that he was an early advocate of the bicycle, the machine on which he made his *début* being an old " boneshaker." Cycling he valued highly both for its practical usefulness and for the healthy recreation it provided. He used to tell, with a gleeful twinkle in his eye, of the discomfiture of a venerated colleague in the Hierarchy, a suffragan of his own, who, in the early days of cycling, had resolved, after much anxious thought, to issue a mandate forbidding his priests to use the wheel. Before coming to a final decision, however, the Bishop determined to consult his Metropolitan, who advised him to talk the matter over with his Vicar-General. As the prelate approached the Vicar's house with this object, he saw on the road an athletic figure in shirt-sleeves wobbling from side to side, and mounted on a bicycle. It was the Vicar, taking his first lessons. The Bishop chatted—about the weather—and nothing more was heard of the mandate.

He was an expert photographer, and in his leisure moments he sorted and arranged in albums with his own hand a most interesting collection of some thousands of photographs

---

* *The Catholic Bulletin.* May 1921. (M. H. Gill & Son.)

taken by himself when travelling in various parts of Europe. He also prepared an index of the photographs, giving the subject, place, time-exposure, and the rest.

The Archbishop's private life was simple and most methodical. In his later years, at least, he passed the greater part of the day in his study. His interests were manifold, his energy untiring, his capacity for work marvellous. Unless when actually ill, he was never seen to sit in an easy chair. He read a great deal, and he always read pen in hand. He was never slipshod. Casual statements were constantly checked by appeal to books of reference, of which he had a goodly number in his own well-stocked and carefully arranged library. He was a constant reader at King's Inns Library, occasionally he read at Trinity College, and sometimes at the National Library of Ireland, and at the British Museum.

He was familiar with the Bible in the Latin and in the various English versions. The Latin classics he knew well; Dante intimately. His reading in general European literature was wide and varied; but he was more interested in literary problems than in literary form, although he admired the *curiosa felicitas* of a neatly-turned phrase. On fancy he set little store, and flights of imagination did not allure him. His own imagination, though not poetic, helped him enormously by enabling him to visualise a complex problem in all its bearings and details. He was a firm believer in apperception as a powerful aid to memory, and he valued highly *memoria technica* and all such artificial helps as the systems of Leibniz, Feinaigle and Loisette afforded. His mind was well-stocked with literary allusions and quotations, but though his conversation was marked by apposite quotations from English and foreign classics, I cannot recall a single such quotation in anything he published.

Dr. Walsh was an admirable host, unaffected and plain, and he liked a small dinner party. He always retained a boyish *joie de vivre*, and even in old age he laughed so heartily that tears would run down his cheeks. He talked well, yet he was no autocrat of the dinner table, and never monopolised, or even directed the conversation. He was a conversationist, not a mere raconteur, nor yet an " expounder," like a famous friend of his. Dr. Mahaffy, late Provost of Trinity College, has left on record that Dr. Walsh was one of the most brilliant talkers he had ever met. " The tongue of the Archbishop," he says, " is the pen of a ready writer." His conversation was direct and pointed ; he had a clear deep voice and a most distinct utterance, with, in some words, the faintest suggestion of a lisp. He was a most attentive and appreciative listener, and his accurately informed mind and powerful memory enabled him without difficulty to take his full share in discussing any subject which might casually arise. Though he did not suffer fools gladly, the youngest and most inexperienced person in his company felt quite at ease, and there was always the greatest toleration shown by him for the views of others, no matter how divergent. True, he was some-what difficult of access, yet he was affable to those whom he received. He was an adept at returning a polite but decisive "No" to an impossible request. Once he had made up his mind, neither importunity nor blandishment could move him to depart from the course he believed to be right. And when urged to do so, even by the most influential and exalted persons, he could, and on occasion did, *trancher le mot* definitively.

He talked much better than he wrote. When he put his thoughts on paper, the first draft of the document was generally plain and clear. But no sooner was a proposition penned than its whole bearings flashed before him. Forth-with provisos and restricting clauses were added, and the overweighted statement which finally emerged was guarded by a network of precautionary qualifications. Yet, though his style was, in consequence, not attractive, and though he lacked intuition in choosing *l'epithète rare*, he generally held the reader's attention, he never lost grip of his argument, his logic was unassailable, his phrases were often telling. He sought out the *mot juste* with exquisite care. He was a very painstaking writer, a clever, reliable, accurate literary craftsman, but not a literary artist. In fact, the only arts in which he excelled were the art of music and the art of conversation.

He brought to the consideration of a question an unusual freshness of mind, calmness of outlook, concentrated attention, and a rare judicial detachment. He possessed, too, in a remarkable degree, the advocate's power of marshalling the facts of a complicated case, and of presenting them in clear, orderly, telling array. He was severely logical in presenting an issue. Once he was much amused by a controversial opponent, who, on being hard pressed by him and sorely bestead, turned at bay and flung at his Grace the taunt levelled by one American editor at another : " The Archbishop's logic is like the peace of God; it passeth all understanding."

In controversy he was alert and nimble. He hardly ever overstated his case. He often purposely left loopholes for attack, and prepared pitfalls for the unwary. He generally managed to lead a discussion along lines which he had clearly foreseen and carefully selected. Sometimes, however, his zest for argument and his delight in playing an opponent, misled him into tediously prolonging a discussion.

From time to time, during his long life, his pronouncements on questions of the day met with vigorous censures in the Press, and provoked the acute hostility of some Irish public men. His own language was sometimes severe, and his attitude towards his opponents was unflinching and, at times, relentless. But he entertained no personal rancour for his public foes, and, in conversation, he was scrupulously careful to bear generous testimony to the high personal character and the private and social virtues of men who were the objects of his most trenchant public denunciations.

A wag once said of the Archbishop that his most pleasurable recreation was writing impish postscripts. Be that as it may, he had other more conventional forms of relaxation. He walked and cycled a good deal, played the piano frequently, billiards and cards occasionally. He was but an indifferent billiard-player, and his knowledge of card-playing was acquired very late in life. When the game of bridge first came into vogue, the problems published in the papers so aroused his interest that he procured Dalton, Foster, and other standard books on the subject, and quickly mastered the principles of the game. He seldom failed to solve a bridge problem on paper, but on the rare occasions on which he played a rubber, the theorist was outdistanced by more practised if less intellectual devotees. Indeed, a player who was noted more for skill at the game than for professional knowledge or mental acumen, once said to him : " You will never be a card-player, your Grace; your early education was shamefully neglected."

This enthusiasm for bridge and the thoroughness with which he learned the game was typical of the man. His comprehensive mind and his persistent and untiring energy enabled him rapidly to master the most complex subject, in principle as in detail, and, having mastered it, he possessed the faculty of clear and orderly exposition. Making up a case was, in fact, a recreation with him. When the Dreyfus *affaire* was at its height, the Archbishop, who happened to be in France at the time, acquired a singularly accurate knowledge of the details of that intricate case. Later, he keenly enjoyed reading Mr. Dooley's humorous presentation of the same *affaire*, beginning, " *J'accuse*," says Zola, " and they thrun him out."

His chief relaxation indoors he found at his piano. In his study he kept a Steinway grand piano, on which, sometimes for hours, he would play Mendelssohn, Chopin, etc. In later years he had a pianola fitted on to the piano, by which means he continued to enjoy his favourite composers. He had a choice selection of music rolls, and was constantly adding to the list. Not infrequently he analysed, or got a competent musician to analyse for him, a piece in which he was particularly interested. He read an orchestral score with ease. On a wet afternoon, when he was unable to walk or drive out, he would exercise himself at the pianola till he became quite heated. When playing, he always liked to have the music before him, and it was remarkable how much expression he could put into a piece played by this mechanical contrivance.

In connection with this piano, a very pathetic incident occurred some hours before his death. About 2.30 p.m. on Friday, April 8th, it was evident that the Archbishop was dying. His voice had become faint and his eyes were becoming dim. He asked for paper and a pencil, and endeavoured to write, but the writing was illegible. It was then suggested to him that he should try to speak the message he wished to convey. He strove to do so, but his utterance was inarticulate and almost inaudible. After a while he took up the pencil again, and for the last time his fingers moved at the behest of his strong will and clear mind. In a very faltering hand he wrote the following message :

" I wish to leave my grand piano to the Convent, Merrion Blind Asylum, as an addition to the enjoyment of the all but hopeless affliction of the blindness of the young, and with the piano the pianola and the music rolls. And it is my desire that the Sister Superior should exempt from this gift any roll, or rolls, which she does not consider suitable for this purpose."

The words " all but " were undecipherable. On the document being read over to him, however, he managed to pronounce the missing words, which were then inserted in the MS. The amended version being then read to him he nodded assent to each part of the statement, and even suggested the insertion of commas and other punctuation marks. This kindly concern for the afflicted blind, whose sad condition always elicited his deep commiseration, was evidently suggested by the perceptible failure of his own sight at the approach of death. With Merrion he had close personal associations. There, as a young priest, he had celebrated his first Masses, having acted as chaplain to the Blind Asylum while living at home, in Booterstown, for some weeks after ordination.

It may be mentioned that this direction of the Archbishop's was not, nor was it intended to be, a last will. He had made his will soon after he took possession of the See, and practically the only subsequent change made in it was the appointment of new executors and trustees according as the executors and trustees originally appointed passed away. The will was short and simple. Everything in and about Archbishop's House was given upon trust for the person who should first succeed him as Roman Catholic Archbishop of the Archdiocese of Dublin and in communion with the Holy See if he should be appointed as such Archbishop within twenty-one years of the date of his decease. All the residue of his property he left upon trust to be applied for such charitable purposes in Ireland as the said Archbishop should in his absolute and sole discretion think fit. The Archbishop's personal assets, apart from his books and furniture, did not amount to more than a few hundred pounds. The considerable amount of money left to him by his parents, and all other personal income, he spent during his life, for he gave generously to charity each year.

Walking was a favourite pastime and recreation of the Archbishop, and he had a preference for the streets and byways and suburbs of his native city. He was well-known in the slums, especially in those on the north side of the city. Frequently he might be seen returning home through Lower or Middle Gardiner Street, where the teeming juvenile population is very much in evidence. The children always recognised him, greeting him with the familiar " God bless you, Father !" Boys doffed their caps, and those who had none to doff were duly reminded to " rise your hair"; the little girls gracefully bowed their heads as their teachers had instructed them, or curtsied, or even genuflected while they repeated the " form." Many stories are told of his kindly interest in and affection for the younger members of his flock, and his special regard for manly, chatty boys. On the mantelpiece of his study the photograph of Jim Treacy occupied for twenty years an honoured place. Jim was a fair, curly-headed, bare-footed boy, who " read" an address to his Grace on the occasion of a visit to the schools in Dorset Street. At the time, compulsory school attendance was being much talked of. When the Archbishop entered the schools Jim stepped forward, and, getting on a chair, proceeded to read with great aplomb and deliberation the address which he had carefully rehearsed beforehand, following the text with his eye, line by line, from left to right. The burden of Jim's statement was a demand for educational equality. " He and his likes" wanted only a fair field and no favour; they did not want to be "compulsed." When he had finished he solemnly handed the address to his Grace, who was amused to find, what he had already suspected, that Jim had been holding the address upside down. The poor little fellow, though so bright and intelligent, was unable to read.

The Archbishop frequently chatted with the children whom he met in his rounds. Walking along Dorset Street one evening he noticed some structural alterations being carried out at the Bethesda Church, and he asked a little boy, who was busily engaged whipping his top, what was being done with the church. The lad lashed his top, lifted his cap, and replied : " They're making a picture-house out of it." " A picture-house?" " Yes, Father," he continued, " and maybe 'tis better than what it was." On another occasion he saw a very small boy standing smiling in Belvedere Road, while an April shower poured down on his unprotected head. The Archbishop offered him the protection of his umbrella. " Ah, it's alright, Father, thank you," the boy replied, " my father says the rain is good for man and baste." The father was a cabman.

Added to his great liking for children was a deep faith in the efficacy of their prayers. Before he left for hospital, he quietly requested that the children of the Sacred Heart Home, Drumcondra, should offer their Holy Communions for him, and on the evening before his operation, his last request to his trusted and most devoted valet, William Kelly, was that the valet's three children should offer their Holy Communions for his intention the following morning. On hearing that they had already intended to do so unsolicited, the Archbishop broke down—the only occasion, as far as the writer knows, on which his emotions so overcame him. It will be recollected that the Sacred Heart Home and the Catholic Working Boys' Home were founded by Dr. Walsh, and the two institutions were always special objects of his patronage.

Behind a mask of outward reserve Dr. Walsh concealed great bashfulness, a kindly heart, and solid piety. Religiously and socially he led a life apart. It was only those who had intimate friendly intercourse with him who were aware of his social charm and deep piety. A friend of his —a man of shrewd character and deep insight, and of most wide and varied experience (Cardinal Logue)—who had known Dr. Walsh intimately for over sixty years, told the writer that he had never known so pureminded a man; that he was an angelic boy, and that, as a man, his high ideals of propriety, and his constitutional repugnance to anything that was coarse, or even unrefined, were so well known that

nobody would ever venture in his presence to give utterance
to the slightest unseemly word.

His faith was the simple faith of the most unsophisticated
Irish Catholic, and the piety he had been schooled in from
childhood remained with him in all its pristine simplicity
to the end. It was a hidden piety. If anything, it was
perhaps, too jealously hidden. Even at home his devotions
were mainly private. At Mass in his oratory, he wished
for no other attendant than his valet, who always served
the Mass. The Divine Office he used to say in the privacy
of his bedroom, and before retiring at night it was
his practice to anticipate Matins and Lauds for the following
day. His crucifix and scapulars he loved. The Rosary
and Litany of the Blessed Virgin he prized most highly.
On the day of his death, when the Litany was being recited,
he asked that it should be said more slowly, so that he
might join with greater deliberation in the responses.

Perhaps the most striking feature of his religious life was
his serene and unclouded faith. Several times during his
last illness he had the Act of Faith read for him, and when
the end was near at hand, as his life ebbed slowly away,
clasping the hand of the priest who was reading, he pressed
it in token of assent after each article of the Creed. When
about to receive the Viaticum on Friday morning he said it
would be his last Holy Communion, and he tried to prepare
with especial care for the worthy reception of our Lord.
Up to the last moments of consciousness he continued to
make Acts of faith, hope, and contrition, resignation and
gratitude to God for granting him a comparatively painless
death.

Dr. Walsh's heraldic motto—appropriate surely—was

Fide et Labore.

APPENDICES

I

SIR JAMES O'CONNOR'S "HISTORY OF IRELAND."

THE pages of this Biography were already in print when, on August 20, 1928, a friend called my attention to a *History of Ireland, 1798-1924* by the Right Hon. Sir James O'Connor. This History was published in 1925, but somehow I had neglected to look into it owing to an impression of its worthlessness left on my mind by the reading of certain articles or extracts made by the author and printed in an English newspaper prior to its publication. In the index I found half a dozen references to Archbishop Walsh; they occur in Vol. II. at pp. 103, 124, 127, 175, 285, 325.

On reading through the pages mentioned in the index I was surprised to discover that almost every statement made regarding Dr. Walsh was ill-informed, inaccurate, or incorrect. In the interests of truth I deem it a duty to comment on the relevant statements. All the passages will be found in Vol. II. at the pages indicated.

1. At page 103 the author writes :

" Dr. Walsh [in May 1885] wanted to be Archbishop [of Dublin] very badly."*

---

* " Something will be said of Archbishop Walsh in connection with the ' Anglo-Irish ' War. At this time (May, 1885) he was president of Maynooth College, and highly placed people were at variance in their estimation of him. Cardinal Manning wrote to Sir Charles Dilke on April 26, 1885 : ' I have an impression that efforts have been made to represent Dr. Walsh as an Nationalist. He is no more so than I am; and whether that is excessive or obstructive you will judge.' Spencer, however, took another view. ' The Cardinal is wrong in his estimation of Dr. Walsh.' Dr. Walsh had no false modesty. He wanted to be Archbishop very badly, and thanked Dilke ' for the part I had in trying to prevent the opposition to the choice.' *United Ireland* got hold of Errington's letter and published it, this made the appointment of Dr. Walsh secure."—Vol. II., p. 103.

(D 700)　　　　　　　587　　　　　　　U 3

This statement is far from the truth. His commendation by the clergy of the archdiocese had been a foregone conclusion. Dr. Walsh did not want to be Archbishop. He resented the attempt to exercise English influence at the Vatican, but this was altogether apart from his own selection. Cf. *supra* pp. 158, 160-1, 168, 171.

2. At page 284 the author writes :

[Dr. Walsh] " had thanked Dilke for his efforts to help him towards the vacancy [in the See of Dublin]"; and again at page 103 he refers to an entry in Sir Charles Dilke's Diary (*Life of Dilke*, by Gwynn and Tuckwell, p. 131) in which it is stated that Dilke had been thanked by Archbishop Walsh " for the part I had in trying to prevent opposition to the choice" [of Dr. Walsh to be Archbishop of Dublin].

The statements both of Dilke and of Sir James O'Connor are inaccurate (Cf. *supra* p. 165). A reviewer of the *Life of Dilke*, writing in the *Tablet* (December 8, 1917) quoted two passages taken from Dilke's diary, under dates May 26 and July 4, which left on the mind of the reader an impression unfavourable to Dr. Walsh. After reading the *Tablet*, I at once drew his attention to the review; but the Archbishop, who had already seen the *Life*, remarked to me that Dilke was in error with regard to the facts, and that it was not worth while correcting him in the *Tablet*. The full entry in Dilke's diary is : " May, 1885.—On Tuesday evening, May 26, the Commission dined with Gray, and met Dr. Walsh, the new Archbishop : but at Dr. Walsh's wish I had gone to Gray's house half an hour before dinner to see the Archbishop privately, and to be thanked by him for the part I had taken in trying to prevent opposition to the choice." This meeting between Dilke and Dr. Walsh took place in Dublin. Dilke, who had come to Ireland as chairman of the Royal Commission on the Housing of the Working Classes, had been recommended by Manning to see Dr. Walsh. They met at Pembroke House, the residence of E. Dwyer Gray, on May 26. On May 26, Dr. Walsh was not Archbishop. He was not appointed till June 23, i.e. till nearly a *month after*. Clearly the entry in the diary was not made by Dilke on May 26. It could not have been made till June 24, when the news of Dr. Walsh's appointment was first published. Dr. Walsh did not thank Dilke for the part he had taken in " trying to prevent opposition to the choice." He expressed his and the country's appreciation of the firm attitude taken by Dilke in the Cabinet against the British Government's support of the Errington intrigue at the Vatican. I am not concerned to say, nor do I suggest, that Dilke wilfully misrepresented Dr. Walsh, but the entry in his diary under date May 26 is erroneous. I refer the reader to the account of the activities of Sir G. Errington and certain members of the Government, and of Dilke's opposition to their manœuvres given at pp. 139-142, 149-153, 164-165, 175-178. This misstatement of Dilke's is the origin of the flimsy legend, afloat since the publication of the *Life of Dilke*, that Dr. Walsh had managed to scramble into the Archbishopric of Dublin by the help of Dilke and Manning. To this myth Sir James O'Connor would give currency in the pages of his *History*.

How closely analogous is the story of the Haldane myth, which is being told in the Press just now (August 1928). For years Lord Haldane suffered eclipse because he was supposed to have stated that Germany was his spiritual home. Sir Arthur Spurgeon (cf. *Irish Times*, August 23, 1928) explains the origin of the myth.

"One day, three or four years after the war, I asked Lord Haldane if he ever really said that Germany was his spiritual home. He replied emphatically ' Never !' and he told me how the legend had arisen.

"Some time prior to the war, he was dining with Mr. and Mrs. Humphrey Ward. Professor Oncken was present, and the conversation turned to German philosophy. When the name of Lotze was mentioned, Lord Haldane casually observed, ' to Lotze I owe much of my spiritual education.' Professor Oncken, writing later in a German publication, used the words ' spiritual home,' and the mischief was done.

"An unfortunate misinterpretation of a remark let fall at a private dinner party led to results that were disastrous to Lord Haldane in the early years of the war. It would be better, I think, if he had corrected this error publicly, but he was indifferent to what people thought at the time."

Quite so ! The Haldane myth has been already exploded. I hope we have heard the last of the Archbishop Walsh myth.

3. At page 325 the author writes : " Archbishop Walsh sent a telegram of congratulation to Lord French [on the occasion of his escape from the attempt on his life at Ashtown, December 19, 1919], and *soon after* sent £100

to the funds of the Irish Republic." This statement also is untrue. Cf. *supra* pp. 574-576.

The facts are these. The Archbishop, after fruitless endeavours to bring home to the Irish Government the recklessness, and, indeed, the purblind and criminal folly, of its military régime, and the grave danger to the country of the policy of wholesale repression of every manifestation of discontent, took the only course which he then saw open to him, and addressed to a brother prelate, Cardinal O'Connell, Archbishop of Boston, a letter of protest and warning for publication in the U.S.A. The letter, written on November 10, 1919, was published in America towards the end of November, about a *month before* the attempt on Lord French's life. Had the Archbishop's wise and timely protests been heeded by the Irish Government, there would probably have been no bloodshed at Ashtown, and much subsequent crime and misery would have been prevented. The letter is printed in full above, p. 572. I quote from the last two paragraphs :

" Freedom of the Press, the right to public meeting, the right of personal liberty, the right of trial by jury, no longer exist in this country . . .

" All this has had its natural effect—the driving of disaffection underground, with the no less natural result that disaffection driven underground finds an outlet in crime. The ' competent military authority' does not seem to realise that there is no possible remedy for this lamentable state of things, so long as the source of all the evil, the present system of military rule, is maintained."

Sir James O'Connor is also inaccurate in stating that Dr. Walsh sent a telegram of congratulation to Lord French. I was secretary to the Archbishop at the time, and I have no recollection of any such telegram having been sent; nor can I find any reference to it in the published list of telegrams received by the Viceroy on the occasion. The Archbishop addressed to the clergy a letter condemning the outrage. The incident at Ashtown occurred on Friday, December 19. On that (Friday) evening the Archbishop wrote the letter denouncing the crime. The letter which was printed and despatched to the clergy on Saturday was read publicly on Sunday in all the churches and chapels throughout the diocese of Dublin (cf. *supra* p. 573). What is in Sir James O'Connor's mind when he complains that, " Archbishop Walsh sent a telegram of congratulation to Lord French and

soon after sent £100 to the funds of the Irish Republic"?
Does he charge the Archbishop with hypocrisy or inconsistency? A charge of hypocrisy will find little credence in
Ireland. The facts are a sufficient answer to a charge of
inconsistency.

4. At page 204 the author writes:

"Archbishop Walsh of Dublin, who, when the See of
Dublin was in the balance, had given Cardinal Manning the
impression of being, at least, a lukewarm Nationalist . . .
had now [1917] become a Sinn Féiner."

This statement is reckless and inaccurate. The innuendo
conveyed by the words " *had given Cardinal Manning the
impression*" is mean and unjust. To me, and I think to
most plain people, Sir James O'Connor's words obviously
and necessarily convey the impression that Dr. Walsh
dissembled his Nationalism in order to enlist Cardinal
Manning's active co-operation to secure the archbishopric.
What grounds had Sir James O'Connor for making this
charge? Throughout the whole life of the Archbishop there
is nothing to support such a suggestion.

5. At page 124 the author writes:

" Dr. Walsh, Archbishop of Dublin, had come up to the
expectations of his supporters [in 1887-8]; he was a fully-
fledged ' patriot-Archbishop,' almost rivalling in zeal
Archbishop Croke."

The words " patriot-Archbishop" in this passage are
printed in inverted commas. Elsewhere in this *History*
(pp. 284, 289, etc.) Sir James O'Connor classes Dr. Walsh
with Dr. Fogarty and other " patriot" bishops. And he
informs his readers that " the workings of the mind of the
' patriot' bishops of Ireland pass human understanding."
The use of inverted commas conveys to ordinary readers
that the writer questions or denies the patriotism of the
" patriot-Archbishop" Walsh. Does Sir James O'Connor
doubt or deny that Dr. Walsh was a patriot? Does he
insinuate that Dr. Walsh was a mere political opportunist?
Political opportunism is an odious charge. Can Sir James
O'Connor substantiate it?

6. At page 176 the author writes:

" The celebrant of the Mass [*the Votive Mass pro
Quacumque Necessitate*, celebrated in the Pro-Cathedral,
Dublin, on the occasion of King Edward VII's death]
invoked a blessing on the new King [George V]."

This statement is also incorrect. The celebrant did not
invoke a blessing on the new King.

7. At page 175 the author writes :

" Manning, who was deeply disappointed in his protégé [Dr. Walsh] was lucky in being spared the agonies of self-reproach that would have assailed him had he survived to see, in 1919, the man whom he supported for the See of Dublin supporting the Irish Republic by noble subscriptions and every other process of encouragment."

Was Manning disappointed in his protégé ? Will Sir James O'Connor produce evidence of his assertion ? Manning's biographers, Purcell and Mr. Leslie, give no hint of any such disappointment. Manning was not disappointed in Dr. Walsh. On the contrary, as is abundantly clear even from the Cardinal's letters published in this volume, Manning's regard and esteem and affection for Dr. Walsh were enhanced as the years went by.

8. At page 278 the author writes :

" Dr. Walsh, Archbishop of Dublin, expressed *his detestation* of it [the Rising of 1916] in an interview I had with him on Easter Monday of 1916."

Dr. Walsh did not express detestation of the Rising in this interview with Mr. O'Connor. Sir James's memory has misled him. The circumstances of the interview were these. On Easter Monday Mr. James O'Connor, who was then a law officer of the Crown, was attending the races at Fairyhouse when he heard of the Rising. He at once hurried back to Dublin, and at about six o'clock in the afternoon he called on the Archbishop. The Archbishop, who was then confined to his house recovering from a grave illness, received Mr. O'Connor in a room adjoining his bedroom. The interview was brief. When Mr. O'Connor was driving away on an outside car I met him near Archbishop's House, where I then lived, and exchanged a word with him. On my entering the House I immediately went upstairs to see the Archbishop, who gave me an account of the interview. This was his account. Mr. O'Connor, he said, was excited and panicky. He asked the Archbishop to write a letter calling on the insurgents to desist from their mad enterprise, etc., etc. The Archbishop declined to do so, and declared the suggestion preposterous. He characterised as absurd and foolish the proposal to call on men who had actually taken up arms to lay them down unconditionally. He spoke of the effrontery of Sir James O'Connor and his Government in trying to make a cat's-paw of him. He roundly denounced the incompetence of the Government, which, with the ample resources of military and police at their disposal had allowed blood to be spilt. He spoke of the *folly* of the rising, which, he believed, could only end in defeat. And finally, he told Mr. O'Connor that he and his Government should resign, and that, if they did not, they ought to be superseded.

Such was the Archbishop's account of the interview to me, and I have a very clear recollection of it.

More than once the Archbishop expressed to me and to others his resentment of the mentality which prompted Mr. O'Connor's visit to him on that Easter Monday. The English Government's idea, as represented by Sir James O'Connor, was apparently that the Rising, which had taken those in authority quite unawares, was to be suppressed by *spiritual weapons*, and the Catholic Law Officer was to be the medium by which the desired condemnation should be secretly obtained. Dr. Walsh did not fall in with the Government's views. Is Sir James O'Connor justified in suggesting inconsistency or weakness in the action of the Archbishop on this occasion?

9. At page 284 the author writes :

" Dr. Walsh wrote to the Press [May 8, 1917] on the eve of the Longford election, in the following terms : ' From information which has just reached me, I am fairly satisfied that the mischief [of making Partition inevitable] has been already done, and that the country is .practically sold.' This *slander* on the Irish Party carried the Sinn Féin candidate for South Longford."

An indictment of slander is a very grave charge to level against any man. An ex-judge especially ought not rashly or lightly to prefer such a charge. Can Sir James O'Connor justify his indictment? Would any impartial jury of Irishmen have convicted Dr. Walsh of slander for the statements contained in his letter? Does Sir James O'Connor intend to convey to his readers that the Archbishop wrote his letter not from a sense of duty (as he stated) but in order to publish a malicious libel? Does Sir James O'Connor doubt the knowledge and the sincerity of the informant who supplied the information which fairly satisfied the Archbishop that the mischief had been already done, and that the country was practically sold?

10. At page 292-3 the author writes :

" In July [1918] a Military Service Bill was introduced raising the age for compulsory service to fifty ... The Military Service Bill included Ireland, and Mr. Bonar Law intimated that it would be enforced ... Since the day of

O'Connell, no such intense and widespread movement had taken place as that which this mistaken policy produced . . . The occasion brought together all classes of thought; political enemies met together to decide on concerted action . . . An interview took place between the political leaders and the Irish Bishops at Maynooth; a solemn episcopal appeal to the nation was the result. Funds were collected at every Catholic church and chapel in Ireland; over £200,000 is said to have been subscribed . . . Where this money went I do not know. I surmise that it, or some of it, went to the Republican War Chest."

The surmise is reckless and shameless; and as far as regards the money contributed in the diocese of Dublin, I know it to be unjust and unfounded. The Archbishop directed that the money should be returned to the contributors, and his directions were carried out.

Much might be written controverting this egregious *History of Ireland* by Sir James O'Connor. In the foregoing remarks I have confined myself to those statements which refer particularly to Dr. Walsh, and I have noted the passages in question lest some inference should be drawn from passing over them in silence.

II

EXTRACT FROM SPEECH OF LORD SALISBURY
At Birmingham, November 24, 1891.

Supra p. 430.

" Nothing in modern history had been shown equal to the influence of Archbishops Croke and Walsh in the recent history of Ireland.

" They have turned the whole of that organisation that seemed to embarrass and baffle the British Government—they have turned it clear away from the man [Parnell] in whose hands it was, with as much ease as a man turns a boat by leaning on the rudder.

" What (he asked) will be the state of the loyal minority in Ireland supposing you hand them over to such an ecclesiastical government? I carefully say ' ecclesiastical'; I do not believe I should be right in saying ' Roman Catholic,' because I believe these Archbishops are defying not only their own country, *but the Head of their own religion*."

III

INTERVIEW ON BIMETALLISM.

Supra p. 438.

" The most remarkable experience I ever had in regard to interviews was the result of a cablegram from ' Hearst, New York,' to ' interview his Grace the Archbishop of Dublin on the subject of Bimetallism as applied to the forthcoming Presidential election.' Yielding to no man in my absolute ignorance of the subject, I regarded the duty with fear and trembling, and it was with natural diffidence and hesitation I even undertook the responsibility which had to be discharged at once or not at all. Knowing so well by personal experience the graciousness and kindly nature of Dr. Walsh, who was, if I may say so, my personal friend, I waited upon him, and in his study was about to explain my mission when he smilingly said : .' I know, you want to interview the Archbishop on the subject of Bimetallism, etc.'—repeating the exact terms of the cablegram which I held in my hand. I was amazed, but the explanation was simple enough. He, too, had received a wire intimating that he would be waited on, and repeating the purpose in the same phraseology and with a respectful and appealing request. And then his Grace, taking compassion on my invincible ignorance, dictated an ' interview' which afterwards appeared on the front page with startling headlines in the New York paper. I certainly gained great commendation and kudos and some coin, though not one word of the vastly important and illuminating ' interview' was, in fact, due to ' Our Special Representative.' "

J. B. HALL in *Random Records of a Reporter.*
(Simpkin Marshall, Ltd., London, 1928).

INDEX

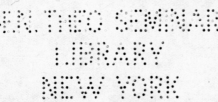